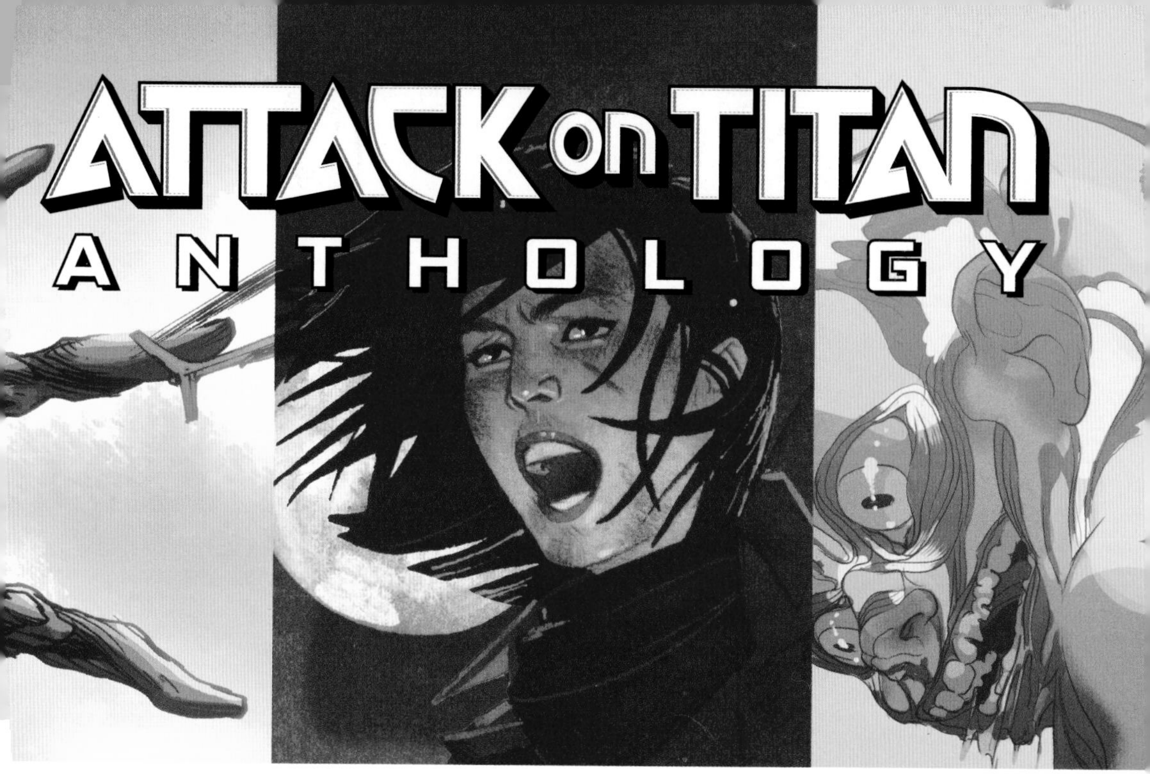
ATTACK on TITAN
ANTHOLOGY

This book is an official collection of stories based on Hajime Isayama's *Attack on Titan*. Some are set in the continuity of the actual *Attack on Titan* series. In others, the authors reimagine the Titans in entirely new settings. All the stories strive to combine the unique elements that made *Attack on Titan* the biggest hit manga in a generation with the sophisticated and beautiful storytelling of the best Western comics. On behalf of all the creators involved with this book, we hope you enjoy reading it.

Kodansha Comics

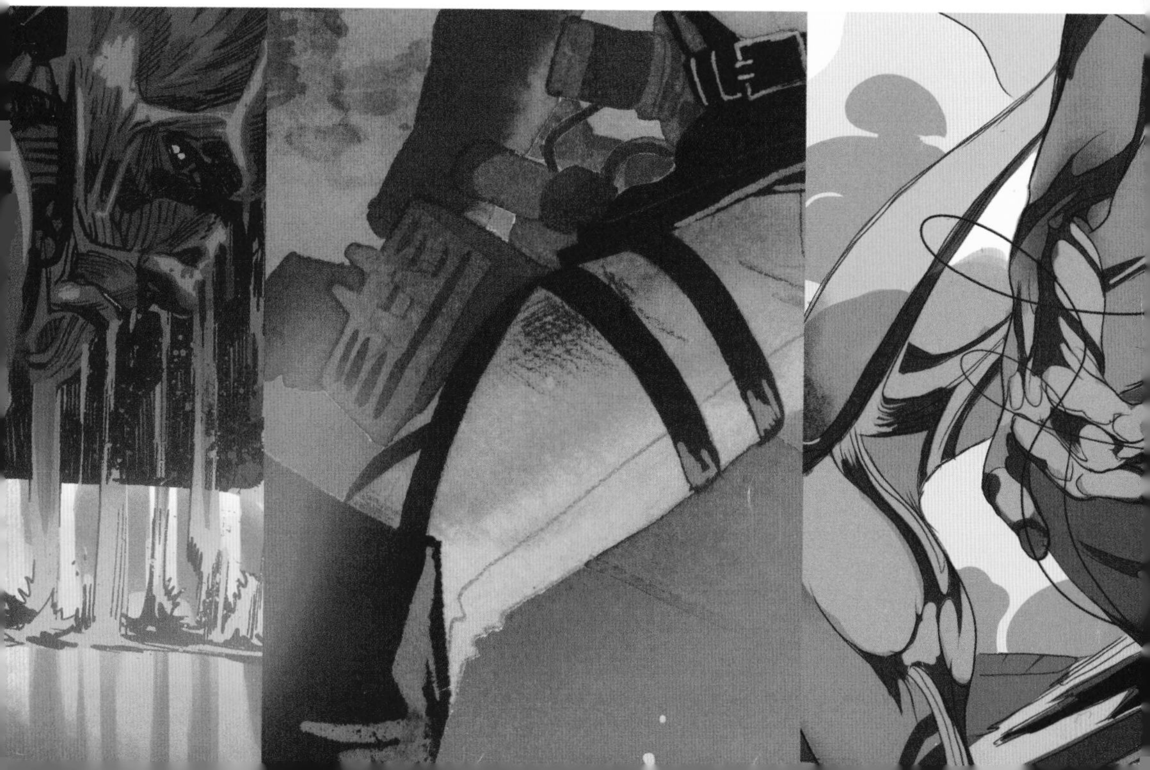

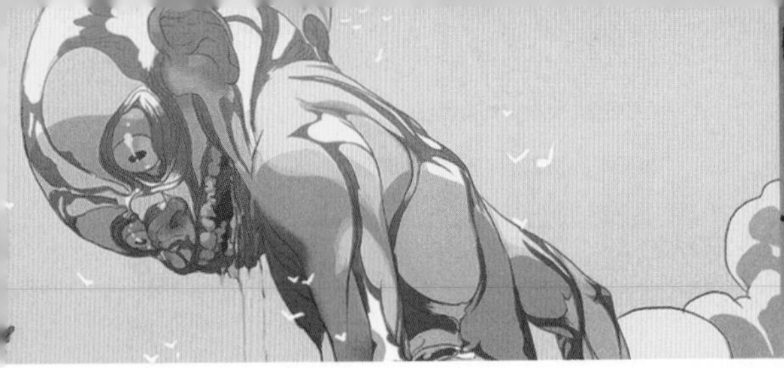

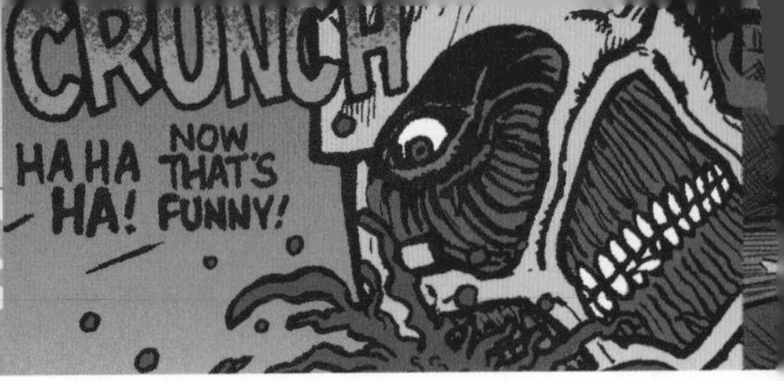

CRUNCH
HA HA -HA!
NOW THAT'S FUNNY!

Attack on Titan created by Hajime Isayama

Edited by Ben Applegate and Jeanine Schaefer
Cover, logo, and interior design by Phil Balsman
Lettering and interior design by Steve Wands

Standard edition cover by Paolo Rivera
ISBN 978-1-63236-258-2
New York Comic Con edition cover by Paolo Rivera
ISBN 978-1-63236-417-3
Barnes & Noble edition cover by Faith Erin Hicks and Noreen Rana
ISBN 978-1-63236-413-5
Diamond edition cover by Phil Jimenez
ISBN 978-1-63236-411-1
Fried Pie Comics variant edition cover by Paul Pope and Paul Maybury
ISBN 978-1-63236-412-8

Published by Kodansha Comics, an imprint of Kodansha USA Publishing, LLC, New York.
Printed in the United States of America.

www.kodanshacomics.com

9 8 7 6 5 4 3 2 1

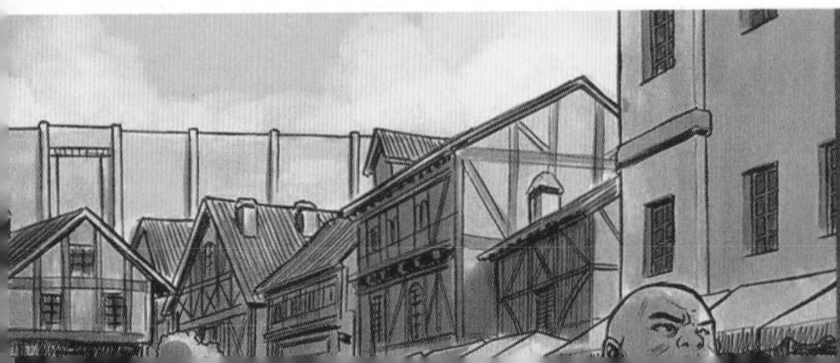

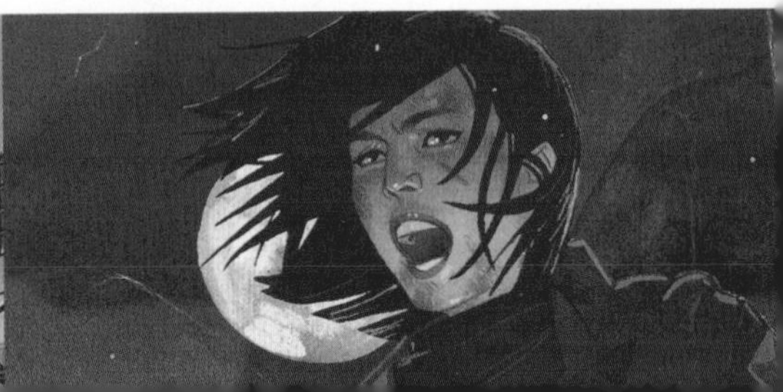

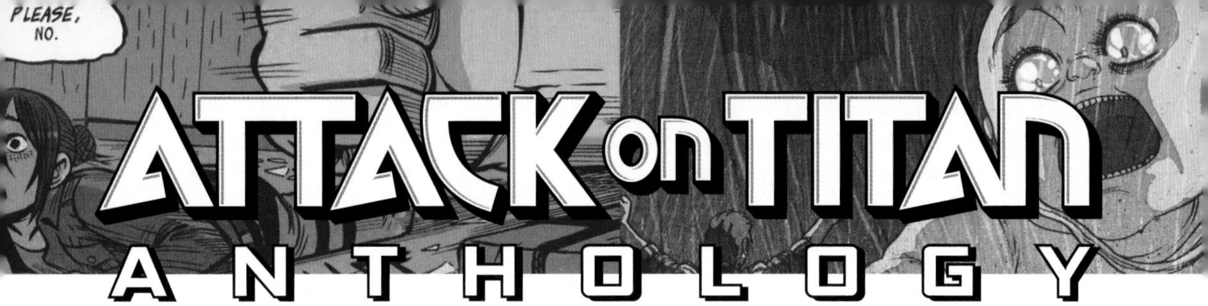
PLEASE,
NO.

ATTACK on TITAN ANTHOLOGY

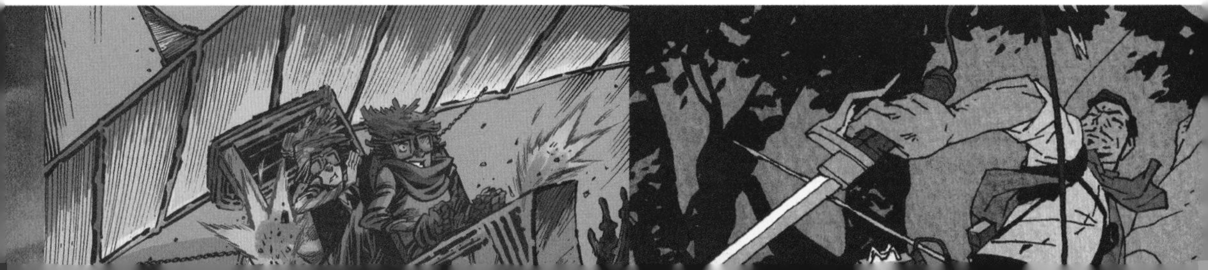

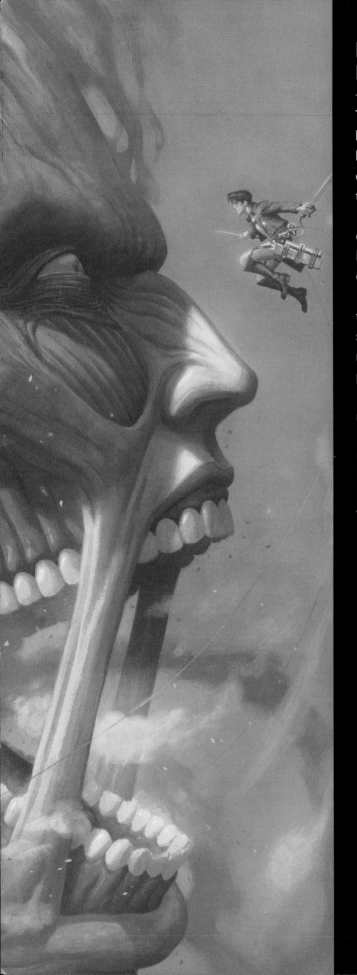

NOTE FROM THE EDITOR OF THE ORIGINAL SERIES

The artists who contributed to this book were all fascinated by the beings known as "Titans," and they have all expressed the charm of the Titans in their own unique ways.

This precise situation has been a dream of *Attack on Titan* creator Hajime Isayama since he started drawing the original comic.

He always said to me, "I want giants to became a popular genre unto themselves, on par with zombies, and it'd make me happy if even one more person understood their appeal."

This book is Hajime Isayama's dream made reality. I hope you enjoy it.

Back-san
Editor, *Attack on Titan*
Kodansha, Ltd.
Tokyo

An Introduction to *Attack on Titan*

One hundred years ago, the Titans appeared. These giant, grotesque parodies of the human form knew only a hunger for our flesh. They could not be starved, they could not be outrun, and they could not even be killed, except by a precision strike with a blade to the back of the neck.

Victims of a sudden genocide, the few remaining humans retreated behind three concentric Walls, encircling all that remained of humanity's territory. As years became decades, we lost all hope of beating them and instead grew contented with our circumscribed existence. As our fear of the Titans faded, we became complacent and weak, like birds in a cage.

Then, five years ago, the Colossus Titan appeared. The largest Titan ever encountered, it destroyed our outermost wall, and threatened to make our species extinct at last. The only people standing in its way are the Survey Corps, humanity's only Titan-fighting force, and three cadets: strategic prodigy Armin, born soldier Mikasa, and Eren, who harbors the mysterious power to transform into a Titan.

The Survey Corps, and these three young people, are humanity's last hope to understand and destroy the Titan threat.

But the world is cruel, and they soon discover that, even in the face of extinction, humanity may be its own worst enemy...

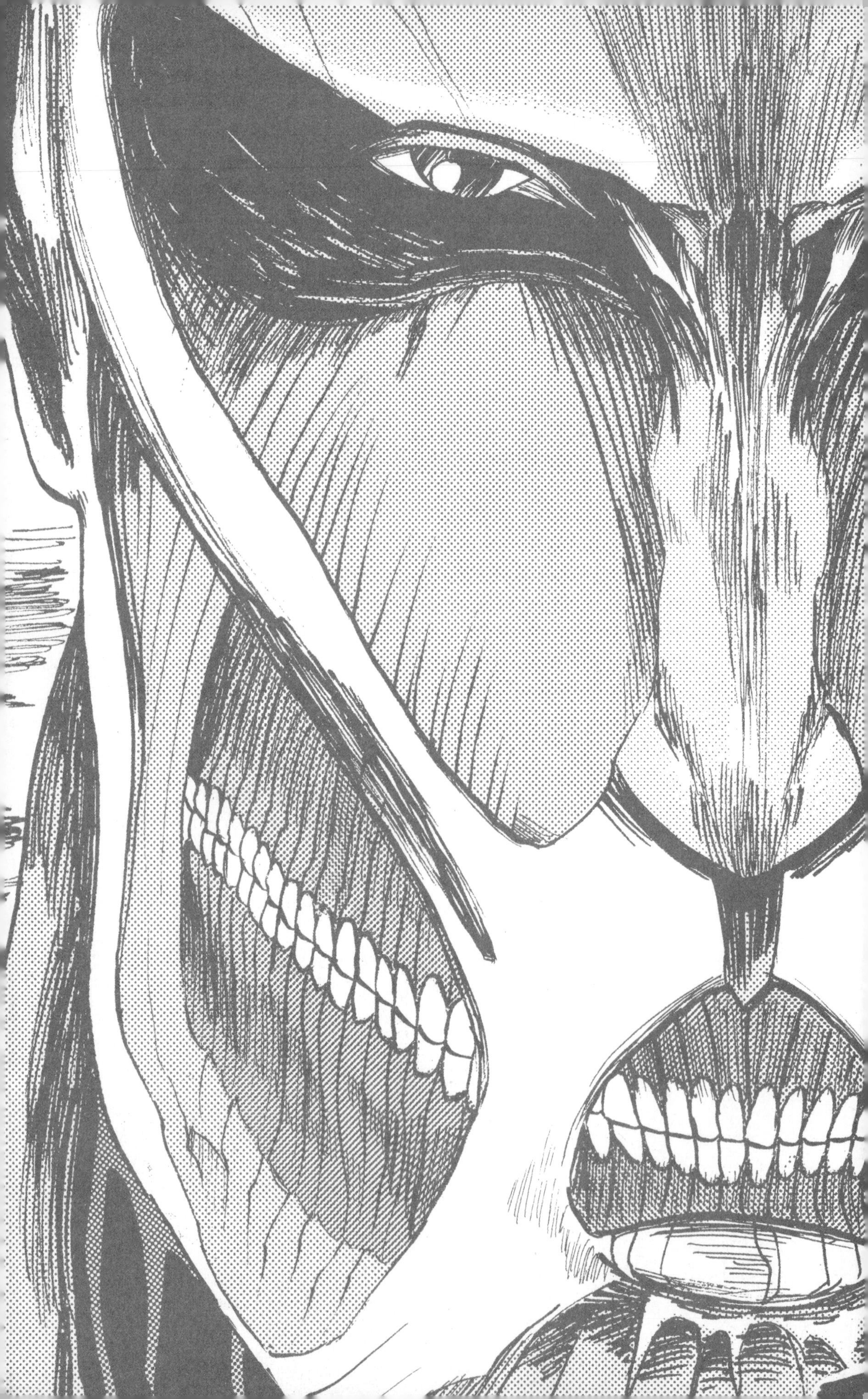

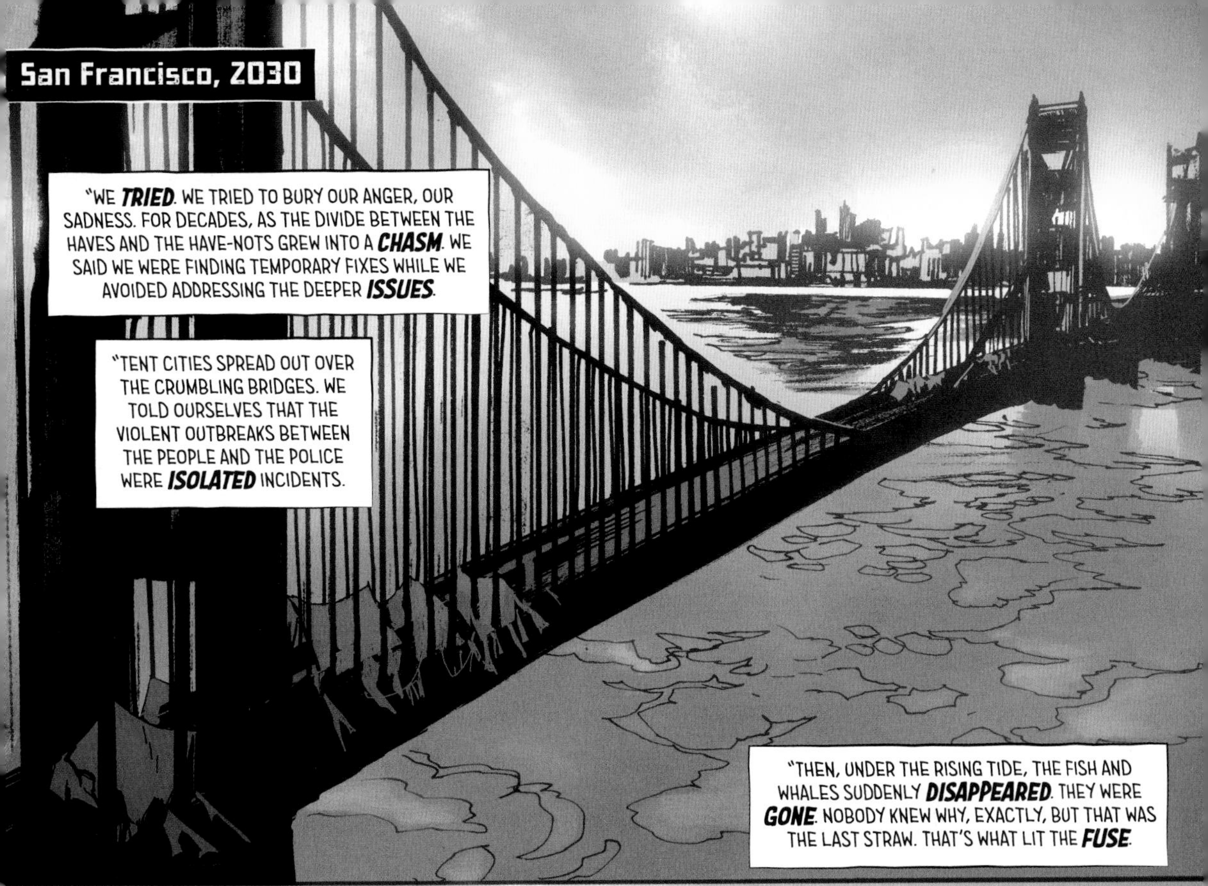
San Francisco, 2030
"WE TRIED. WE TRIED TO BURY OUR ANGER, OUR SADNESS. FOR DECADES, AS THE DIVIDE BETWEEN THE HAVES AND THE HAVE-NOTS GREW INTO A CHASM. WE SAID WE WERE FINDING TEMPORARY FIXES WHILE WE AVOIDED ADDRESSING THE DEEPER ISSUES.
"TENT CITIES SPREAD OUT OVER THE CRUMBLING BRIDGES. WE TOLD OURSELVES THAT THE VIOLENT OUTBREAKS BETWEEN THE PEOPLE AND THE POLICE WERE ISOLATED INCIDENTS.
"THEN, UNDER THE RISING TIDE, THE FISH AND WHALES SUDDENLY DISAPPEARED. THEY WERE GONE. NOBODY KNEW WHY, EXACTLY, BUT THAT WAS THE LAST STRAW. THAT'S WHAT LIT THE FUSE.
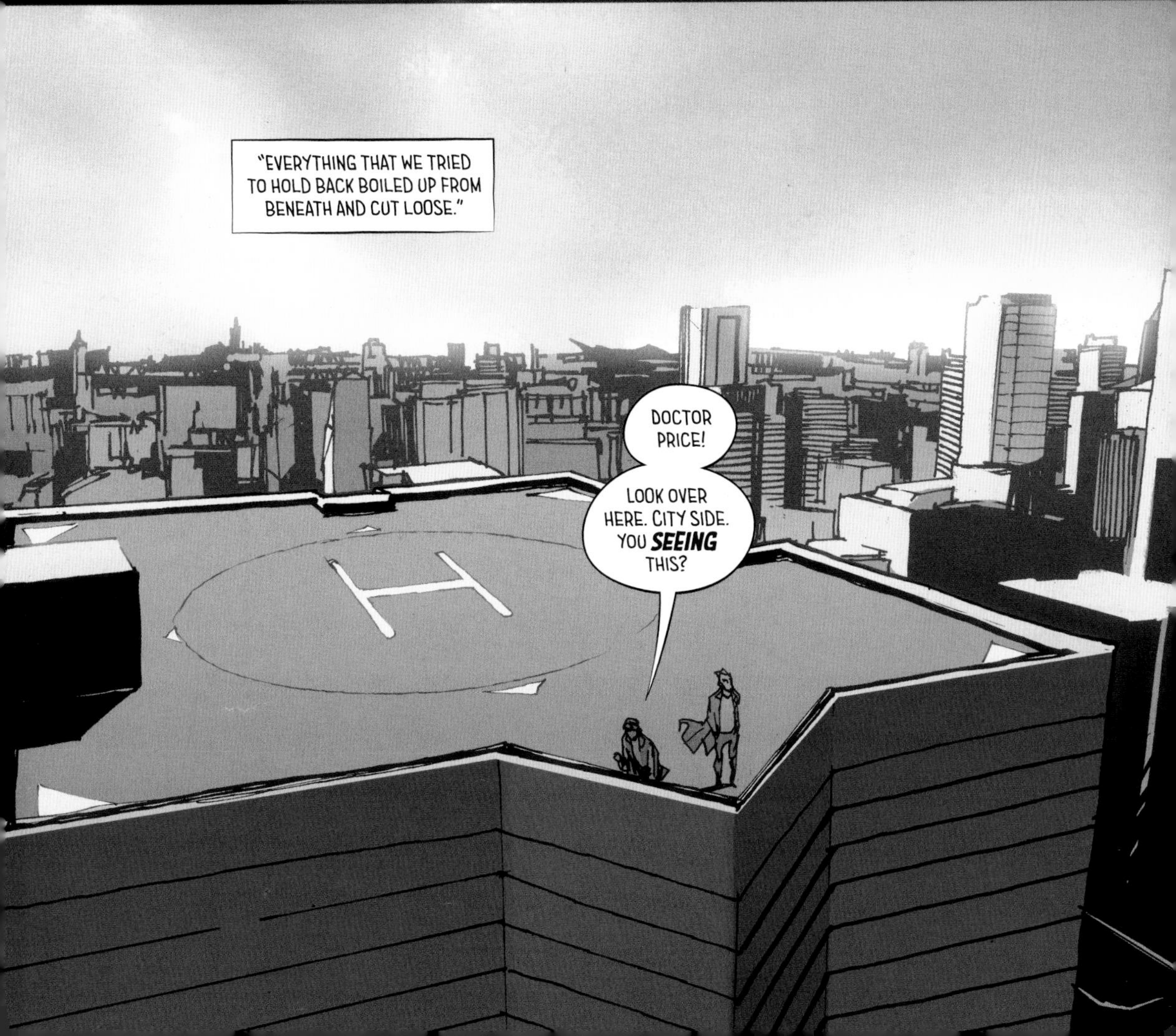
"EVERYTHING THAT WE TRIED TO HOLD BACK BOILED UP FROM BENEATH AND CUT LOOSE."
DOCTOR PRICE!
LOOK OVER HERE. CITY SIDE. YOU SEEING THIS?

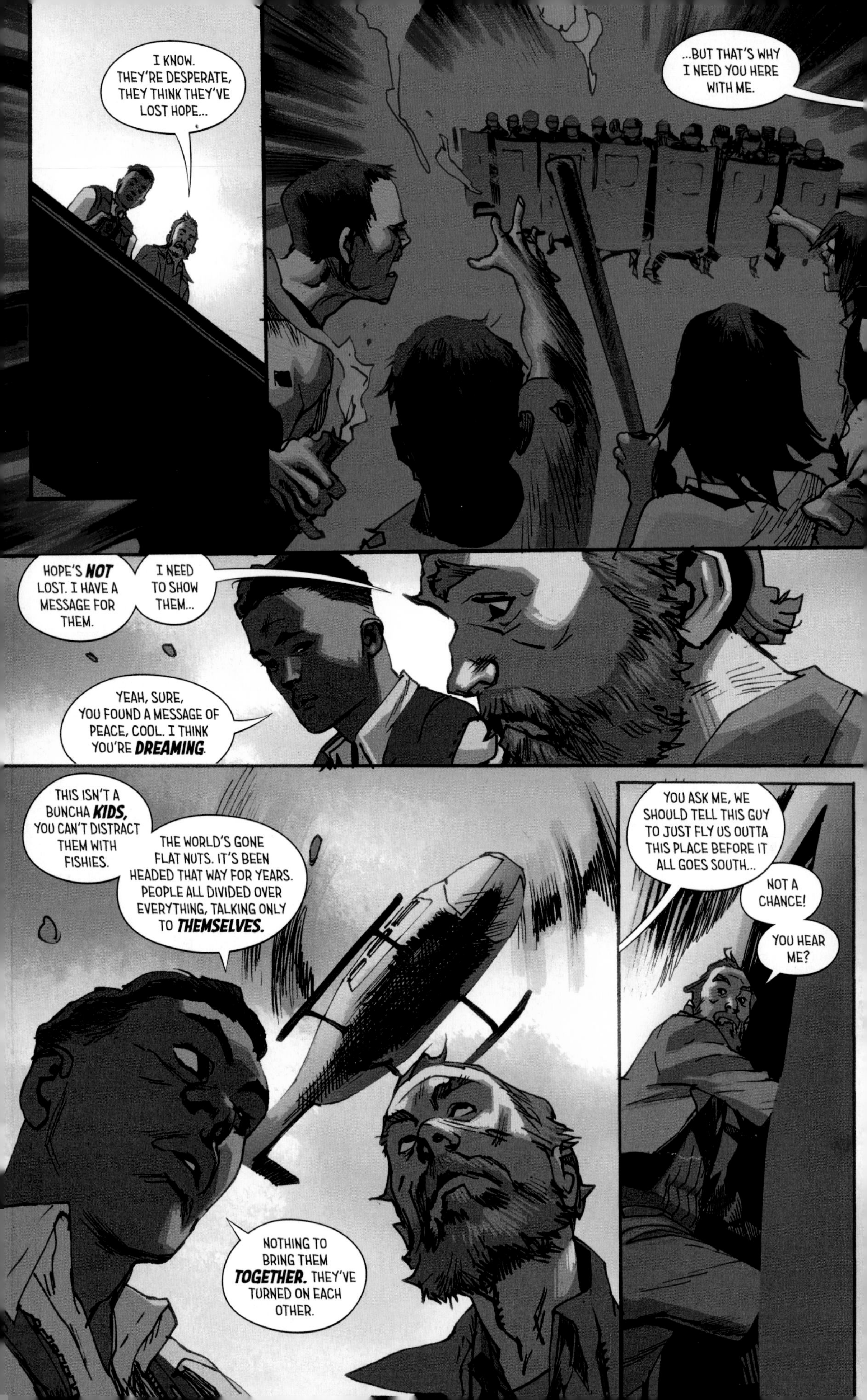
I KNOW. THEY'RE DESPERATE, THEY THINK THEY'VE LOST HOPE...
...BUT THAT'S WHY I NEED YOU HERE WITH ME.
HOPE'S **NOT** LOST. I HAVE A MESSAGE FOR THEM.
I NEED TO SHOW THEM...
YEAH, SURE, YOU FOUND A MESSAGE OF PEACE, COOL. I THINK YOU'RE ***DREAMING***.
THIS ISN'T A BUNCHA ***KIDS,*** YOU CAN'T DISTRACT THEM WITH FISHIES.
THE WORLD'S GONE FLAT NUTS. IT'S BEEN HEADED THAT WAY FOR YEARS. PEOPLE ALL DIVIDED OVER EVERYTHING, TALKING ONLY TO ***THEMSELVES.***
NOTHING TO BRING THEM ***TOGETHER.*** THEY'VE TURNED ON EACH OTHER.
YOU ASK ME, WE SHOULD TELL THIS GUY TO JUST FLY US OUTTA THIS PLACE BEFORE IT ALL GOES SOUTH...
NOT A CHANCE!
YOU HEAR ME?

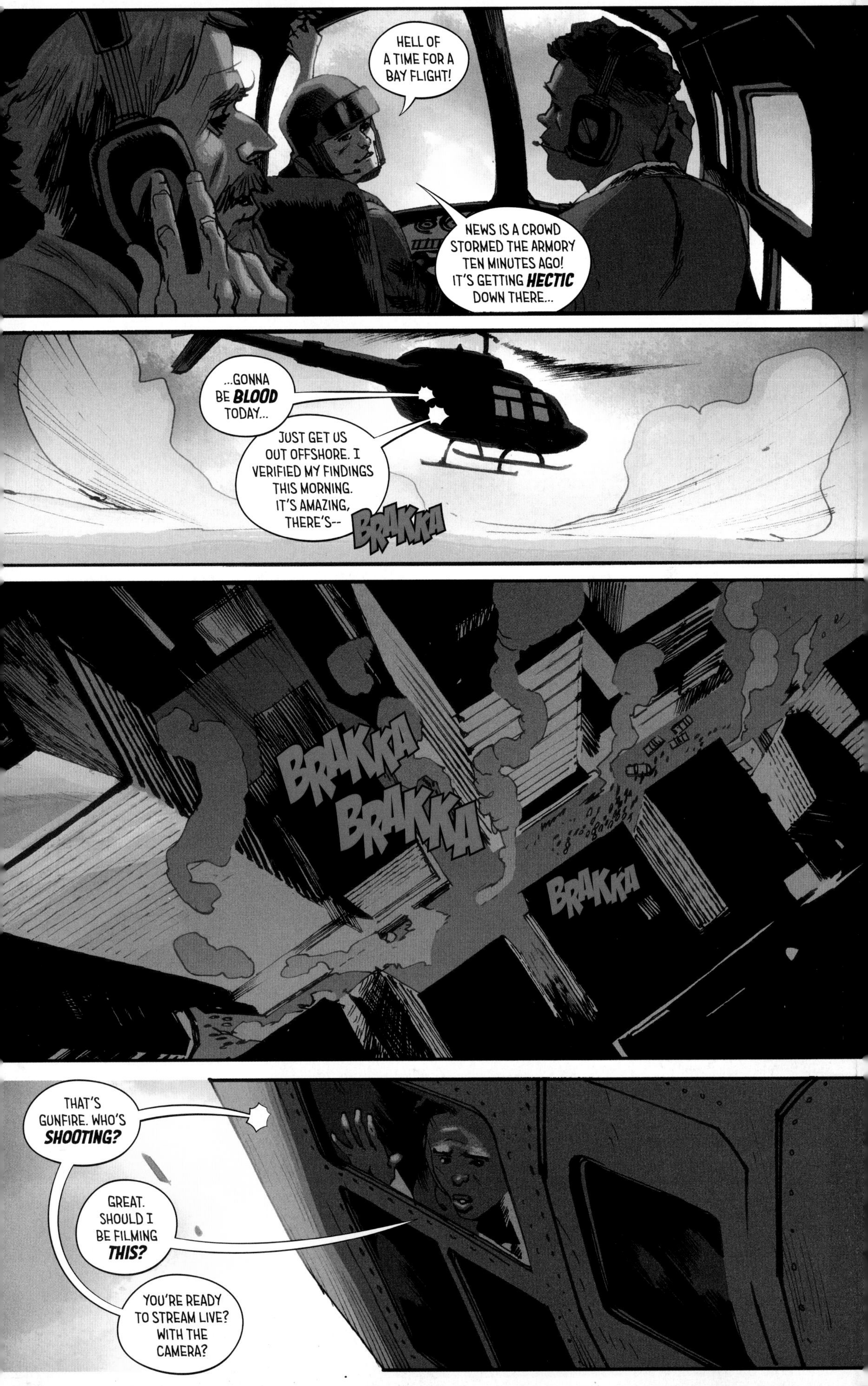
HELL OF A TIME FOR A BAY FLIGHT!
NEWS IS A CROWD STORMED THE ARMORY TEN MINUTES AGO! IT'S GETTING **HECTIC** DOWN THERE...
...GONNA BE **BLOOD** TODAY...
JUST GET US OUT OFFSHORE. I VERIFIED MY FINDINGS THIS MORNING. IT'S AMAZING, THERE'S--
BRAKKA
BRAKKA
BRAKKA
BRAKKA
THAT'S GUNFIRE. WHO'S **SHOOTING?**
GREAT. SHOULD I BE FILMING **THIS?**
YOU'RE READY TO STREAM LIVE? WITH THE CAMERA?

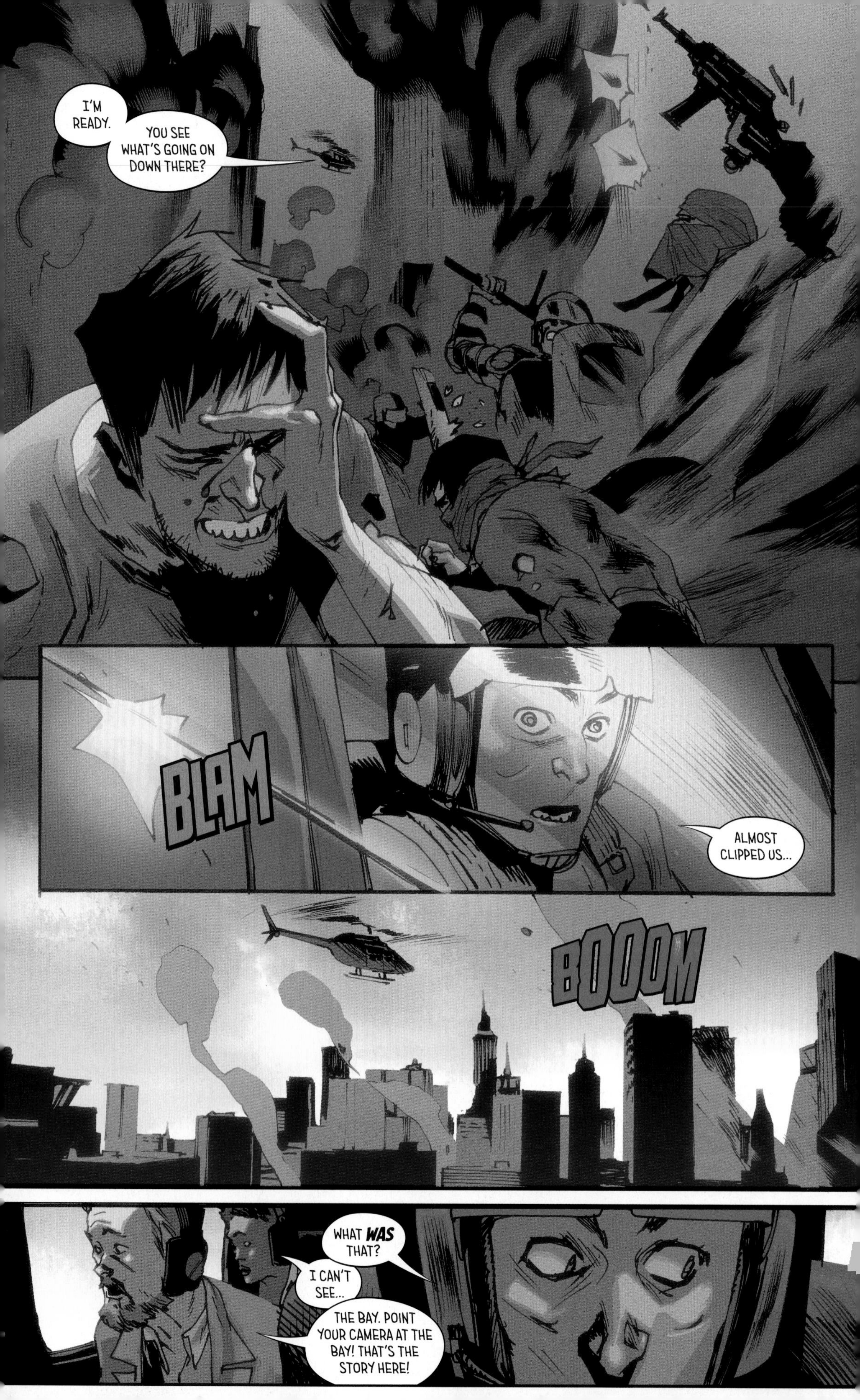
I'M READY.
YOU SEE WHAT'S GOING ON DOWN THERE?
BLAM
ALMOST CLIPPED US...
BOOOM
WHAT **WAS** THAT?
I CAN'T SEE...
THE BAY. POINT YOUR CAMERA AT THE BAY! THAT'S THE STORY HERE!

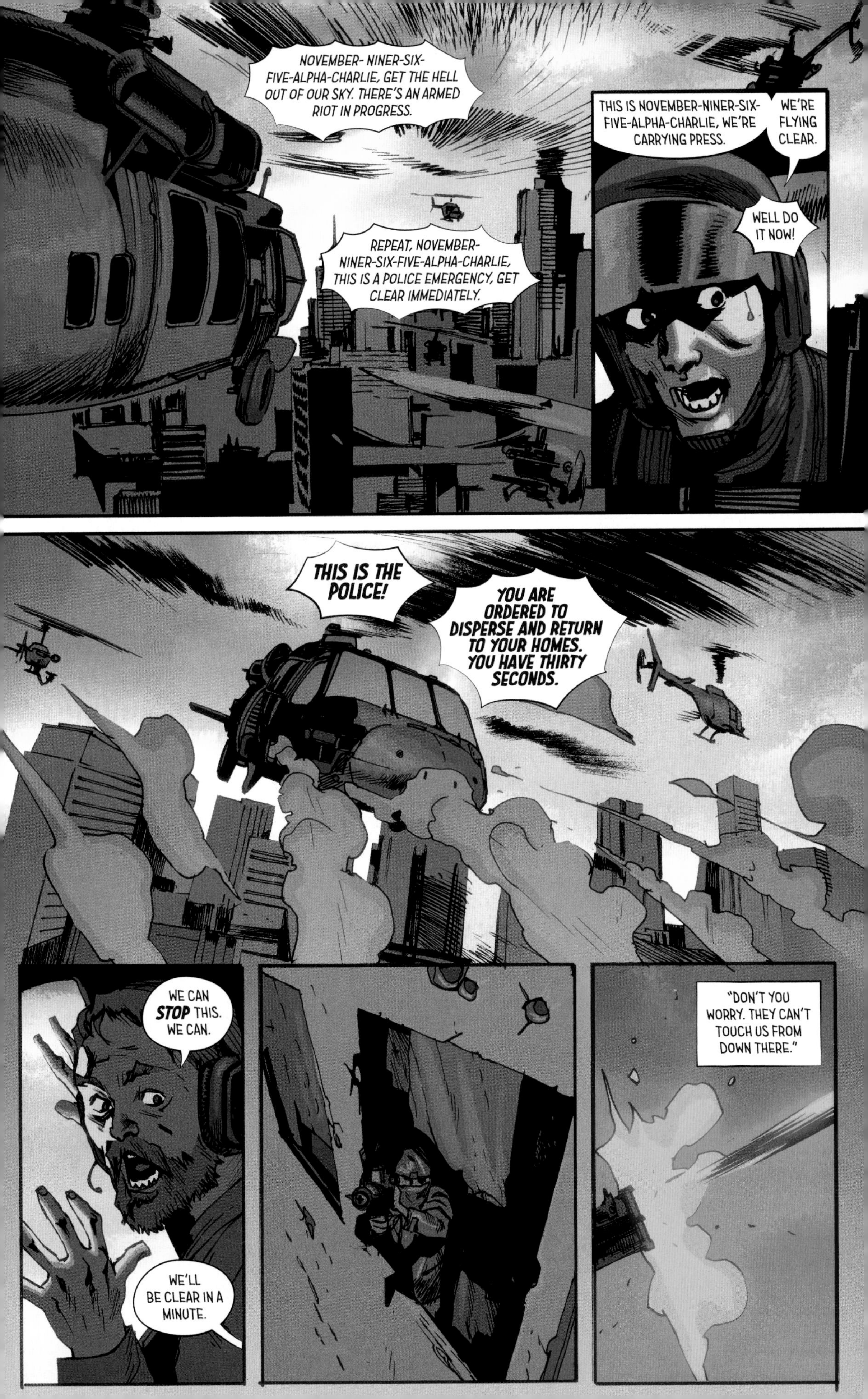
NOVEMBER- NINER-SIX-FIVE-ALPHA-CHARLIE, GET THE HELL OUT OF OUR SKY. THERE'S AN ARMED RIOT IN PROGRESS.
REPEAT, NOVEMBER-NINER-SIX-FIVE-ALPHA-CHARLIE, THIS IS A POLICE EMERGENCY, GET CLEAR IMMEDIATELY.
THIS IS NOVEMBER-NINER-SIX-FIVE-ALPHA-CHARLIE, WE'RE CARRYING PRESS.
WE'RE FLYING CLEAR.
WELL DO IT NOW!
THIS IS THE POLICE!
YOU ARE ORDERED TO DISPERSE AND RETURN TO YOUR HOMES. YOU HAVE THIRTY SECONDS.
WE CAN **STOP** THIS. WE CAN.
WE'LL BE CLEAR IN A MINUTE.
"DON'T YOU WORRY. THEY CAN'T TOUCH US FROM DOWN THERE."

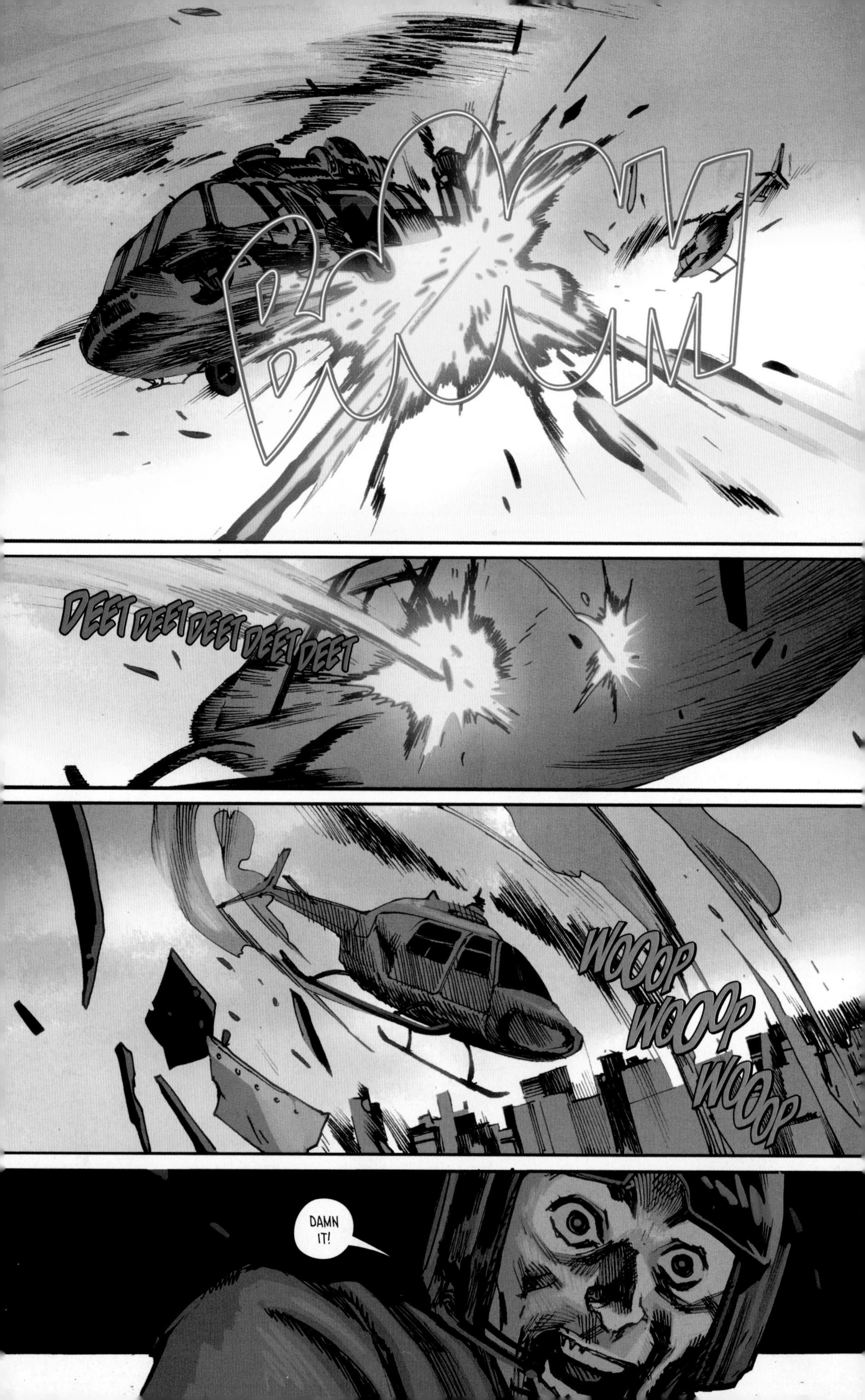
BOOM
DEET DEET DEET DEET DEET
WOOOP WOOOP WOOOP
DAMN IT!

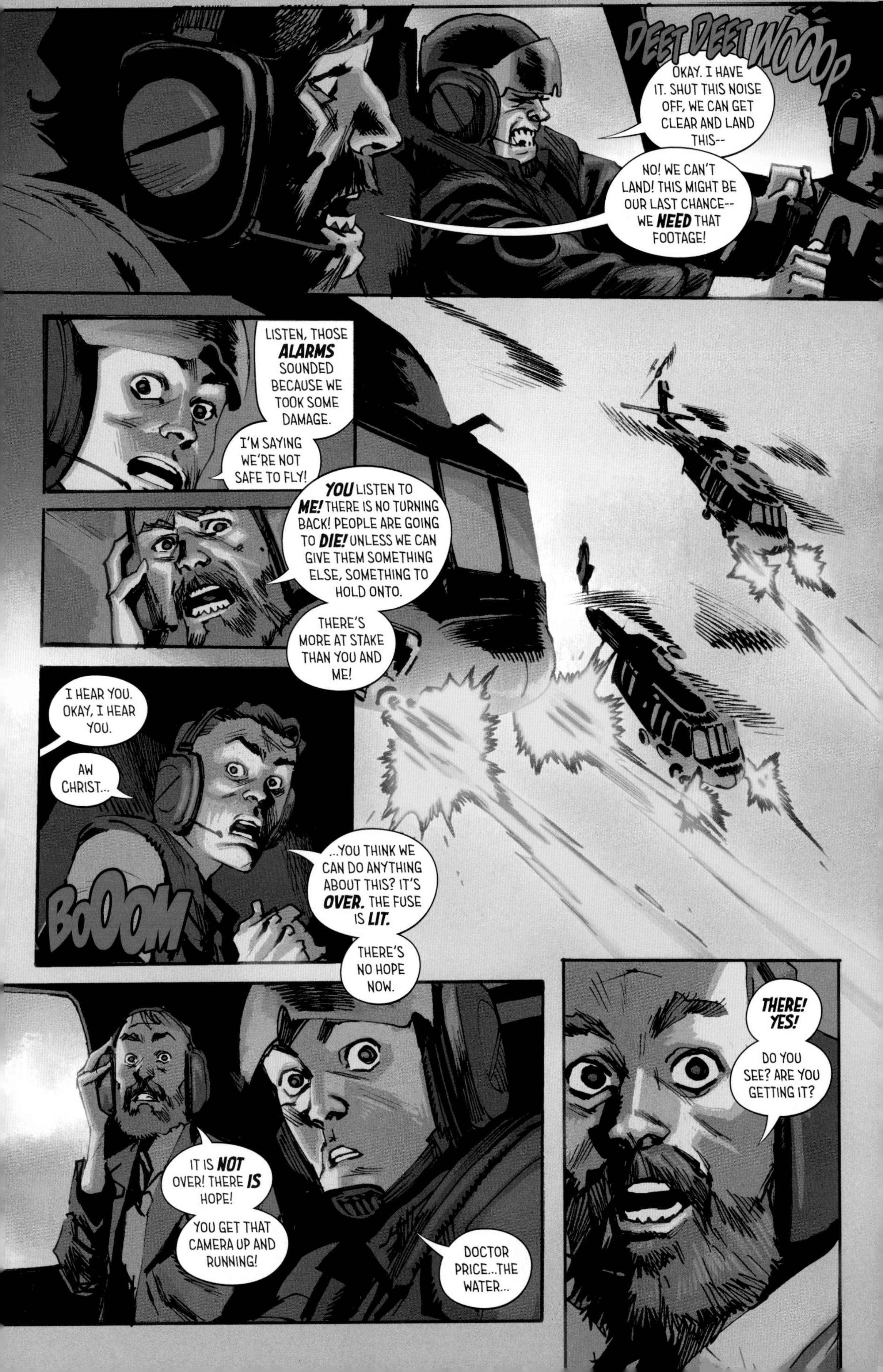
DEET DEET WOOOP
OKAY. I HAVE IT. SHUT THIS NOISE OFF, WE CAN GET CLEAR AND LAND THIS--
NO! WE CAN'T LAND! THIS MIGHT BE OUR LAST CHANCE-- WE NEED THAT FOOTAGE!
LISTEN, THOSE ALARMS SOUNDED BECAUSE WE TOOK SOME DAMAGE.
I'M SAYING WE'RE NOT SAFE TO FLY!
YOU LISTEN TO ME! THERE IS NO TURNING BACK! PEOPLE ARE GOING TO DIE! UNLESS WE CAN GIVE THEM SOMETHING ELSE, SOMETHING TO HOLD ONTO.
THERE'S MORE AT STAKE THAN YOU AND ME!
I HEAR YOU. OKAY, I HEAR YOU.
AW CHRIST...
BOOOM
...YOU THINK WE CAN DO ANYTHING ABOUT THIS? IT'S OVER. THE FUSE IS LIT.
THERE'S NO HOPE NOW.
IT IS NOT OVER! THERE IS HOPE!
YOU GET THAT CAMERA UP AND RUNNING!
DOCTOR PRICE...THE WATER...
THERE! YES!
DO YOU SEE? ARE YOU GETTING IT?

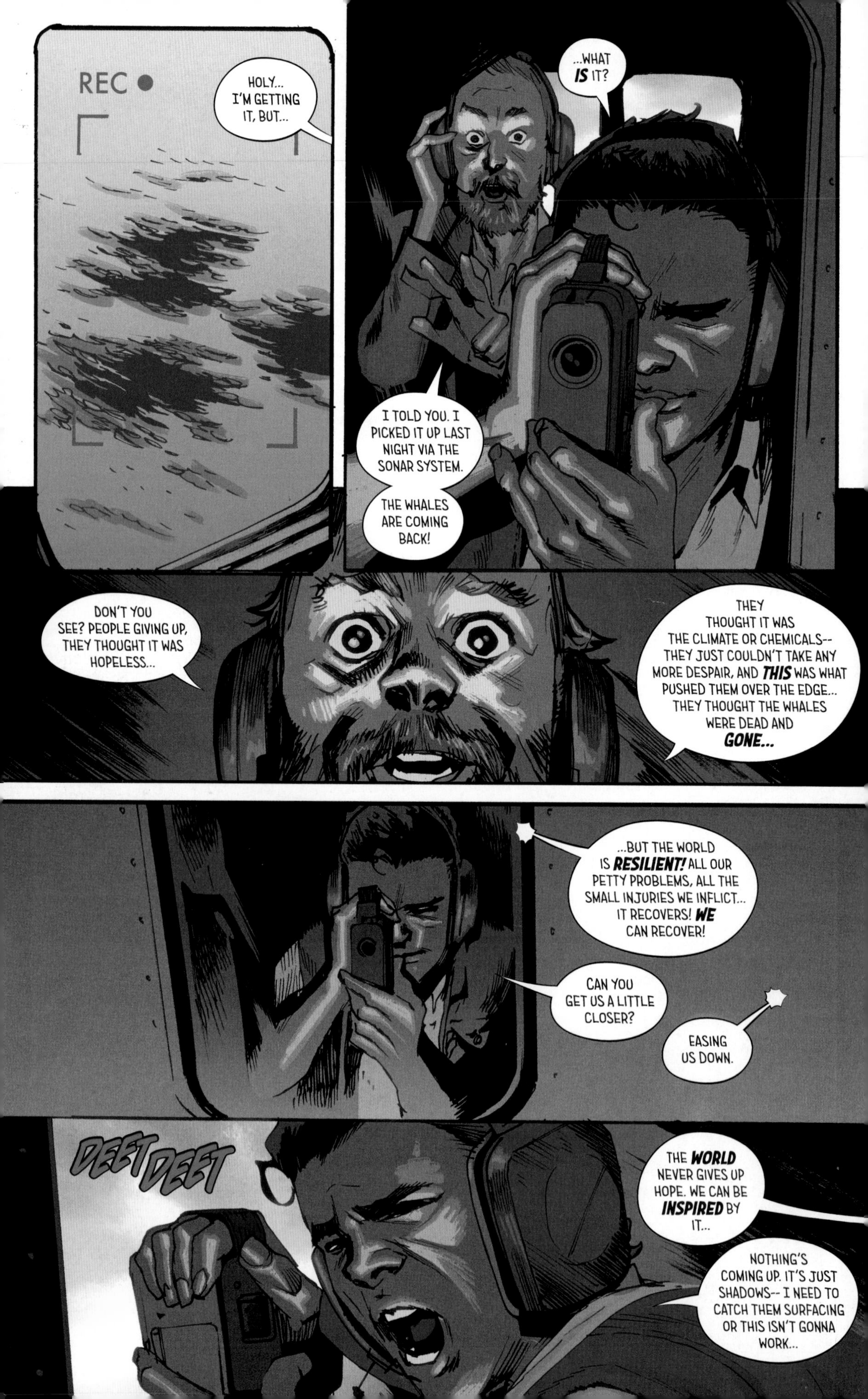
REC
HOLY... I'M GETTING IT, BUT...
...WHAT IS IT?
I TOLD YOU. I PICKED IT UP LAST NIGHT VIA THE SONAR SYSTEM.
THE WHALES ARE COMING BACK!
DON'T YOU SEE? PEOPLE GIVING UP, THEY THOUGHT IT WAS HOPELESS...
THEY THOUGHT IT WAS THE CLIMATE OR CHEMICALS-- THEY JUST COULDN'T TAKE ANY MORE DESPAIR, AND THIS WAS WHAT PUSHED THEM OVER THE EDGE... THEY THOUGHT THE WHALES WERE DEAD AND GONE...
...BUT THE WORLD IS RESILIENT! ALL OUR PETTY PROBLEMS, ALL THE SMALL INJURIES WE INFLICT... IT RECOVERS! WE CAN RECOVER!
CAN YOU GET US A LITTLE CLOSER?
EASING US DOWN.
DEET DEET
THE WORLD NEVER GIVES UP HOPE. WE CAN BE INSPIRED BY IT...
NOTHING'S COMING UP. IT'S JUST SHADOWS-- I NEED TO CATCH THEM SURFACING OR THIS ISN'T GONNA WORK...

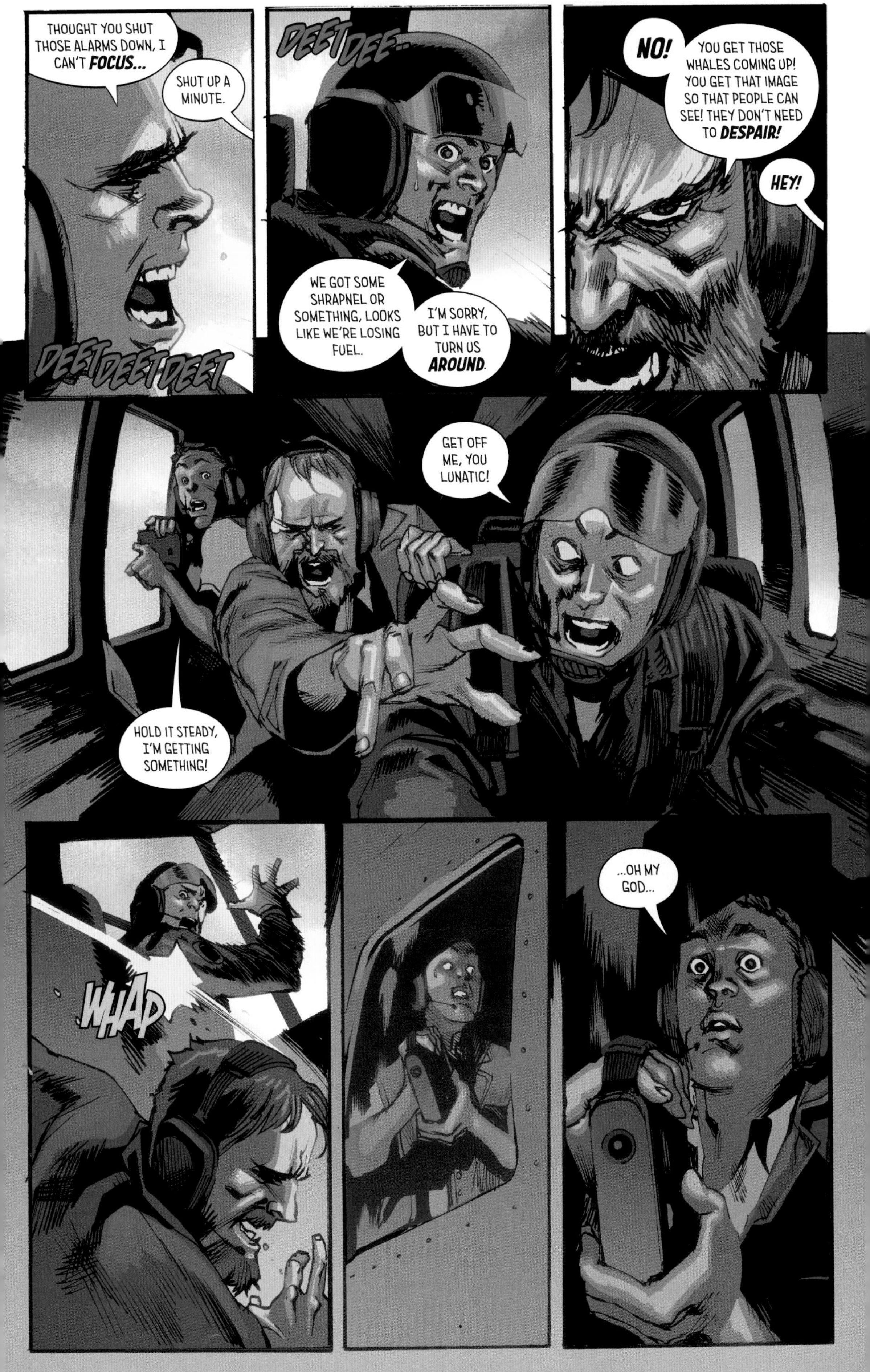
THOUGHT YOU SHUT THOSE ALARMS DOWN, I CAN'T **FOCUS...**
SHUT UP A MINUTE.
DEET DEET DEET DEET
DEET DEE...
WE GOT SOME SHRAPNEL OR SOMETHING, LOOKS LIKE WE'RE LOSING FUEL.
I'M SORRY, BUT I HAVE TO TURN US **AROUND**.
NO!
YOU GET THOSE WHALES COMING UP! YOU GET THAT IMAGE SO THAT PEOPLE CAN SEE! THEY DON'T NEED TO **DESPAIR!**
HEY!
GET OFF ME, YOU LUNATIC!
HOLD IT STEADY, I'M GETTING SOMETHING!
WHAP
...OH MY GOD...

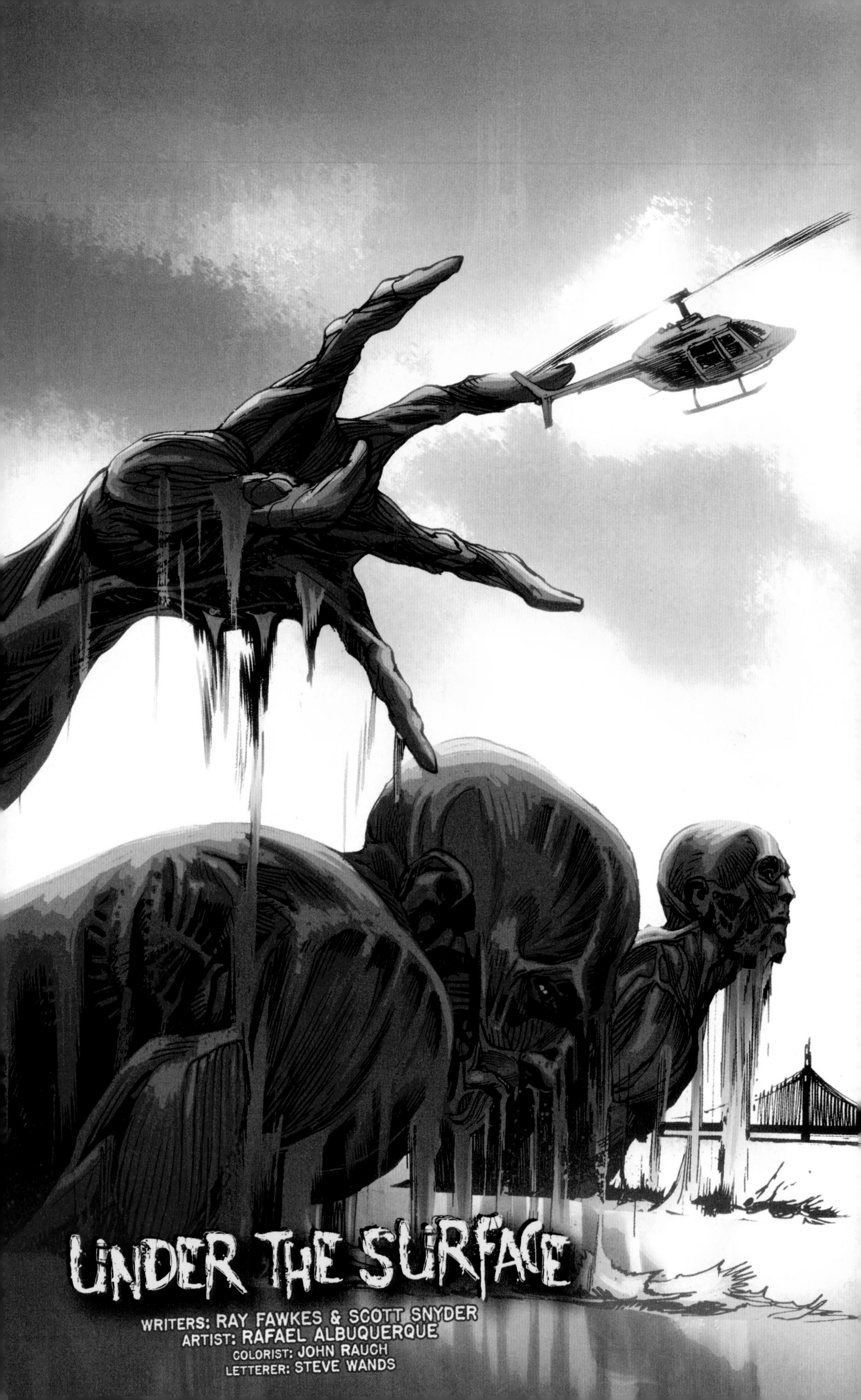
UNDER THE SURFACE
WRITERS: RAY FAWKES & SCOTT SNYDER
ARTIST: RAFAEL ALBUQUERQUE
COLORIST: JOHN RAUCH
LETTERER: STEVE WANDS

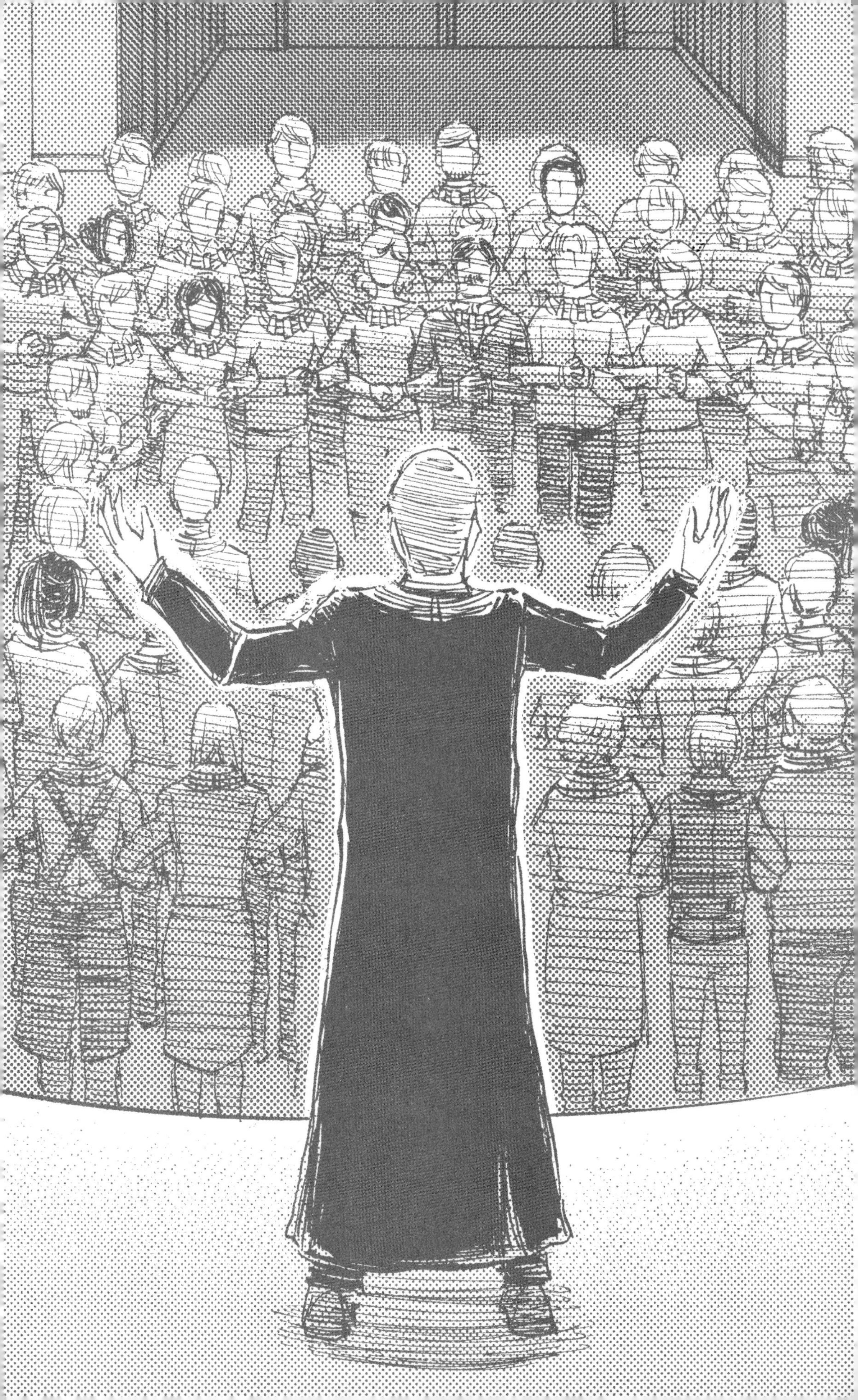

ATTACK on ATTACK on

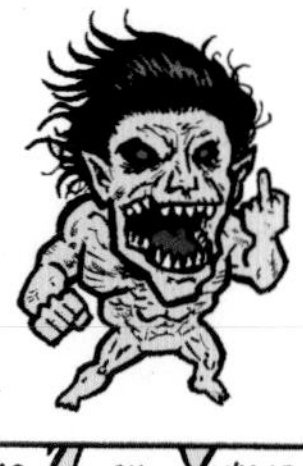

By Evan Dorkin and Sarah Dyer
Flatted and additional colors by Bill Mudron

BITE CLUB

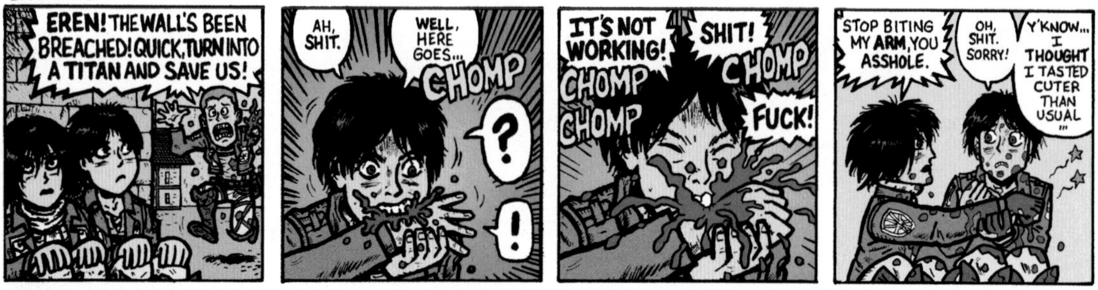

EREN! THE WALL'S BEEN BREACHED! QUICK, TURN INTO A TITAN AND SAVE US!
AH, SHIT.
WELL, HERE GOES...
CHOMP
?
!
IT'S NOT WORKING!
SHIT!
CHOMP
CHOMP
CHOMP
FUCK!
STOP BITING MY ARM, YOU ASSHOLE.
OH, SHIT. SORRY!
Y'KNOW... I THOUGHT I TASTED CUTER THAN USUAL ...

INSECURITY ISSUES

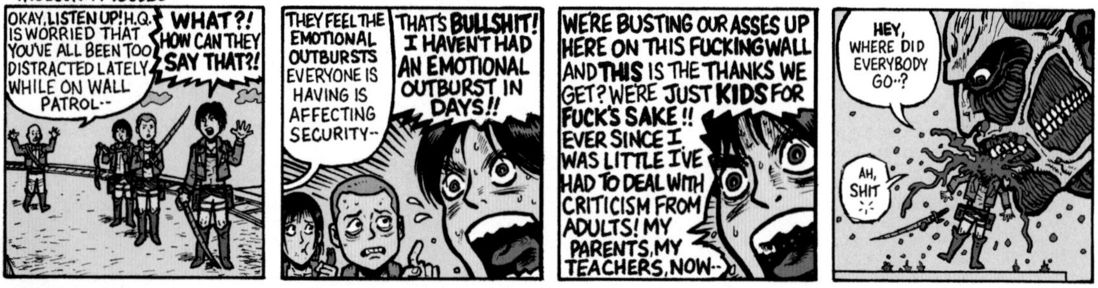

OKAY, LISTEN UP! H.Q. IS WORRIED THAT YOU'VE ALL BEEN TOO DISTRACTED LATELY WHILE ON WALL PATROL--
WHAT?! HOW CAN THEY SAY THAT?!
THEY FEEL THE EMOTIONAL OUTBURSTS EVERYONE IS HAVING IS AFFECTING SECURITY--
THAT'S BULLSHIT! I HAVEN'T HAD AN EMOTIONAL OUTBURST IN DAYS!!
WE'RE BUSTING OUR ASSES UP HERE ON THIS FUCKING WALL AND THIS IS THE THANKS WE GET? WE'RE JUST KIDS FOR FUCK'S SAKE!! EVER SINCE I WAS LITTLE I'VE HAD TO DEAL WITH CRITICISM FROM ADULTS! MY PARENTS, MY TEACHERS, NOW--
HEY, WHERE DID EVERYBODY GO..?
AH, SHIT

THE #1 QUESTION

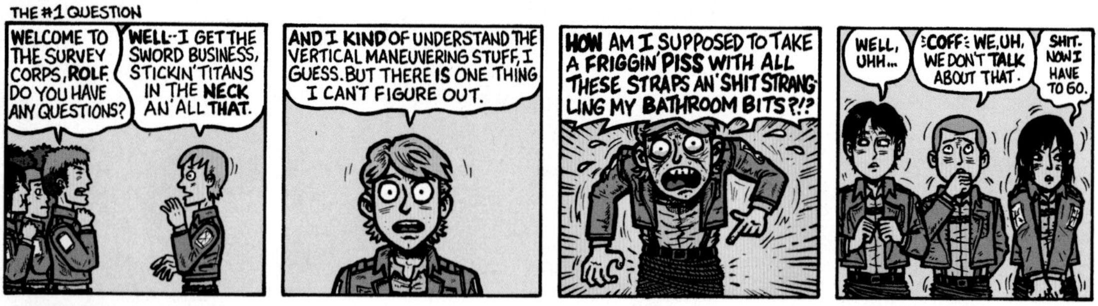

WELCOME TO THE SURVEY CORPS, ROLF. DO YOU HAVE ANY QUESTIONS?
WELL-- I GET THE SWORD BUSINESS, STICKIN' TITANS IN THE NECK AN' ALL THAT.
AND I KIND OF UNDERSTAND THE VERTICAL MANEUVERING STUFF, I GUESS. BUT THERE IS ONE THING I CAN'T FIGURE OUT.
HOW AM I SUPPOSED TO TAKE A FRIGGIN' PISS WITH ALL THESE STRAPS AN' SHIT STRANGLING MY BATHROOM BITS?!?
WELL, UHH...
COFF WE, UH, WE DON'T TALK ABOUT THAT.
SHIT- NOW I HAVE TO GO.

ANOTHER SHTICK IN THE WALL

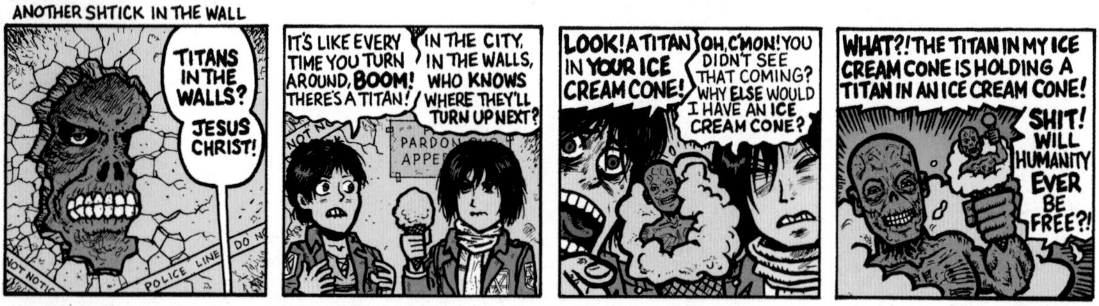

TITANS IN THE WALLS?
JESUS CHRIST!
POLICE LINE
IT'S LIKE EVERY TIME YOU TURN AROUND, BOOM! THERE'S A TITAN!
IN THE CITY, IN THE WALLS, WHO KNOWS WHERE THEY'LL TURN UP NEXT?
LOOK! A TITAN IN YOUR ICE CREAM CONE!
OH, C'MON! YOU DIDN'T SEE THAT COMING? WHY ELSE WOULD I HAVE AN ICE CREAM CONE?
WHAT?! THE TITAN IN MY ICE CREAM CONE IS HOLDING A TITAN IN AN ICE CREAM CONE!
SHIT! WILL HUMANITY EVER BE FREE?!

LESSER-KNOWN ABNORMAL TITANS

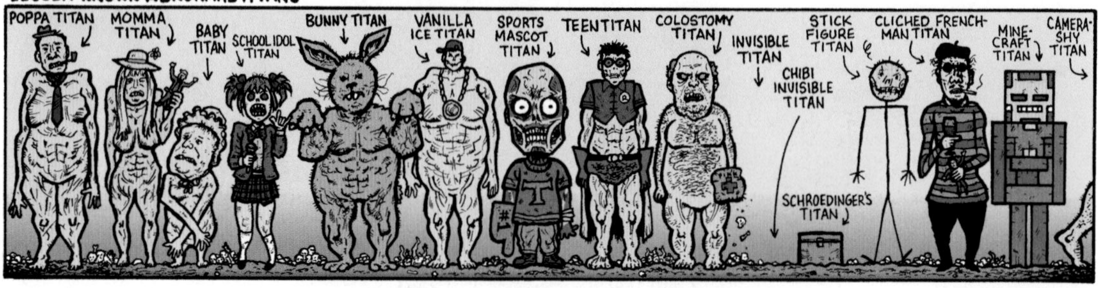

POPPA TITAN
MOMMA TITAN
BABY TITAN
SCHOOL IDOL TITAN
BUNNY TITAN
VANILLA ICE TITAN
SPORTS MASCOT TITAN
TEEN TITAN
COLOSTOMY TITAN
INVISIBLE TITAN
CHIBI INVISIBLE TITAN
STICK FIGURE TITAN
CLICHED FRENCH-MAN TITAN
MINE-CRAFT TITAN
CAMERA-SHY TITAN
SCHROEDINGER'S TITAN

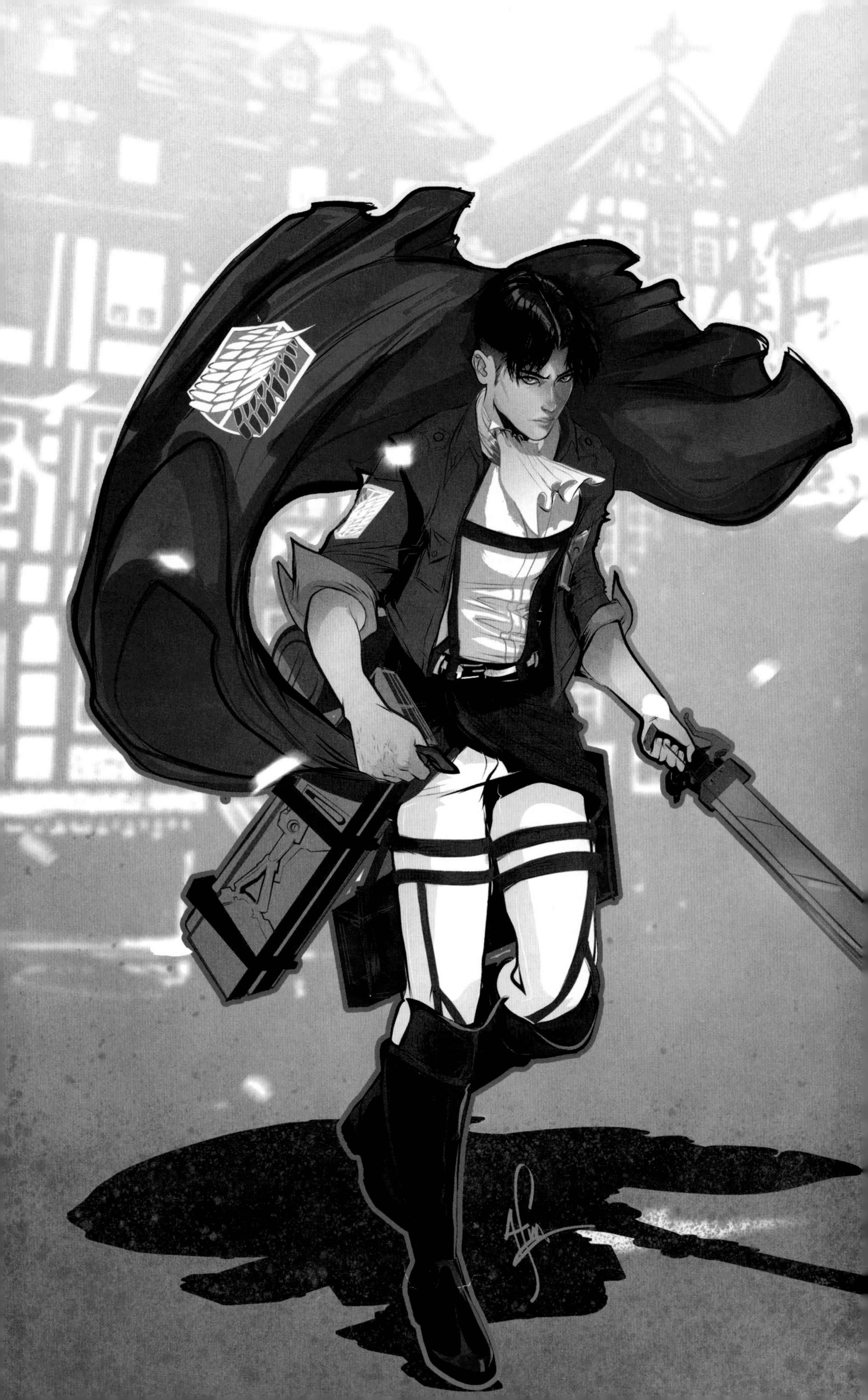

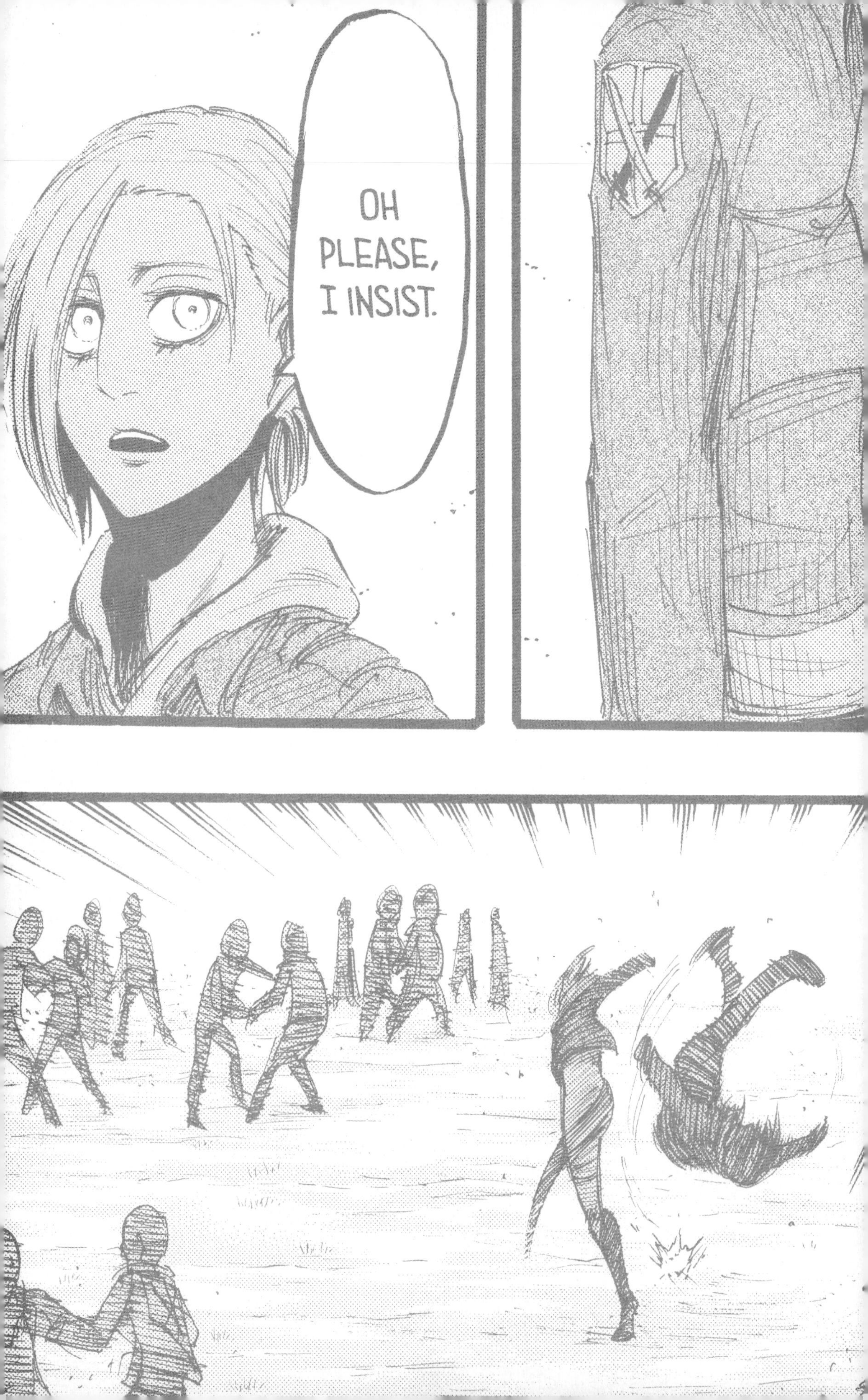
OH PLEASE, I INSIST.

An Illustrated Guide to the Glorious Walled Cities

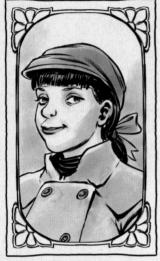

THE AUTHOR, a young adventurer of excellent reputation

By Hilde Gartner

MITRAS QUARTERLY proudly offers this GUIDE from a fearless traveler, the finest serial ever assembled, for your reading pleasure. —Paul Bergen, Editor

I was just a girl when my father took us to celebrate the seventy-fifth year safe within the Walls. We lived in a small village; it took a week just to reach Wall Maria.

Here I touched a Wall for the first time - feeling brave, with my father to protect me from the rumbling footsteps of Titans far beyond! - but my mother drew me aside and bade me look at the valley below us, with villages and the comforting green forest and, so far off I could hardly see it, Wall Rose.

"Remember," she told me, "the miracle of the Walls is not what they are, but what they make possible."

I have taken her words to heart; this travel guide is a study of the world within the Walls.

—FOR MY FAMILY

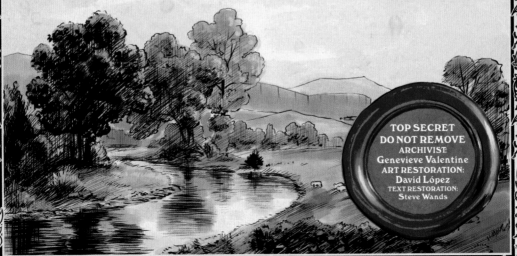

TOP SECRET
DO NOT REMOVE
ARCHIVIST:
Genevieve Valentine
ART RESTORATION:
David López
TEXT RESTORATION:
Steve Wands

The Glorious

WALL MARIA

Klorva

Yarckel

The Joys of Wall Maria

It pains me to hear the outer wall spoken of merely as a perimeter. (Your humble author must admit some partiality here, from her own youth in Merseburg in the Western plain.) However, more objective eyes than mine have sung the praises of the Marian miles; anyone who has laid eyes on the rolling hills and vast forests inside Wall Maria can attest that these lands are unparalleled for their untamed appeal.

True, the traveler here must be prepared to ride long hours and to sleep beneath the stars when villages are scarce, but what is life without risk – what is a night without stars?

Discover Wall Maria for yourself!

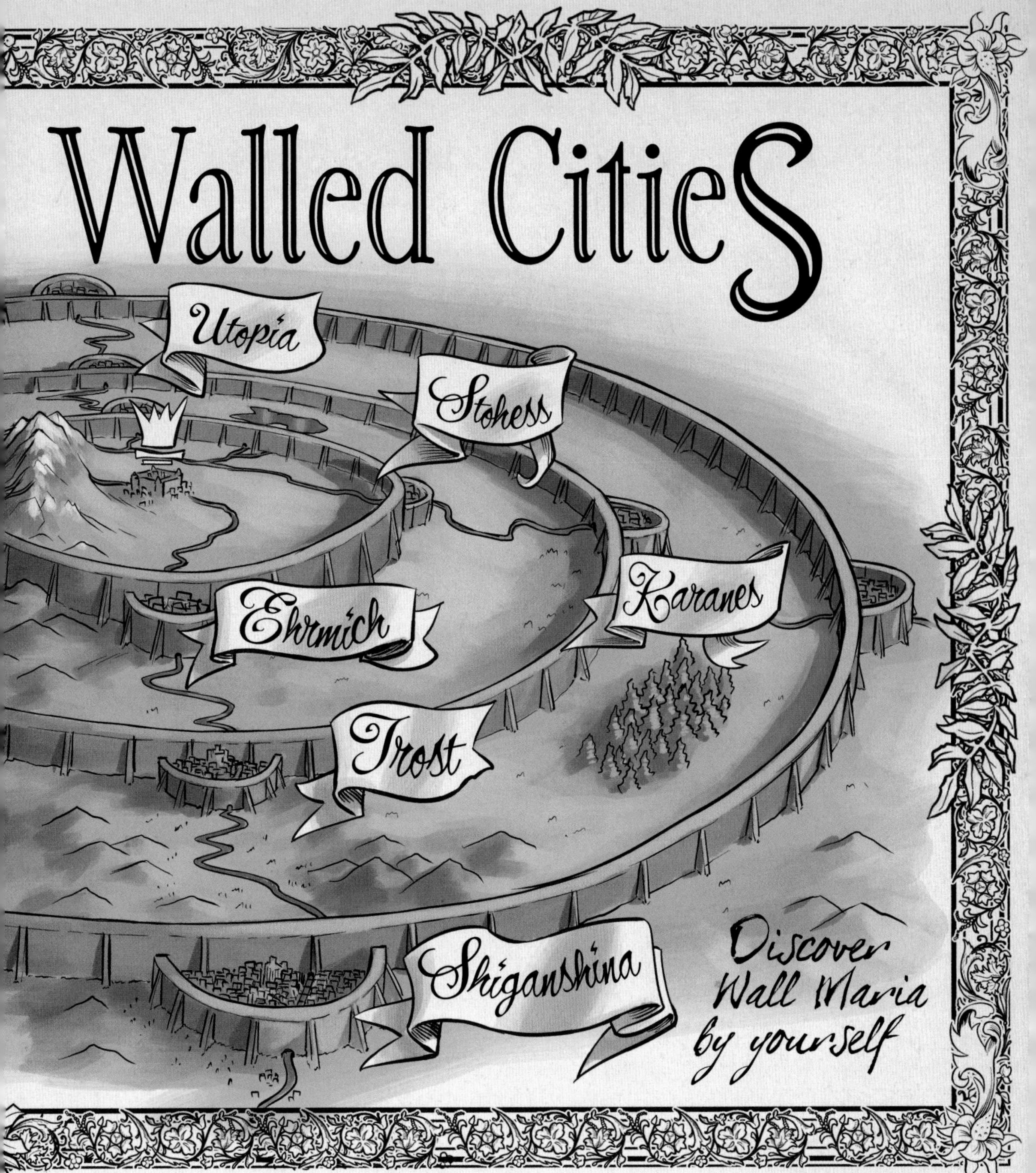
Walled Cities
Utopia
Stohess
Ehrmich
Karanes
Trost
Shiganshina
Discover Wall Maria by yourself

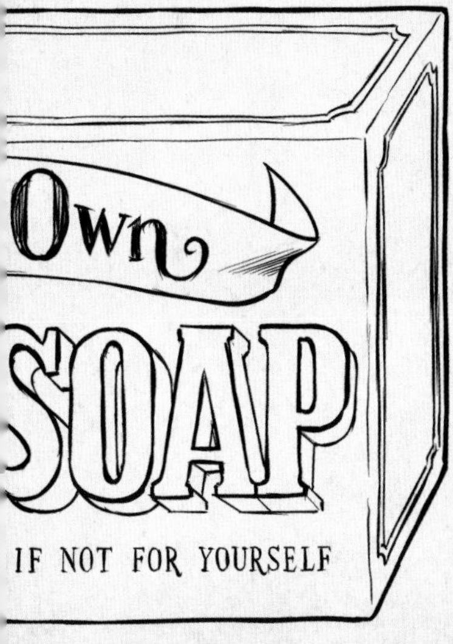
Own
SOAP
IF NOT FOR YOURSELF

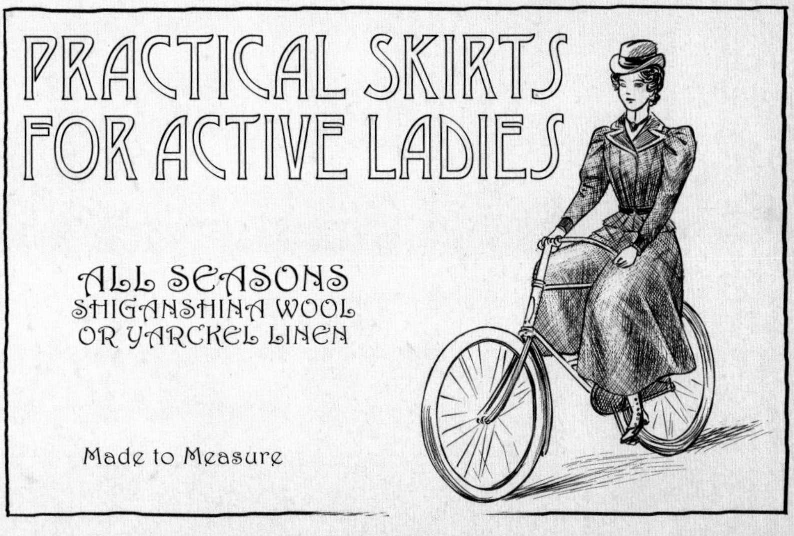
PRACTICAL SKIRTS FOR ACTIVE LADIES
ALL SEASONS
SHIGANSHINA WOOL
OR YARCKEL LINEN
Made to Measure

SHIGANSHINA

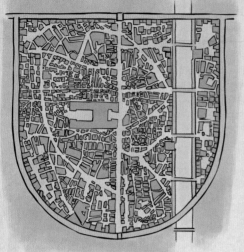

Shiganshina Market began from necessity, but a century later, this is the best shopping in the outer districts.

The discerning traveler will notice fine woodwork, and wool – as delicate as in our capital, Mitras, for a tenth of the price! (Some merchants, it must be said, will put on airs. Avoid them without regret – there are far better around the corner!)

And when you get fatigued, a cider stand beneath the clocktower refreshes like a magic spring.

Open daily, rain or shine, but the archways of this District are narrow – go early to avoid traffic.

The remoteness of the north is matched only by its wild beauty. The sharp hills past Utopia are rocky in summer and troublesome in winter (your intrepid writer, without a nearby village to hire a sledge, snowshoed ten miles to reach the gates), but sledding quickly restores the spirits.

In the fall months, after first snow, one can even arrange to scale Mount Aegil. For courageous travelers only, to be sure, but oh, what awaits you!

[This is, it must be noted, not a destination for children easily frightened; Ms. Gartner records the roar of far-off Titans mingling with the winds. - Ed.]

But the most beautiful landscape inside the Walls is yet to come...

The Forest Of Giant Trees

For any who can manage the journey, the Forest should not be missed. Its size, the surroundings and their eternal spring, the deep stillness found under its trees; it is unlike anywhere else in the world.

Tent accommodations are available year-round. Buy your food from open-air vendors – pine-smoked river fish is without equal! – and join one of the many public excursions. Don't neglect lamps for your party; the forest is always in twilight! (Public tours only, kind readers; going alone is forbidden.)

Charming Karanes

For more cosmopolitan holidays, visit Karanes, Eastern jewel! Its quaint riverside is matched only by the hospitality of its people.

The TWO LAMBS INN offers old-world charm; the Quarterly recommends the dormer-window room, which looks out over the canal and the city center.

A taste of Stohess luxury on the outer wall, The QUEEN MARIA offers full suites with private balconies. Forest tours offered daily.

And THE FOREST TOWER INN provides a view of the whole inner city; soar like a bird even within district walls!

Next issue: Hilde Journeys To Adventures in Wall Rose!

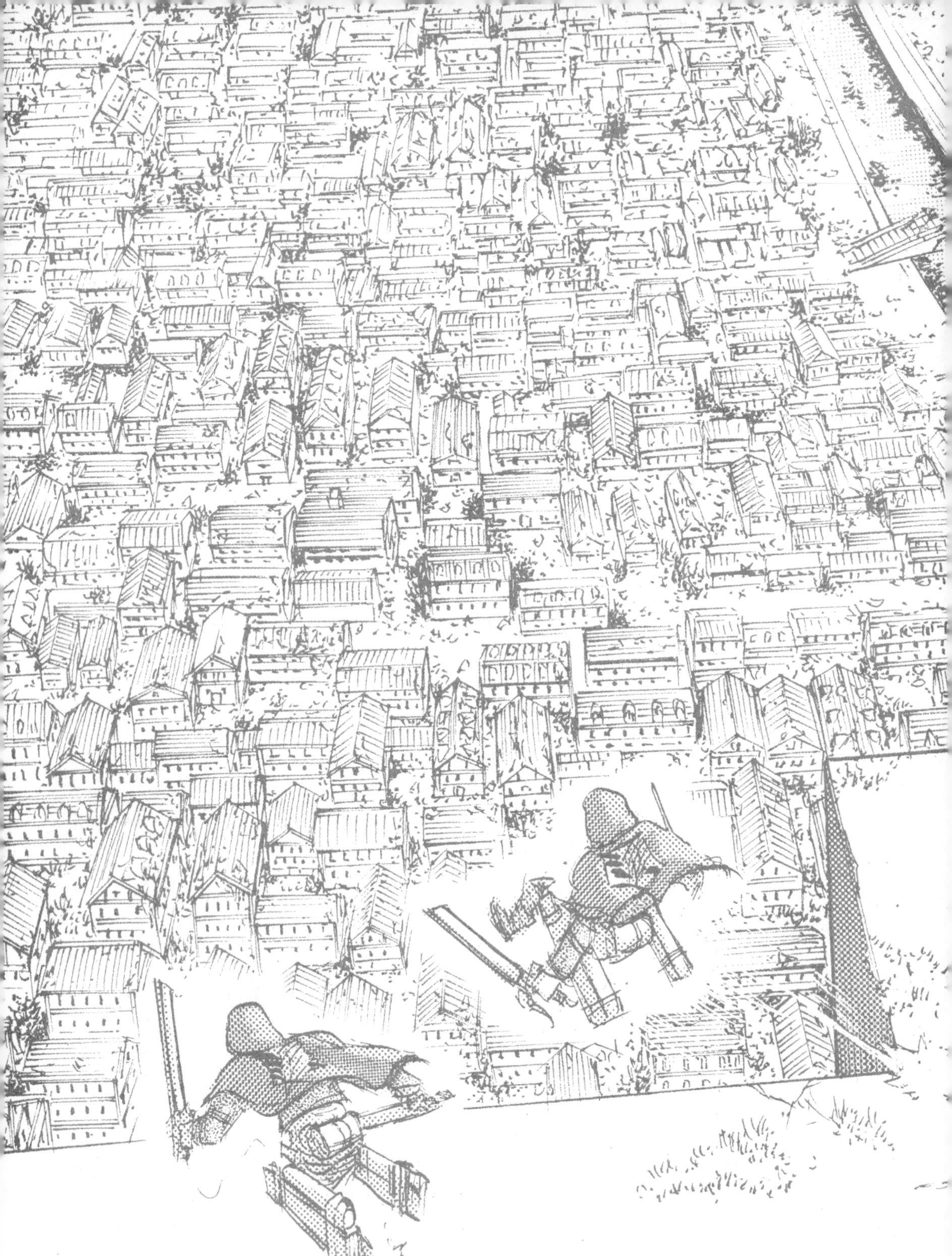

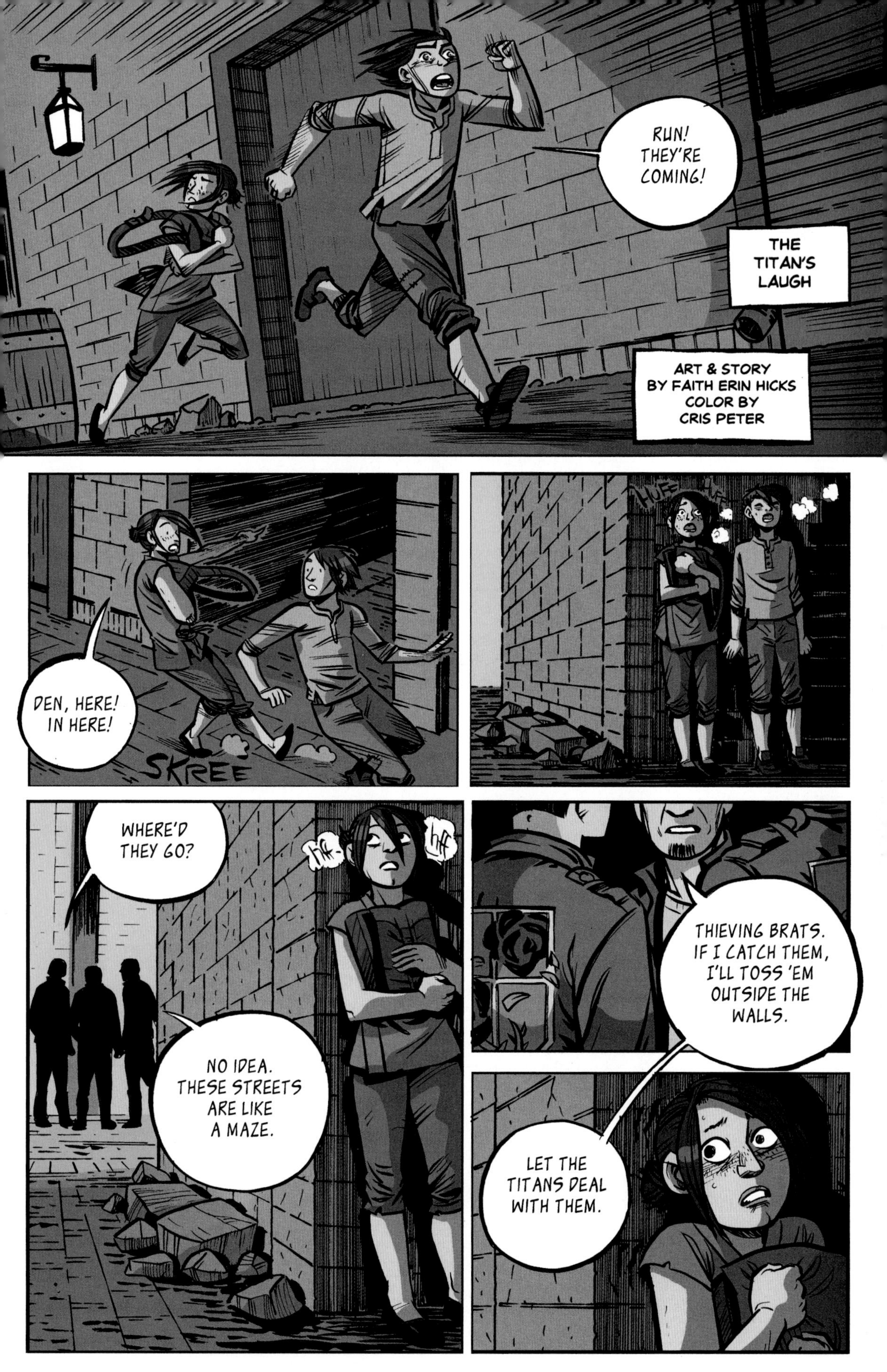
RUN! THEY'RE COMING!
THE TITAN'S LAUGH
ART & STORY BY FAITH ERIN HICKS COLOR BY CRIS PETER
DEN, HERE! IN HERE!
SKREE
HUFF HUFF
WHERE'D THEY GO?
hff hff
NO IDEA. THESE STREETS ARE LIKE A MAZE.
THIEVING BRATS. IF I CATCH THEM, I'LL TOSS 'EM OUTSIDE THE WALLS.
LET THE TITANS DEAL WITH THEM.

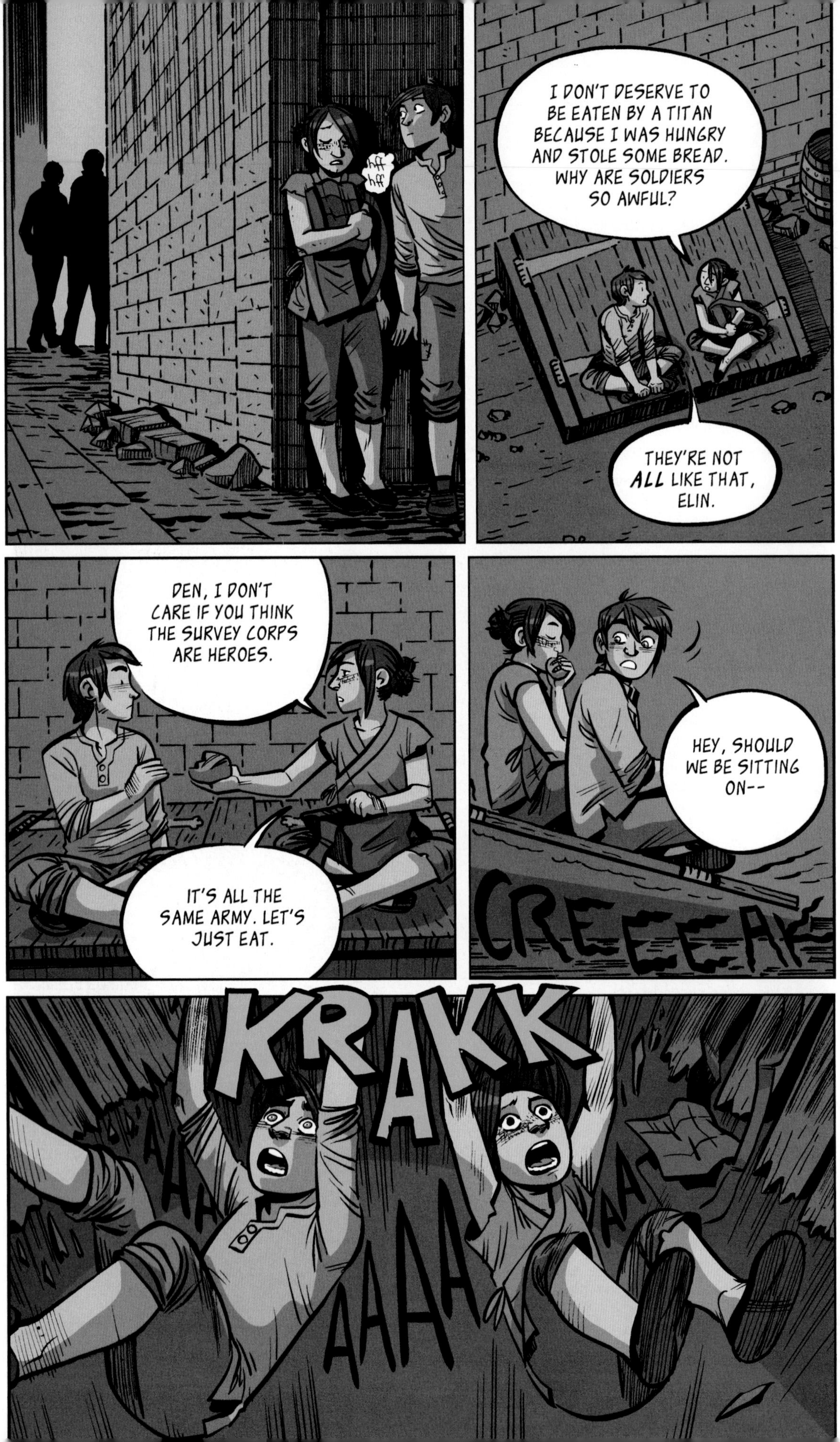
hff hff
I DON'T DESERVE TO BE EATEN BY A TITAN BECAUSE I WAS HUNGRY AND STOLE SOME BREAD. WHY ARE SOLDIERS SO AWFUL?
THEY'RE NOT **ALL** LIKE THAT, ELIN.
DEN, I DON'T CARE IF YOU THINK THE SURVEY CORPS ARE HEROES.
IT'S ALL THE SAME ARMY. LET'S JUST EAT.
HEY, SHOULD WE BE SITTING ON--
CREEEAK
KRAKK
AAAA

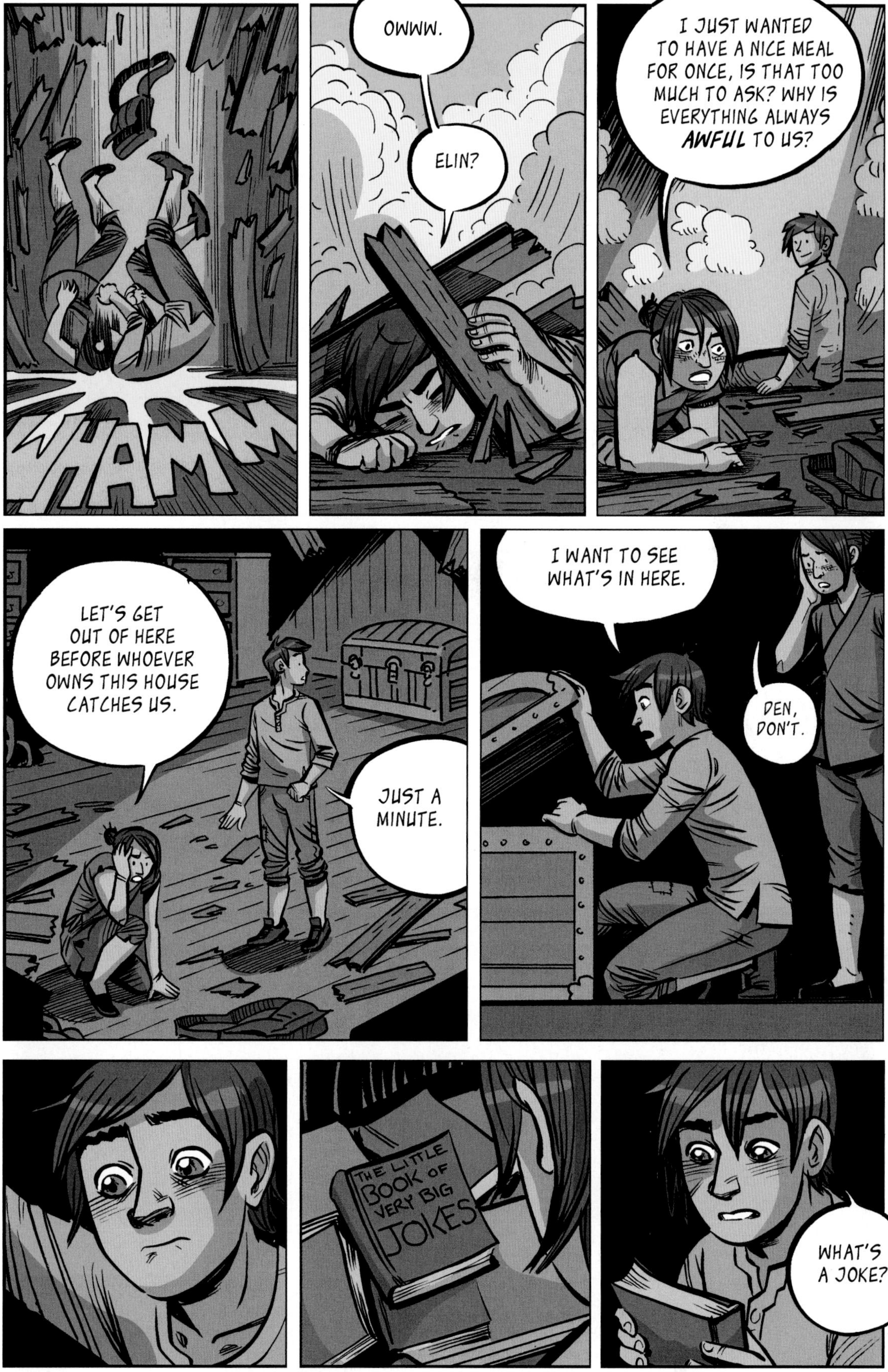
WHAMM
OWWW.
ELIN?
I JUST WANTED TO HAVE A NICE MEAL FOR ONCE, IS THAT TOO MUCH TO ASK? WHY IS EVERYTHING ALWAYS AWFUL TO US?
LET'S GET OUT OF HERE BEFORE WHOEVER OWNS THIS HOUSE CATCHES US.
JUST A MINUTE.
I WANT TO SEE WHAT'S IN HERE.
DEN, DON'T.
THE LITTLE BOOK OF VERY BIG JOKES
WHAT'S A JOKE?

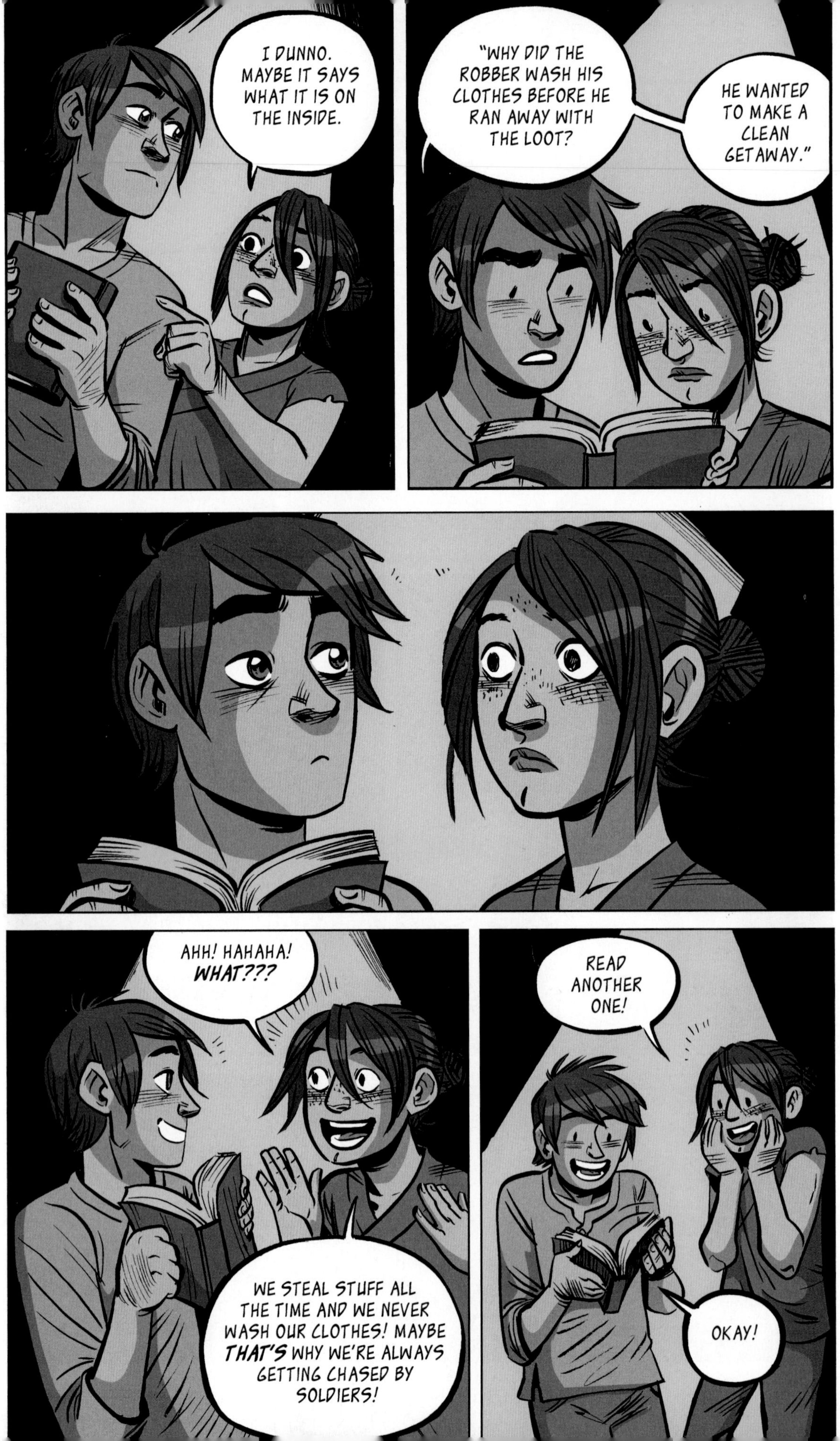
I DUNNO. MAYBE IT SAYS WHAT IT IS ON THE INSIDE.
"WHY DID THE ROBBER WASH HIS CLOTHES BEFORE HE RAN AWAY WITH THE LOOT?
HE WANTED TO MAKE A CLEAN GETAWAY."
AHH! HAHAHA! ***WHAT???***
WE STEAL STUFF ALL THE TIME AND WE NEVER WASH OUR CLOTHES! MAYBE ***THAT'S*** WHY WE'RE ALWAYS GETTING CHASED BY SOLDIERS!
READ ANOTHER ONE!
OKAY!

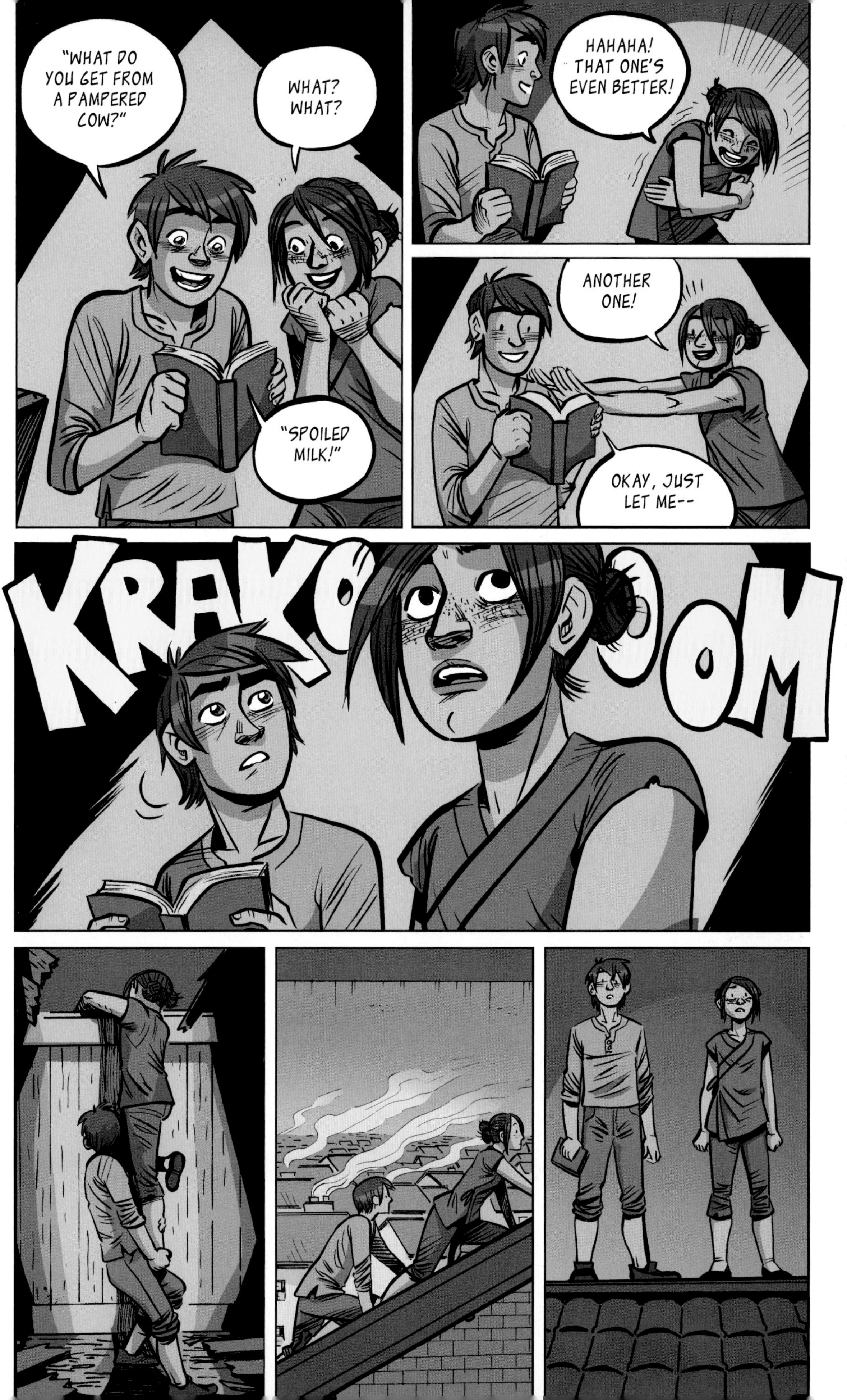
"WHAT DO YOU GET FROM A PAMPERED COW?"
WHAT? WHAT?
"SPOILED MILK!"
HAHAHA! THAT ONE'S EVEN BETTER!
ANOTHER ONE!
OKAY, JUST LET ME--
KRAKOOOM

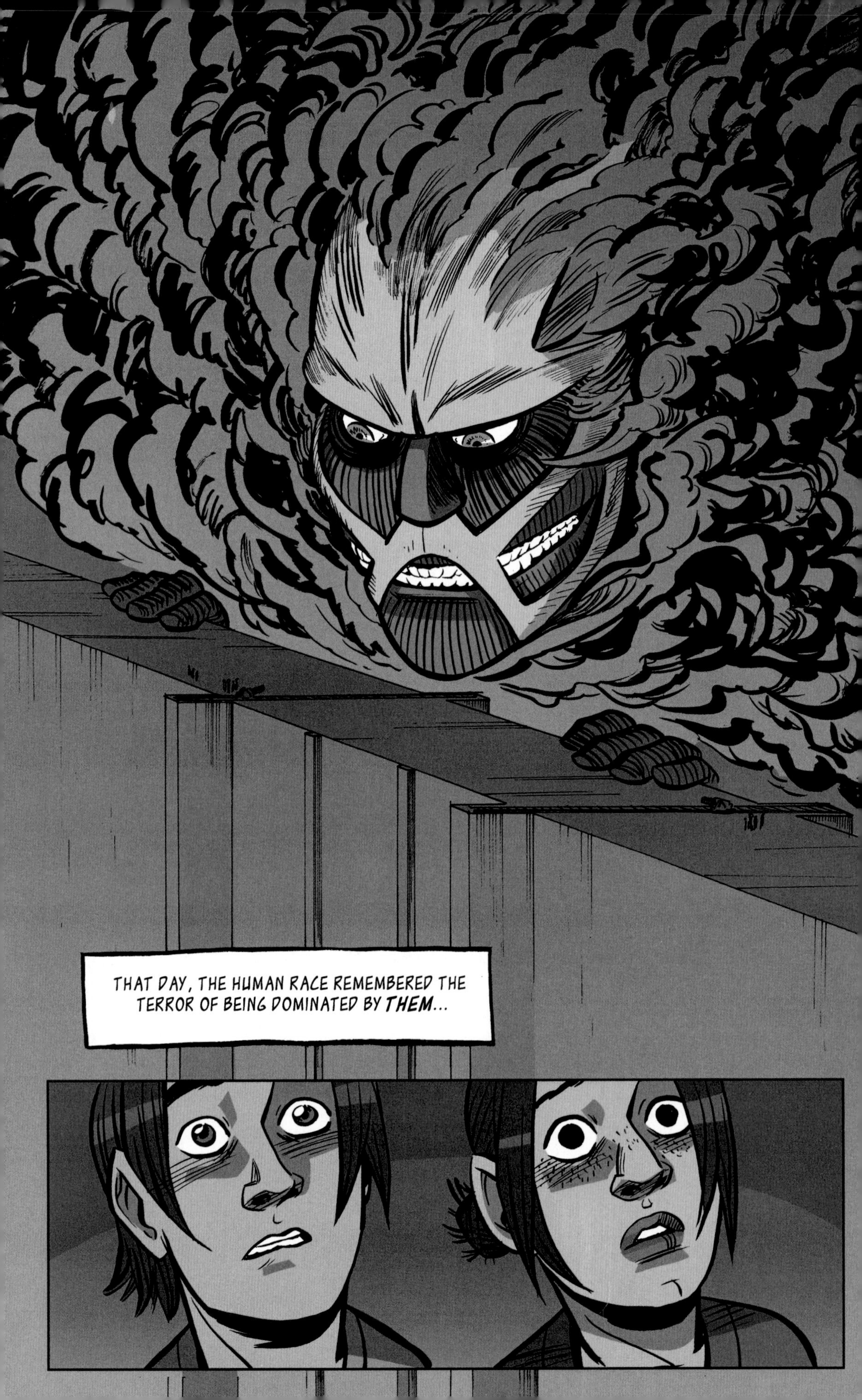
THAT DAY, THE HUMAN RACE REMEMBERED THE TERROR OF BEING DOMINATED BY *THEM*...

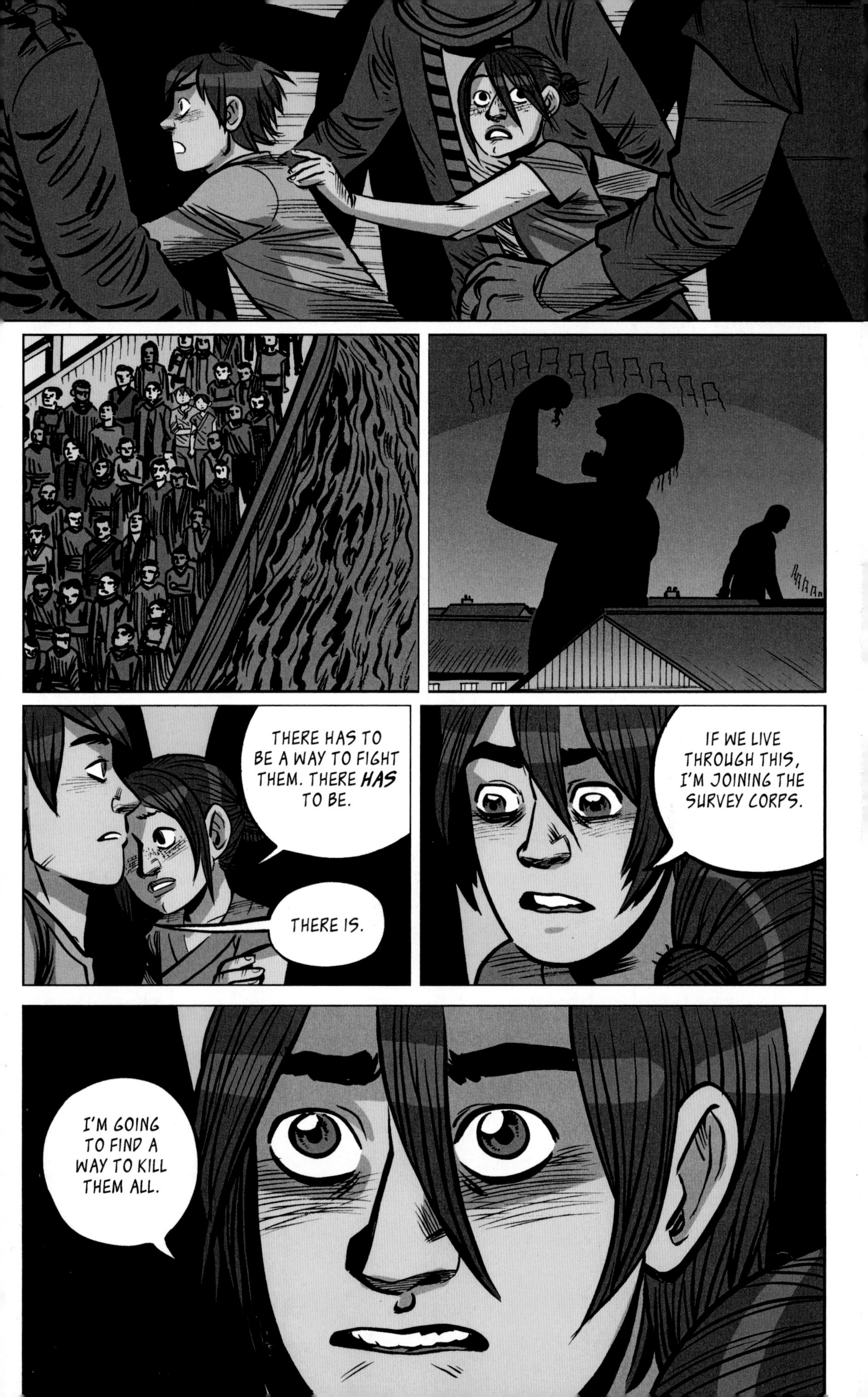
THERE HAS TO BE A WAY TO FIGHT THEM. THERE *HAS* TO BE.
THERE IS.
IF WE LIVE THROUGH THIS, I'M JOINING THE SURVEY CORPS.
I'M GOING TO FIND A WAY TO KILL THEM ALL.

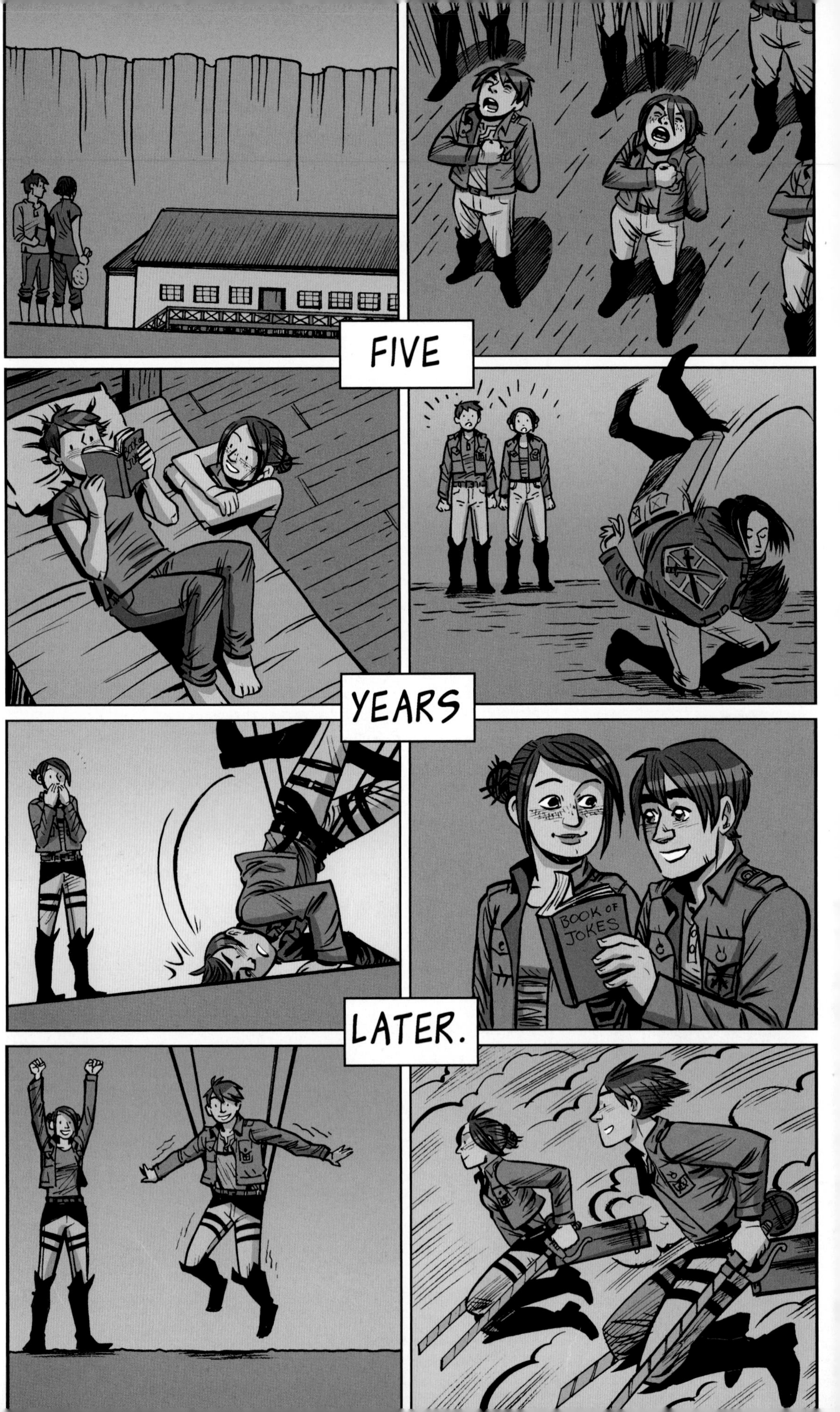
FIVE
YEARS
BOOK OF JOKES
LATER.

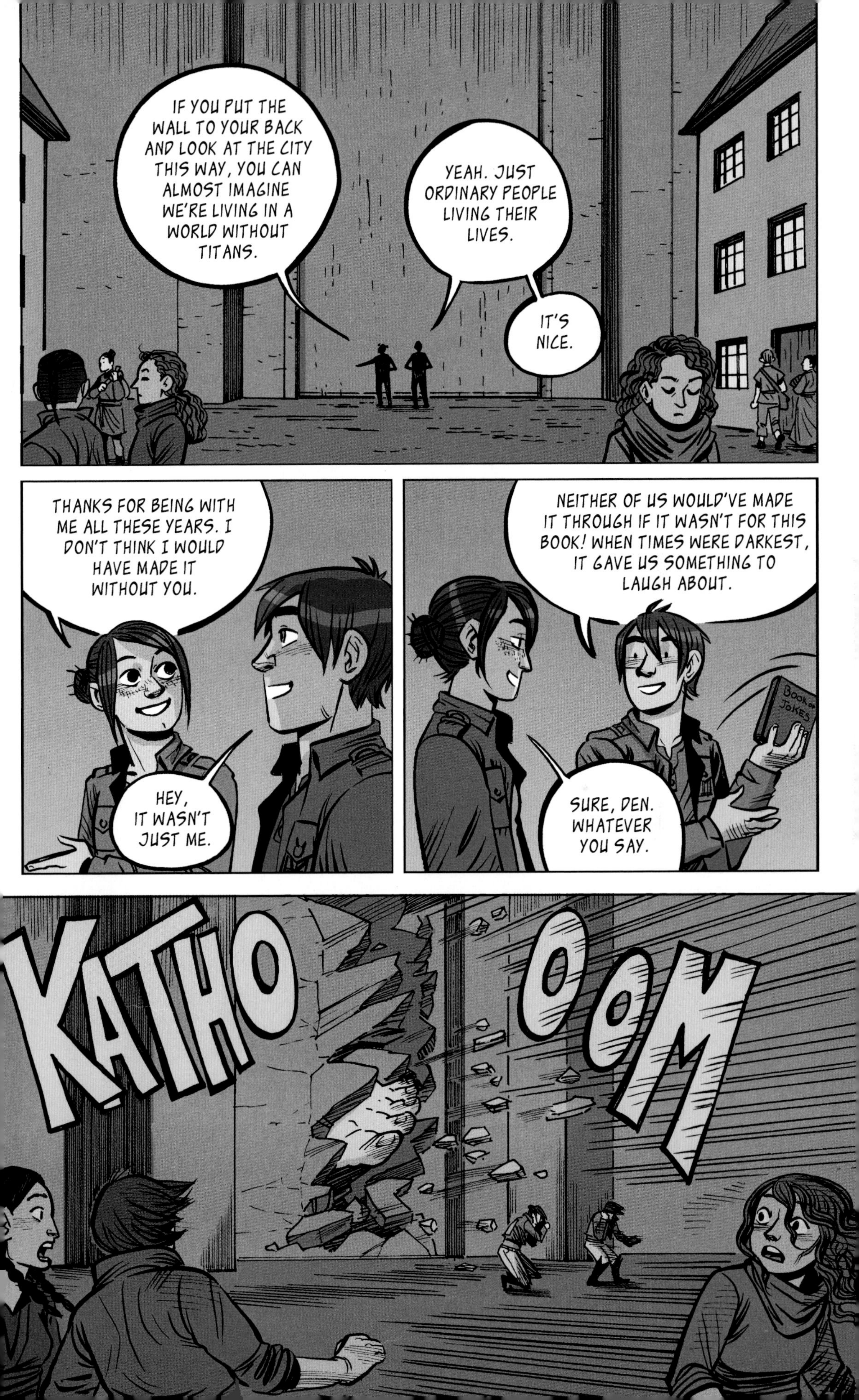
IF YOU PUT THE WALL TO YOUR BACK AND LOOK AT THE CITY THIS WAY, YOU CAN ALMOST IMAGINE WE'RE LIVING IN A WORLD WITHOUT TITANS.
YEAH. JUST ORDINARY PEOPLE LIVING THEIR LIVES.
IT'S NICE.
THANKS FOR BEING WITH ME ALL THESE YEARS. I DON'T THINK I WOULD HAVE MADE IT WITHOUT YOU.
HEY, IT WASN'T JUST ME.
NEITHER OF US WOULD'VE MADE IT THROUGH IF IT WASN'T FOR THIS BOOK! WHEN TIMES WERE DARKEST, IT GAVE US SOMETHING TO LAUGH ABOUT.
BOOK OF JOKES
SURE, DEN. WHATEVER YOU SAY.
KATHOOOM

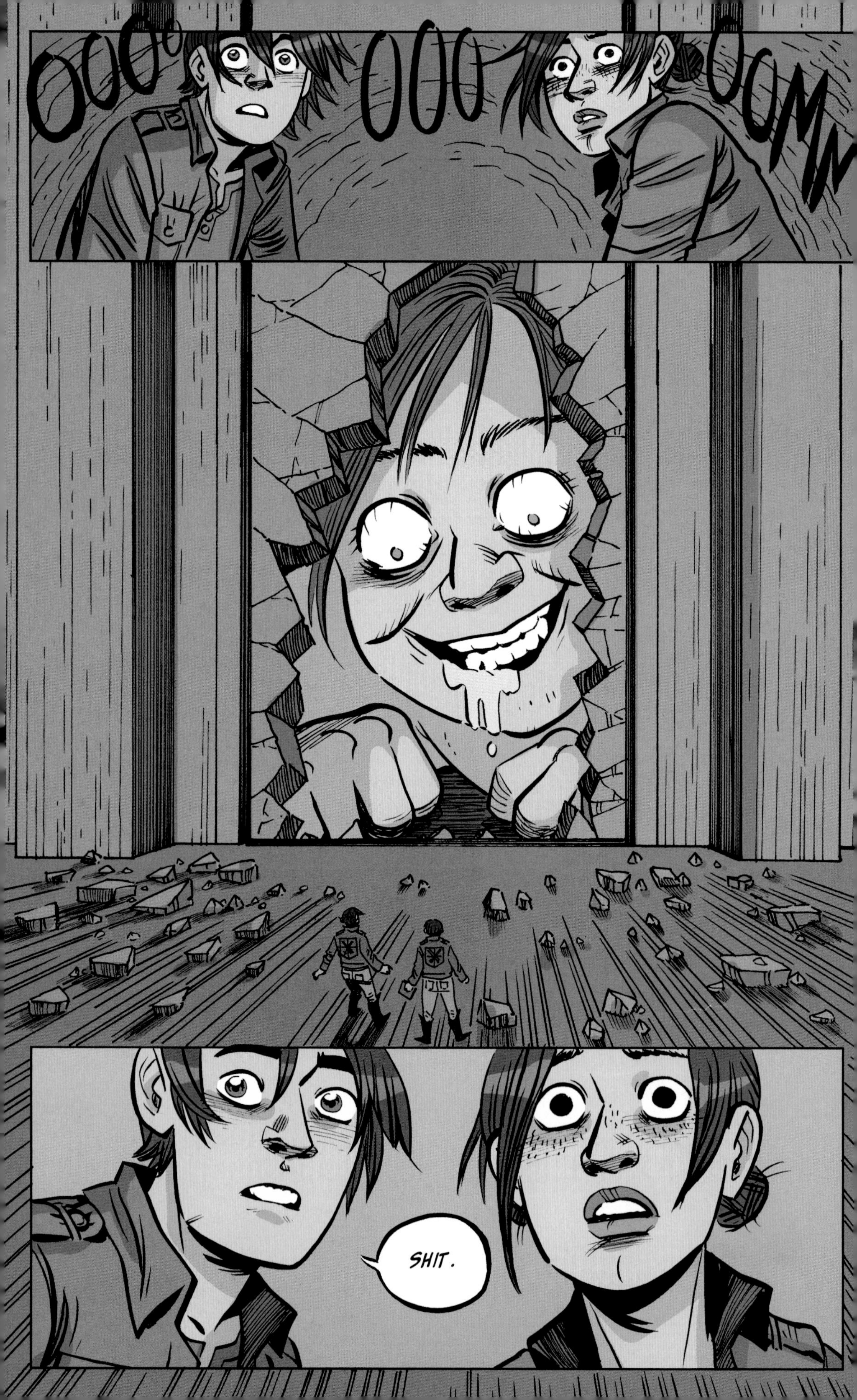
OOOOOOOOOMM
SHIT.

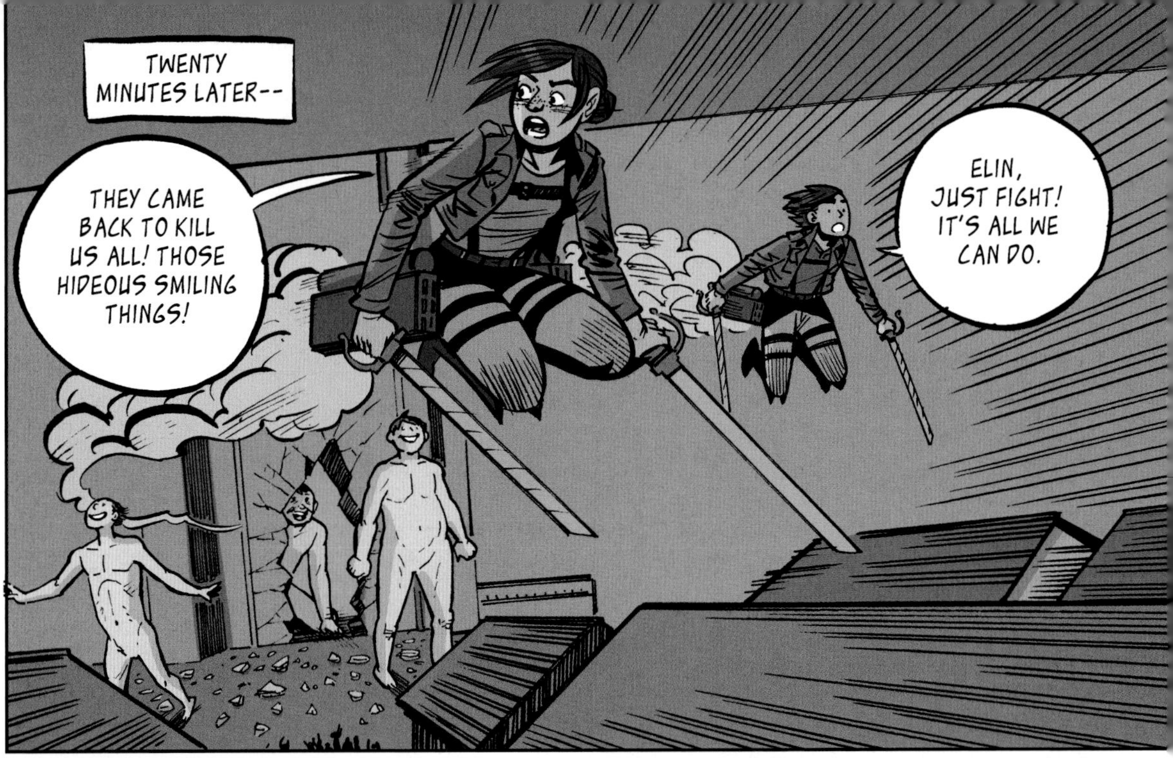
TWENTY MINUTES LATER--
THEY CAME BACK TO KILL US ALL! THOSE HIDEOUS SMILING THINGS!
ELIN, JUST FIGHT! IT'S ALL WE CAN DO.

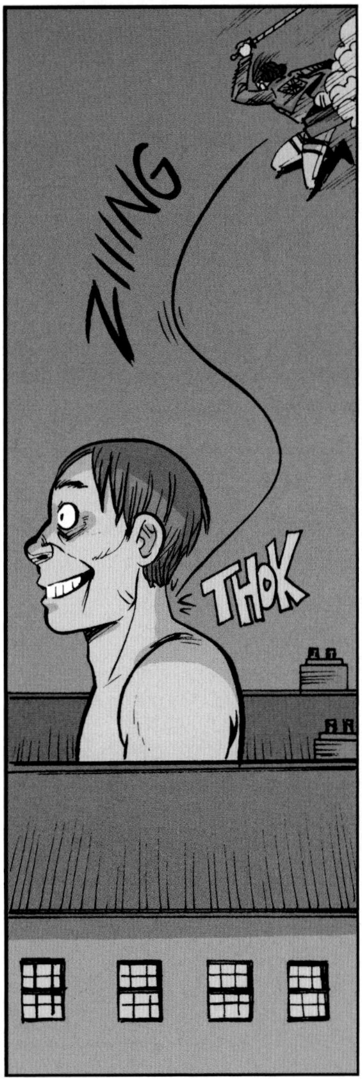
ZIIING
THOK

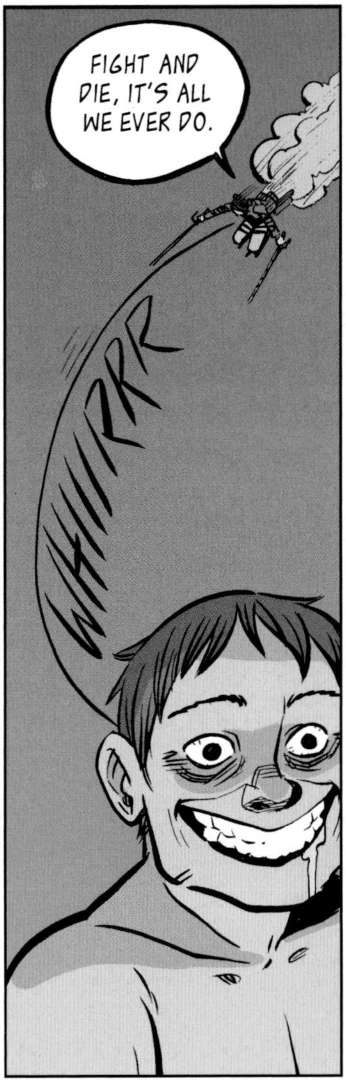
FIGHT AND DIE, IT'S ALL WE EVER DO.
WHIRRR

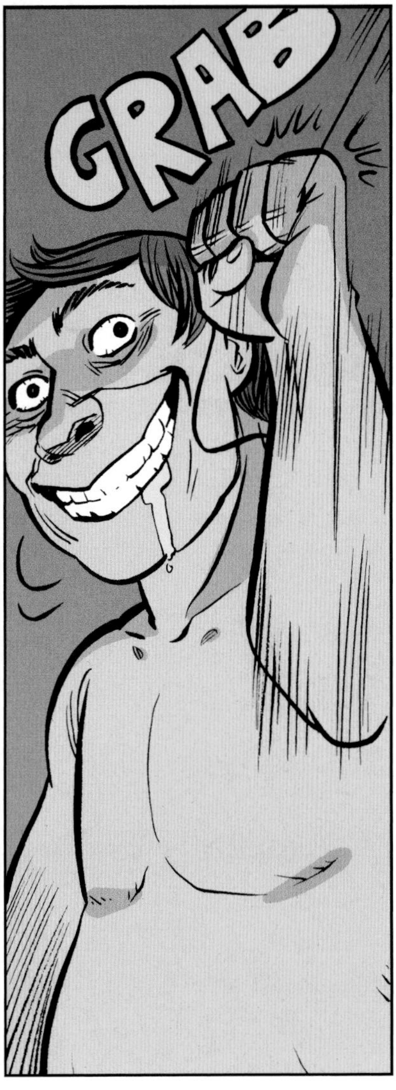
GRAB

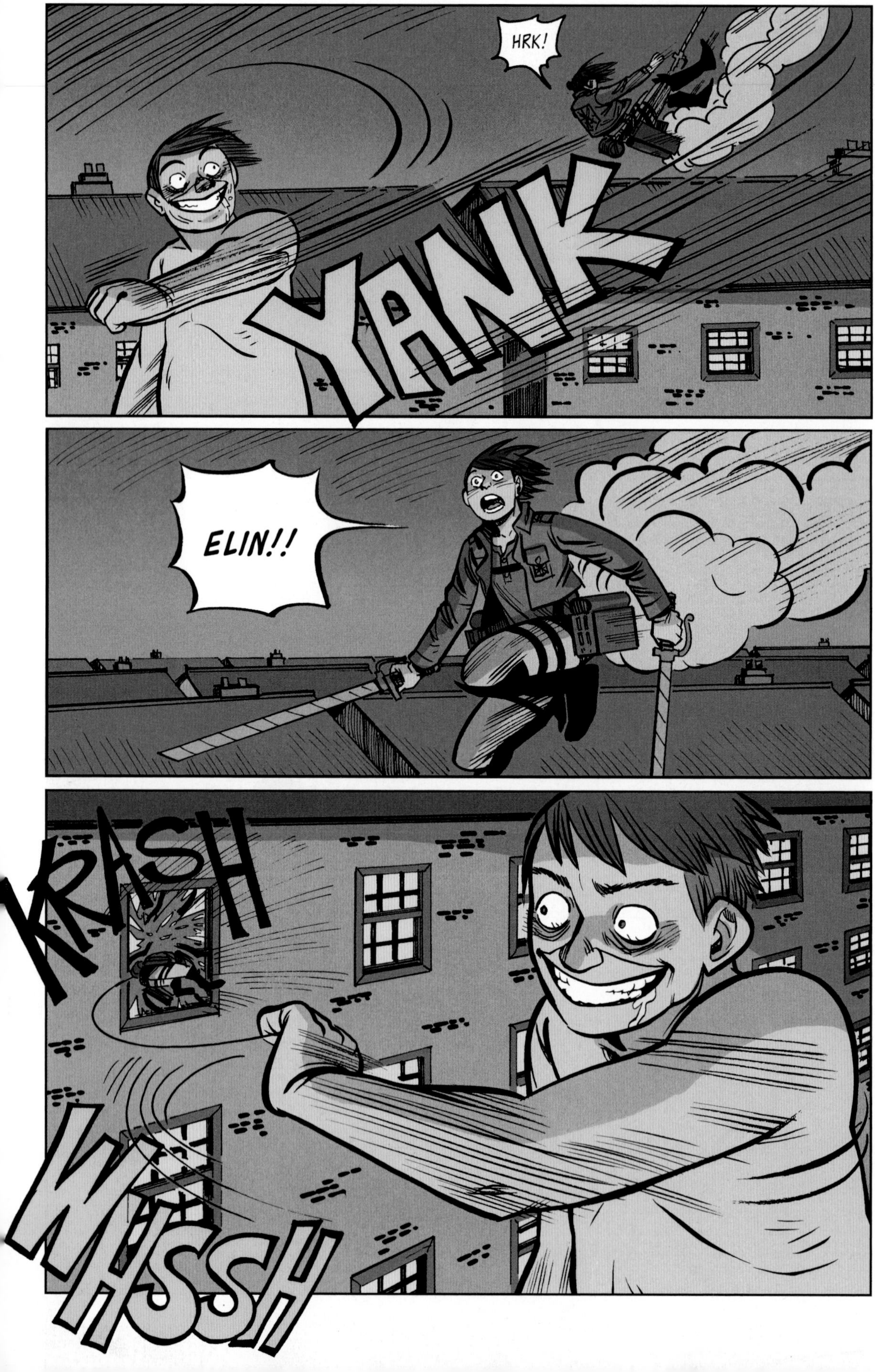
HRK!
YANK
ELIN!!
KRASH
WHSSH

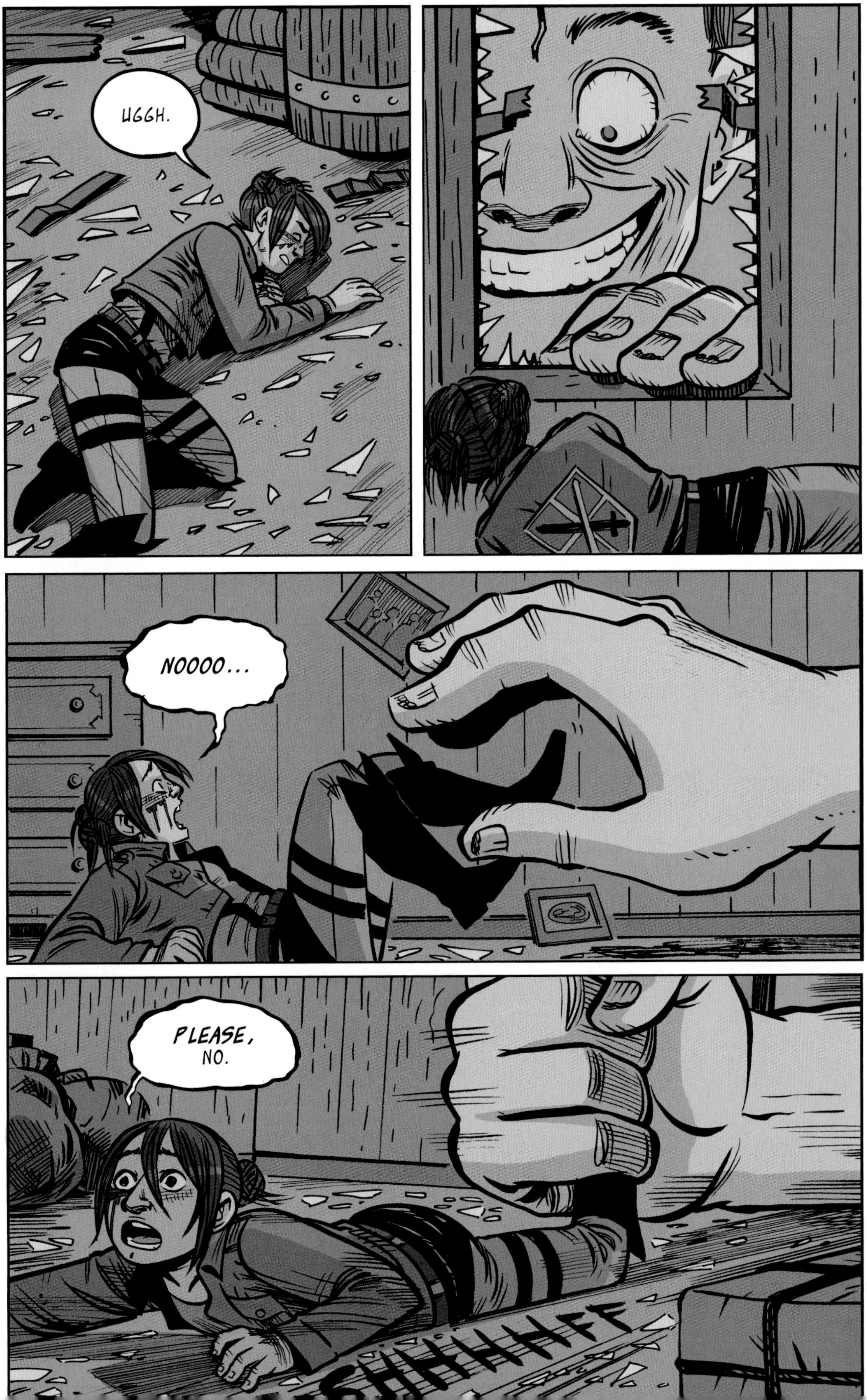
UGGH.
NOOOO...
PLEASE, NO.
SHHHHFF

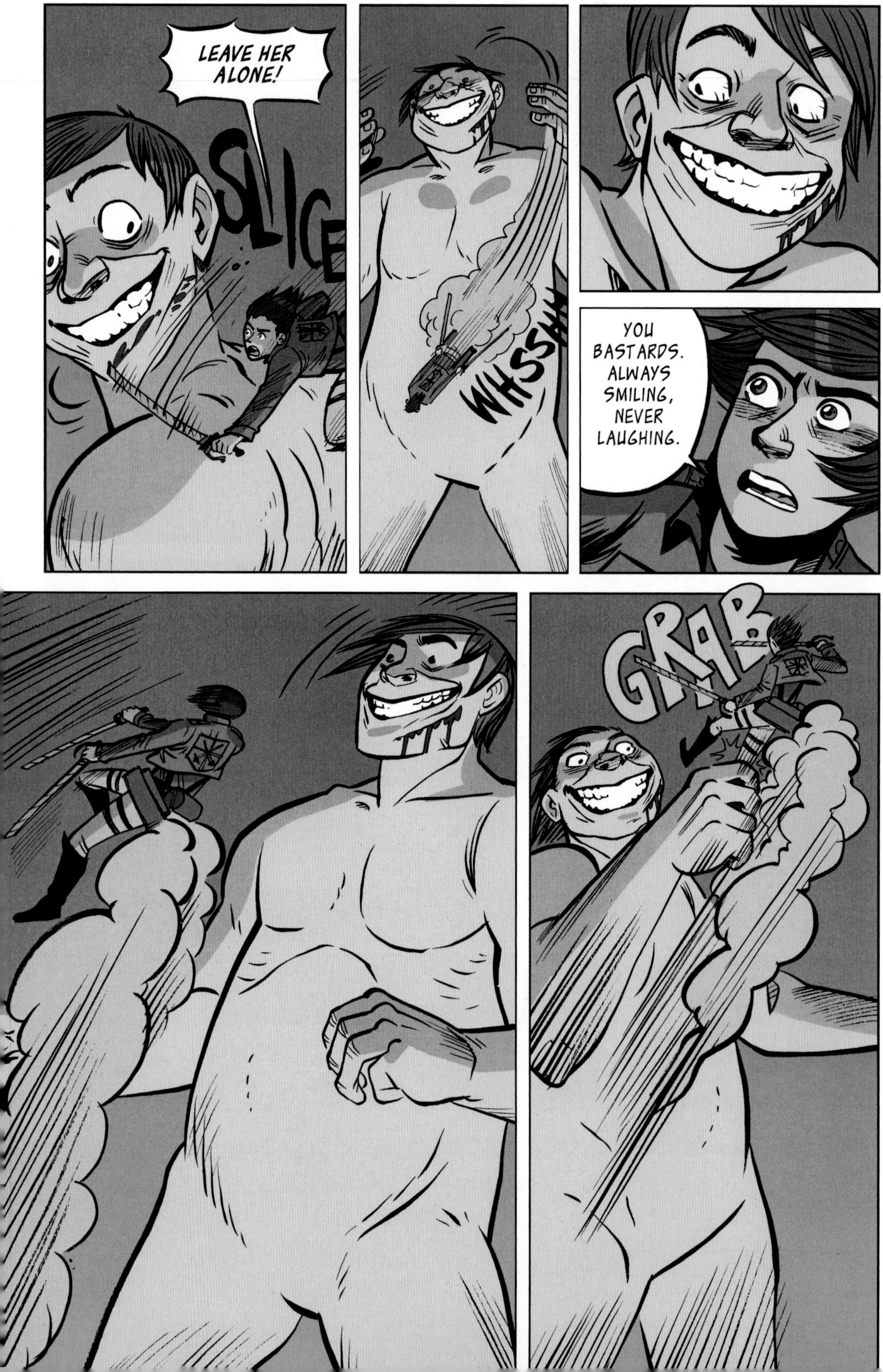
LEAVE HER ALONE!
SLICE
WHSSHH
YOU BASTARDS. ALWAYS SMILING, NEVER LAUGHING.
GRAB

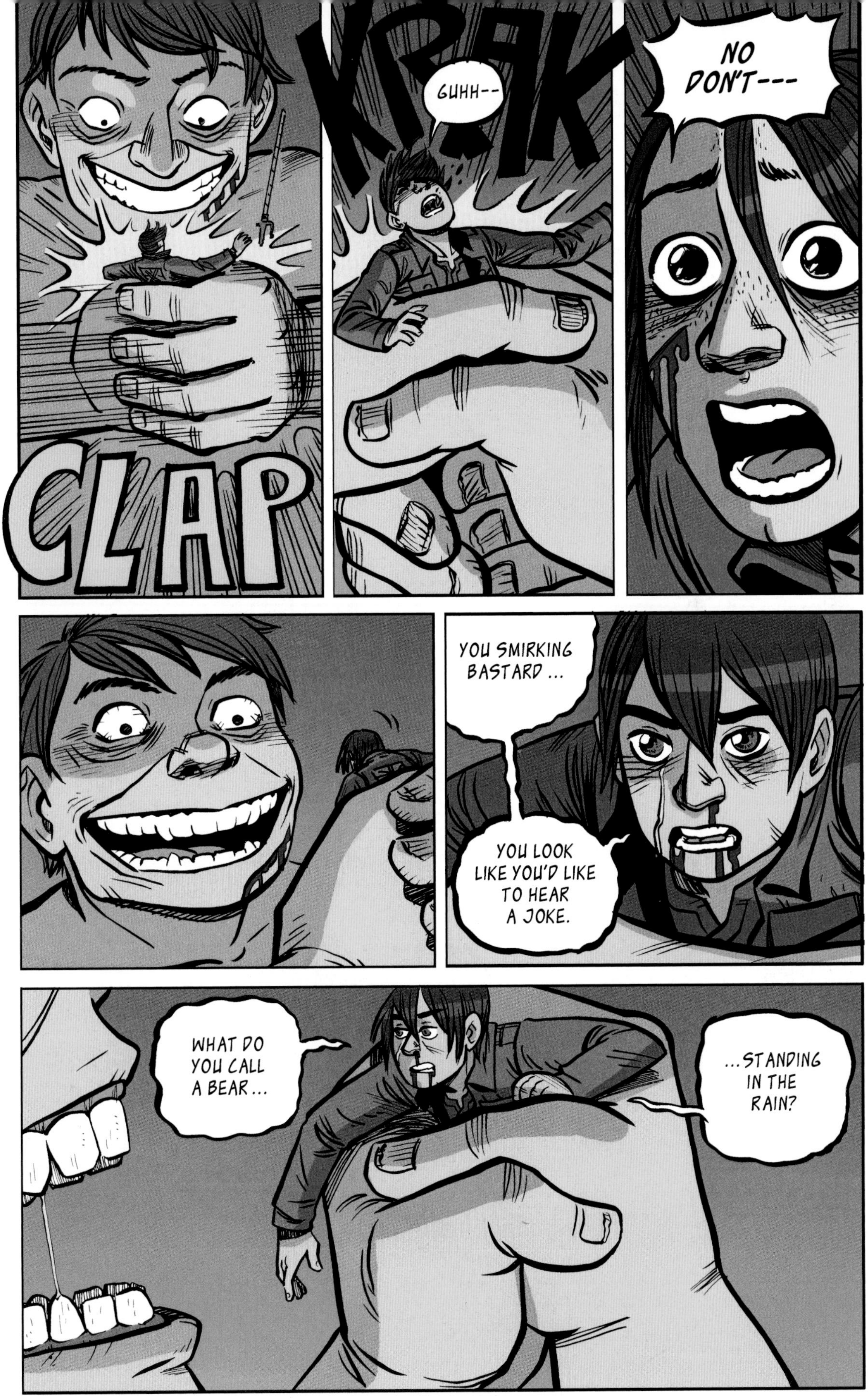

CLAP
KRAK
GUHH--
NO DON'T---
YOU SMIRKING BASTARD ...
YOU LOOK LIKE YOU'D LIKE TO HEAR A JOKE.
WHAT DO YOU CALL A BEAR ...
... STANDING IN THE RAIN?

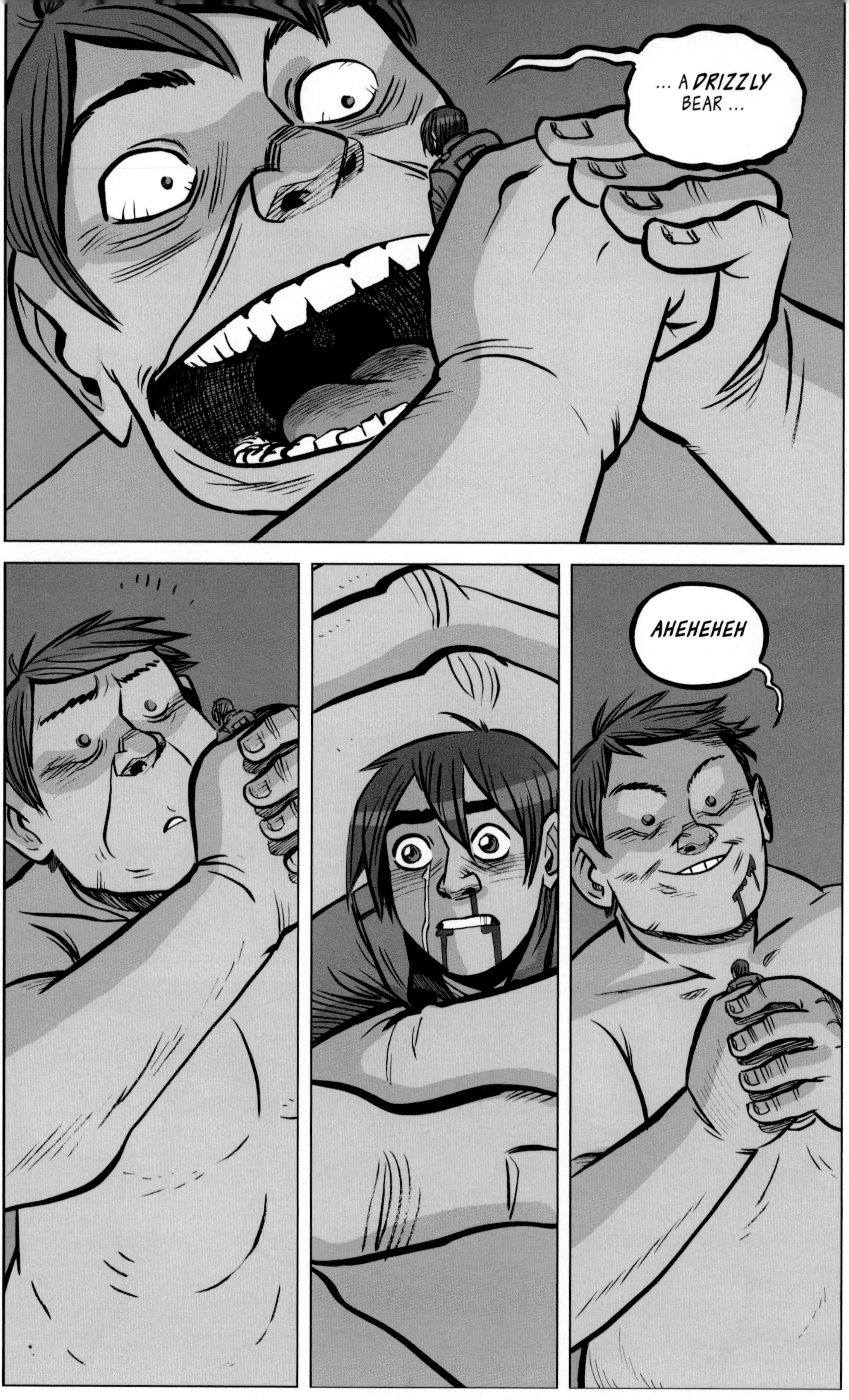
... A DRIZZLY BEAR ...
AHEHEHEH

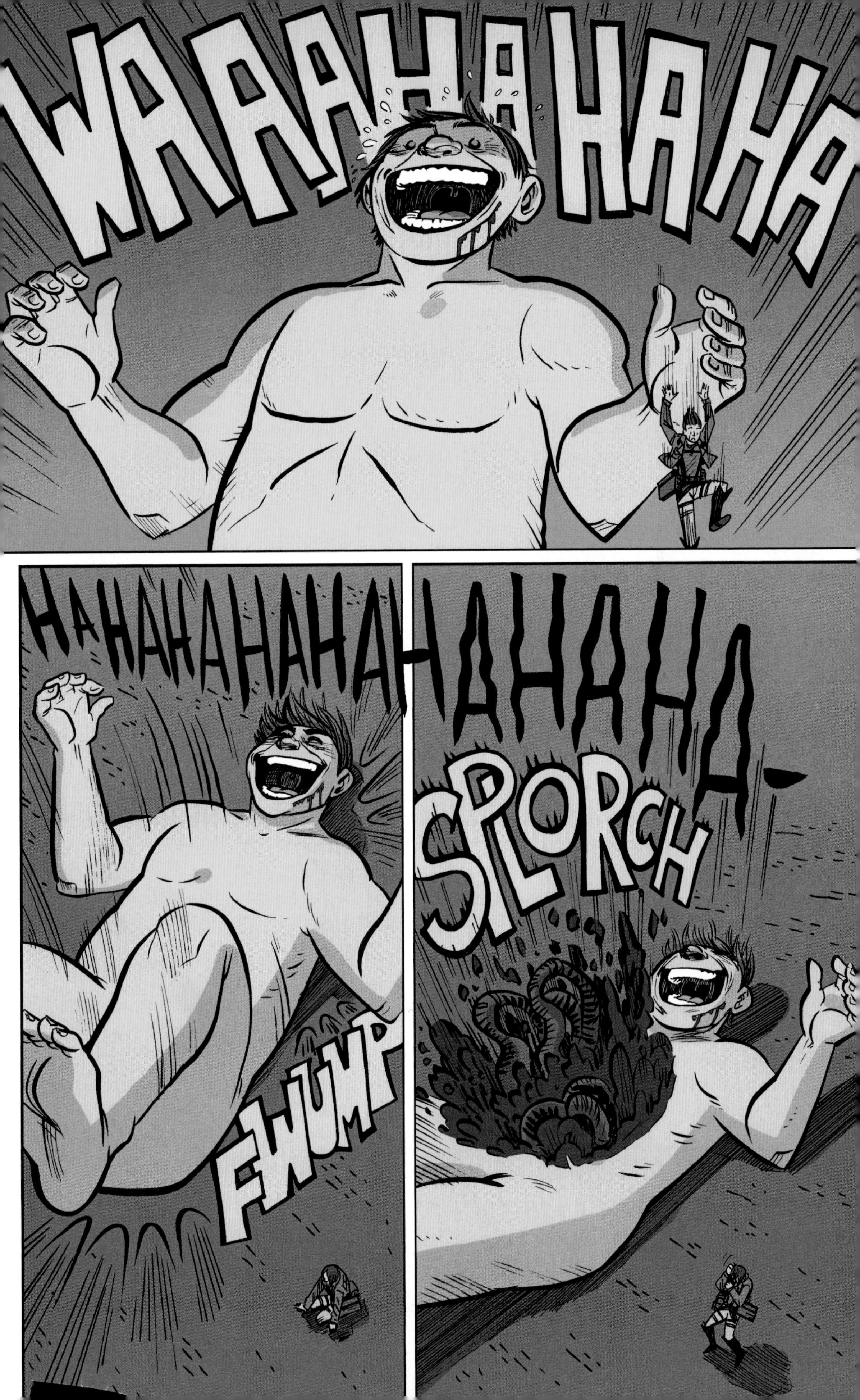
WAAAHAHAHA
HAHAHAHAHAH
FWUMP
AHAHA-
SPLORCH

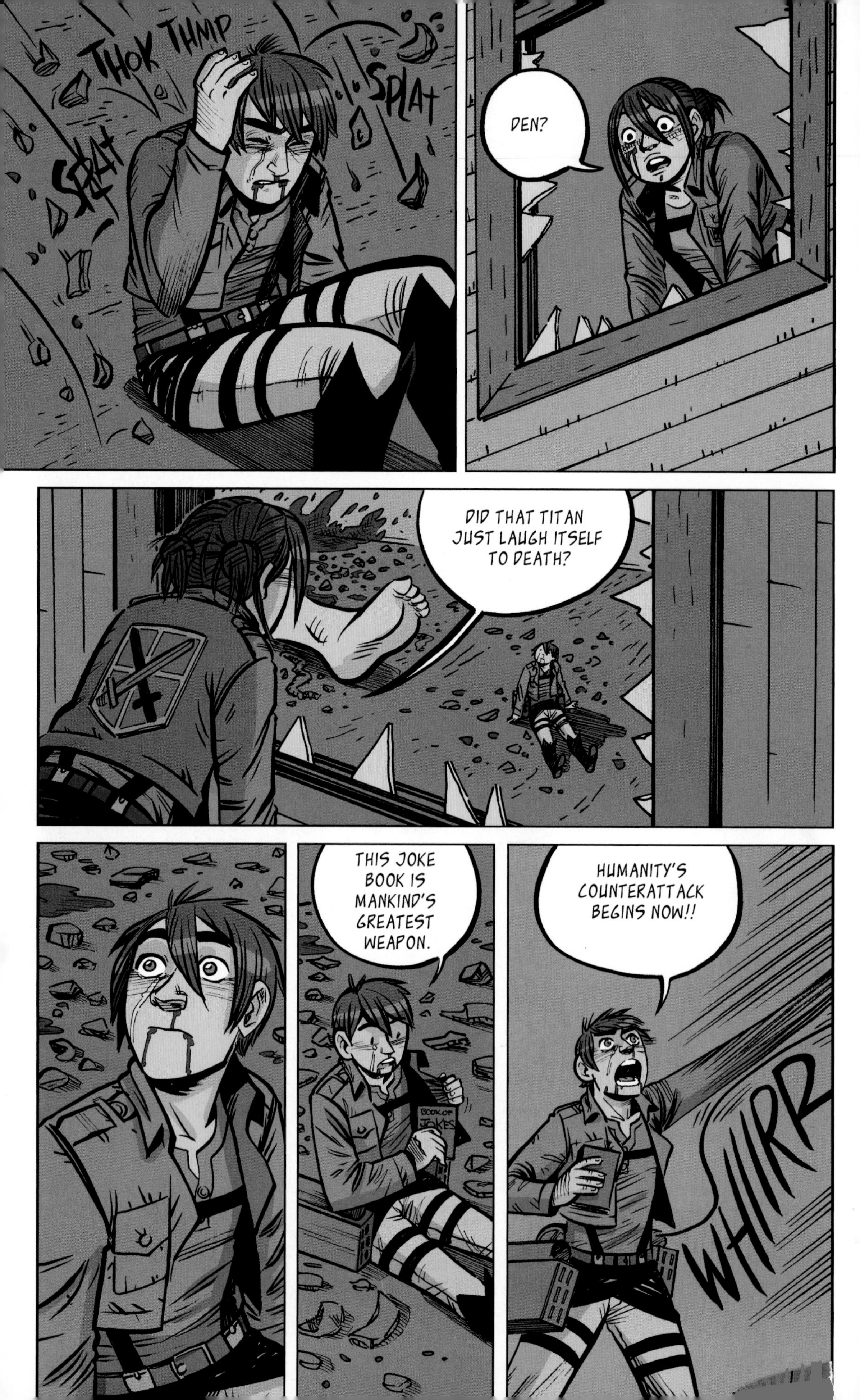
THOK THMP
SPLAT
SPLAT
DEN?
DID THAT TITAN JUST LAUGH ITSELF TO DEATH?
THIS JOKE BOOK IS MANKIND'S GREATEST WEAPON.
BOOK OF JOKES
HUMANITY'S COUNTERATTACK BEGINS NOW!!
WHIRR

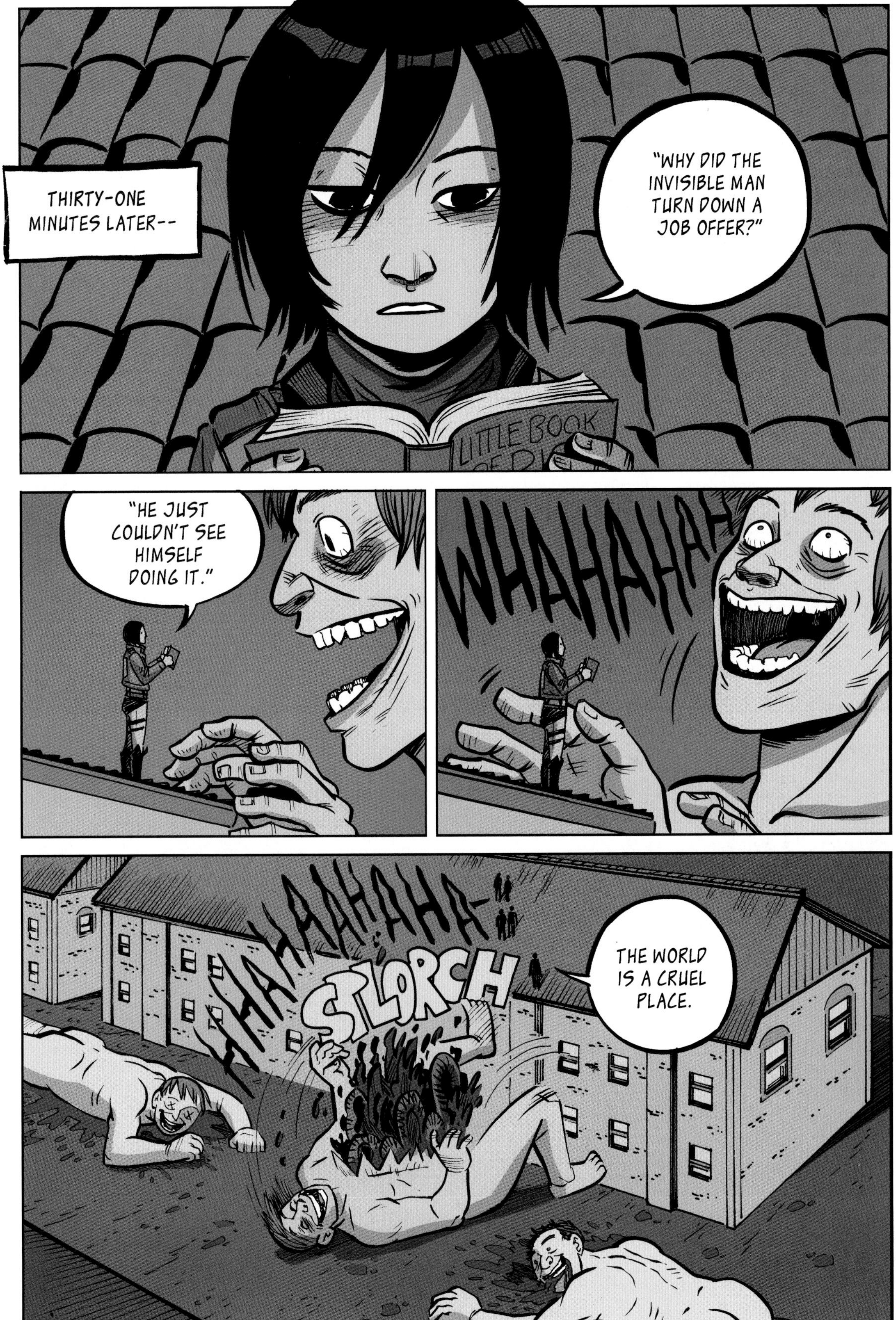
THIRTY-ONE MINUTES LATER--
"WHY DID THE INVISIBLE MAN TURN DOWN A JOB OFFER?"
LITTLE BOOK
"HE JUST COULDN'T SEE HIMSELF DOING IT."
WHAHAHAH
HAHAHAHAHA-
SPLORCH
THE WORLD IS A CRUEL PLACE.

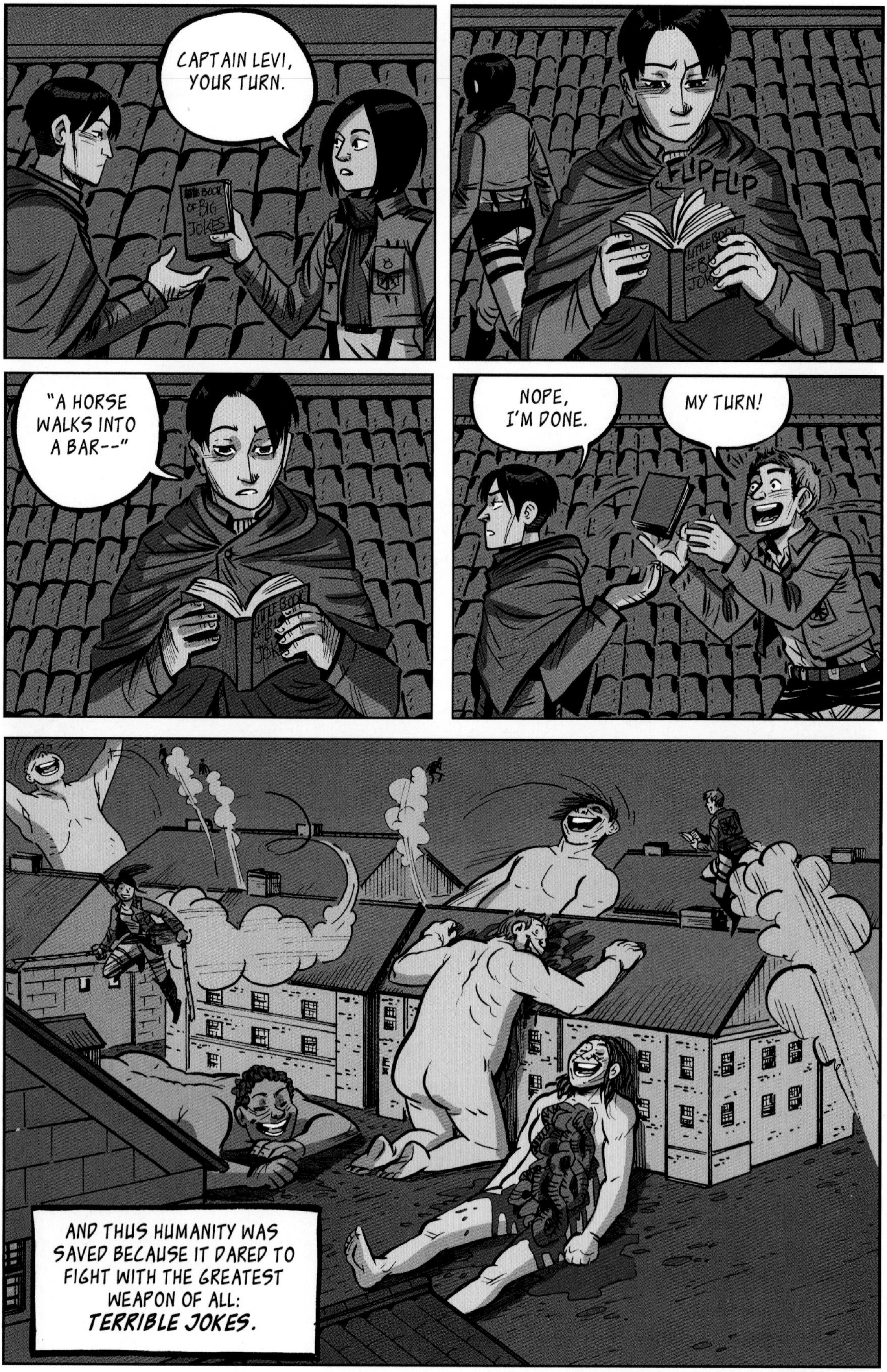
CAPTAIN LEVI, YOUR TURN.
FLIP FLIP
"A HORSE WALKS INTO A BAR--"
NOPE, I'M DONE.
MY TURN!
AND THUS HUMANITY WAS SAVED BECAUSE IT DARED TO FIGHT WITH THE GREATEST WEAPON OF ALL: TERRIBLE JOKES.

ATTACK on ATTACK on

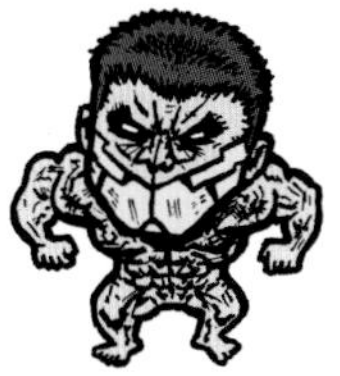

By Evan Dorkin and Sarah Dyer
Flatted and additional colors by Bill Mudron

OUTMANEUVERED

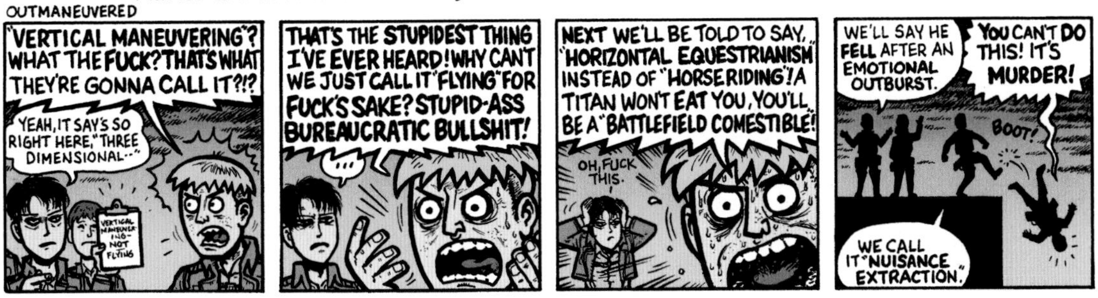

"VERTICAL MANEUVERING"? WHAT THE FUCK? THAT'S WHAT THEY'RE GONNA CALL IT?!?
YEAH, IT SAYS SO RIGHT HERE, "THREE DIMENSIONAL--"
VERTICAL MANEUVER-ING NOT FLYING
THAT'S THE STUPIDEST THING I'VE EVER HEARD! WHY CAN'T WE JUST CALL IT "FLYING" FOR FUCK'S SAKE? STUPID-ASS BUREAUCRATIC BULLSHIT!
...
NEXT WE'LL BE TOLD TO SAY, "HORIZONTAL EQUESTRIANISM" INSTEAD OF "HORSE RIDING"! A TITAN WON'T EAT YOU, YOU'LL BE A "BATTLEFIELD COMESTIBLE"!
OH, FUCK THIS.
WE'LL SAY HE FELL AFTER AN EMOTIONAL OUTBURST.
YOU CAN'T DO THIS! IT'S MURDER!
BOOT!
WE CALL IT "NUISANCE EXTRACTION."

POISON IDEA

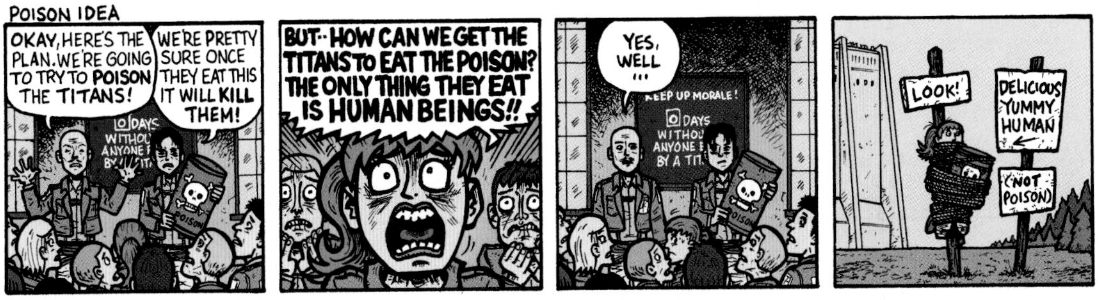

OKAY, HERE'S THE PLAN. WE'RE GOING TO TRY TO POISON THE TITANS!
WE'RE PRETTY SURE ONCE THEY EAT THIS IT WILL KILL THEM!
POISON
BUT-- HOW CAN WE GET THE TITANS TO EAT THE POISON? THE ONLY THING THEY EAT IS HUMAN BEINGS!!
YES, WELL ...
KEEP UP MORALE!
LOOK!
DELICIOUS YUMMY HUMAN
(NOT POISON)

THE RESULTS ARE IN

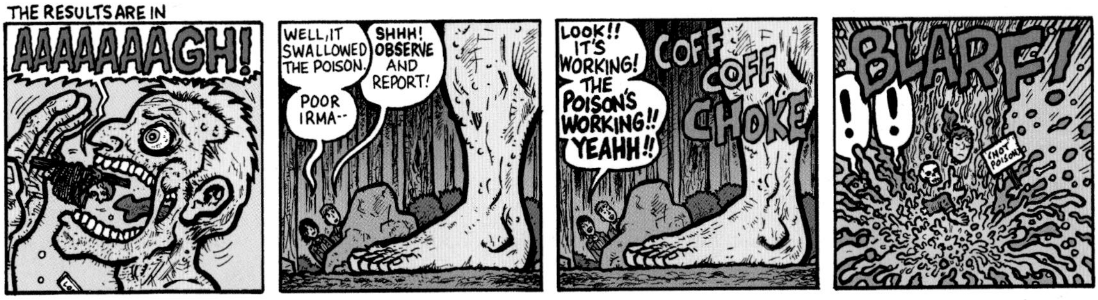

AAAAAAAGH!
WELL, IT SWALLOWED THE POISON.
SHHH! OBSERVE AND REPORT!
POOR IRMA--
LOOK!! IT'S WORKING! THE POISON'S WORKING!! YEAHH!!
COFF COFF CHOKE
BLARF!
! !
NOT POISON

SPOILS OF WAR

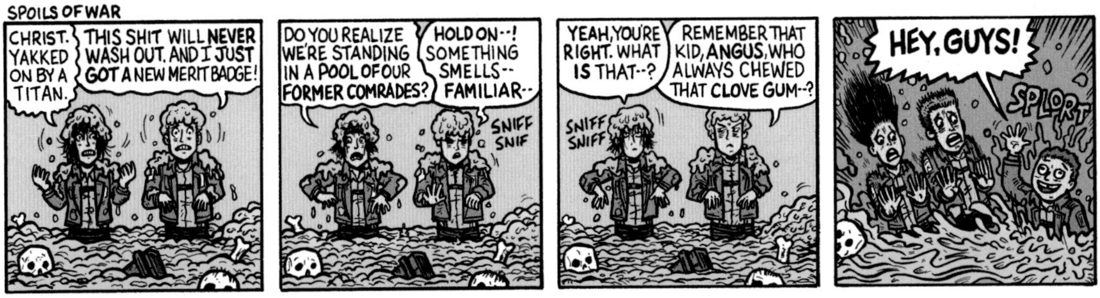

CHRIST. YAKKED ON BY A TITAN.
THIS SHIT WILL NEVER WASH OUT. AND I JUST GOT A NEW MERIT BADGE!
DO YOU REALIZE WE'RE STANDING IN A POOL OF OUR FORMER COMRADES?
HOLD ON--! SOMETHING SMELLS-- FAMILIAR--
SNIFF SNIF
YEAH, YOU'RE RIGHT. WHAT IS THAT--?
SNIFF SNIFF
REMEMBER THAT KID, ANGUS, WHO ALWAYS CHEWED THAT CLOVE GUM--?
HEY, GUYS!
SPLORT

NEVER LEAVE A MAN BEHIND

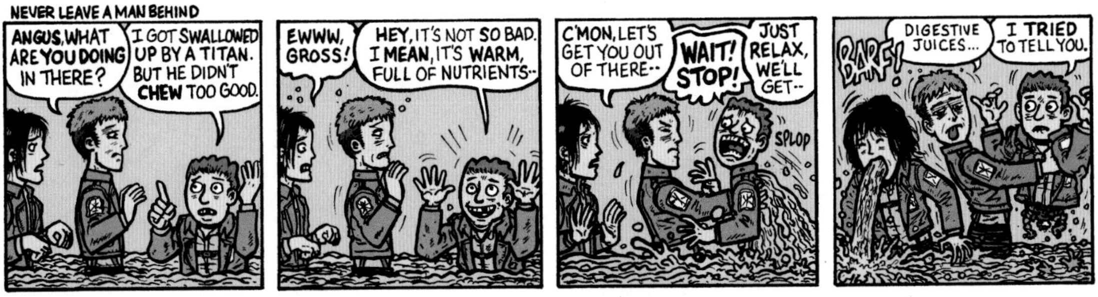

ANGUS, WHAT ARE YOU DOING IN THERE?
I GOT SWALLOWED UP BY A TITAN. BUT HE DIDN'T CHEW TOO GOOD.
EWWW, GROSS!
HEY, IT'S NOT SO BAD. I MEAN, IT'S WARM, FULL OF NUTRIENTS--
C'MON, LET'S GET YOU OUT OF THERE--
WAIT! STOP!
JUST RELAX, WE'LL GET--
SPLOP
BARF!
DIGESTIVE JUICES...
I TRIED TO TELL YOU.

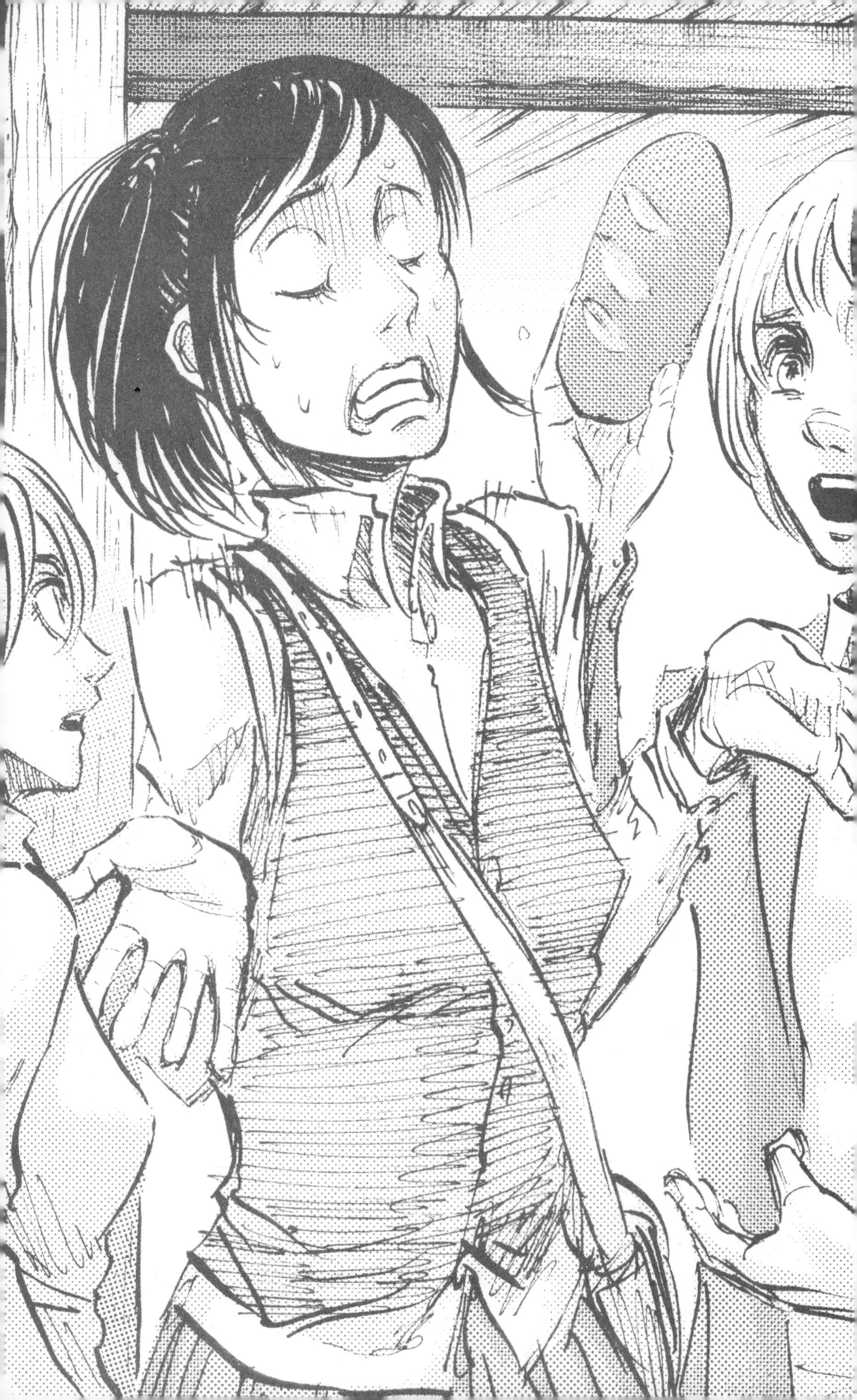

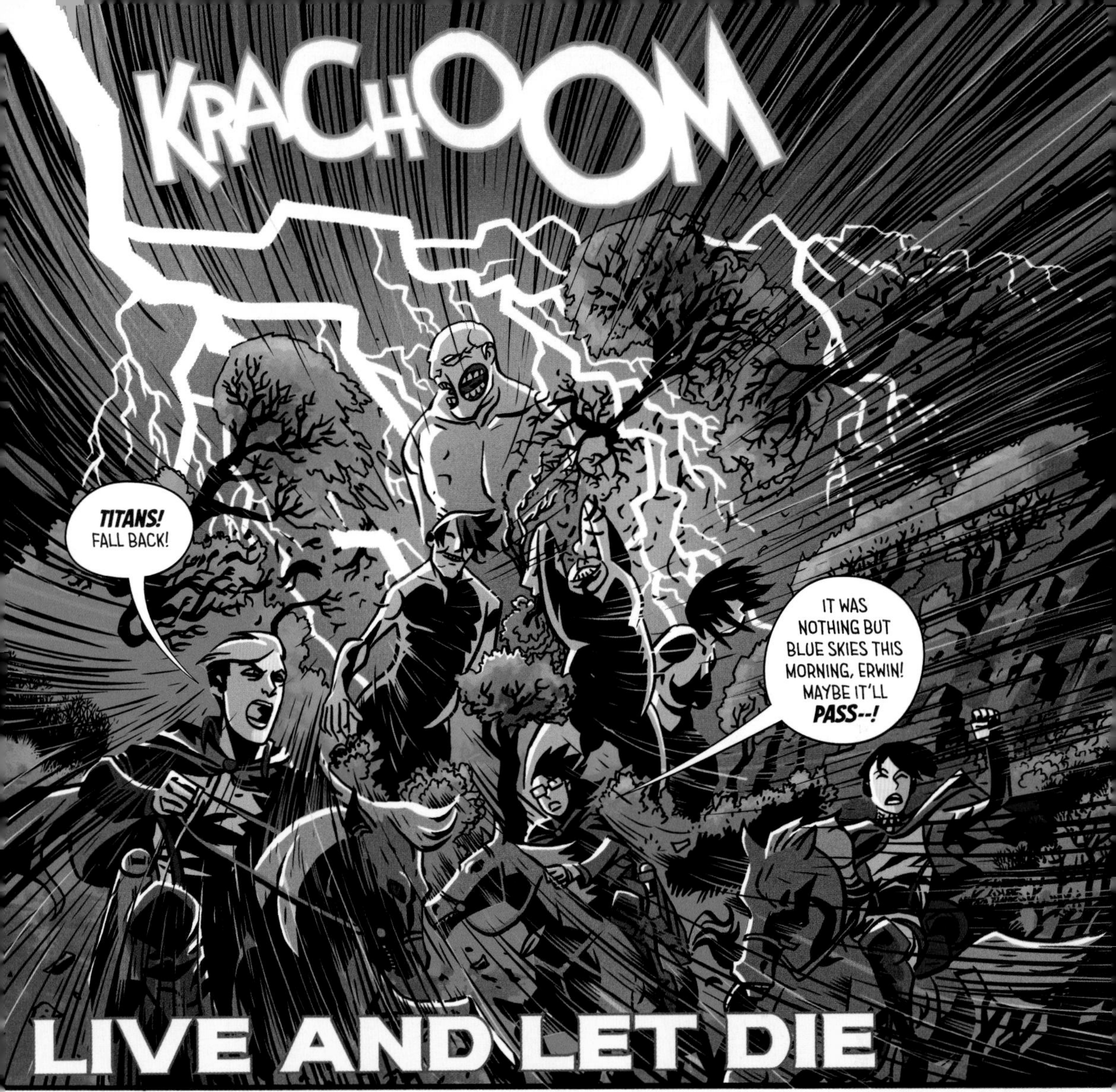
KRACHOOM
TITANS! FALL BACK!
IT WAS NOTHING BUT BLUE SKIES THIS MORNING, ERWIN! MAYBE IT'LL PASS--!
LIVE AND LET DIE

STORY and ART by Michael Avon Oeming · COLORS by Michael Avon Oeming and Taki Soma · LETTERING by Steve Wands

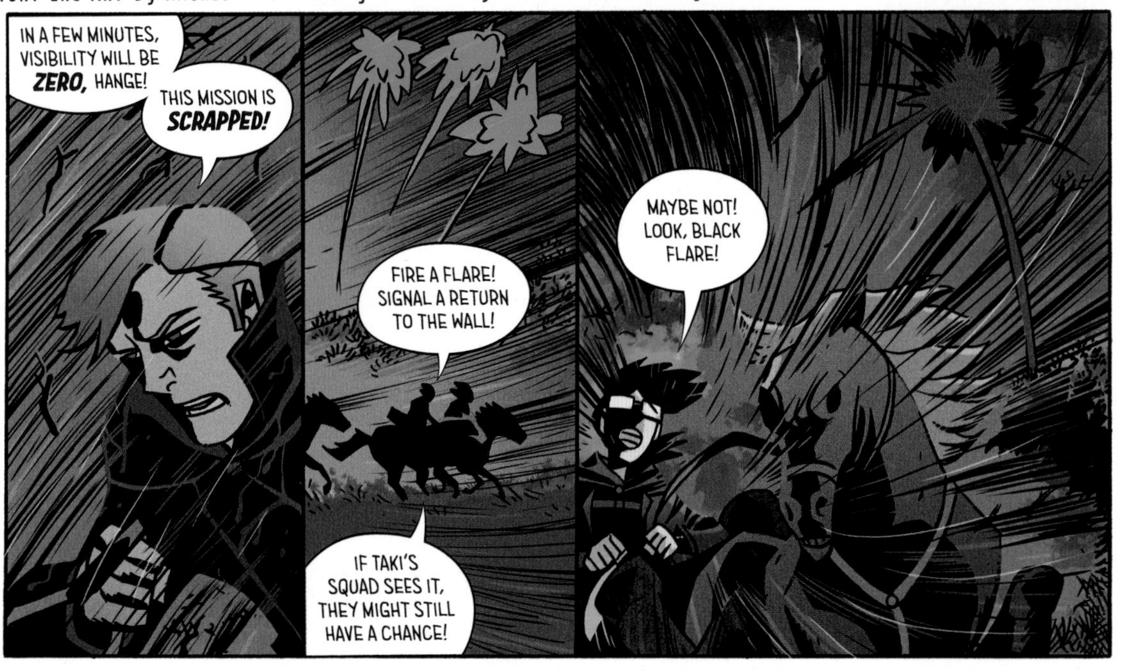
IN A FEW MINUTES, VISIBILITY WILL BE ZERO, HANGE!
THIS MISSION IS SCRAPPED!
FIRE A FLARE! SIGNAL A RETURN TO THE WALL!
IF TAKI'S SQUAD SEES IT, THEY MIGHT STILL HAVE A CHANCE!
MAYBE NOT! LOOK, BLACK FLARE!

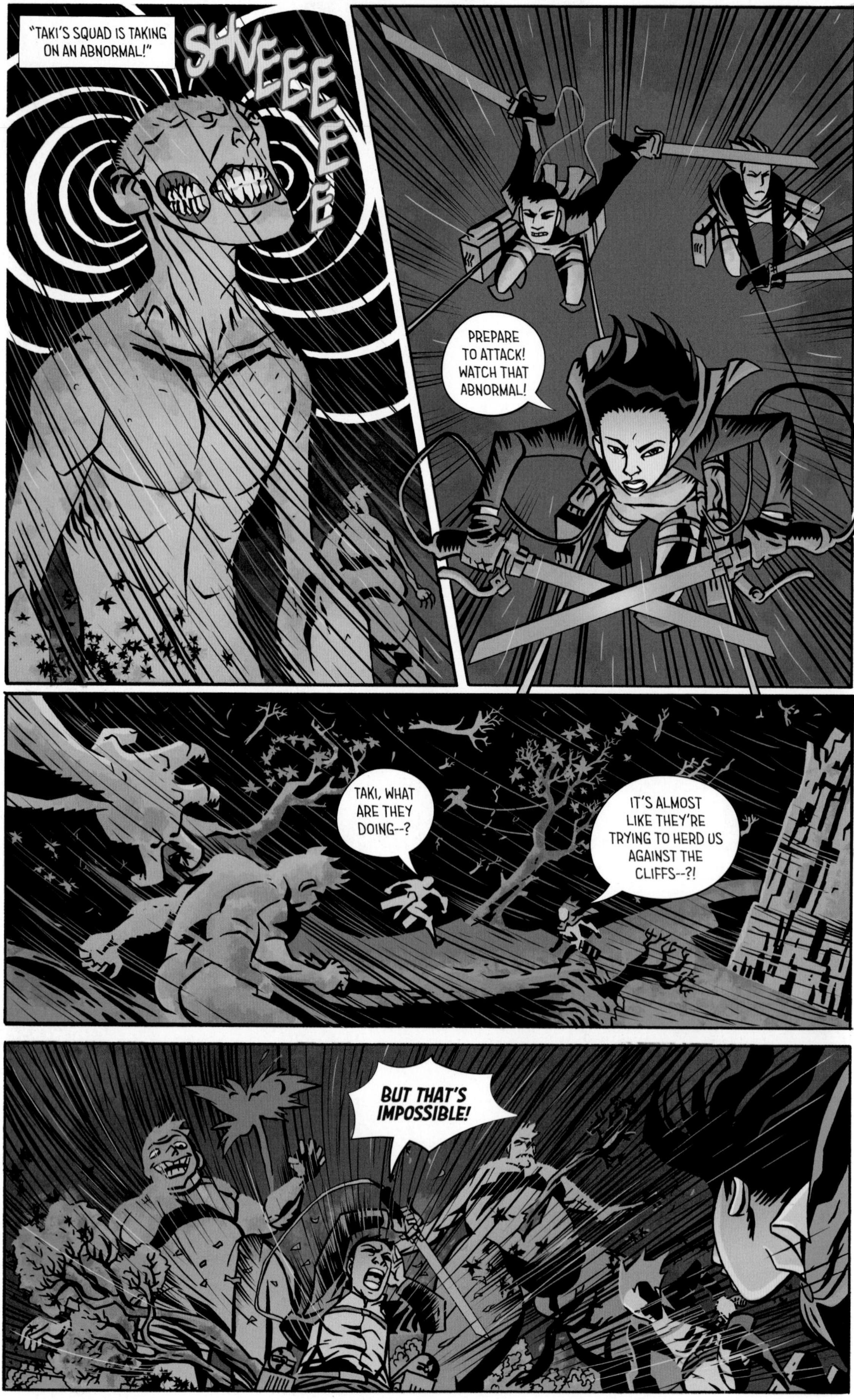
"TAKI'S SQUAD IS TAKING ON AN ABNORMAL!"
SHVEEEEEE
PREPARE TO ATTACK! WATCH THAT ABNORMAL!
TAKI, WHAT ARE THEY DOING--?
IT'S ALMOST LIKE THEY'RE TRYING TO HERD US AGAINST THE CLIFFS--?!
BUT THAT'S IMPOSSIBLE!

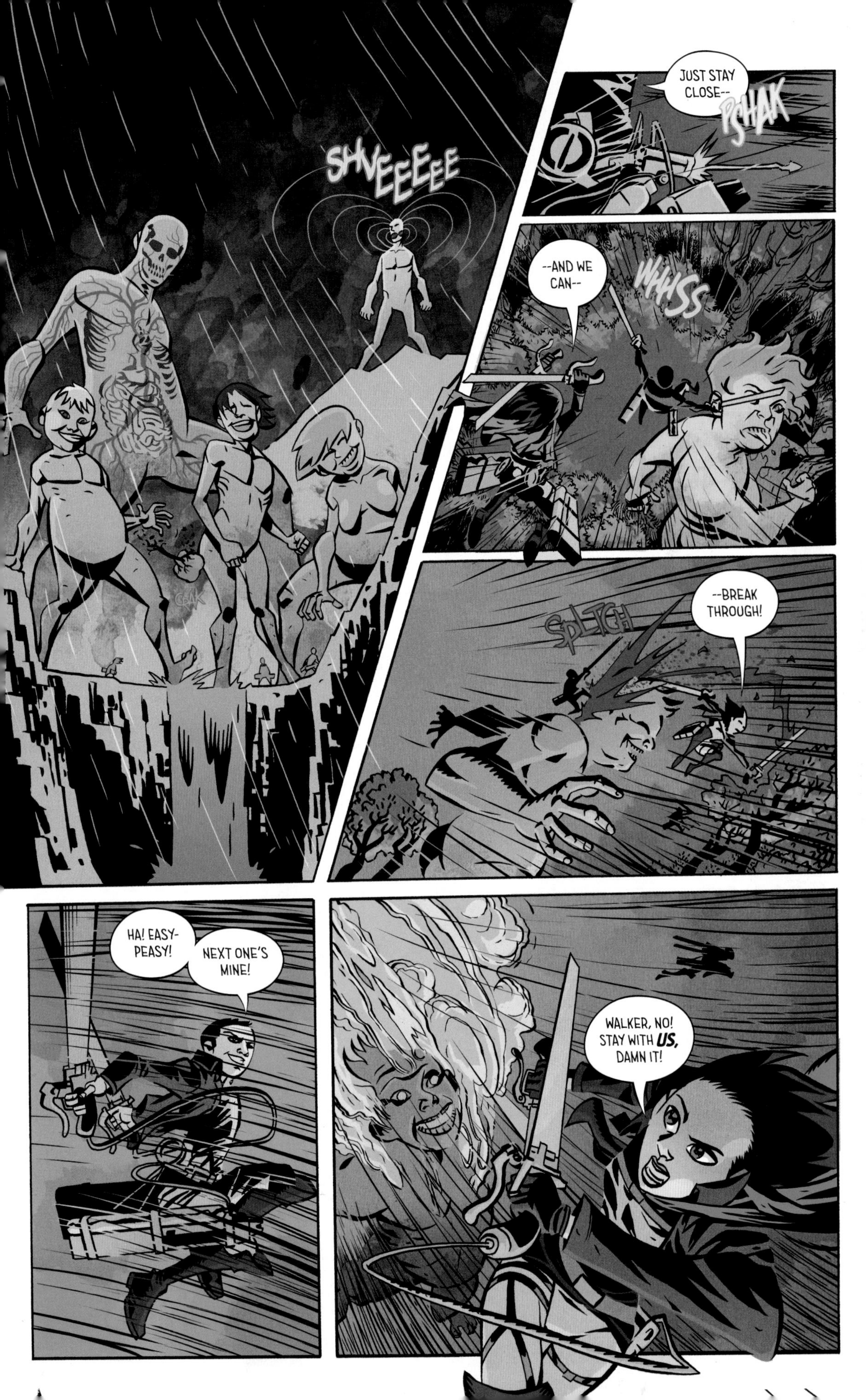
SHVEEEEEE
JUST STAY CLOSE--
PSHAK
--AND WE CAN--
WHHSS
SPLTCH
--BREAK THROUGH!
HA! EASY-PEASY!
NEXT ONE'S MINE!
WALKER, NO! STAY WITH **US,** DAMN IT!

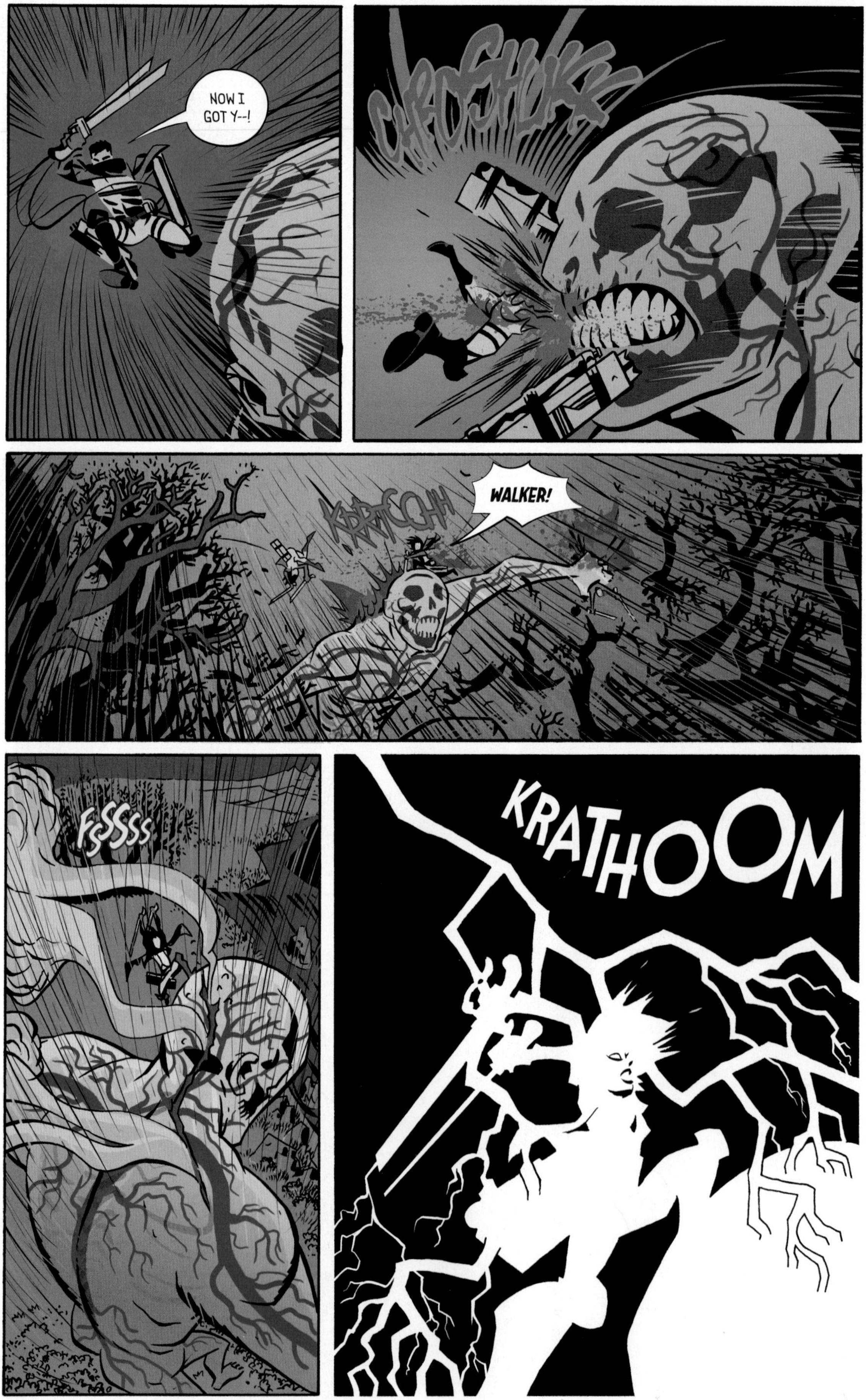
NOW I GOT Y--!
CHROGHUKK
KRRTCHH
WALKER!
FSSSSS
KRATHOOM

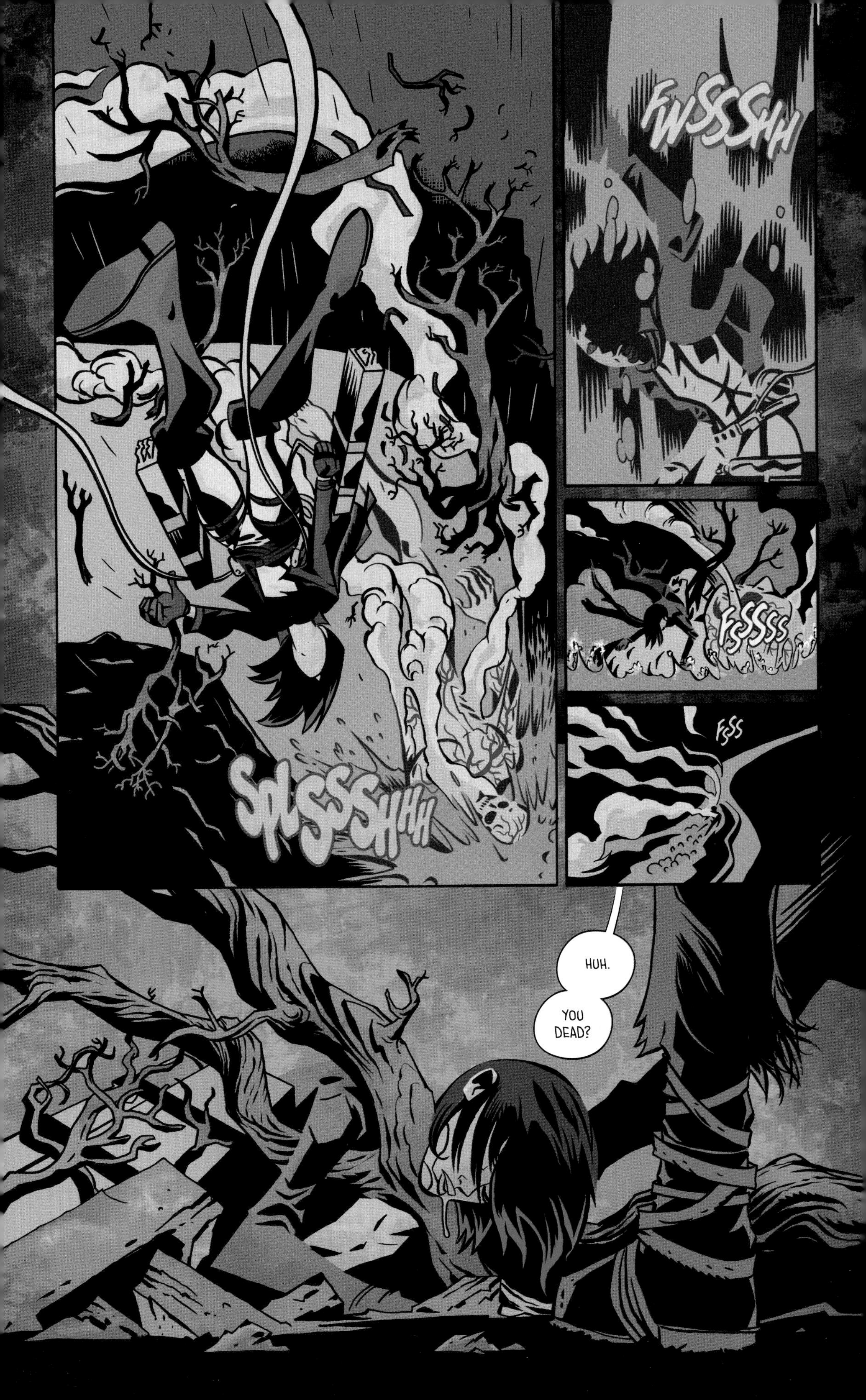
SPLSSSHHH
FWSSSHH
FSSSS
FSSS
HUH.
YOU DEAD?

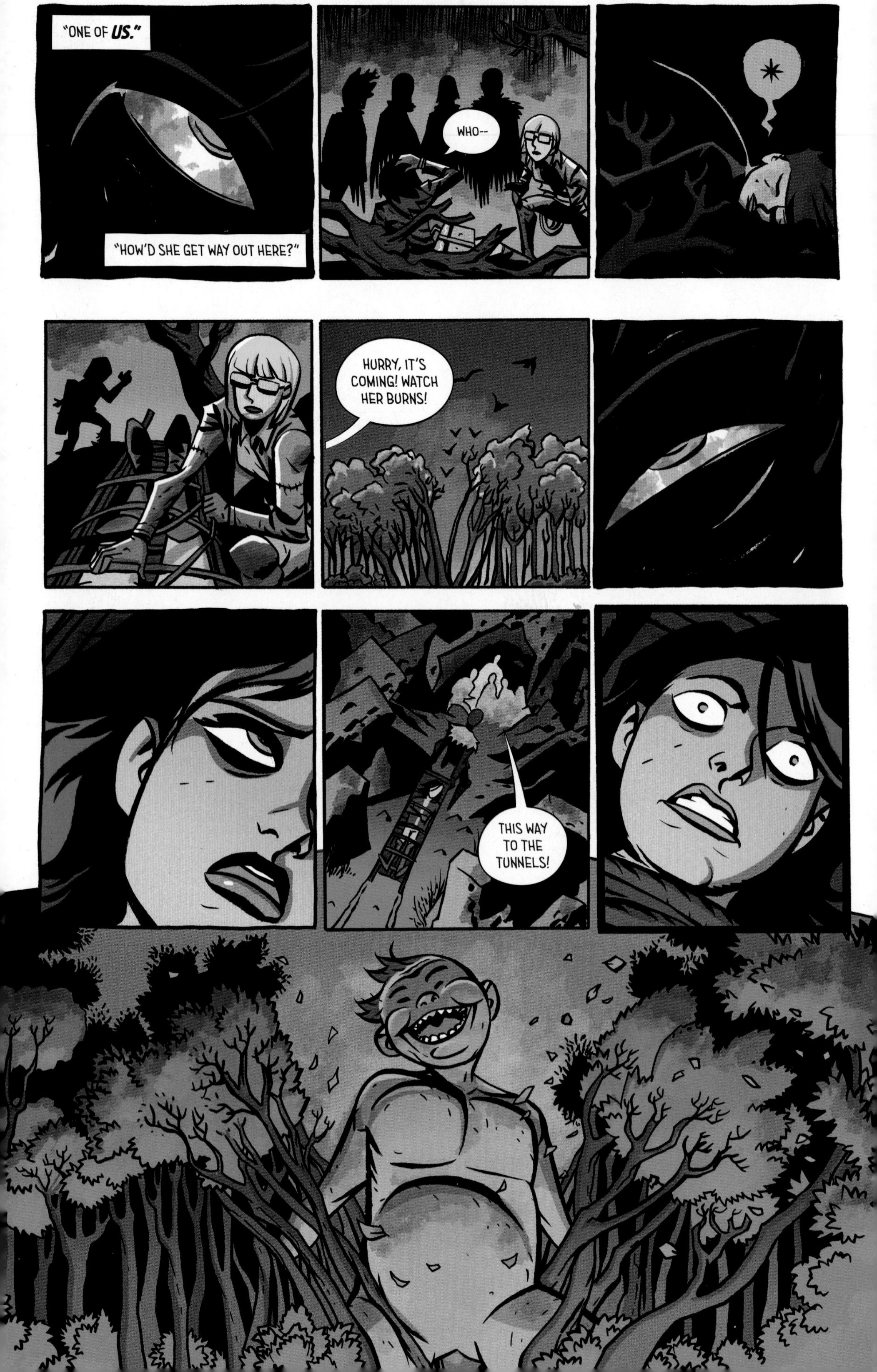
"ONE OF US."
"HOW'D SHE GET WAY OUT HERE?"
WHO--
*
HURRY, IT'S COMING! WATCH HER BURNS!
THIS WAY TO THE TUNNELS!

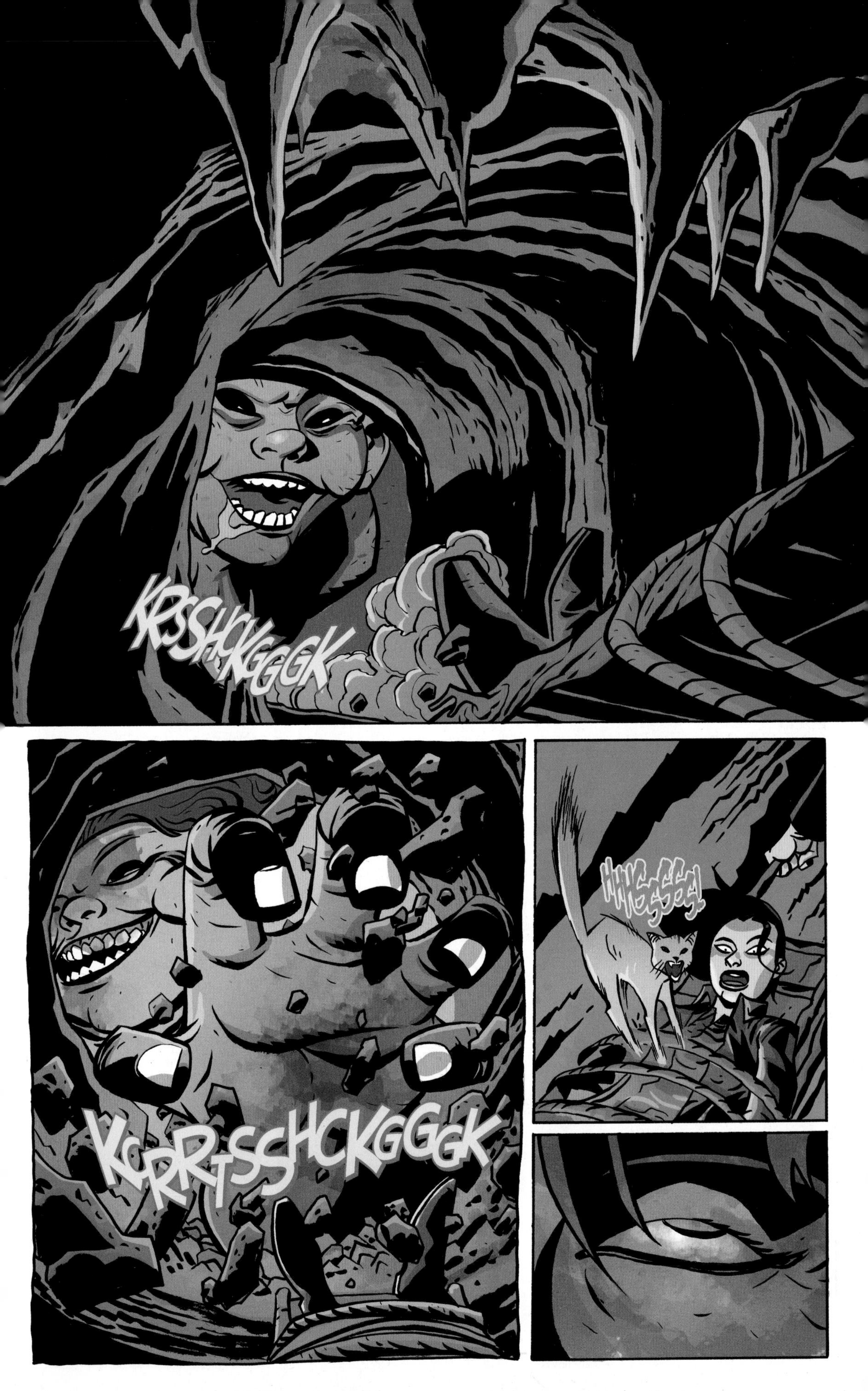
KRSSHCKGGGK
KCRRTSSHCKGGGK
HHHSSSS!

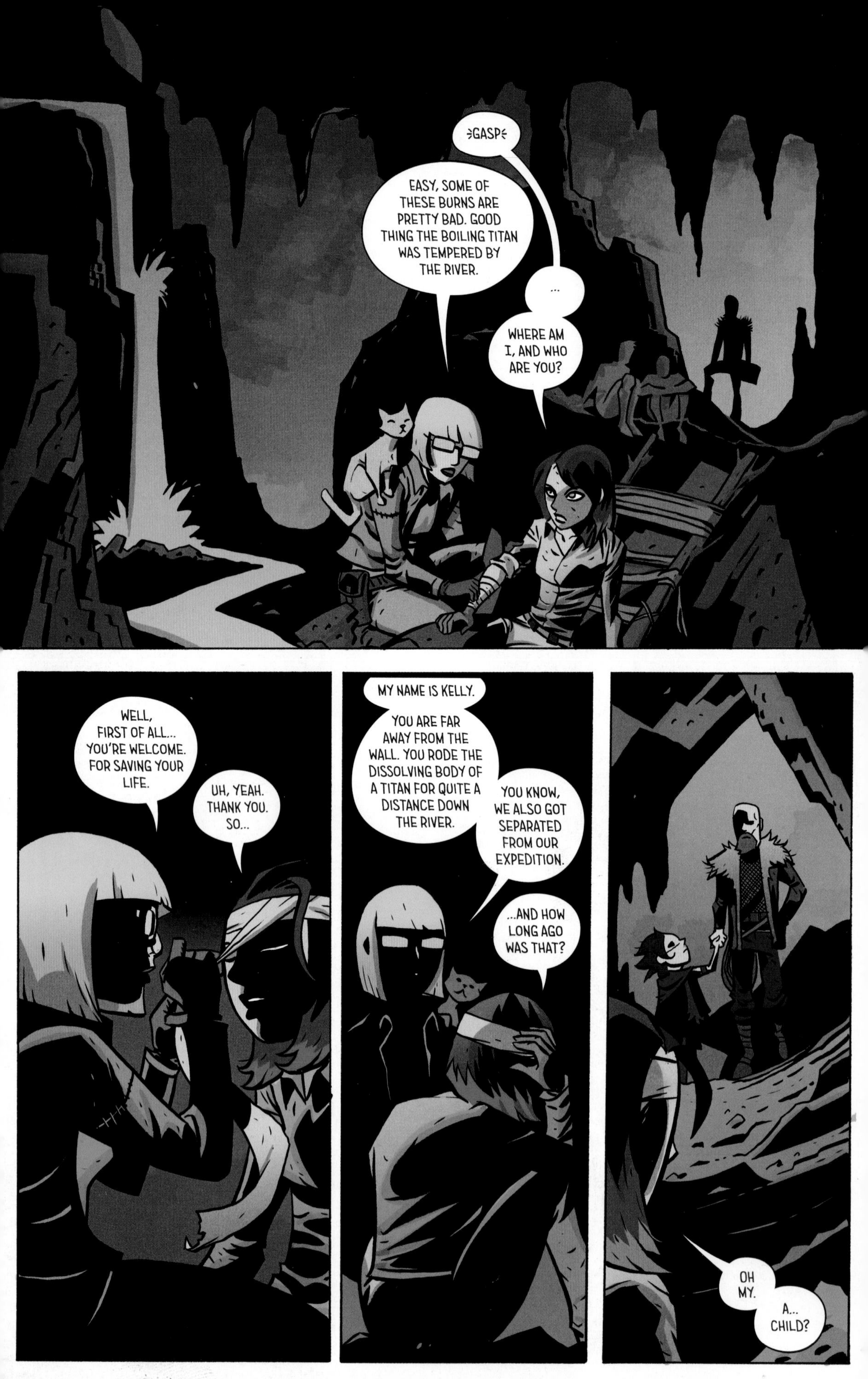

GASP
EASY, SOME OF THESE BURNS ARE PRETTY BAD. GOOD THING THE BOILING TITAN WAS TEMPERED BY THE RIVER.
...
WHERE AM I, AND WHO ARE YOU?
WELL, FIRST OF ALL... YOU'RE WELCOME. FOR SAVING YOUR LIFE.
UH, YEAH. THANK YOU. SO...
MY NAME IS KELLY.
YOU ARE FAR AWAY FROM THE WALL. YOU RODE THE DISSOLVING BODY OF A TITAN FOR QUITE A DISTANCE DOWN THE RIVER.
YOU KNOW, WE ALSO GOT SEPARATED FROM OUR EXPEDITION.
...AND HOW LONG AGO WAS THAT?
OH MY.
A... CHILD?

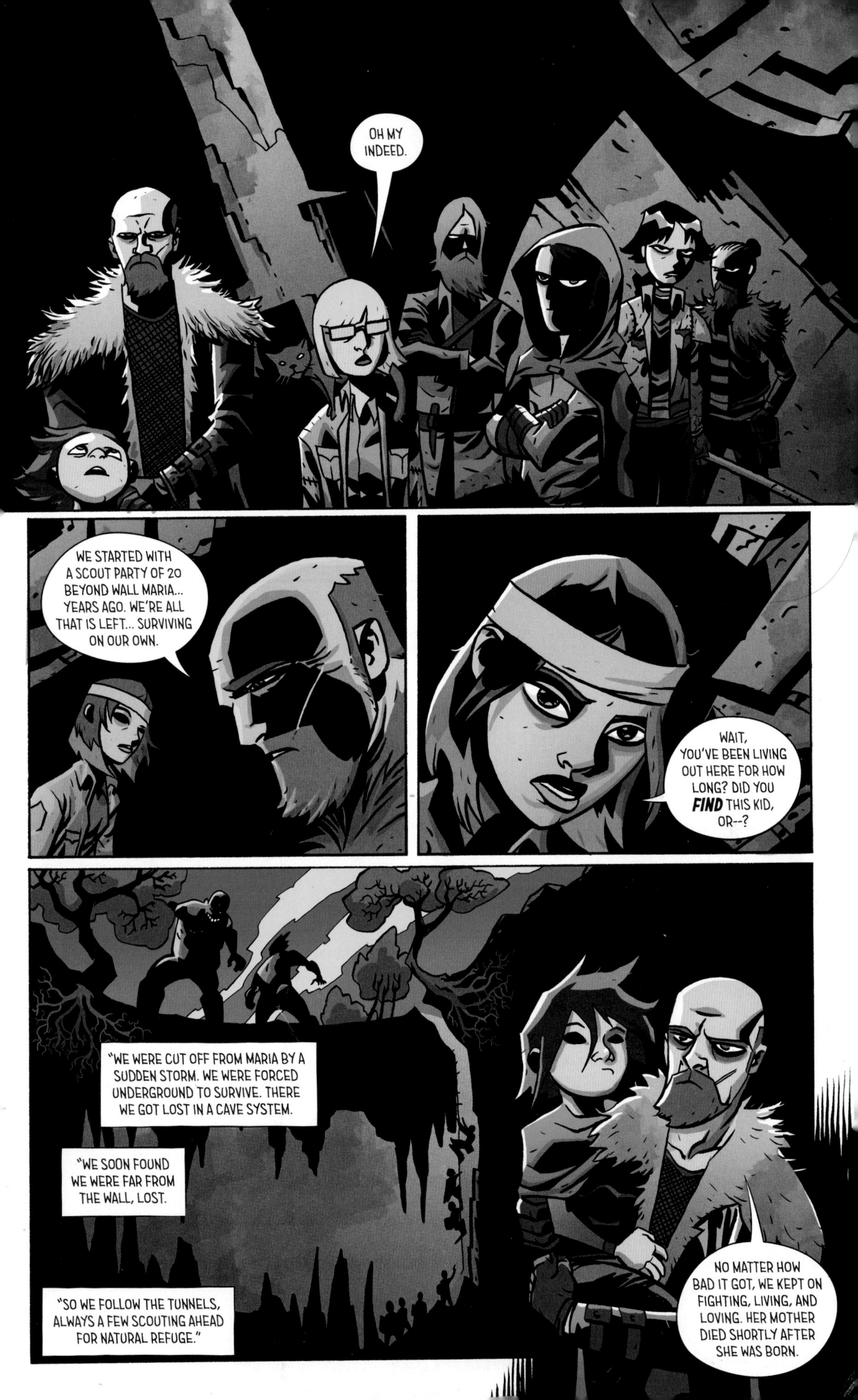
OH MY INDEED.
WE STARTED WITH A SCOUT PARTY OF 20 BEYOND WALL MARIA... YEARS AGO. WE'RE ALL THAT IS LEFT... SURVIVING ON OUR OWN.
WAIT, YOU'VE BEEN LIVING OUT HERE FOR HOW LONG? DID YOU **FIND** THIS KID, OR--?
"WE WERE CUT OFF FROM MARIA BY A SUDDEN STORM. WE WERE FORCED UNDERGROUND TO SURVIVE. THERE WE GOT LOST IN A CAVE SYSTEM.
"WE SOON FOUND WE WERE FAR FROM THE WALL, LOST.
"SO WE FOLLOW THE TUNNELS, ALWAYS A FEW SCOUTING AHEAD FOR NATURAL REFUGE."
NO MATTER HOW BAD IT GOT, WE KEPT ON FIGHTING, LIVING, AND LOVING. HER MOTHER DIED SHORTLY AFTER SHE WAS BORN.

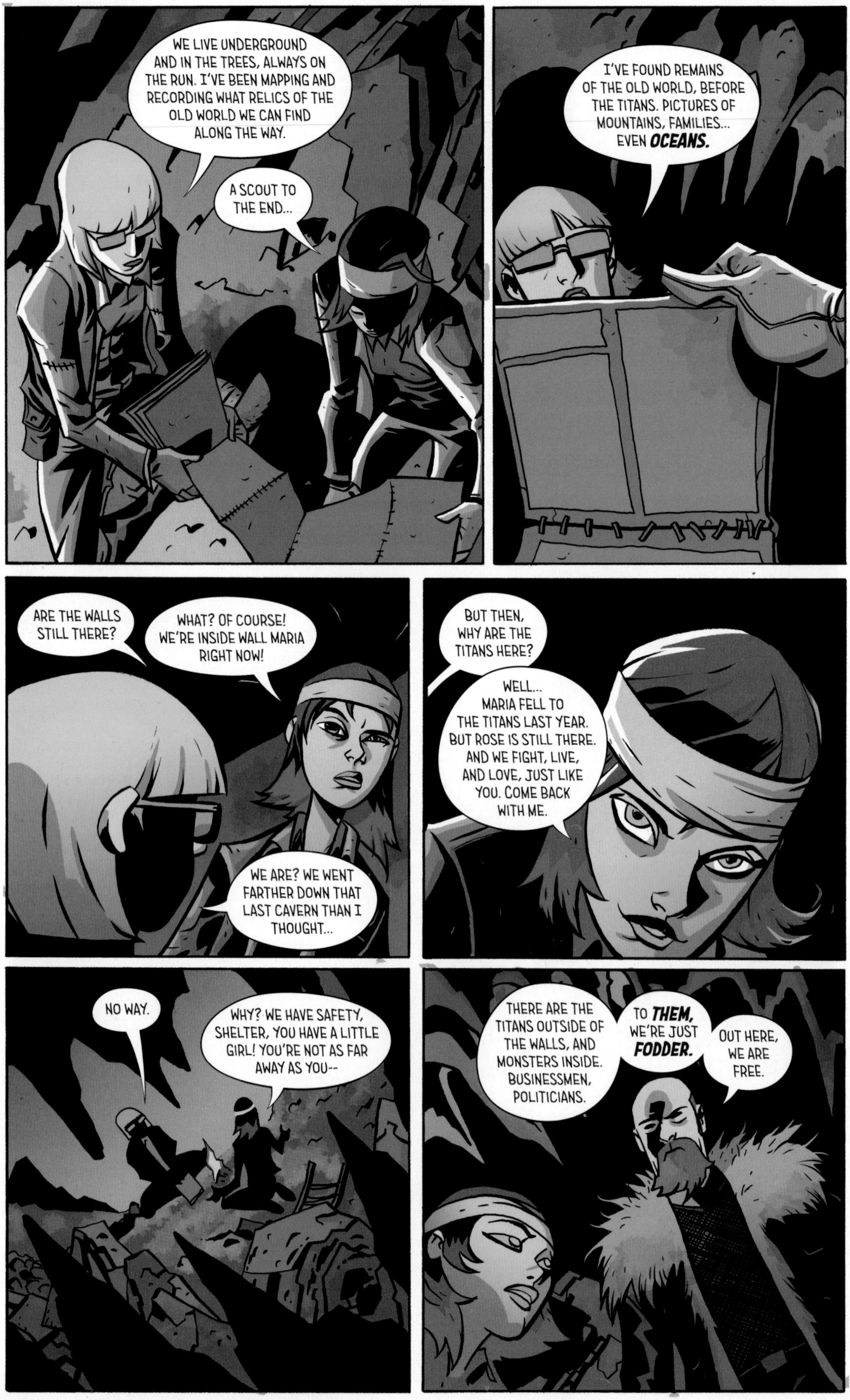
WE LIVE UNDERGROUND AND IN THE TREES, ALWAYS ON THE RUN. I'VE BEEN MAPPING AND RECORDING WHAT RELICS OF THE OLD WORLD WE CAN FIND ALONG THE WAY.
A SCOUT TO THE END...
I'VE FOUND REMAINS OF THE OLD WORLD, BEFORE THE TITANS. PICTURES OF MOUNTAINS, FAMILIES... EVEN **OCEANS.**
ARE THE WALLS STILL THERE?
WHAT? OF COURSE! WE'RE INSIDE WALL MARIA RIGHT NOW!
WE ARE? WE WENT FARTHER DOWN THAT LAST CAVERN THAN I THOUGHT...
BUT THEN, WHY ARE THE TITANS HERE?
WELL... MARIA FELL TO THE TITANS LAST YEAR. BUT ROSE IS STILL THERE. AND WE FIGHT, LIVE, AND LOVE, JUST LIKE YOU. COME BACK WITH ME.
NO WAY.
WHY? WE HAVE SAFETY, SHELTER, YOU HAVE A LITTLE GIRL! YOU'RE NOT AS FAR AWAY AS YOU--
THERE ARE THE TITANS OUTSIDE OF THE WALLS, AND MONSTERS INSIDE. BUSINESSMEN, POLITICIANS.
TO ***THEM,*** WE'RE JUST ***FODDER.***
OUT HERE, WE ARE FREE.

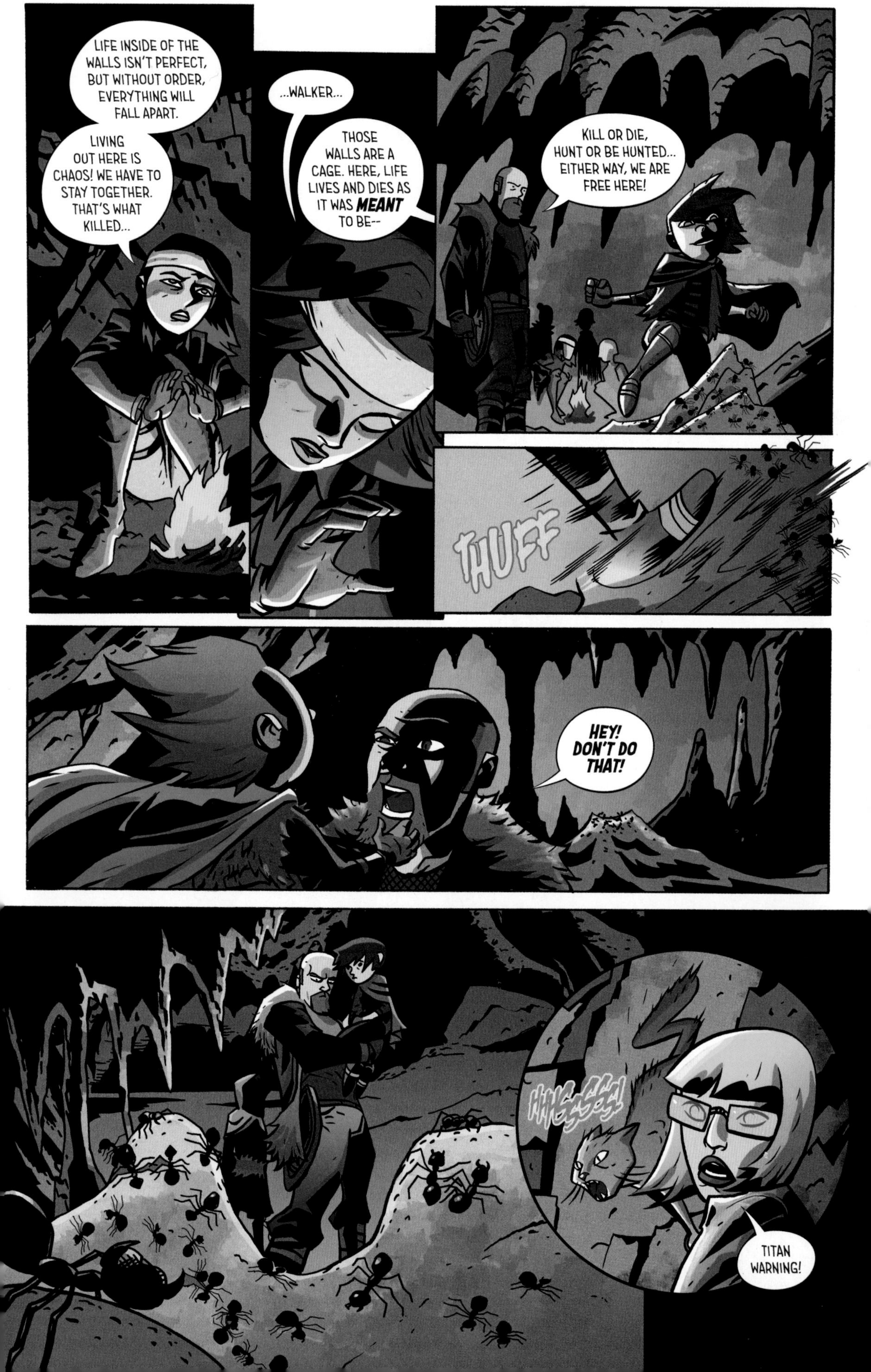
LIFE INSIDE OF THE WALLS ISN'T PERFECT, BUT WITHOUT ORDER, EVERYTHING WILL FALL APART.
LIVING OUT HERE IS CHAOS! WE HAVE TO STAY TOGETHER. THAT'S WHAT KILLED...
...WALKER...
THOSE WALLS ARE A CAGE. HERE, LIFE LIVES AND DIES AS IT WAS **MEANT** TO BE--
KILL OR DIE, HUNT OR BE HUNTED... EITHER WAY, WE ARE FREE HERE!
THUFF
HEY! DON'T DO THAT!
HHHSSSSS!
TITAN WARNING!

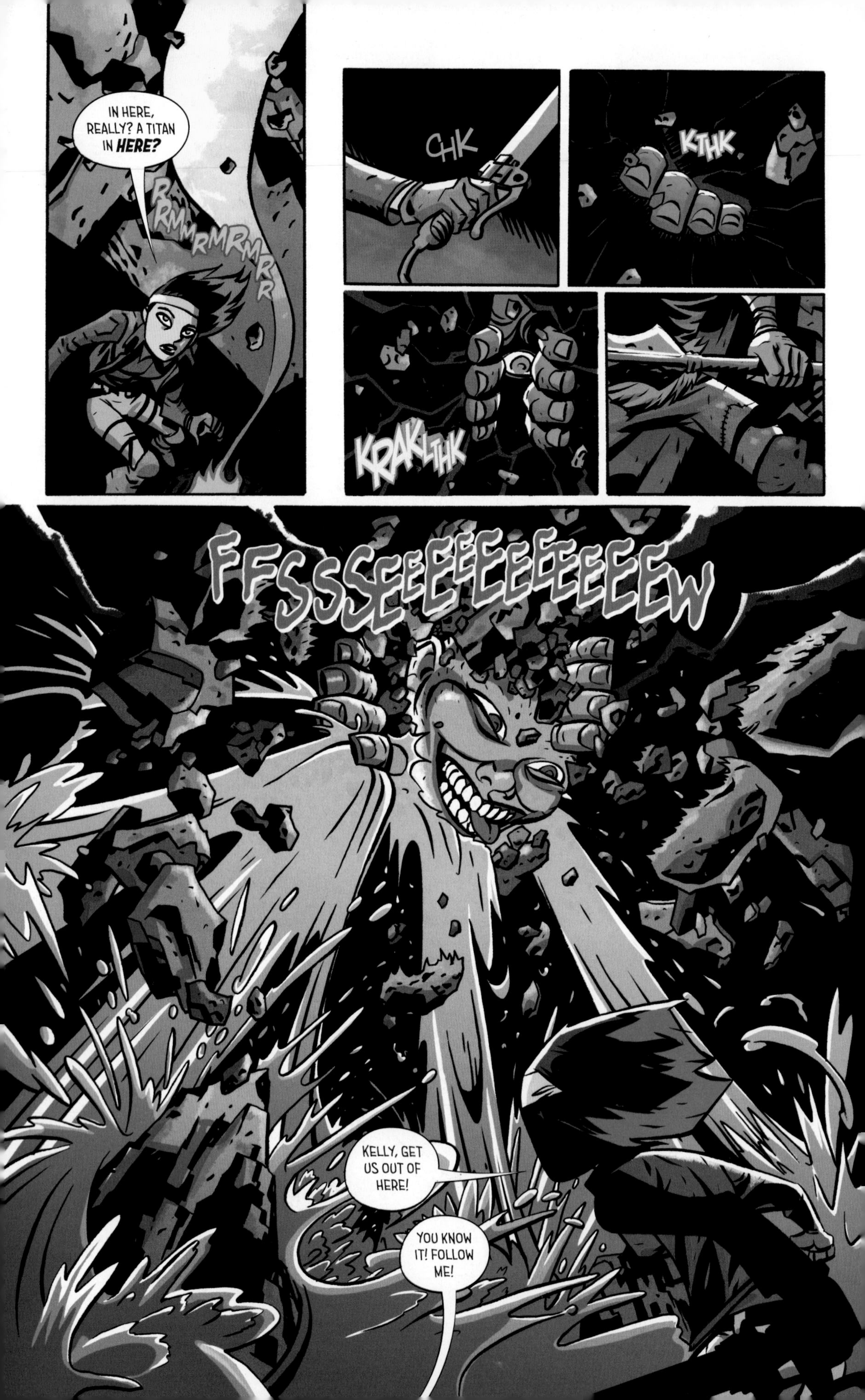
IN HERE, REALLY? A TITAN IN **HERE?**
RRMMRMRMRRR
CHK
KTHK
KRAKLTHK
FFSSSEEEEEEEEEEEEW
KELLY, GET US OUT OF HERE!
YOU KNOW IT! FOLLOW ME!

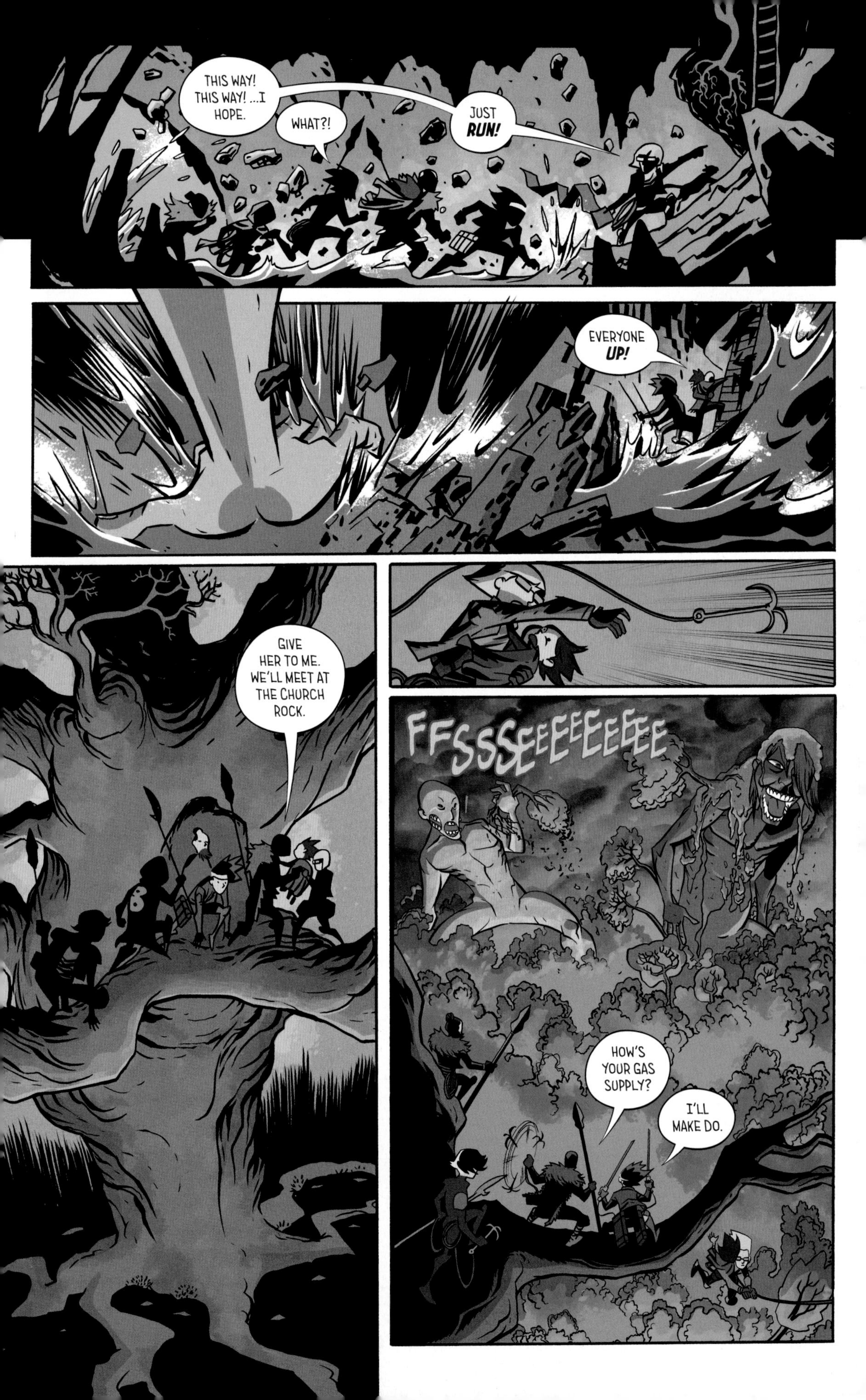
THIS WAY! THIS WAY! ...I HOPE.
WHAT?!
JUST **RUN!**
EVERYONE **UP!**
GIVE HER TO ME. WE'LL MEET AT THE CHURCH ROCK.
FFSSSEEEEEEEE
HOW'S YOUR GAS SUPPLY?
I'LL MAKE DO.

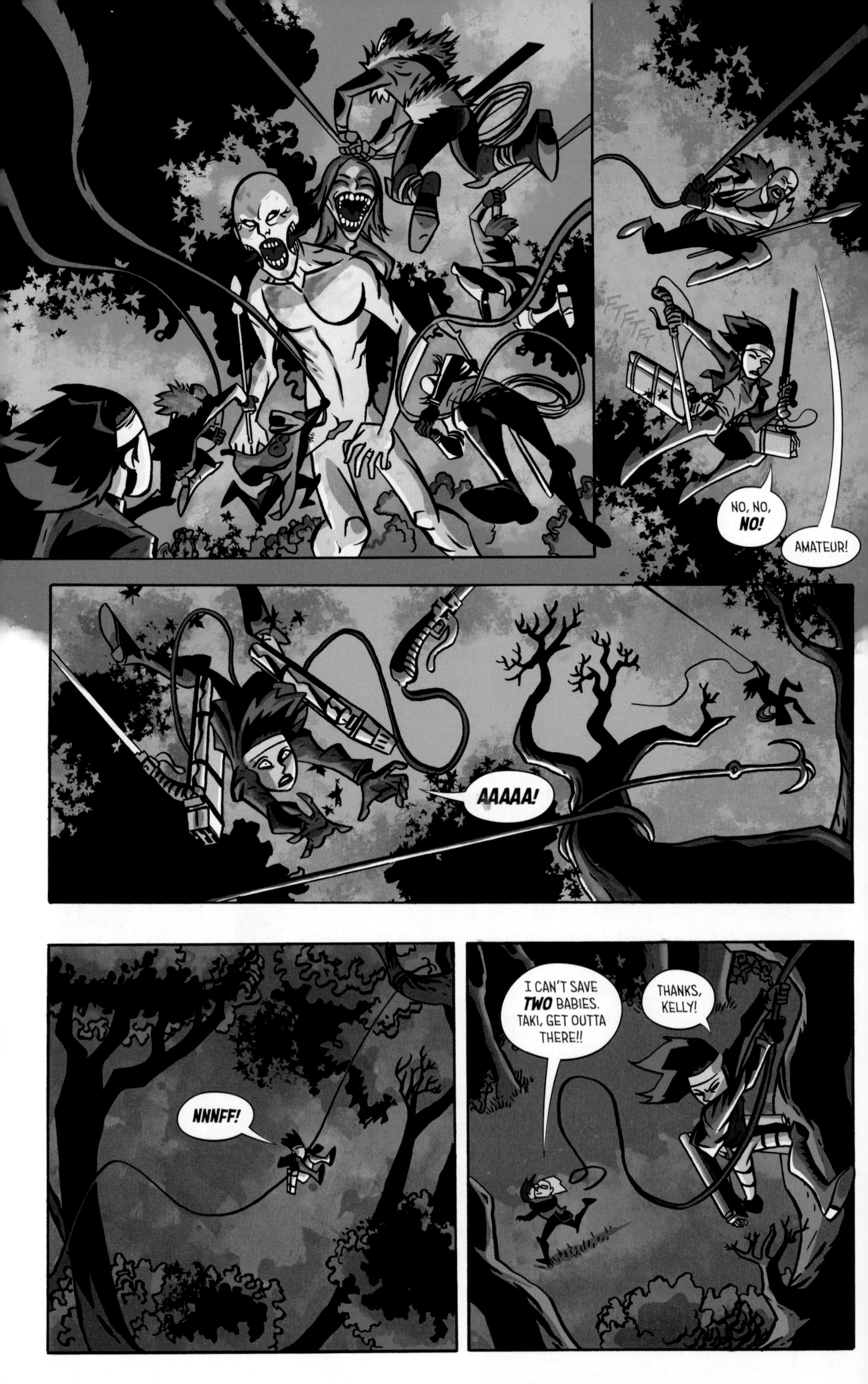
NO, NO, **NO!**
AMATEUR!
AAAAA!
NNNFF!
I CAN'T SAVE **TWO** BABIES. TAKI, GET OUTTA THERE!!
THANKS, KELLY!

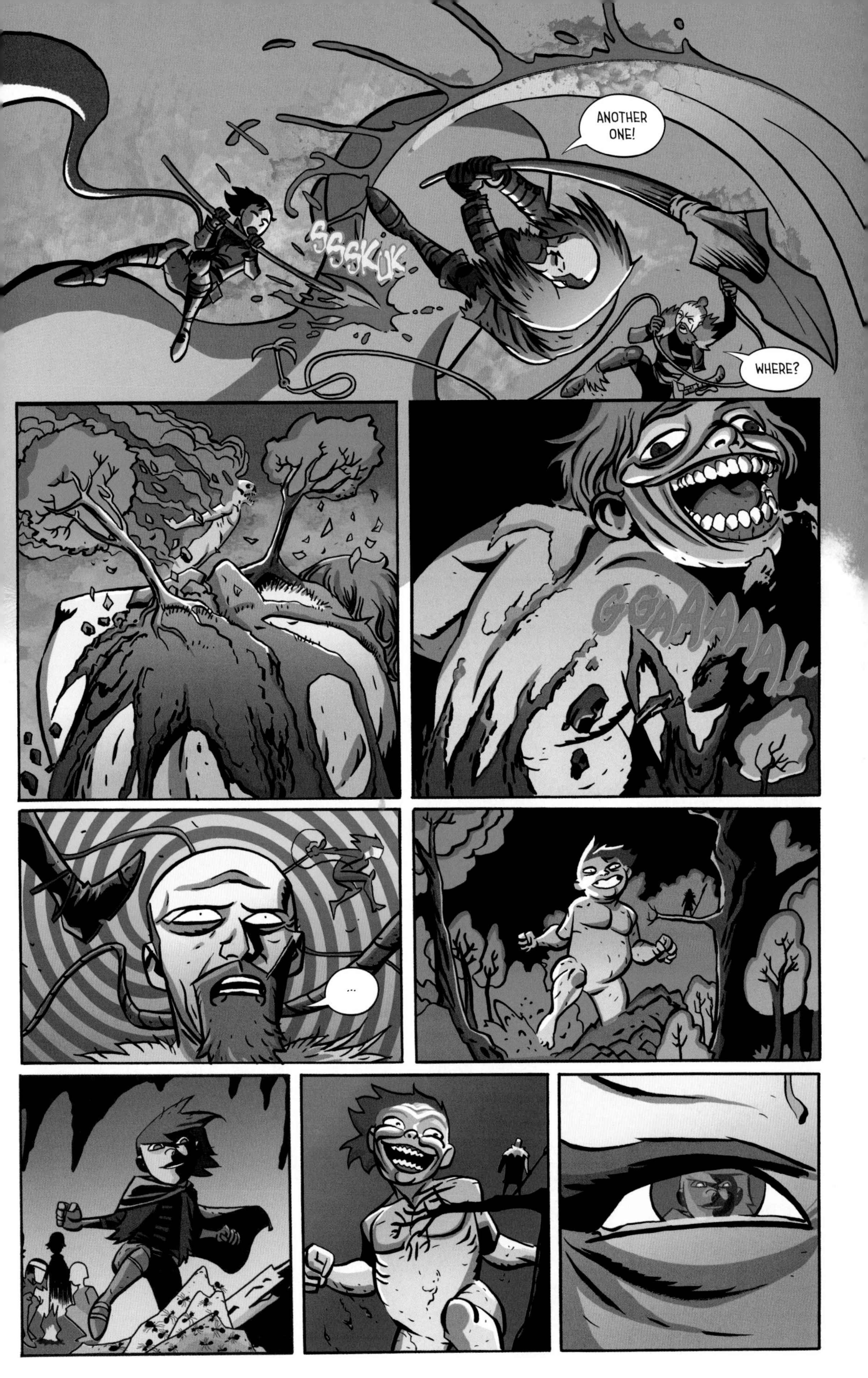
ANOTHER ONE!
SSSKUK
WHERE?
GGAAAAAA!
...

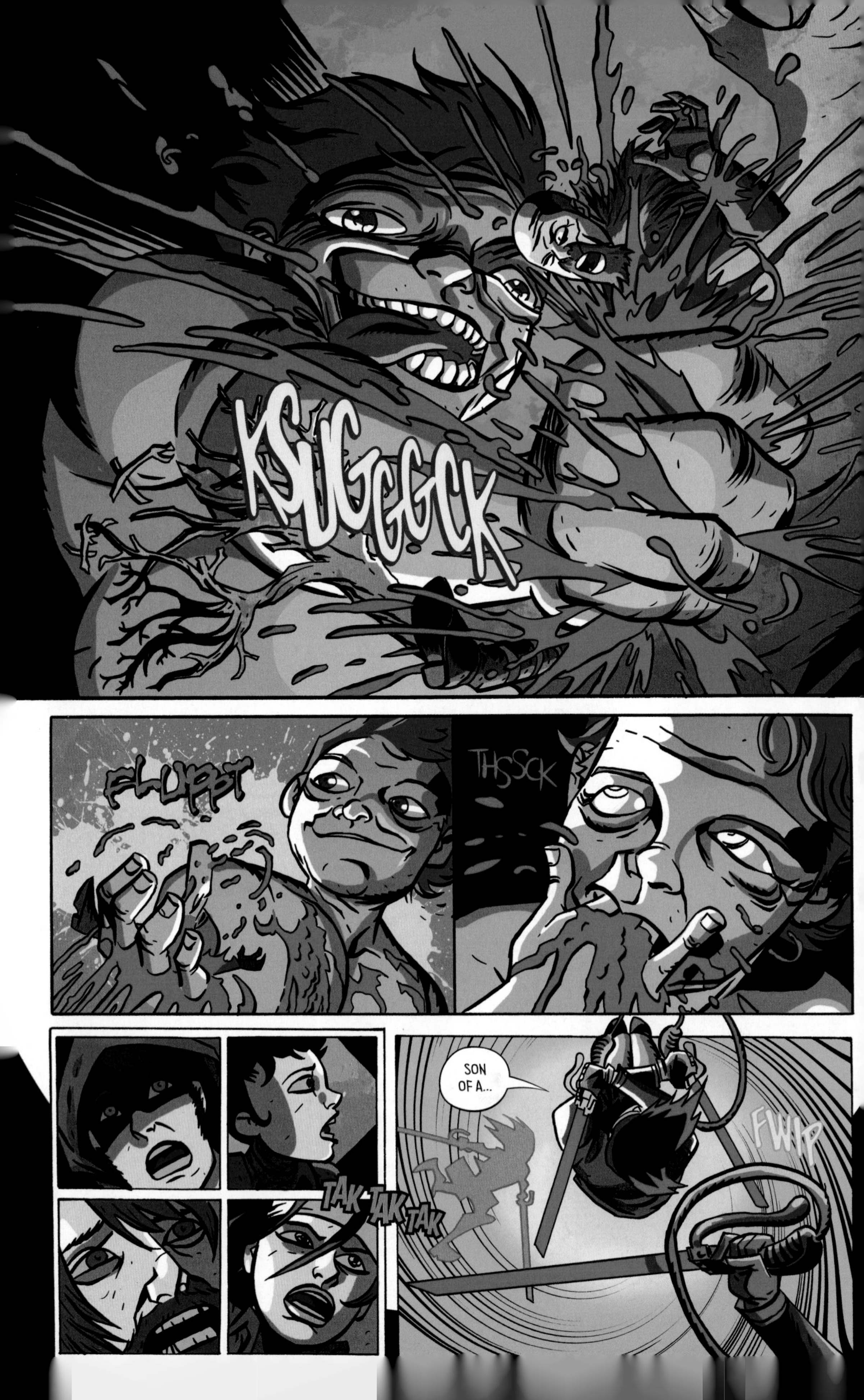
KSUGGCK
FLUBBT
THSSCK
SON OF A...
FWIP
TAK TAK TAK

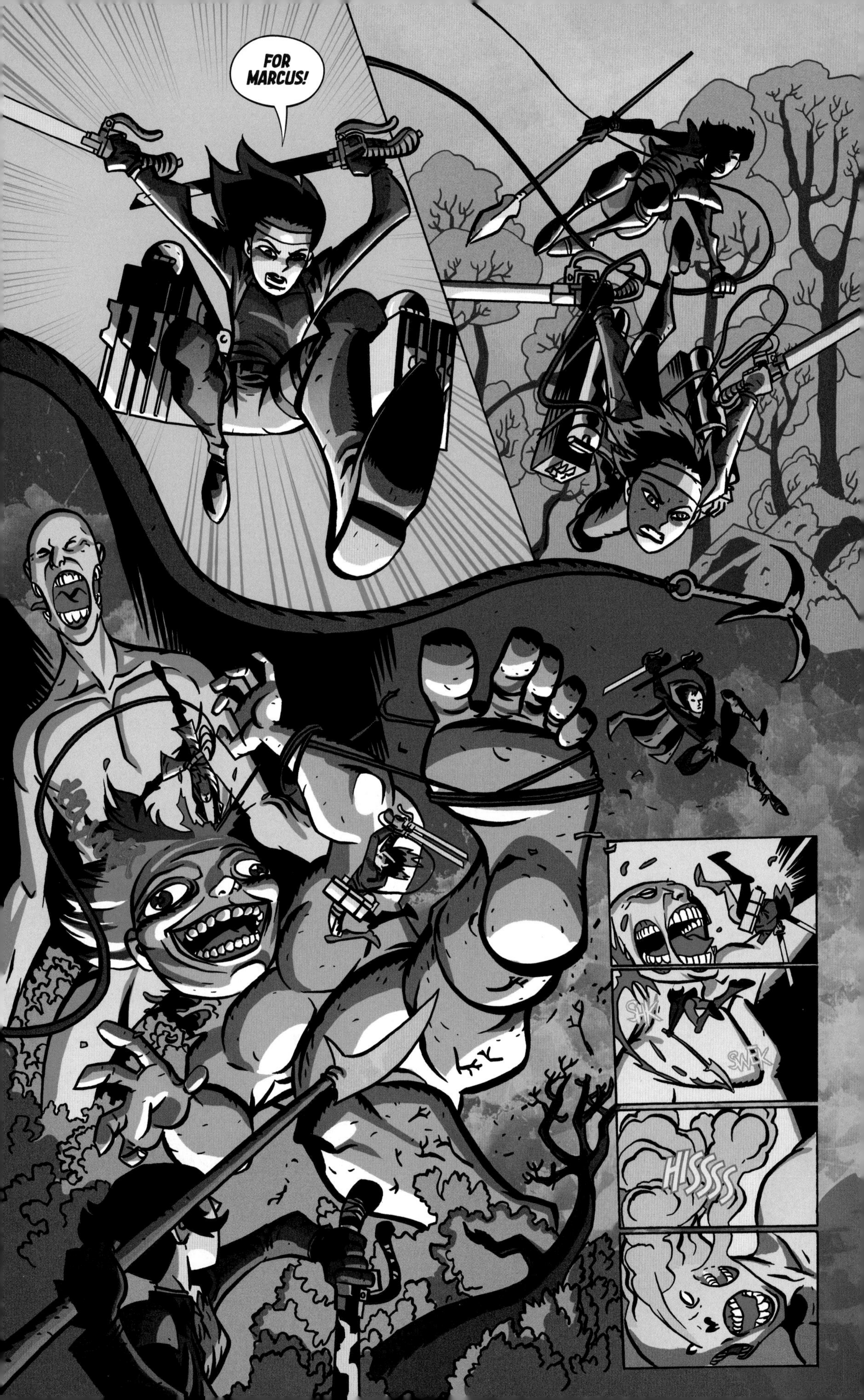
FOR MARCUS!
SHK
SWEK
HISSSS

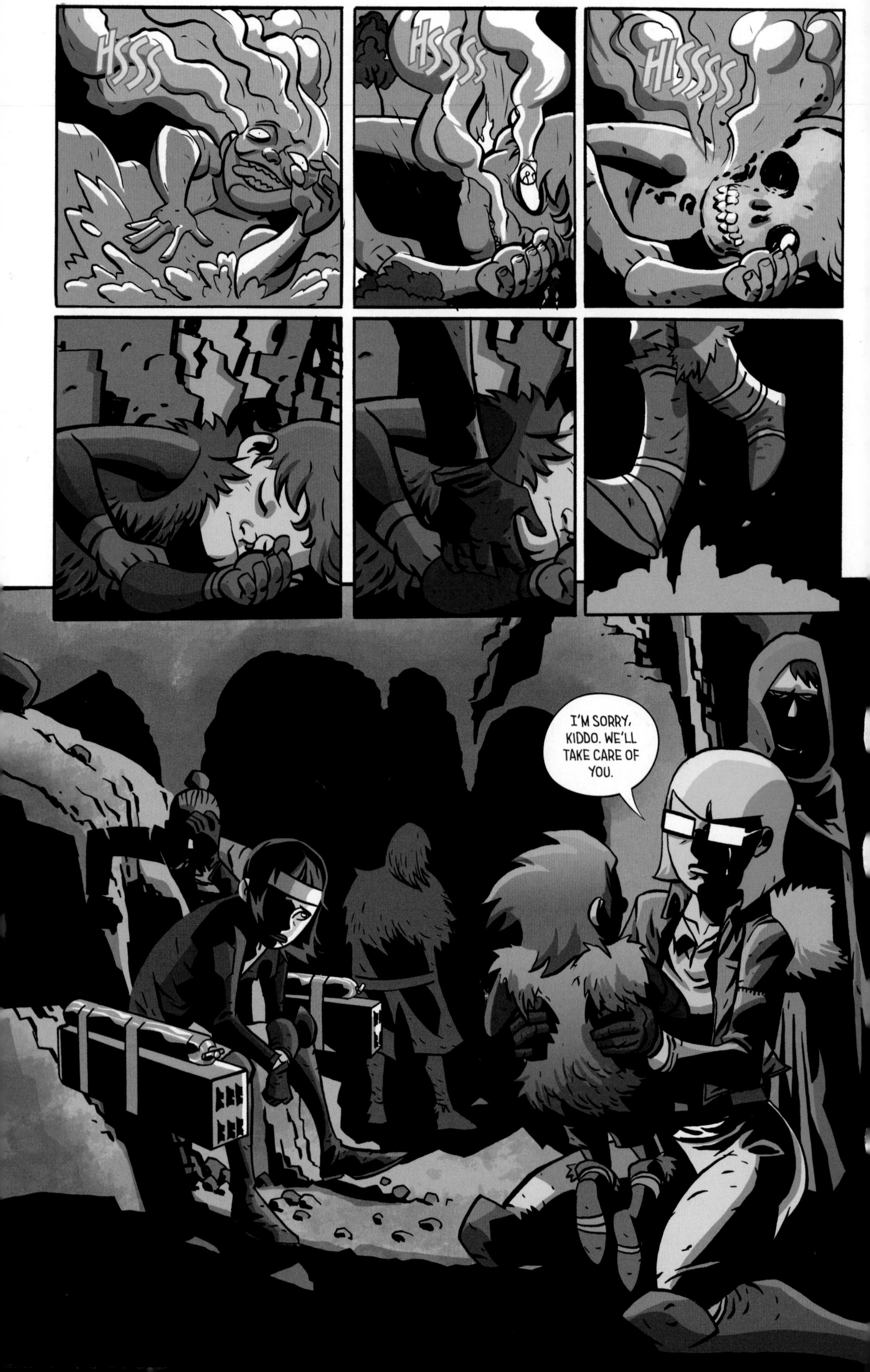
HSSS
HSSSS
HISSSS
I'M SORRY, KIDDO. WE'LL TAKE CARE OF YOU.

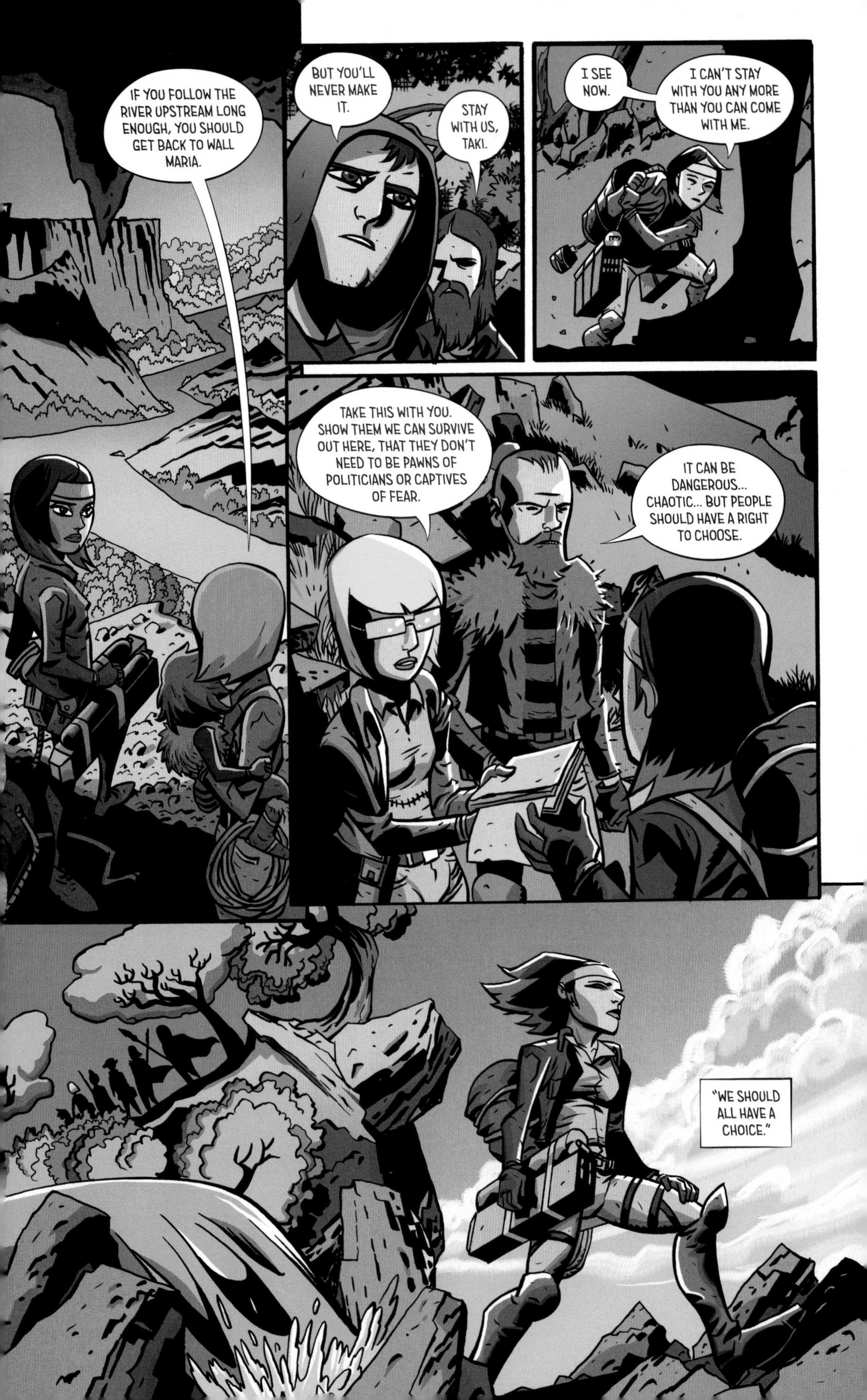
IF YOU FOLLOW THE RIVER UPSTREAM LONG ENOUGH, YOU SHOULD GET BACK TO WALL MARIA.
BUT YOU'LL NEVER MAKE IT.
STAY WITH US, TAKI.
I SEE NOW.
I CAN'T STAY WITH YOU ANY MORE THAN YOU CAN COME WITH ME.
TAKE THIS WITH YOU. SHOW THEM WE CAN SURVIVE OUT HERE, THAT THEY DON'T NEED TO BE PAWNS OF POLITICIANS OR CAPTIVES OF FEAR.
IT CAN BE DANGEROUS... CHAOTIC... BUT PEOPLE SHOULD HAVE A RIGHT TO CHOOSE.
"WE SHOULD ALL HAVE A CHOICE."

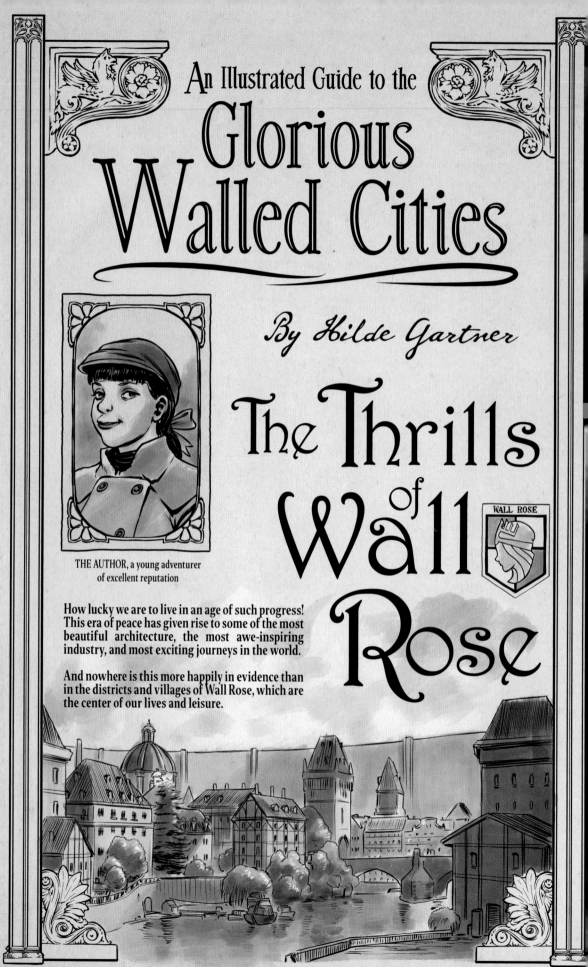

An Illustrated Guide to the

Glorious Walled Cities

By Hilde Gartner

The Thrills of Wall Rose

WALL ROSE

THE AUTHOR, a young adventurer
of excellent reputation

How lucky we are to live in an age of such progress!
This era of peace has given rise to some of the most
beautiful architecture, the most awe-inspiring
industry, and most exciting journeys in the world.

And nowhere is this more happily in evidence than
in the districts and villages of Wall Rose, which are
the center of our lives and leisure.

How to be Fashionable

In outer districts, practicality rules; she is always admired whose skirt can withstand the cold, whose boots the mud, and whose coat the rain. At Wall Rose, however, are the makers of such textiles as are the envy of every city, and thus Lady Fashion must be obeyed.

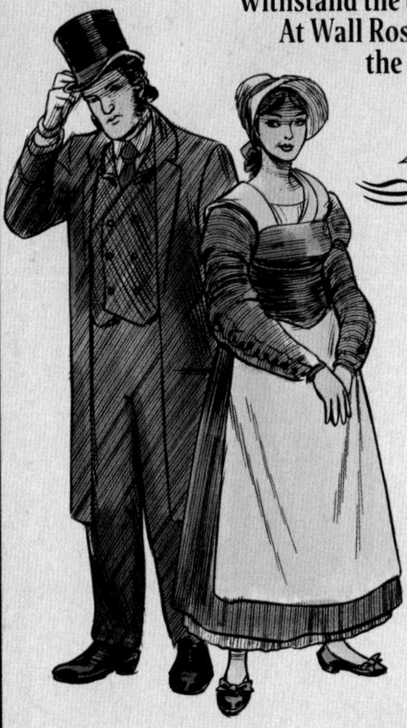

As the sun sets on Klorva and Yarckel, a wise lady traveler will prepare for weather: independent sleeves, colorful petticoats, and tuckers. For gentlemen, coats here are as long as the winter nights.

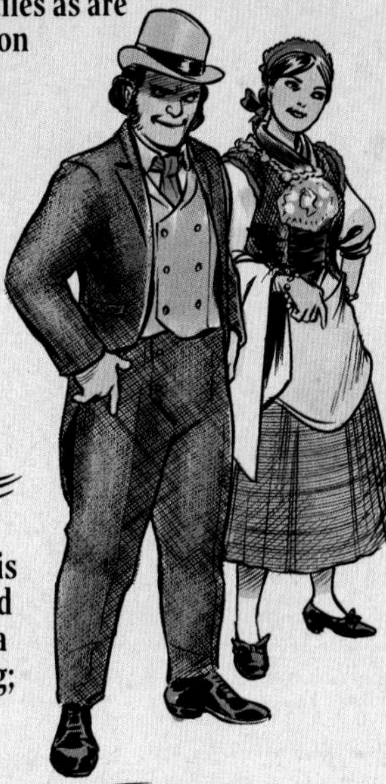

For ladies, no bodice can have too many laces, and no spring day is complete without a shawl trimmed with embroidery. For gentlemen, a short jacket to the waist is dashing; a waistcoat divine.

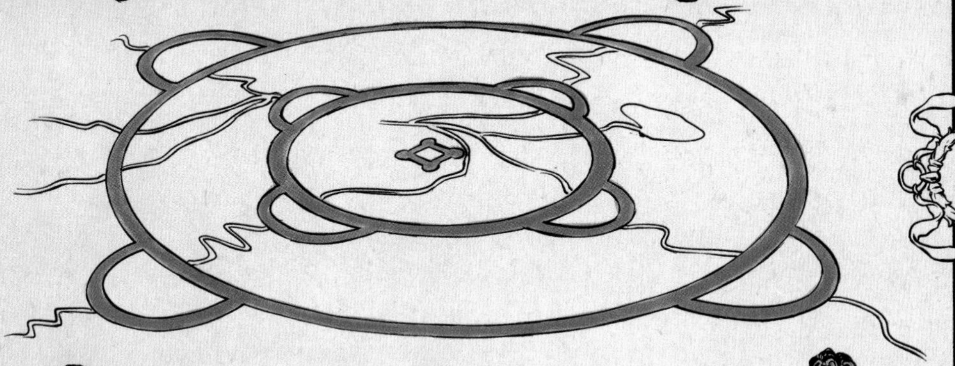

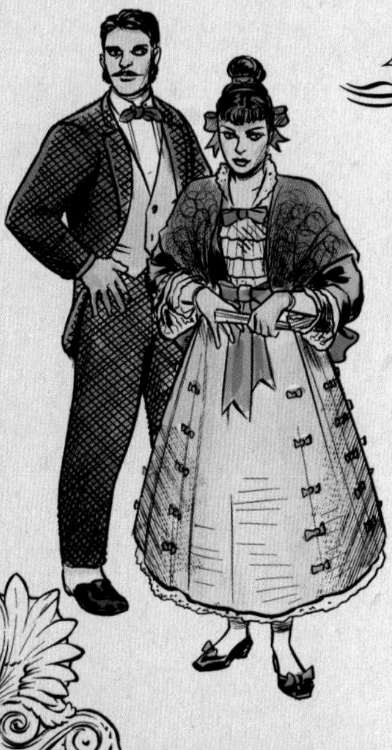

A mining town ruled by a single edict from Dame Fashion. In Utopia, dress as you choose, so long as there is room for silver upon it!

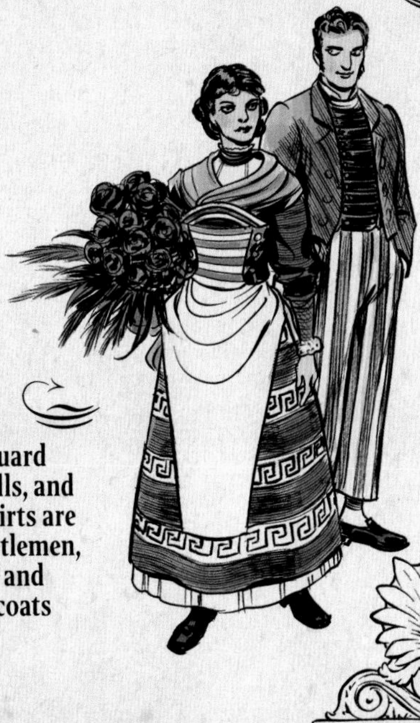

Stohess and Karanes stand guard over the muslin mills, and so bright double skirts are all the rage. For gentlemen, striped trousers and colorfully-lined coats with tails.

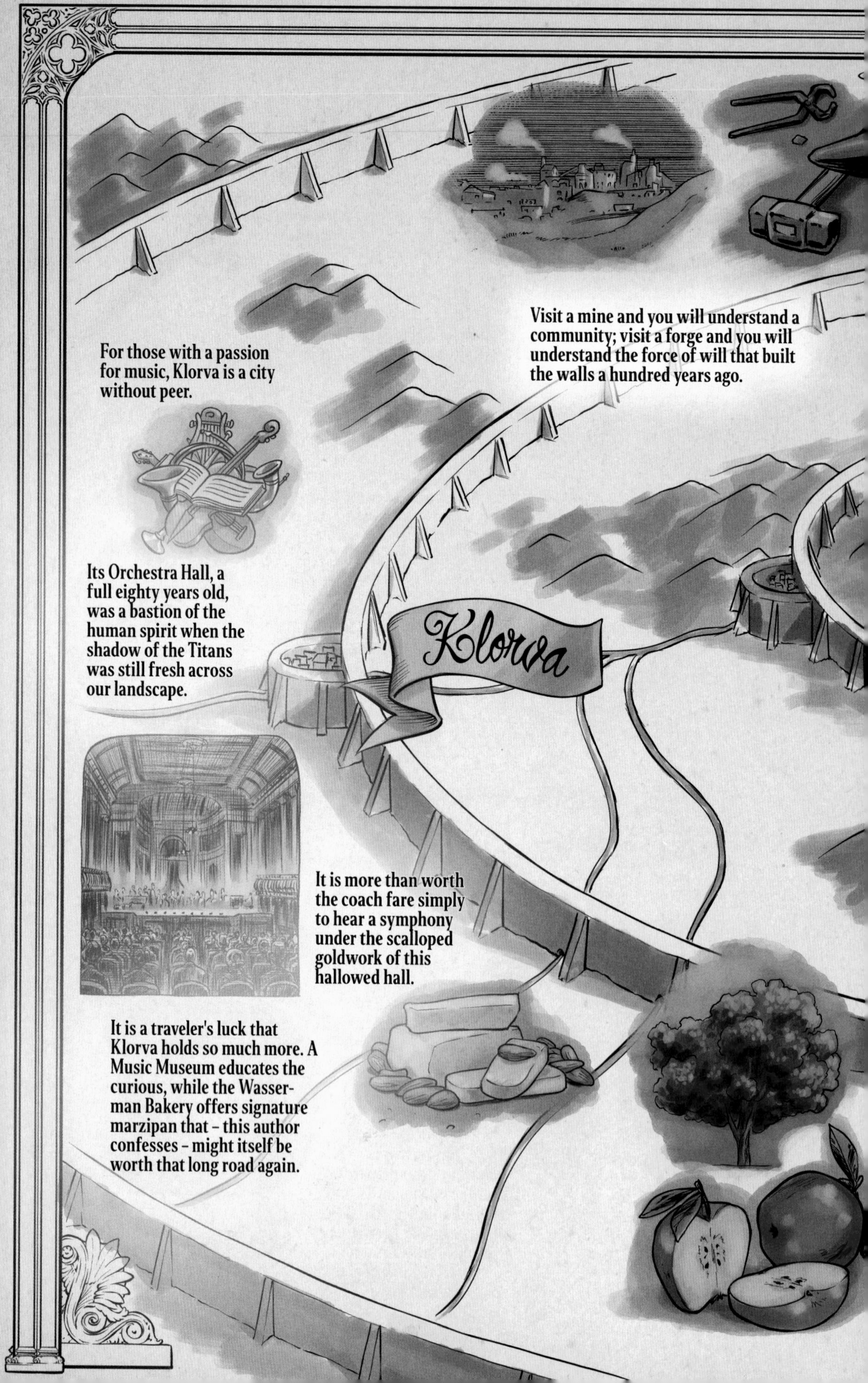
Klorva

Visit a mine and you will understand a community; visit a forge and you will understand the force of will that built the walls a hundred years ago.

For those with a passion for music, Klorva is a city without peer.

Its Orchestra Hall, a full eighty years old, was a bastion of the human spirit when the shadow of the Titans was still fresh across our landscape.

It is more than worth the coach fare simply to hear a symphony under the scalloped goldwork of this hallowed hall.

It is a traveler's luck that Klorva holds so much more. A Music Museum educates the curious, while the Wasserman Bakery offers signature marzipan that – this author confesses – might itself be worth that long road again.

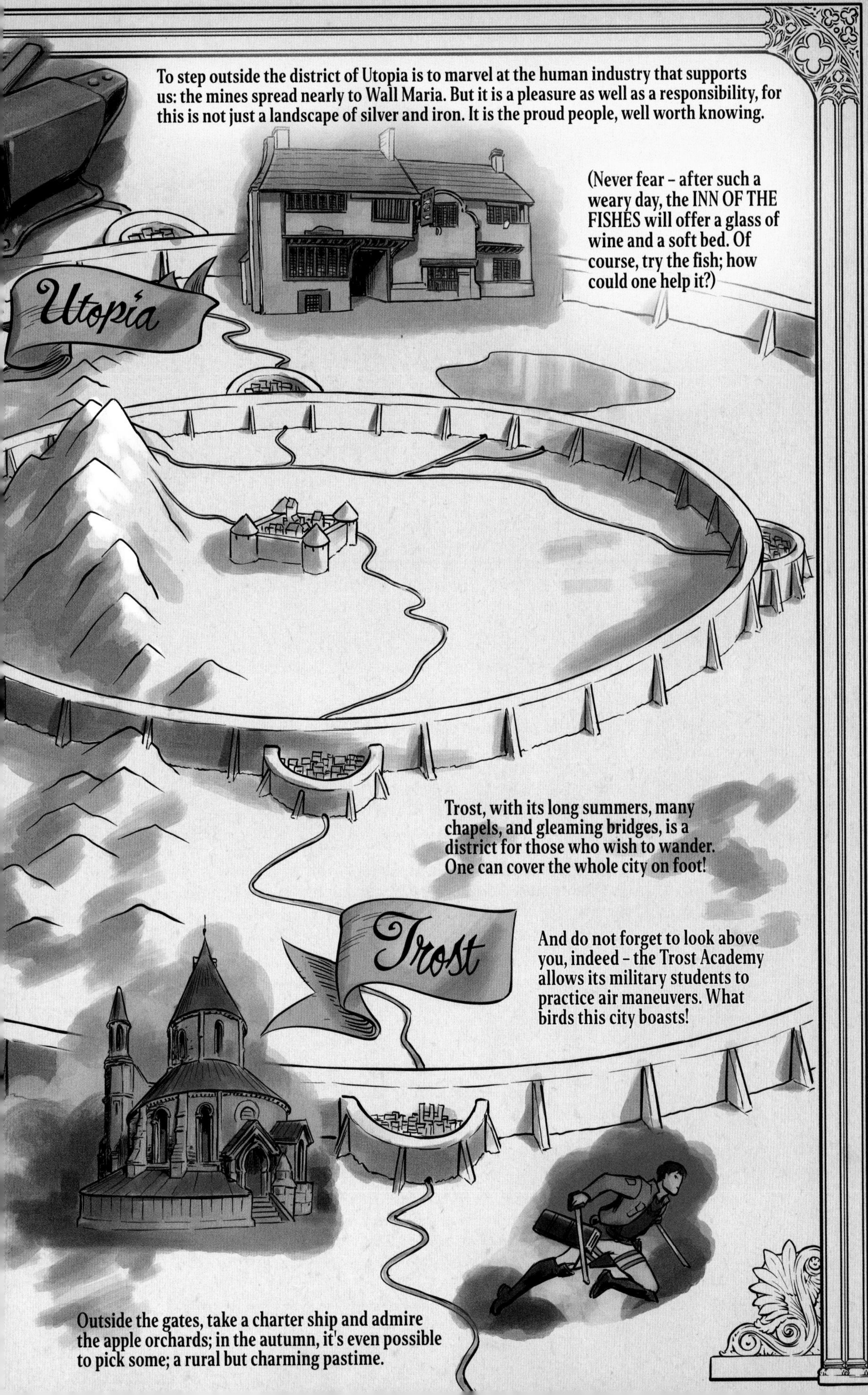
To step outside the district of Utopia is to marvel at the human industry that supports us: the mines spread nearly to Wall Maria. But it is a pleasure as well as a responsibility, for this is not just a landscape of silver and iron. It is the proud people, well worth knowing.
(Never fear – after such a weary day, the INN OF THE FISHES will offer a glass of wine and a soft bed. Of course, try the fish; how could one help it?)
Utopia
Trost, with its long summers, many chapels, and gleaming bridges, is a district for those who wish to wander. One can cover the whole city on foot!
Trost
And do not forget to look above you, indeed – the Trost Academy allows its military students to practice air maneuvers. What birds this city boasts!
Outside the gates, take a charter ship and admire the apple orchards; in the autumn, it's even possible to pick some; a rural but charming pastime.

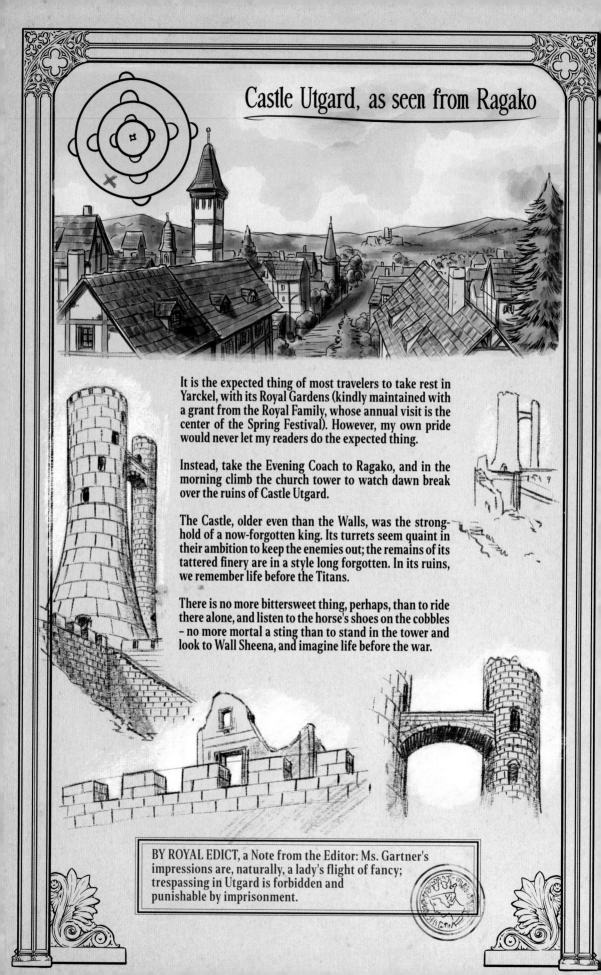

Castle Utgard, as seen from Ragako

It is the expected thing of most travelers to take rest in Yarckel, with its Royal Gardens (kindly maintained with a grant from the Royal Family, whose annual visit is the center of the Spring Festival). However, my own pride would never let my readers do the expected thing.

Instead, take the Evening Coach to Ragako, and in the morning climb the church tower to watch dawn break over the ruins of Castle Utgard.

The Castle, older even than the Walls, was the stronghold of a now-forgotten king. Its turrets seem quaint in their ambition to keep the enemies out; the remains of its tattered finery are in a style long forgotten. In its ruins, we remember life before the Titans.

There is no more bittersweet thing, perhaps, than to ride there alone, and listen to the horse's shoes on the cobbles – no more mortal a sting than to stand in the tower and look to Wall Sheena, and imagine life before the war.

BY ROYAL EDICT, a Note from the Editor: Ms. Gartner's impressions are, naturally, a lady's flight of fancy; trespassing in Utgard is forbidden and punishable by imprisonment.

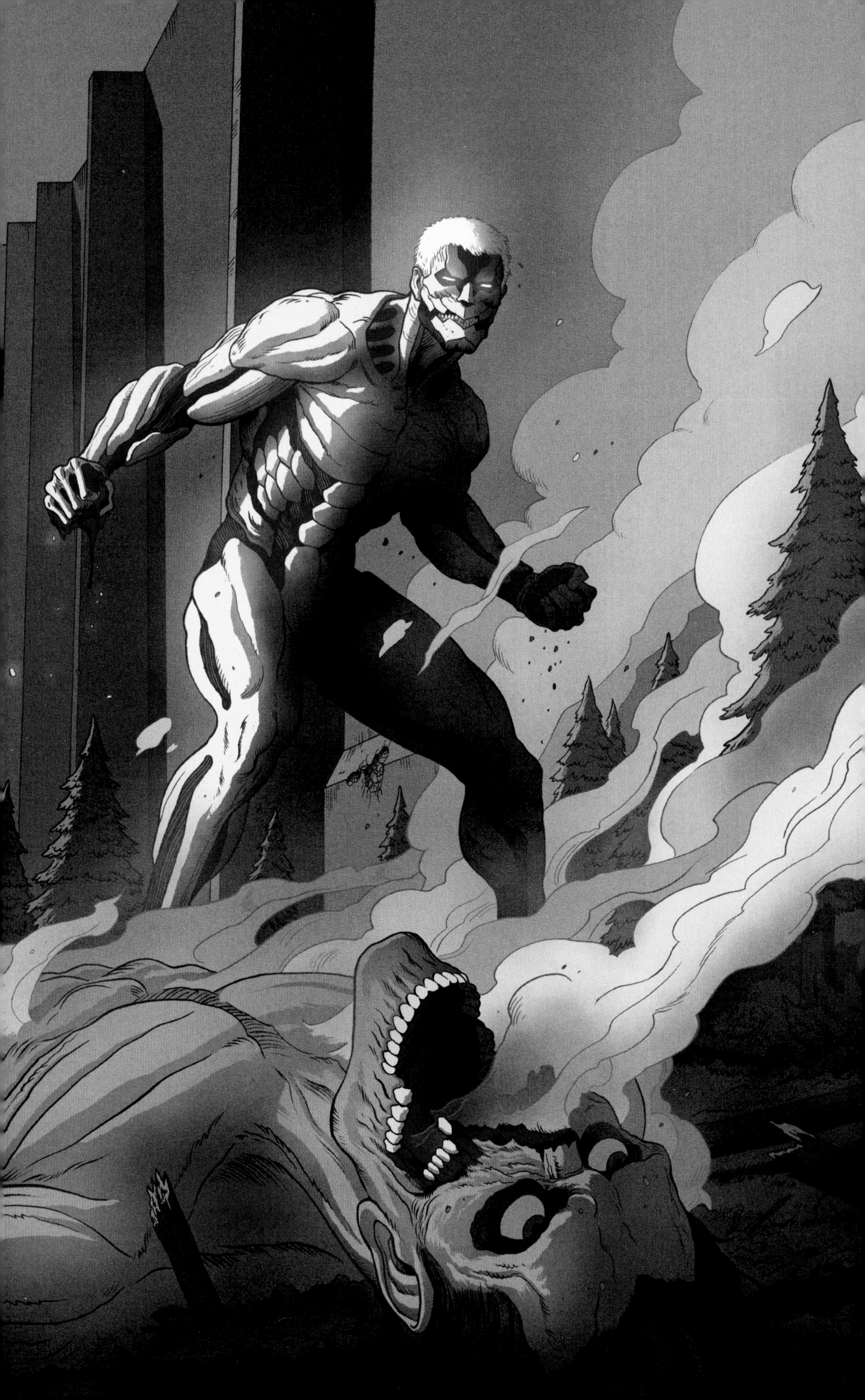

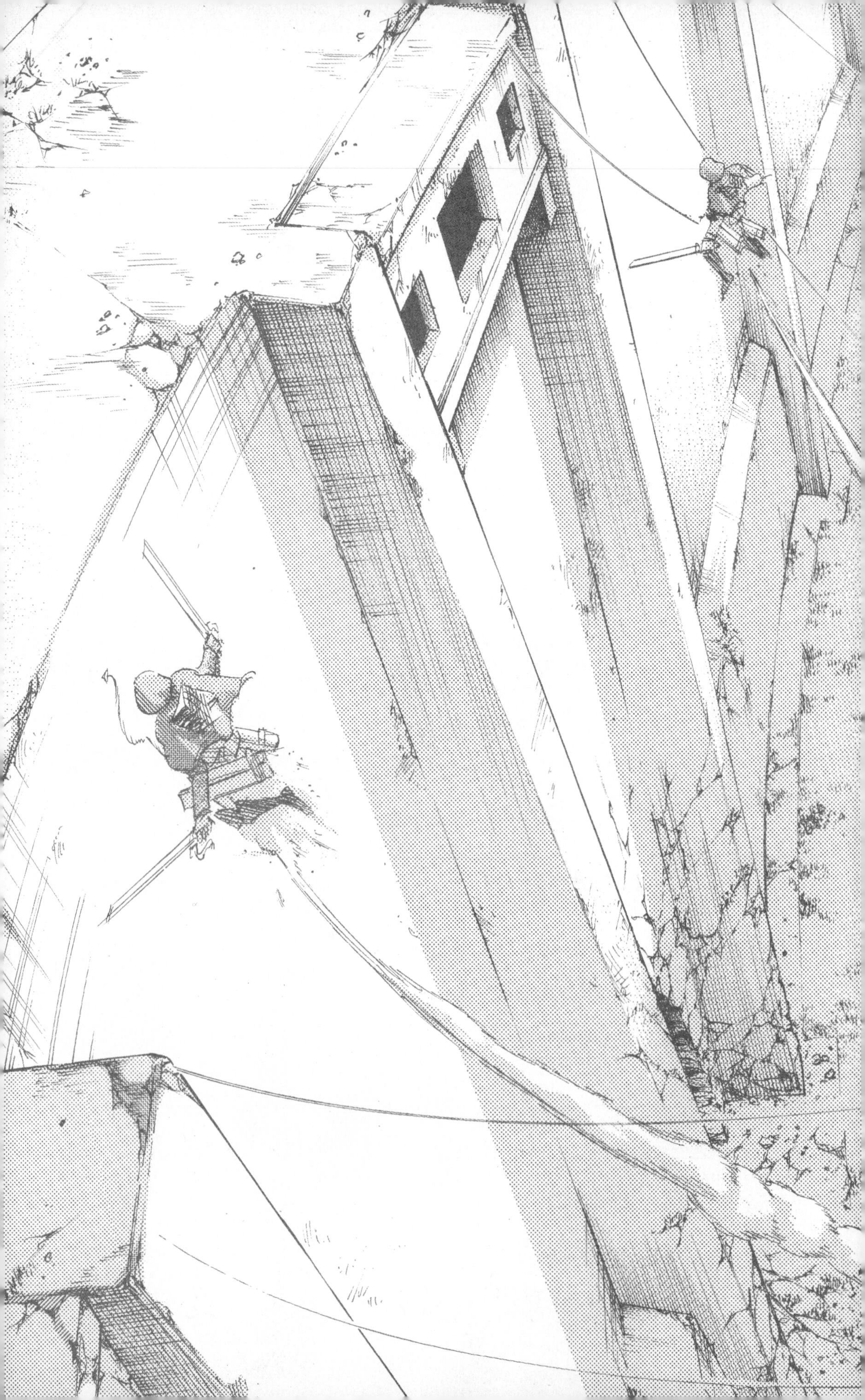

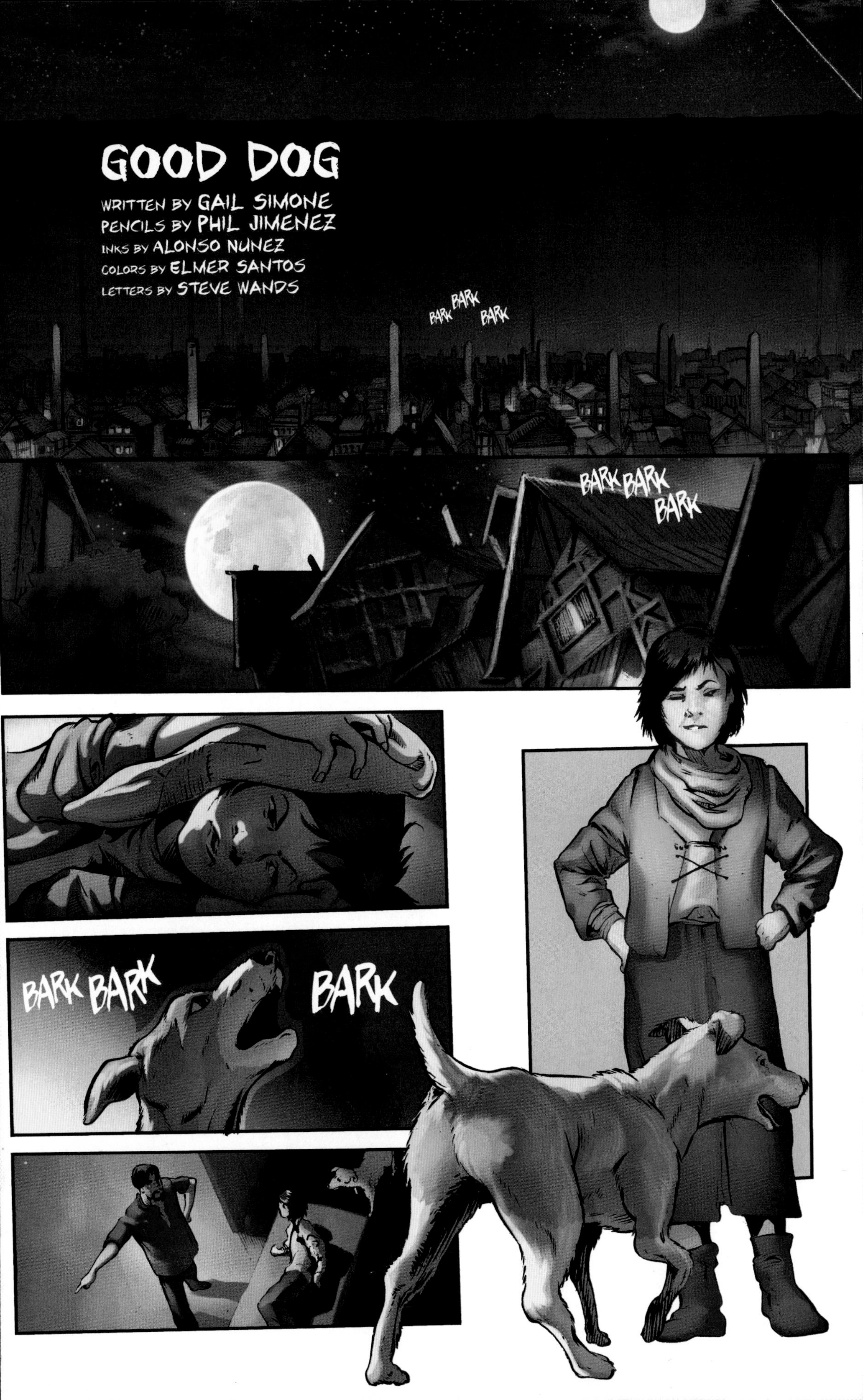
GOOD DOG
WRITTEN BY GAIL SIMONE
PENCILS BY PHIL JIMENEZ
INKS BY ALONSO NUNEZ
COLORS BY ELMER SANTOS
LETTERS BY STEVE WANDS
BARK BARK BARK
BARK BARK BARK
BARK BARK
BARK

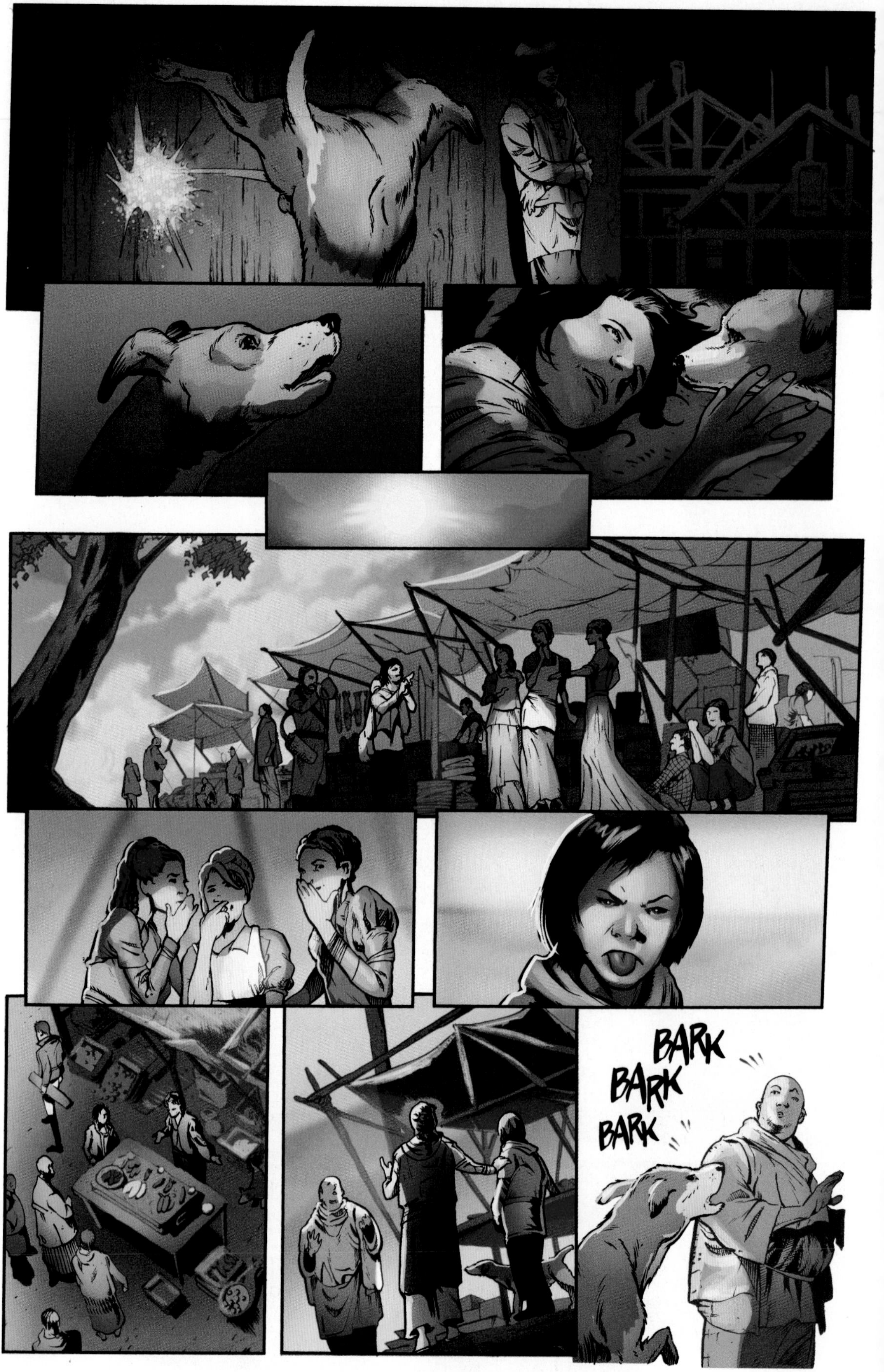
BARK
BARK
BARK

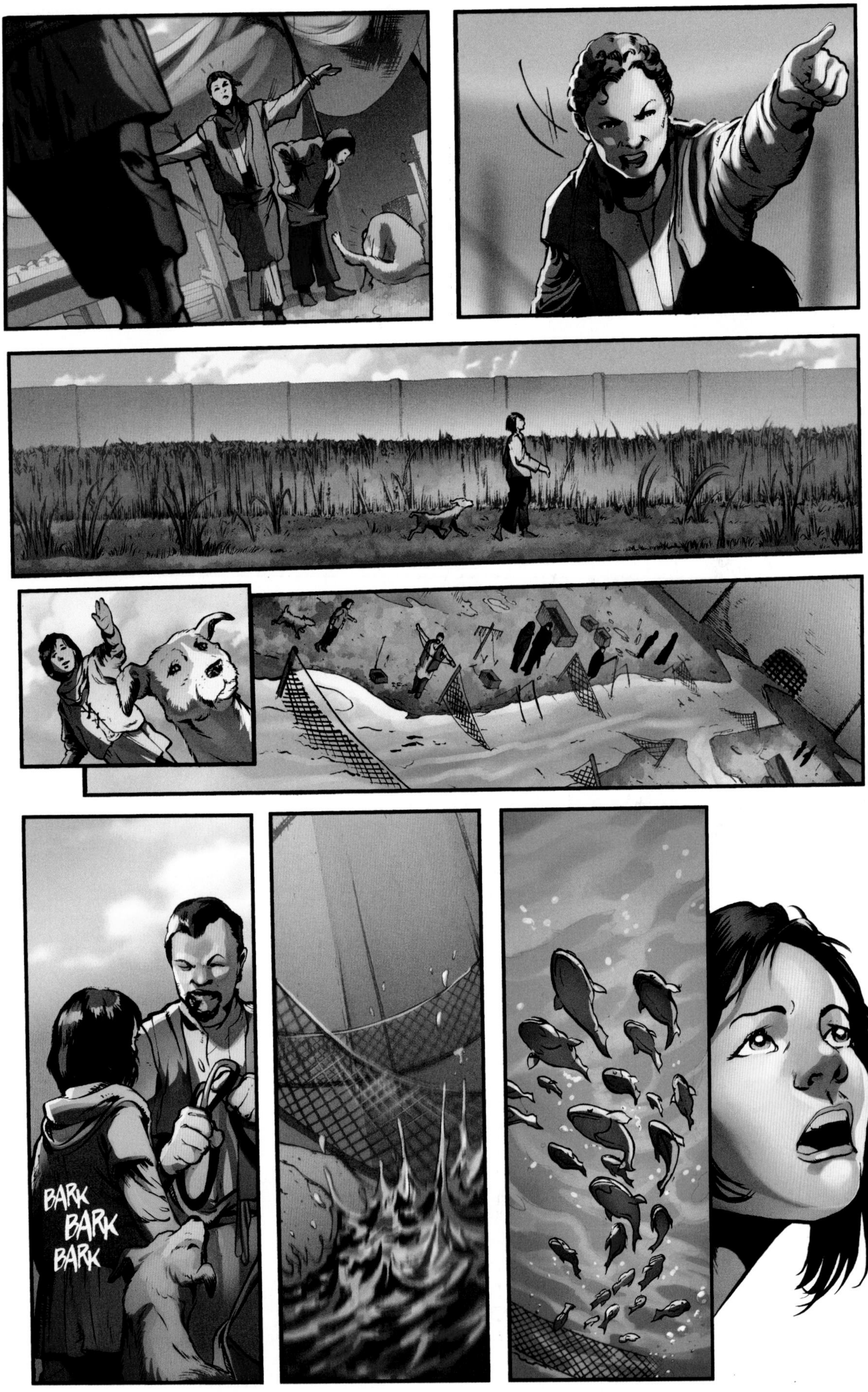
BARK
BARK
BARK

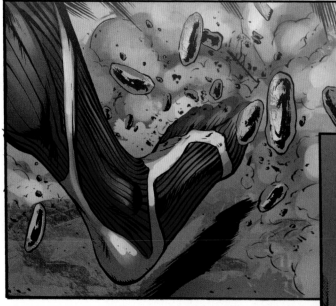

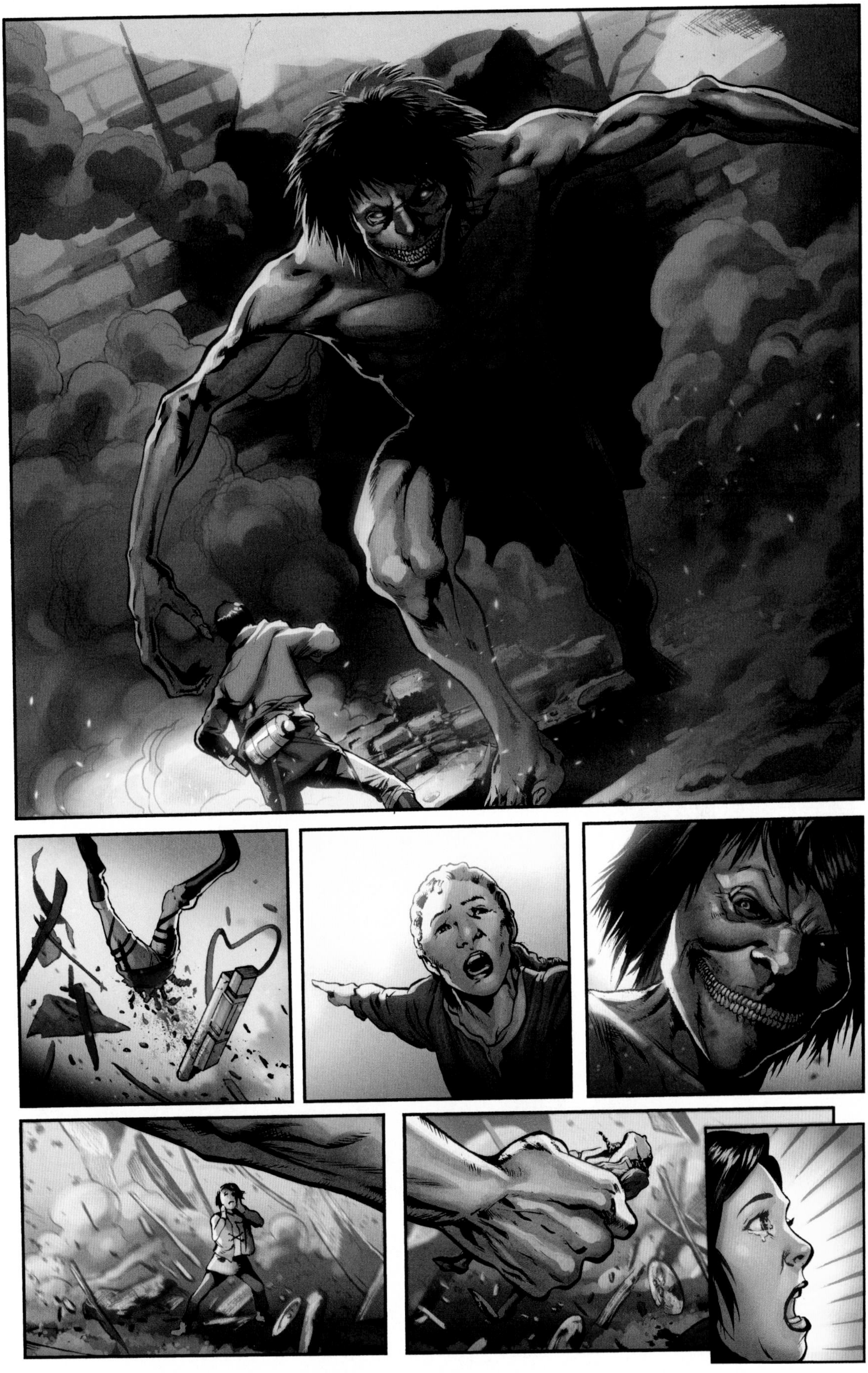

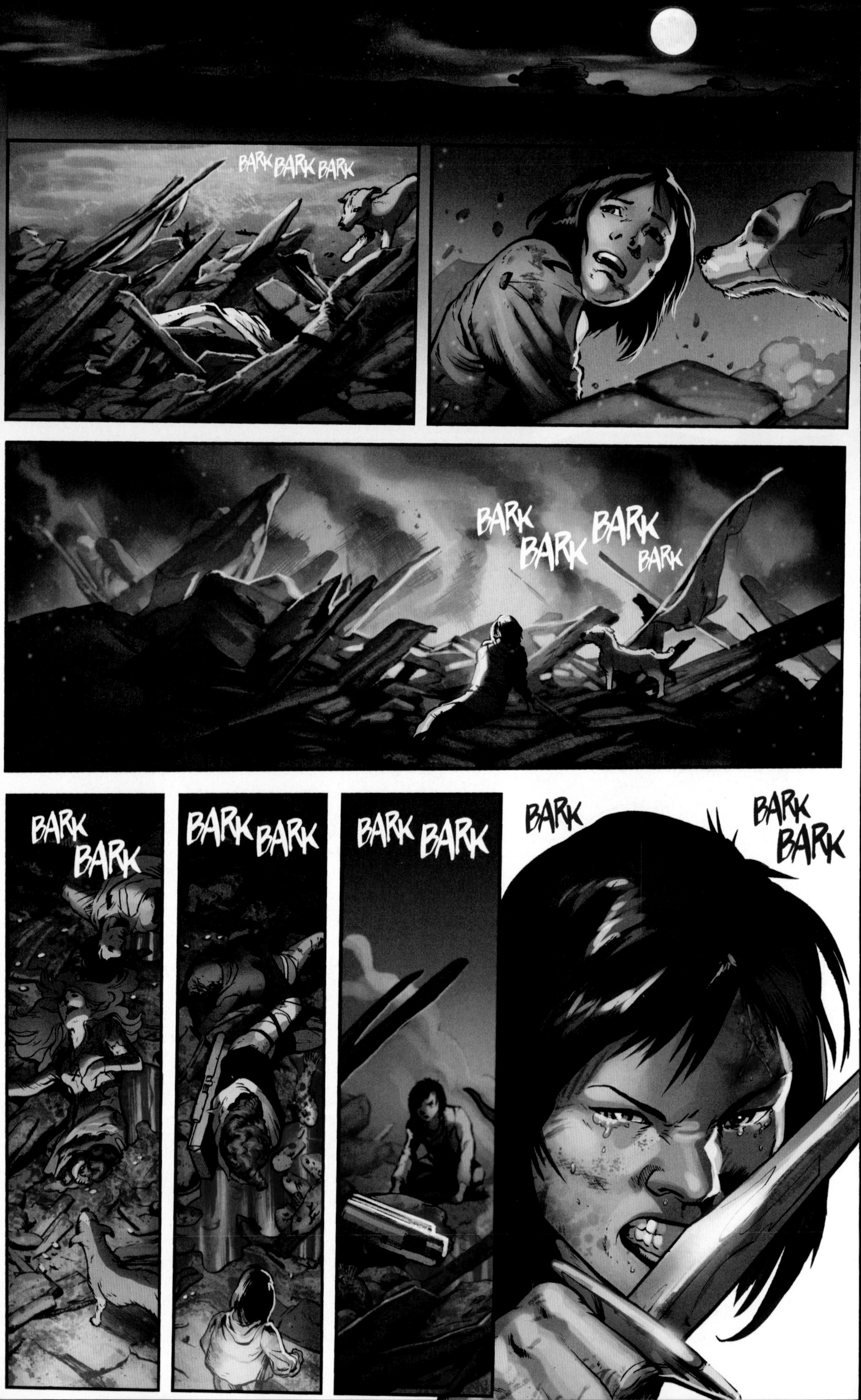
BARK BARK BARK
BARK BARK BARK BARK
BARK BARK
BARK BARK
BARK BARK
BARK BARK BARK

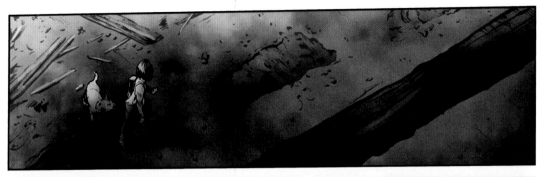

BARK
BARK BARK
BARK

BARK BARK

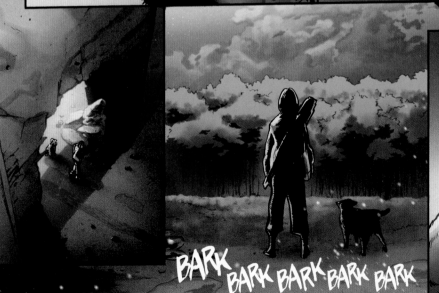

BARK
BARK BARK BARK BARK

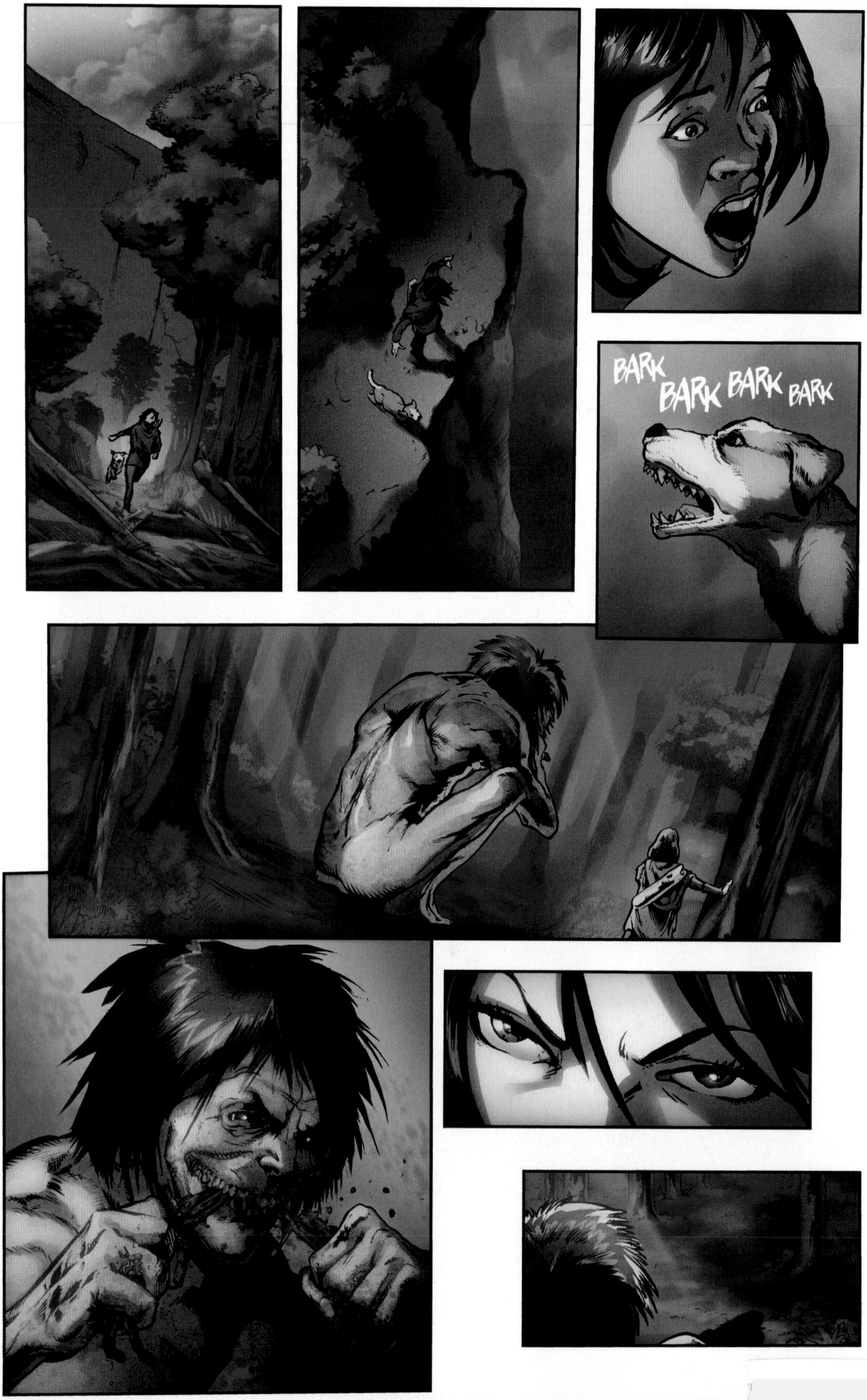
BARK
BARK BARK BARK

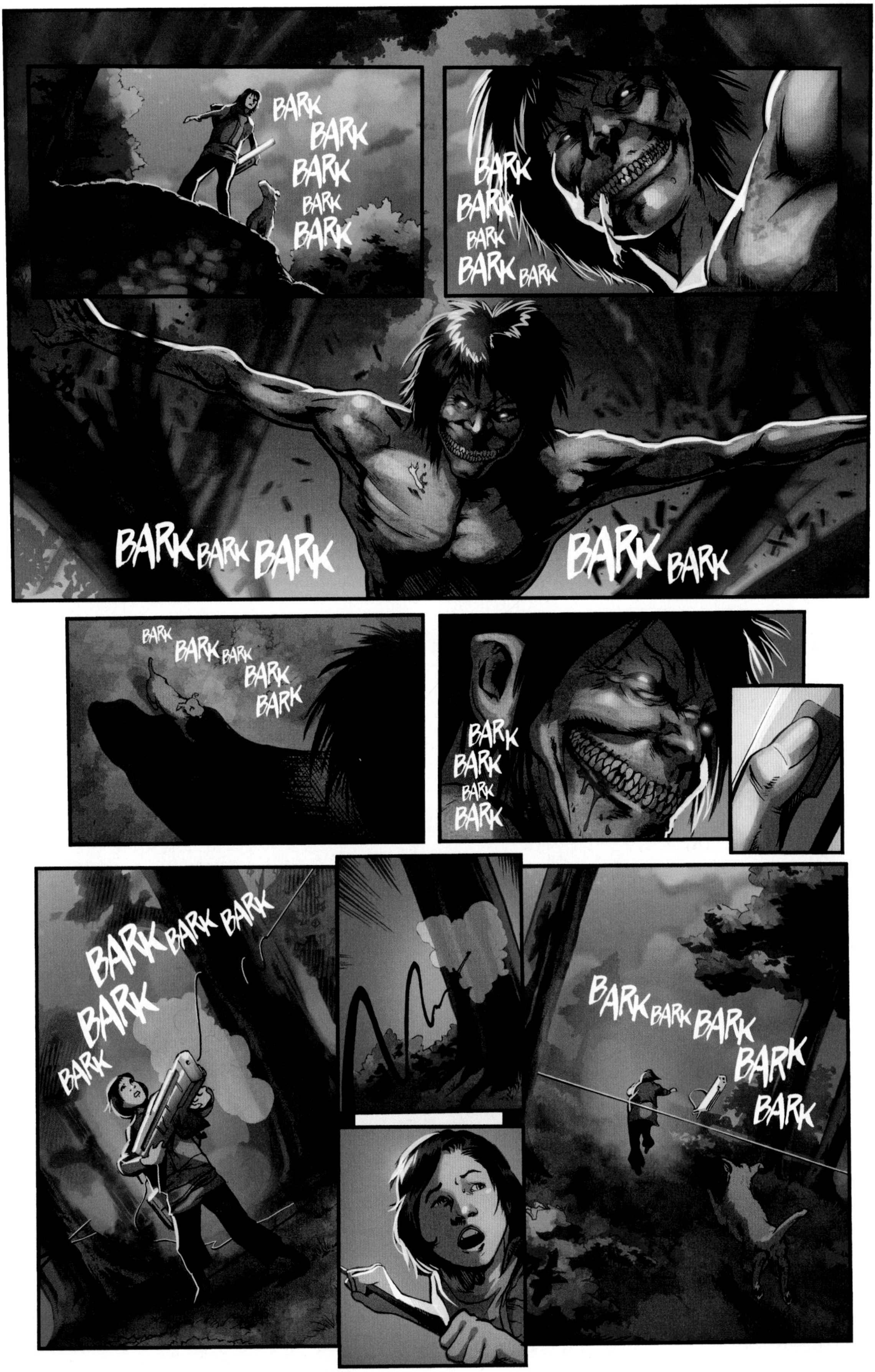
BARK
BARK
BARK
BARK
BARK
BARK
BARK
BARK
BARK BARK
BARK BARK BARK
BARK BARK
BARK
BARK BARK
BARK
BARK
BARK
BARK
BARK
BARK
BARK BARK BARK
BARK
BARK
BARK BARK BARK
BARK
BARK

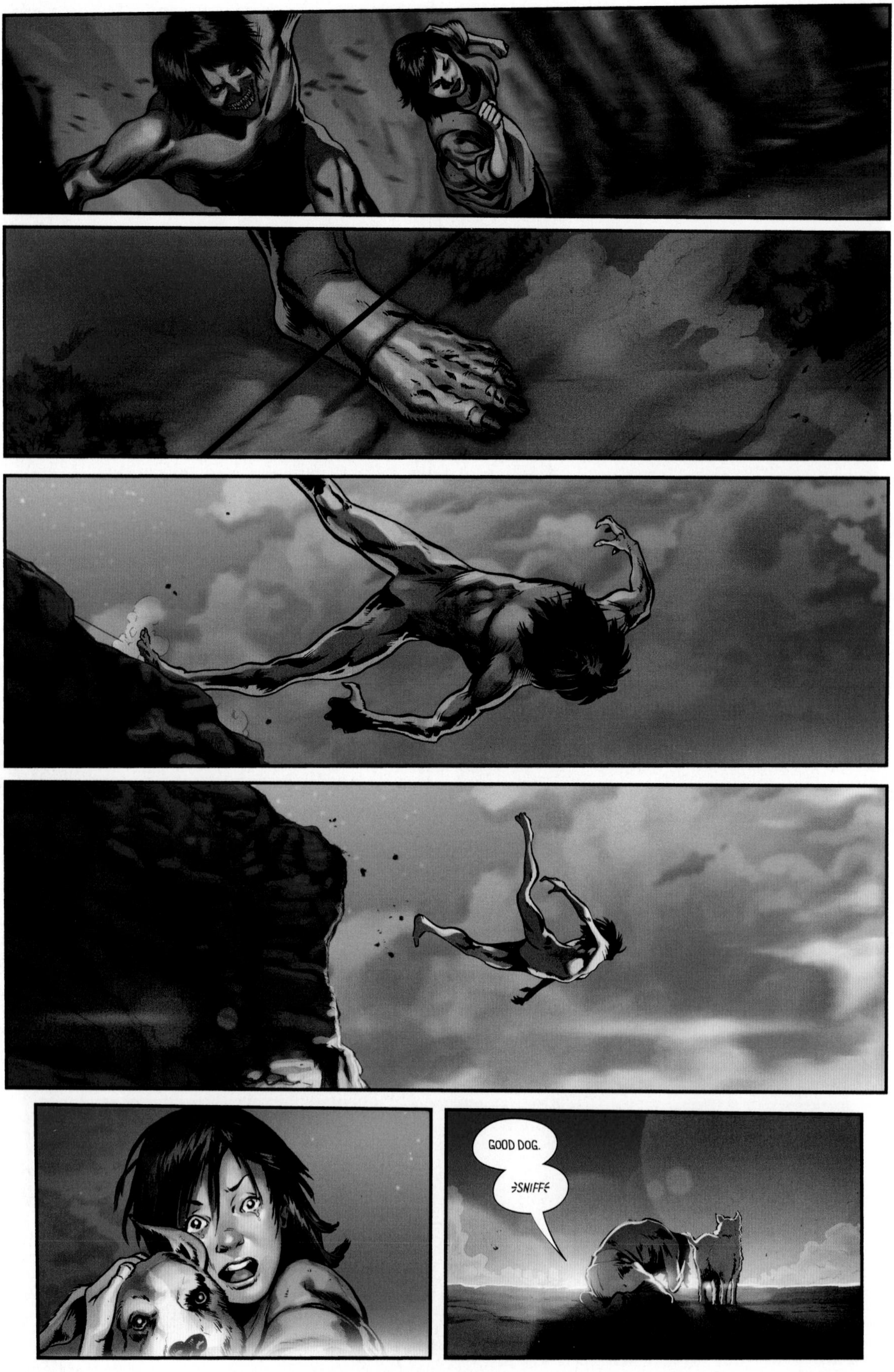
GOOD DOG.
≯SNIFF≮

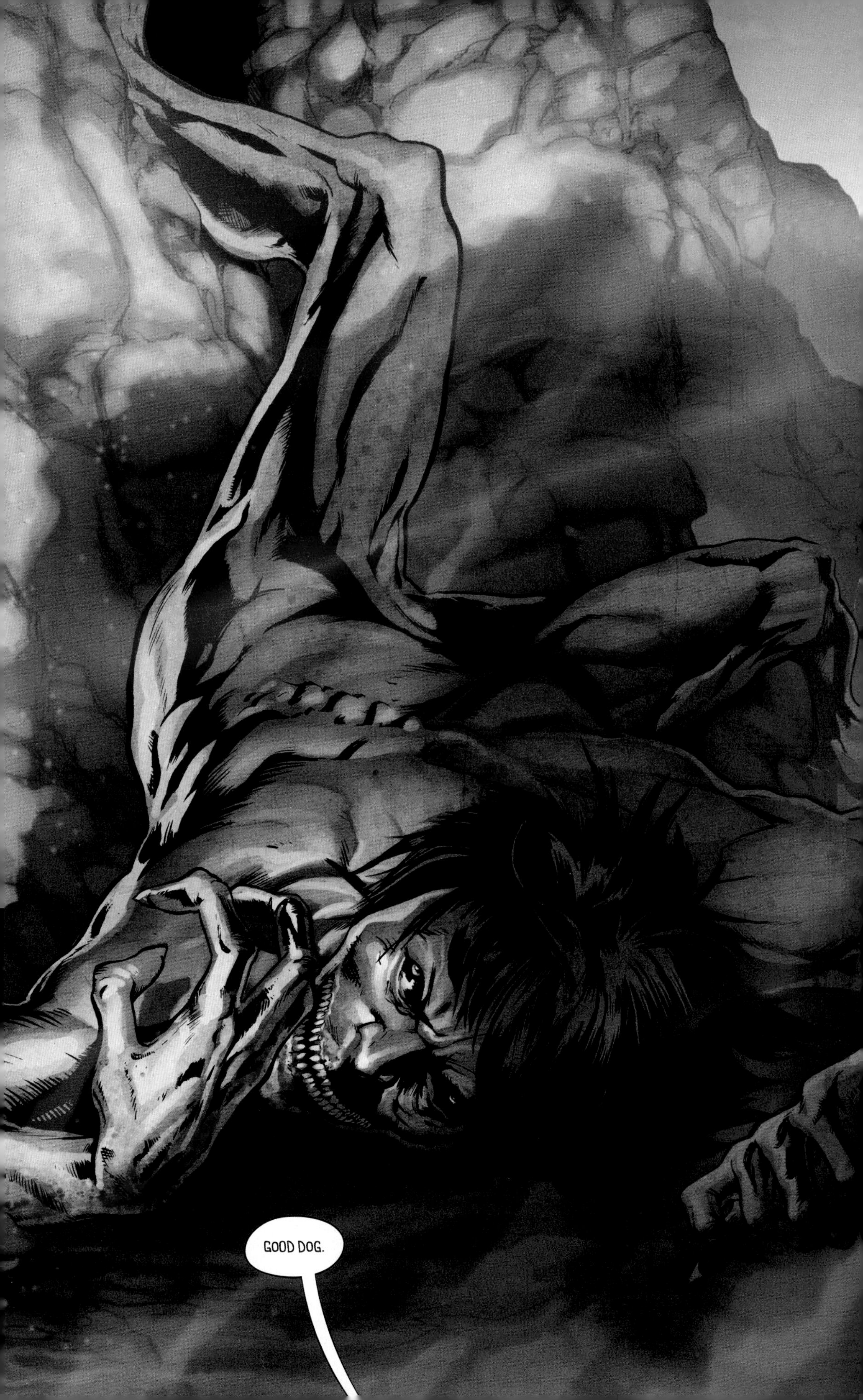
GOOD DOG.

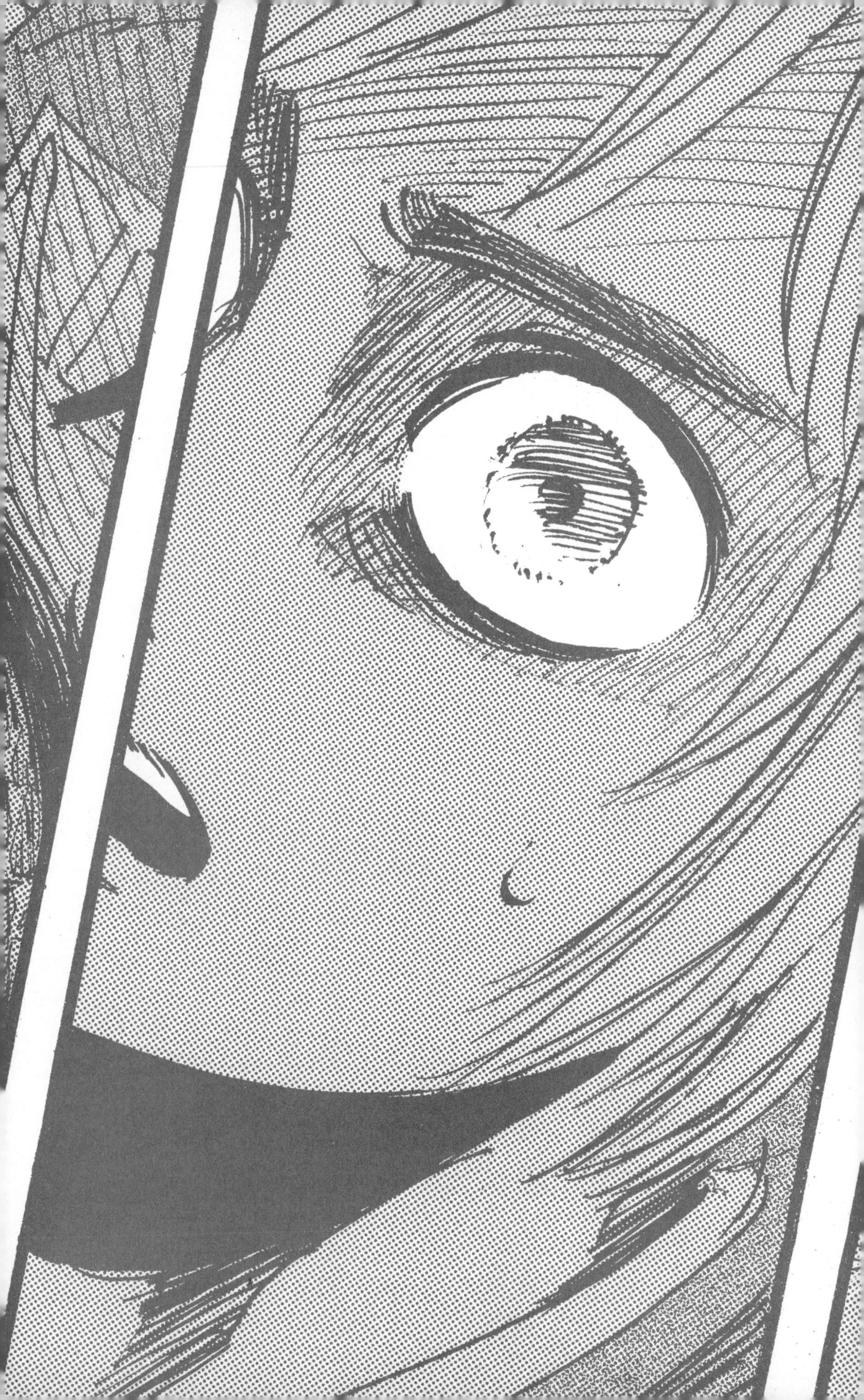

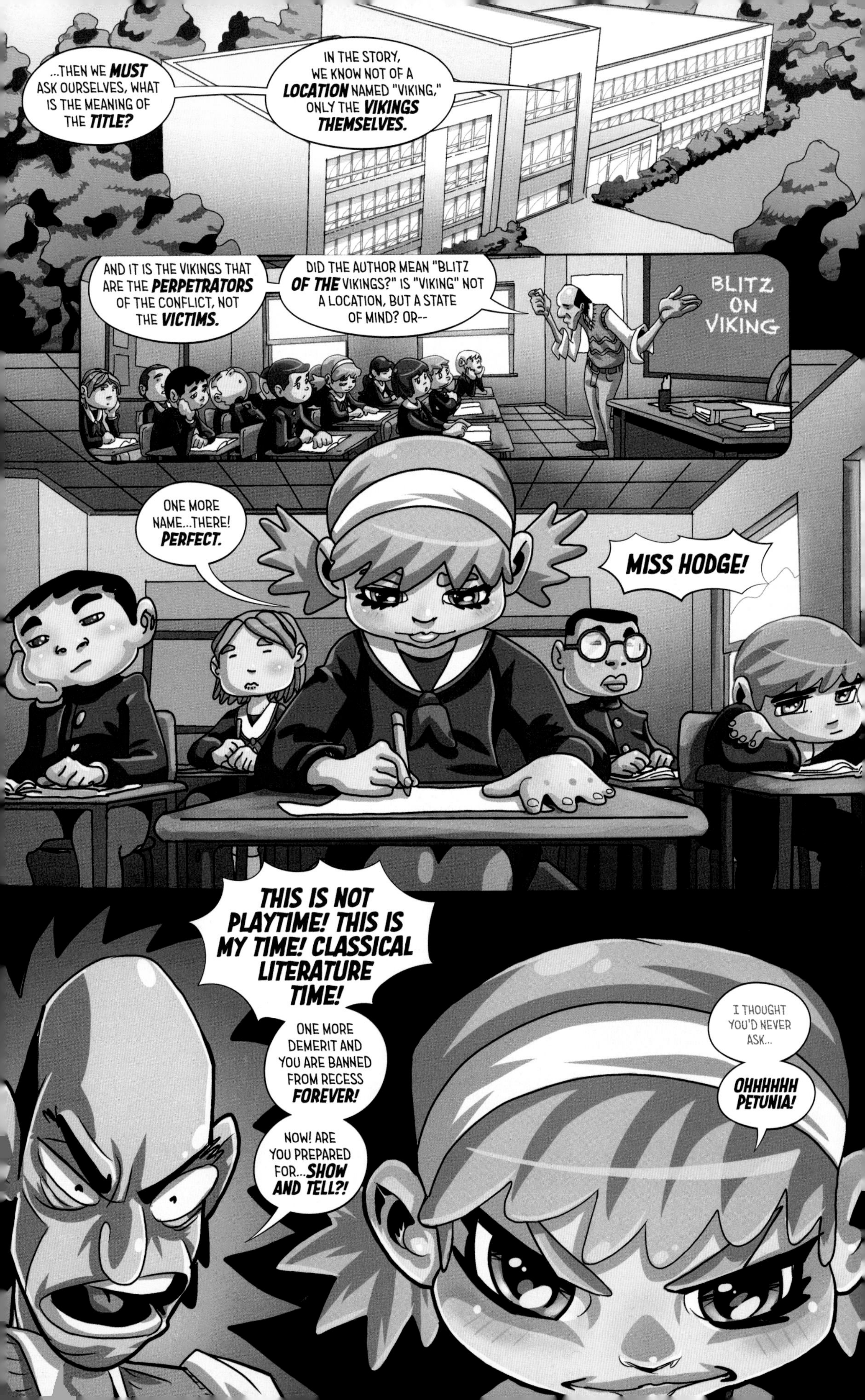
...THEN WE **MUST** ASK OURSELVES, WHAT IS THE MEANING OF THE **TITLE?**
IN THE STORY, WE KNOW NOT OF A **LOCATION** NAMED "VIKING," ONLY THE **VIKINGS THEMSELVES.**
AND IT IS THE VIKINGS THAT ARE THE **PERPETRATORS** OF THE CONFLICT, NOT THE **VICTIMS.**
DID THE AUTHOR MEAN "BLITZ **OF THE** VIKINGS?" IS "VIKING" NOT A LOCATION, BUT A STATE OF MIND? OR--
BLITZ ON VIKING
ONE MORE NAME...THERE! **PERFECT.**
MISS HODGE!
THIS IS NOT PLAYTIME! THIS IS MY TIME! CLASSICAL LITERATURE TIME!
ONE MORE DEMERIT AND YOU ARE BANNED FROM RECESS **FOREVER!**
NOW! ARE YOU PREPARED FOR...**SHOW AND TELL?!**
I THOUGHT YOU'D NEVER ASK...
OHHHHHH PETUNIA!

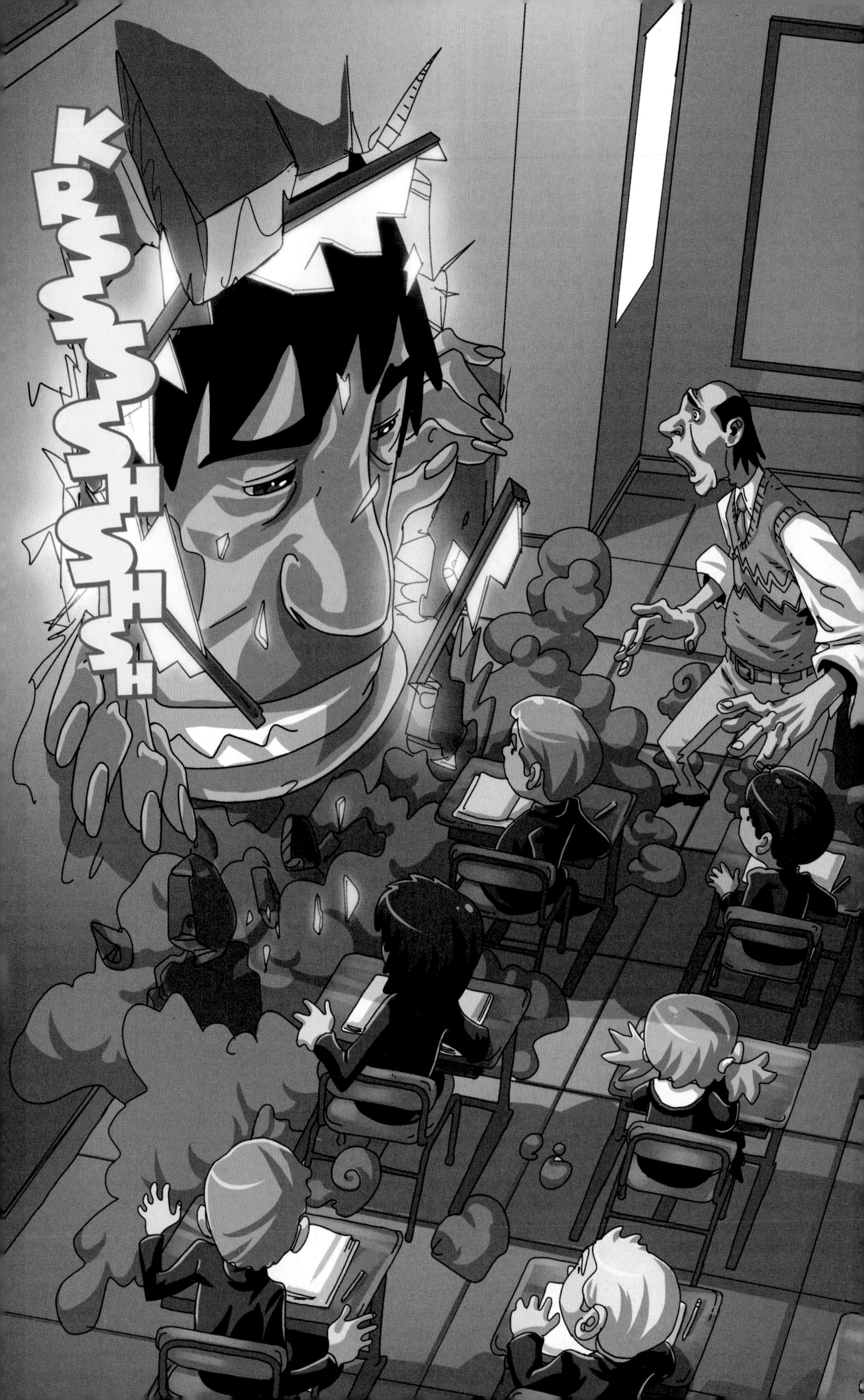
KRSSSHSHSH

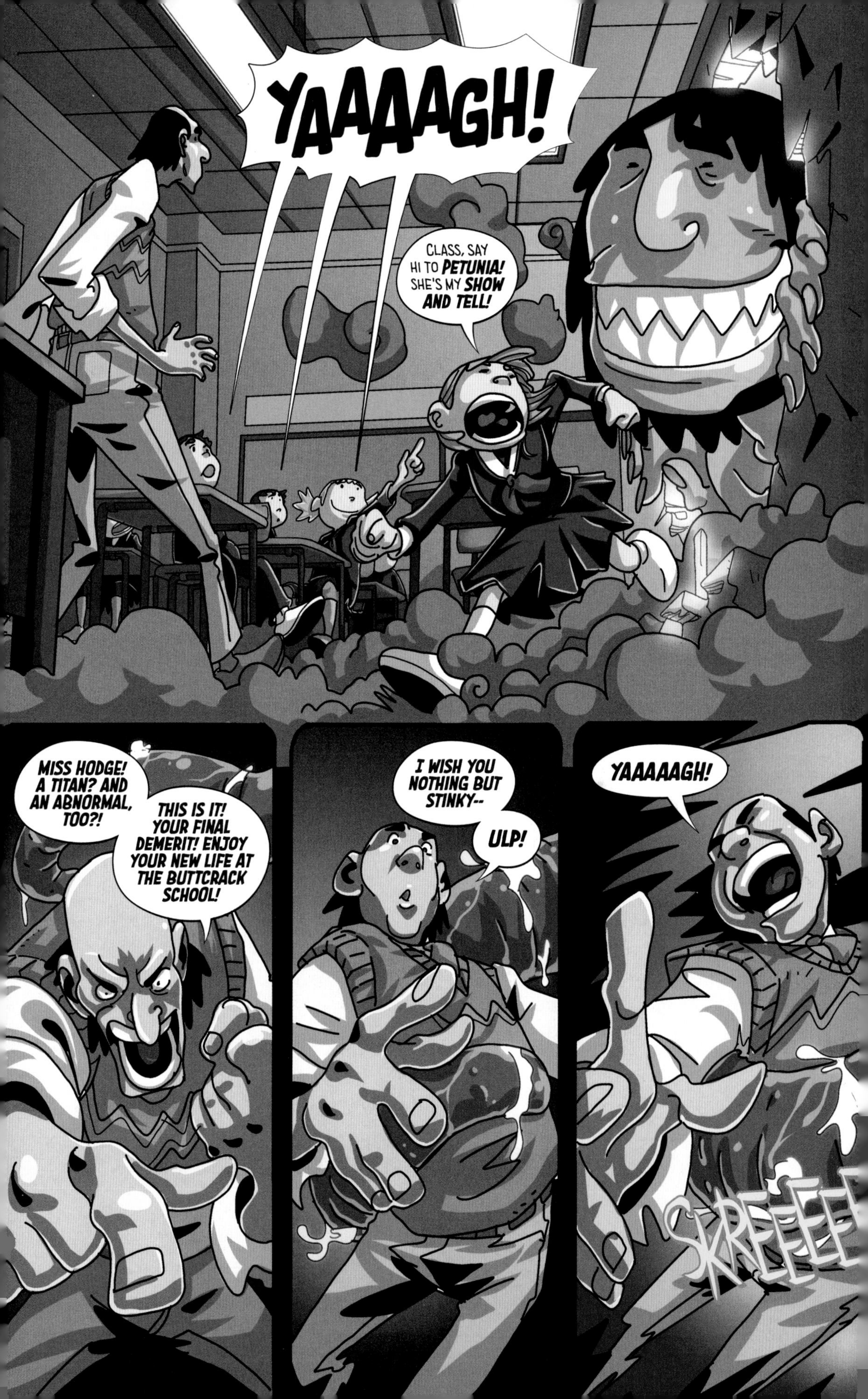
YAAAAGH!
CLASS, SAY HI TO PETUNIA! SHE'S MY SHOW AND TELL!
MISS HODGE! A TITAN? AND AN ABNORMAL, TOO?!
THIS IS IT! YOUR FINAL DEMERIT! ENJOY YOUR NEW LIFE AT THE BUTTCRACK SCHOOL!
I WISH YOU NOTHING BUT STINKY--
ULP!
YAAAAAGH!
SKREEEEE

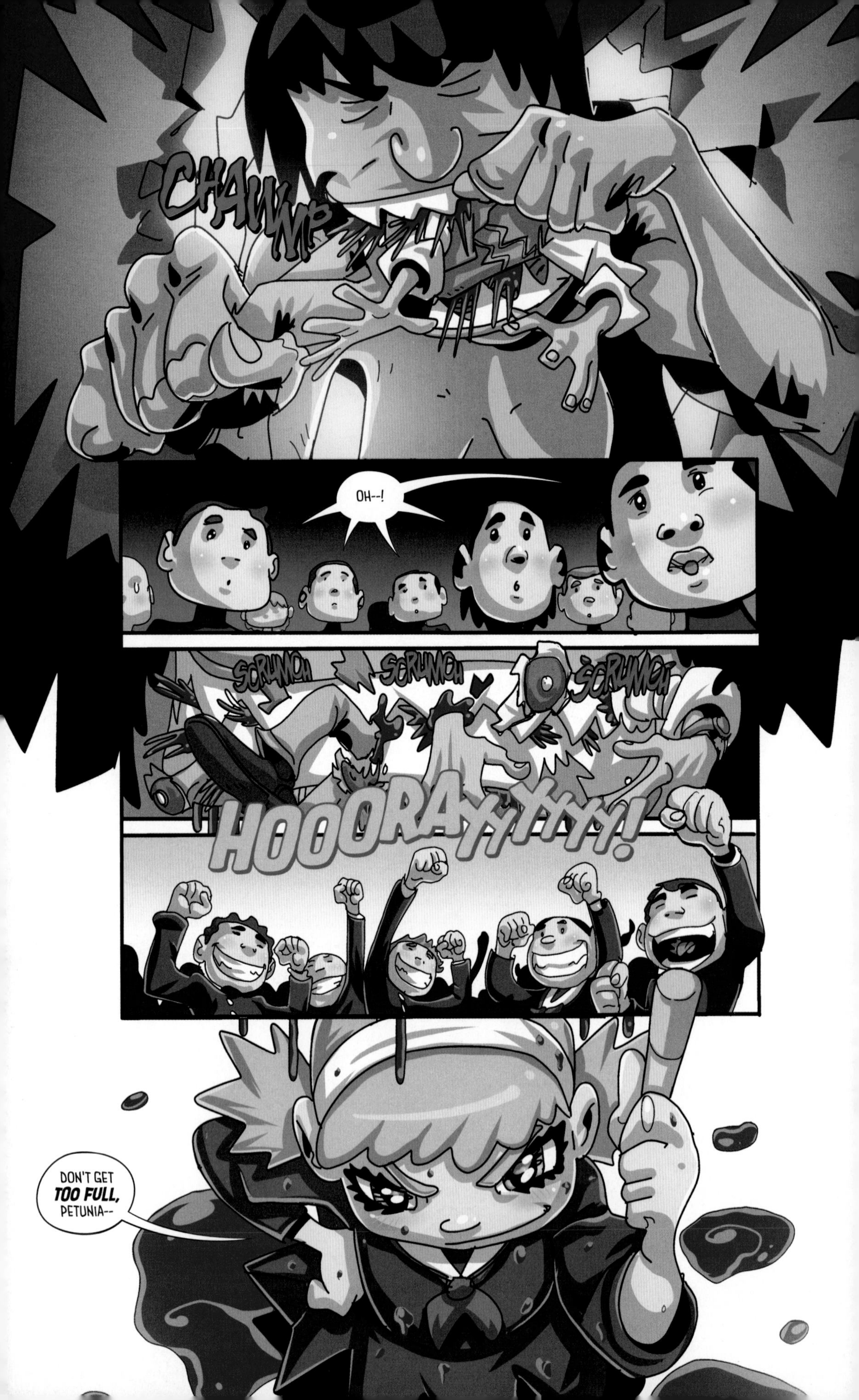
CHAWMP
OH--!
SCRUNCH
SCRUNCH
SCRUNCH
HOOORAYYYYYY!
DON'T GET **TOO FULL,** PETUNIA--

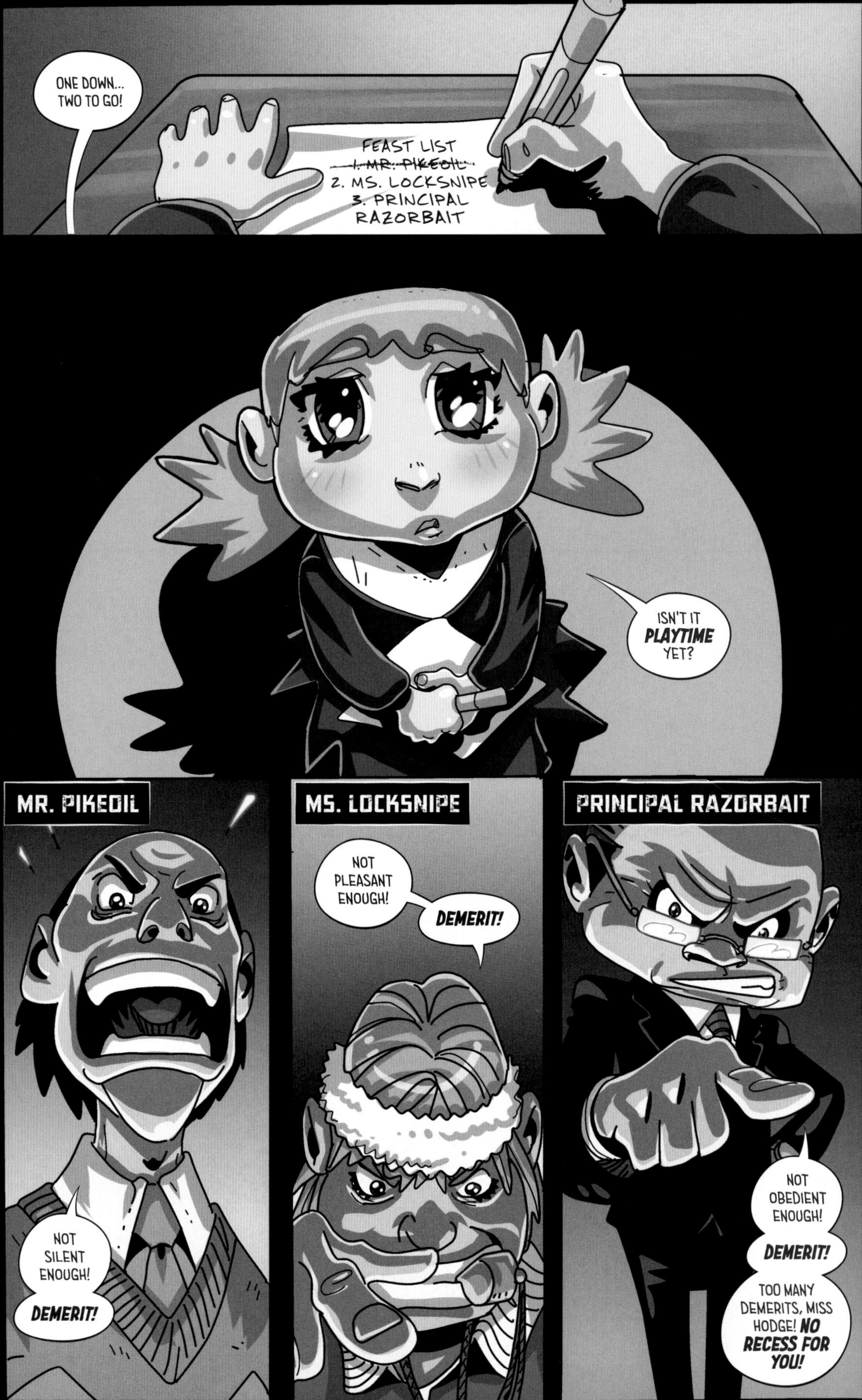

ONE DOWN... TWO TO GO!
FEAST LIST
1. MR. PIKEOIL
2. MS. LOCKSNIPE
3. PRINCIPAL RAZORBAIT
ISN'T IT PLAYTIME YET?
MR. PIKEOIL
NOT SILENT ENOUGH!
DEMERIT!
MS. LOCKSNIPE
NOT PLEASANT ENOUGH!
DEMERIT!
PRINCIPAL RAZORBAIT
NOT OBEDIENT ENOUGH!
DEMERIT!
TOO MANY DEMERITS, MISS HODGE! NO RECESS FOR YOU!

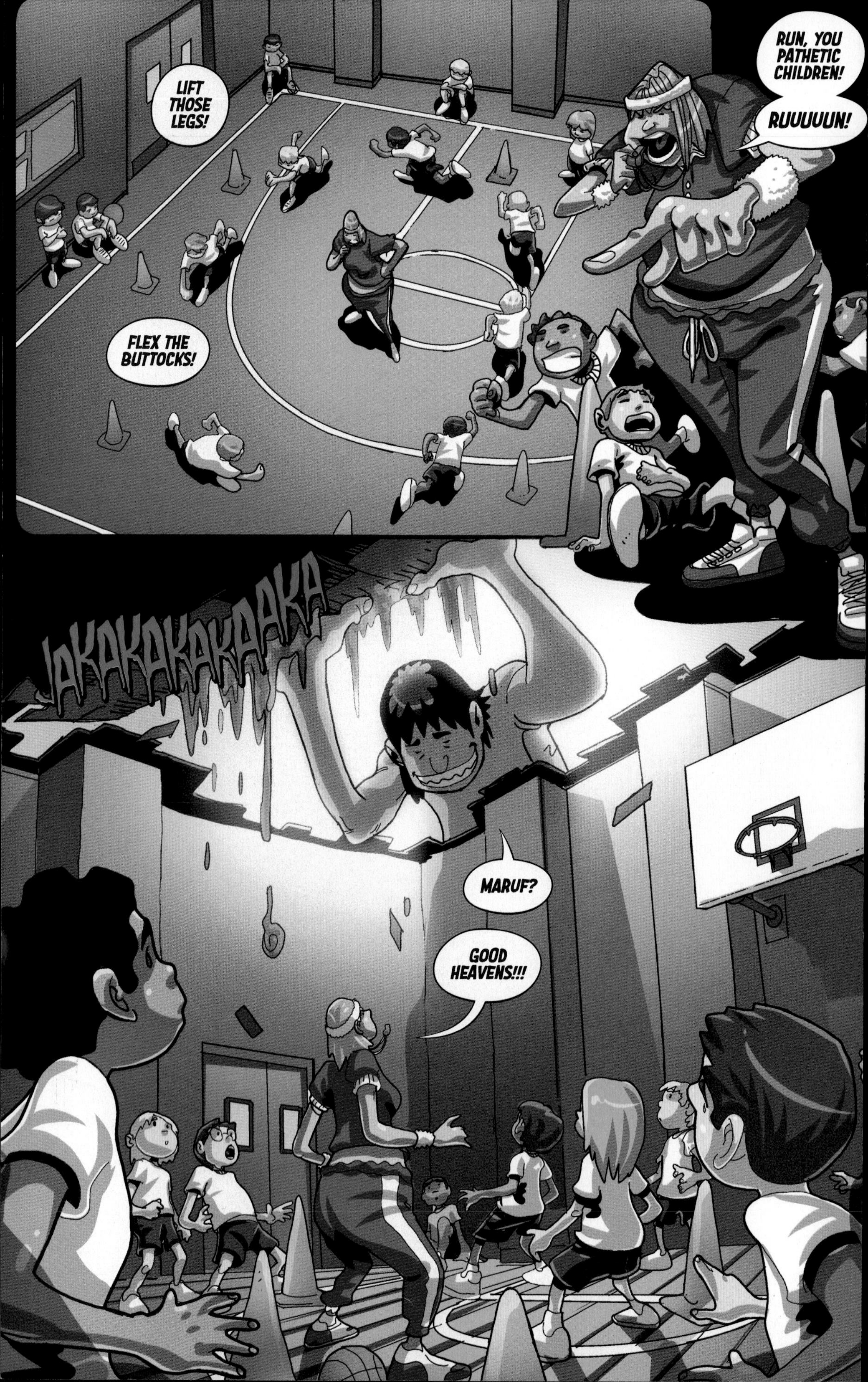
LIFT THOSE LEGS!
FLEX THE BUTTOCKS!
RUN, YOU PATHETIC CHILDREN!
RUUUUUN!
JAKAKAKAKAKAAKA
MARUF?
GOOD HEAVENS!!!

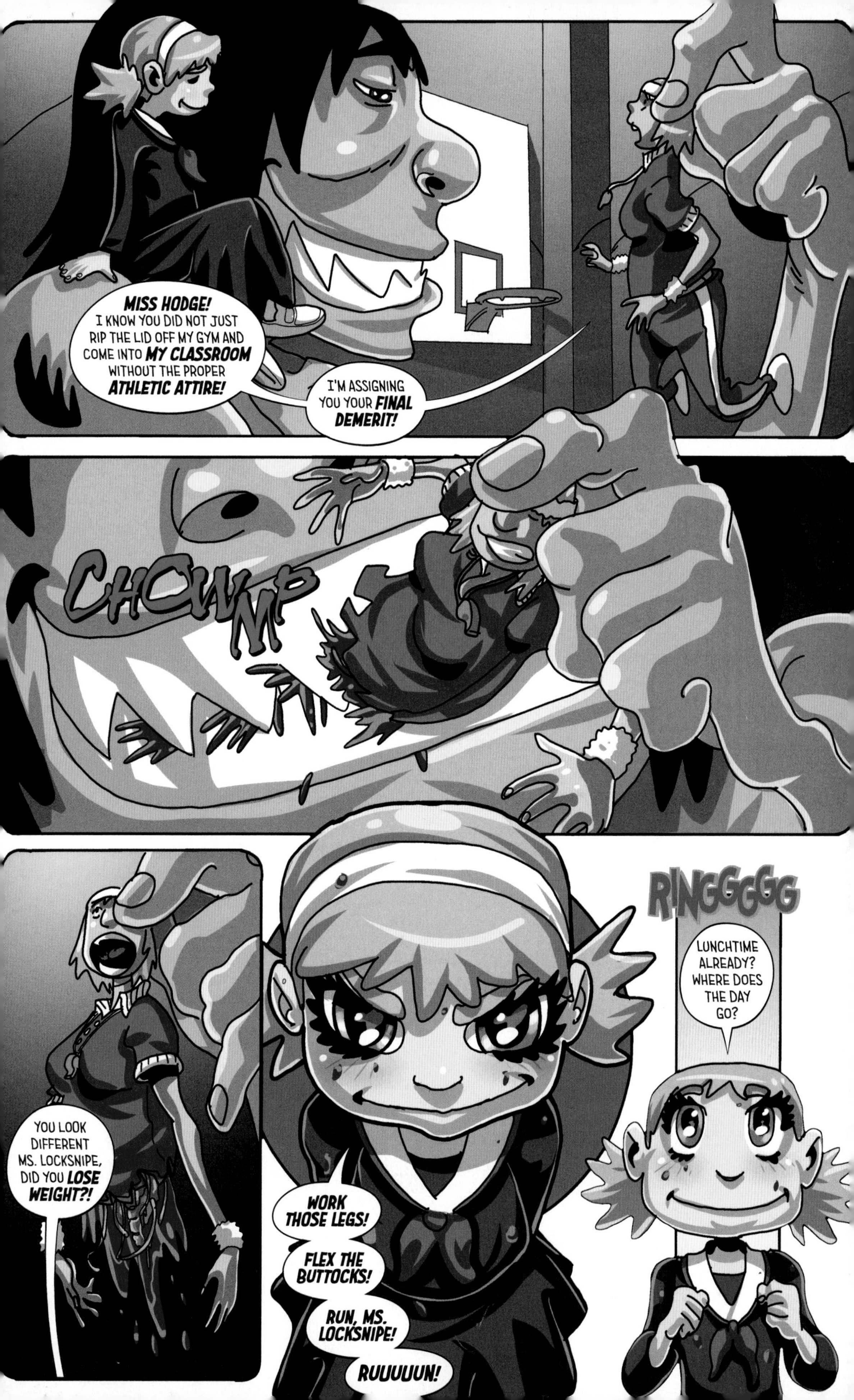
MISS HODGE! I KNOW YOU DID NOT JUST RIP THE LID OFF MY GYM AND COME INTO MY CLASSROOM WITHOUT THE PROPER ATHLETIC ATTIRE!
I'M ASSIGNING YOU YOUR FINAL DEMERIT!
CHOWMP
YOU LOOK DIFFERENT MS. LOCKSNIPE, DID YOU LOSE WEIGHT?!
WORK THOSE LEGS!
FLEX THE BUTTOCKS!
RUN, MS. LOCKSNIPE!
RUUUUUN!
RINGGGGG
LUNCHTIME ALREADY? WHERE DOES THE DAY GO?

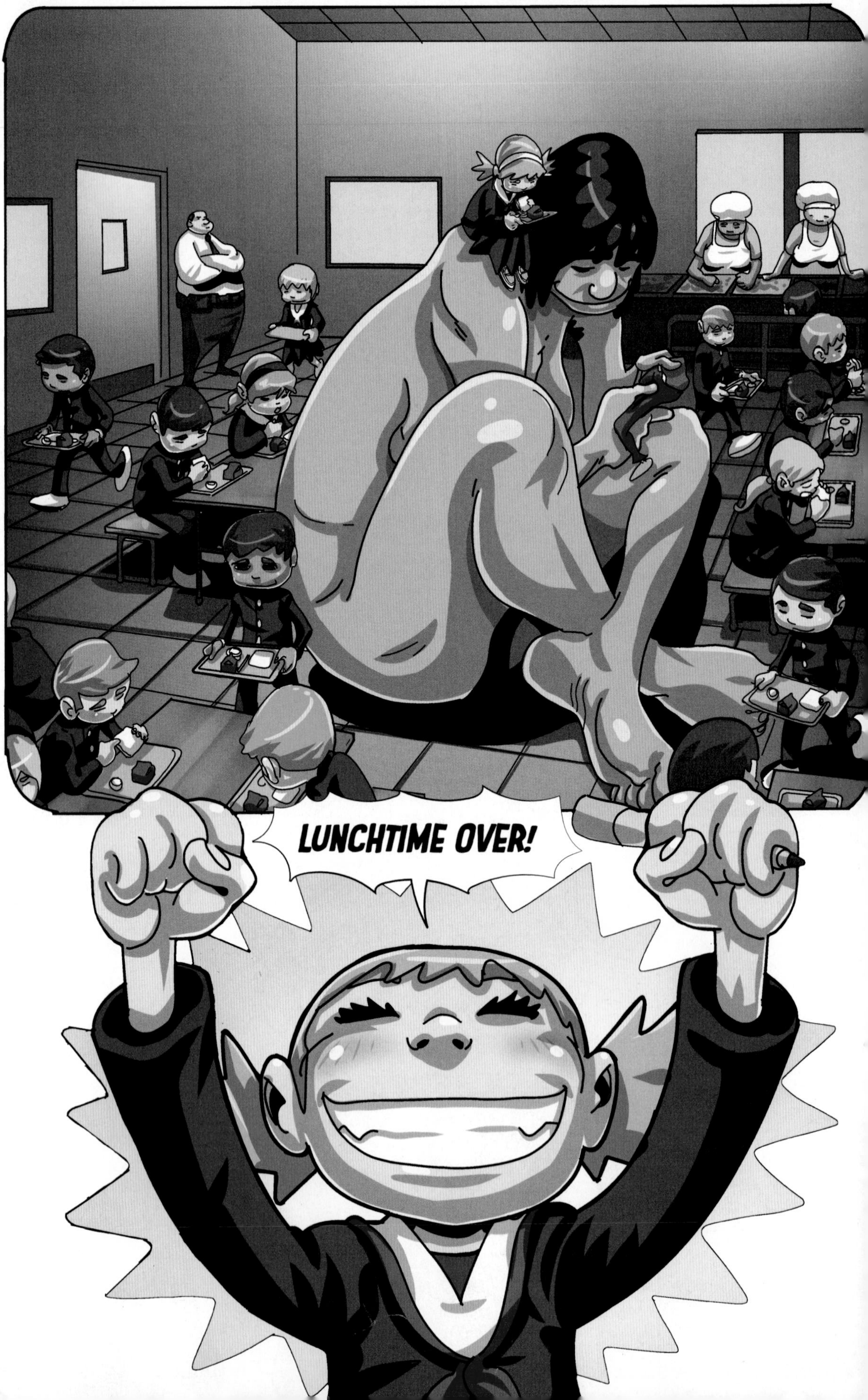
LUNCHTIME OVER!

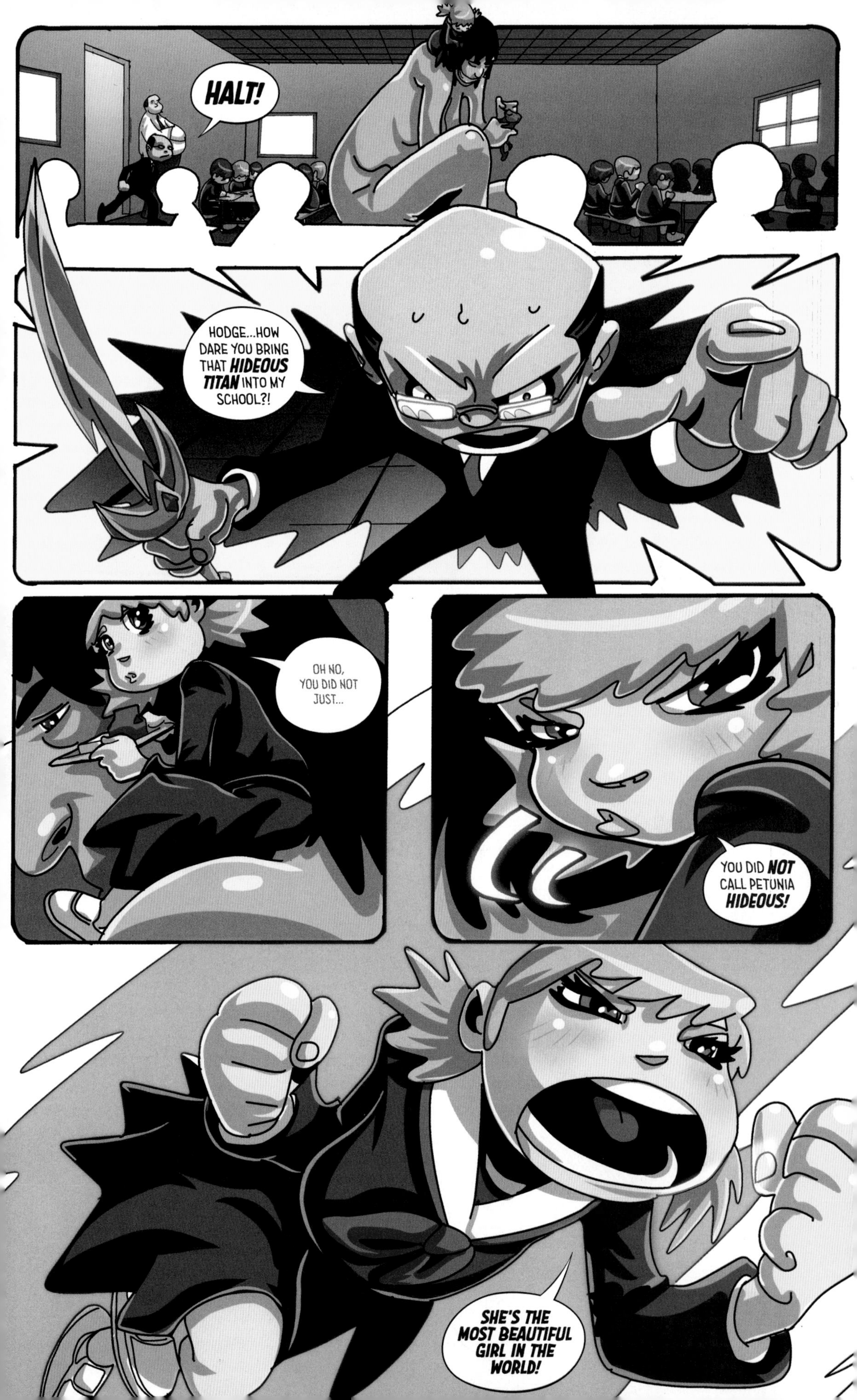
HALT!
HODGE...HOW DARE YOU BRING THAT HIDEOUS TITAN INTO MY SCHOOL?!
OH NO, YOU DID NOT JUST...
YOU DID NOT CALL PETUNIA HIDEOUS!
SHE'S THE MOST BEAUTIFUL GIRL IN THE WORLD!

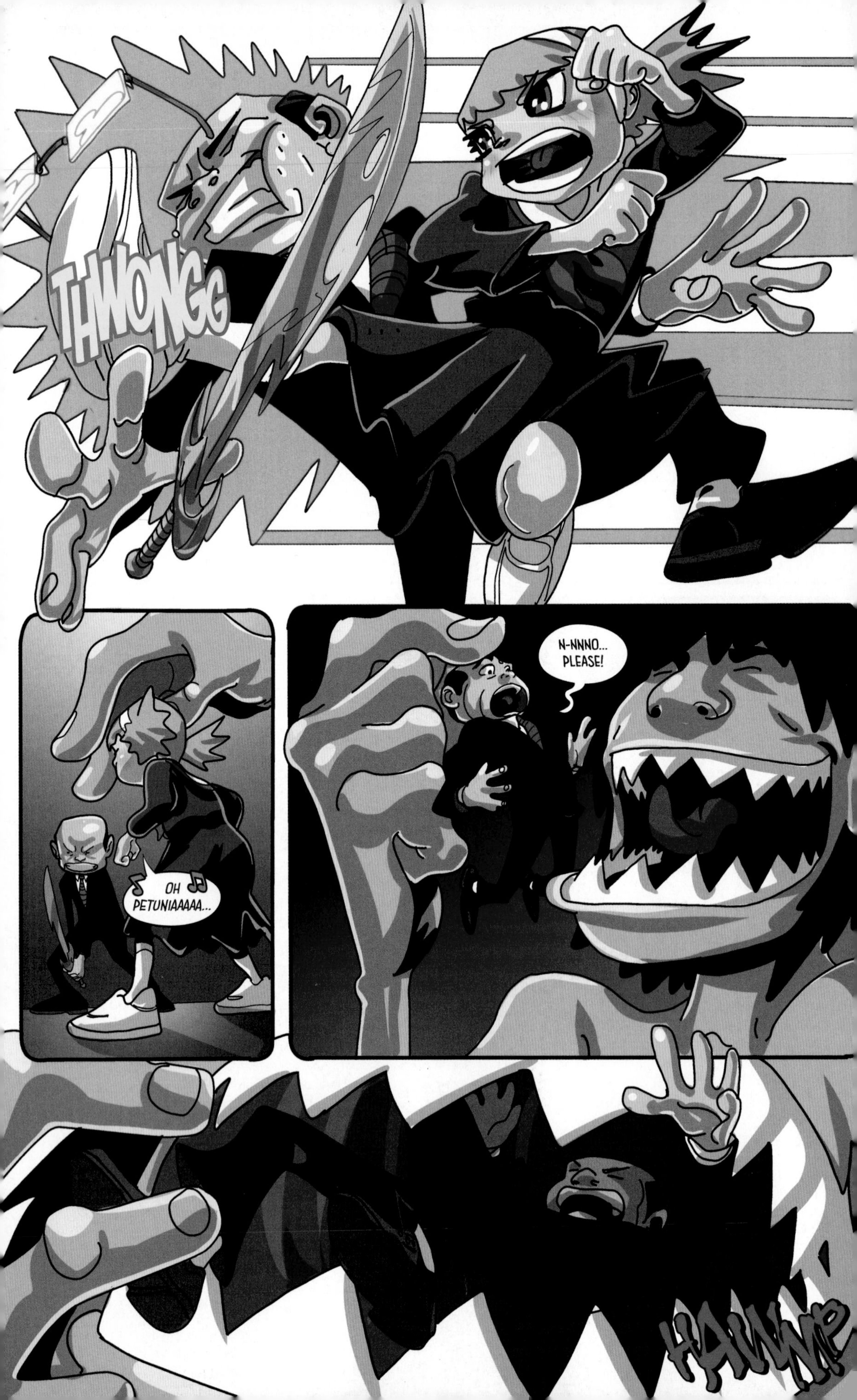
THWONGG
OH PETUNIAAAAA...
N-NNNO... PLEASE!
HAWWMP

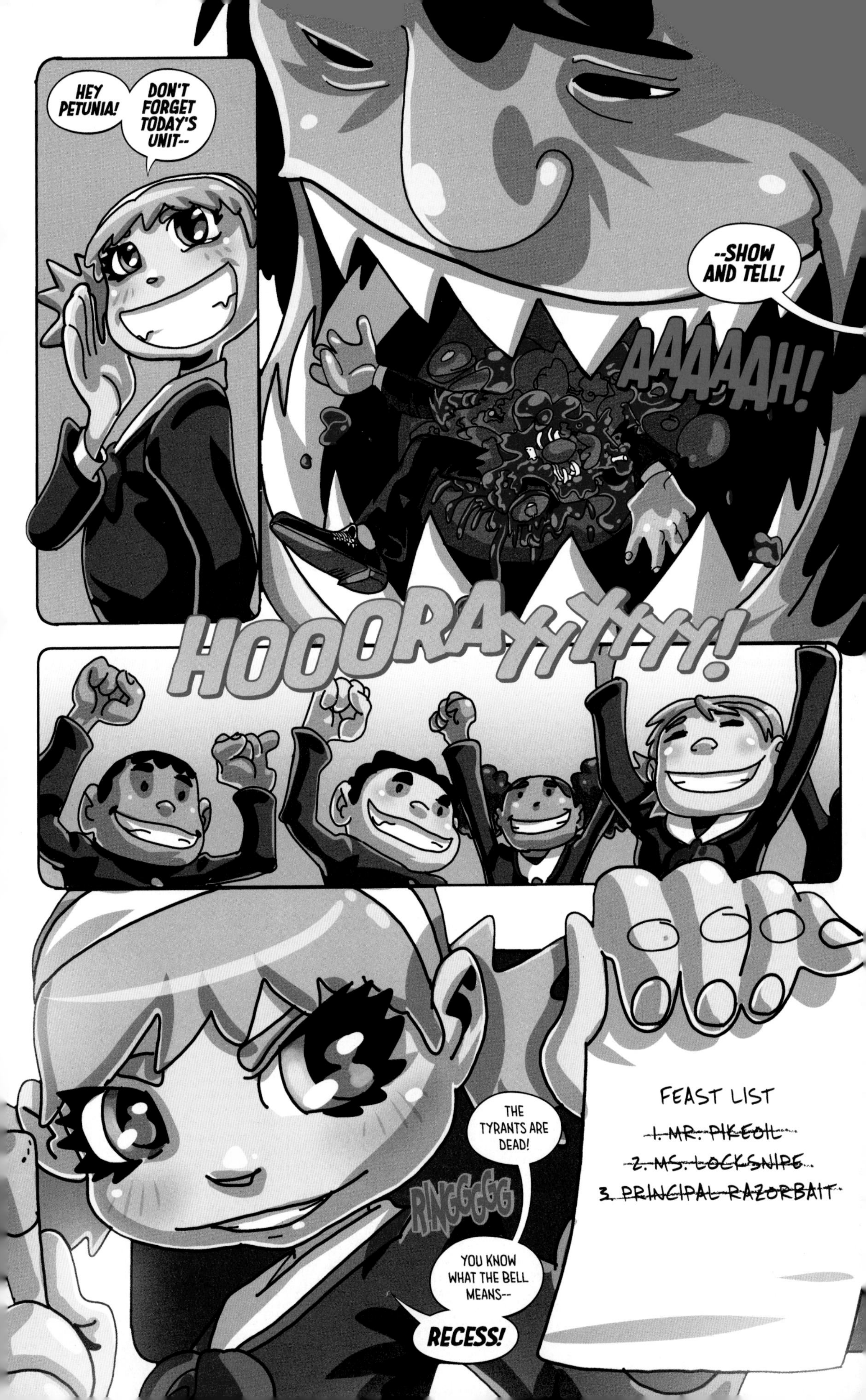
HEY PETUNIA!
DON'T FORGET TODAY'S UNIT--
--SHOW AND TELL!
AAAAAH!
HOOORAYYYYYY!
THE TYRANTS ARE DEAD!
RINGGGGG
YOU KNOW WHAT THE BELL MEANS--
RECESS!
FEAST LIST
1. MR. PIKEOIL
2. MS. LOCKSNIPE
3. PRINCIPAL RAZORBAIT

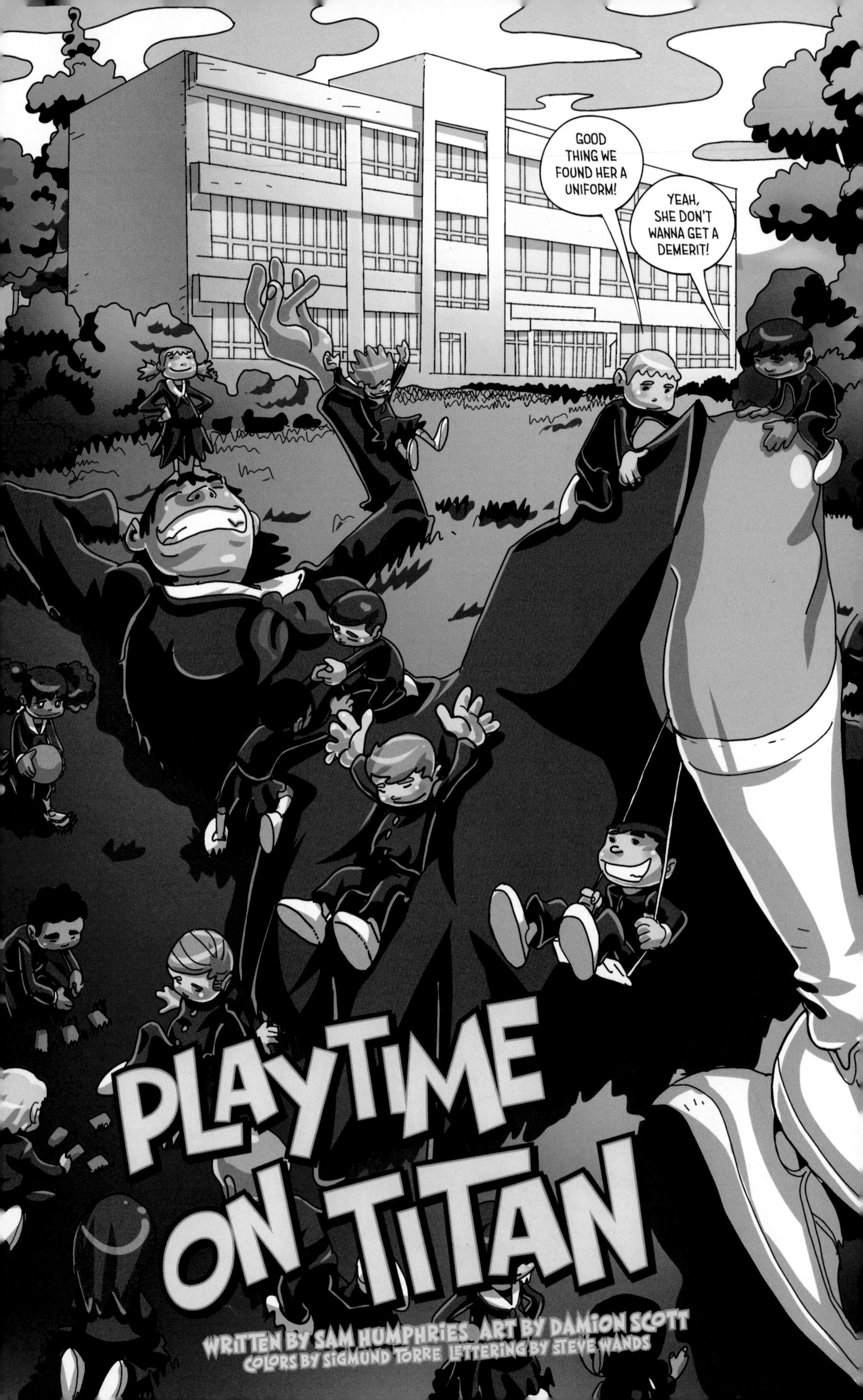
GOOD THING WE FOUND HER A UNIFORM!
YEAH, SHE DON'T WANNA GET A DEMERIT!
PLAYTIME ON TITAN
WRITTEN BY SAM HUMPHRIES ART BY DAMION SCOTT
COLORS BY SIGMUND TORRE LETTERING BY STEVE WANDS

ATTACK on ATTACK on 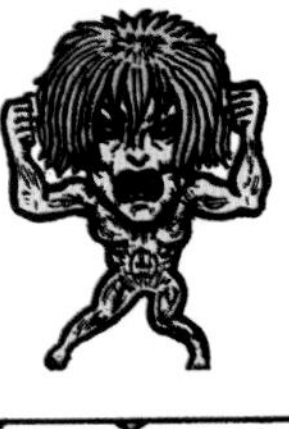

By Evan Dorkin and Sarah Dyer
Flatted and additional colors by Bill Mudron

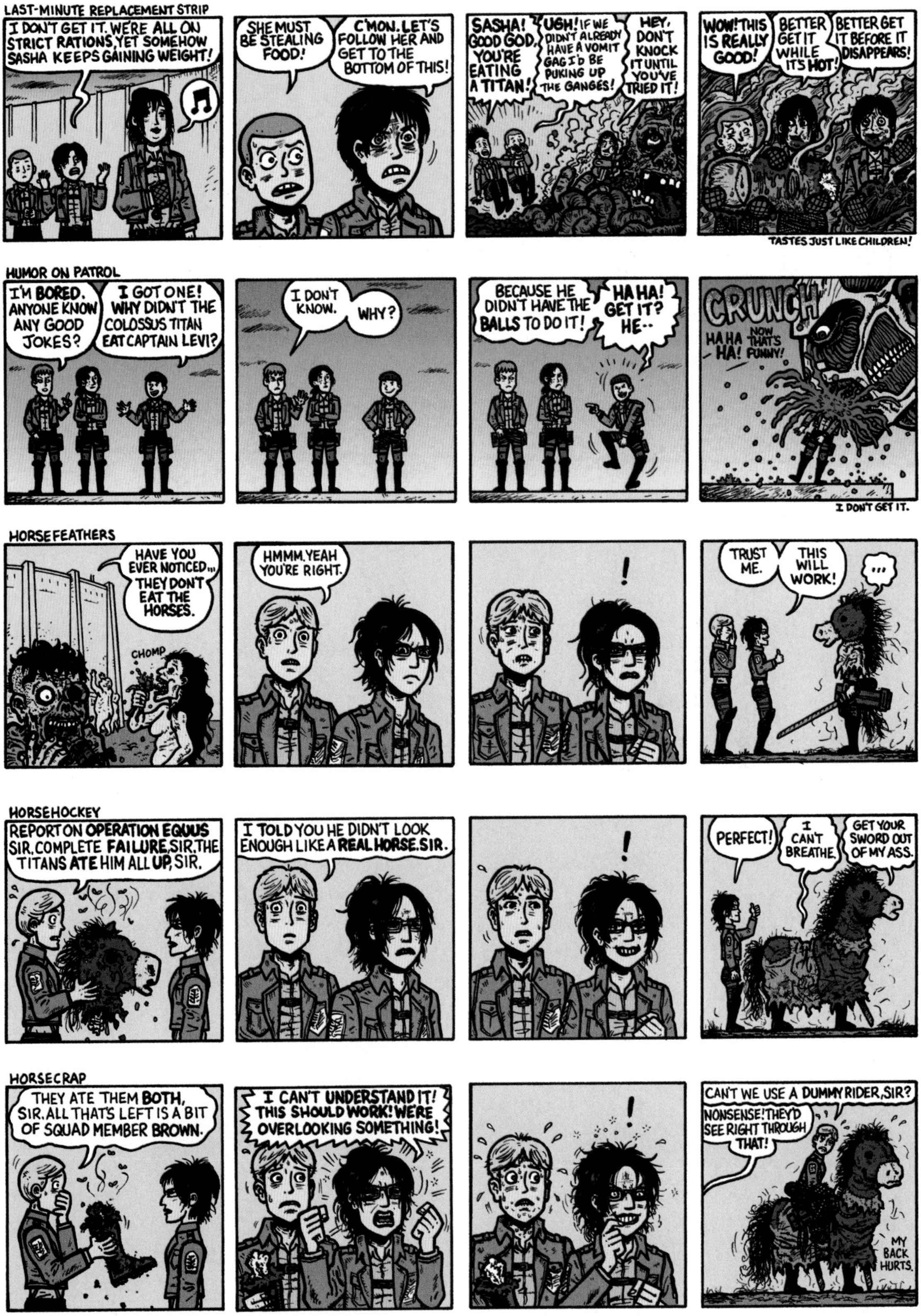
LAST-MINUTE REPLACEMENT STRIP
I DON'T GET IT. WE'RE ALL ON STRICT RATIONS, YET SOMEHOW SASHA KEEPS GAINING WEIGHT!
SHE MUST BE STEALING FOOD!
C'MON, LET'S FOLLOW HER AND GET TO THE BOTTOM OF THIS!
SASHA! GOOD GOD, YOU'RE EATING A TITAN!
UGH! IF WE DIDN'T ALREADY HAVE A VOMIT GAG I'D BE PUKING UP THE GANGES!
HEY, DON'T KNOCK IT UNTIL YOU'VE TRIED IT!
WOW! THIS IS REALLY GOOD!
BETTER GET IT WHILE IT'S HOT!
BETTER GET IT BEFORE IT DISAPPEARS!
TASTES JUST LIKE CHILDREN!
HUMOR ON PATROL
I'M BORED. ANYONE KNOW ANY GOOD JOKES?
I GOT ONE! WHY DIDN'T THE COLOSSUS TITAN EAT CAPTAIN LEVI?
I DON'T KNOW.
WHY?
BECAUSE HE DIDN'T HAVE THE BALLS TO DO IT!
HA HA! GET IT? HE--
CRUNCH
HA HA HA!
NOW THAT'S FUNNY!
I DON'T GET IT.
HORSEFEATHERS
HAVE YOU EVER NOTICED... THEY DON'T EAT THE HORSES.
CHOMP
HMMM. YEAH YOU'RE RIGHT.
!
TRUST ME.
THIS WILL WORK!
...
HORSEHOCKEY
REPORT ON OPERATION EQUUS SIR. COMPLETE FAILURE, SIR. THE TITANS ATE HIM ALL UP, SIR.
I TOLD YOU HE DIDN'T LOOK ENOUGH LIKE A REAL HORSE, SIR.
!
PERFECT!
I CAN'T BREATHE.
GET YOUR SWORD OUT OF MY ASS.
HORSECRAP
THEY ATE THEM BOTH, SIR. ALL THAT'S LEFT IS A BIT OF SQUAD MEMBER BROWN.
I CAN'T UNDERSTAND IT! THIS SHOULD WORK! WE'RE OVERLOOKING SOMETHING!
!
CAN'T WE USE A DUMMY RIDER, SIR?
NONSENSE! THEY'D SEE RIGHT THROUGH THAT!
MY BACK HURTS.

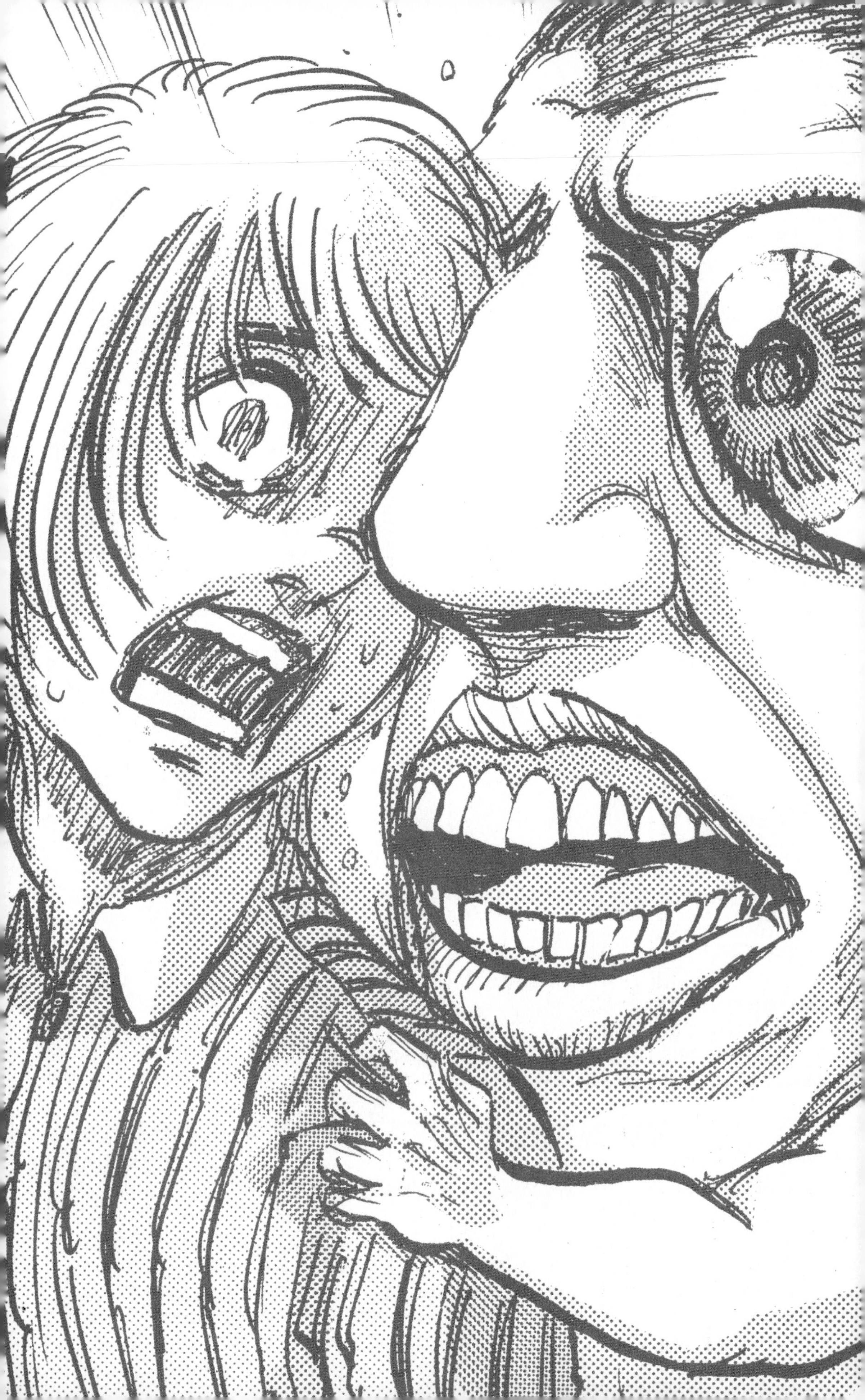

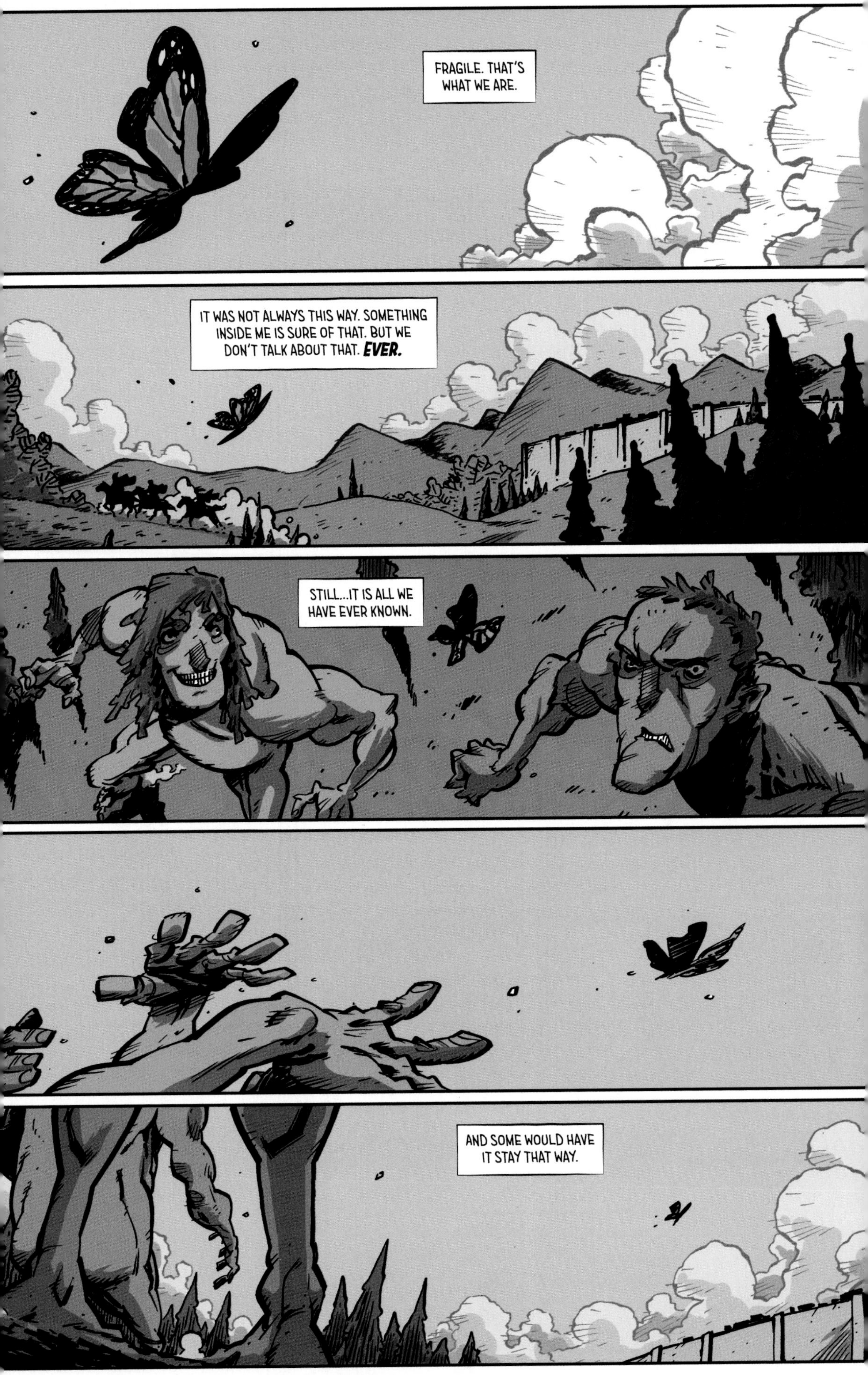
FRAGILE. THAT'S WHAT WE ARE.
IT WAS NOT ALWAYS THIS WAY. SOMETHING INSIDE ME IS SURE OF THAT. BUT WE DON'T TALK ABOUT THAT. ***EVER.***
STILL...IT IS ALL WE HAVE EVER KNOWN.
AND SOME WOULD HAVE IT STAY THAT WAY.

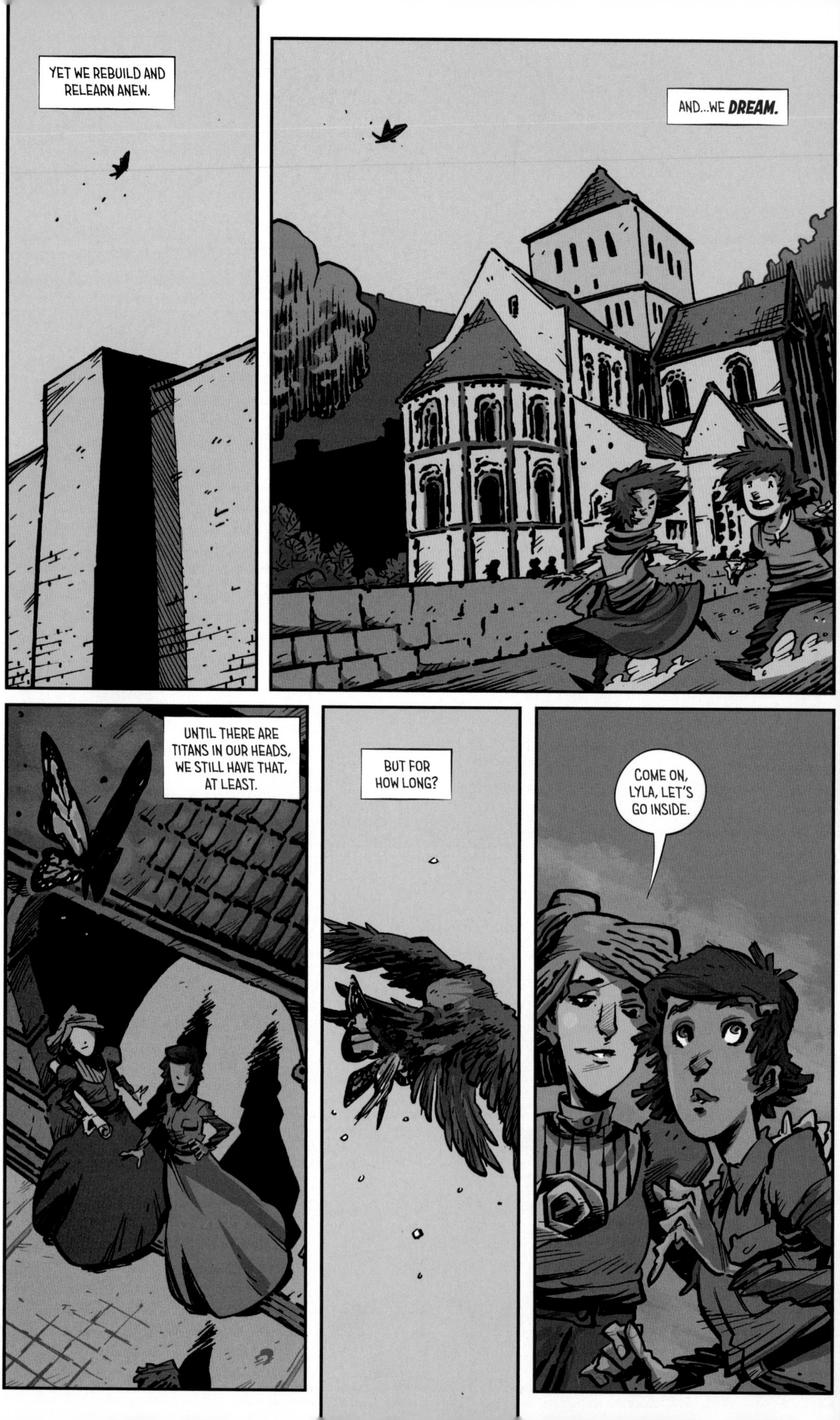
YET WE REBUILD AND RELEARN ANEW.
AND...WE **DREAM.**
UNTIL THERE ARE TITANS IN OUR HEADS, WE STILL HAVE THAT, AT LEAST.
BUT FOR HOW LONG?
COME ON, LYLA, LET'S GO INSIDE.

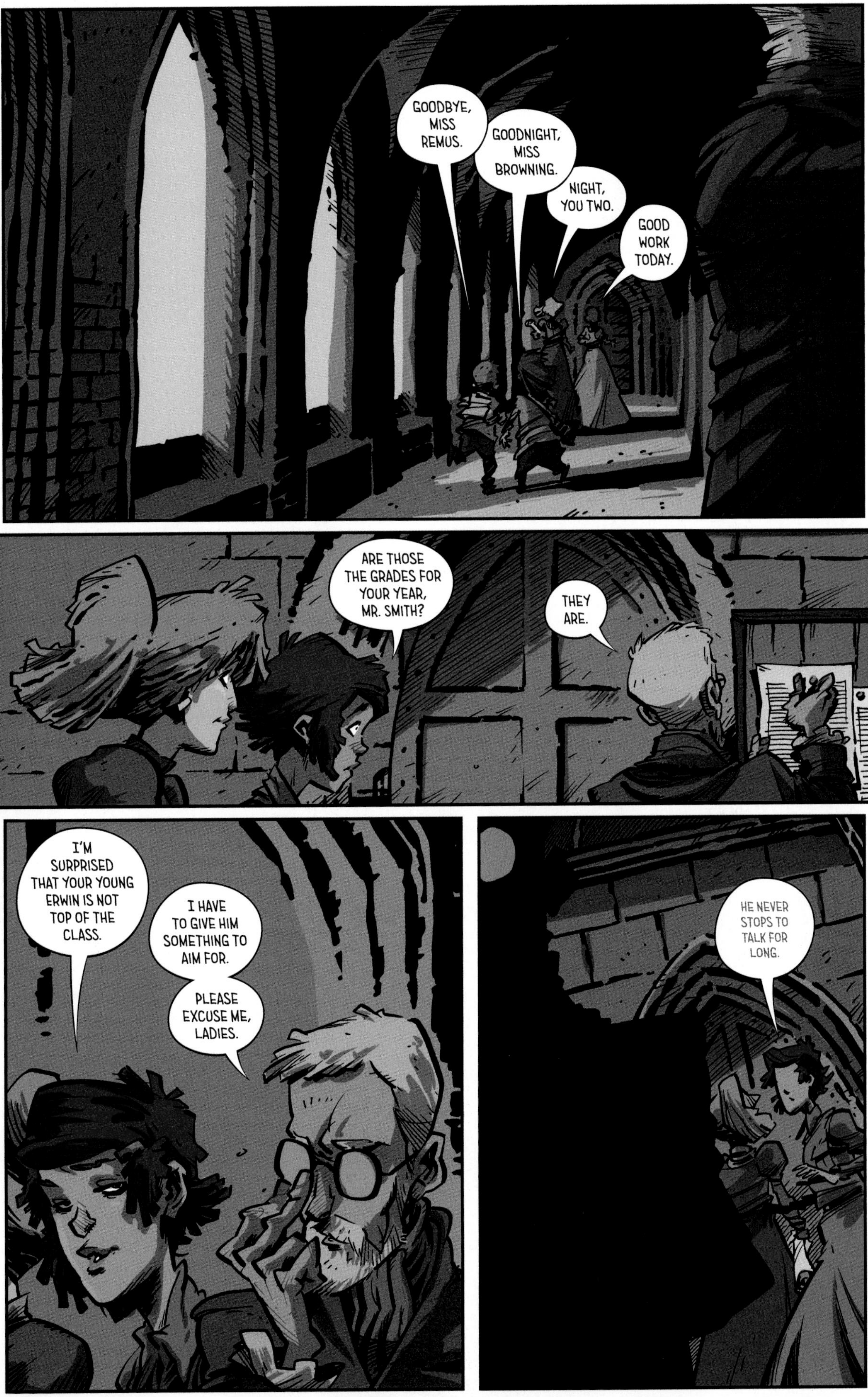
GOODBYE, MISS REMUS.
GOODNIGHT, MISS BROWNING.
NIGHT, YOU TWO.
GOOD WORK TODAY.
ARE THOSE THE GRADES FOR YOUR YEAR, MR. SMITH?
THEY ARE.
I'M SURPRISED THAT YOUR YOUNG ERWIN IS NOT TOP OF THE CLASS.
I HAVE TO GIVE HIM SOMETHING TO AIM FOR.
PLEASE EXCUSE ME, LADIES.
HE NEVER STOPS TO TALK FOR LONG.

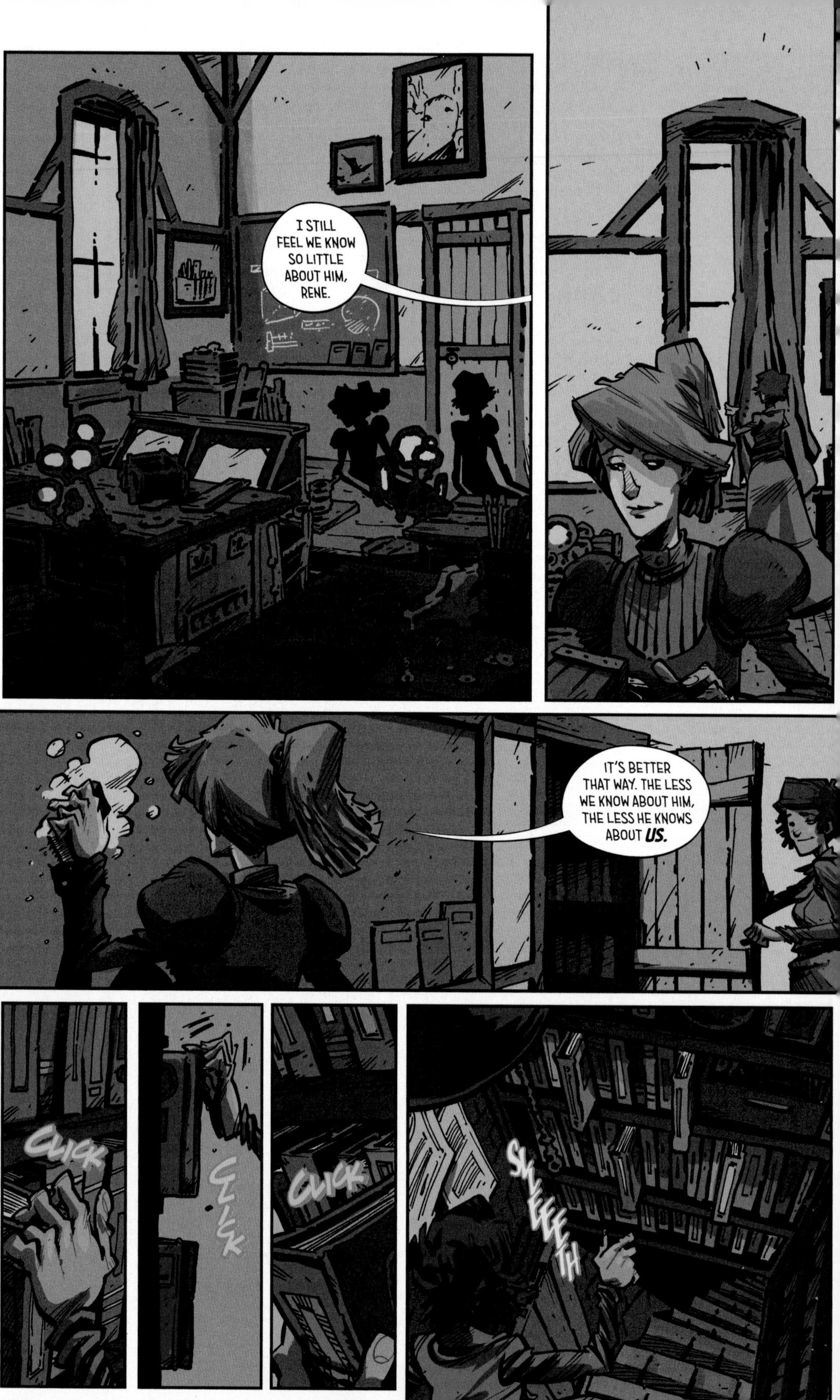
I STILL FEEL WE KNOW SO LITTLE ABOUT HIM, RENE.
IT'S BETTER THAT WAY. THE LESS WE KNOW ABOUT HIM, THE LESS HE KNOWS ABOUT **US.**
CLICK
CLICK
CLICK
SKLEEETH

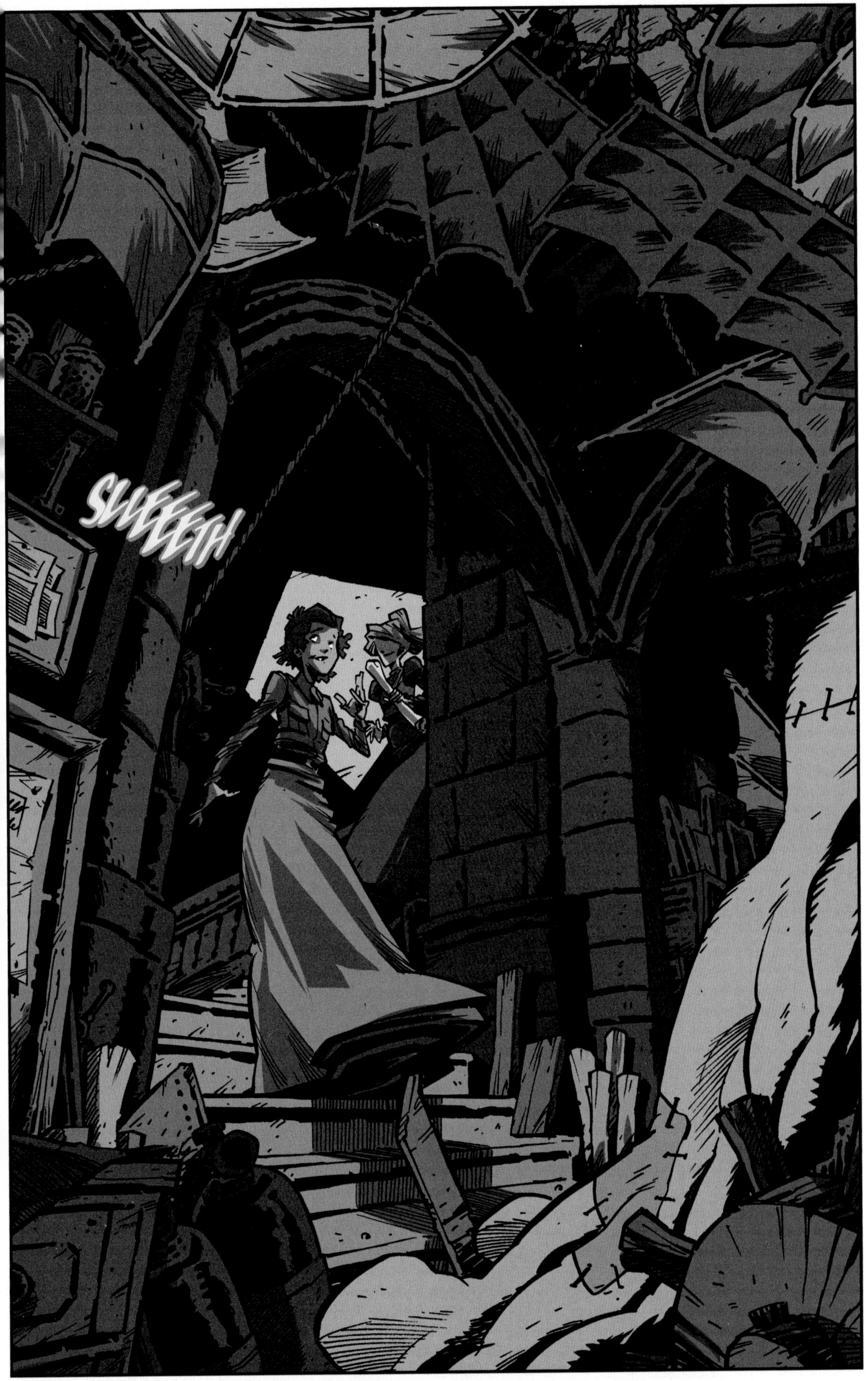
SLLEEETH

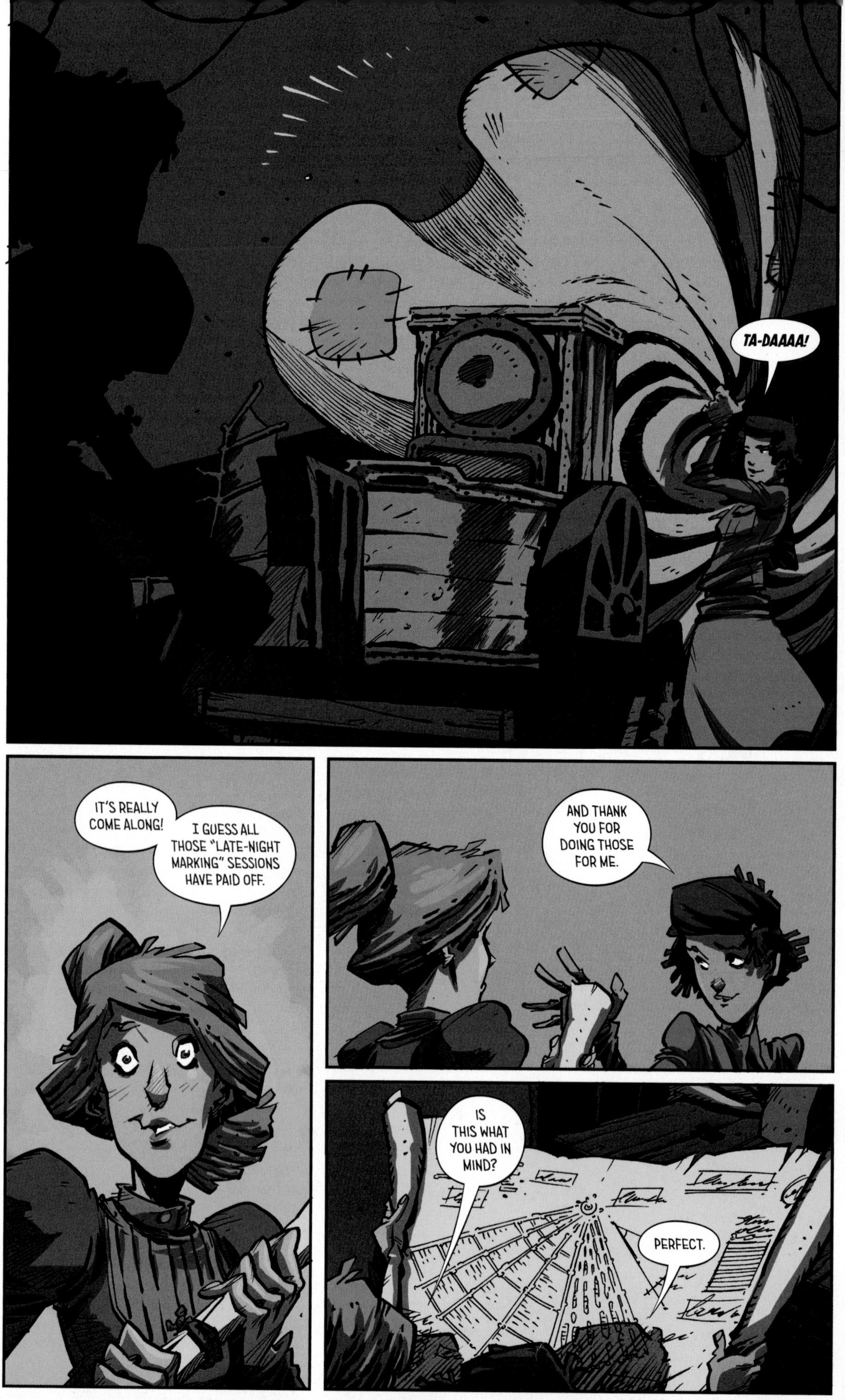
TA-DAAAA!
IT'S REALLY COME ALONG!
I GUESS ALL THOSE "LATE-NIGHT MARKING" SESSIONS HAVE PAID OFF.
AND THANK YOU FOR DOING THOSE FOR ME.
IS THIS WHAT YOU HAD IN MIND?
PERFECT.

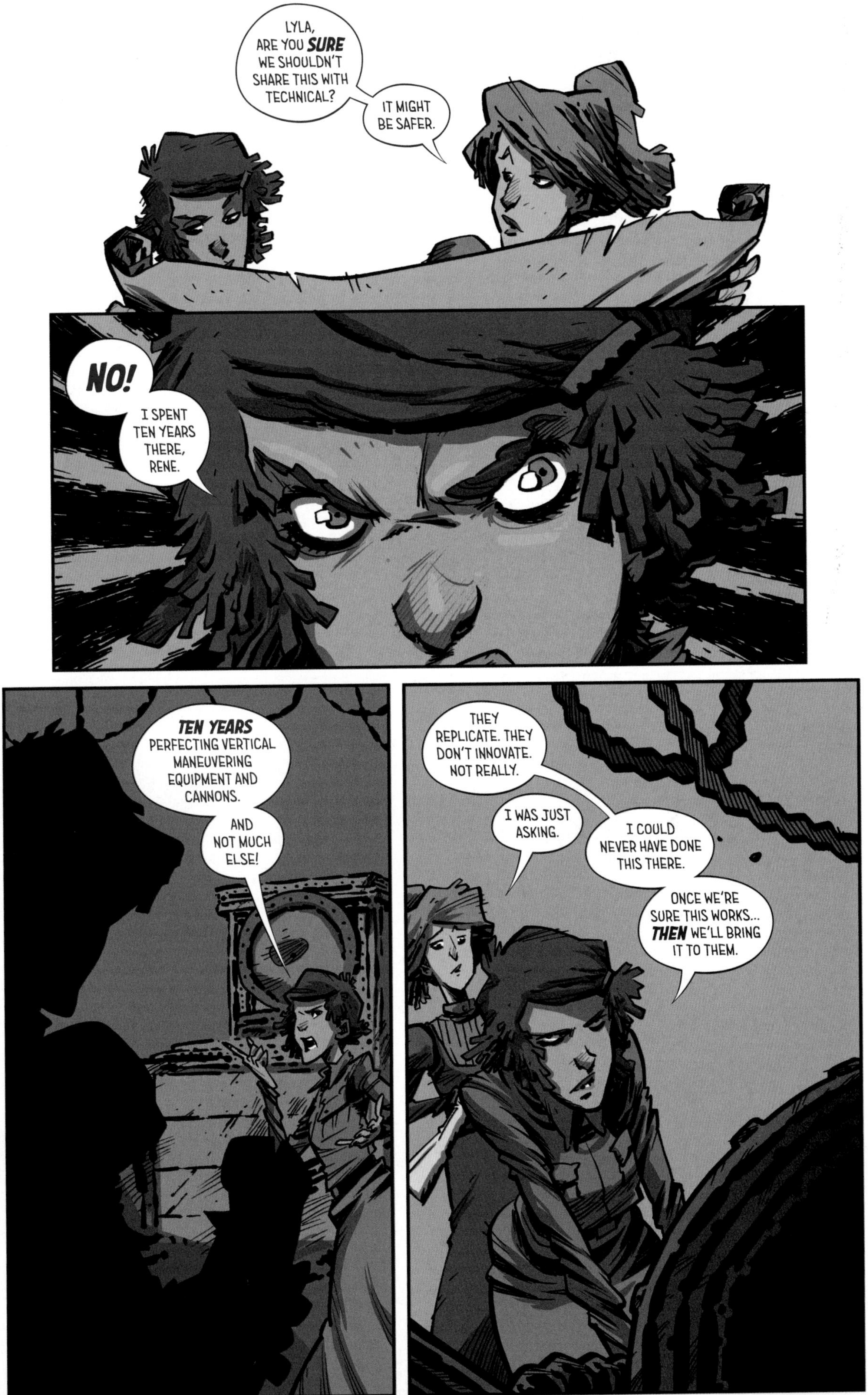
LYLA, ARE YOU **SURE** WE SHOULDN'T SHARE THIS WITH TECHNICAL?
IT MIGHT BE SAFER.
NO!
I SPENT TEN YEARS THERE, RENE.
TEN YEARS PERFECTING VERTICAL MANEUVERING EQUIPMENT AND CANNONS.
AND NOT MUCH ELSE!
THEY REPLICATE. THEY DON'T INNOVATE. NOT REALLY.
I WAS JUST ASKING.
I COULD NEVER HAVE DONE THIS THERE.
ONCE WE'RE SURE THIS WORKS... **THEN** WE'LL BRING IT TO THEM.

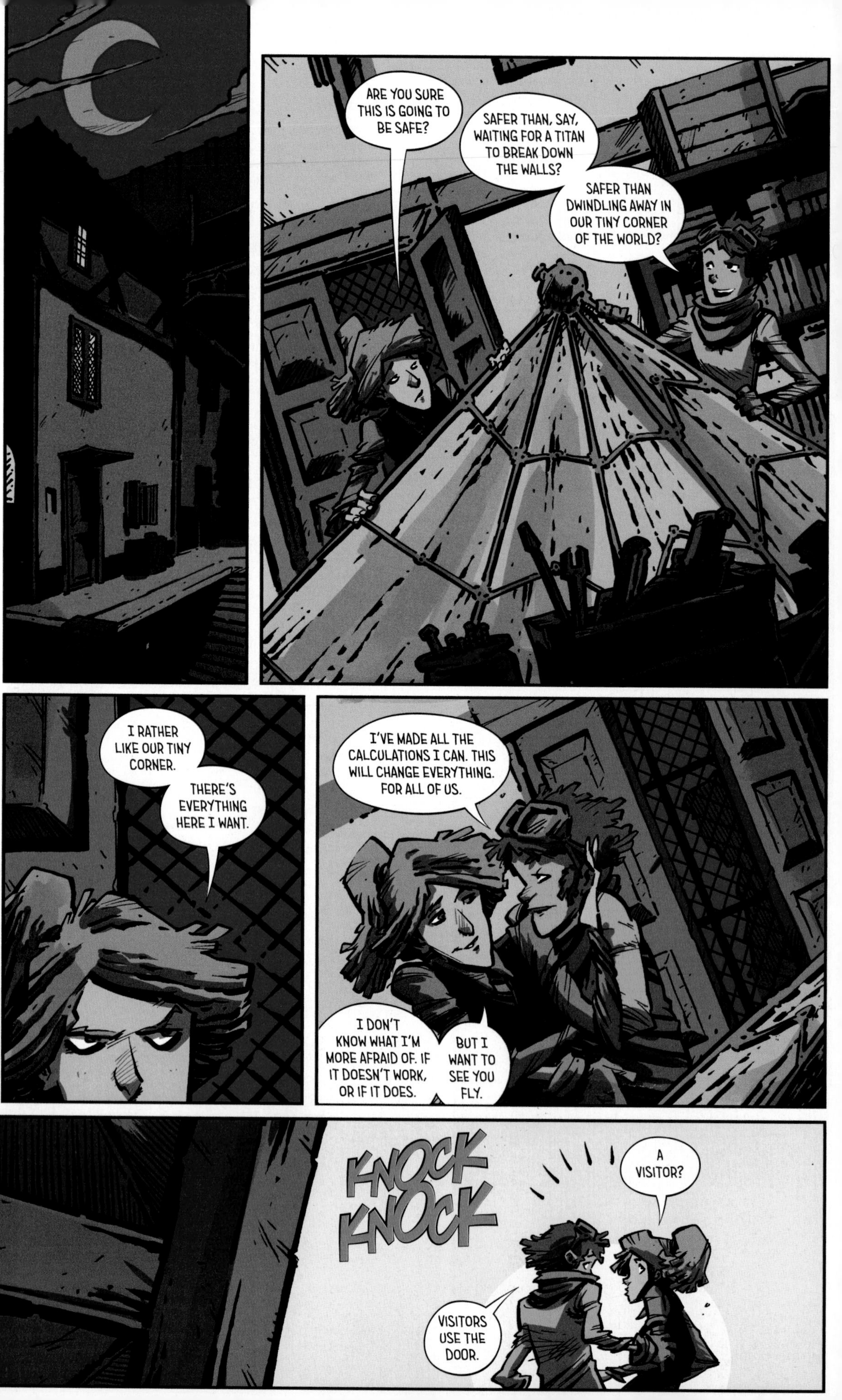

ARE YOU SURE THIS IS GOING TO BE SAFE?
SAFER THAN, SAY, WAITING FOR A TITAN TO BREAK DOWN THE WALLS?
SAFER THAN DWINDLING AWAY IN OUR TINY CORNER OF THE WORLD?
I RATHER LIKE OUR TINY CORNER.
THERE'S EVERYTHING HERE I WANT.
I'VE MADE ALL THE CALCULATIONS I CAN. THIS WILL CHANGE EVERYTHING. FOR ALL OF US.
I DON'T KNOW WHAT I'M MORE AFRAID OF. IF IT DOESN'T WORK, OR IF IT DOES.
BUT I WANT TO SEE YOU FLY.
KNOCK KNOCK
A VISITOR?
VISITORS USE THE DOOR.

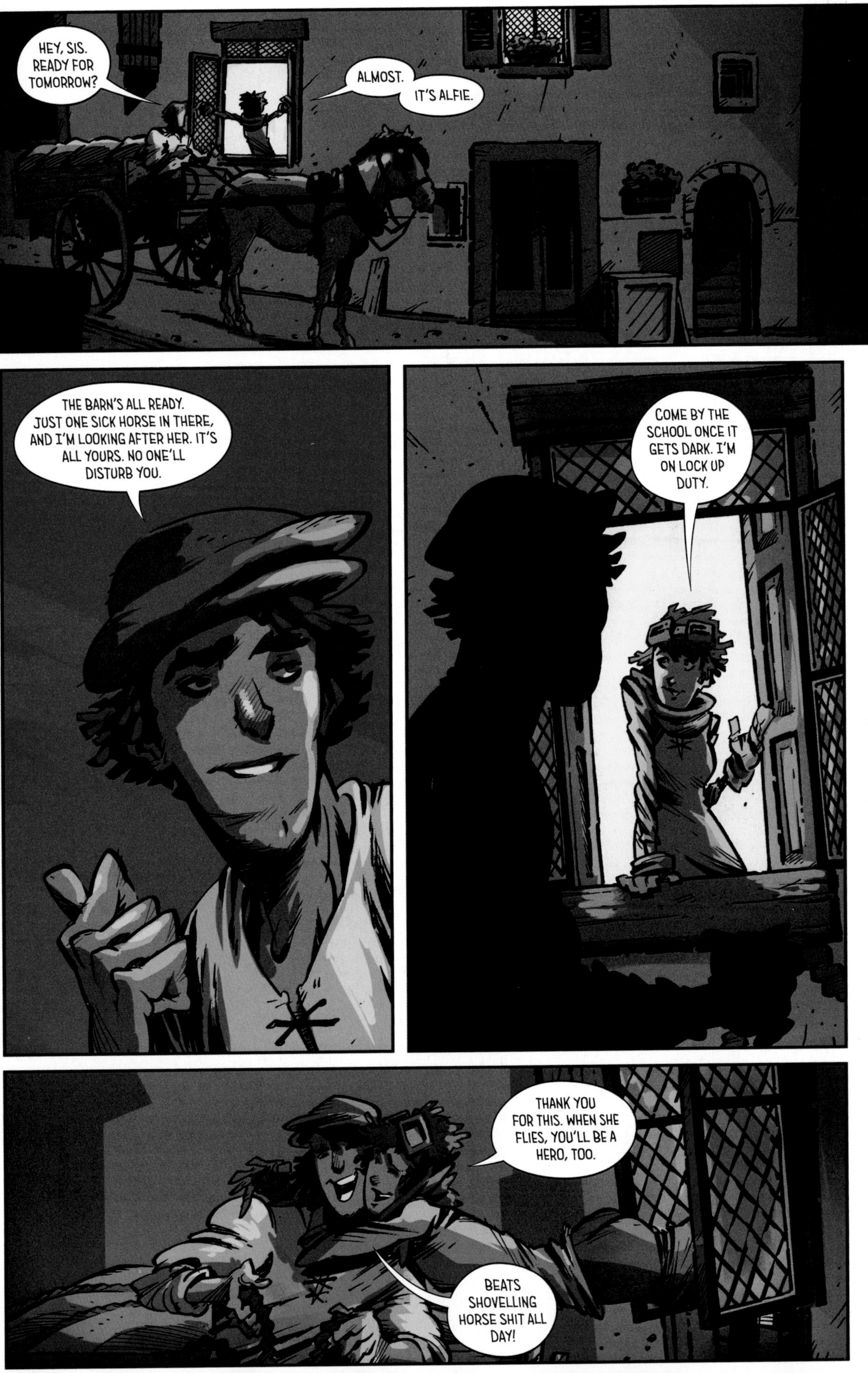
HEY, SIS. READY FOR TOMORROW?
ALMOST.
IT'S ALFIE.
THE BARN'S ALL READY. JUST ONE SICK HORSE IN THERE, AND I'M LOOKING AFTER HER. IT'S ALL YOURS. NO ONE'LL DISTURB YOU.
COME BY THE SCHOOL ONCE IT GETS DARK. I'M ON LOCK UP DUTY.
THANK YOU FOR THIS. WHEN SHE FLIES, YOU'LL BE A HERO, TOO.
BEATS SHOVELLING HORSE SHIT ALL DAY!

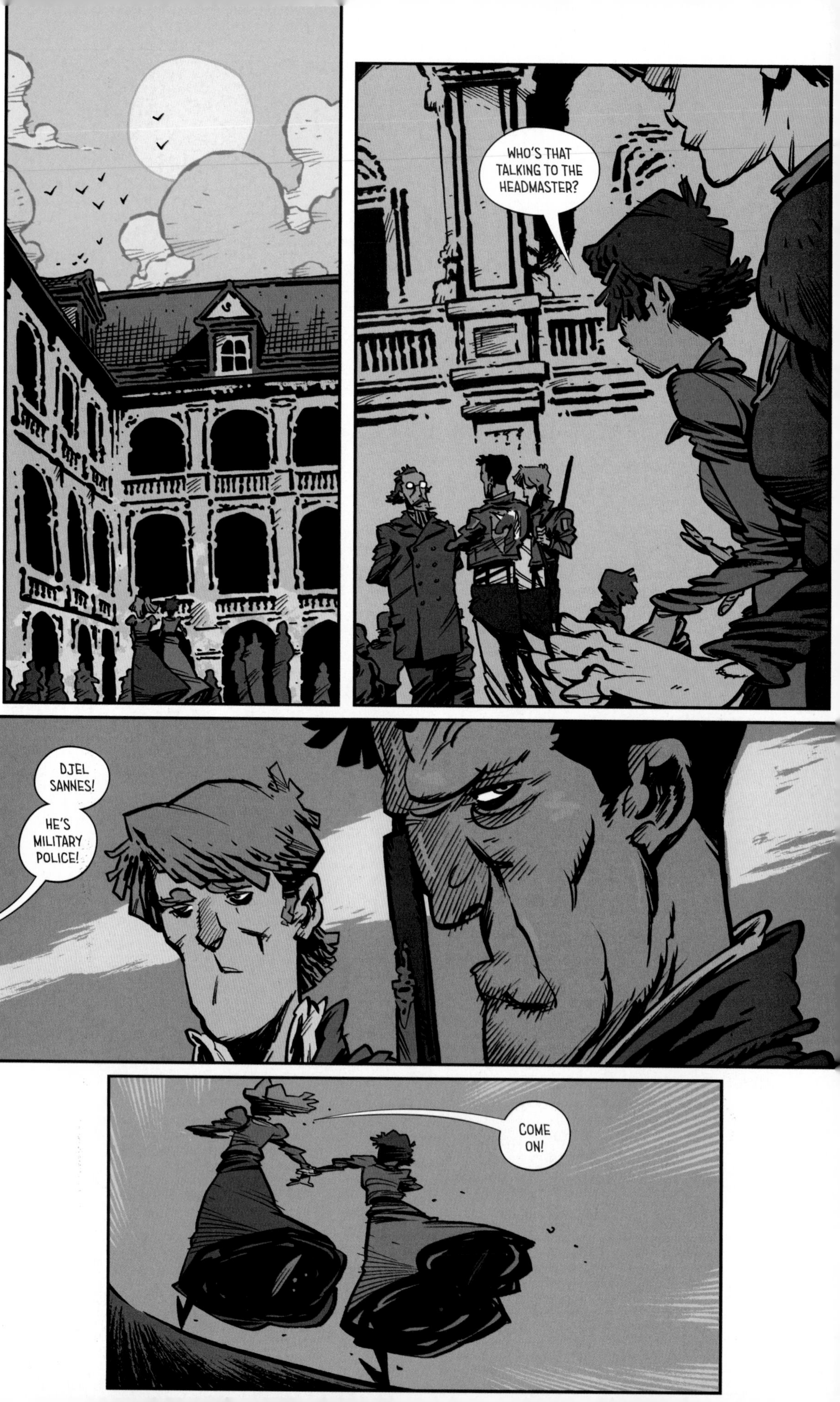
WHO'S THAT TALKING TO THE HEADMASTER?
DJEL SANNES!
HE'S MILITARY POLICE!
COME ON!

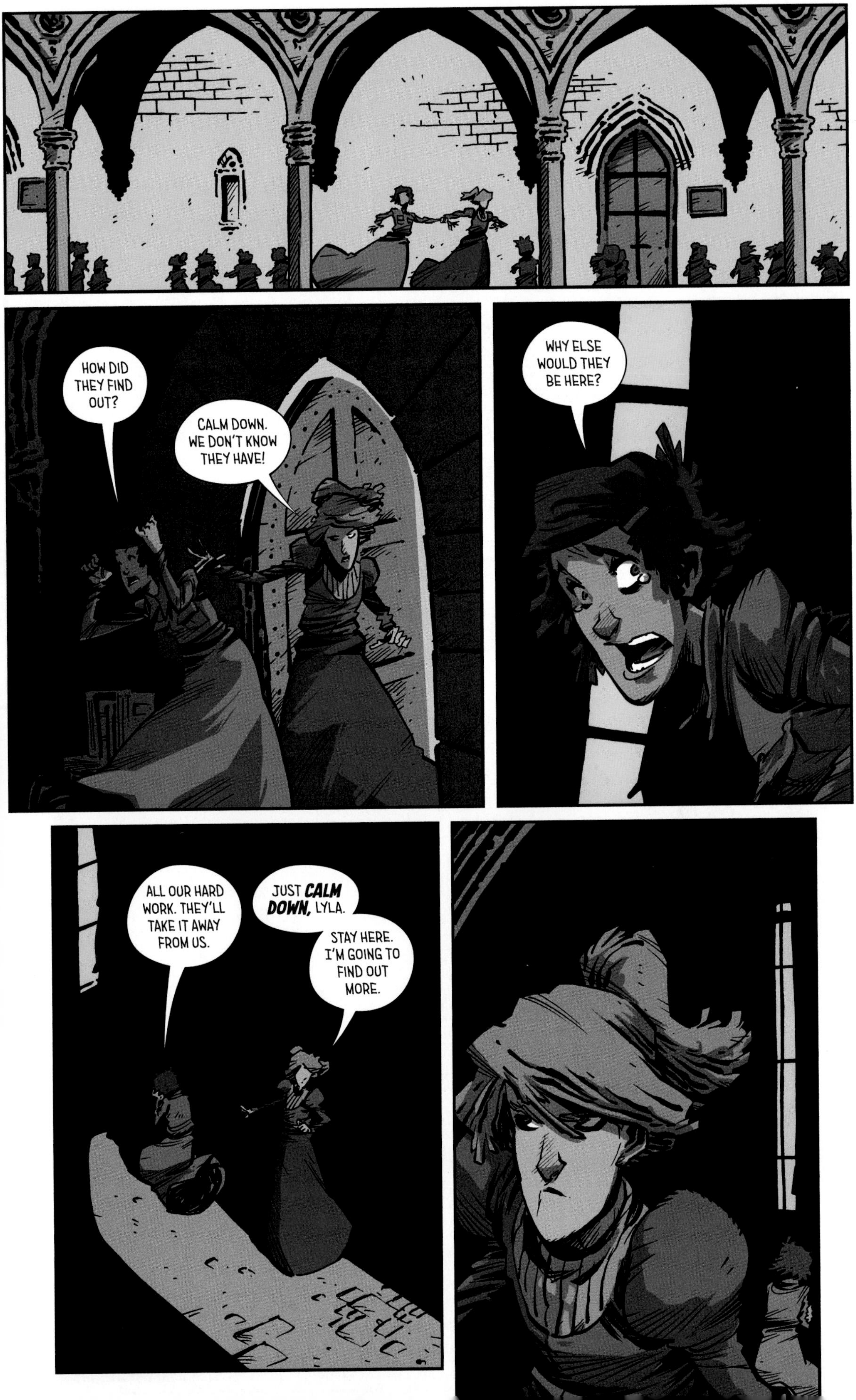
HOW DID THEY FIND OUT?
CALM DOWN. WE DON'T KNOW THEY HAVE!
WHY ELSE WOULD THEY BE HERE?
ALL OUR HARD WORK. THEY'LL TAKE IT AWAY FROM US.
JUST **CALM DOWN,** LYLA.
STAY HERE. I'M GOING TO FIND OUT MORE.

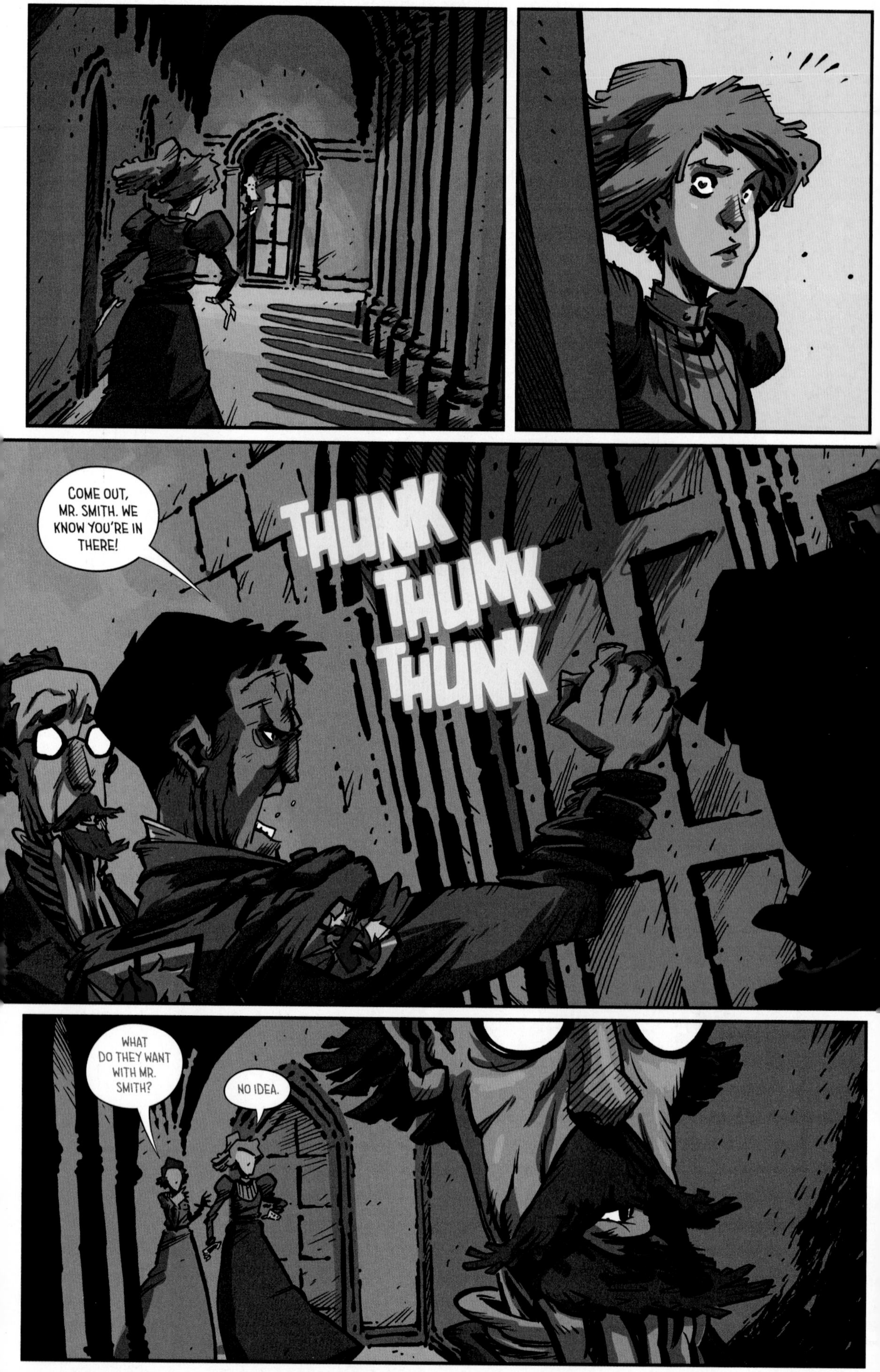
COME OUT, MR. SMITH. WE KNOW YOU'RE IN THERE!
THUNK THUNK THUNK
WHAT DO THEY WANT WITH MR. SMITH?
NO IDEA.

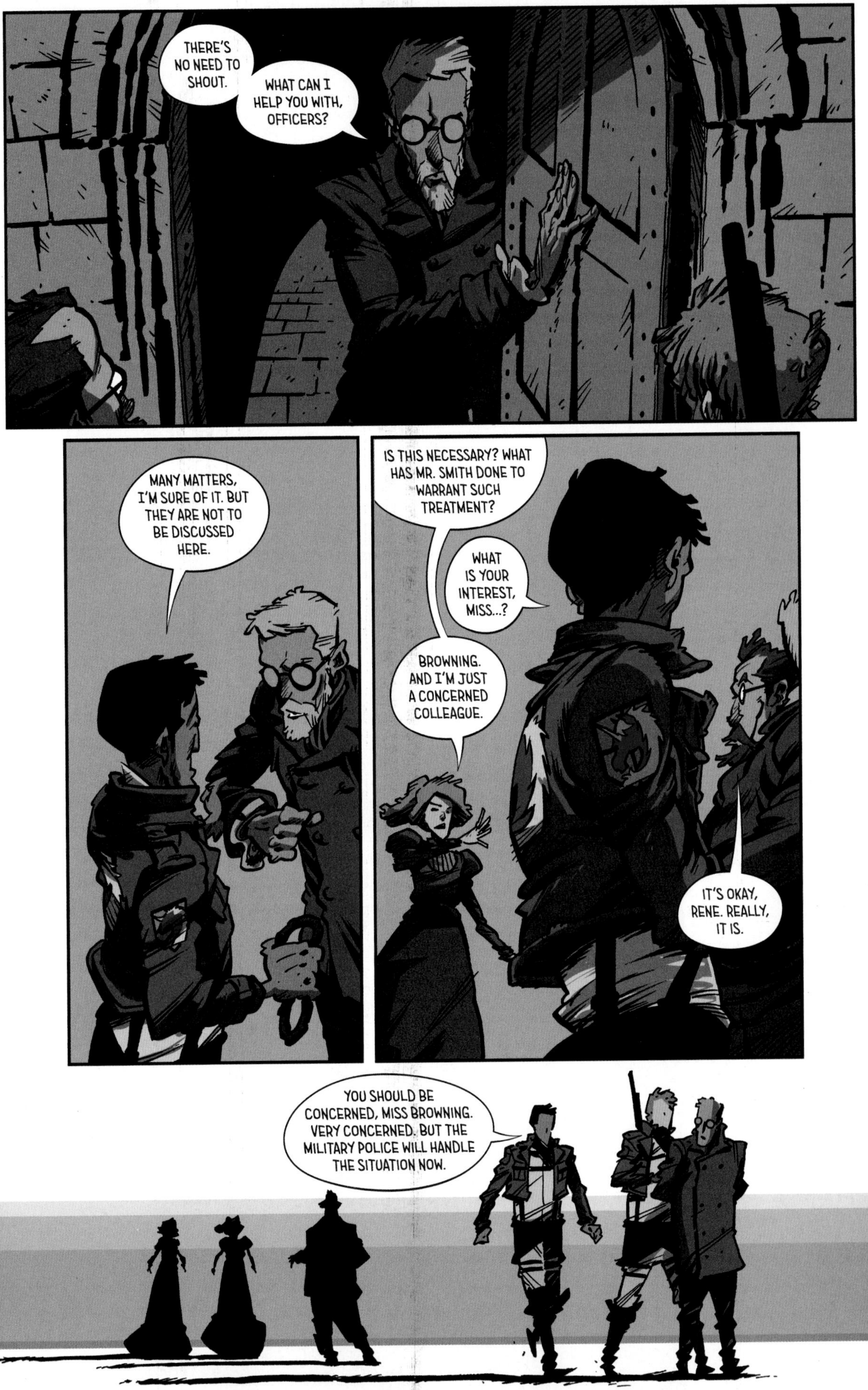
THERE'S NO NEED TO SHOUT.
WHAT CAN I HELP YOU WITH, OFFICERS?
MANY MATTERS, I'M SURE OF IT. BUT THEY ARE NOT TO BE DISCUSSED HERE.
IS THIS NECESSARY? WHAT HAS MR. SMITH DONE TO WARRANT SUCH TREATMENT?
WHAT IS YOUR INTEREST, MISS...?
BROWNING. AND I'M JUST A CONCERNED COLLEAGUE.
IT'S OKAY, RENE. REALLY, IT IS.
YOU SHOULD BE CONCERNED, MISS BROWNING. VERY CONCERNED. BUT THE MILITARY POLICE WILL HANDLE THE SITUATION NOW.

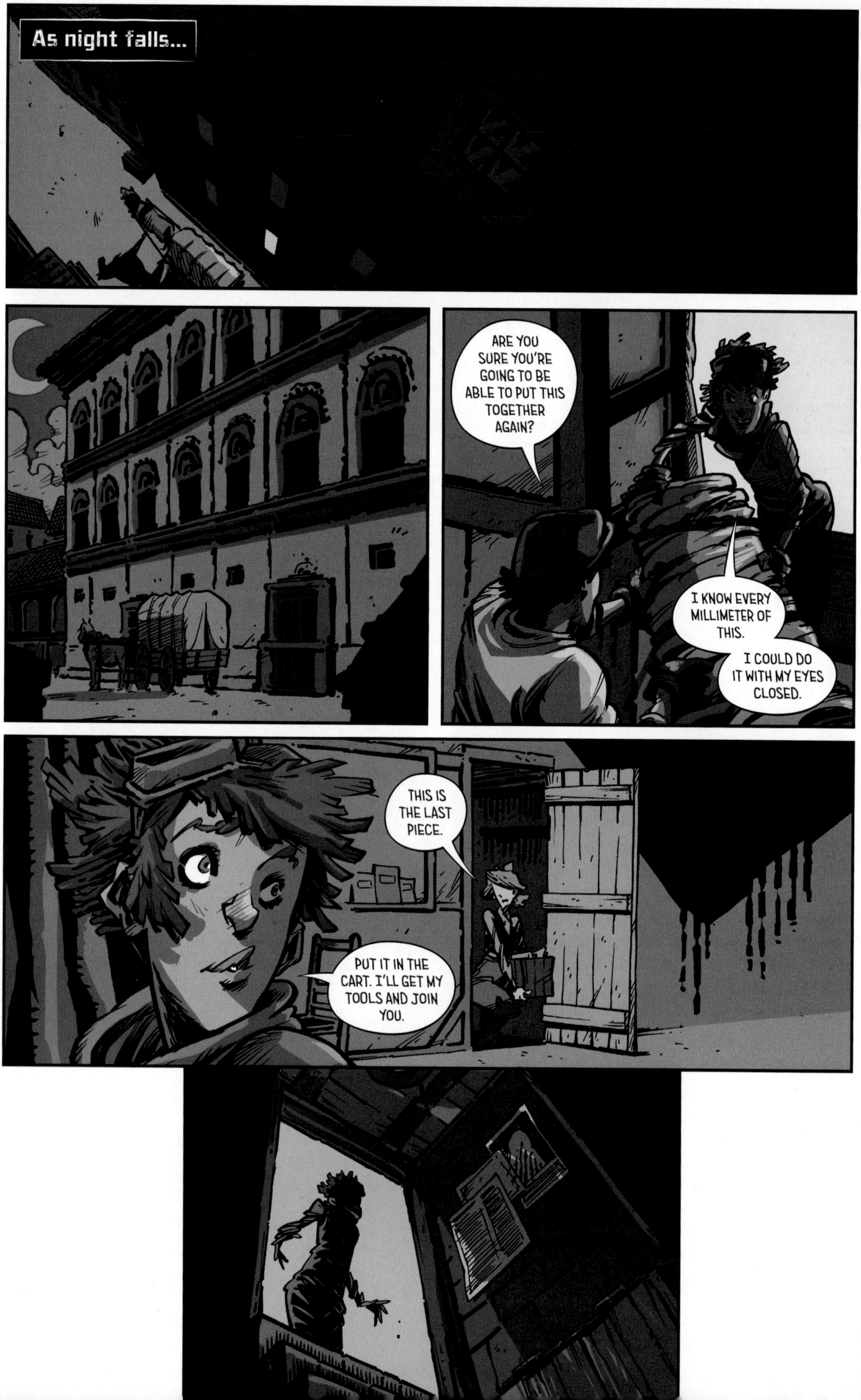
As night falls...
ARE YOU SURE YOU'RE GOING TO BE ABLE TO PUT THIS TOGETHER AGAIN?
I KNOW EVERY MILLIMETER OF THIS.
I COULD DO IT WITH MY EYES CLOSED.
THIS IS THE LAST PIECE.
PUT IT IN THE CART. I'LL GET MY TOOLS AND JOIN YOU.

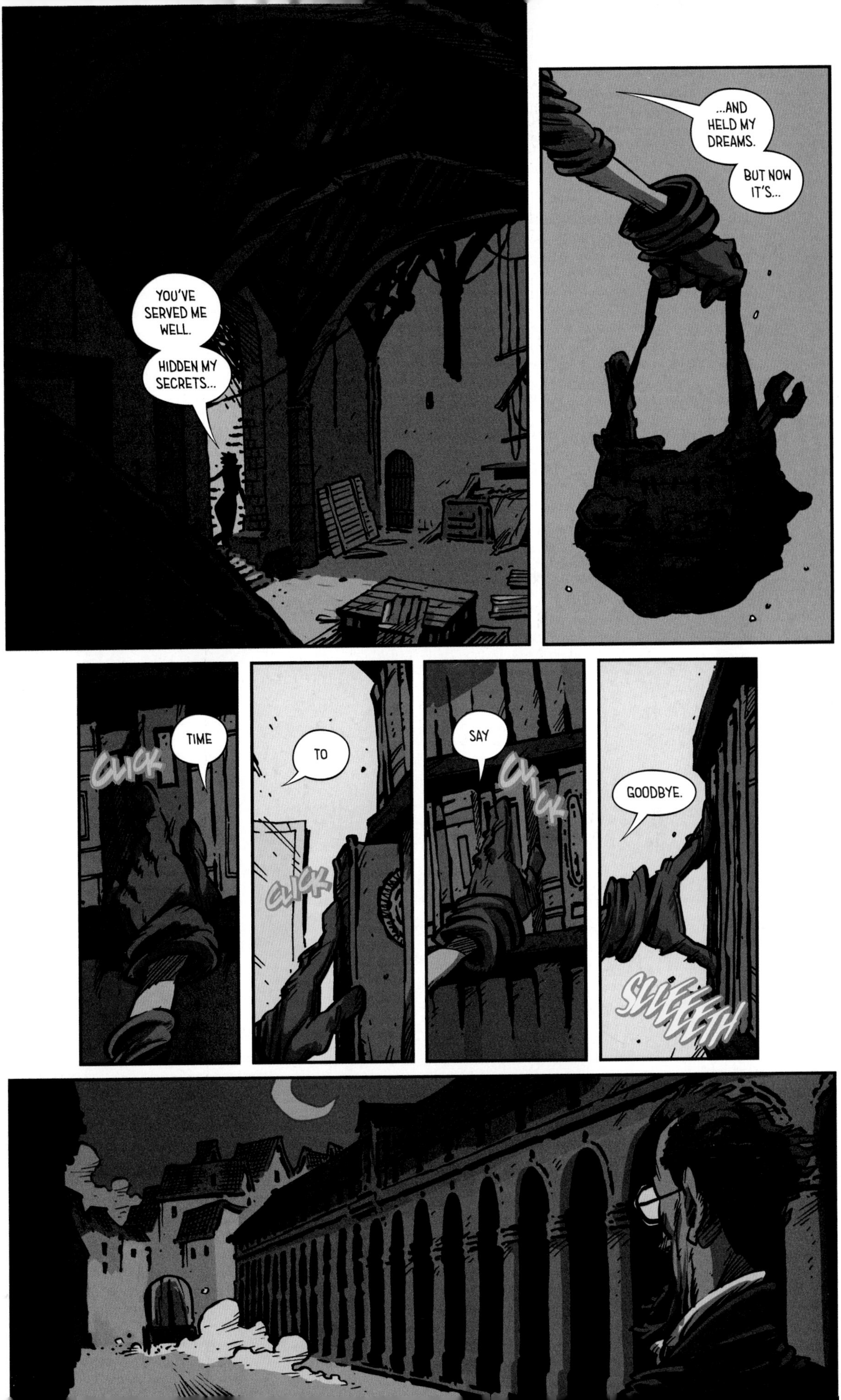
YOU'VE SERVED ME WELL.
HIDDEN MY SECRETS...
...AND HELD MY DREAMS.
BUT NOW IT'S...
CLICK
TIME
TO
CLICK
SAY
CLICK
GOODBYE.
SLLEEEETH

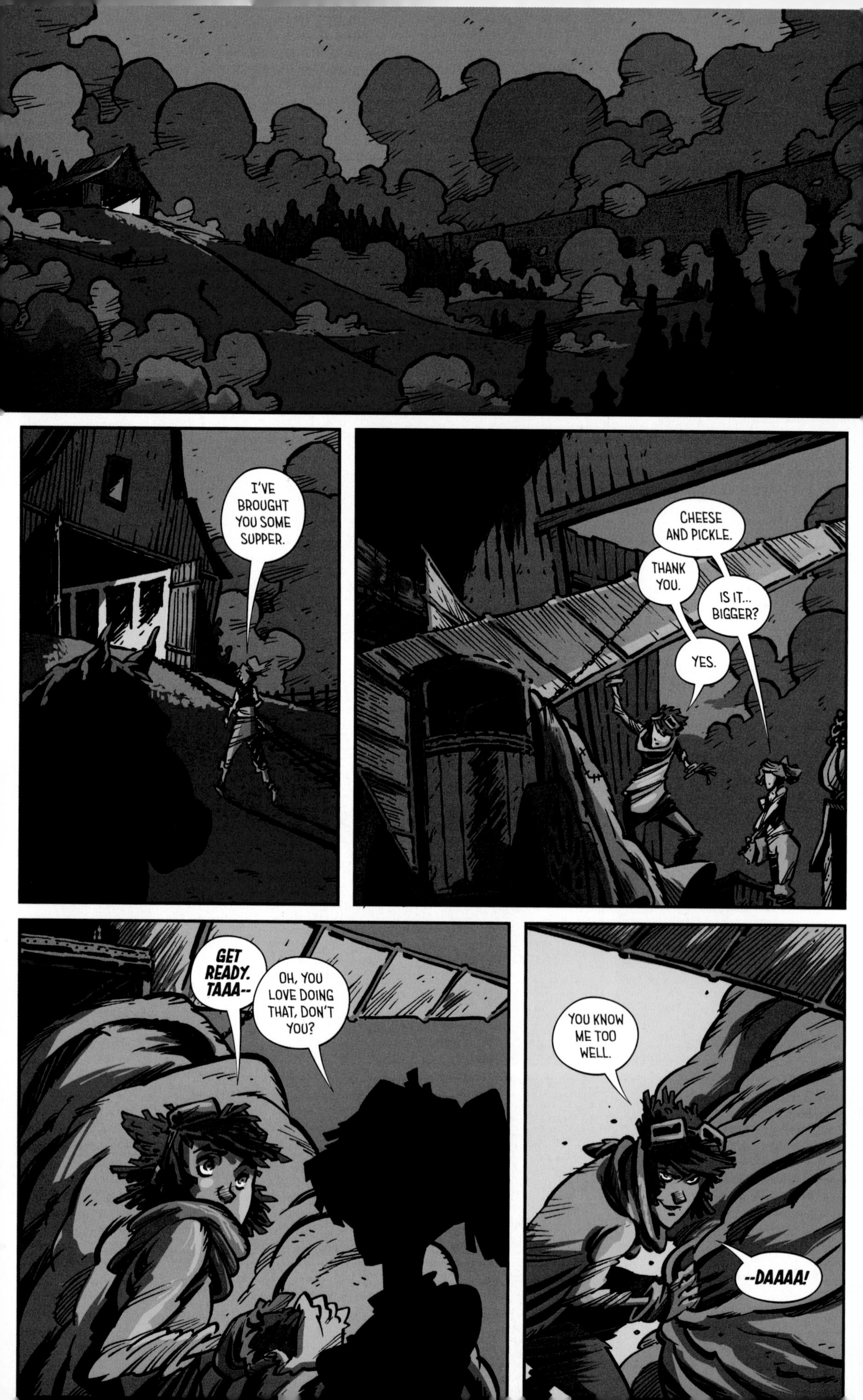
I'VE BROUGHT YOU SOME SUPPER.
CHEESE AND PICKLE.
THANK YOU.
IS IT... BIGGER?
YES.
GET READY. TAAA--
OH, YOU LOVE DOING THAT, DON'T YOU?
YOU KNOW ME TOO WELL.
--DAAAA!

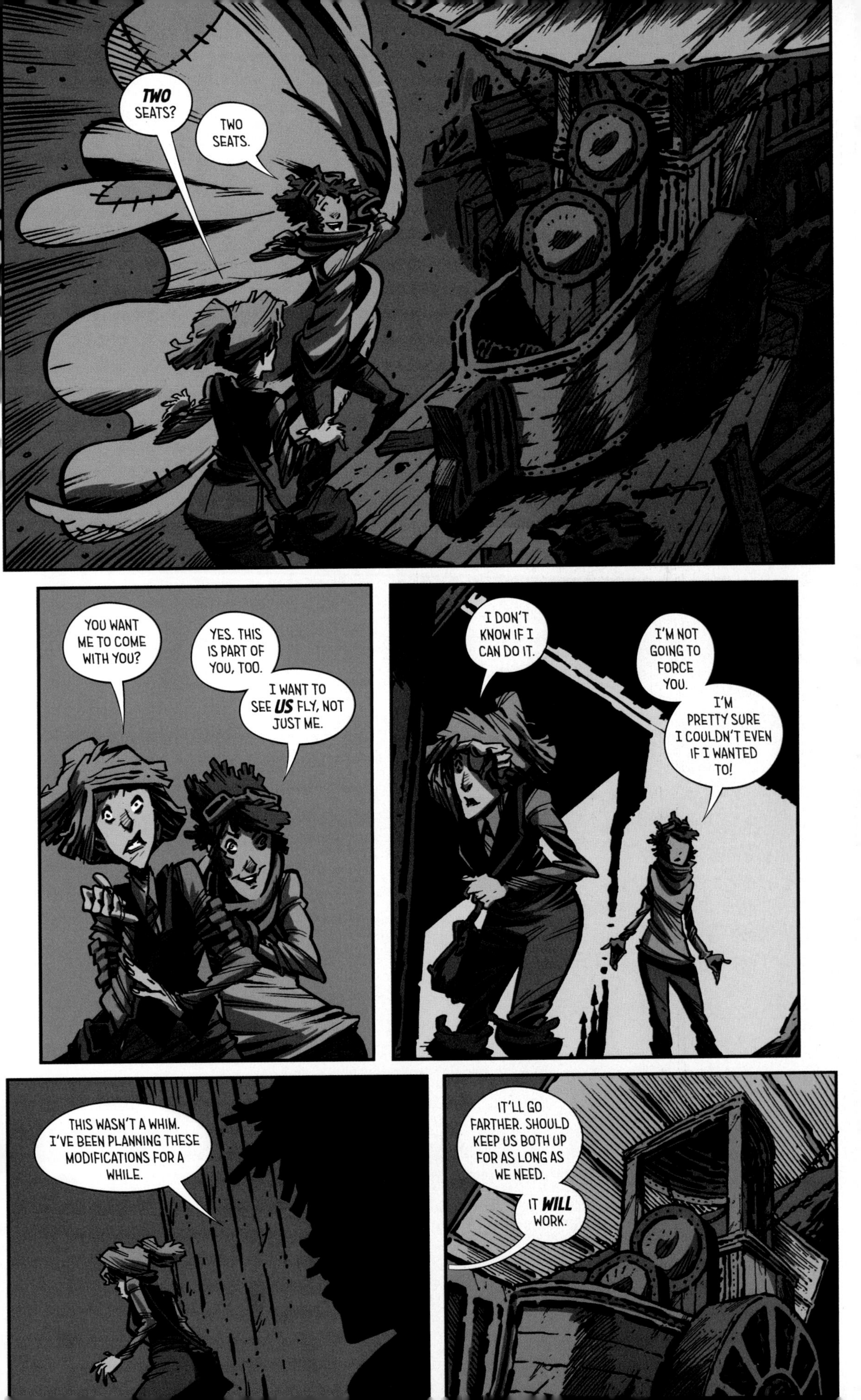
TWO SEATS?
TWO SEATS.
YOU WANT ME TO COME WITH YOU?
YES. THIS IS PART OF YOU, TOO.
I WANT TO SEE US FLY, NOT JUST ME.
I DON'T KNOW IF I CAN DO IT.
I'M NOT GOING TO FORCE YOU.
I'M PRETTY SURE I COULDN'T EVEN IF I WANTED TO!
THIS WASN'T A WHIM. I'VE BEEN PLANNING THESE MODIFICATIONS FOR A WHILE.
IT'LL GO FARTHER. SHOULD KEEP US BOTH UP FOR AS LONG AS WE NEED.
IT WILL WORK.

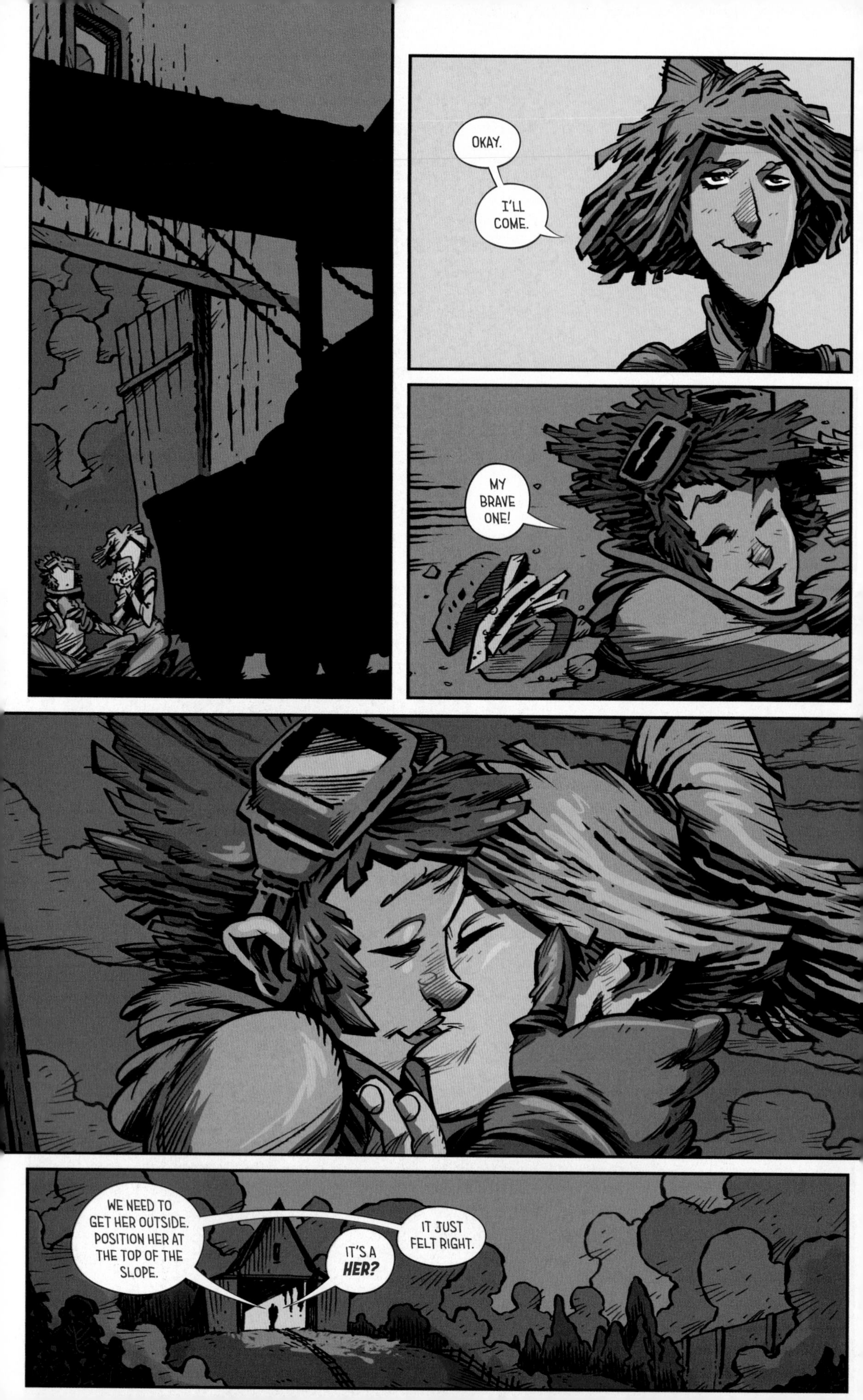
OKAY.
I'LL COME.
MY BRAVE ONE!
WE NEED TO GET HER OUTSIDE. POSITION HER AT THE TOP OF THE SLOPE.
IT'S A HER?
IT JUST FELT RIGHT.

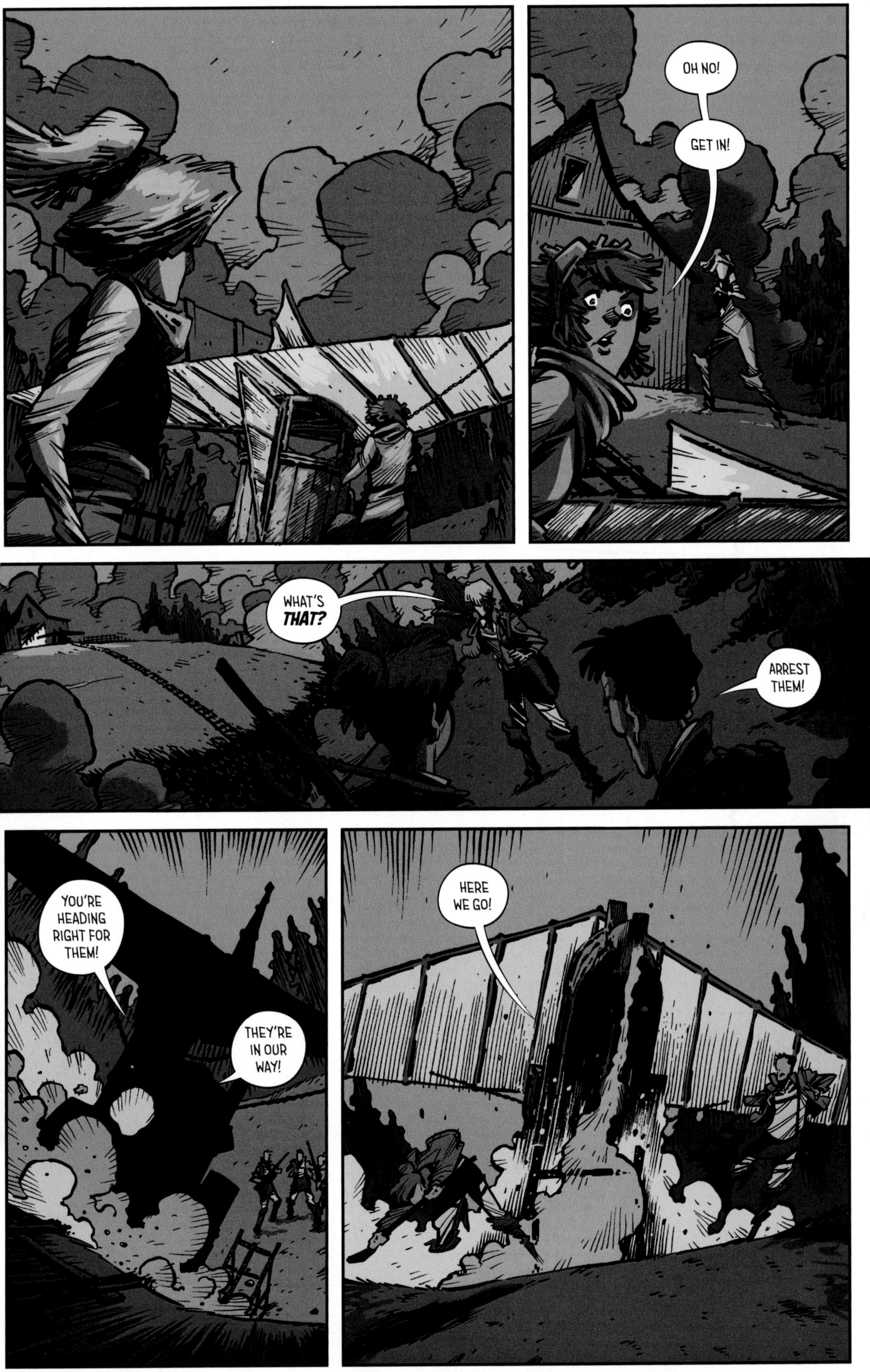
OH NO!
GET IN!
WHAT'S THAT?
ARREST THEM!
YOU'RE HEADING RIGHT FOR THEM!
THEY'RE IN OUR WAY!
HERE WE GO!

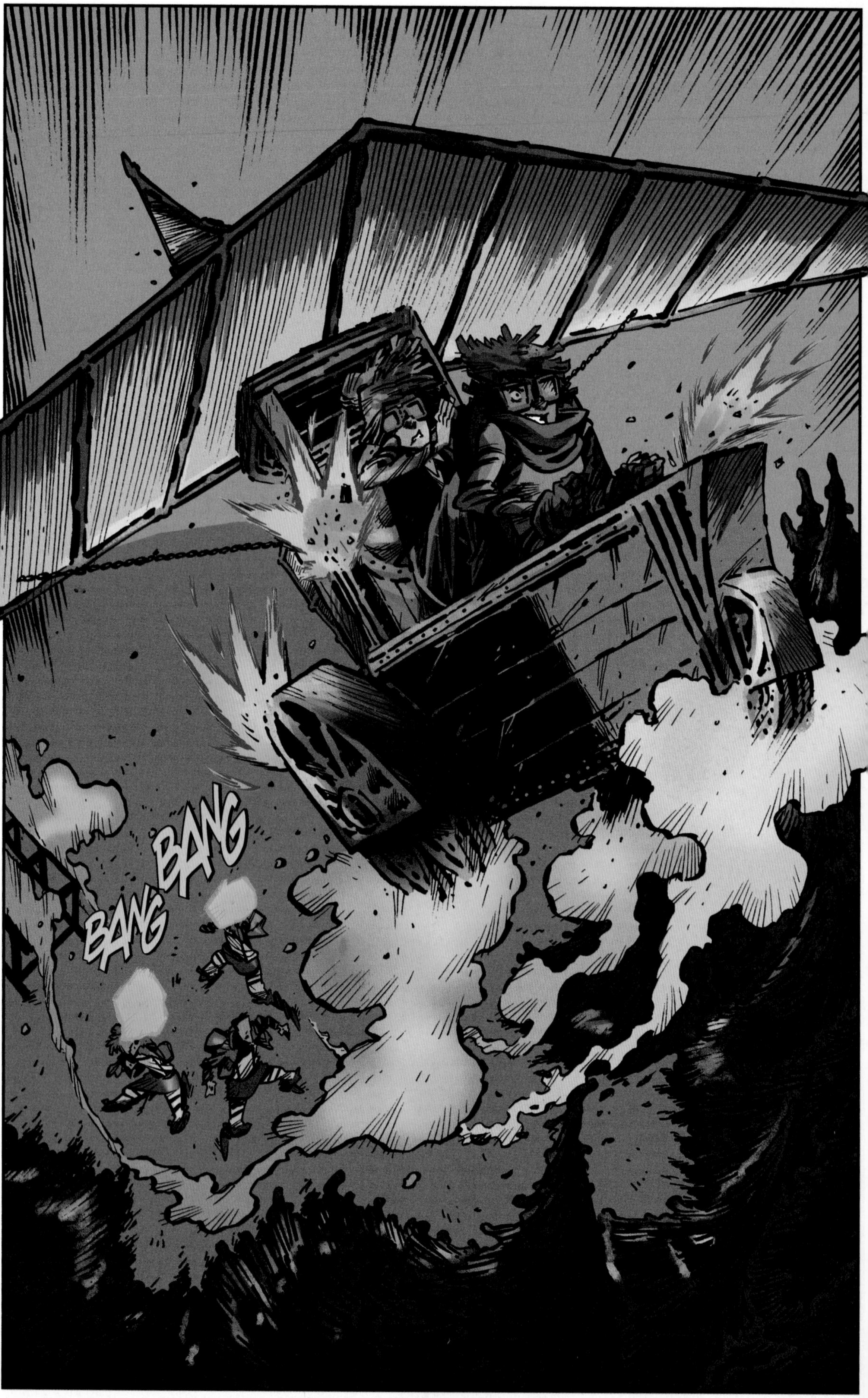
BANG
BANG

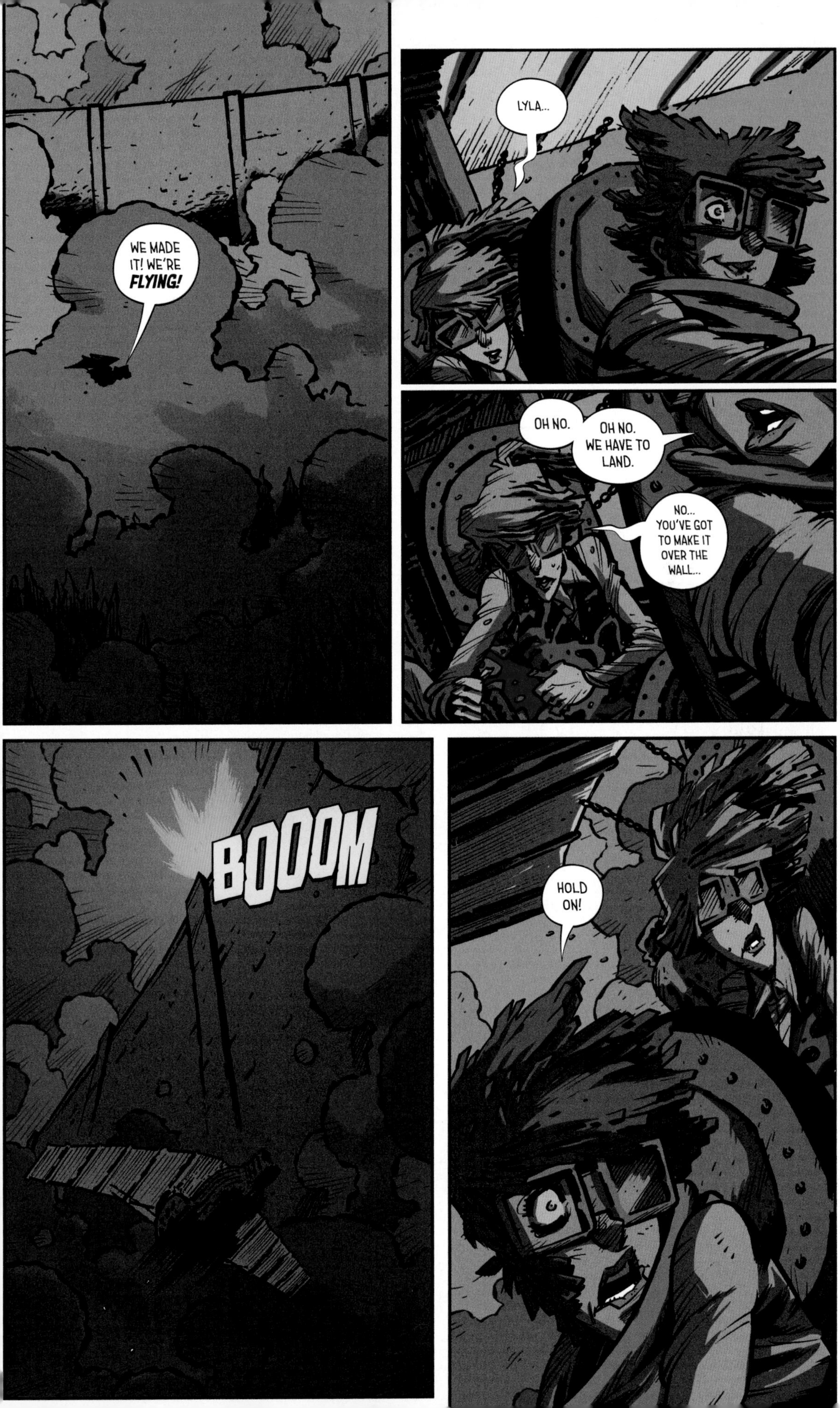
WE MADE IT! WE'RE **FLYING!**
LYLA...
OH NO.
OH NO. WE HAVE TO LAND.
NO... YOU'VE GOT TO MAKE IT OVER THE WALL...
BOOOM
HOLD ON!

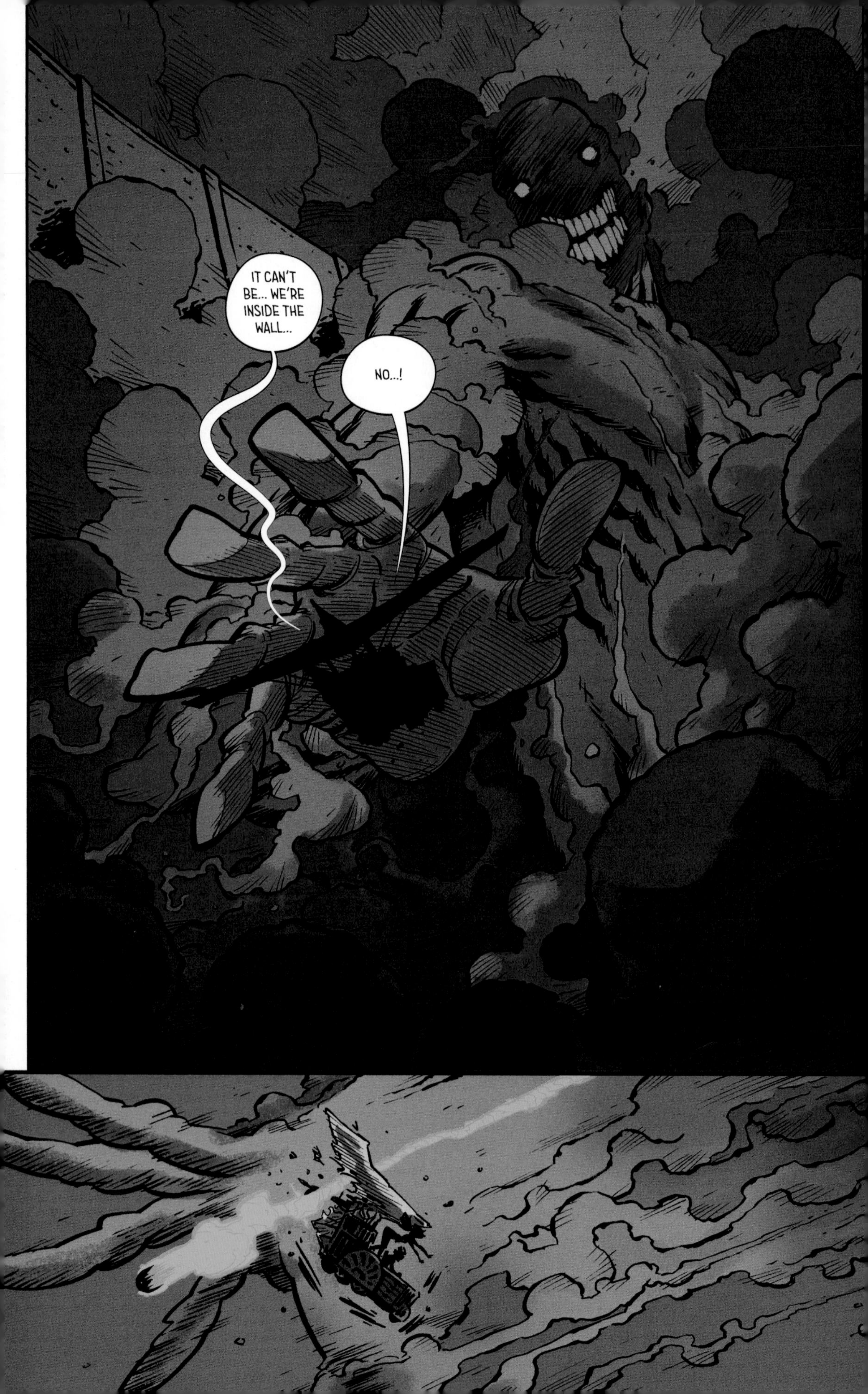
IT CAN'T BE... WE'RE INSIDE THE WALL...
NO...!

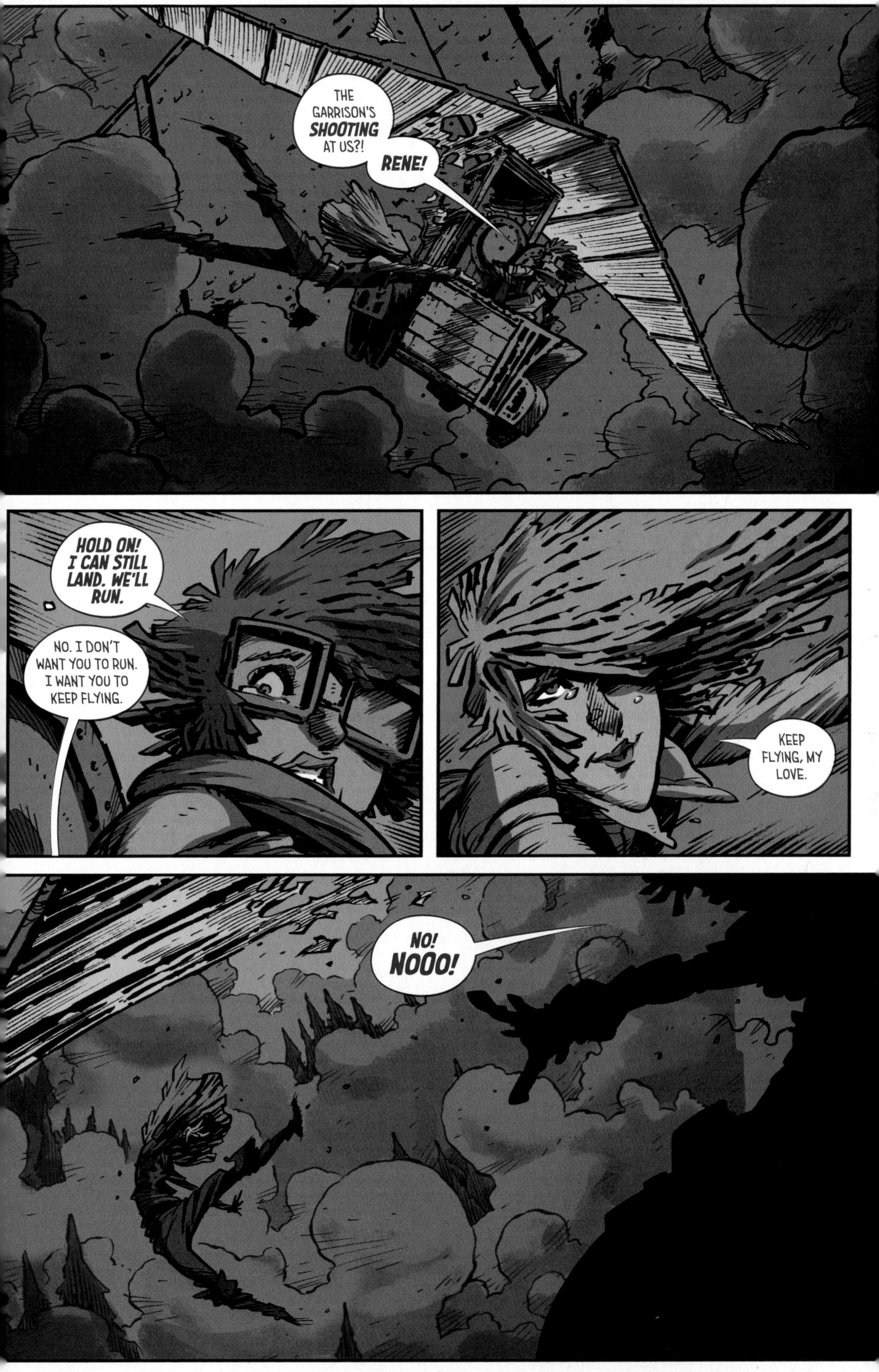
THE GARRISON'S SHOOTING AT US?!
RENE!
HOLD ON! I CAN STILL LAND. WE'LL RUN.
NO. I DON'T WANT YOU TO RUN. I WANT YOU TO KEEP FLYING.
KEEP FLYING, MY LOVE.
NO! NOOO!

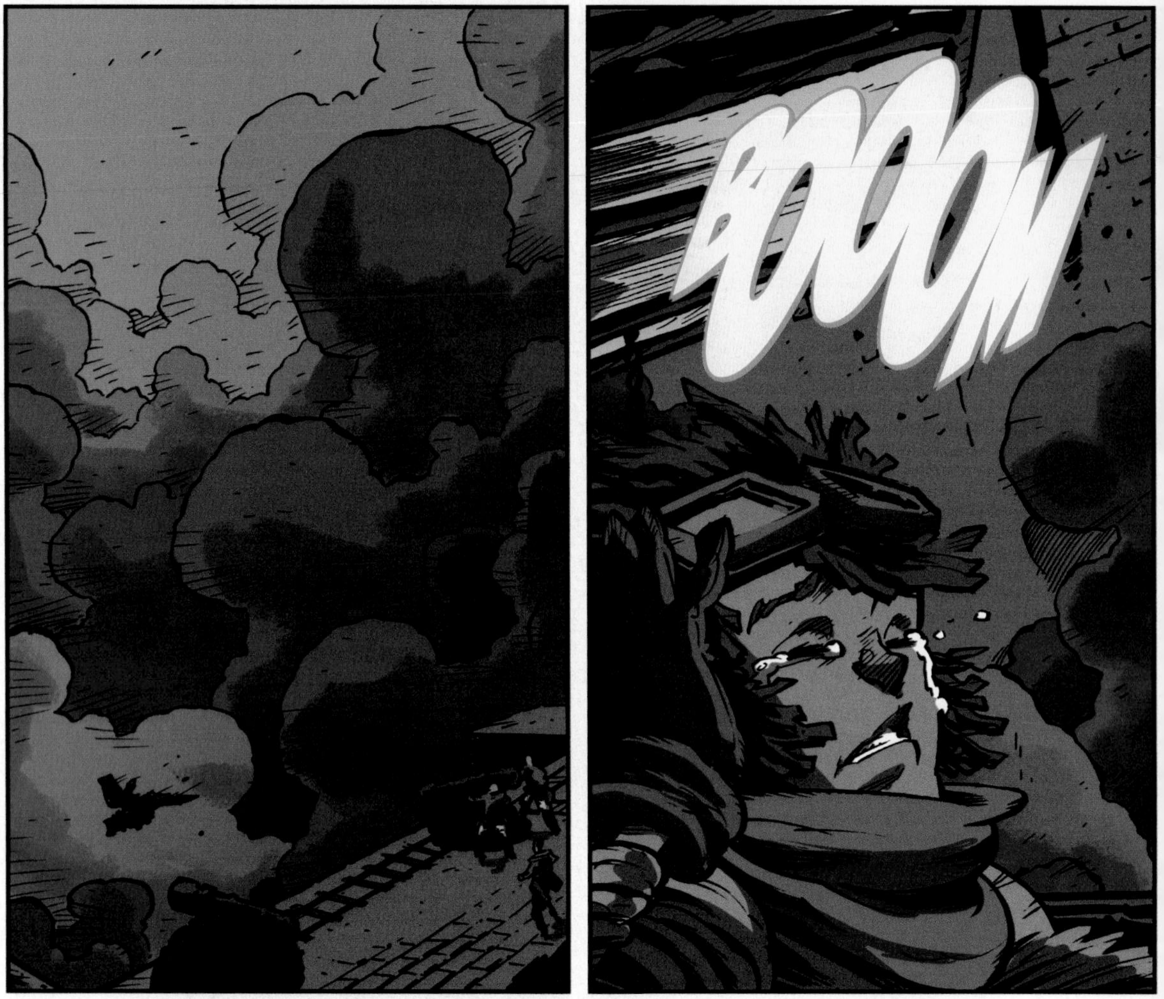
BOOOM

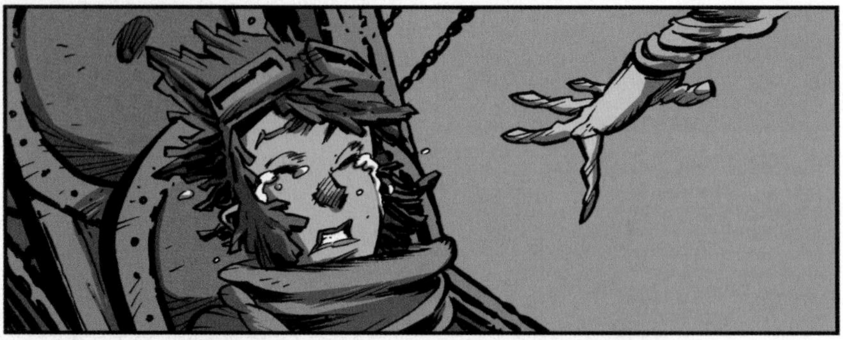

SKIES ABOVE

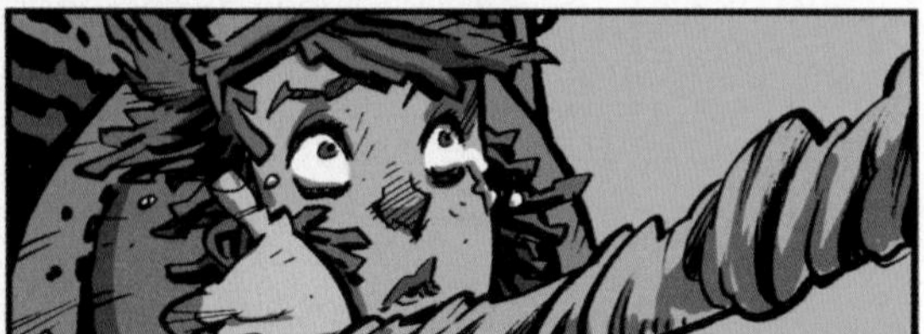

WRITTEN BY RHIANNA PRATCHETT
AND BEN APPLEGATE
PENCILS AND INKS BY JORGE CORONA
COLORS BY JENNIFER HICKMAN
LETTERING BY STEVE WANDS

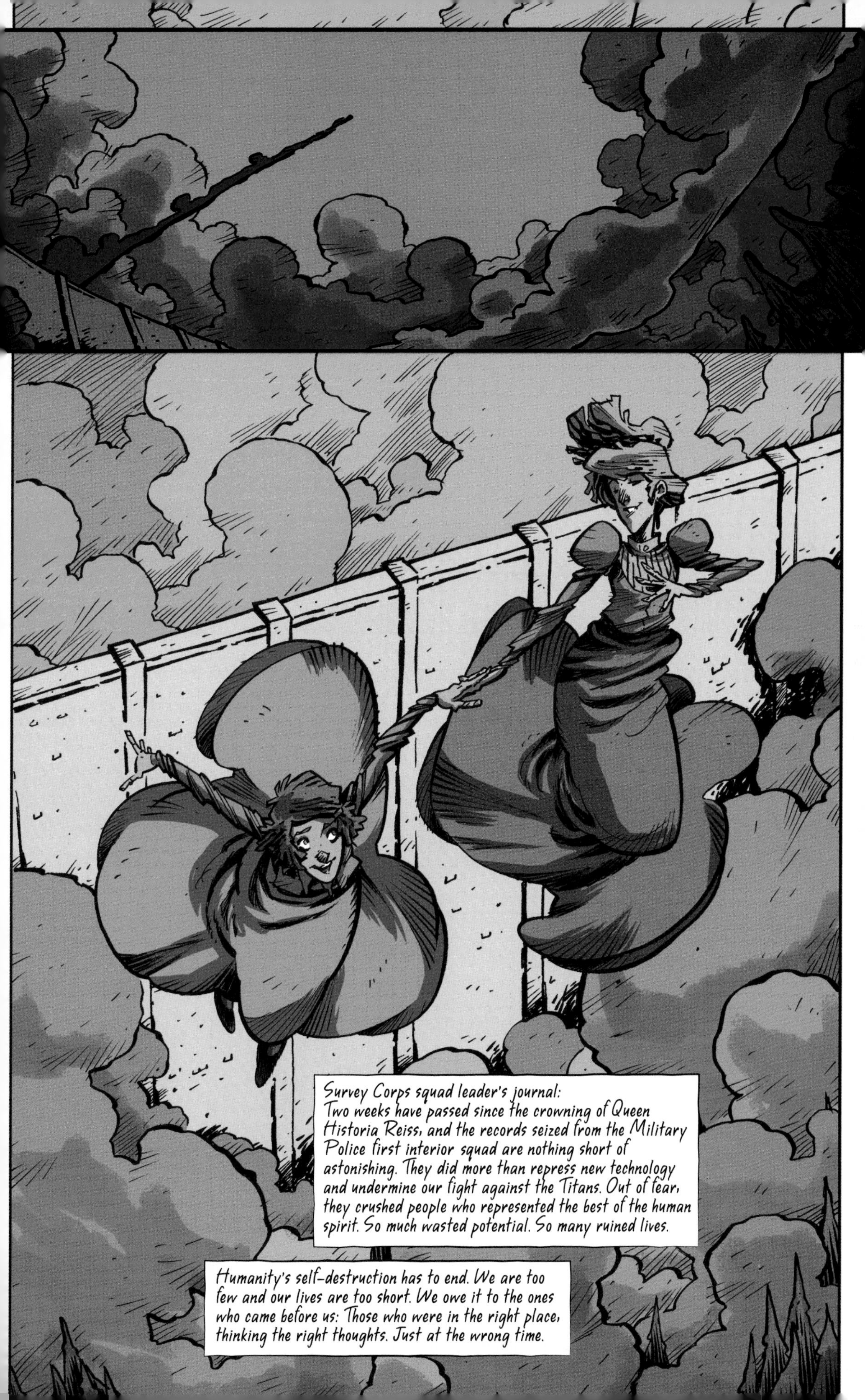
Survey Corps squad leader's journal:
Two weeks have passed since the crowning of Queen Historia Reiss, and the records seized from the Military Police first interior squad are nothing short of astonishing. They did more than repress new technology and undermine our fight against the Titans. Out of fear, they crushed people who represented the best of the human spirit. So much wasted potential. So many ruined lives.
Humanity's self-destruction has to end. We are too few and our lives are too short. We owe it to the ones who came before us: Those who were in the right place, thinking the right thoughts. Just at the wrong time.

ATTACK on ATTACK on 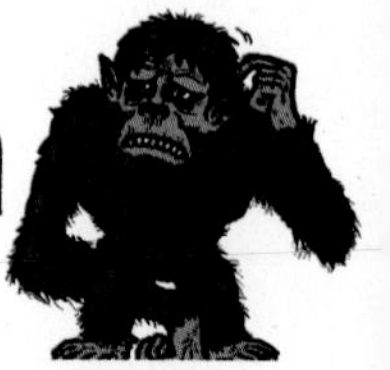

By Evan Dorkin and Sarah Dyer
Flatted and additional colors by Bill Mudron

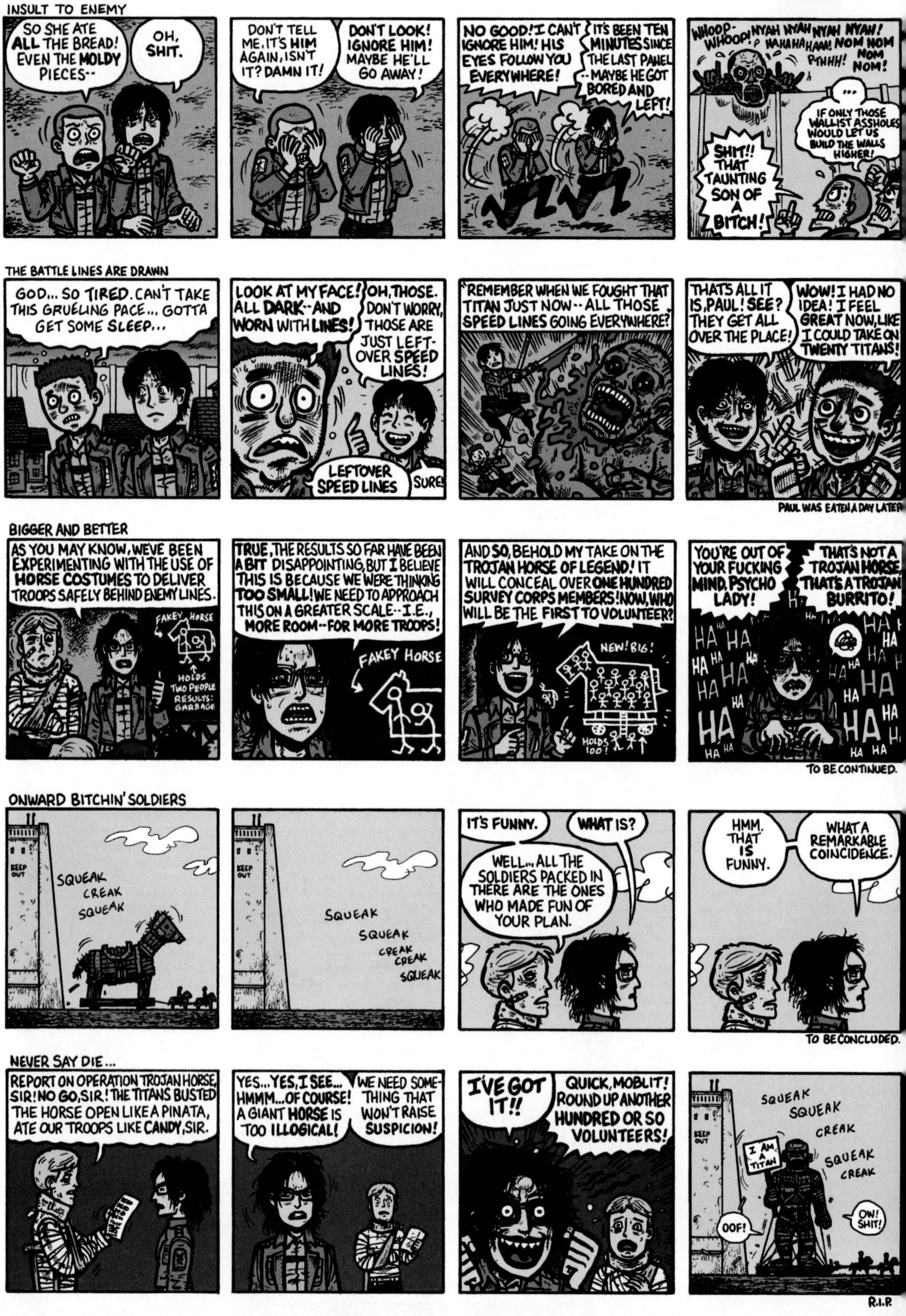
INSULT TO ENEMY
SO SHE ATE ALL THE BREAD! EVEN THE MOLDY PIECES--
OH, SHIT.
DON'T TELL ME. IT'S HIM AGAIN, ISN'T IT? DAMN IT!
DON'T LOOK! IGNORE HIM! MAYBE HE'LL GO AWAY!
NO GOOD! I CAN'T IGNORE HIM! HIS EYES FOLLOW YOU EVERYWHERE!
IT'S BEEN TEN MINUTES SINCE THE LAST PANEL--MAYBE HE GOT BORED AND LEFT!
WHOOP-WHOOP! NYAH NYAH HAHAHA HAAA! NYAH NYAH! PTHHH! NOM NOM NOM NOM!
...
IF ONLY THOSE WALLIST ASSHOLES WOULD LET US BUILD THE WALLS HIGHER!
SHIT!! THAT TAUNTING SON OF A BITCH!
THE BATTLE LINES ARE DRAWN
GOD... SO TIRED. CAN'T TAKE THIS GRUELING PACE... GOTTA GET SOME SLEEP...
LOOK AT MY FACE! ALL DARK--AND WORN WITH LINES!
OH, THOSE. DON'T WORRY, THOSE ARE JUST LEFT-OVER SPEED LINES!
LEFTOVER SPEED LINES
SURE!
"REMEMBER WHEN WE FOUGHT THAT TITAN JUST NOW--ALL THOSE SPEED LINES GOING EVERYWHERE?
THAT'S ALL IT IS, PAUL! SEE? THEY GET ALL OVER THE PLACE!
WOW! I HAD NO IDEA! I FEEL GREAT NOW, LIKE I COULD TAKE ON TWENTY TITANS!
PAUL WAS EATEN A DAY LATER
BIGGER AND BETTER
AS YOU MAY KNOW, WE'VE BEEN EXPERIMENTING WITH THE USE OF HORSE COSTUMES TO DELIVER TROOPS SAFELY BEHIND ENEMY LINES.
FAKEY HORSE
HOLDS TWO PEOPLE RESULTS: GARBAGE
TRUE, THE RESULTS SO FAR HAVE BEEN A BIT DISAPPOINTING, BUT I BELIEVE THIS IS BECAUSE WE WERE THINKING TOO SMALL! WE NEED TO APPROACH THIS ON A GREATER SCALE--I.E., MORE ROOM--FOR MORE TROOPS!
FAKEY HORSE
AND SO, BEHOLD MY TAKE ON THE TROJAN HORSE OF LEGEND! IT WILL CONCEAL OVER ONE HUNDRED SURVEY CORPS MEMBERS! NOW, WHO WILL BE THE FIRST TO VOLUNTEER?
NEW! BIG!
HOLDS 100!
YOU'RE OUT OF YOUR FUCKING MIND, PSYCHO LADY!
THAT'S NOT A TROJAN HORSE, THAT'S A TROJAN BURRITO!
HA HA HA HA HA HA HA HA HA HA HA HA HA HA HA HA HA HA HA HA
TO BE CONTINUED.
ONWARD BITCHIN' SOLDIERS
KEEP OUT
SQUEAK CREAK SQUEAK
KEEP OUT
SQUEAK SQUEAK CREAK CREAK SQUEAK
IT'S FUNNY.
WHAT IS?
WELL... ALL THE SOLDIERS PACKED IN THERE ARE THE ONES WHO MADE FUN OF YOUR PLAN.
HMM. THAT IS FUNNY.
WHAT A REMARKABLE COINCIDENCE.
TO BE CONCLUDED.
NEVER SAY DIE...
REPORT ON OPERATION TROJAN HORSE, SIR! NO GO, SIR! THE TITANS BUSTED THE HORSE OPEN LIKE A PINATA, ATE OUR TROOPS LIKE CANDY, SIR.
YES... YES, I SEE... HMMM... OF COURSE! A GIANT HORSE IS TOO ILLOGICAL!
WE NEED SOMETHING THAT WON'T RAISE SUSPICION!
I'VE GOT IT!!
QUICK, MOBLIT! ROUND UP ANOTHER HUNDRED OR SO VOLUNTEERS!
KEEP OUT
SQUEAK SQUEAK CREAK SQUEAK CREAK
I AM A TITAN
OOF!
OW! SHIT!
R.I.P.

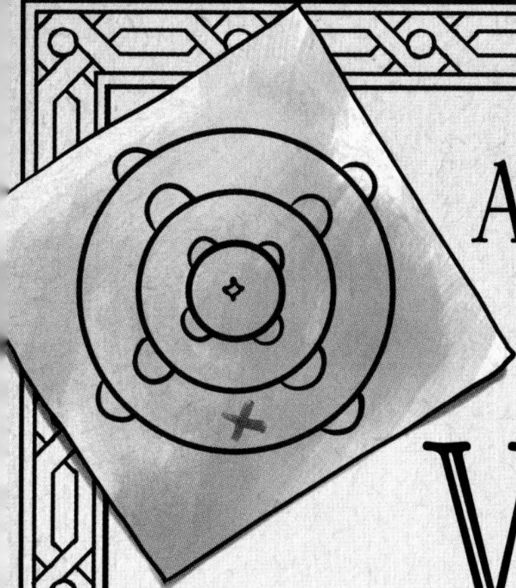

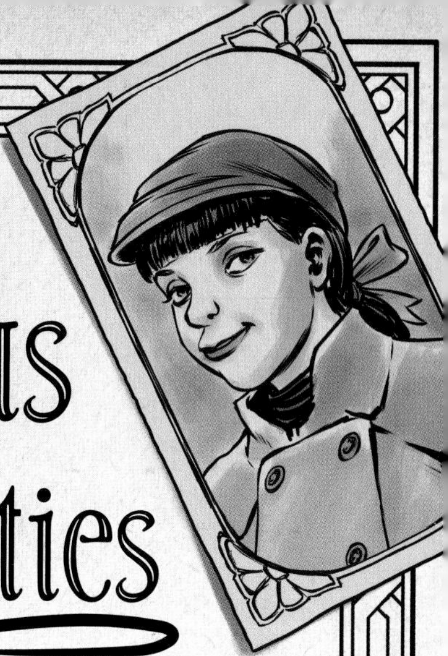

An Illustrated Guide to the Glorious Walled Cities

By Hilde Gartner

THE AUTHOR, a young adventurer of excellent reputation

The Center Cities

The discerning readers of Mitras Quarterly will, of course, be assured that in my last report I did not intend to neglect Yarckel. As my editor has noted, a flight of fancy is no substitute for a journey that is possible. My apologies.

Yarckel, then, must be considered at the top of any traveler's list of conquests. Of the Center Cities, it boasts the finest gardens in the world. With the Royal Pavilion at its center to protect those seeds from before the war that need more tropical care, the hundred acres of plants are carefully tended.

And for those of a scientific mind, let me extol the many virtues of the Botanical Initiative, which works tirelessly to farm the spices that season our food, preserve all the seeds necessary to safeguard our crops, our flowers, and the insects that pollinate them. (For those who are very brave, it is possible to see the bees – do not fear, ladies, for your author has done so herself, and got no stings for her trouble!)

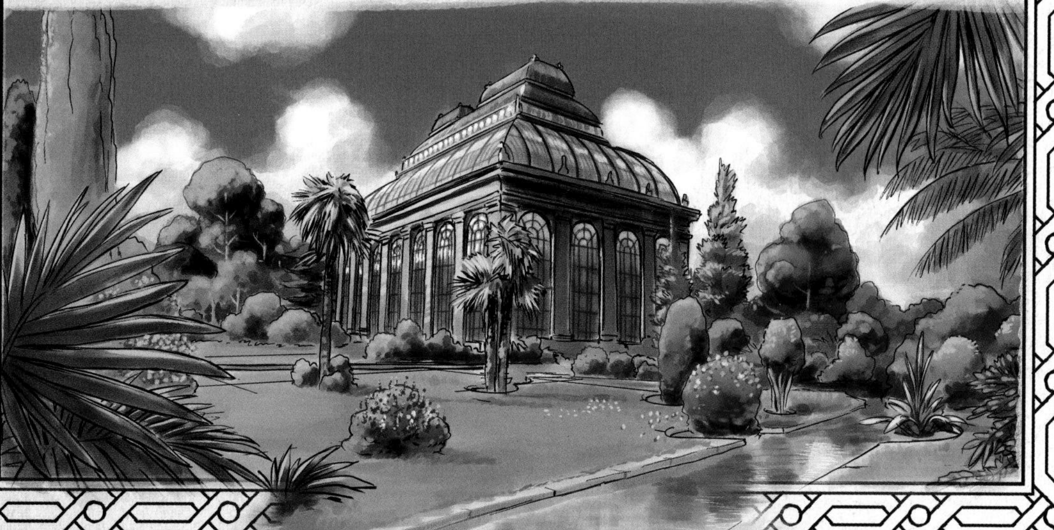

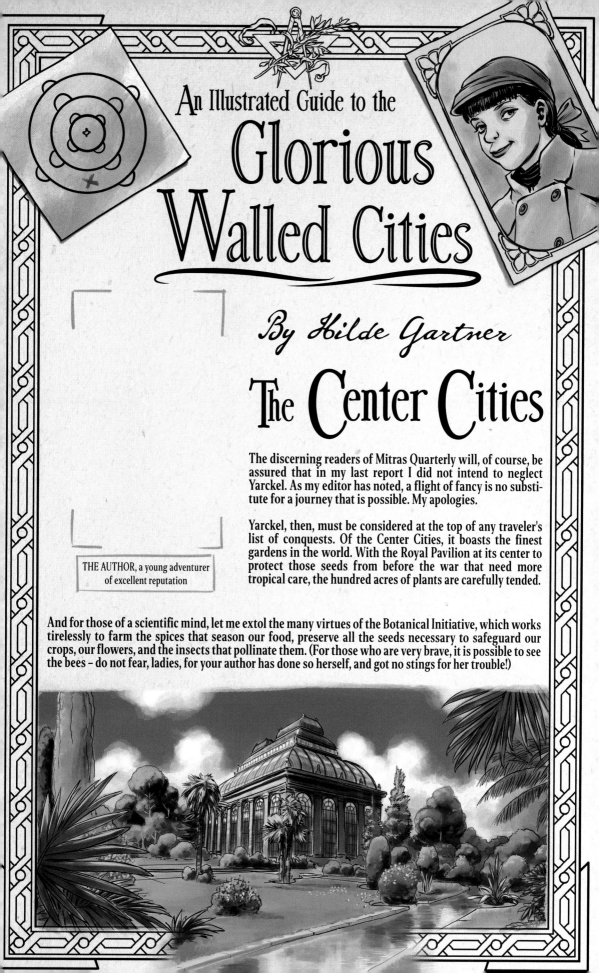

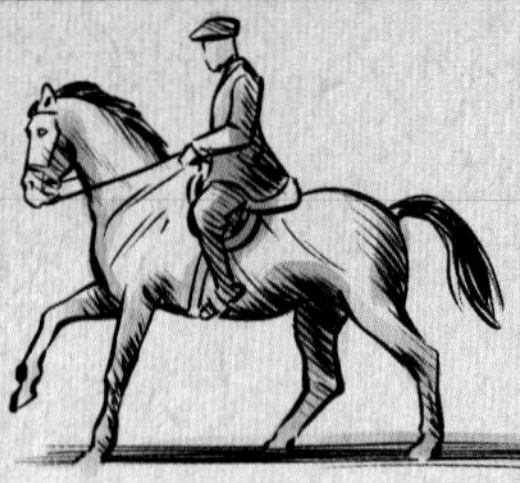

EHRMICH

the Horsemaster City

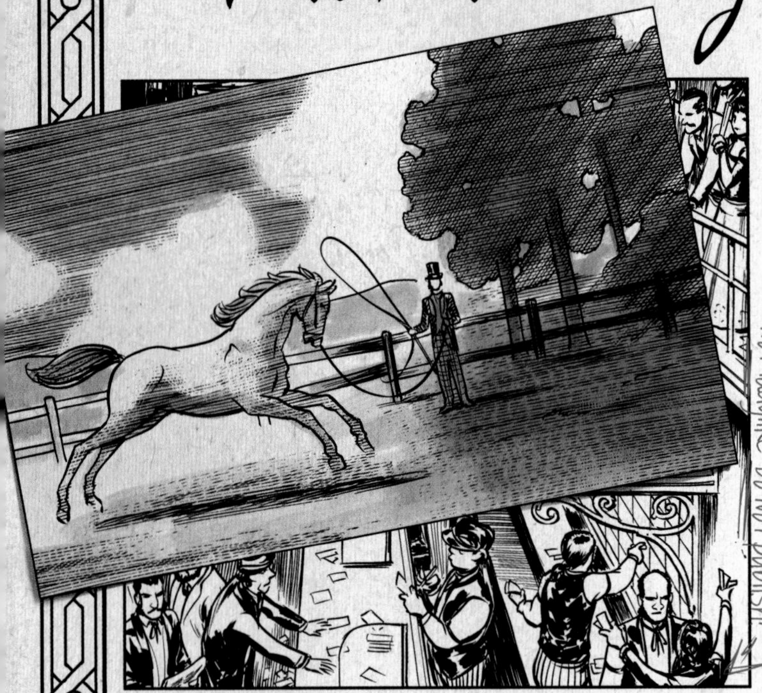
NOT ladylike—DO NOT publish!

Like the horsemaster Ehrmich of legend, this district prides itself on these beautiful beasts. Hunter's Horn stables provide for nothing less than the Survey Corps; something to boast, indeed, when a district's racetrack holds only its second-best animals!

The Three-Length Racetrack is but a small part of the finest gambling house any of the walled cities can boast. For cards and dice alike, the Three-Length is a test of skill, of patience, and (dear reader, beware) of finance.

For those with a fondness for either the military or for horseflesh, the only fashionable time to visit Ehrmich is the autumn, when the Garrison drives them toward Trost and Stohess for the Survey Corps.

Such majestic creatures, trained in the defense of our nation; it brings a tear to the eye of every patriot.

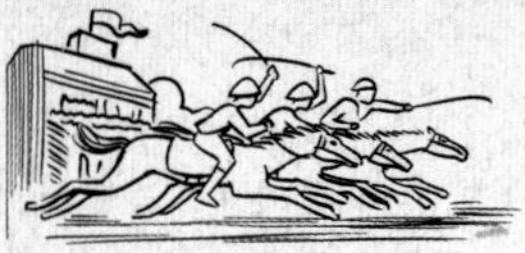

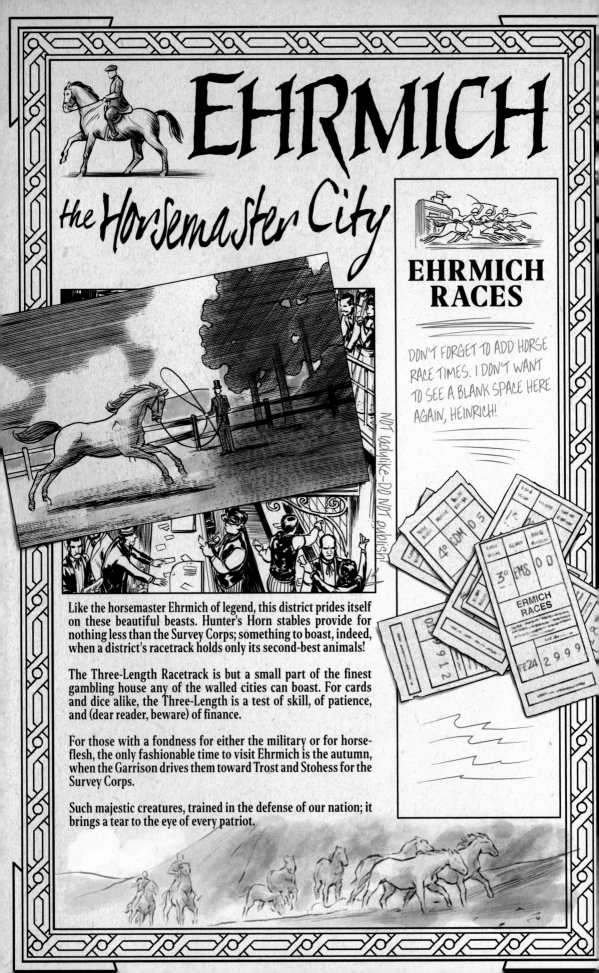

EHRMICH RACES

DON'T FORGET TO ADD HORSE RACE TIMES. I DON'T WANT TO SEE A BLANK SPACE HERE AGAIN, HEINRICH!

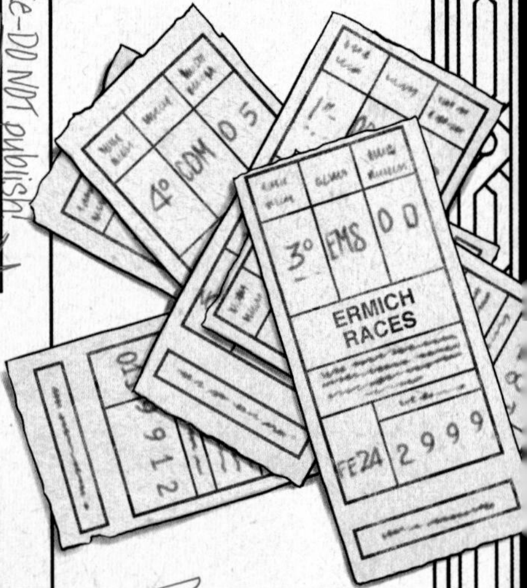
ERMICH RACES

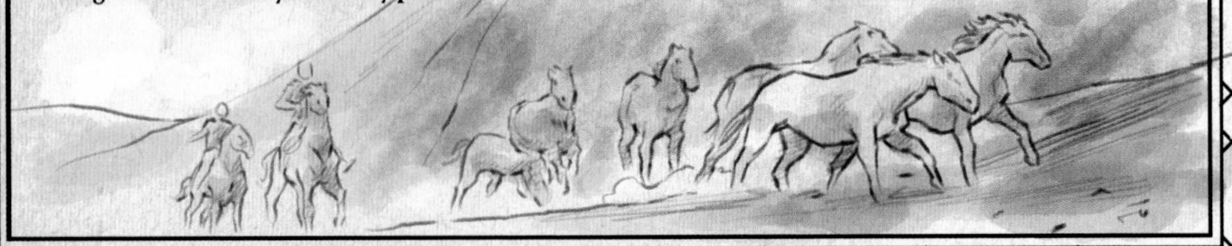

The Traveler

Mitras Quarterly has received letters asking how I find travel – not new places, which my readers have guessed suit me very well, but travel itself.

As a small girl in Merseburg, I knew how wide the world was: wider than a wagon could travel in a week, to the celebration at the Wall. Wider than that.

One may imagine my surprise when school drew me past Wall Rose, with three coaches a day from one district to another. With Garrison outposts on the roads, with wider roads – how small the world suddenly seemed!

One may also imagine what I thought when I first saw the streets of Mitras.

Travel still seems impossible; it always must, I imagine, to those who know how large the world is. The roads within Wall Maria somehow earn so little consideration; so many will never make it past the villages of home.

Reader, a road is as long as your ability to travel it; no longer than that.

CRITICAL OF GOVERNMENT INFRASTRUCTURE—
REMOVE BEFORE PUBLICATION - P. Bergen

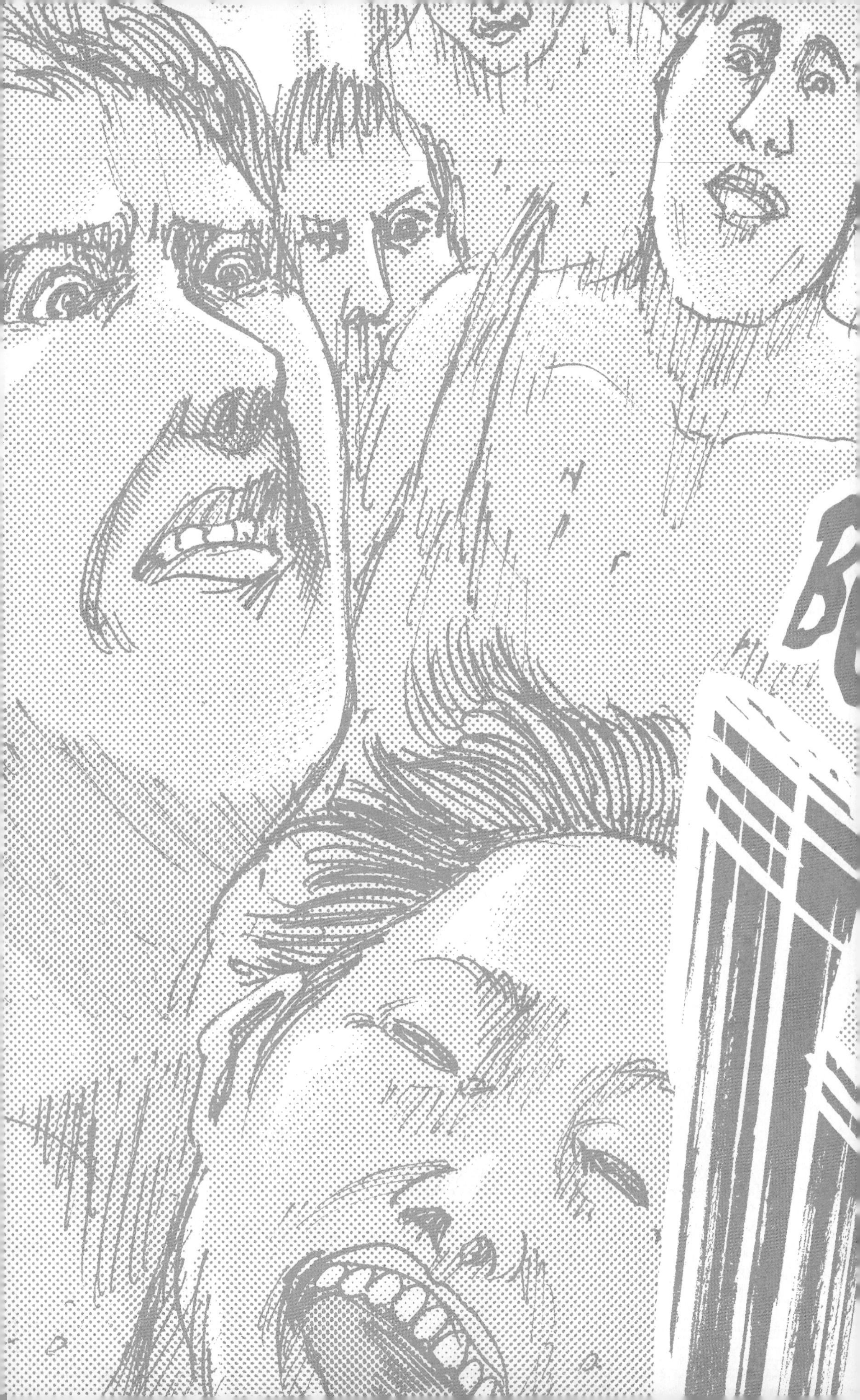

SETH, IT'S ME !
TAKE ME WITH YOU.
DIDN'T WE LOVE EACH-OTHER?!
SETH?
SETH!

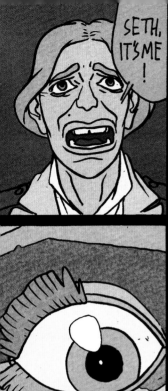

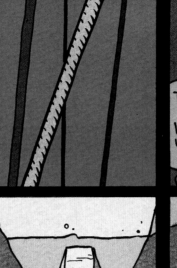

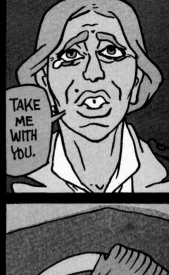

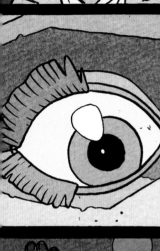

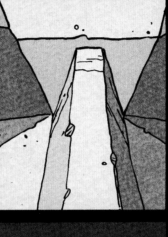

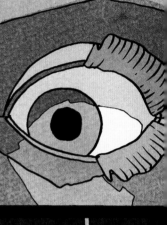

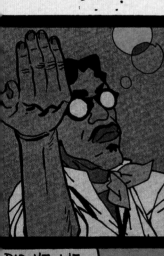

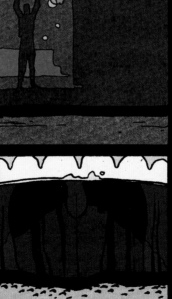

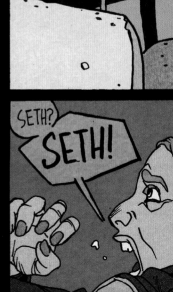

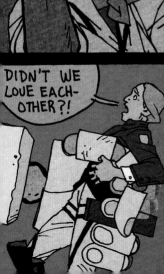

RONALD WIMBERLY PRESENTS

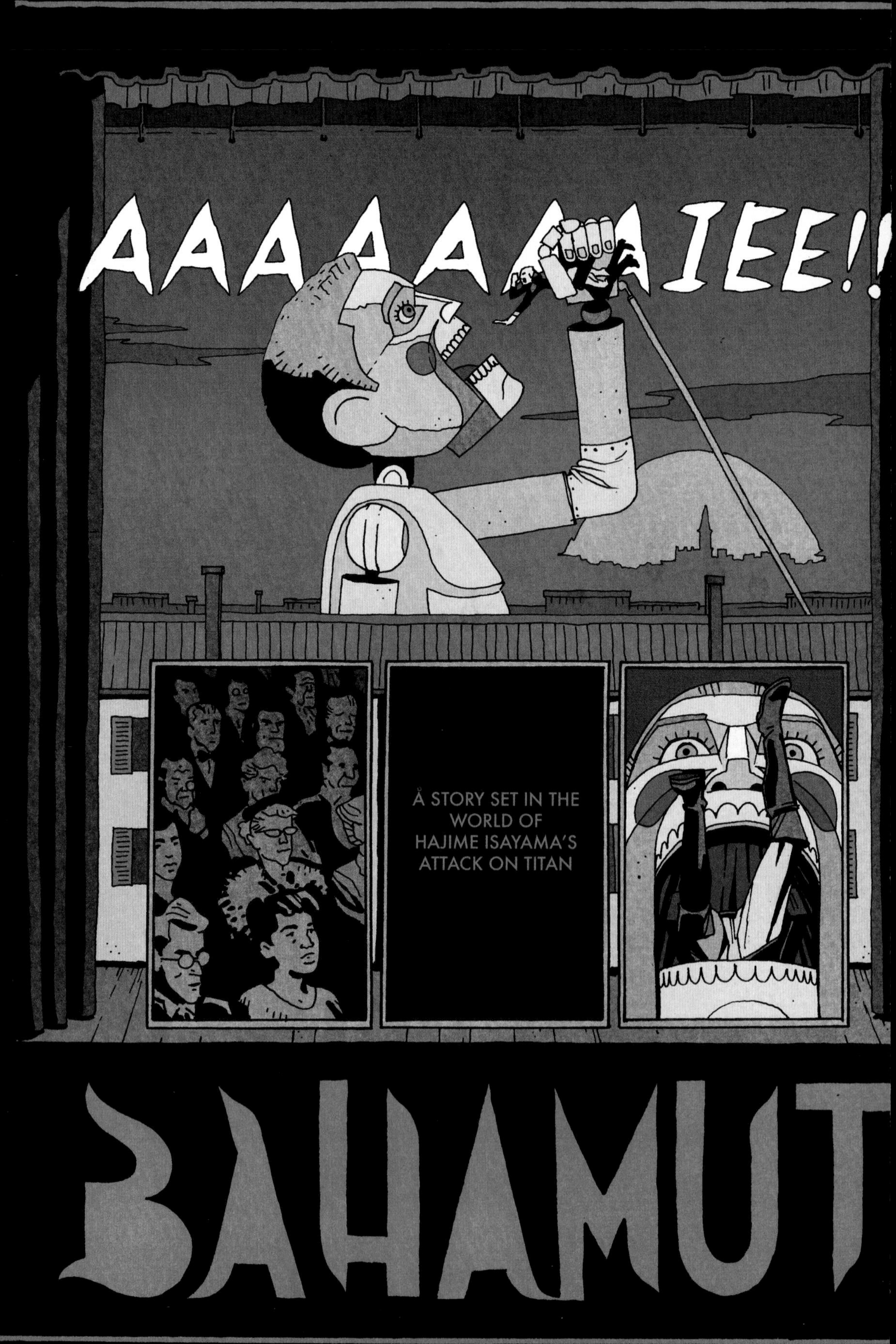
AAAAAAAIEE!!
A STORY SET IN THE WORLD OF HAJIME ISAYAMA'S ATTACK ON TITAN

BAHAMUT

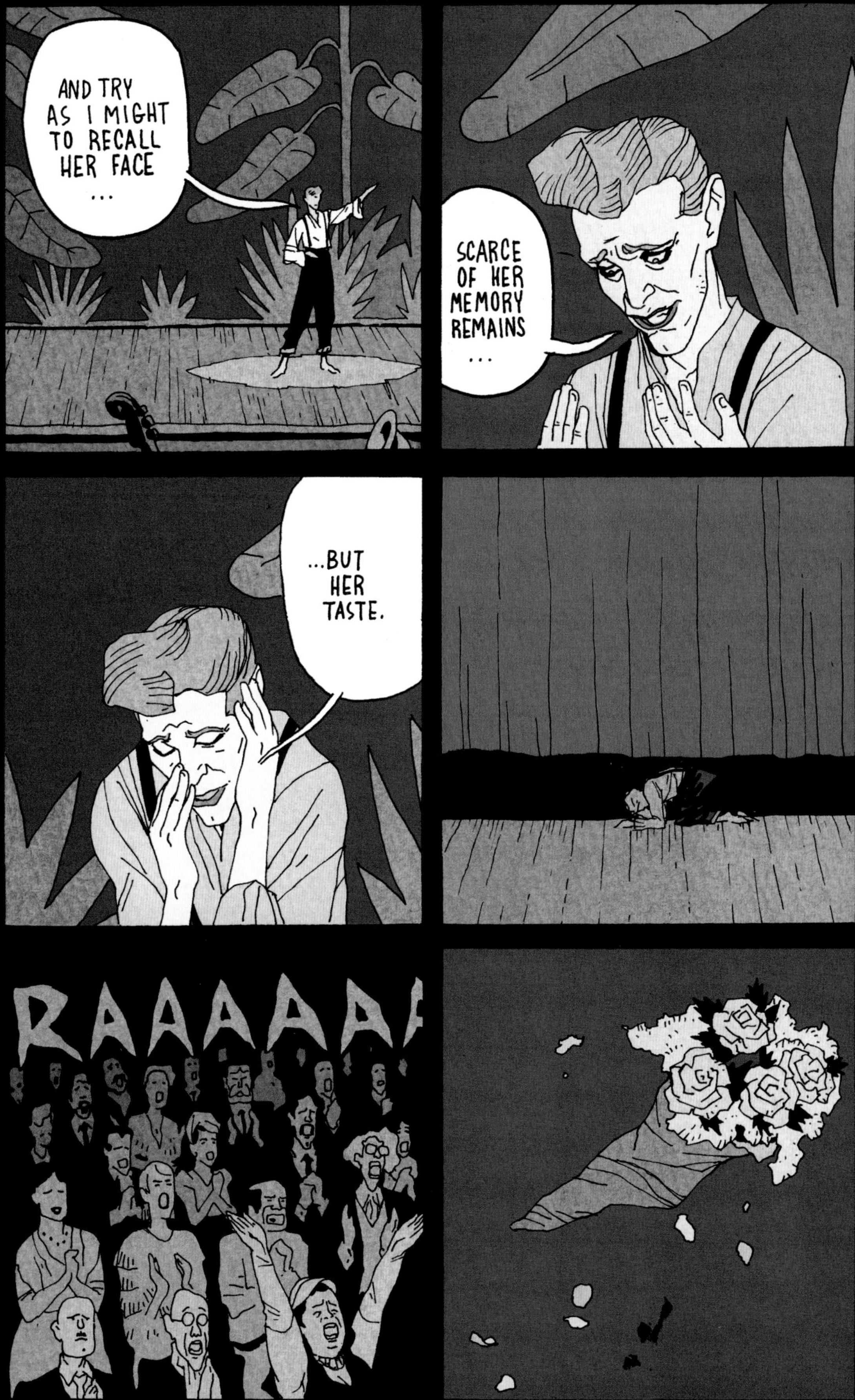
AND TRY AS I MIGHT TO RECALL HER FACE ...
SCARCE OF HER MEMORY REMAINS ...
...BUT HER TASTE.
RAAAAA

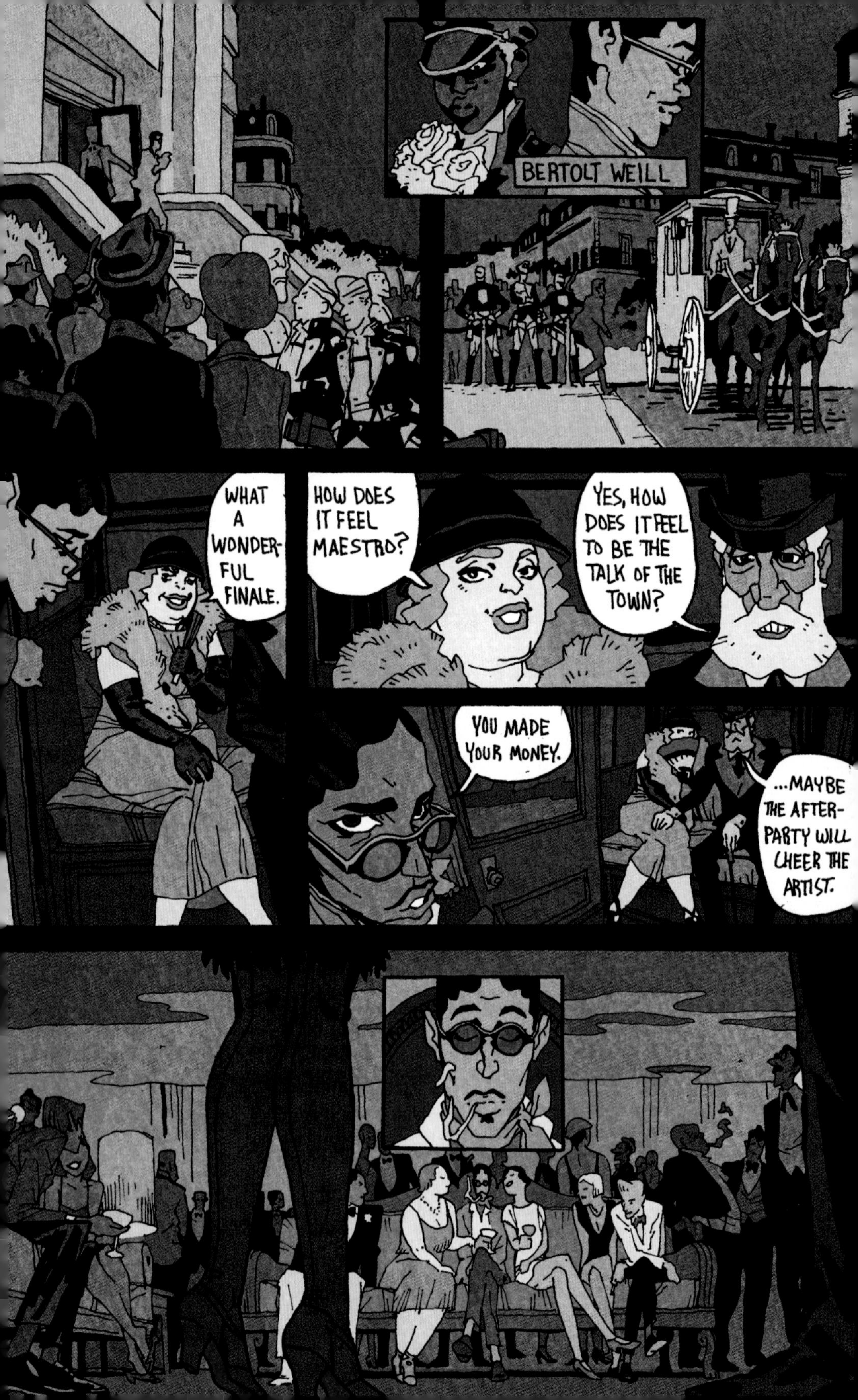
BERTOLT WEILL
WHAT A WONDER-FUL FINALE.
HOW DOES IT FEEL MAESTRO?
YES, HOW DOES IT FEEL TO BE THE TALK OF THE TOWN?
YOU MADE YOUR MONEY.
...MAYBE THE AFTER-PARTY WILL CHEER THE ARTIST.

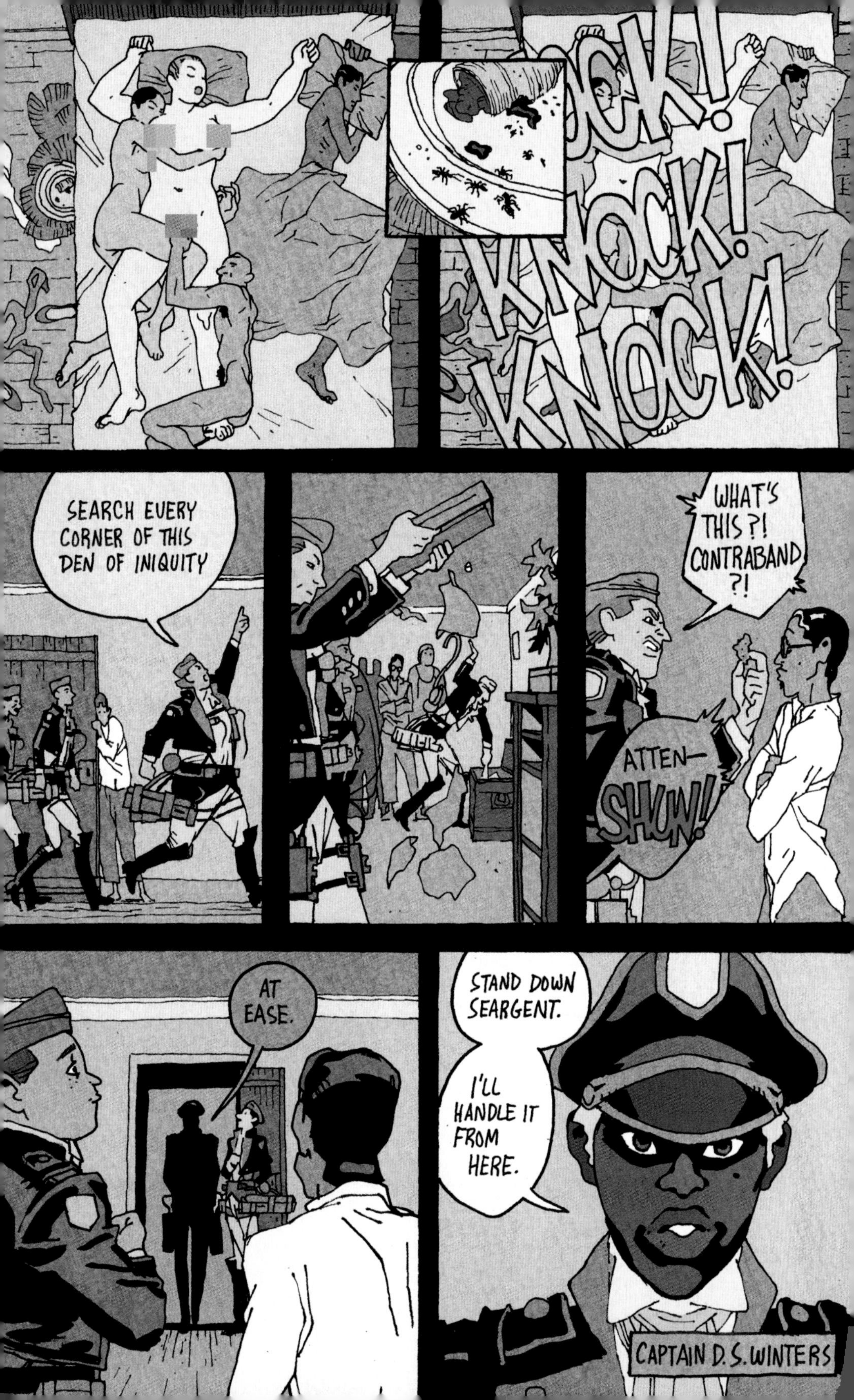
KNOCK! KNOCK! KNOCK!
SEARCH EVERY CORNER OF THIS DEN OF INIQUITY
WHAT'S THIS?! CONTRABAND?!
ATTEN— SHUN!
AT EASE.
STAND DOWN SEARGENT.
I'LL HANDLE IT FROM HERE.
CAPTAIN D. S. WINTERS

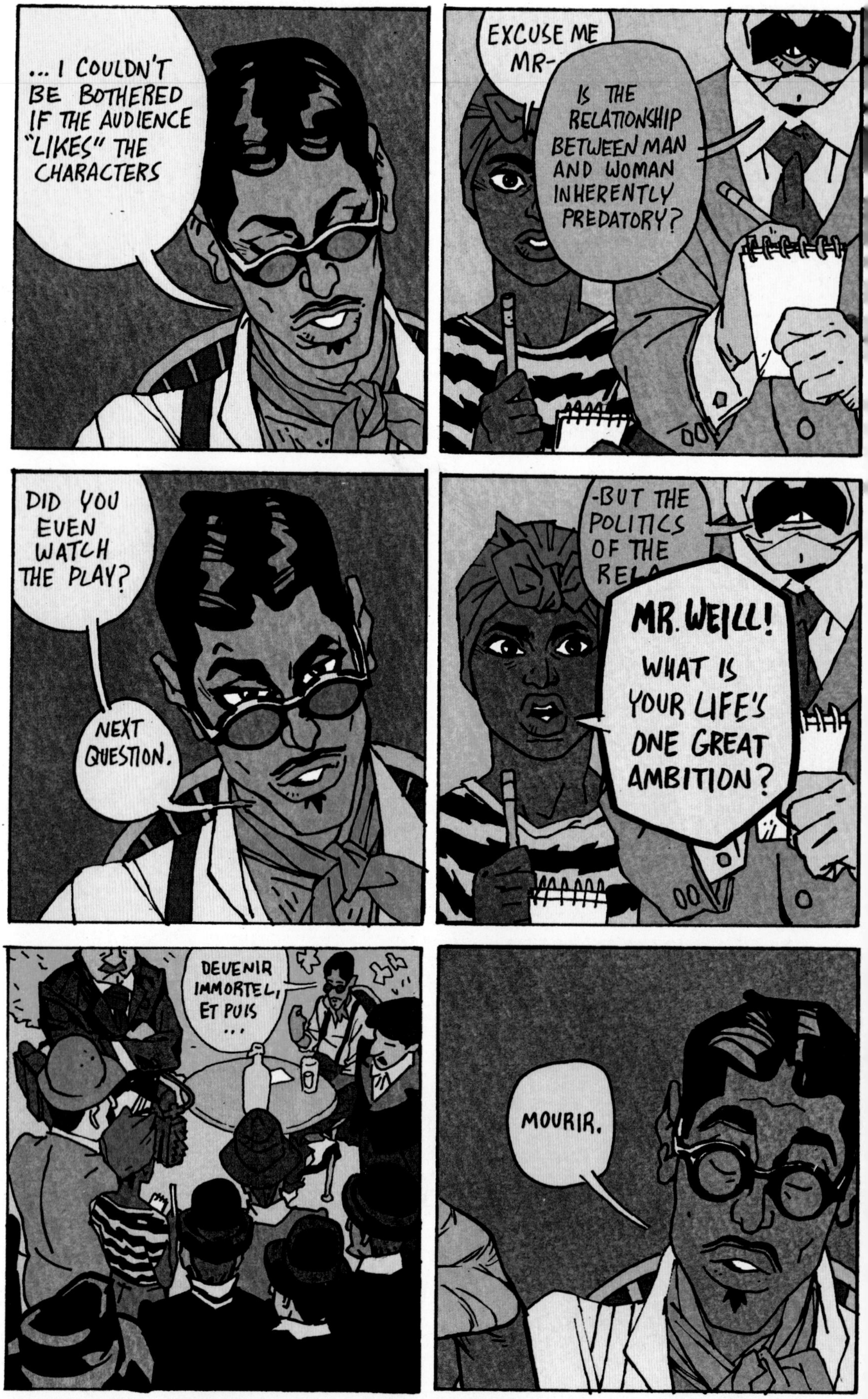

... I COULDN'T BE BOTHERED IF THE AUDIENCE "LIKES" THE CHARACTERS
EXCUSE ME MR-
IS THE RELATIONSHIP BETWEEN MAN AND WOMAN INHERENTLY PREDATORY?
DID YOU EVEN WATCH THE PLAY?
NEXT QUESTION.
-BUT THE POLITICS OF THE RELA
MR. WEILL! WHAT IS YOUR LIFE'S ONE GREAT AMBITION?
DEVENIR IMMORTEL, ET PUIS ...
MOURIR.

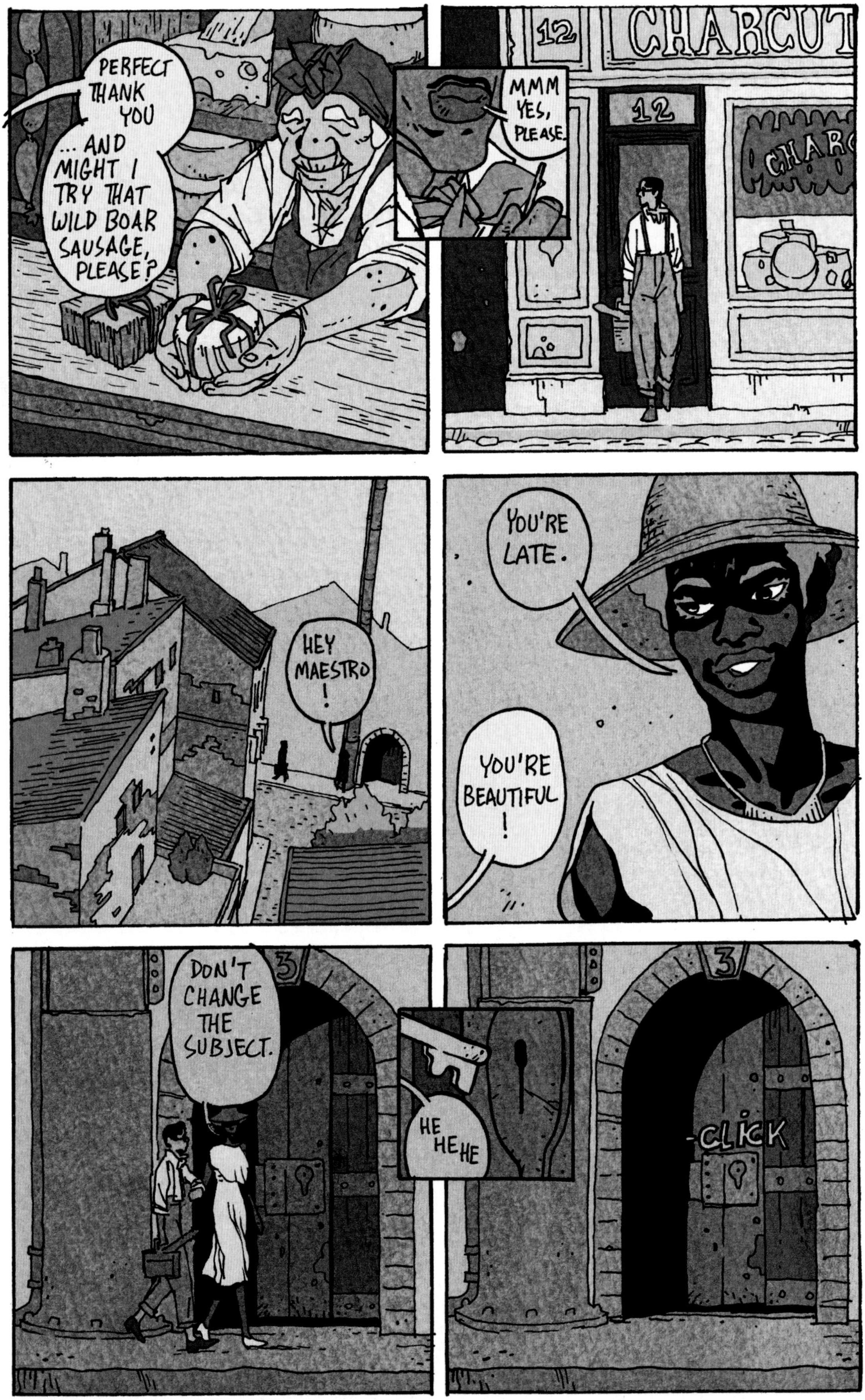
PERFECT THANK YOU
... AND MIGHT I TRY THAT WILD BOAR SAUSAGE, PLEASE?
12
CHARCUT
MMM YES, PLEASE.
12
CHARC
HEY MAESTRO!
YOU'RE LATE.
YOU'RE BEAUTIFUL!
3
DON'T CHANGE THE SUBJECT.
HE HE HE
3
CLICK

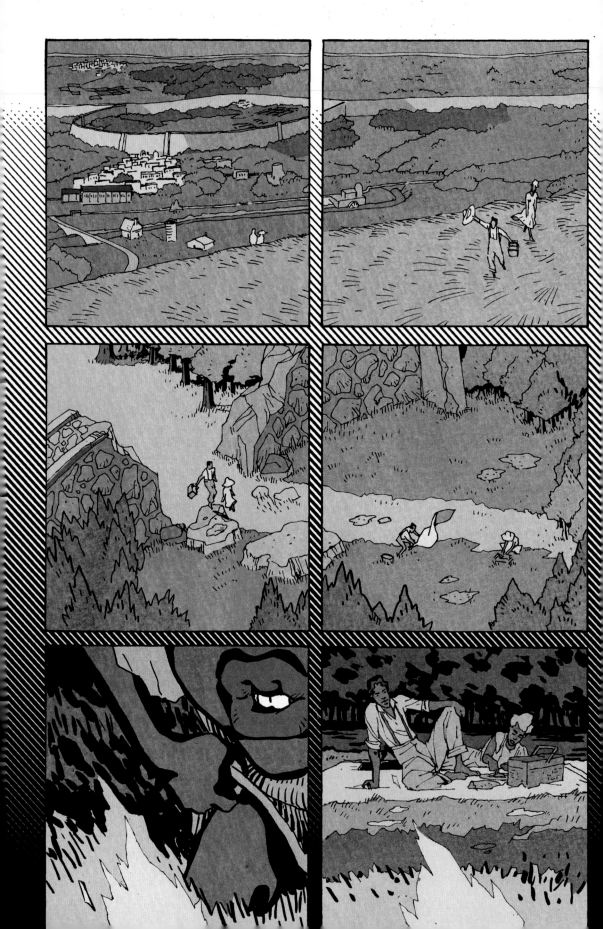

Due to their depiction of a woman's pleasure, this and the following panel have been removed. I assure you it was all very tasteful*, but nevertheless too explicit for this particular book. In place of those drawings, the author humbly offers you Baudelaire's Le Geante.

*tongue in cheek

La Géante

Du temps que la Nature en sa verve puissante
Concevait chaque jour des enfants monstrueux,
J'eusse aimé vivre auprès d'une jeune géante,
Comme aux pieds d'une reine un chat voluptueux.
J'eusse aimé voir son corps fleurir avec son âme
Et grandir librement dans ses terribles jeux;
Deviner si son coeur couve une sombre flamme
Aux humides brouillards qui nagent dans ses yeux;
Parcourir à loisir ses magnifiques formes;
Ramper sur le versant de ses genoux énormes,
Et parfois en été, quand les soleils malsains,
Lasse, la font s'étendre à travers la campagne,
Dormir nonchalamment à l'ombre de ses seins,
Comme un hameau paisible au pied
d'une montagne.

— Charles Baudelaire

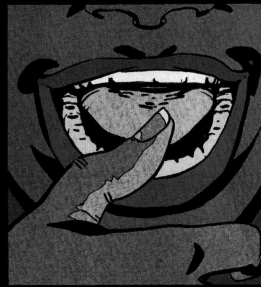

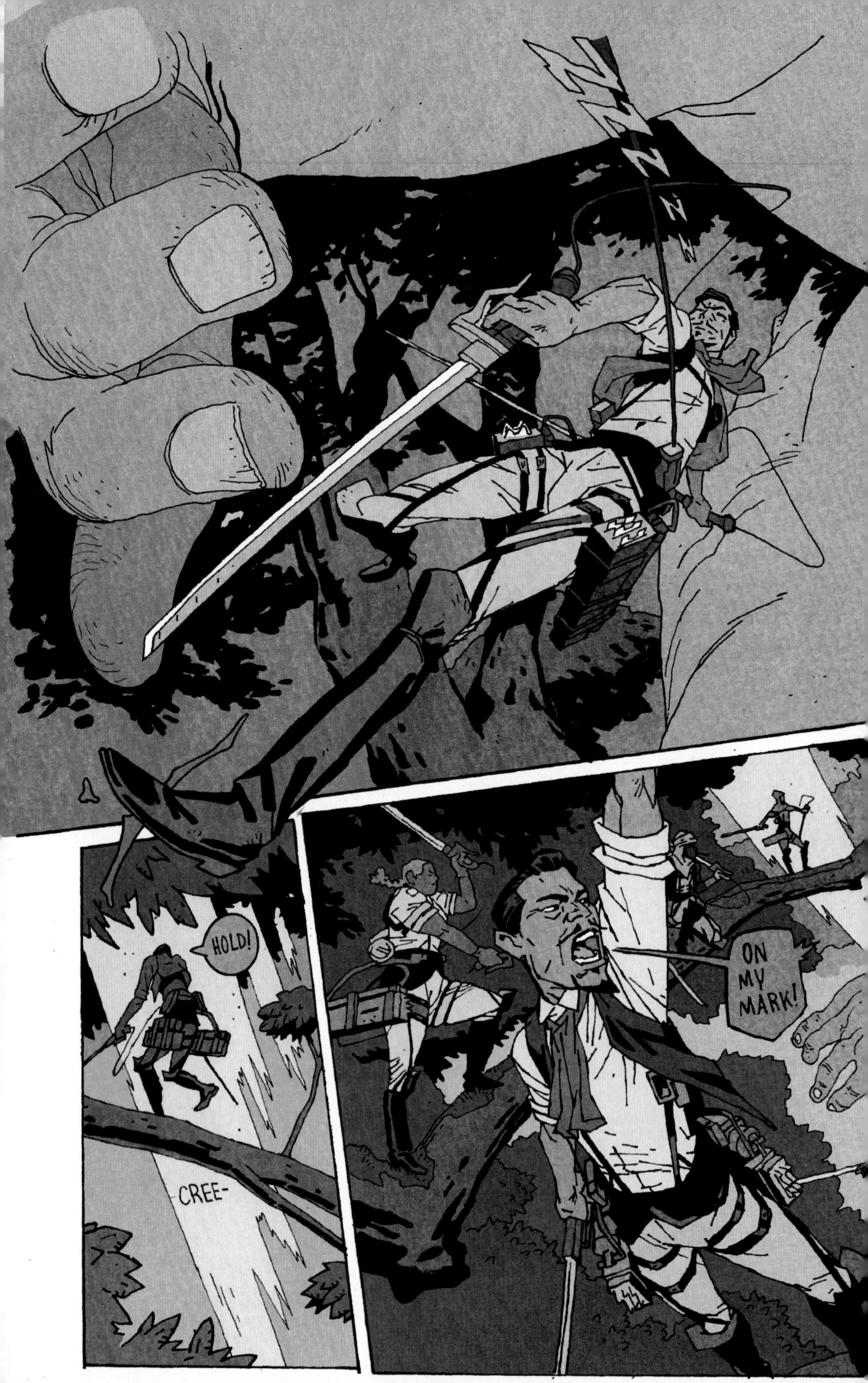
HOLD!
-CREE-
ON MY MARK!

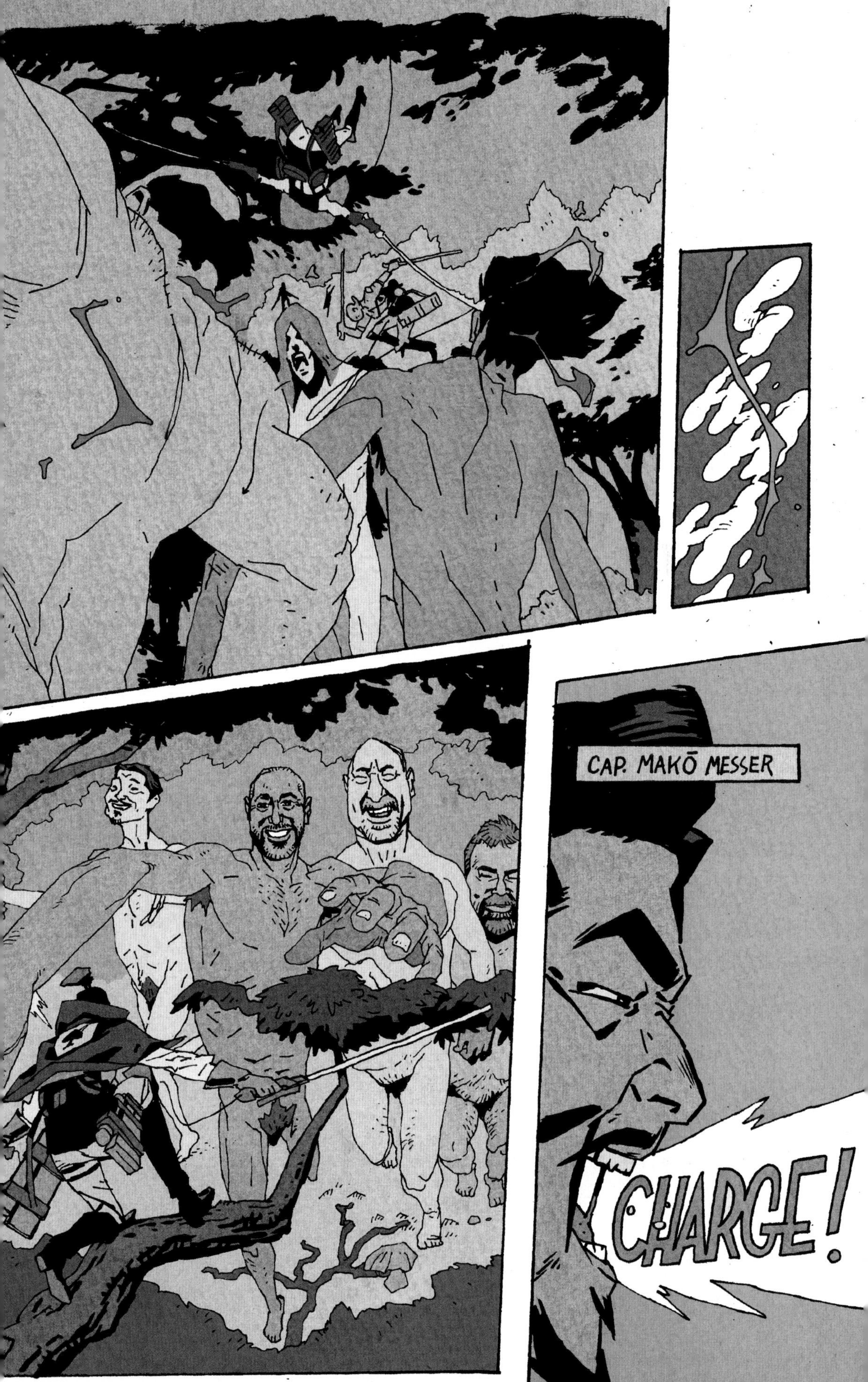
CAP. MAKŌ MESSER
CHARGE!

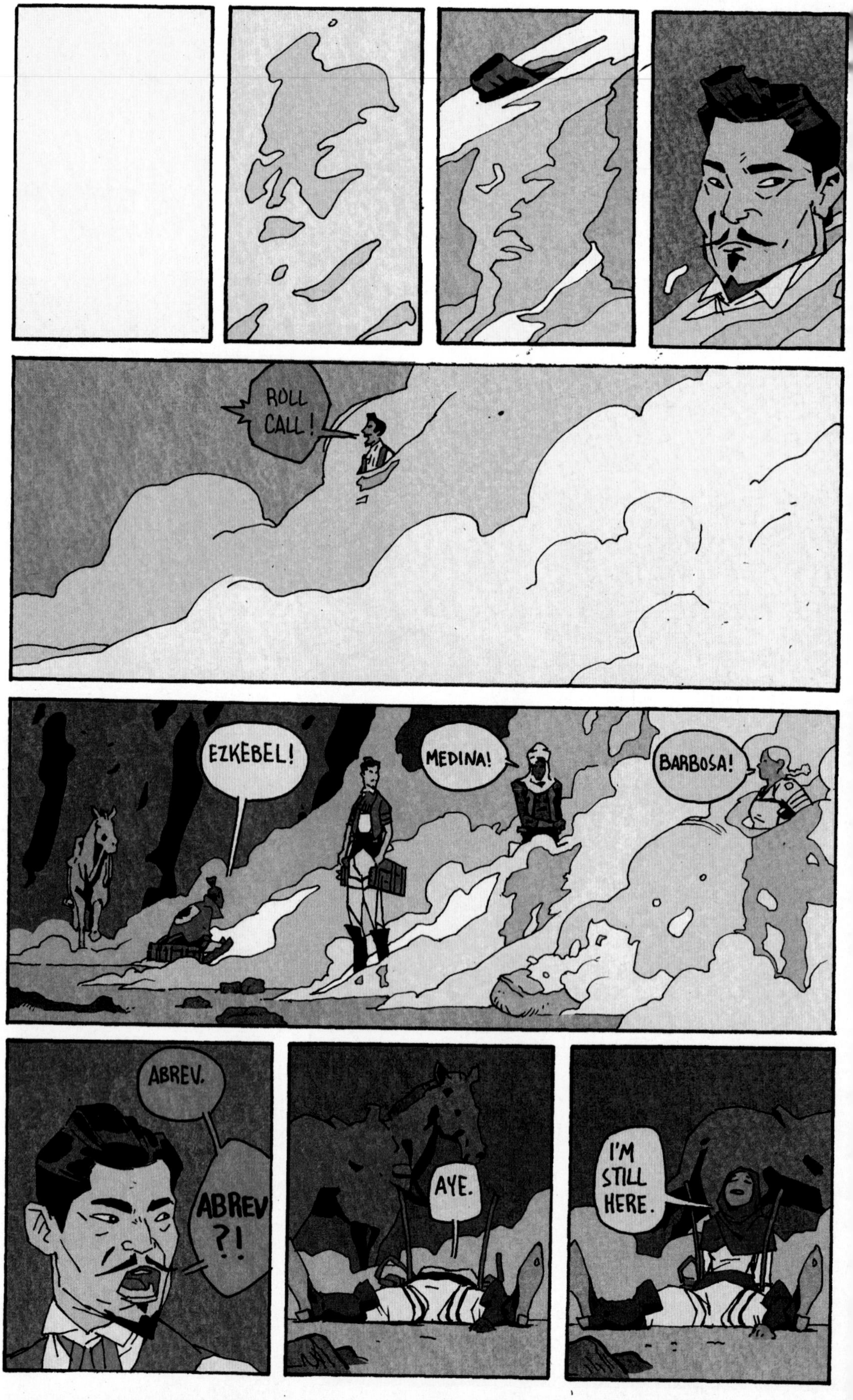
ROLL CALL!
EZKEBEL!
MEDINA!
BARBOSA!
ABREV.
ABREV ?!
AYE.
I'M STILL HERE.

PROBABLY THE LAST WE'LL SEE TILL DAWN...

AND WE ALL MANAGED TO SURVIVE AGAIN! HUZZAH!! TEAM SPADE!

WE CAN KILL'M ALL DAY OUT HERE, BUT WHAT ABOUT THE ONES BEHIND THE WALL?

HERE WE GO AGAIN...

I'M JUST SAYING... IF THAT KID, EREN, CAN CHANGE, CHANCES ARE THERE ARE MORE TITANS DISGUISED AS CITIZENS.

EZZY, YOU AND YOUR CONSPIRACY THEORIES.

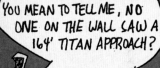

YOU MEAN TO TELL ME, NO ONE ON THE WALL SAW A 164' TITAN APPROACH?

LIGHTNING STRUCK ON A CLEAR DAY.

MAYBE IT WAS A HEAT STORM.

KRA

KOOM!

...AND NOT A CLOUD IN THE SKY.

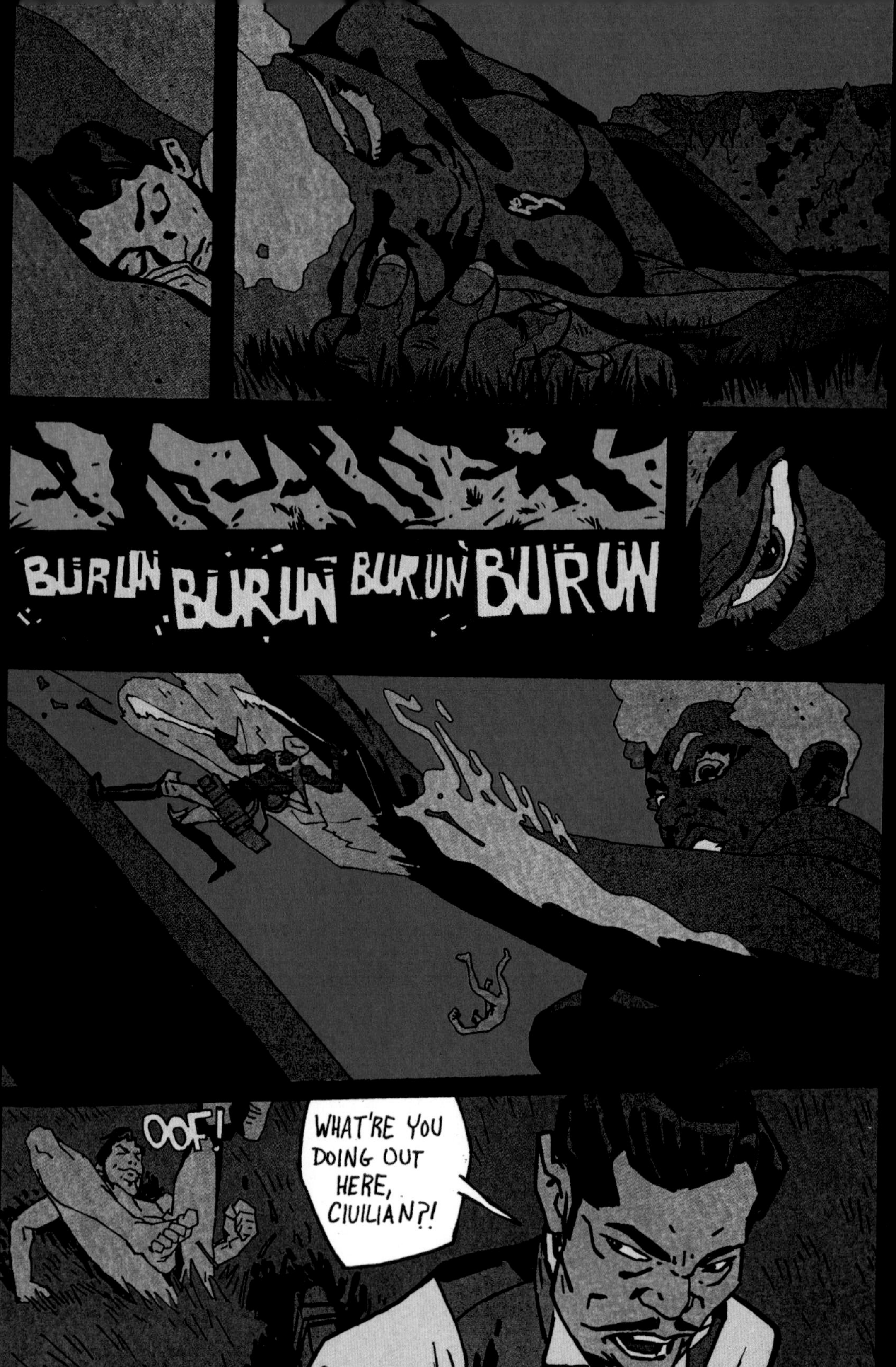
BURUN BURUN BURUN BURUN
OOF!
WHAT'RE YOU DOING OUT HERE, CIVILIAN?!

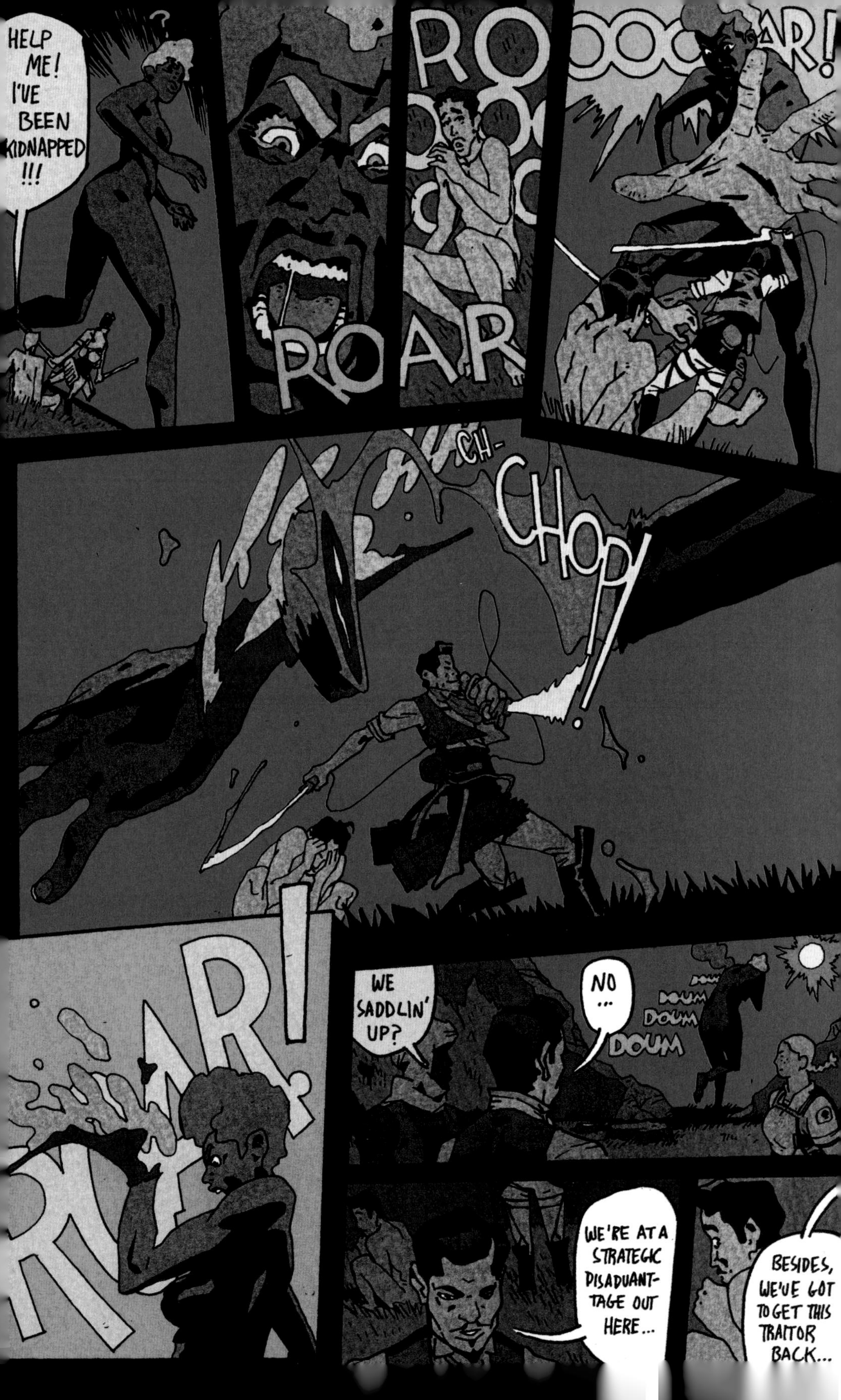
?
HELP ME! I'VE BEEN KIDNAPPED !!!
ROOOOOOAR!
ROAR
CH-
CHOP!
AR!
WE SADDLIN' UP?
NO ...
DOUM DOUM DOUM DOUM
WE'RE AT A STRATEGIC DISADVANT-TAGE OUT HERE...
BESIDES, WE'VE GOT TO GET THIS TRAITOR BACK...

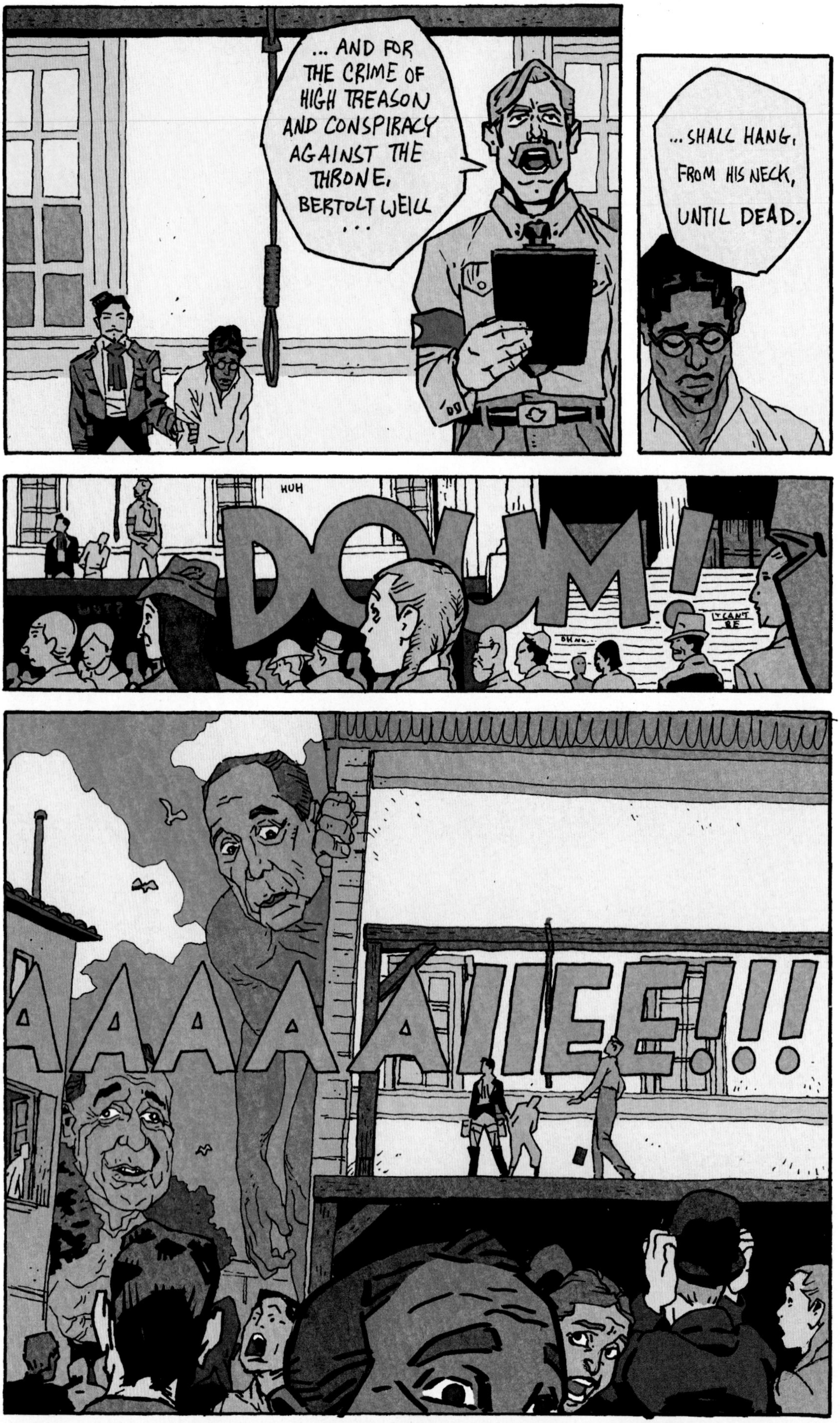
... AND FOR THE CRIME OF HIGH TREASON AND CONSPIRACY AGAINST THE THRONE, BERTOLT WEILL ...
... SHALL HANG, FROM HIS NECK, UNTIL DEAD.
HUH
WUT?
DOUM!
OH NO...
IT CAN'T BE
AAAAAIIEE!!!

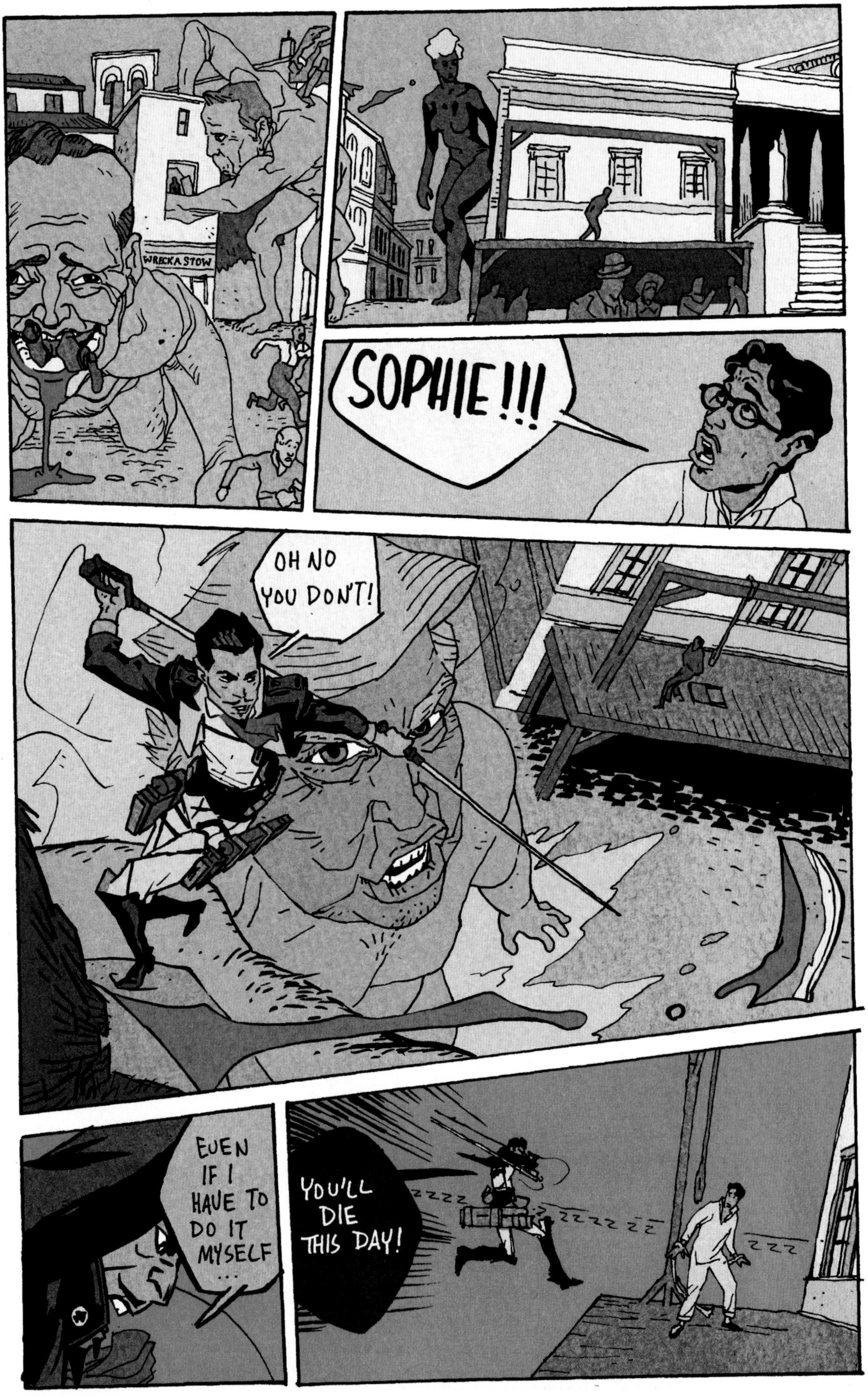
WRECKA STOW
SOPHIE!!!
OH NO YOU DON'T!
EVEN IF I HAVE TO DO IT MYSELF...
YOU'LL DIE THIS DAY!
ZZZZ
ZZZZZZ
ZZZ

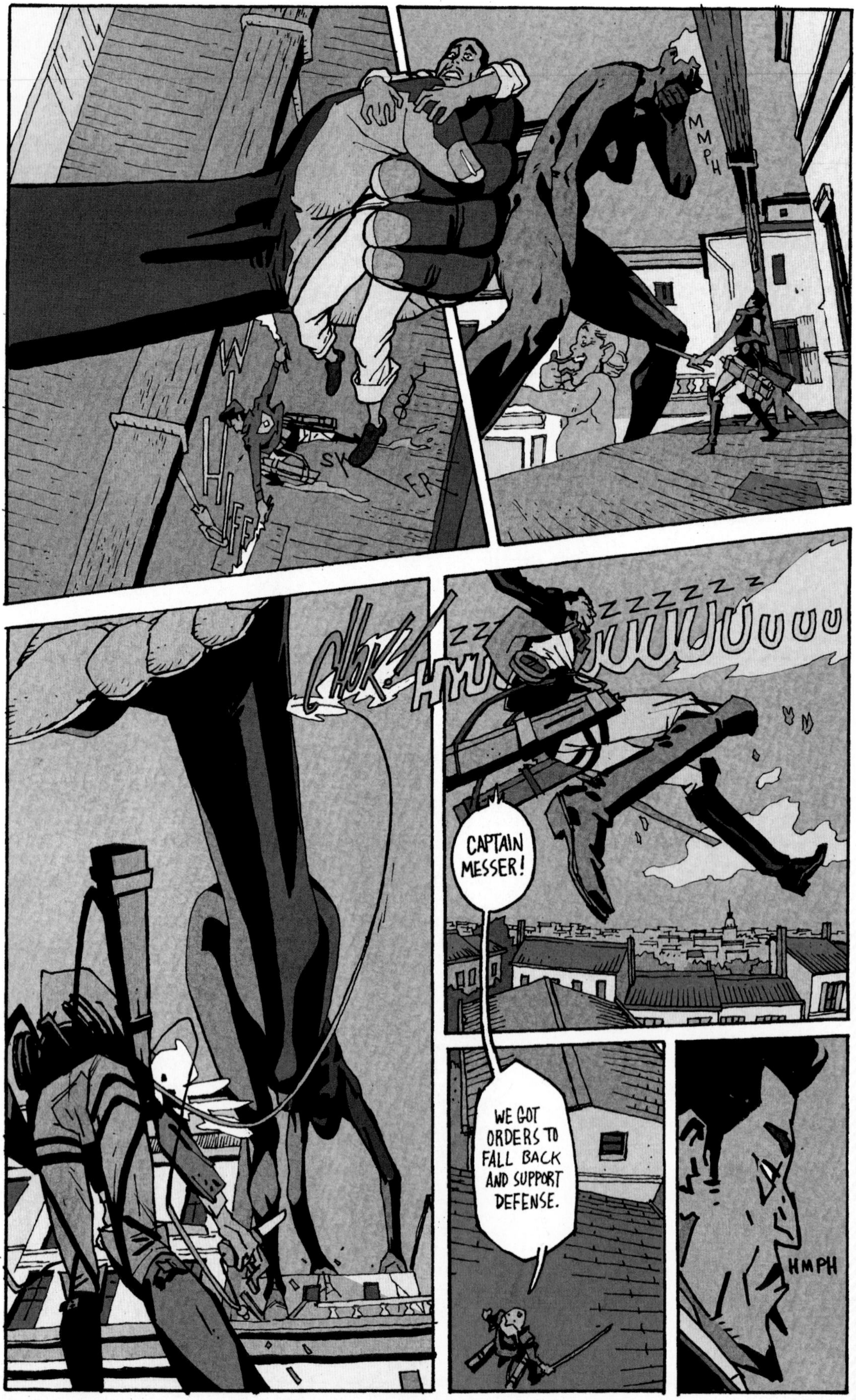
WHIFF
MMPH
CHOK!
HYUUUUUUUUUUU
CAPTAIN MESSER!
WE GOT ORDERS TO FALL BACK AND SUPPORT DEFENSE.
HMPH

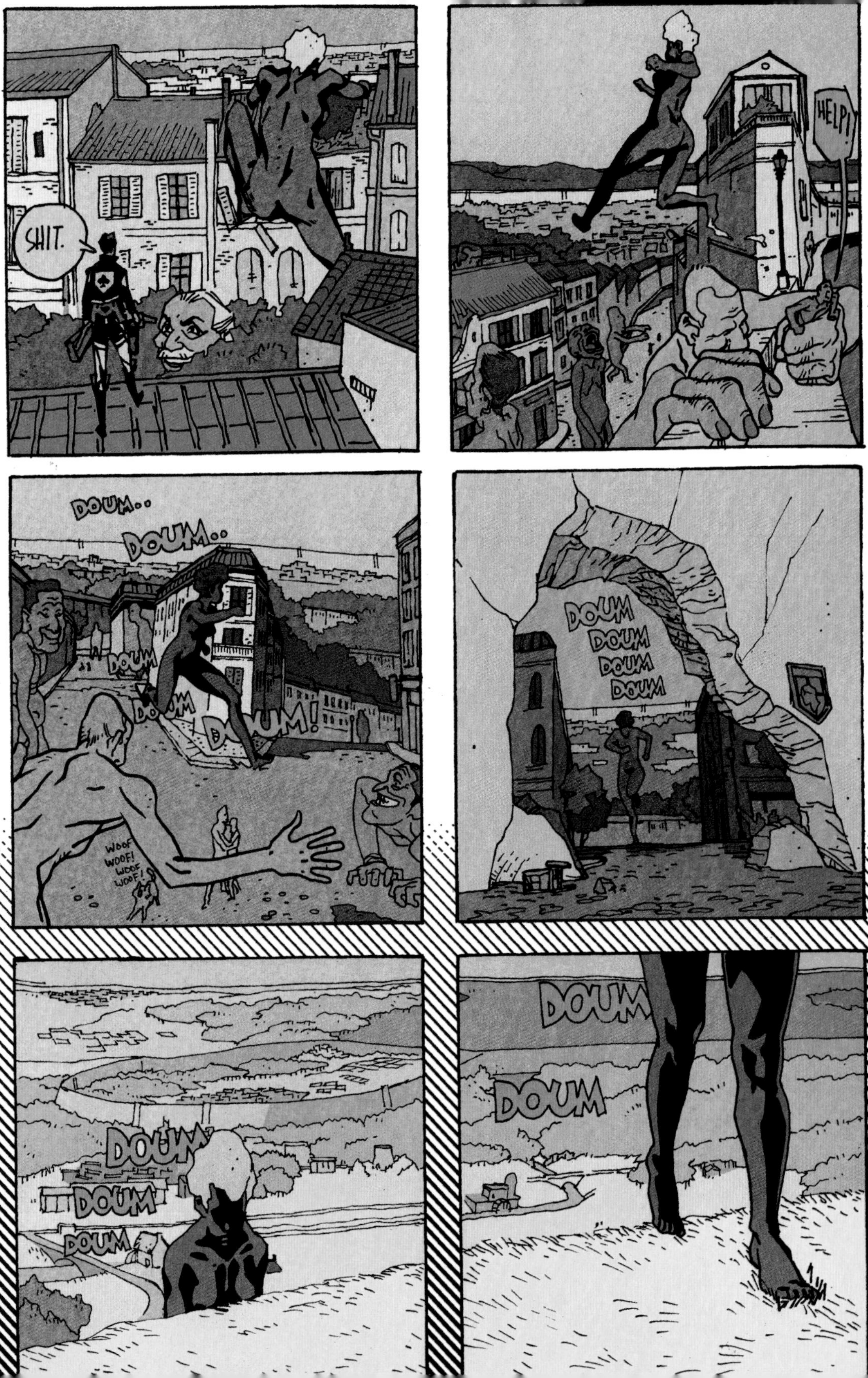
SHIT.
HELP!
DOUM..
DOUM..
DOUM
DOUM!
WOOF WOOF! WOOF WOOF!
DOUM
DOUM
DOUM
DOUM
DOUM
DOUM
DOUM
DOUM
DOUM

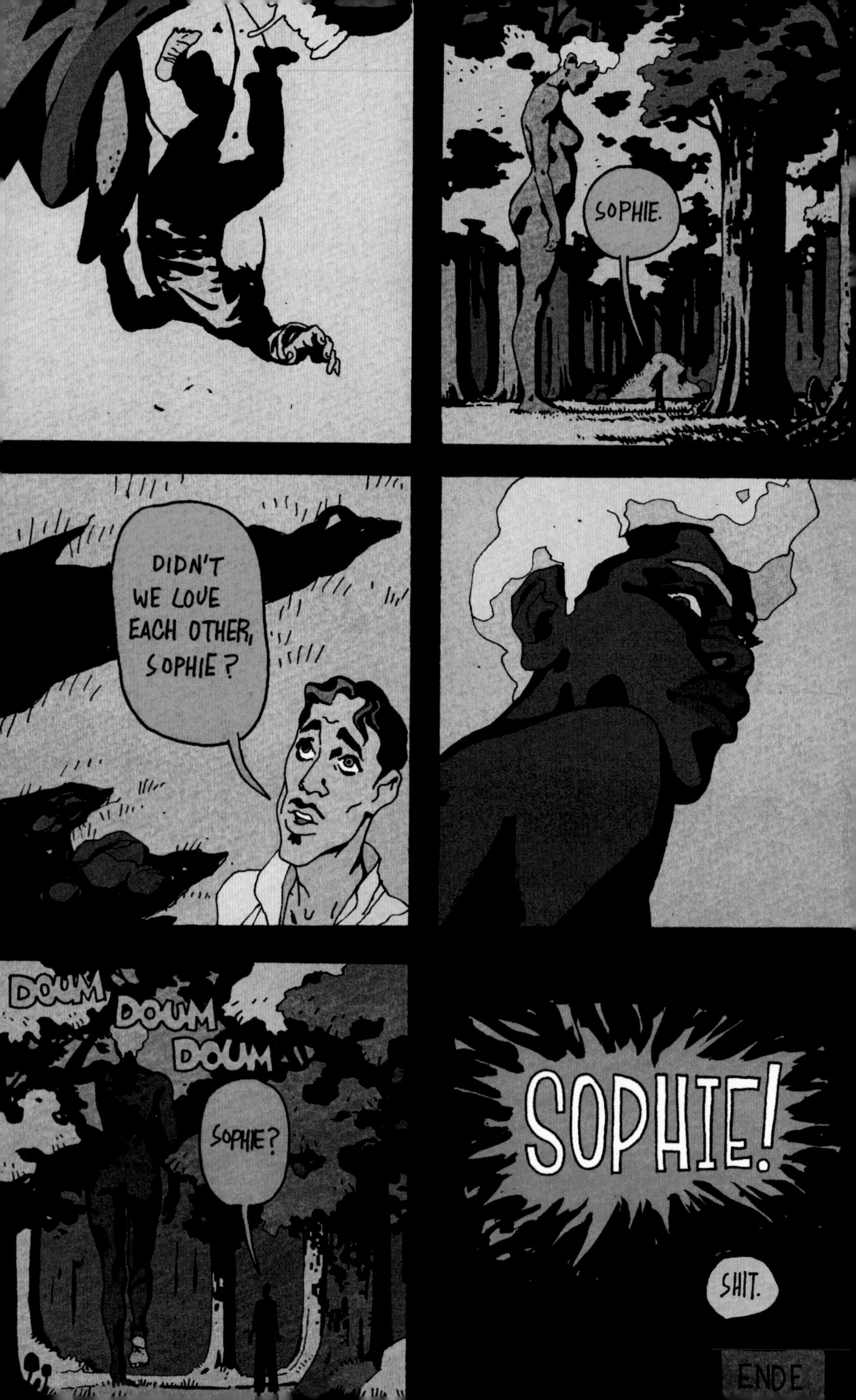
SOPHIE.
DIDN'T WE LOVE EACH OTHER, SOPHIE?
DOUM DOUM DOUM
SOPHIE?
SOPHIE!
SHIT.
ENDE

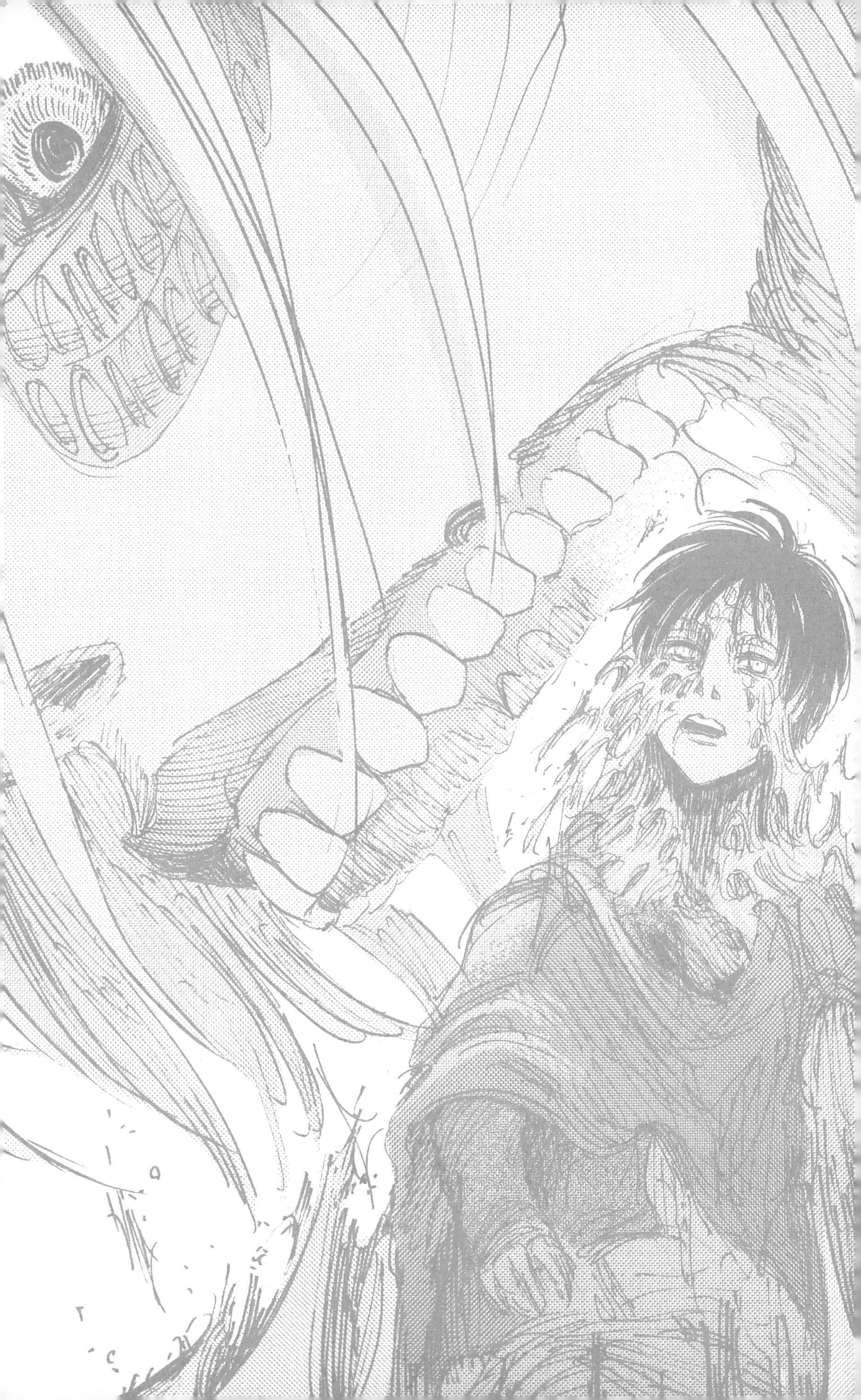

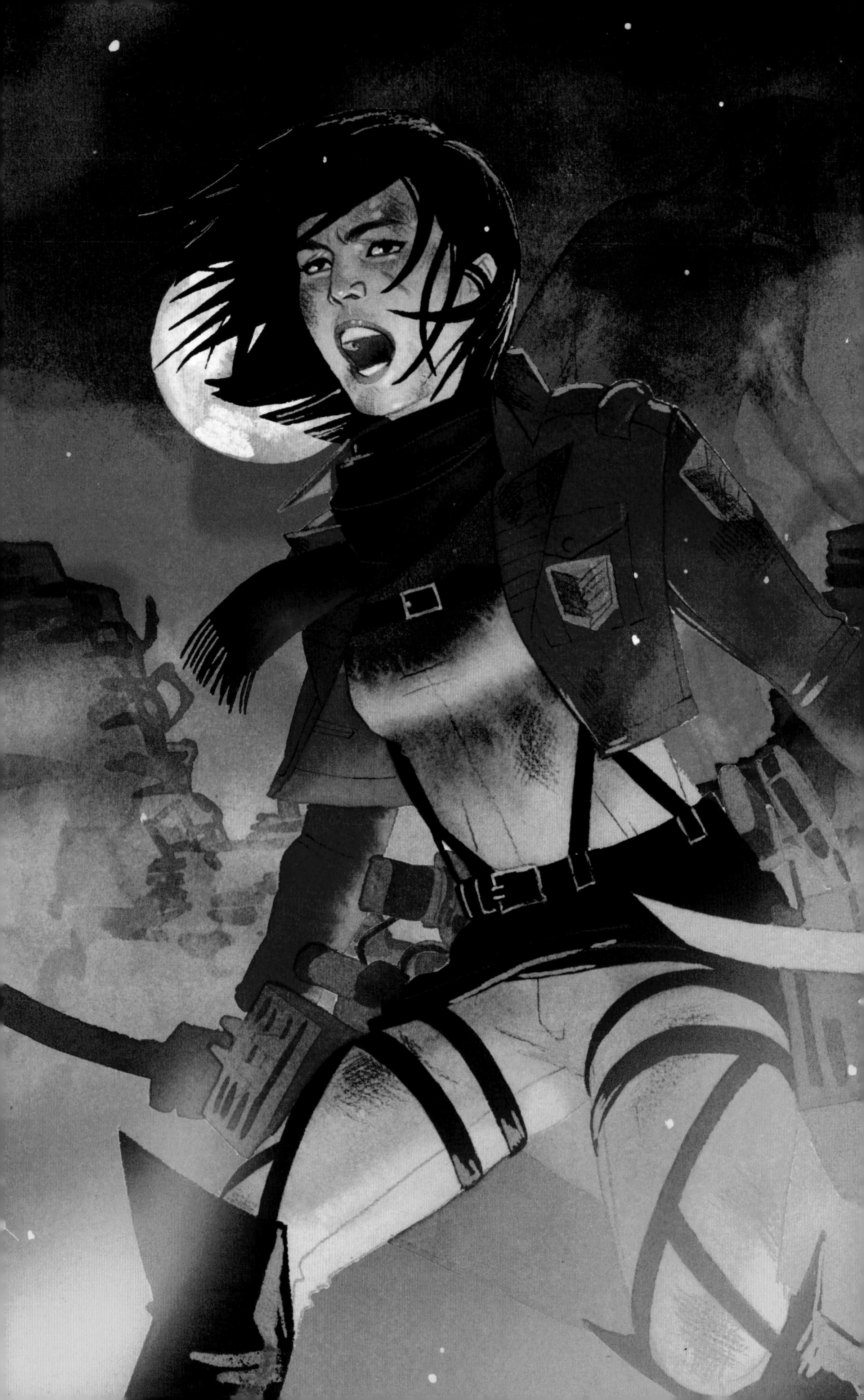

An Illustrated Guide to the
Glorious
Walled Cities

BY HILDE GARTNER

THE ANCIENT WALL SHEENA
MITRAS, CITY OF GOLD

I first visited Mitras years ago, with a jewelry merchant I assisted as the price of my passport; in my village-girl way, I marveled at the cobbled streets as much as the palace. Such is youth!

And how strange, to return to a place one loved that way!

I was granted three days' passport. It was not enough to catalog Mitras's wonders, but enough to realize there the air is clean of coal dust; there the ground shudders not with Titan footsteps, but with carriages for one.

A luxury and a marvel, to be sure, to walk the streets a King walks; but never to feel quite welcome.

A brave traveler might visit the silver mines instead — though perhaps coming here is the real bravery.

Shopping in Stohess

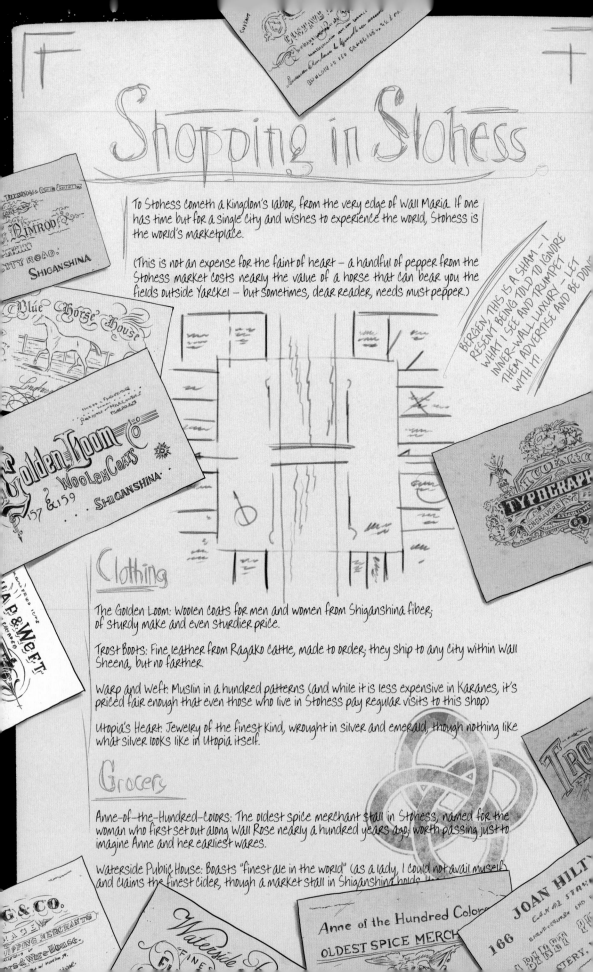

To Stohess cometh a kingdom's labor, from the very edge of Wall Maria. If one has time but for a single city and wishes to experience the world, Stohess is the world's marketplace.

(This is not an expense for the faint of heart – a handful of pepper from the Stohess market costs nearly the value of a horse that can bear you the fields outside Yarckel – but sometimes, dear reader, needs must pepper.)

BERGEN, THIS IS A SHAM – I RESENT BEING TOLD TO IGNORE WHAT I SEE AND TRUMPET INNER-WALL LUXURY – LET THEM ADVERTISE AND BE DONE WITH IT!

NIMROD
CITY ROAD:
SHIGANSHINA

Blue Horse House

Golden Loom Co
WOOLEN COATS
157 & 159
SHIGANSHINA

TYPOGRAPH
ENGRAVERS

Clothing

The Golden Loom: Woolen coats for men and women from Shiganshina fiber; of sturdy make and even sturdier price.

Trost Boots: Fine leather from Ragako cattle, made to order; they ship to any city within Wall Sheena, but no farther.

WARP & WEFT

Warp and Weft: Muslin in a hundred patterns (and while it is less expensive in Karanes, it's priced fair enough that even those who live in Stohess pay regular visits to this shop)

Utopia's Heart: Jewelry of the finest kind, wrought in silver and emerald, though nothing like what silver looks like in Utopia itself.

TRO

Grocers

Anne-of-the-Hundred-Colors: The oldest spice merchant stall in Stohess, named for the woman who first set out along Wall Rose nearly a hundred years ago; worth passing just to imagine Anne and her earliest wares.

Waterside Public House: Boasts "finest ale in the world" (as a lady, I could not avail myself) and claims the finest cider, though a market stall in Shiganshina holds

G & CO.
SHIPPING MERCHANTS
Ware-House

Waterside
FINE

Anne of the Hundred Colors
OLDEST SPICE MERCH

JOAN HILTY
166

A Walking Tour of Stohess

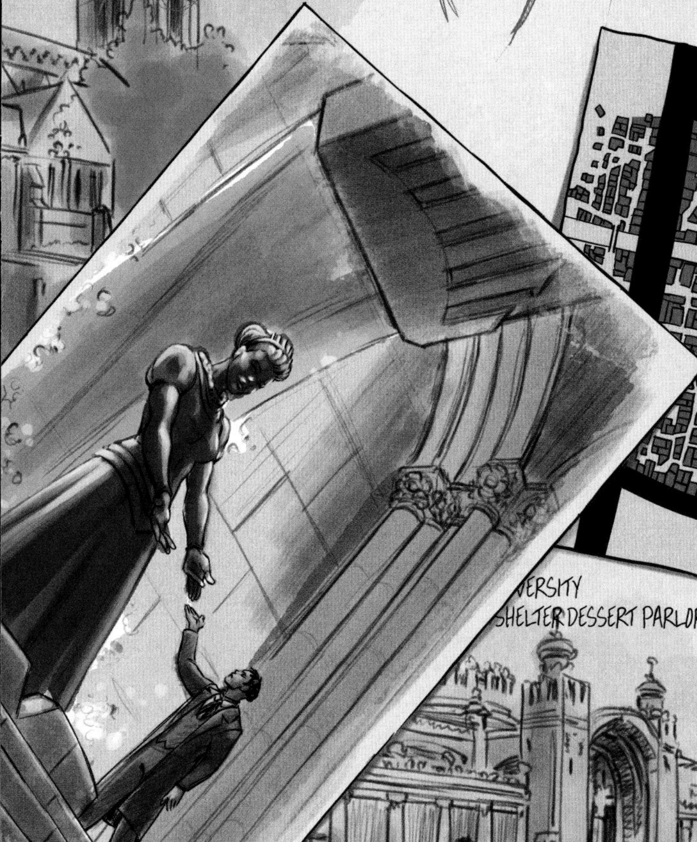

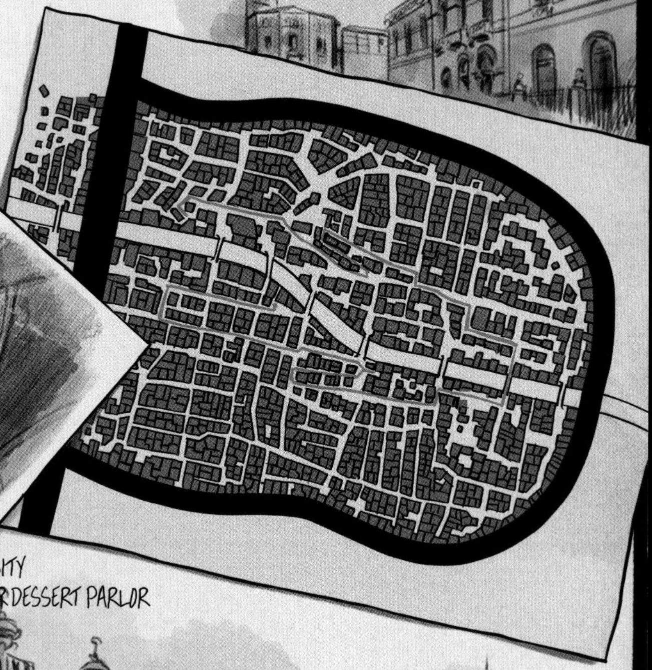

…VERSITY
…SHELTER DESSERT PARLOR

Mr. Bergen – Though it is likely very little of this will make it to the page, given how royal edicts spoken and unspoken seem to interfere in matters of geography (are we a free people or not?), I shall note everything as my conscience dictates.

To walk the Stohess District is to realize how much we have to lose.

The University is as old as Wall Sheena; some records in the Archives suggest it was here before the Wall itself. It is the source of all knowledge: scientists to study Titans, governors to make sure crops never wither.

~~The architecture is pleasing, but I dislike the interior tour. Walls within walls are a cloister, not a school, as the daughter of a farmer – herself ambitious – the students seemed cut from stone.~~ Have they ever seen the Giant Trees? Will they ever set foot outside their manses in the Districts they govern?

After admiring the University grounds, visit the Shrine to Sheena! At the edge of a busy square, this monument somehow creates its own peace. Drop a coin in the fountain for good luck; touch Sheena's outstretched hands for mercy.

~~ADD'L DETAIL~~ AFTER PASTOR
~~ELIMINATE~~ UNIVERSITY? SAFER?

ow to see Wall Sheena

The oldest wall bears some marvelous history. Though the Wall Cult can be very serious to take on one's holiday, truly nothing can be better than talking to an expert. Pay a pastor to guide you, and take a morning in the Stohess District to appreciate the beauty and surprises Wall Sheena has to offer!

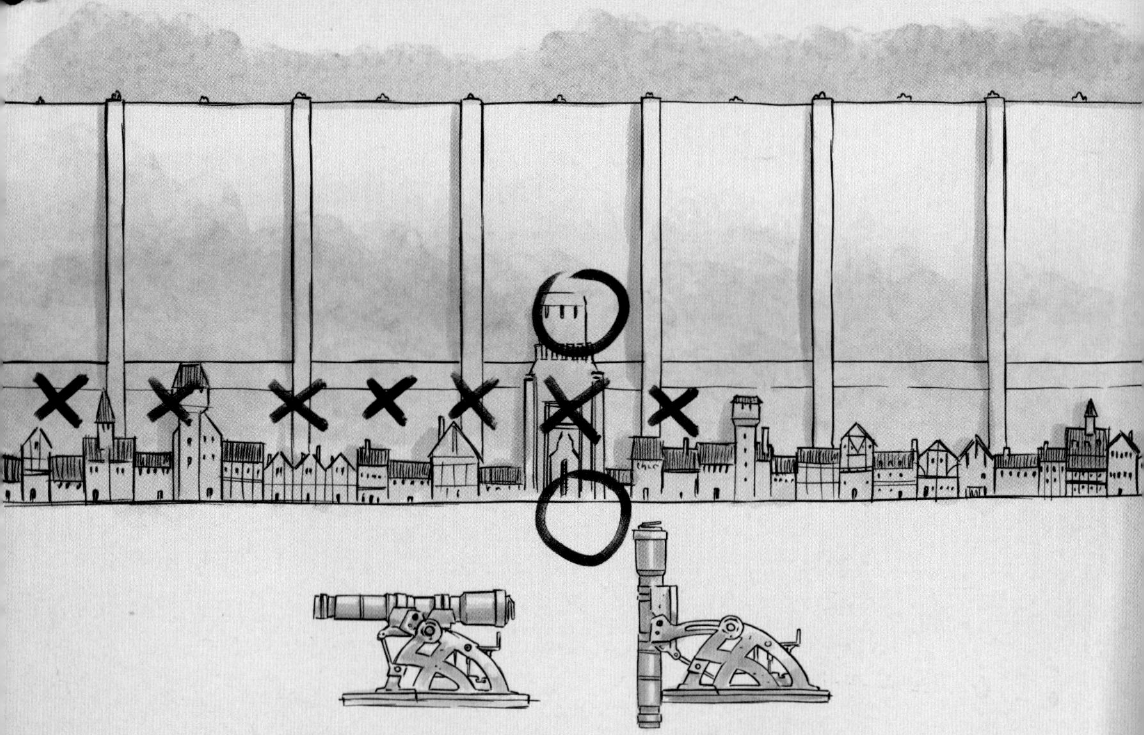

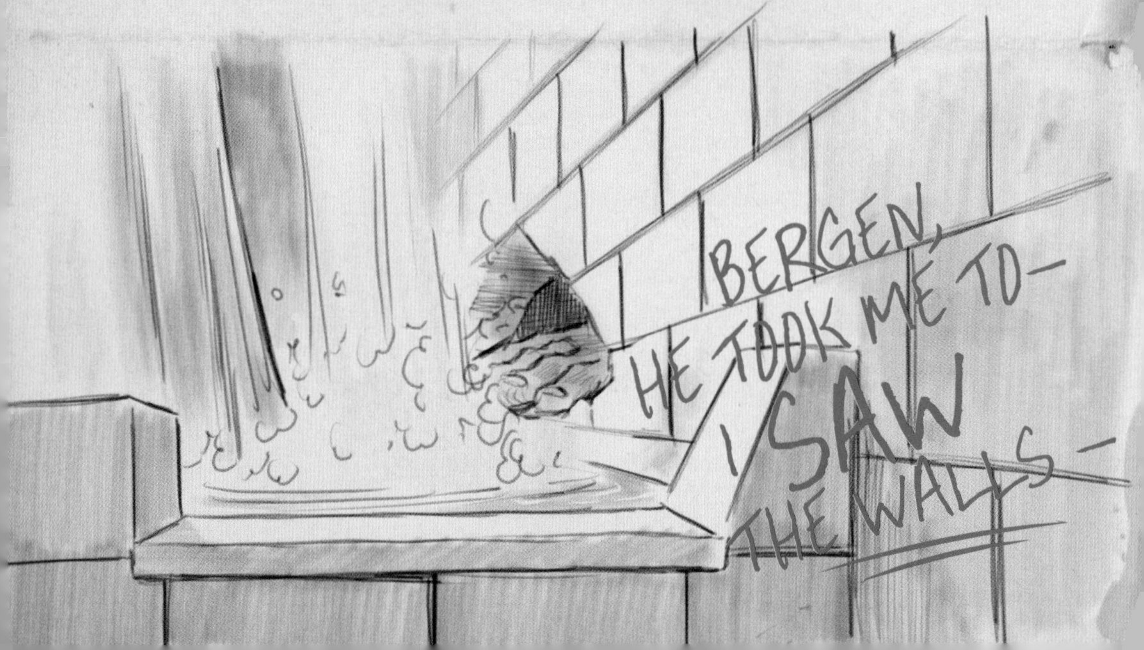
BERGEN,
HE TOOK ME TO—
I SAW
THE WALLS—

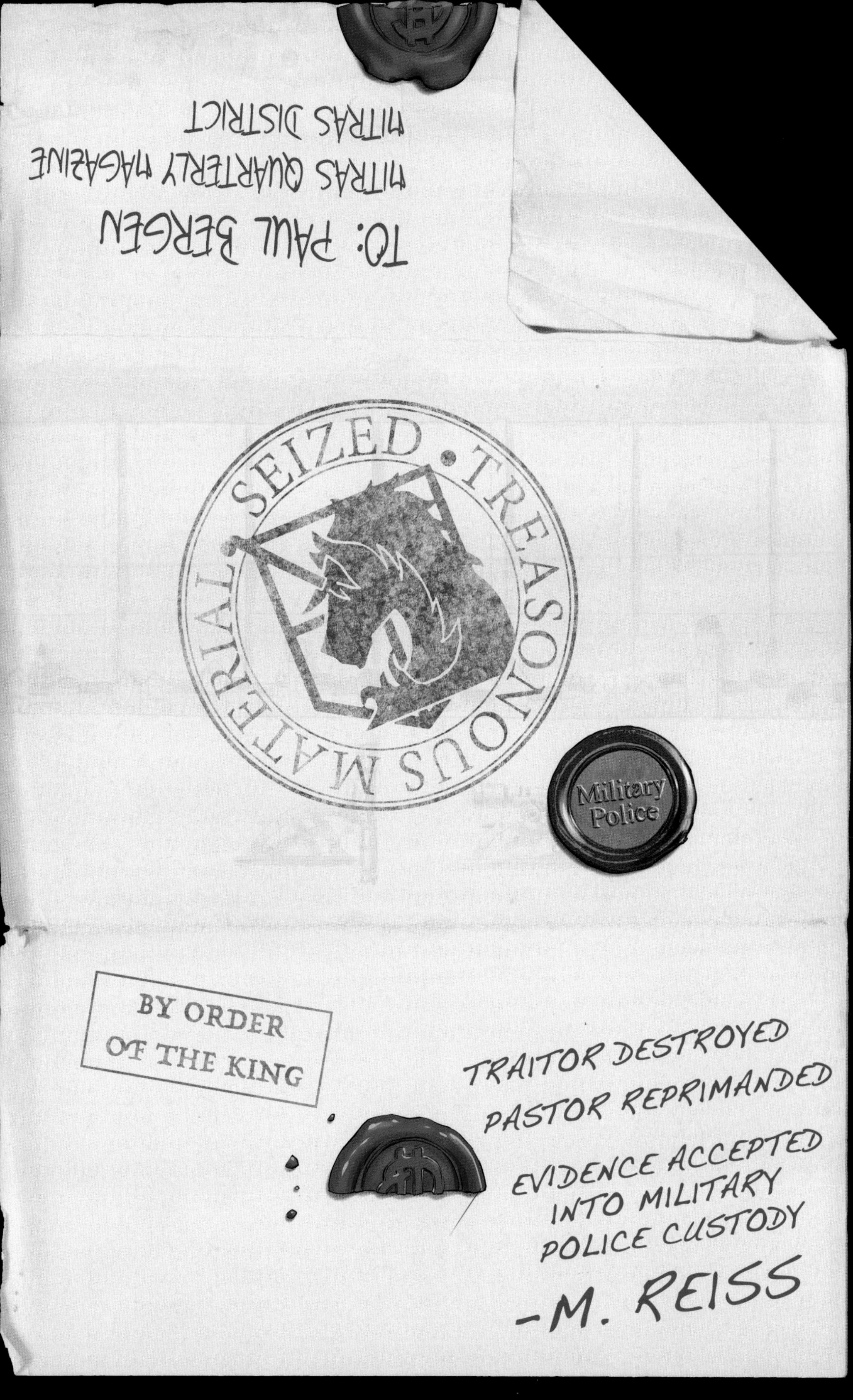
TO: PAUL BERGEN
MITRAS QUARTERLY MAGAZINE
MITRAS DISTRICT
SEIZED • TREASONOUS MATERIAL •
Military Police
BY ORDER OF THE KING
TRAITOR DESTROYED
PASTOR REPRIMANDED
EVIDENCE ACCEPTED INTO MILITARY POLICE CUSTODY
-M. REISS

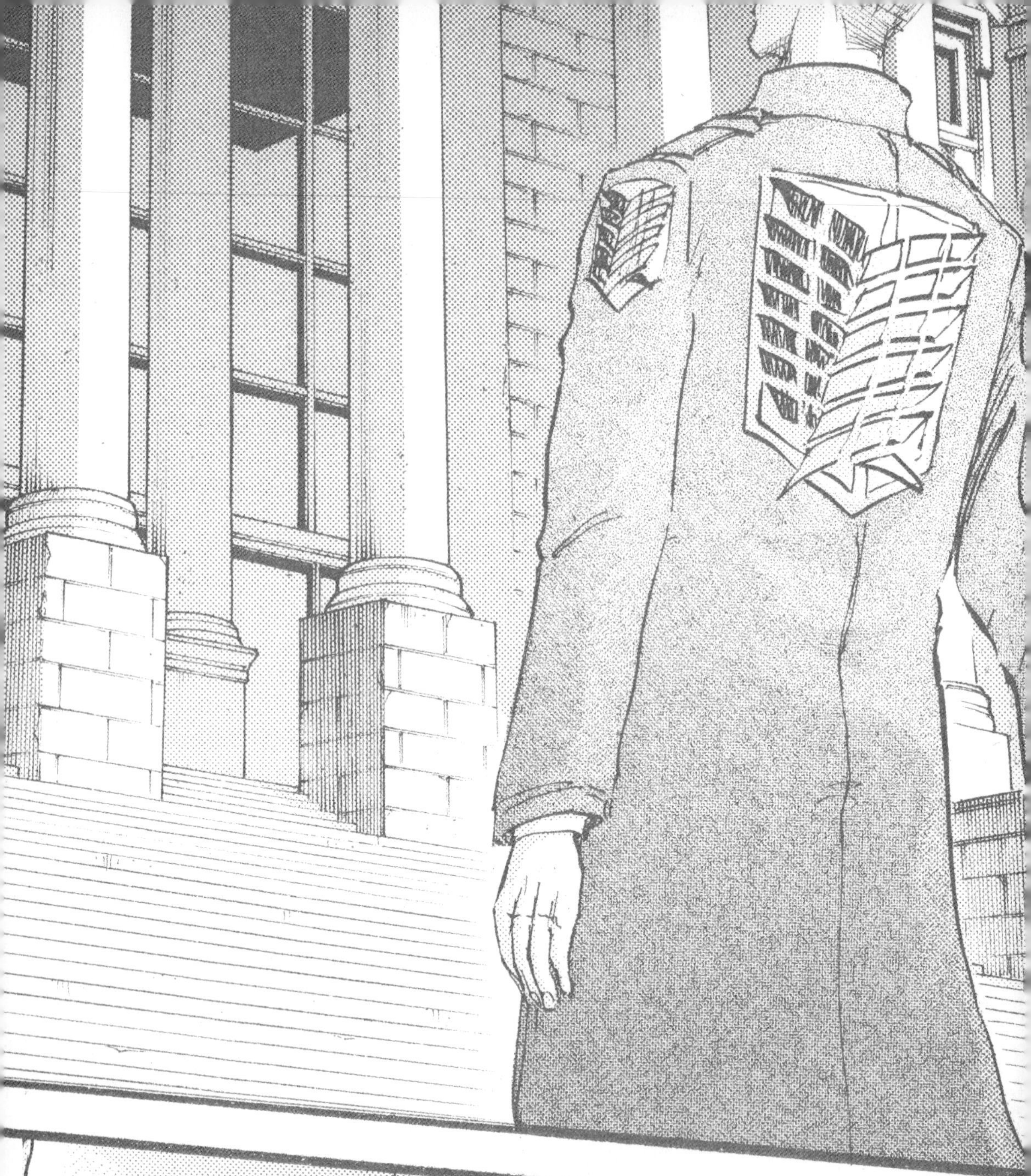
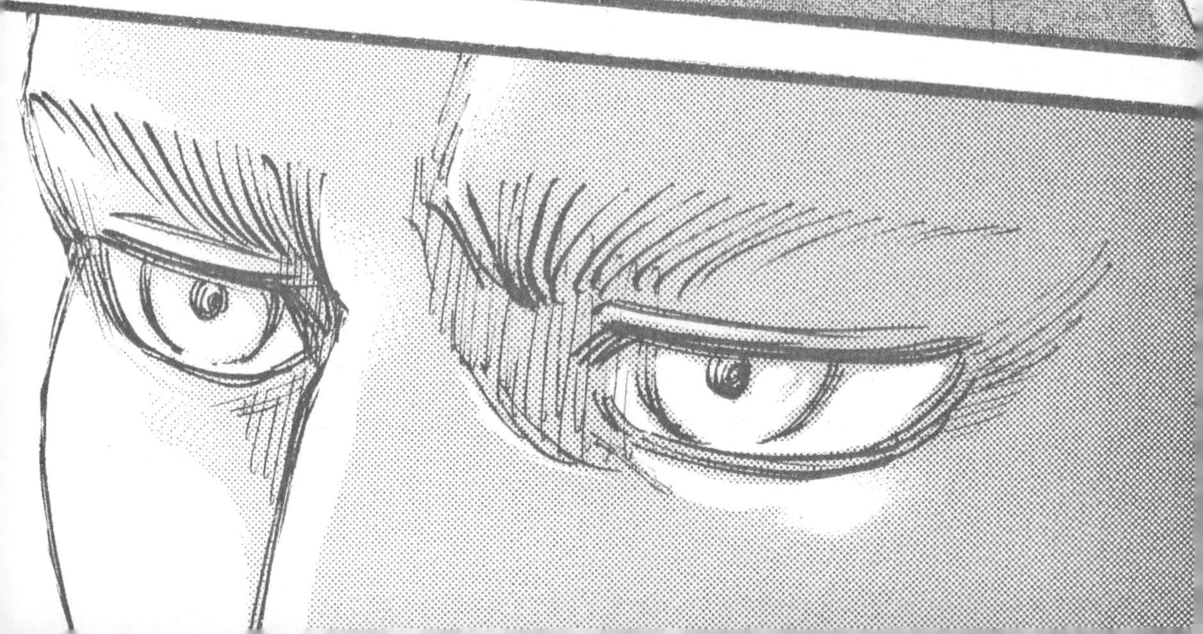

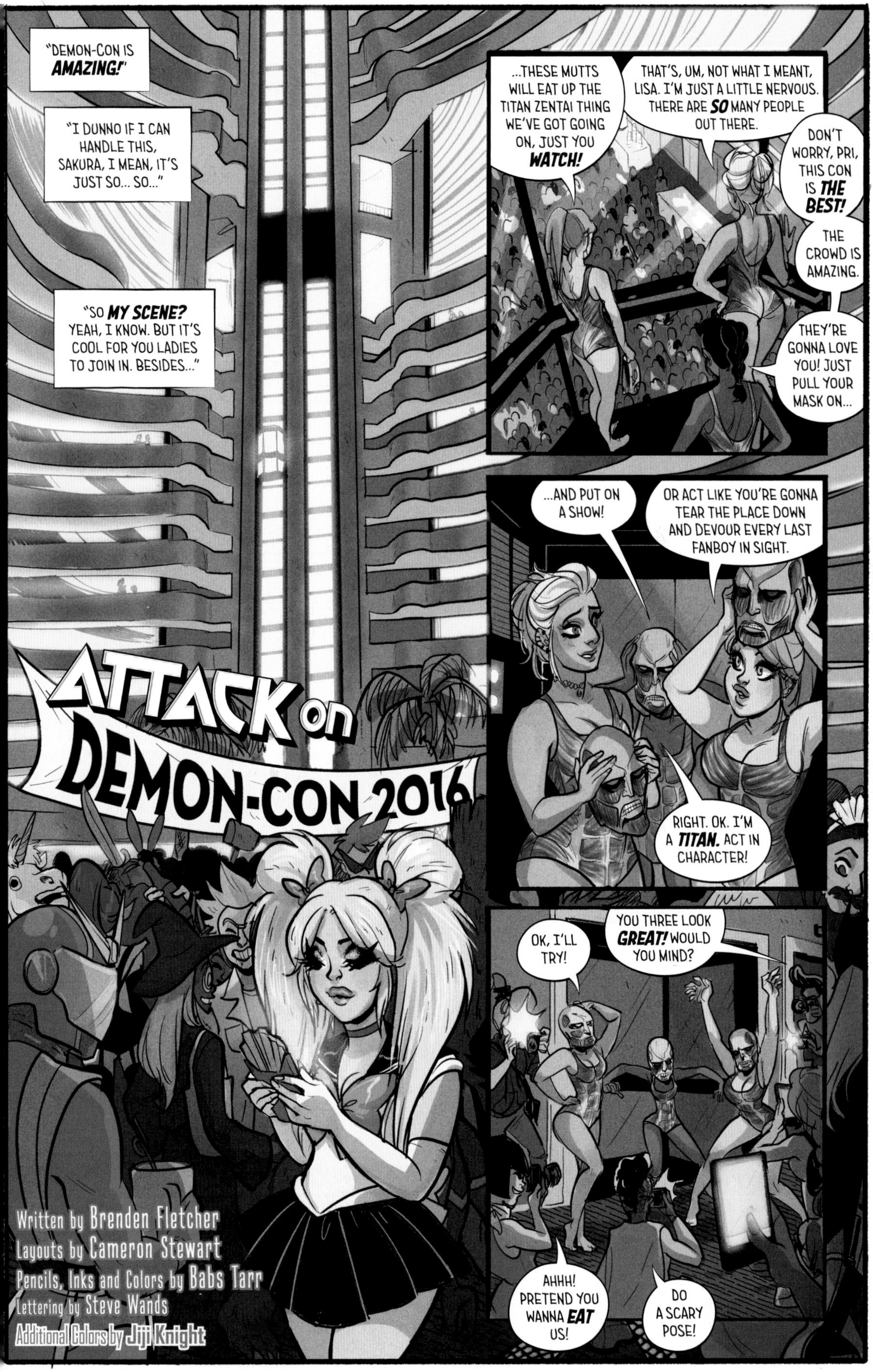
"DEMON-CON IS AMAZING!"
"I DUNNO IF I CAN HANDLE THIS, SAKURA, I MEAN, IT'S JUST SO... SO..."
"SO MY SCENE? YEAH, I KNOW. BUT IT'S COOL FOR YOU LADIES TO JOIN IN. BESIDES..."
ATTACK on DEMON-CON 2016
Written by Brenden Fletcher
Layouts by Cameron Stewart
Pencils, Inks and Colors by Babs Tarr
Lettering by Steve Wands
Additional Colors by Jiji Knight
...THESE MUTTS WILL EAT UP THE TITAN ZENTAI THING WE'VE GOT GOING ON, JUST YOU WATCH!
THAT'S, UM, NOT WHAT I MEANT, LISA. I'M JUST A LITTLE NERVOUS. THERE ARE SO MANY PEOPLE OUT THERE.
DON'T WORRY, PRI, THIS CON IS THE BEST!
THE CROWD IS AMAZING.
THEY'RE GONNA LOVE YOU! JUST PULL YOUR MASK ON...
...AND PUT ON A SHOW!
OR ACT LIKE YOU'RE GONNA TEAR THE PLACE DOWN AND DEVOUR EVERY LAST FANBOY IN SIGHT.
RIGHT. OK. I'M A TITAN. ACT IN CHARACTER!
OK, I'LL TRY!
YOU THREE LOOK GREAT! WOULD YOU MIND?
AHHH! PRETEND YOU WANNA EAT US!
DO A SCARY POSE!

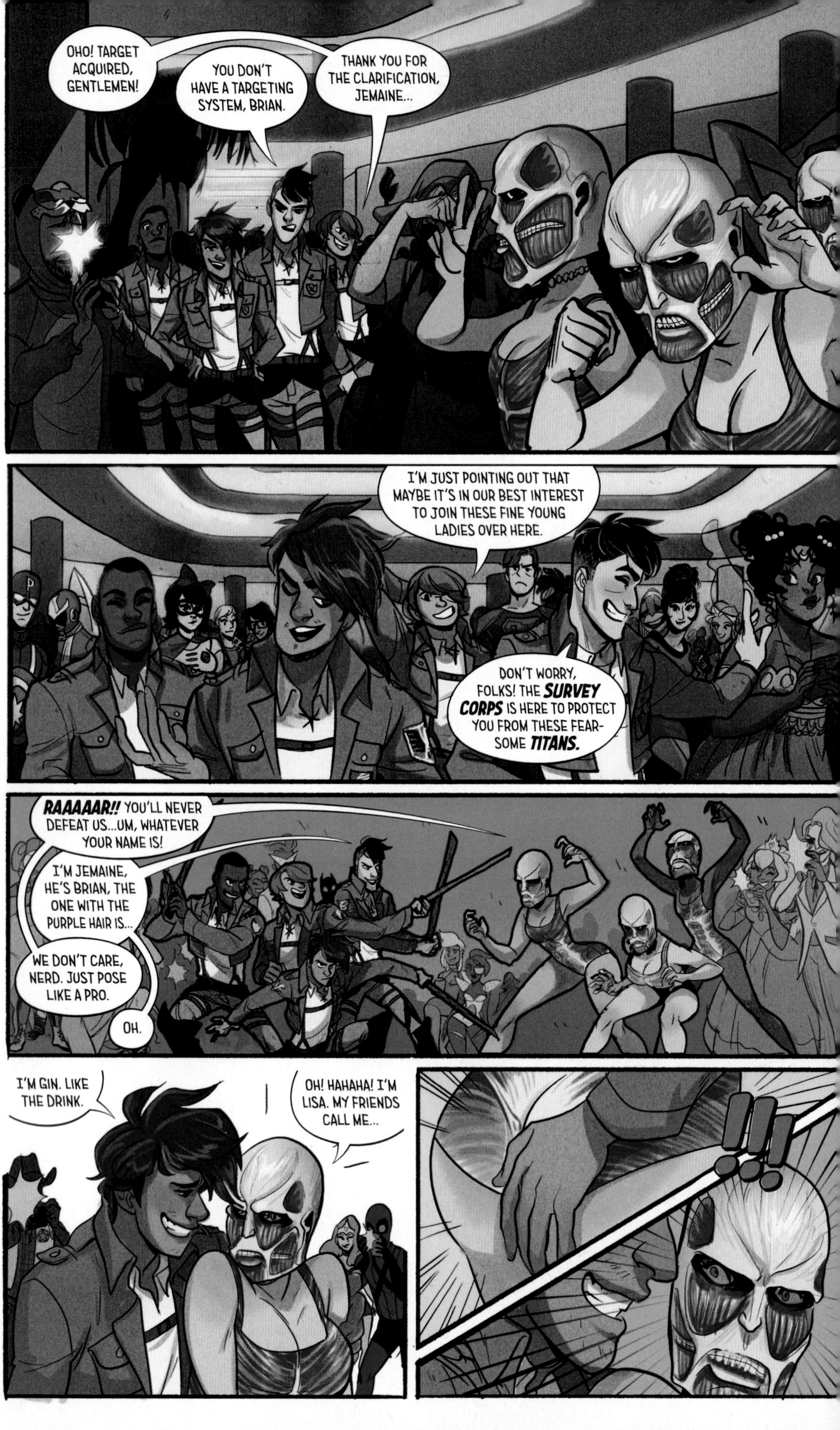
OHO! TARGET ACQUIRED, GENTLEMEN!
YOU DON'T HAVE A TARGETING SYSTEM, BRIAN.
THANK YOU FOR THE CLARIFICATION, JEMAINE...
I'M JUST POINTING OUT THAT MAYBE IT'S IN OUR BEST INTEREST TO JOIN THESE FINE YOUNG LADIES OVER HERE.
DON'T WORRY, FOLKS! THE SURVEY CORPS IS HERE TO PROTECT YOU FROM THESE FEAR-SOME TITANS.
RAAAAAR!! YOU'LL NEVER DEFEAT US...UM, WHATEVER YOUR NAME IS!
I'M JEMAINE, HE'S BRIAN, THE ONE WITH THE PURPLE HAIR IS...
WE DON'T CARE, NERD. JUST POSE LIKE A PRO.
OH.
I'M GIN. LIKE THE DRINK.
OH! HAHAHA! I'M LISA. MY FRIENDS CALL ME...
!!!

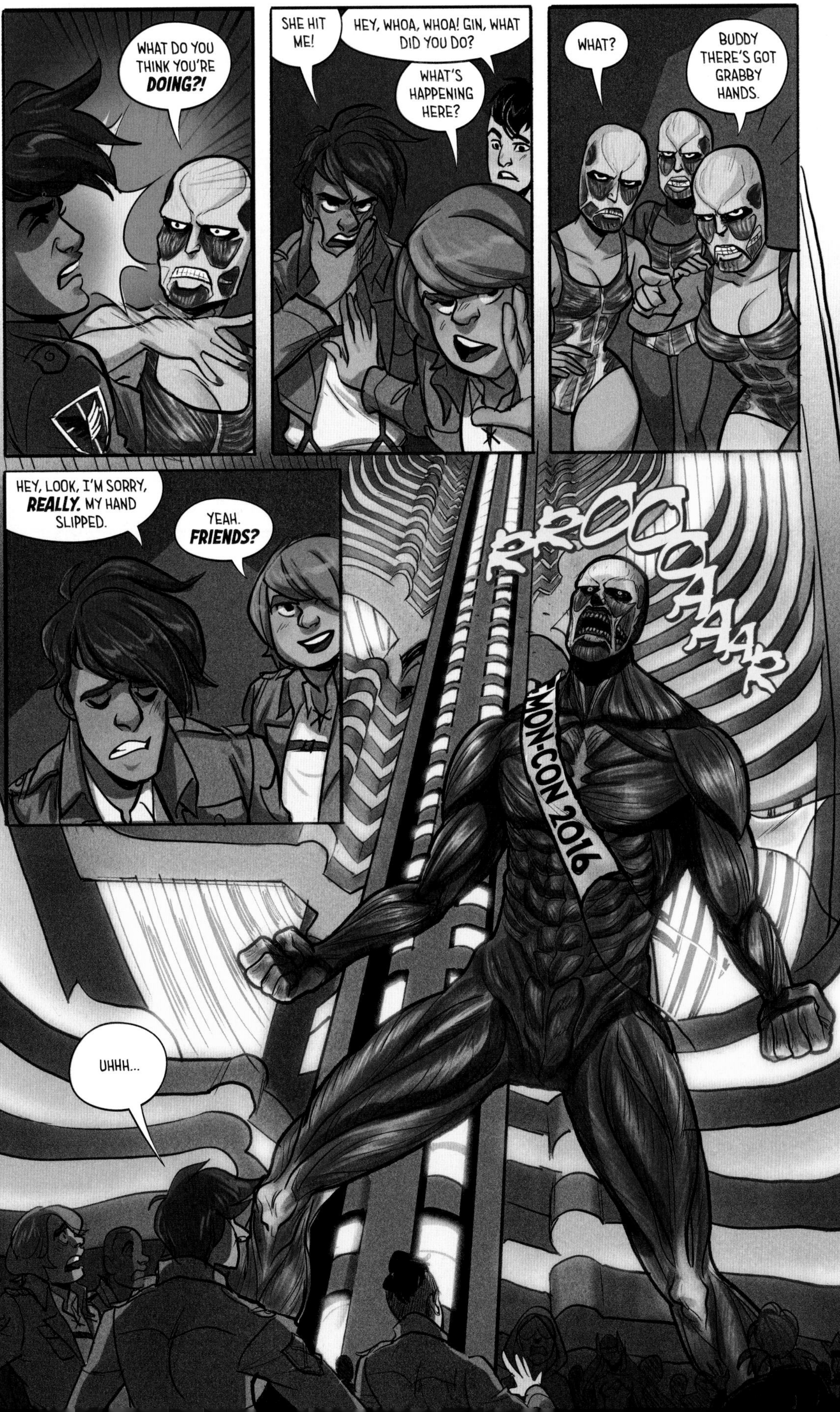
WHAT DO YOU THINK YOU'RE **DOING?!**
SHE HIT ME!
HEY, WHOA, WHOA! GIN, WHAT DID YOU DO?
WHAT'S HAPPENING HERE?
WHAT?
BUDDY THERE'S GOT GRABBY HANDS.
HEY, LOOK, I'M SORRY, **REALLY.** MY HAND SLIPPED.
YEAH. **FRIENDS?**
RROOOAAAR
MON-CON 2016
UHHH...

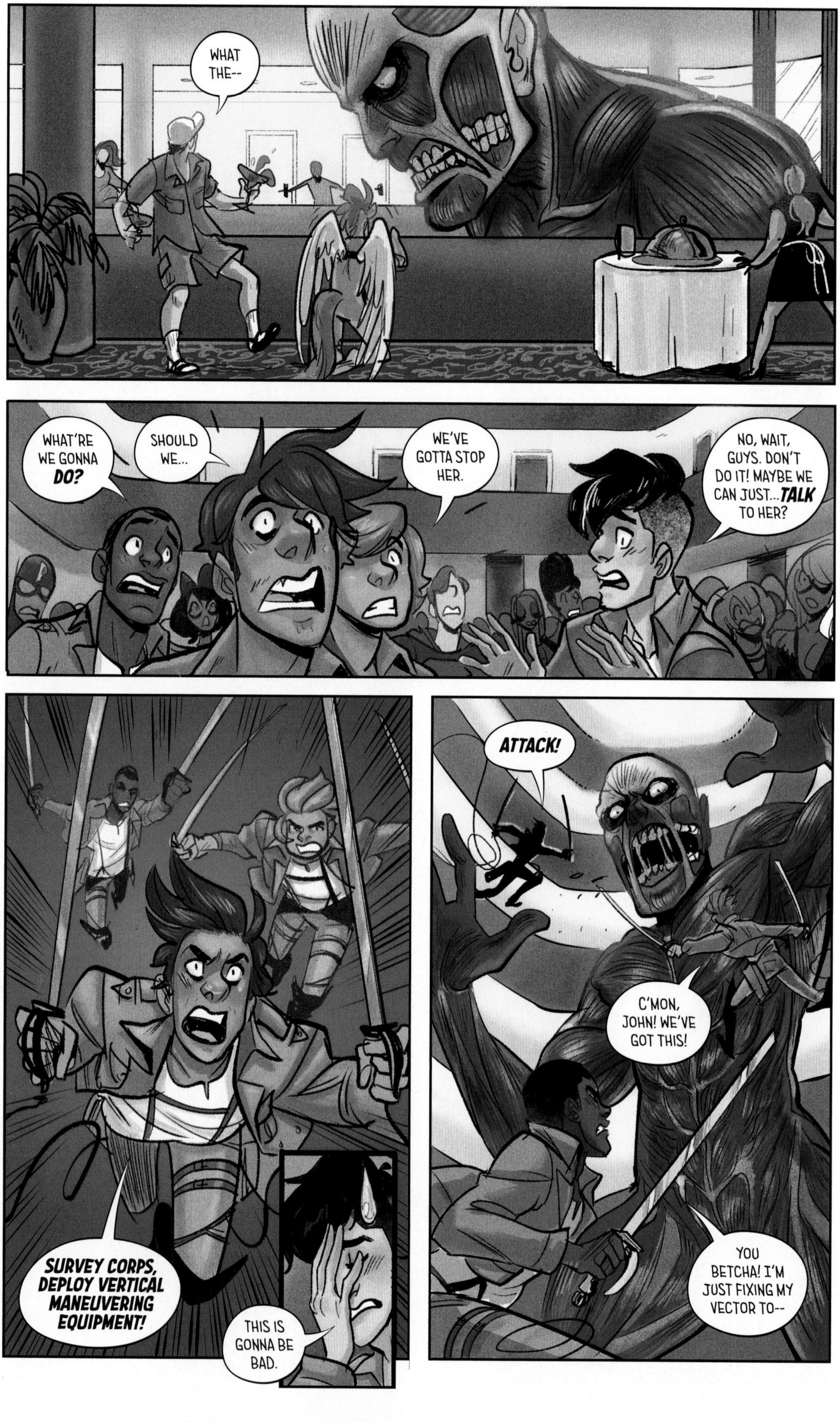
WHAT THE--
WHAT'RE WE GONNA **DO?**
SHOULD WE...
WE'VE GOTTA STOP HER.
NO, WAIT, GUYS. DON'T DO IT! MAYBE WE CAN JUST...**TALK** TO HER?
SURVEY CORPS, DEPLOY VERTICAL MANEUVERING EQUIPMENT!
THIS IS GONNA BE BAD.
ATTACK!
C'MON, JOHN! WE'VE GOT THIS!
YOU BETCHA! I'M JUST FIXING MY VECTOR TO--

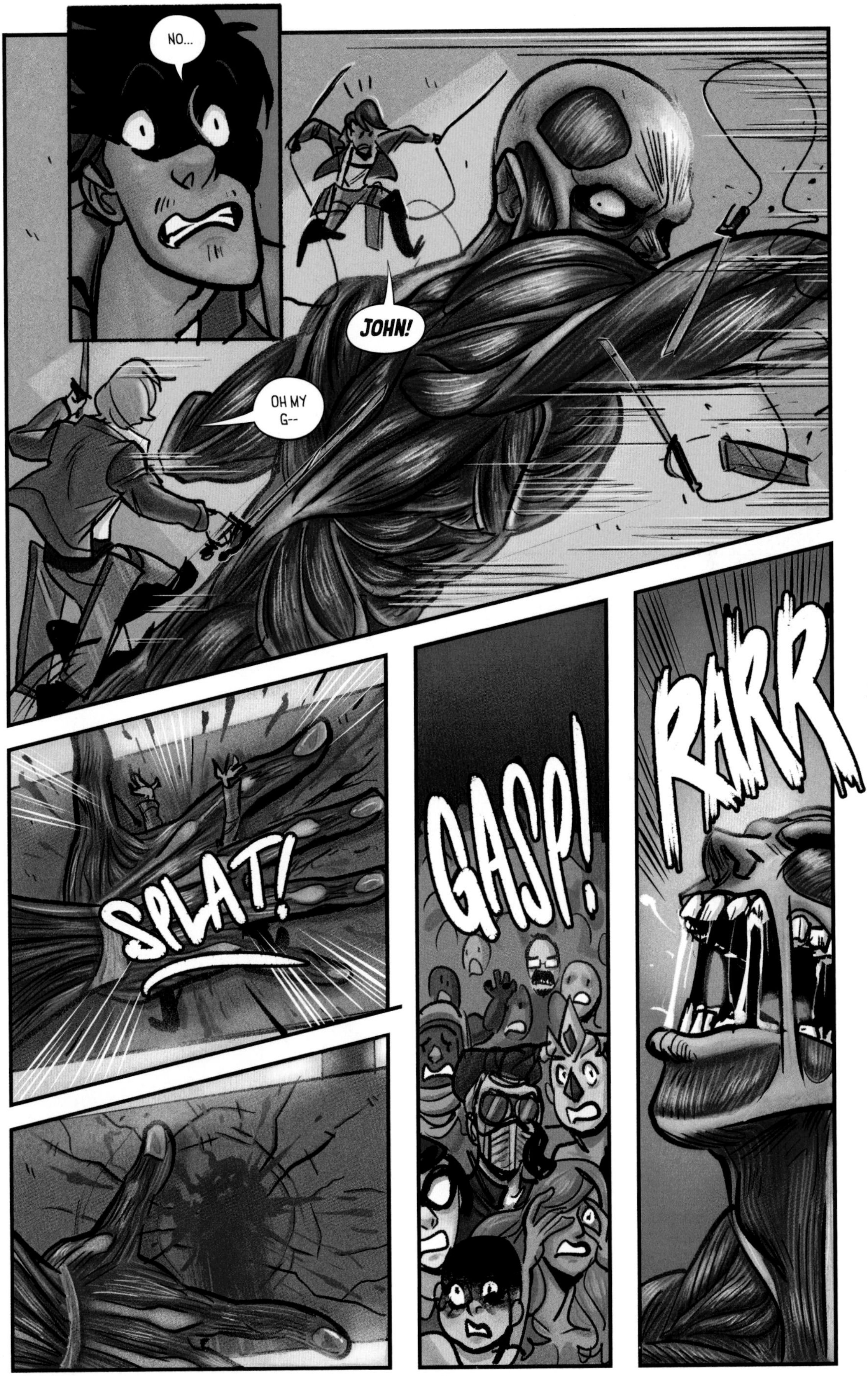
NO...
JOHN!
OH MY G--
SPLAT!
GASP!
RARR

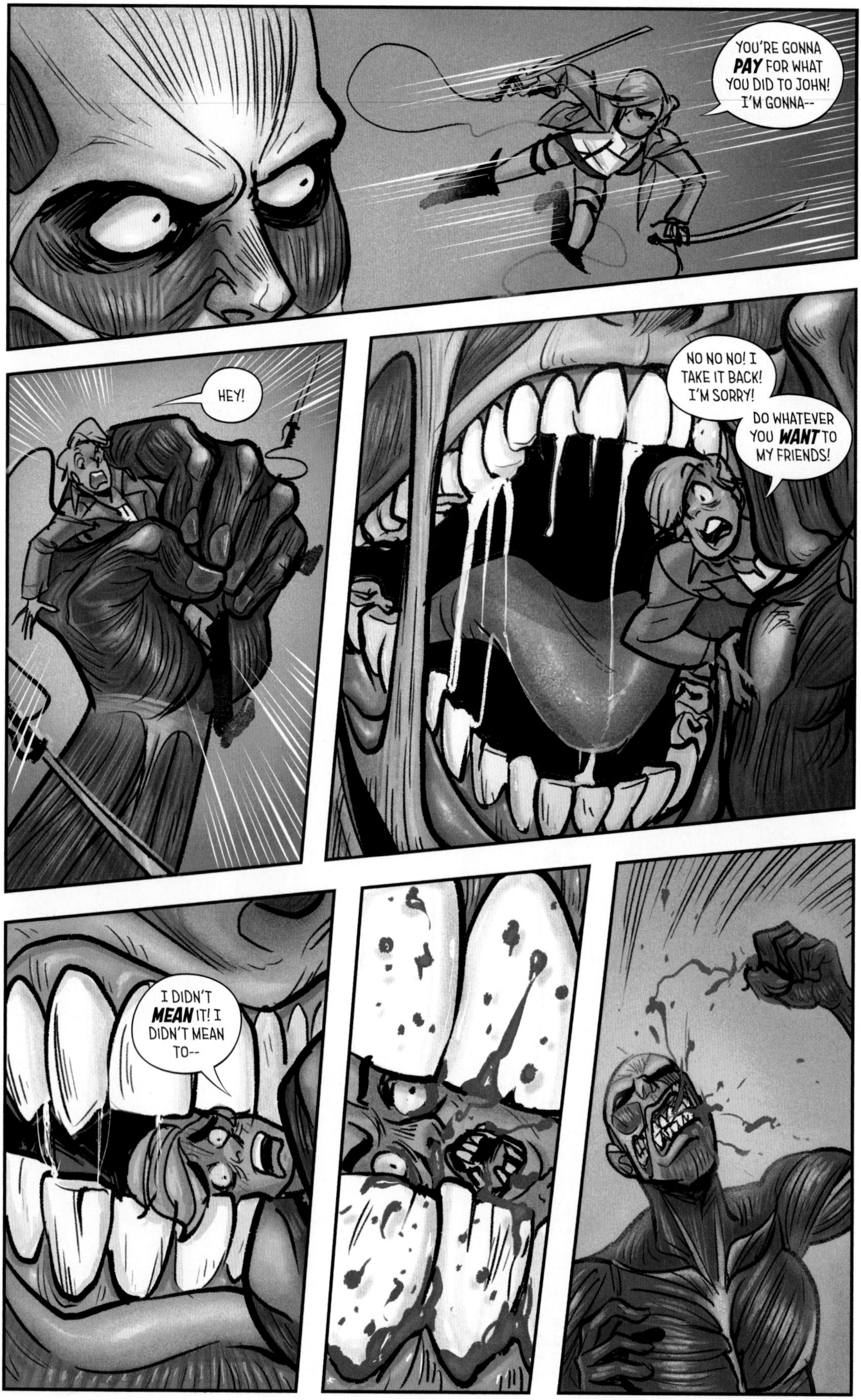
YOU'RE GONNA PAY FOR WHAT YOU DID TO JOHN! I'M GONNA--
HEY!
NO NO NO! I TAKE IT BACK! I'M SORRY!
DO WHATEVER YOU WANT TO MY FRIENDS!
I DIDN'T MEAN IT! I DIDN'T MEAN TO--

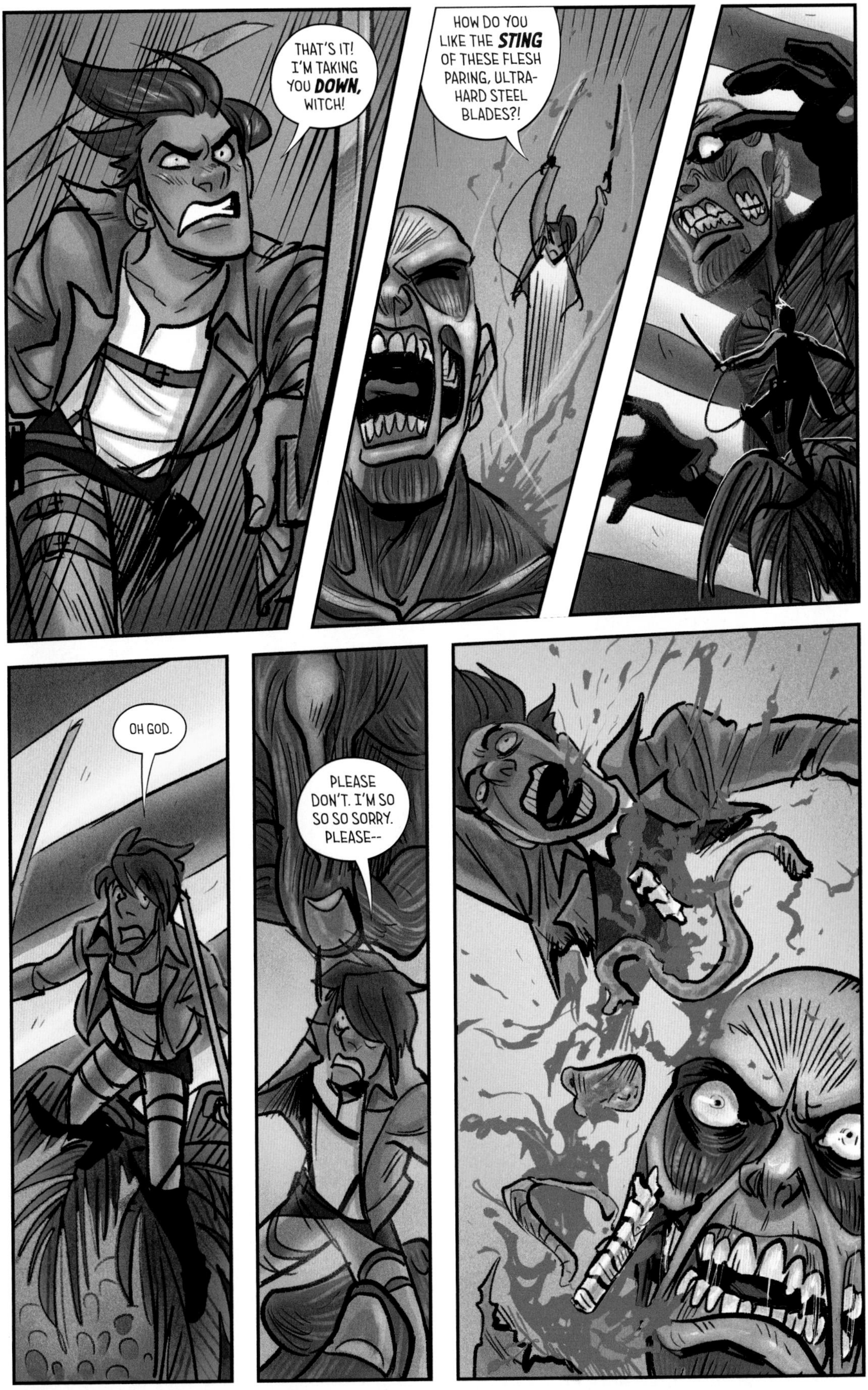
THAT'S IT! I'M TAKING YOU **DOWN,** WITCH!
HOW DO YOU LIKE THE **STING** OF THESE FLESH PARING, ULTRA-HARD STEEL BLADES?!
OH GOD.
PLEASE DON'T. I'M SO SO SO SORRY. PLEASE--

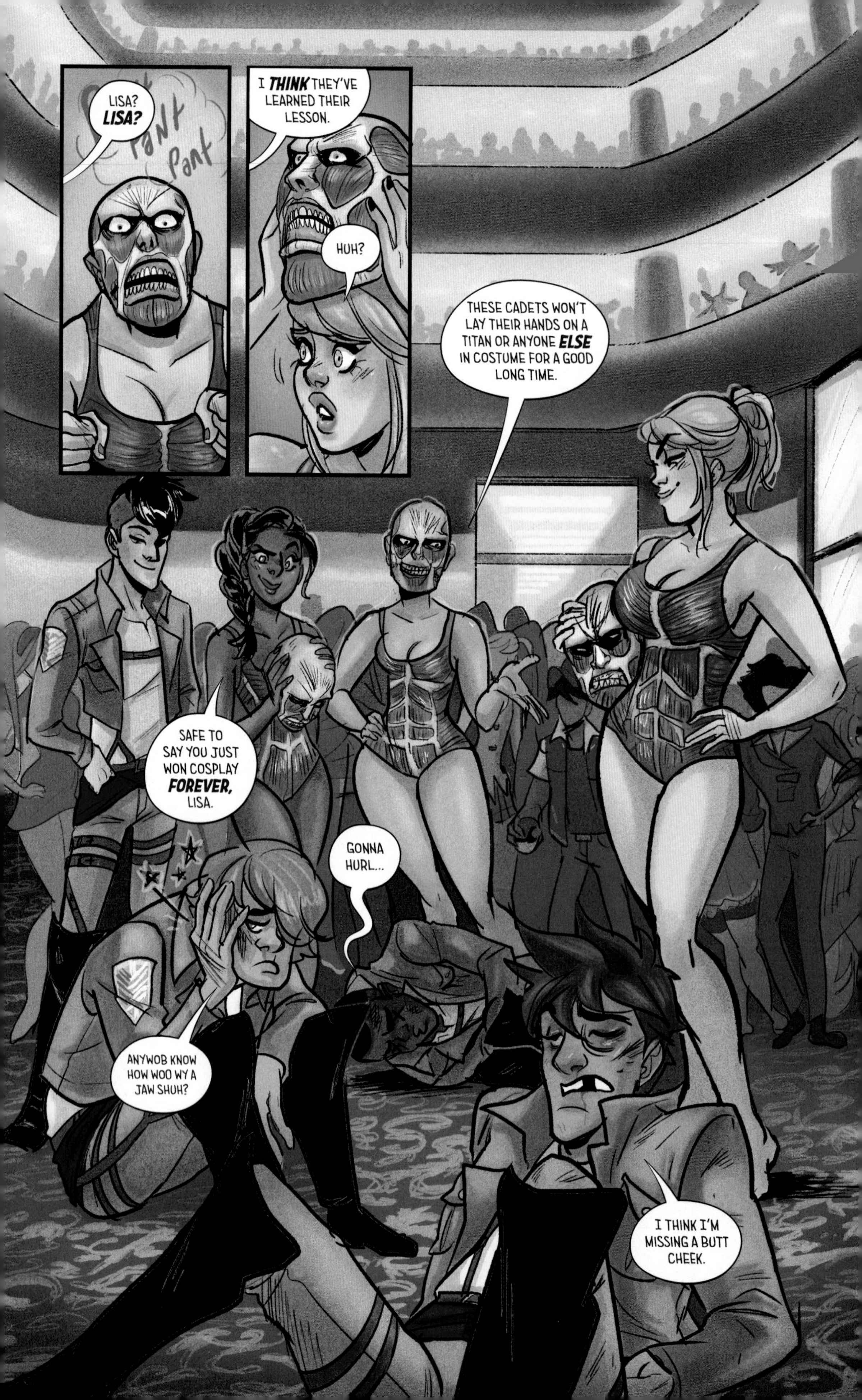
LISA? **LISA?**
pant pant
I **THINK** THEY'VE LEARNED THEIR LESSON.
HUH?
THESE CADETS WON'T LAY THEIR HANDS ON A TITAN OR ANYONE **ELSE** IN COSTUME FOR A GOOD LONG TIME.
SAFE TO SAY YOU JUST WON COSPLAY **FOREVER,** LISA.
GONNA HURL...
ANYWOB KNOW HOW WOO WY A JAW SHUH?
I THINK I'M MISSING A BUTT CHEEK.

ATTACK on ATTACK on

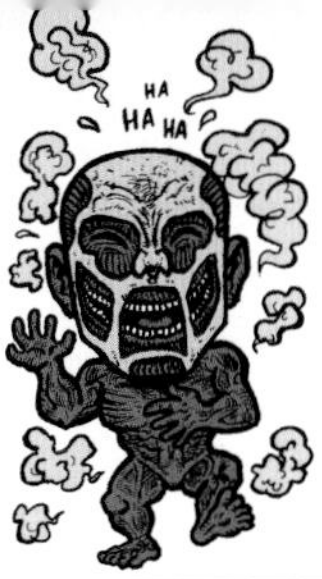

HA
HA HA

By Evan Dorkin and Sarah Dyer
Flatted and additional colors by Bill Mudron

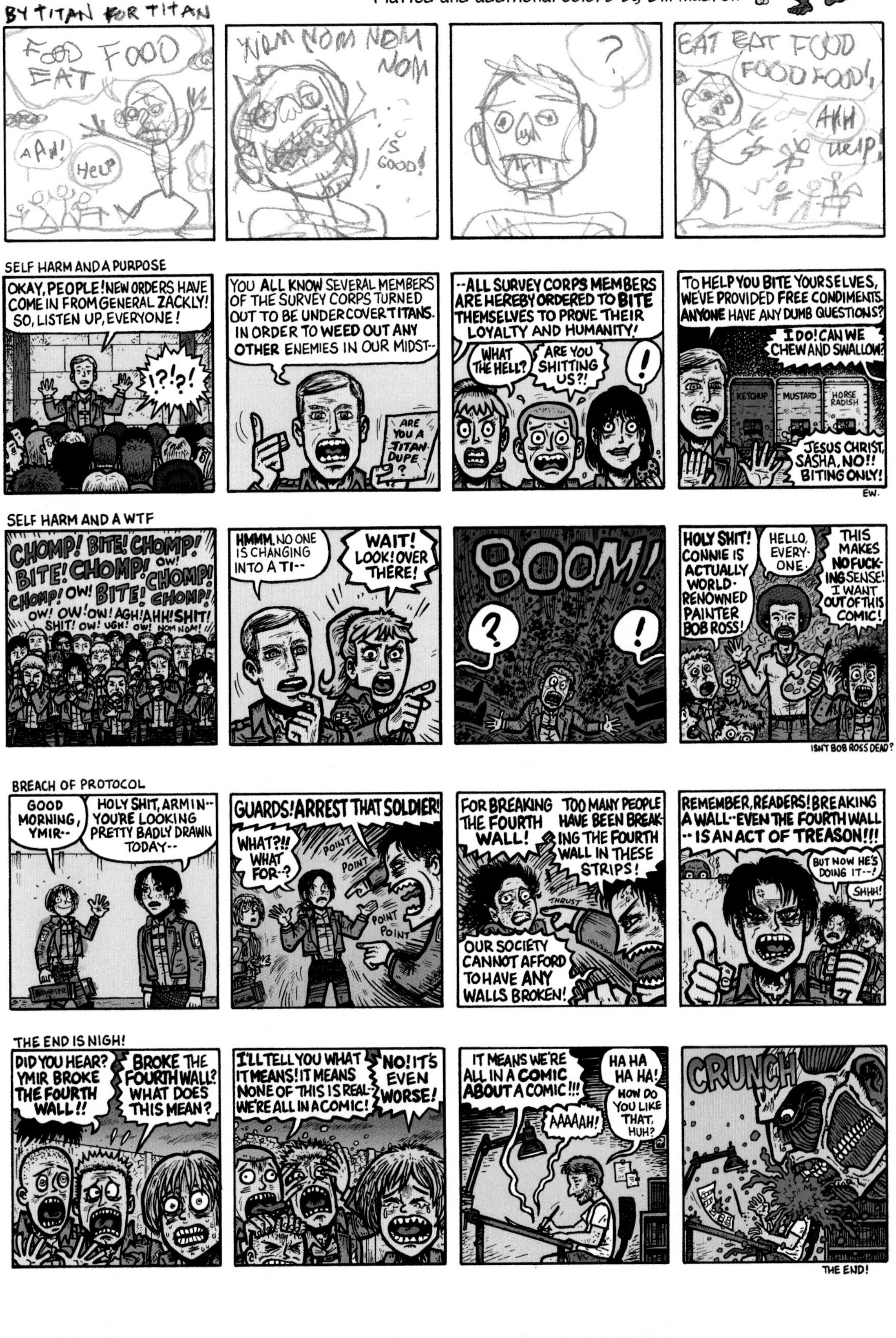

BY TITAN FOR TITAN
FOOD EAT FOOD
AAH!
HELP
NOM NOM NOM NOM
IS GOOD!
?
EAT EAT FOOD FOOD FOOD!
AHH
HELP!
SELF HARM AND A PURPOSE
OKAY, PEOPLE! NEW ORDERS HAVE COME IN FROM GENERAL ZACKLY! SO, LISTEN UP, EVERYONE!
!?!?!
YOU ALL KNOW SEVERAL MEMBERS OF THE SURVEY CORPS TURNED OUT TO BE UNDERCOVER TITANS. IN ORDER TO WEED OUT ANY OTHER ENEMIES IN OUR MIDST--
ARE YOU A TITAN DUPE?
--ALL SURVEY CORPS MEMBERS ARE HEREBY ORDERED TO BITE THEMSELVES TO PROVE THEIR LOYALTY AND HUMANITY!
WHAT THE HELL?
ARE YOU SHITTING US?!
!
TO HELP YOU BITE YOURSELVES, WE'VE PROVIDED FREE CONDIMENTS. ANYONE HAVE ANY DUMB QUESTIONS?
I DO! CAN WE CHEW AND SWALLOW?
KETCHUP
MUSTARD
HORSE RADISH
JESUS CHRIST, SASHA, NO!! BITING ONLY!
EW.
SELF HARM AND A WTF
CHOMP! BITE! CHOMP! BITE! CHOMP! OW! CHOMP! CHOMP! OW! BITE! CHOMP! OW! OW! OW! AGH! AHH! SHIT! SHIT! OW! UGH! OW! NOM NOM!
HMMM. NO ONE IS CHANGING INTO A TI--
WAIT! LOOK! OVER THERE!
BOOM!
?
!
HOLY SHIT! CONNIE IS ACTUALLY WORLD-RENOWNED PAINTER BOB ROSS!
HELLO, EVERY-ONE.
THIS MAKES NO FUCKING SENSE! I WANT OUT OF THIS COMIC!
ISN'T BOB ROSS DEAD?
BREACH OF PROTOCOL
GOOD MORNING, YMIR--
HOLY SHIT, ARMIN-- YOU'RE LOOKING PRETTY BADLY DRAWN TODAY--
GUARDS! ARREST THAT SOLDIER!
WHAT?!! WHAT FOR-?
POINT
POINT
POINT
POINT
FOR BREAKING THE FOURTH WALL!
TOO MANY PEOPLE HAVE BEEN BREAKING THE FOURTH WALL IN THESE STRIPS!
THRUST
OUR SOCIETY CANNOT AFFORD TO HAVE ANY WALLS BROKEN!
REMEMBER, READERS! BREAKING A WALL--EVEN THE FOURTH WALL--IS AN ACT OF TREASON!!!
BUT NOW HE'S DOING IT--!
SHHH!
THE END IS NIGH!
DID YOU HEAR? YMIR BROKE THE FOURTH WALL!!
BROKE THE FOURTH WALL? WHAT DOES THIS MEAN?
I'LL TELL YOU WHAT IT MEANS! IT MEANS NONE OF THIS IS REAL-- WE'RE ALL IN A COMIC!
NO! IT'S EVEN WORSE!
IT MEANS WE'RE ALL IN A COMIC ABOUT A COMIC!!!
HA HA HA HA!
HOW DO YOU LIKE THAT, HUH?
AAAAAH!
CRUNCH
THE END!

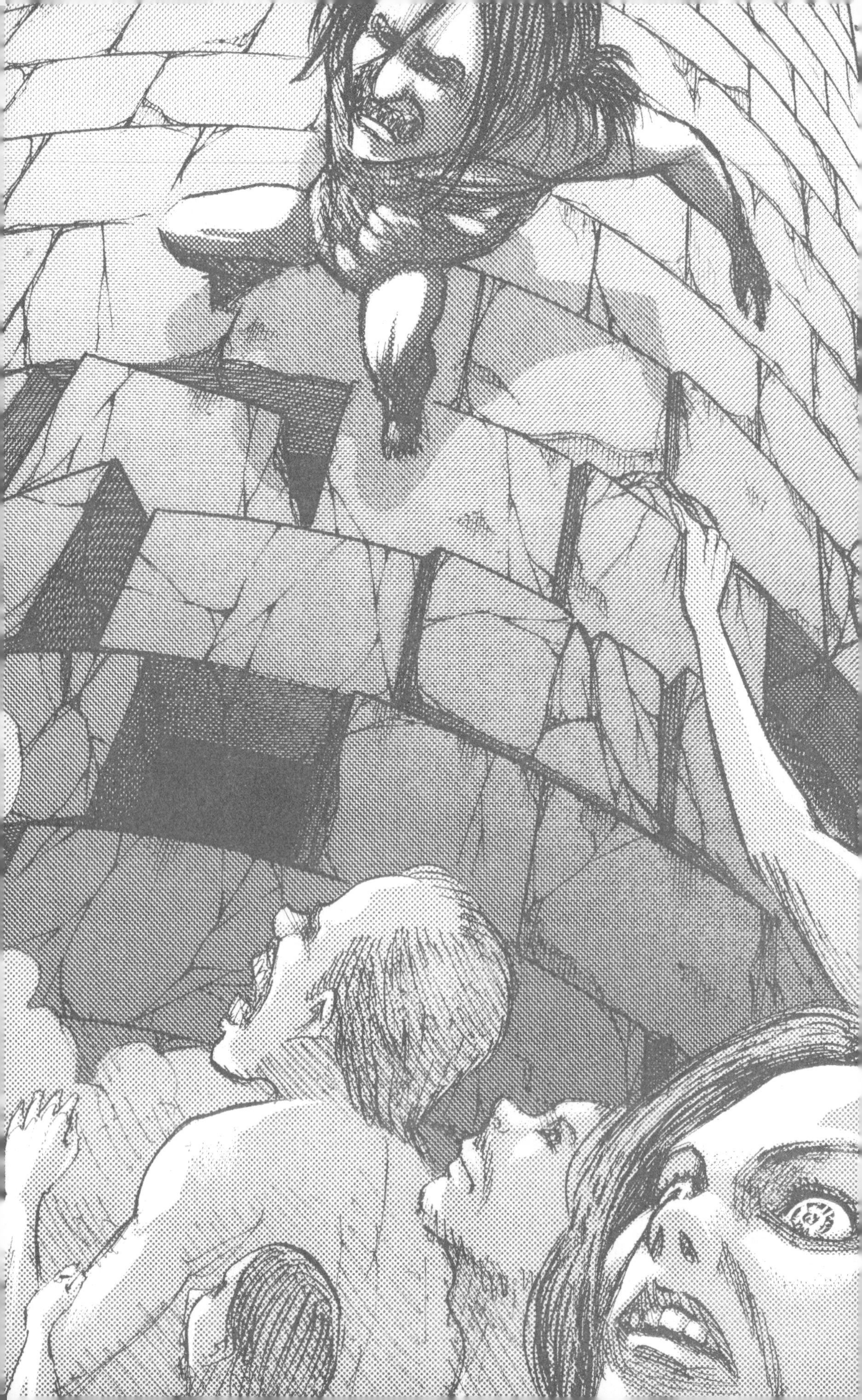

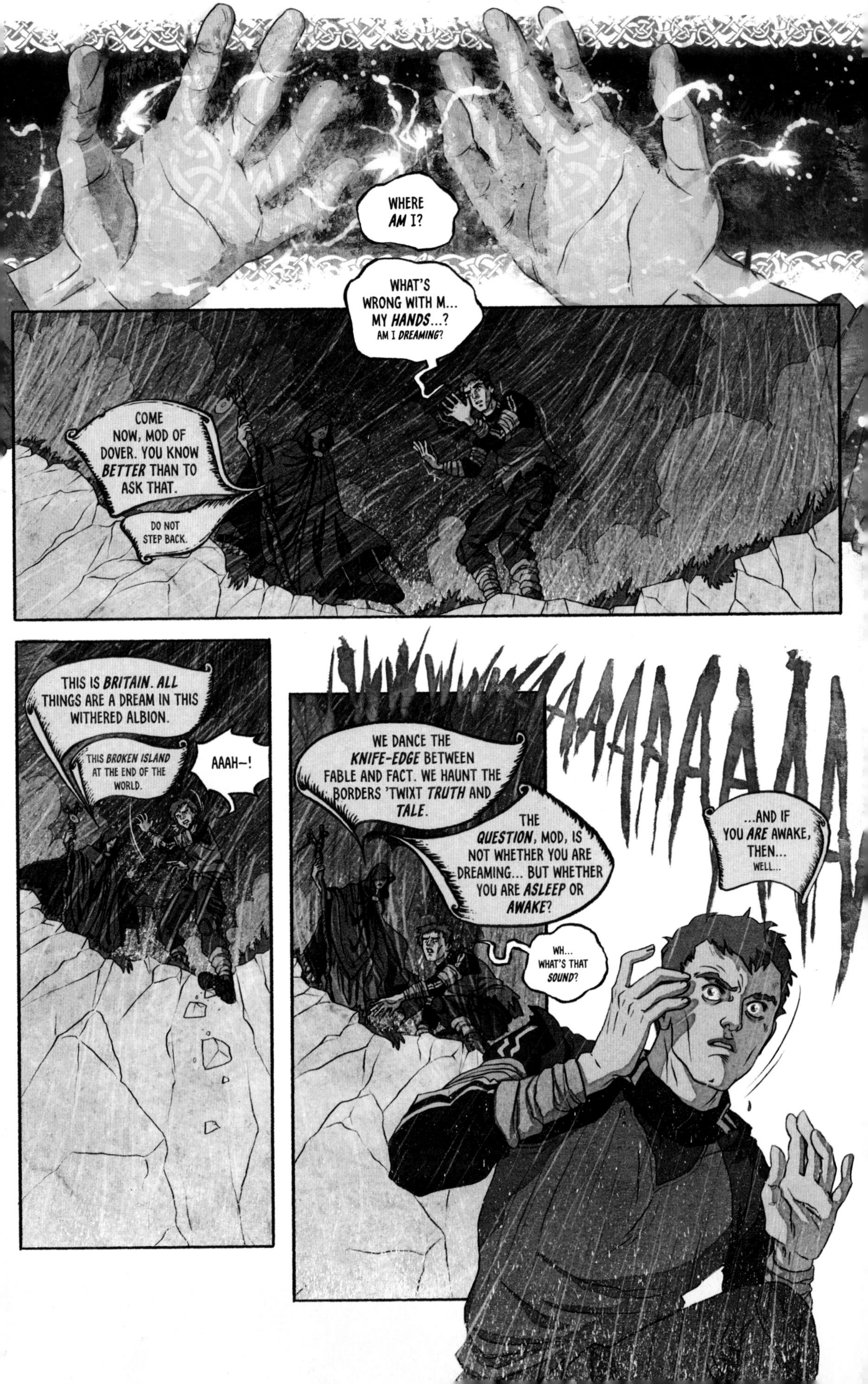

WHERE AM I?
WHAT'S WRONG WITH M... MY HANDS...? AM I DREAMING?
COME NOW, MOD OF DOVER. YOU KNOW BETTER THAN TO ASK THAT.
DO NOT STEP BACK.
THIS IS BRITAIN. ALL THINGS ARE A DREAM IN THIS WITHERED ALBION.
THIS BROKEN ISLAND AT THE END OF THE WORLD.
AAAH—!
WE DANCE THE KNIFE-EDGE BETWEEN FABLE AND FACT. WE HAUNT THE BORDERS 'TWIXT TRUTH AND TALE.
THE QUESTION, MOD, IS NOT WHETHER YOU ARE DREAMING... BUT WHETHER YOU ARE ASLEEP OR AWAKE?
WH... WHAT'S THAT SOUND?
...AND IF YOU ARE AWAKE, THEN... WELL...

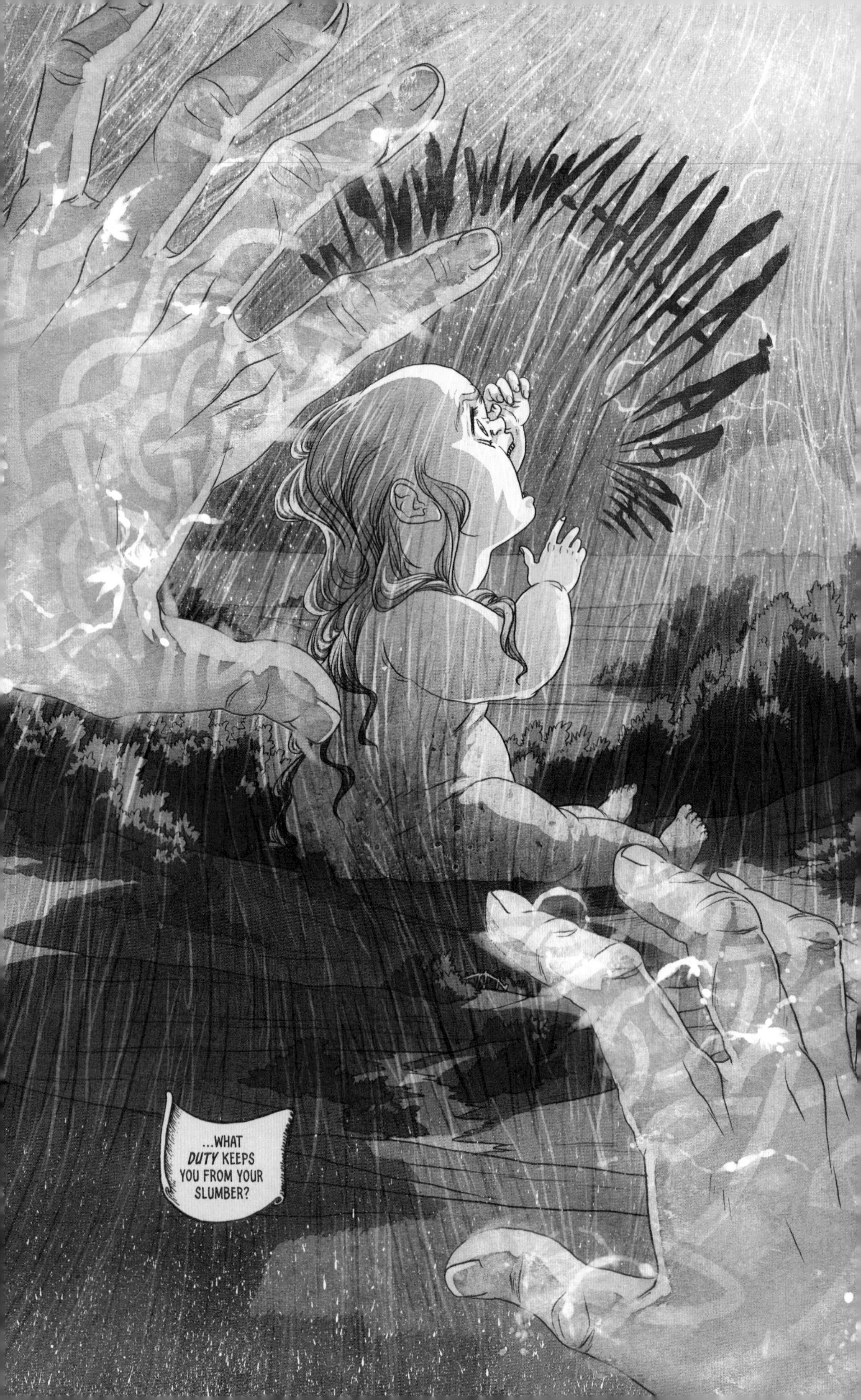
WWWWWAAAAAAAAA
...WHAT *DUTY* KEEPS YOU FROM YOUR SLUMBER?

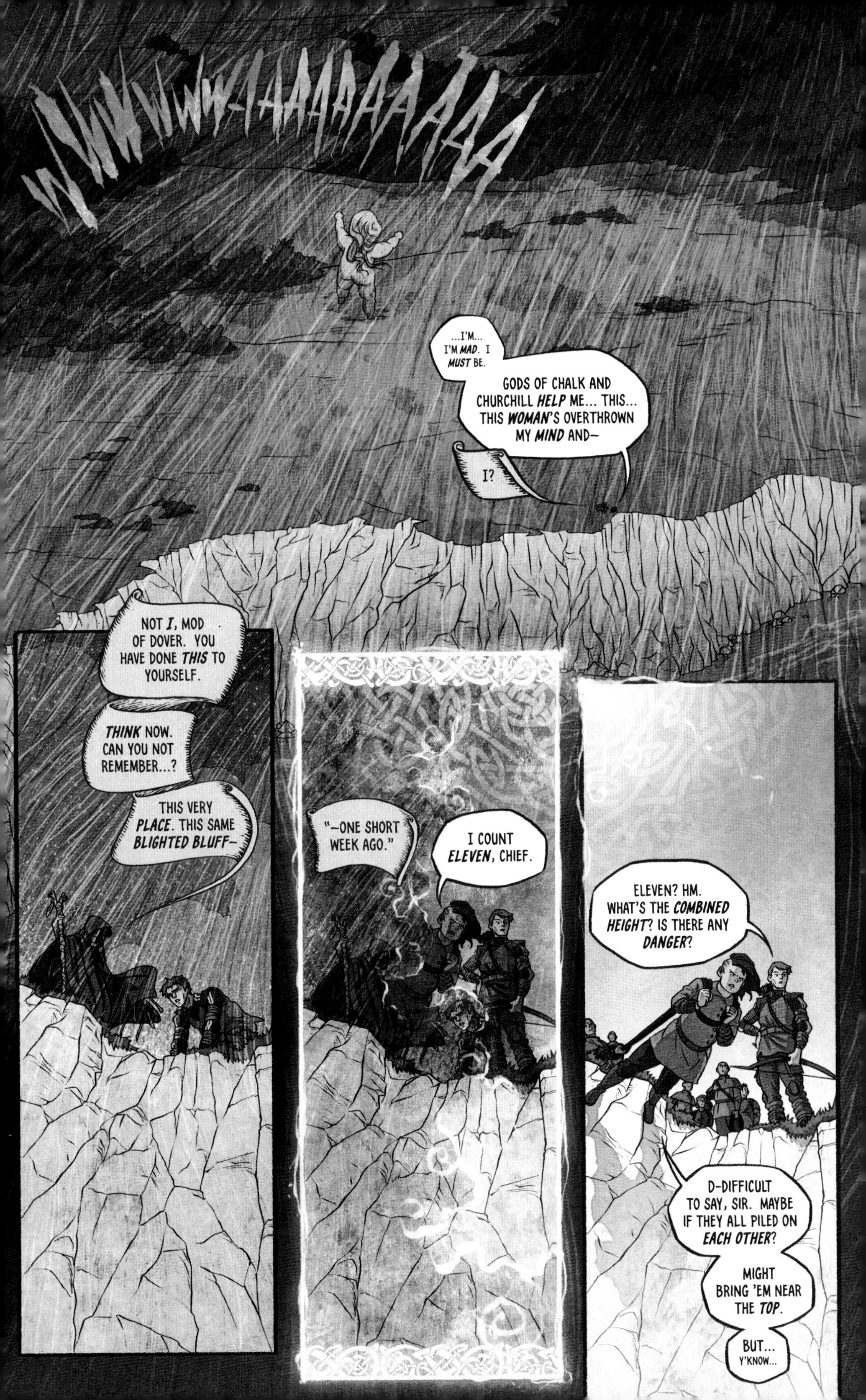
WWWWWW-IAAAAAAAAAA
...I'M... I'M MAD. I MUST BE.
GODS OF CHALK AND CHURCHILL HELP ME... THIS... THIS WOMAN'S OVERTHROWN MY MIND AND—
I?
NOT I, MOD OF DOVER. YOU HAVE DONE THIS TO YOURSELF.
THINK NOW. CAN YOU NOT REMEMBER...?
THIS VERY PLACE. THIS SAME BLIGHTED BLUFF—
"—ONE SHORT WEEK AGO."
I COUNT ELEVEN, CHIEF.
ELEVEN? HM. WHAT'S THE COMBINED HEIGHT? IS THERE ANY DANGER?
D-DIFFICULT TO SAY, SIR. MAYBE IF THEY ALL PILED ON EACH OTHER?
MIGHT BRING 'EM NEAR THE TOP.
BUT... Y'KNOW...

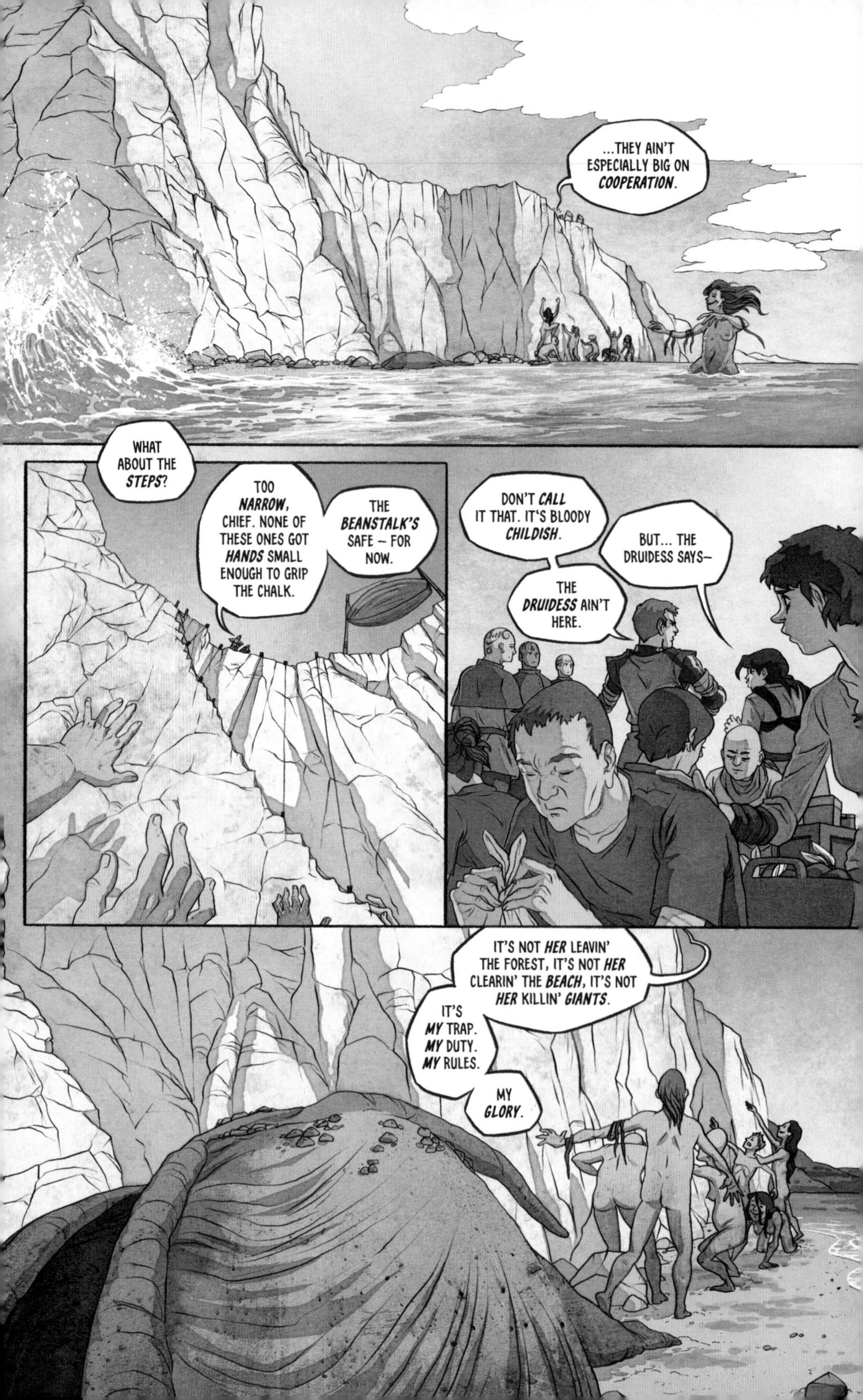
...THEY AIN'T ESPECIALLY BIG ON COOPERATION.
WHAT ABOUT THE STEPS?
TOO NARROW, CHIEF. NONE OF THESE ONES GOT HANDS SMALL ENOUGH TO GRIP THE CHALK.
THE BEANSTALK'S SAFE – FOR NOW.
DON'T CALL IT THAT. IT'S BLOODY CHILDISH.
BUT... THE DRUIDESS SAYS–
THE DRUIDESS AIN'T HERE.
IT'S NOT HER LEAVIN' THE FOREST, IT'S NOT HER CLEARIN' THE BEACH, IT'S NOT HER KILLIN' GIANTS.
IT'S MY TRAP. MY DUTY. MY RULES.
MY GLORY.

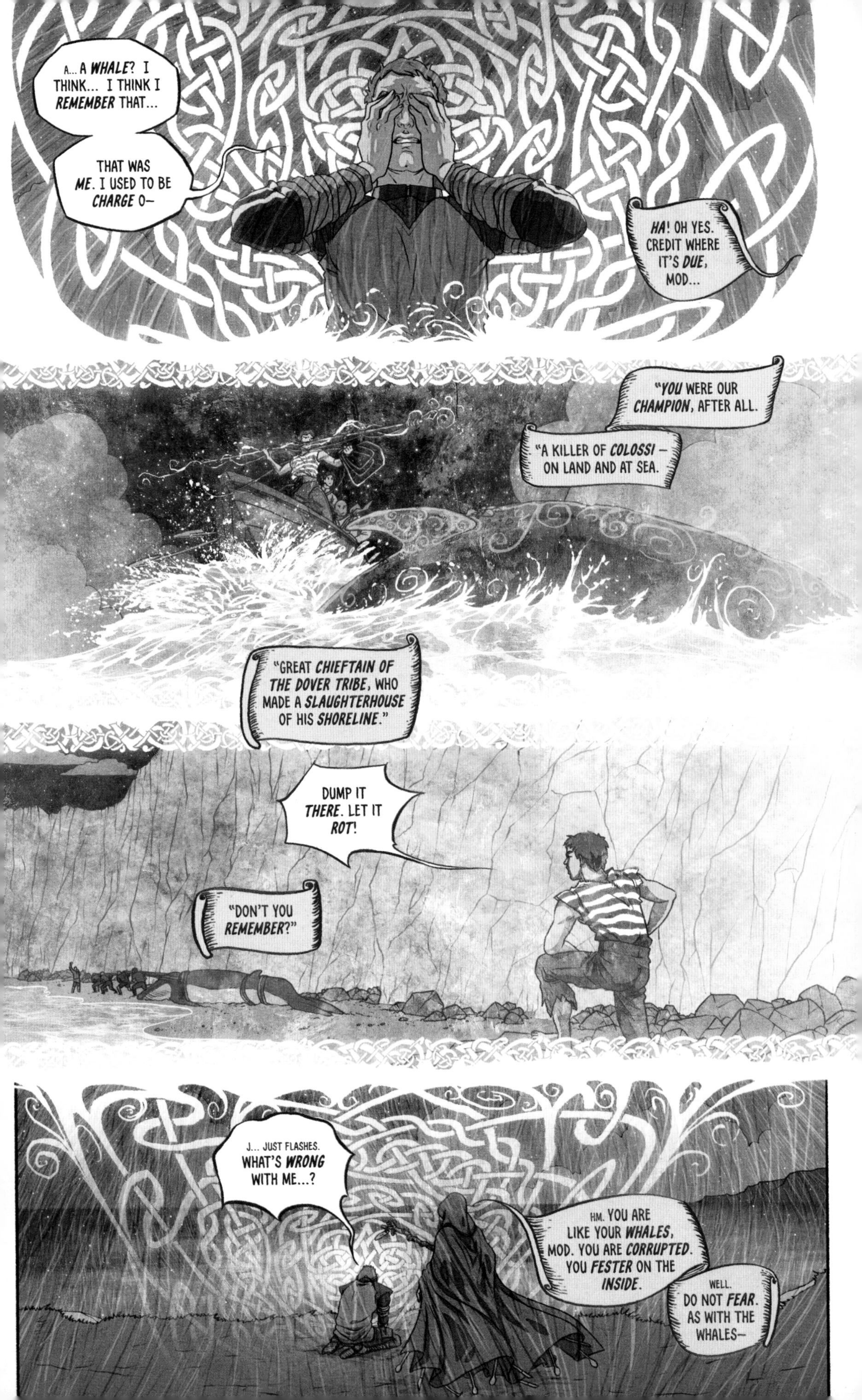

A... A *WHALE*? I THINK... I THINK I *REMEMBER* THAT...
THAT WAS *ME*. I USED TO BE *CHARGE* O—
HA! OH YES. CREDIT WHERE IT'S *DUE*, MOD...
"*YOU* WERE OUR *CHAMPION*, AFTER ALL.
"A KILLER OF *COLOSSI* — ON LAND AND AT SEA.
"GREAT *CHIEFTAIN OF THE DOVER TRIBE*, WHO MADE A *SLAUGHTERHOUSE* OF HIS *SHORELINE*."
DUMP IT *THERE*. LET IT *ROT*!
"DON'T YOU *REMEMBER*?"
J... JUST FLASHES. WHAT'S *WRONG* WITH ME...?
HM. YOU ARE LIKE YOUR *WHALES*, MOD. YOU ARE *CORRUPTED*. YOU *FESTER* ON THE *INSIDE*.
WELL. DO NOT *FEAR*. AS WITH THE WHALES—

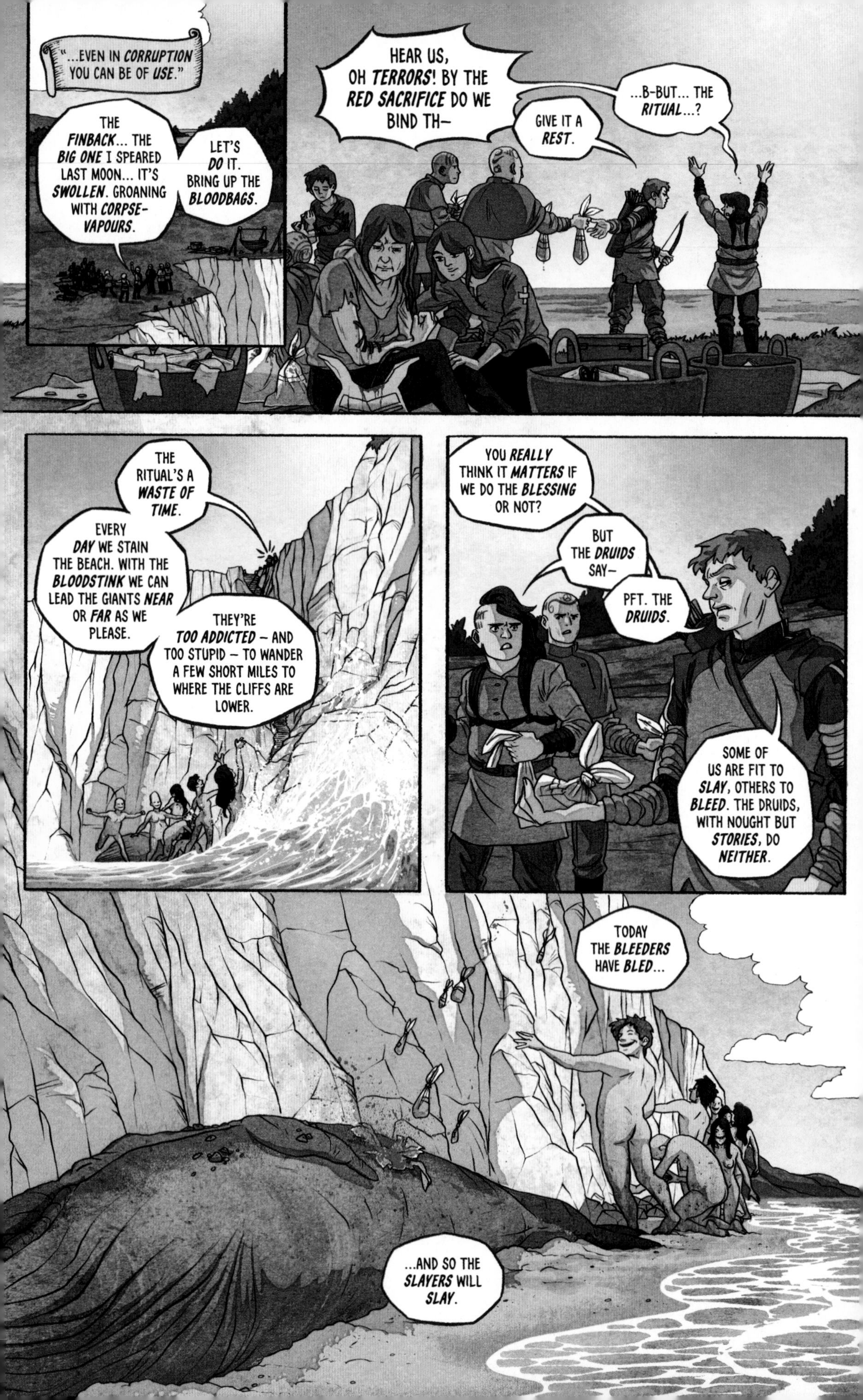
"...EVEN IN *CORRUPTION* YOU CAN BE OF *USE*."
THE *FINBACK*... THE *BIG ONE* I SPEARED LAST MOON... IT'S *SWOLLEN*. GROANING WITH *CORPSE-VAPOURS*.
LET'S *DO* IT. BRING UP THE *BLOODBAGS*.
HEAR US, OH *TERRORS*! BY THE *RED SACRIFICE* DO WE BIND TH—
GIVE IT A *REST*.
...B-BUT... THE *RITUAL*...?
THE RITUAL'S A *WASTE OF TIME*.
EVERY *DAY* WE STAIN THE BEACH. WITH THE *BLOODSTINK* WE CAN LEAD THE GIANTS *NEAR* OR *FAR* AS WE PLEASE.
THEY'RE *TOO ADDICTED* – AND TOO STUPID – TO WANDER A FEW SHORT MILES TO WHERE THE CLIFFS ARE LOWER.
YOU *REALLY* THINK IT *MATTERS* IF WE DO THE *BLESSING* OR NOT?
BUT THE *DRUIDS* SAY—
PFT. THE *DRUIDS*.
SOME OF US ARE FIT TO *SLAY*, OTHERS TO *BLEED*. THE DRUIDS, WITH NOUGHT BUT *STORIES*, DO *NEITHER*.
TODAY THE *BLEEDERS* HAVE *BLED*...
...AND SO THE *SLAYERS* WILL *SLAY*.

SEE? THEY'RE *GATHERING*.

NO *STORIES* NEEDED.

CHIEF, THE... THE *FOLK* WANT TO DO THE *CHANT*.

MORE SUPERSTITIOUS *CRAP*!

A *FIREBOX* AND *CORPSE-GAS*, GRUM — THOSE ARE THE ONLY *TOOLS* WE NEED!

THOSE AND THE *AIM* OF A *HERO*.

OH, FOR CHALK'S *SAKE*. LET THE IDIOTS *DO* IT, IF IT GIVES THEM COMFORT. IT MAKES NO *DIFFERENCE* TO ME.

BUT, SIR—

FEE FIE FOH FFUMMMM

BLOODY RIDICULOUS.

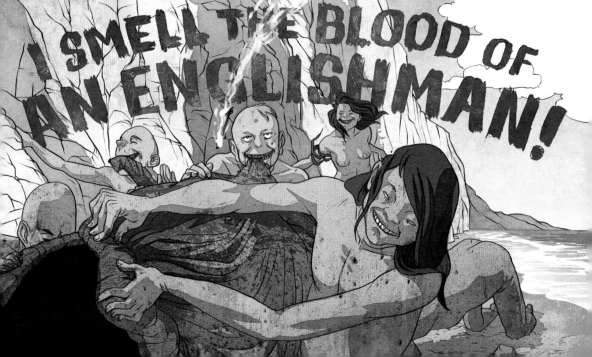

I SMELL THE BLOOD OF AN ENGLISHMAN!

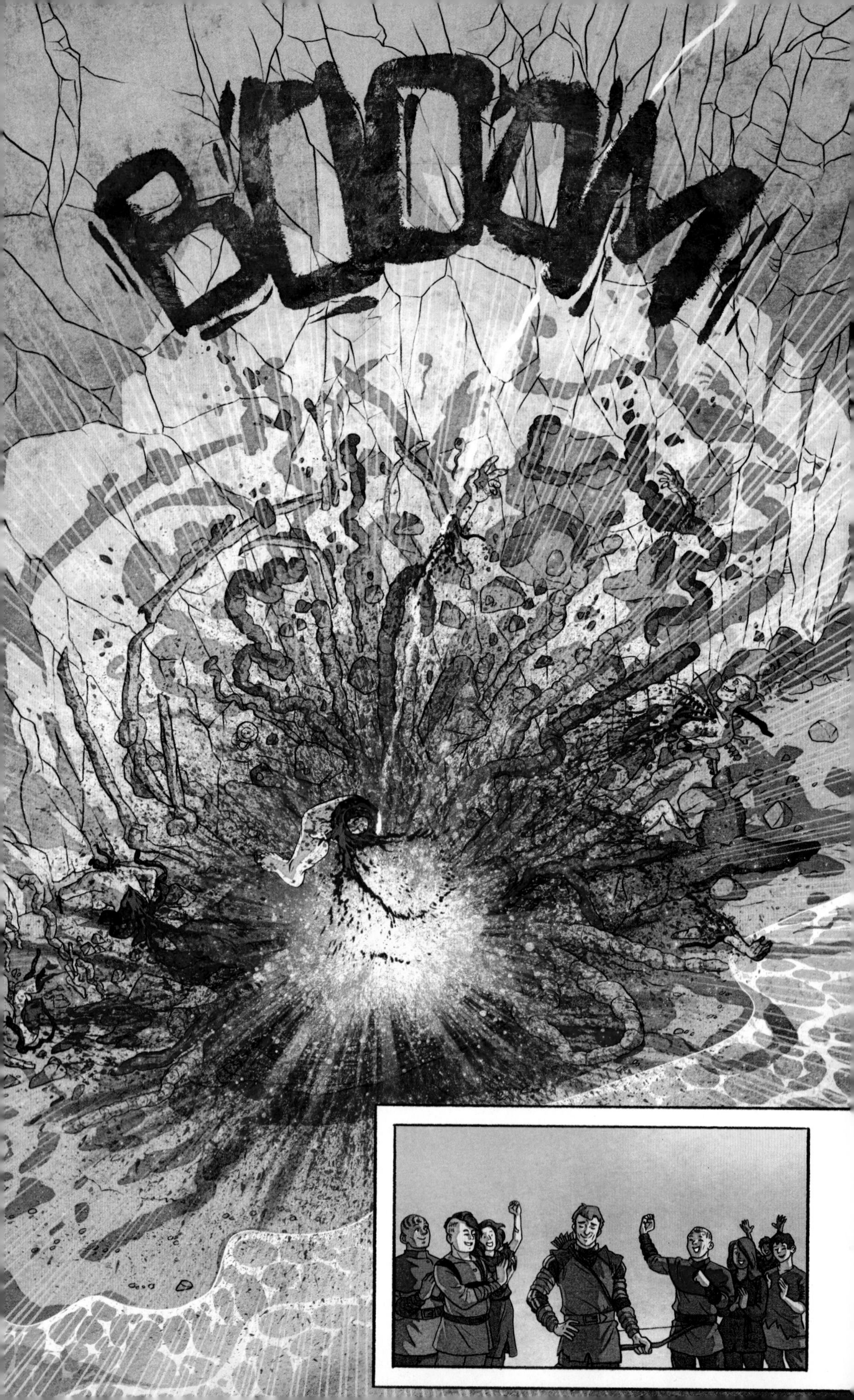
BOOM

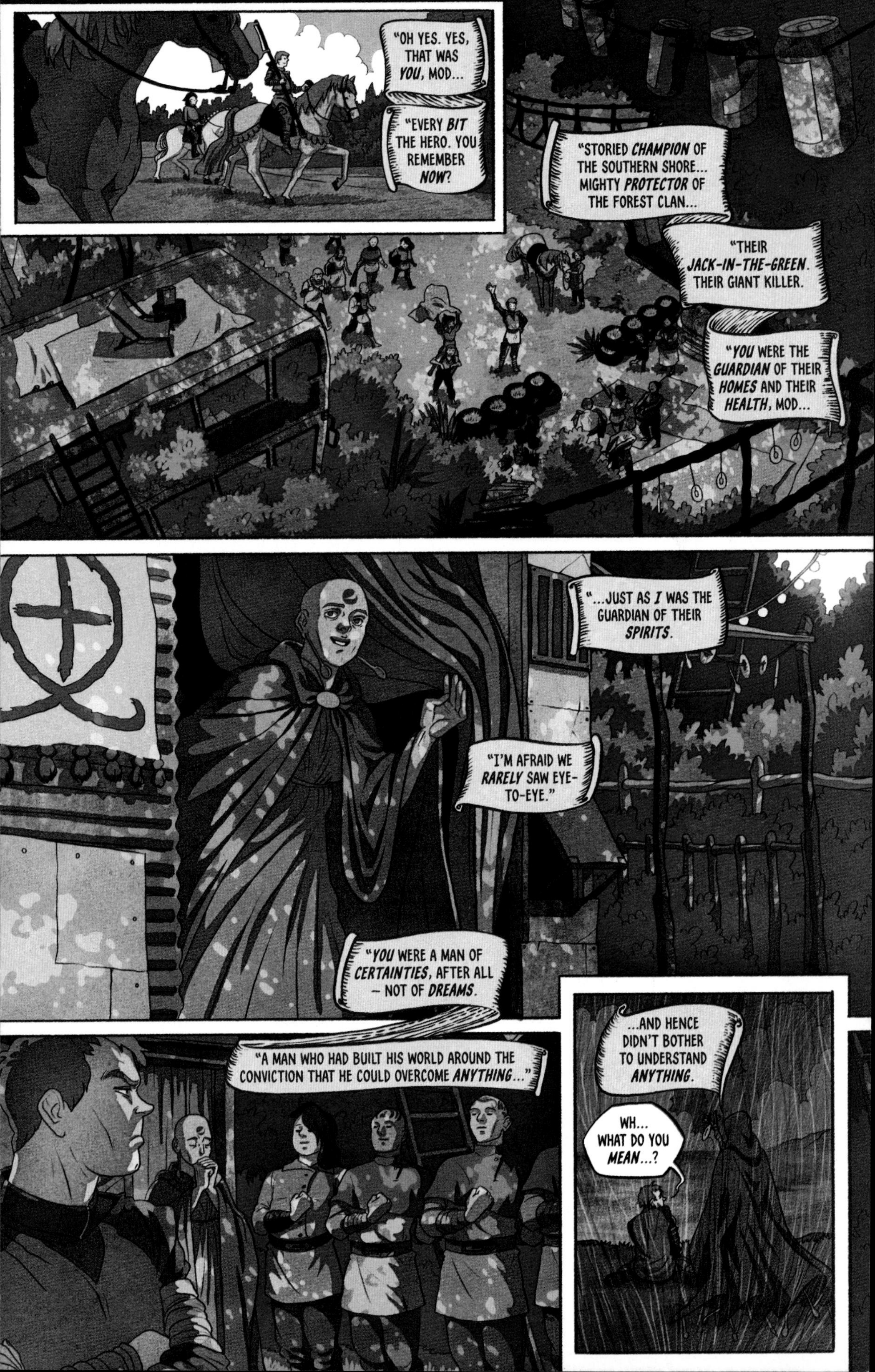
"OH YES. YES, THAT WAS YOU, MOD...
"EVERY BIT THE HERO. YOU REMEMBER NOW?
"STORIED CHAMPION OF THE SOUTHERN SHORE... MIGHTY PROTECTOR OF THE FOREST CLAN...
"THEIR JACK-IN-THE-GREEN. THEIR GIANT KILLER.
"YOU WERE THE GUARDIAN OF THEIR HOMES AND THEIR HEALTH, MOD...
"...JUST AS I WAS THE GUARDIAN OF THEIR SPIRITS.
"I'M AFRAID WE RARELY SAW EYE-TO-EYE."
"YOU WERE A MAN OF CERTAINTIES, AFTER ALL – NOT OF DREAMS.
"A MAN WHO HAD BUILT HIS WORLD AROUND THE CONVICTION THAT HE COULD OVERCOME ANYTHING..."
...AND HENCE DIDN'T BOTHER TO UNDERSTAND ANYTHING.
WH... WHAT DO YOU MEAN...?

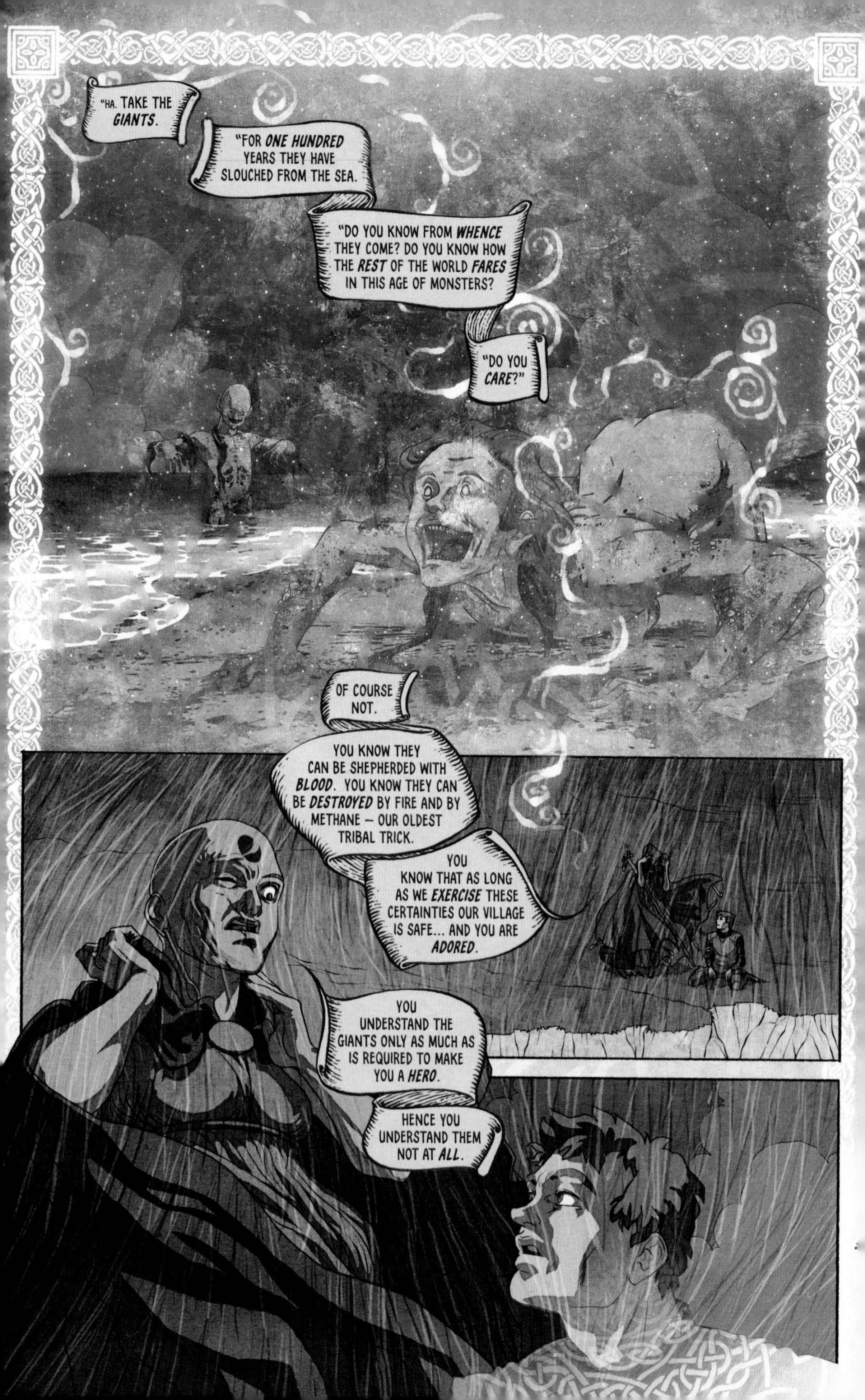
"HA. TAKE THE *GIANTS*.
"FOR *ONE HUNDRED* YEARS THEY HAVE SLOUCHED FROM THE SEA.
"DO YOU KNOW FROM *WHENCE* THEY COME? DO YOU KNOW HOW THE *REST* OF THE WORLD *FARES* IN THIS AGE OF MONSTERS?
"DO YOU *CARE*?"
OF COURSE NOT.
YOU KNOW THEY CAN BE SHEPHERDED WITH *BLOOD*. YOU KNOW THEY CAN BE *DESTROYED* BY FIRE AND BY METHANE — OUR OLDEST TRIBAL TRICK.
YOU KNOW THAT AS LONG AS WE *EXERCISE* THESE CERTAINTIES OUR VILLAGE IS SAFE... AND YOU ARE *ADORED*.
YOU UNDERSTAND THE GIANTS ONLY AS MUCH AS IS REQUIRED TO MAKE YOU A *HERO*.
HENCE YOU UNDERSTAND THEM NOT AT *ALL*.

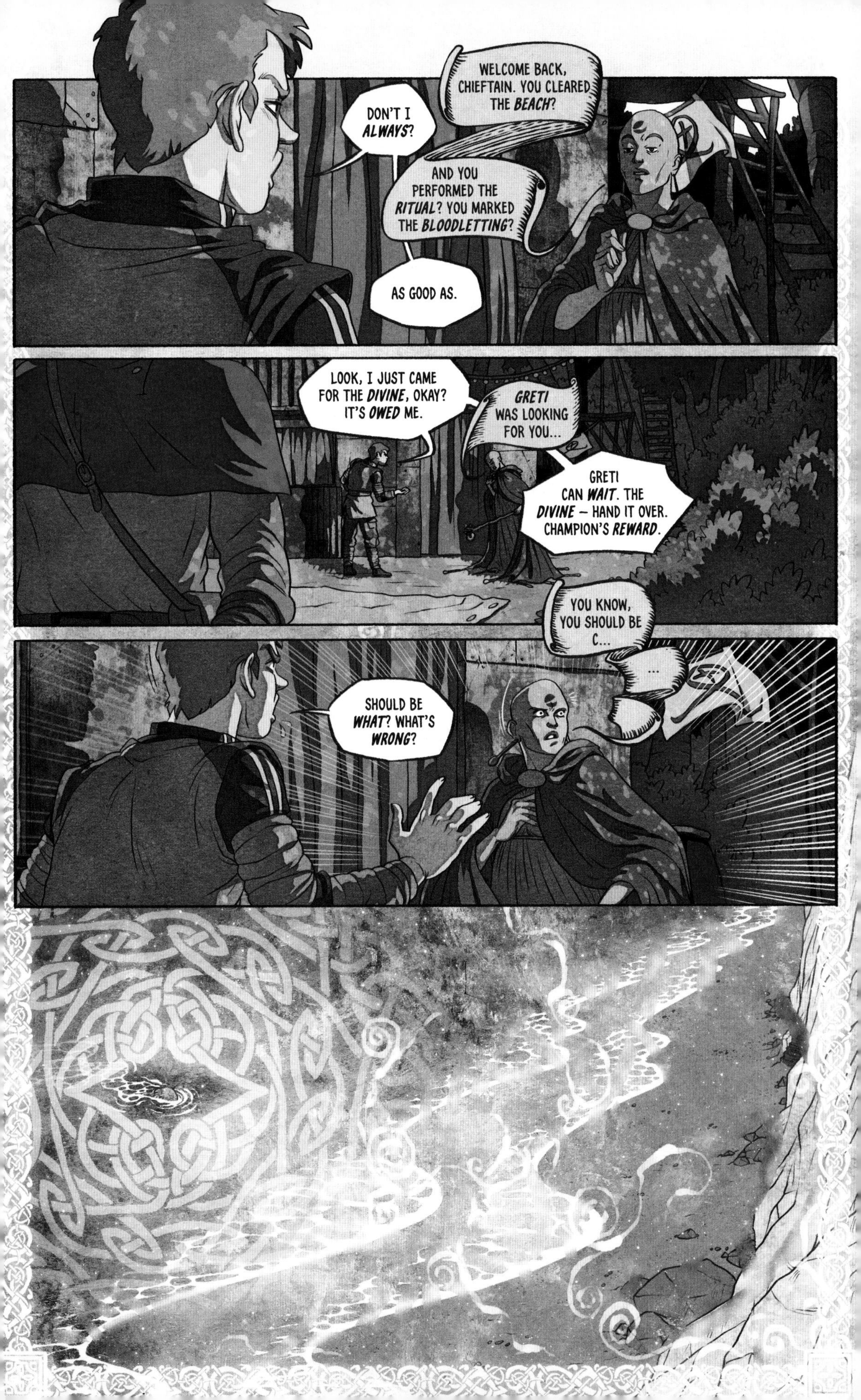
WELCOME BACK, CHIEFTAIN. YOU CLEARED THE BEACH?
DON'T I ALWAYS?
AND YOU PERFORMED THE RITUAL? YOU MARKED THE BLOODLETTING?
AS GOOD AS.
LOOK, I JUST CAME FOR THE DIVINE, OKAY? IT'S OWED ME.
GRETI WAS LOOKING FOR YOU...
GRETI CAN WAIT. THE DIVINE – HAND IT OVER. CHAMPION'S REWARD.
YOU KNOW, YOU SHOULD BE C...
...
SHOULD BE WHAT? WHAT'S WRONG?

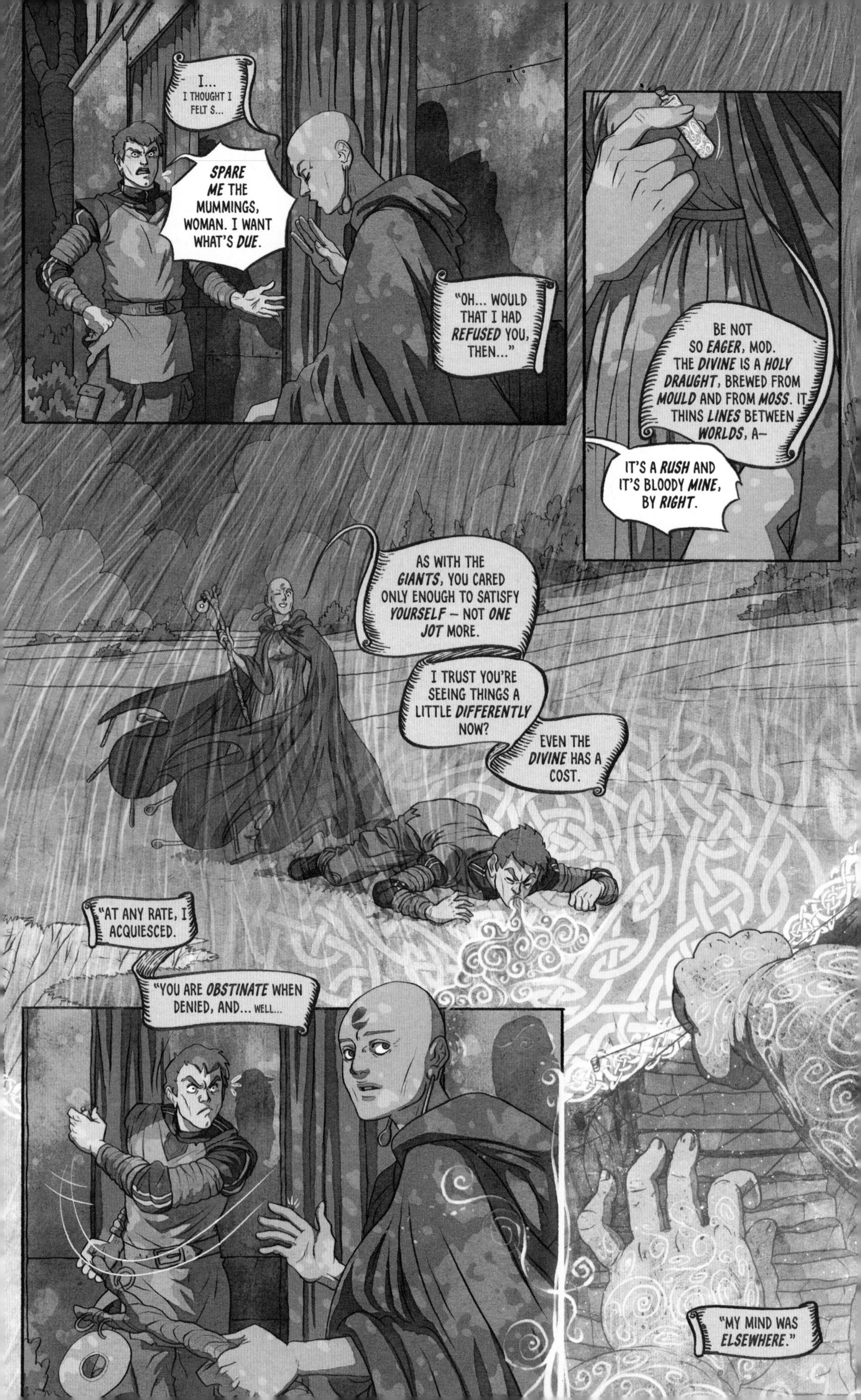
I... I THOUGHT I FELT S...
SPARE ME THE MUMMINGS, WOMAN. I WANT WHAT'S DUE.
"OH... WOULD THAT I HAD REFUSED YOU, THEN..."
BE NOT SO EAGER, MOD. THE DIVINE IS A HOLY DRAUGHT, BREWED FROM MOULD AND FROM MOSS. IT THINS LINES BETWEEN WORLDS, A—
IT'S A RUSH AND IT'S BLOODY MINE, BY RIGHT.
AS WITH THE GIANTS, YOU CARED ONLY ENOUGH TO SATISFY YOURSELF – NOT ONE JOT MORE.
I TRUST YOU'RE SEEING THINGS A LITTLE DIFFERENTLY NOW?
EVEN THE DIVINE HAS A COST.
"AT ANY RATE, I ACQUIESCED.
"YOU ARE OBSTINATE WHEN DENIED, AND... WELL...
"MY MIND WAS ELSEWHERE."

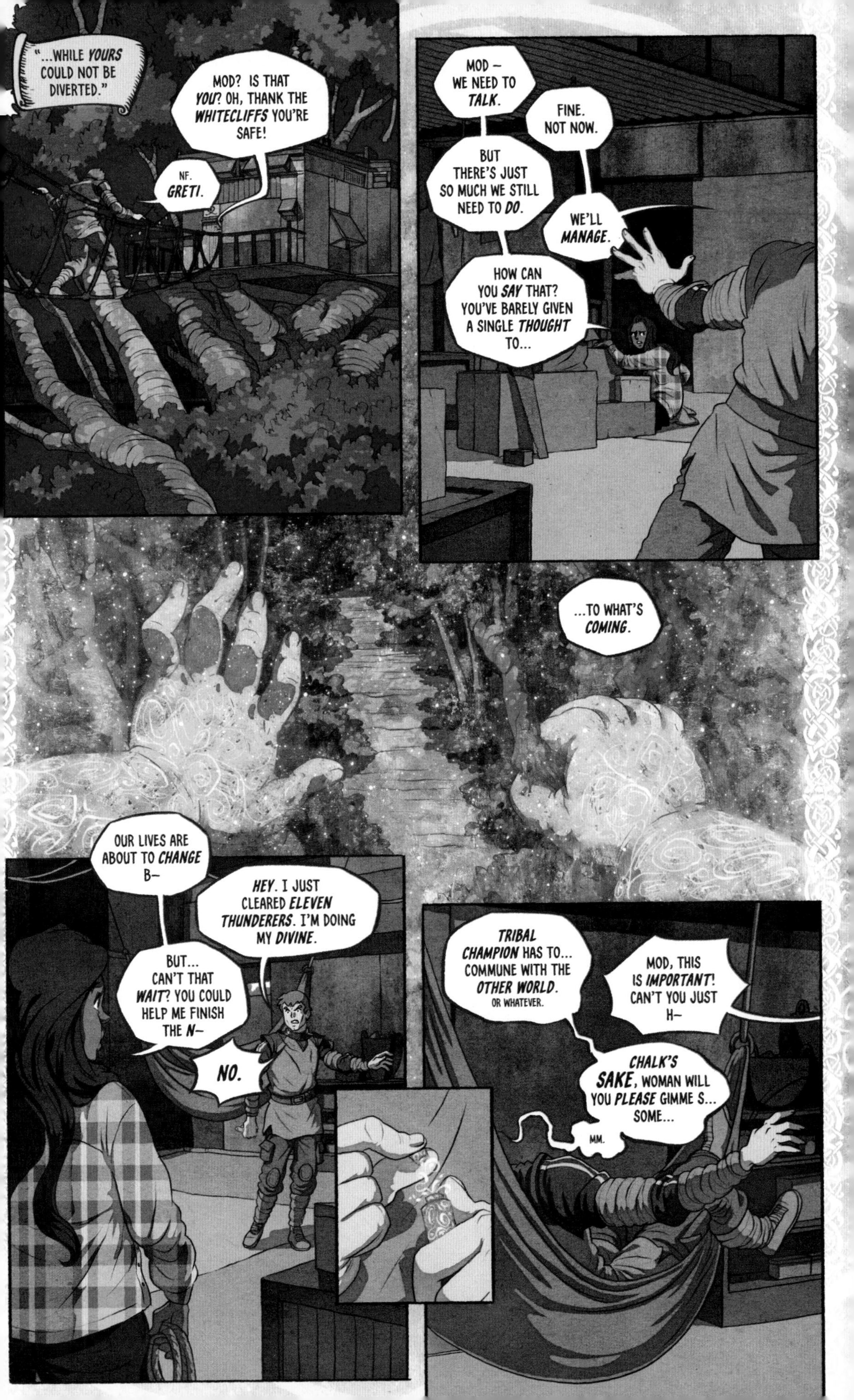
"...WHILE YOURS COULD NOT BE DIVERTED."
MOD? IS THAT YOU? OH, THANK THE WHITECLIFFS YOU'RE SAFE!
NF. GRETI.
MOD — WE NEED TO TALK.
FINE. NOT NOW.
BUT THERE'S JUST SO MUCH WE STILL NEED TO DO.
WE'LL MANAGE.
HOW CAN YOU SAY THAT? YOU'VE BARELY GIVEN A SINGLE THOUGHT TO...
...TO WHAT'S COMING.
OUR LIVES ARE ABOUT TO CHANGE B—
HEY. I JUST CLEARED ELEVEN THUNDERERS. I'M DOING MY DIVINE.
BUT... CAN'T THAT WAIT? YOU COULD HELP ME FINISH THE N—
NO.
TRIBAL CHAMPION HAS TO... COMMUNE WITH THE OTHER WORLD. OR WHATEVER.
MOD, THIS IS IMPORTANT! CAN'T YOU JUST H—
CHALK'S SAKE, WOMAN WILL YOU PLEASE GIMME S... SOME...
MM.

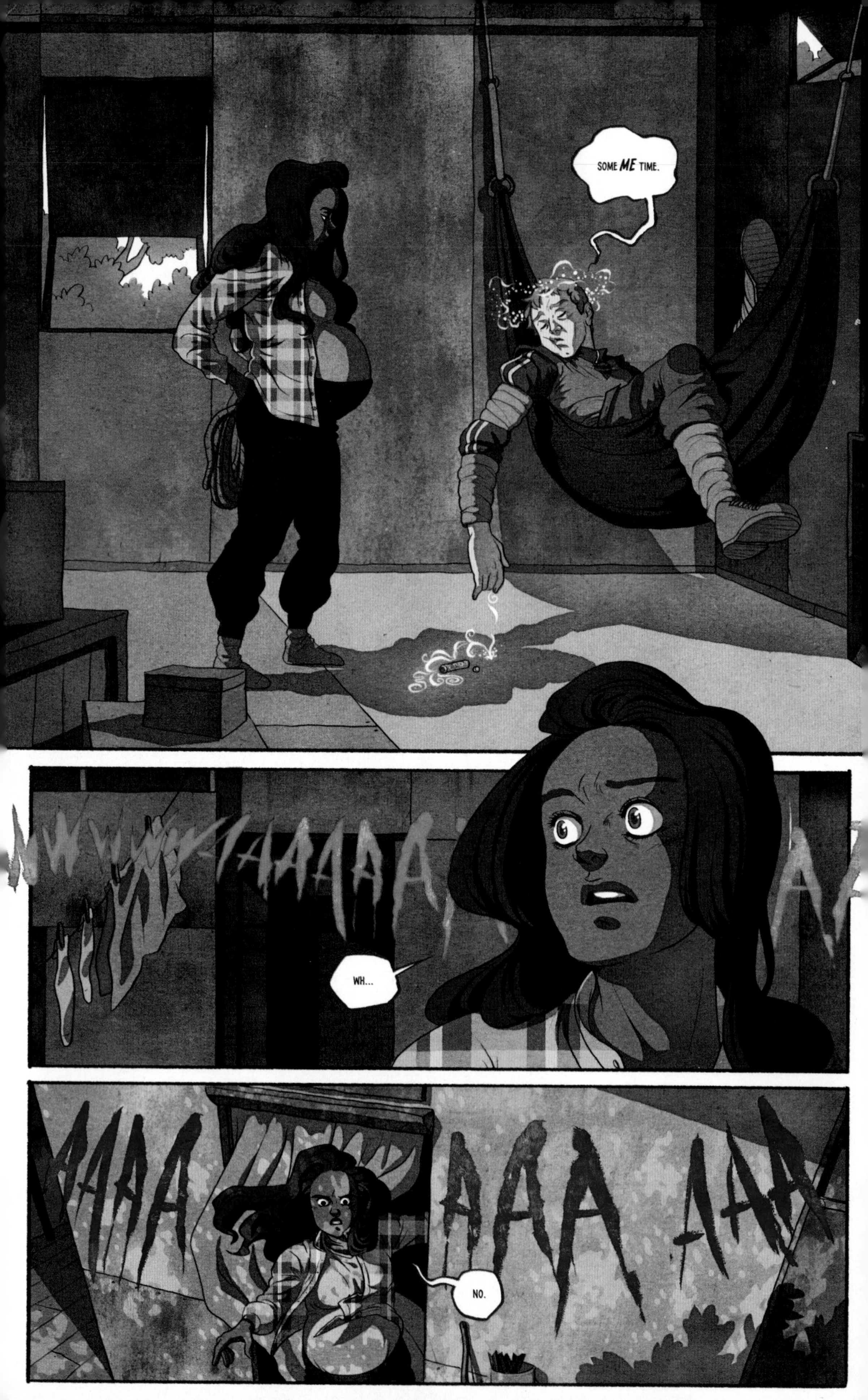
SOME ME TIME.
WH...
NO.

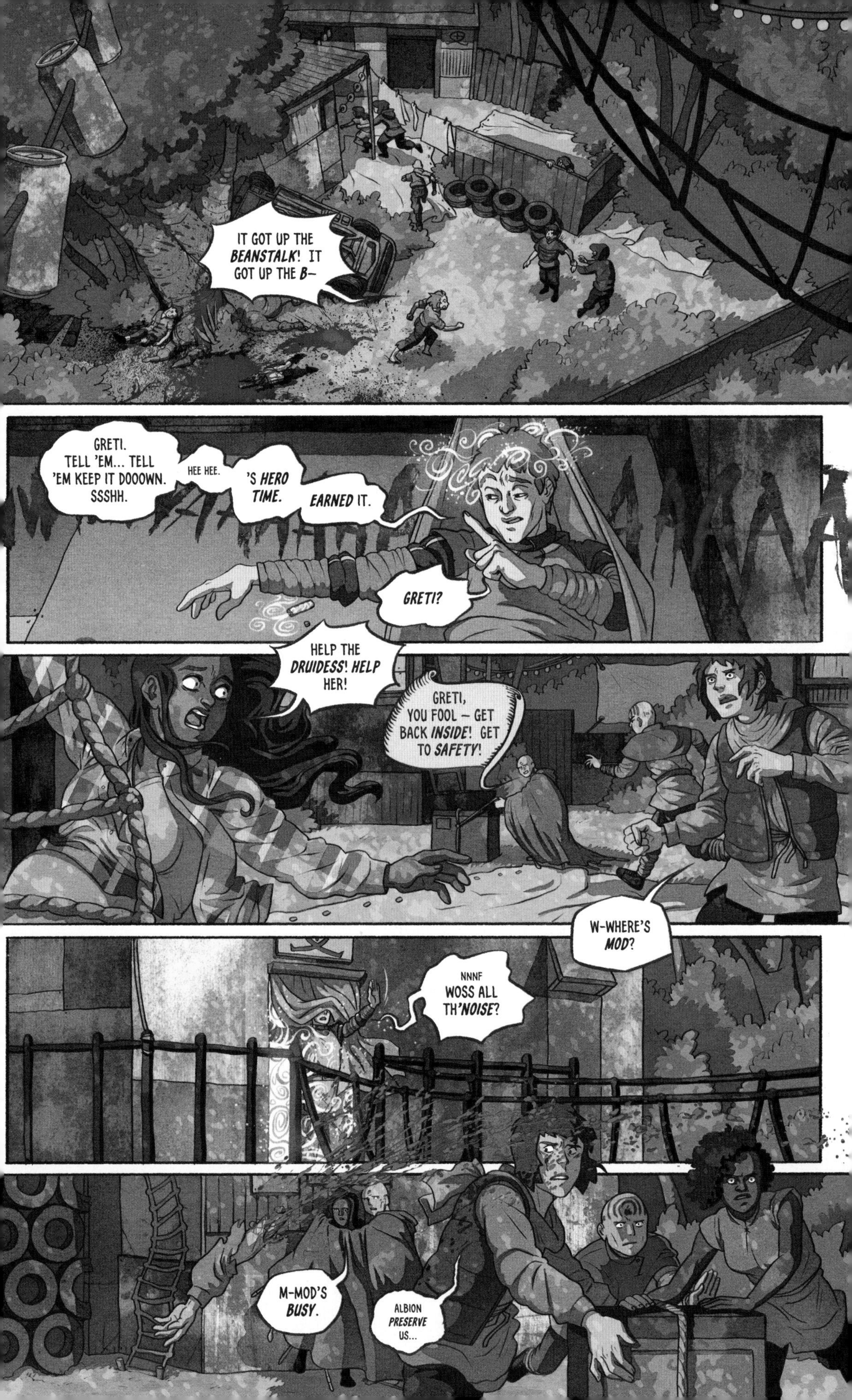

IT GOT UP THE *BEANSTALK*! IT GOT UP THE *B*–
GRETI. TELL 'EM... TELL 'EM KEEP IT DOOOWN. SSSHH.
HEE HEE.
'S *HERO TIME.*
EARNED IT.
GRETI?
HELP THE *DRUIDESS*! *HELP* HER!
GRETI, YOU FOOL – GET BACK *INSIDE*! GET TO *SAFETY*!
W-WHERE'S *MOD*?
NNNF WOSS ALL TH'*NOISE*?
M-MOD'S *BUSY*.
ALBION *PRESERVE* US...

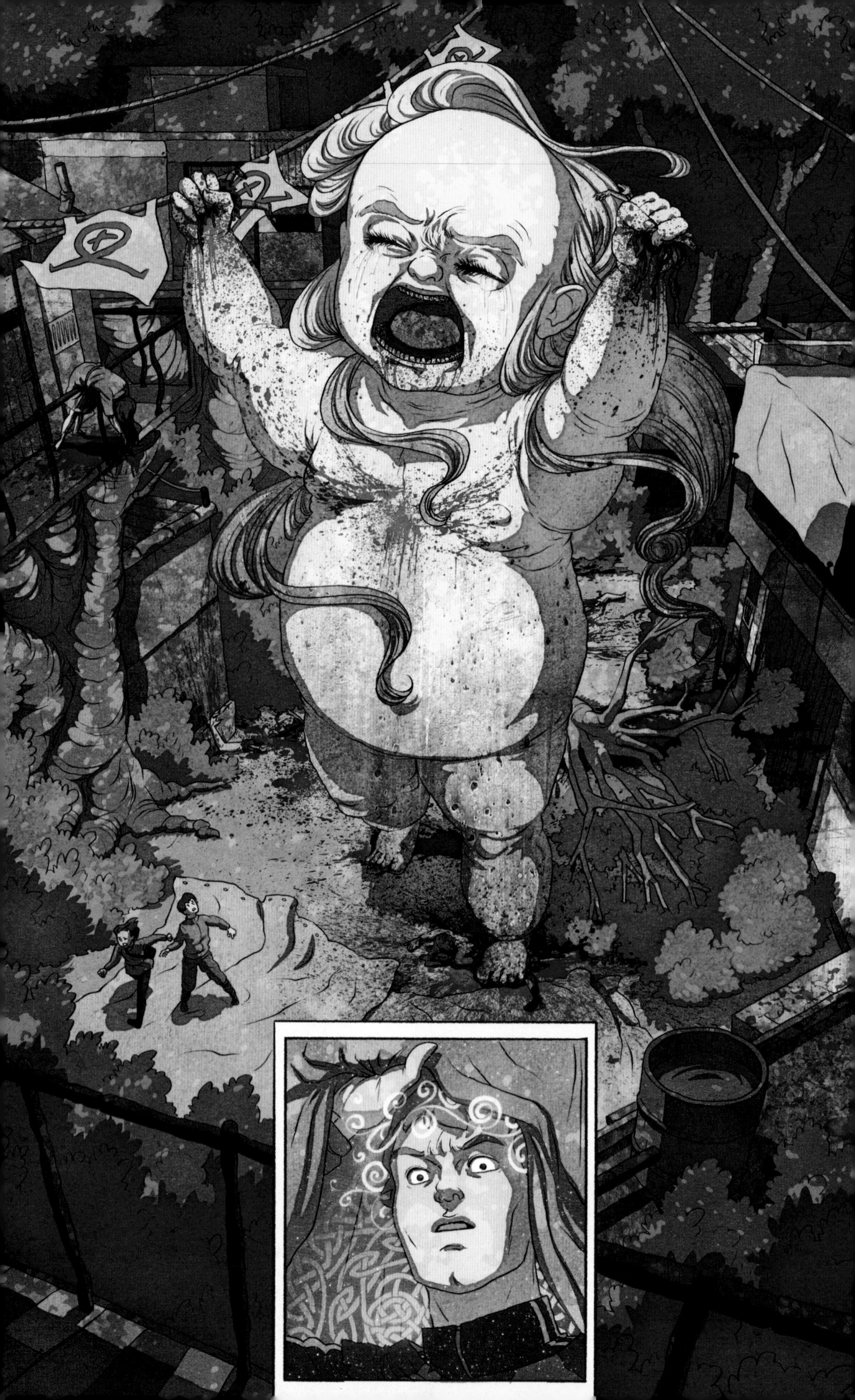

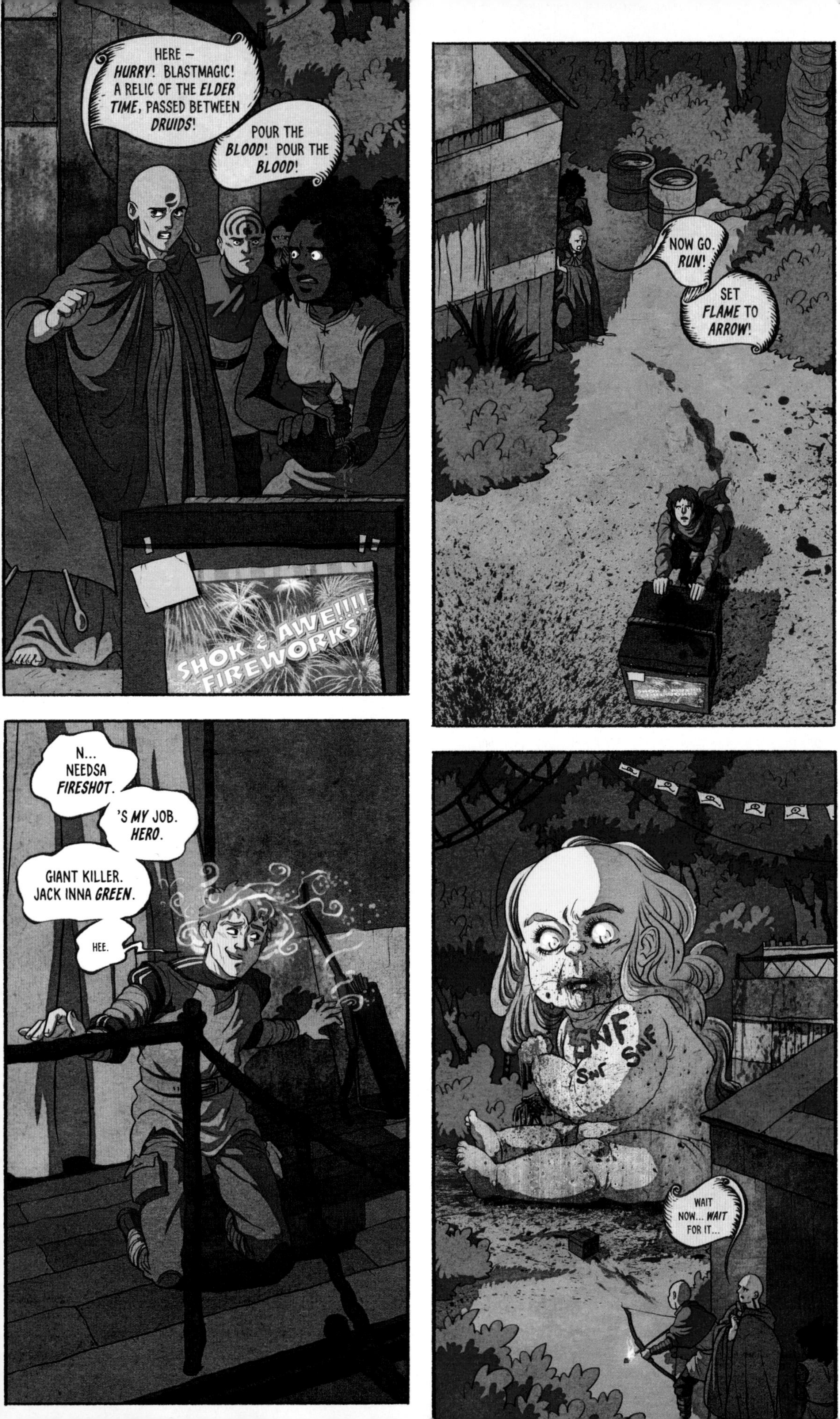
HERE – *HURRY*! BLASTMAGIC! A RELIC OF THE *ELDER TIME*, PASSED BETWEEN *DRUIDS*!
POUR THE *BLOOD*! POUR THE *BLOOD*!
SHOK & AWE!!!! FIREWORKS
NOW GO. *RUN*!
SET *FLAME TO ARROW*!
N... NEEDSA *FIRESHOT*.
'S *MY* JOB. *HERO*.
GIANT KILLER. JACK INNA *GREEN*.
HEE.
SNF
SNF SNF
WAIT NOW... *WAIT* FOR IT...

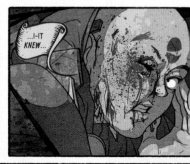

...I-IT KNEW...

THE NURSERY. SWEET CHURCHILL, IT'S GOING FOR THE NURSERY! THE CHILDREN! SOMEBODY DO S—

HEY!!

F-FEE.

FIE.

FOH.

FUMMM...

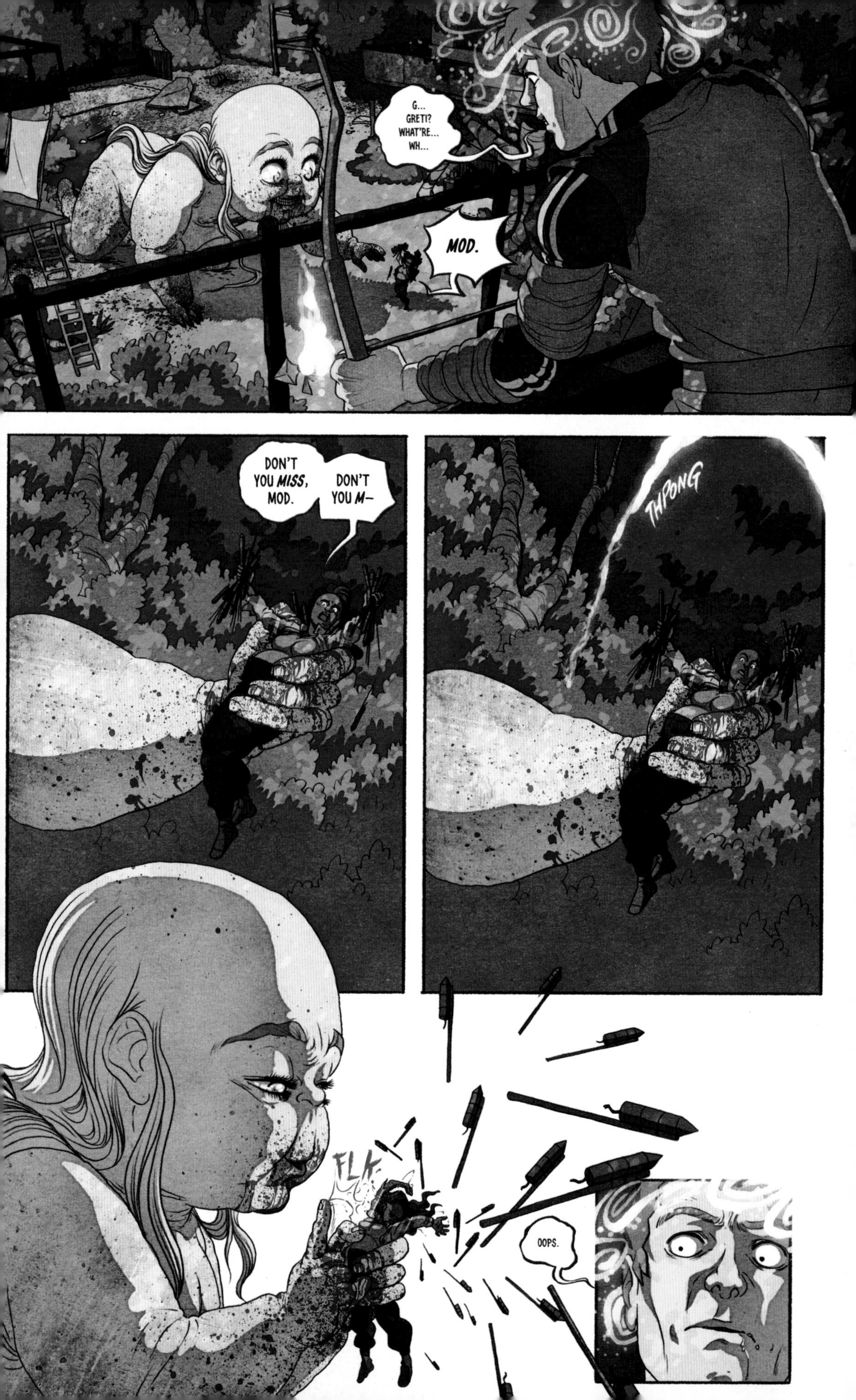
G... GRETI? WHAT'RE... WH...
MOD.
DON'T YOU MISS, MOD.
DON'T YOU M—
THPONG
FLK.
OOPS.

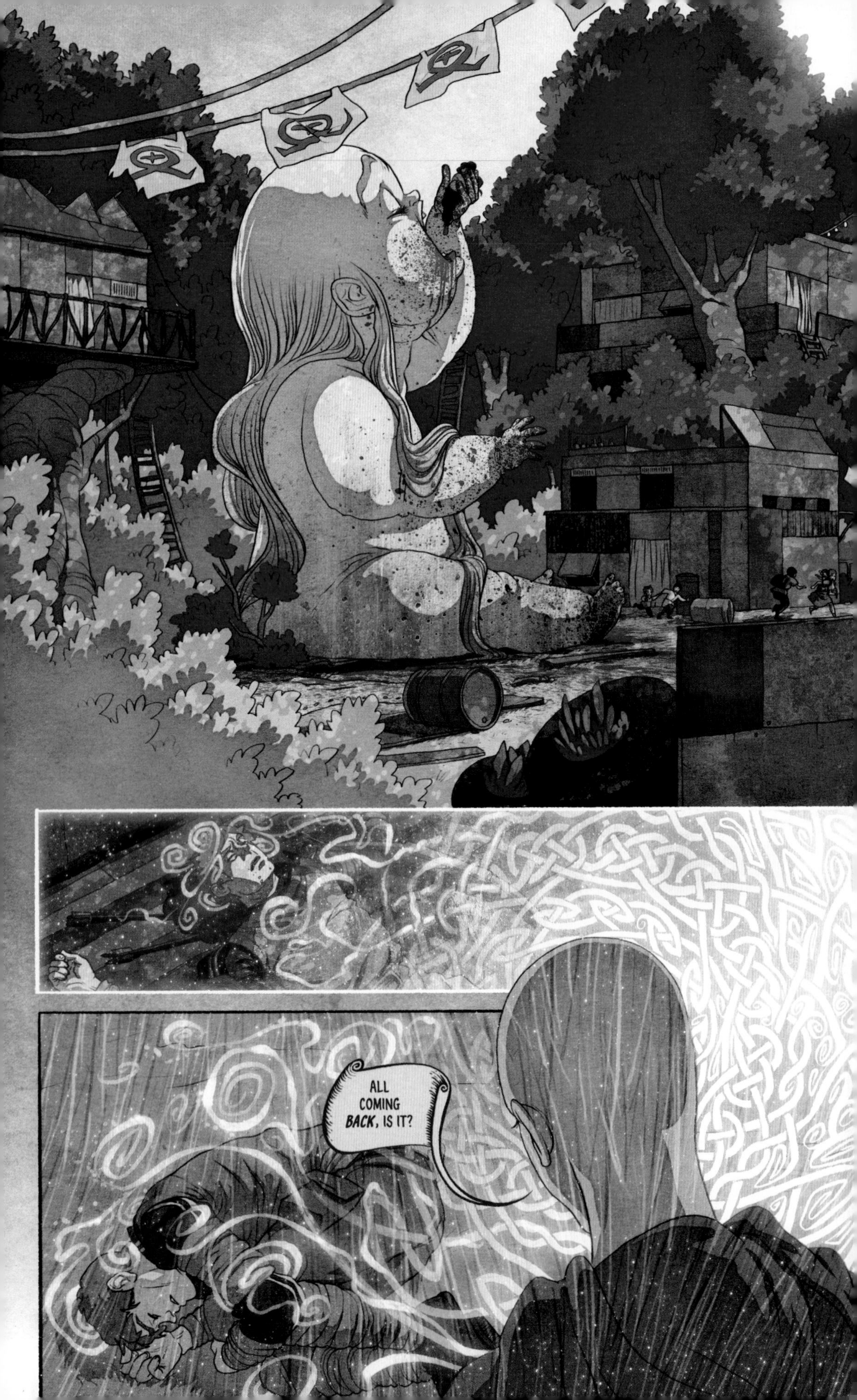
ALL COMING BACK, IS IT?

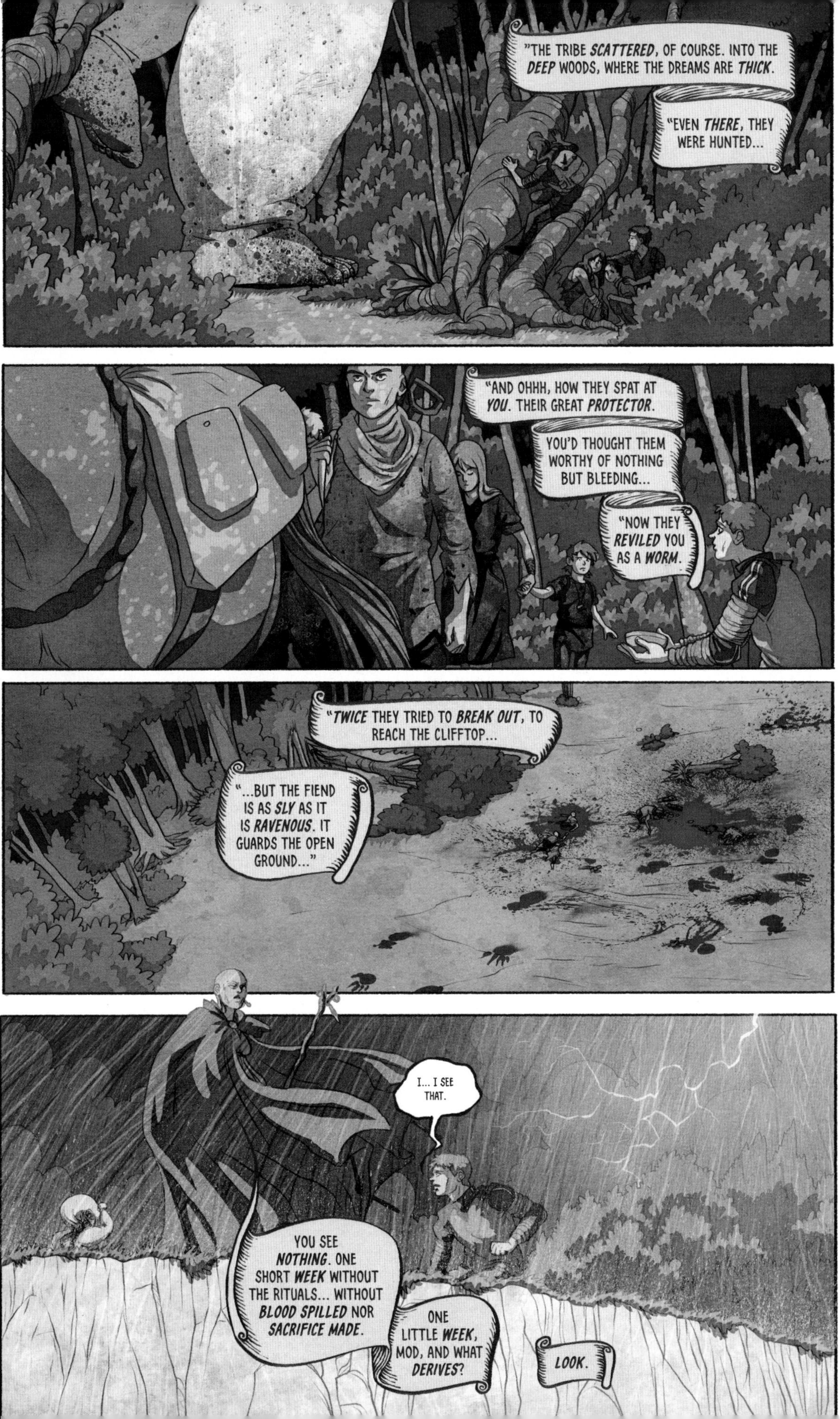
"THE TRIBE *SCATTERED*, OF COURSE. INTO THE *DEEP* WOODS, WHERE THE DREAMS ARE *THICK*.
"EVEN *THERE*, THEY WERE HUNTED...
"AND OHHH, HOW THEY SPAT AT *YOU*. THEIR GREAT *PROTECTOR*.
YOU'D THOUGHT THEM WORTHY OF NOTHING BUT BLEEDING...
"NOW THEY *REVILED* YOU AS A *WORM*.
"*TWICE* THEY TRIED TO *BREAK OUT*, TO REACH THE CLIFFTOP...
"...BUT THE FIEND IS AS *SLY* AS IT IS *RAVENOUS*. IT GUARDS THE OPEN GROUND..."
I... I SEE THAT.
YOU SEE *NOTHING*. ONE SHORT *WEEK* WITHOUT THE RITUALS... WITHOUT *BLOOD SPILLED* NOR *SACRIFICE MADE*.
ONE LITTLE *WEEK*, MOD, AND WHAT *DERIVES*?
LOOK.

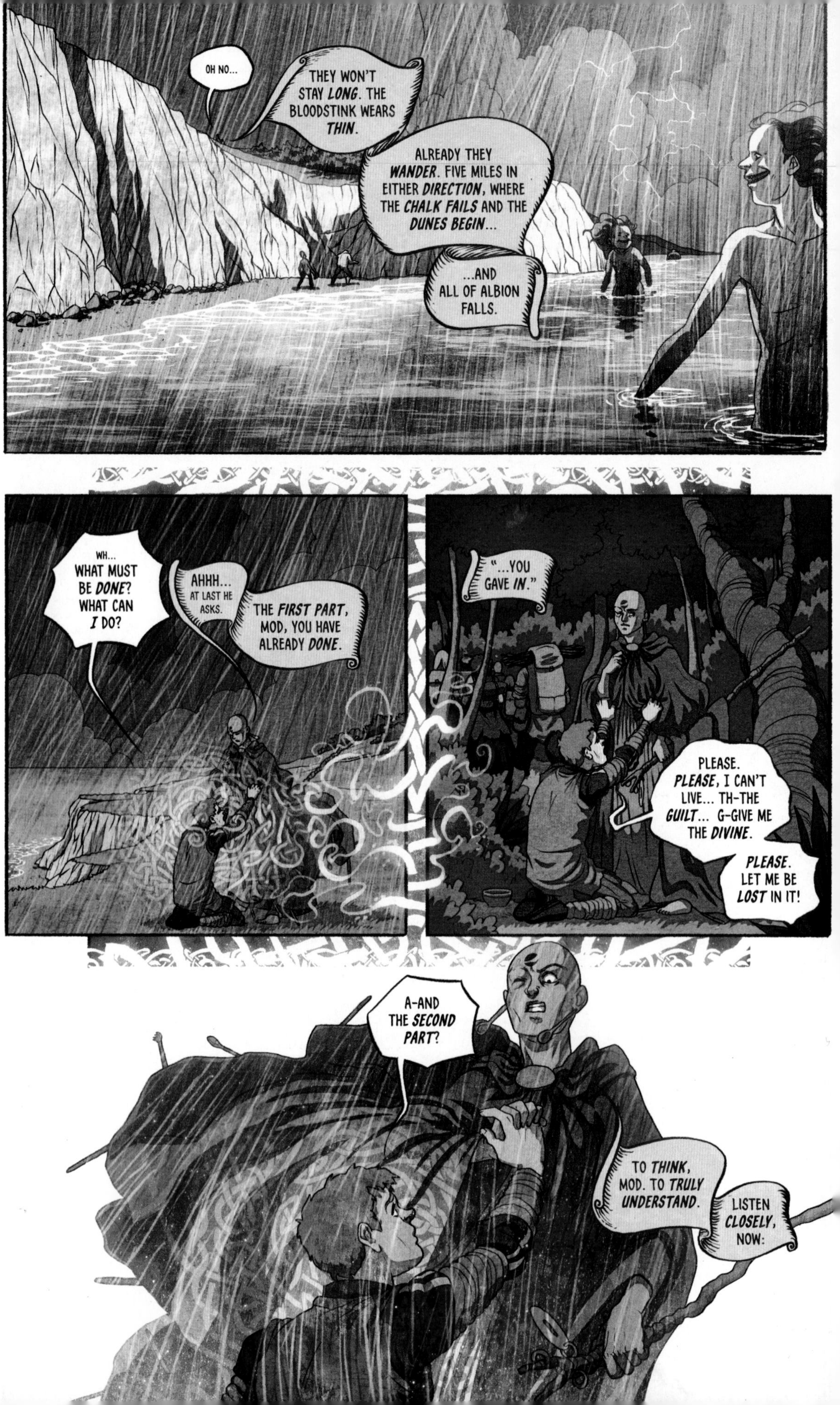
OH NO...
THEY WON'T STAY LONG. THE BLOODSTINK WEARS THIN.
ALREADY THEY WANDER. FIVE MILES IN EITHER DIRECTION, WHERE THE CHALK FAILS AND THE DUNES BEGIN...
...AND ALL OF ALBION FALLS.
WH... WHAT MUST BE DONE? WHAT CAN I DO?
AHHH... AT LAST HE ASKS.
THE FIRST PART, MOD, YOU HAVE ALREADY DONE.
"...YOU GAVE IN."
PLEASE. PLEASE, I CAN'T LIVE... TH-THE GUILT... G-GIVE ME THE DIVINE.
PLEASE. LET ME BE LOST IN IT!
A-AND THE SECOND PART?
TO THINK, MOD. TO TRULY UNDERSTAND.
LISTEN CLOSELY, NOW:

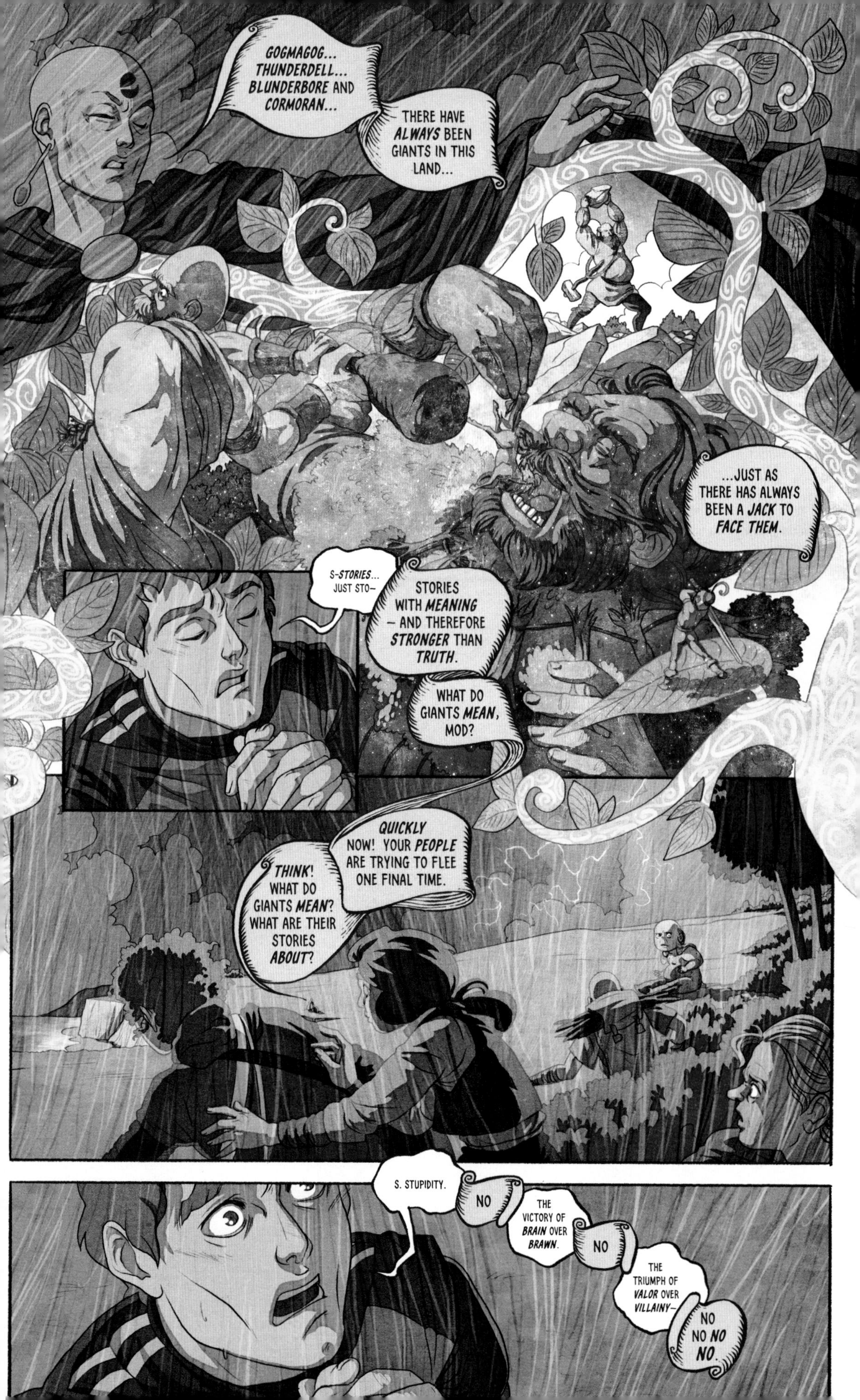
GOGMAGOG... THUNDERDELL... BLUNDERBORE AND CORMORAN...
THERE HAVE ALWAYS BEEN GIANTS IN THIS LAND...
...JUST AS THERE HAS ALWAYS BEEN A JACK TO FACE THEM.
S-STORIES... JUST STO—
STORIES WITH MEANING — AND THEREFORE STRONGER THAN TRUTH.
WHAT DO GIANTS MEAN, MOD?
QUICKLY NOW! YOUR PEOPLE ARE TRYING TO FLEE ONE FINAL TIME.
THINK! WHAT DO GIANTS MEAN? WHAT ARE THEIR STORIES ABOUT?
S. STUPIDITY.
NO
THE VICTORY OF BRAIN OVER BRAWN.
NO
THE TRIUMPH OF VALOR OVER VILLAINY—
NO NO NO NO.

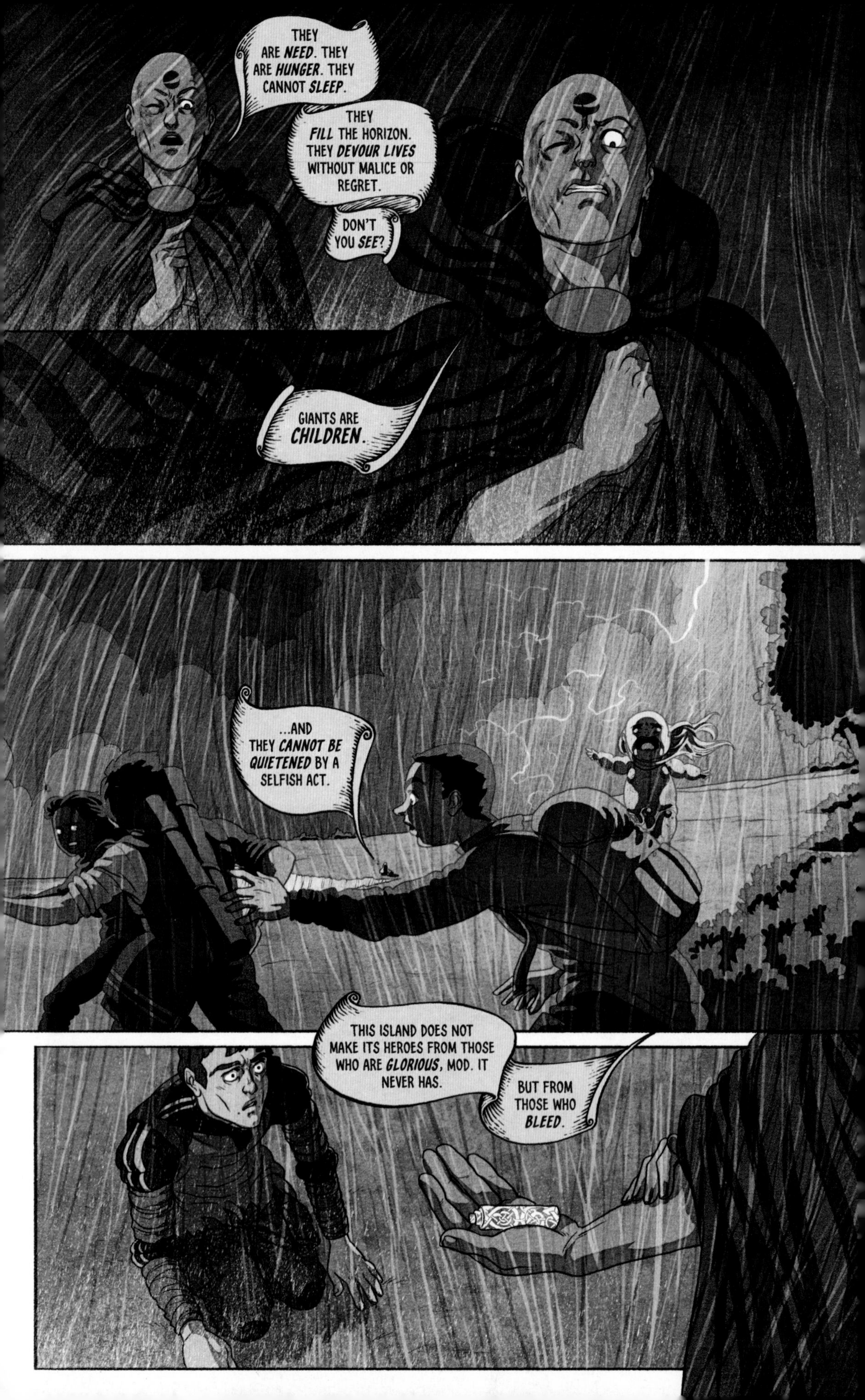
THEY ARE *NEED*. THEY ARE *HUNGER*. THEY CANNOT *SLEEP*.
THEY *FILL* THE HORIZON. THEY *DEVOUR LIVES* WITHOUT MALICE OR REGRET.
DON'T YOU *SEE*?
GIANTS ARE ***CHILDREN***.
...AND THEY *CANNOT BE QUIETENED* BY A SELFISH ACT.
THIS ISLAND DOES NOT MAKE ITS HEROES FROM THOSE WHO ARE *GLORIOUS*, MOD. IT NEVER HAS.
BUT FROM THOSE WHO *BLEED*.

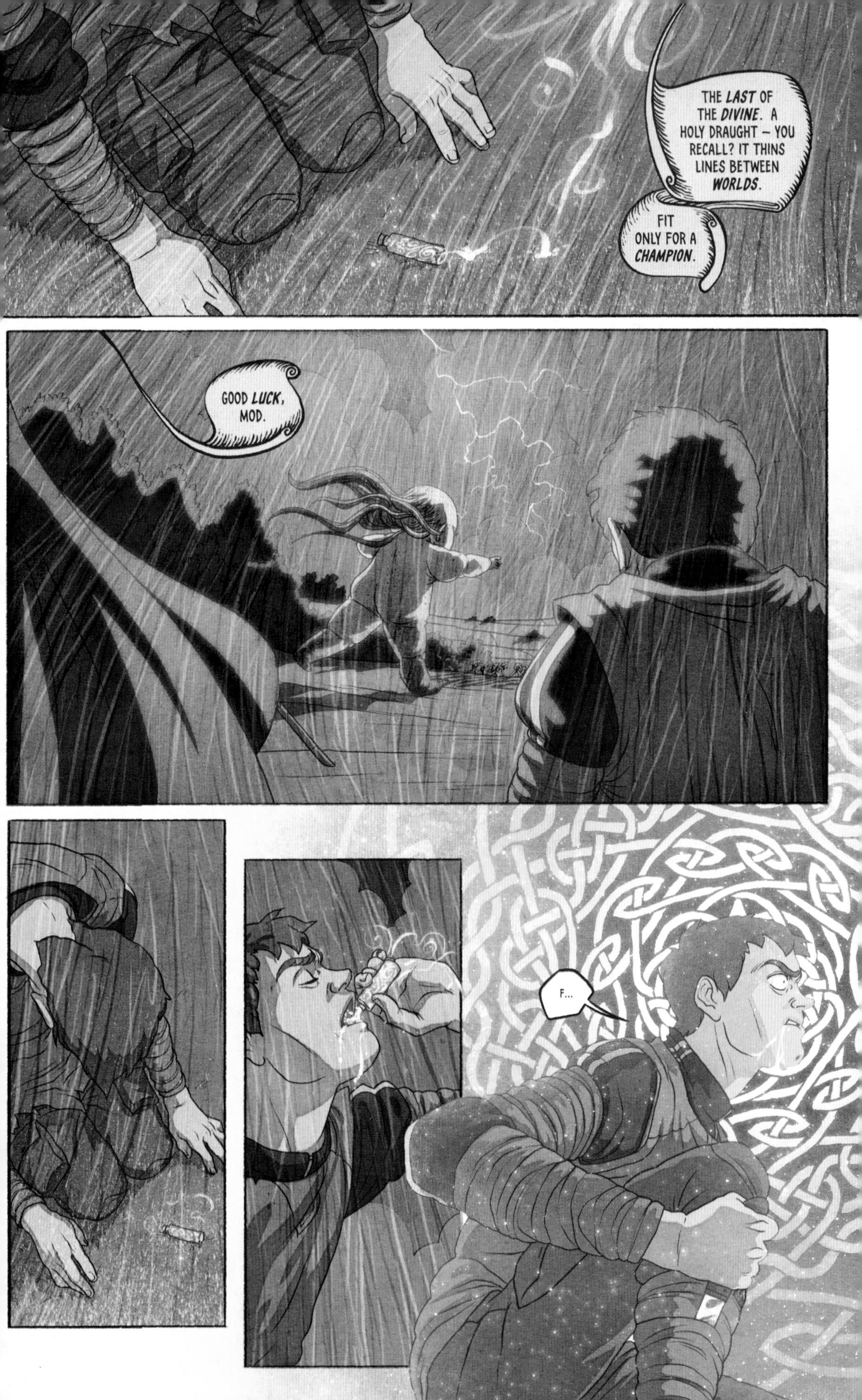
THE LAST OF THE DIVINE. A HOLY DRAUGHT – YOU RECALL? IT THINS LINES BETWEEN WORLDS.
FIT ONLY FOR A CHAMPION.
GOOD LUCK, MOD.
F...

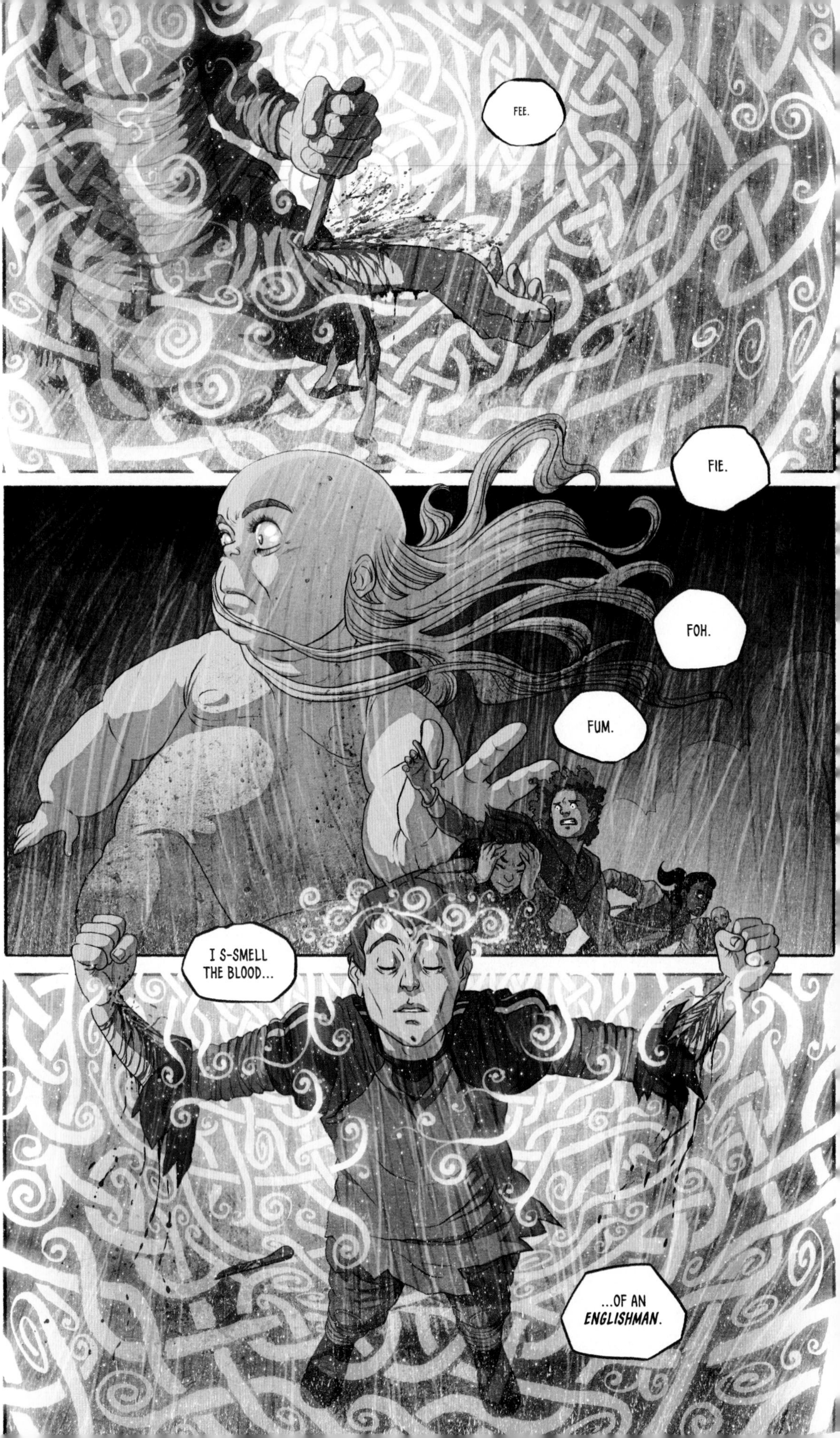
FEE.
FIE.
FOH.
FUM.
I S-SMELL THE BLOOD...
...OF AN *ENGLISHMAN*.

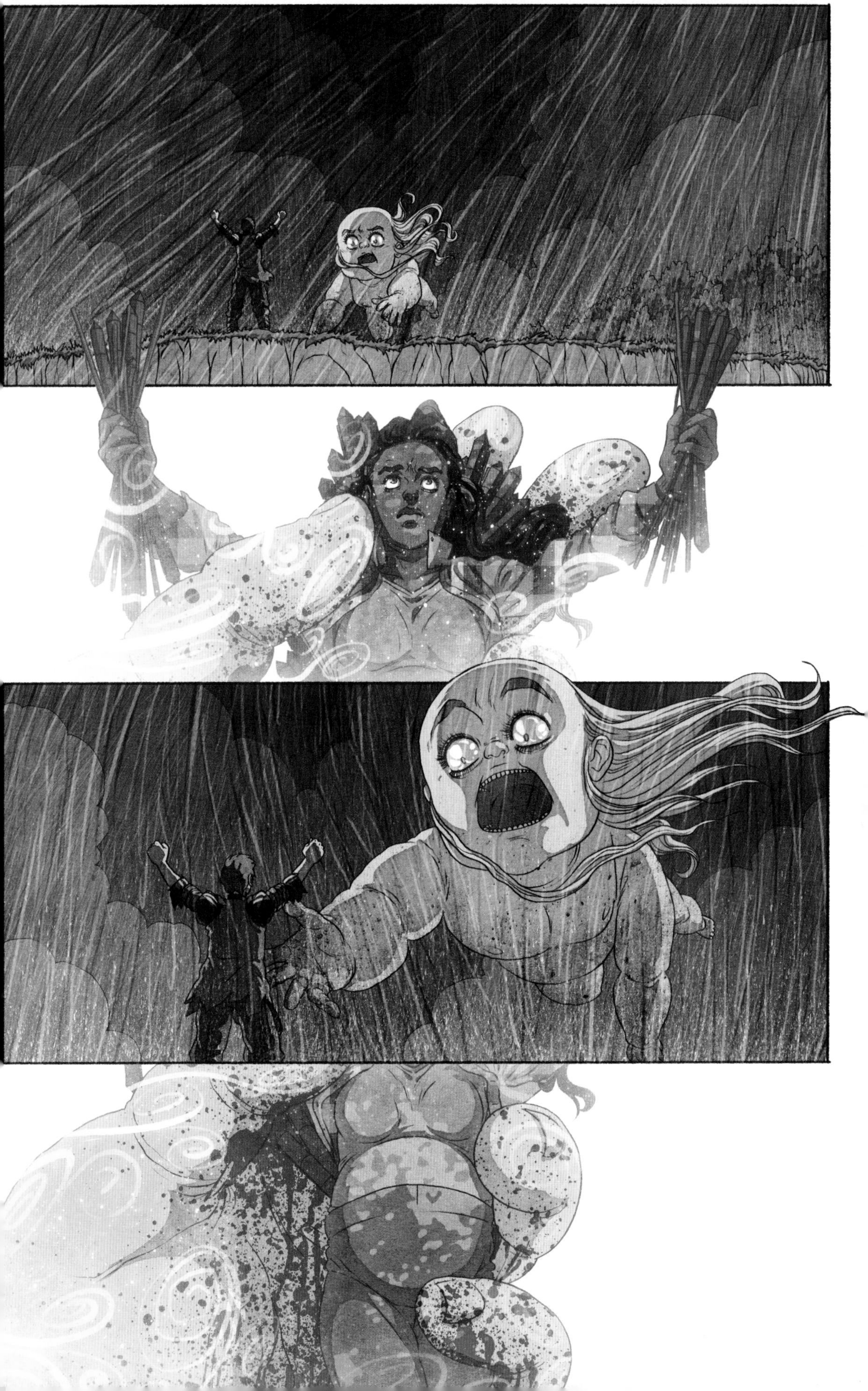

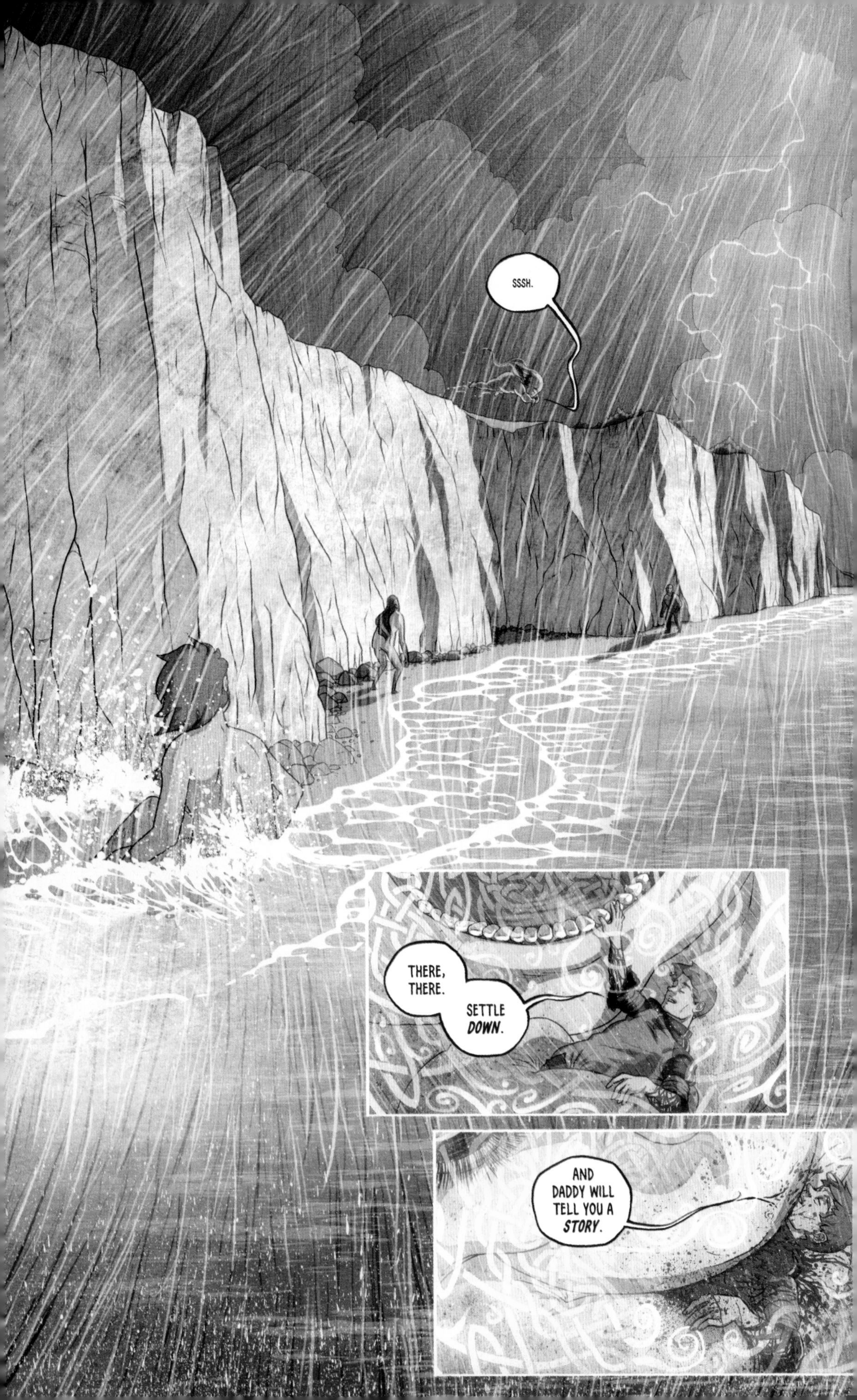
SSSH.
THERE, THERE.
SETTLE *DOWN*.
AND DADDY WILL TELL YOU A *STORY*.

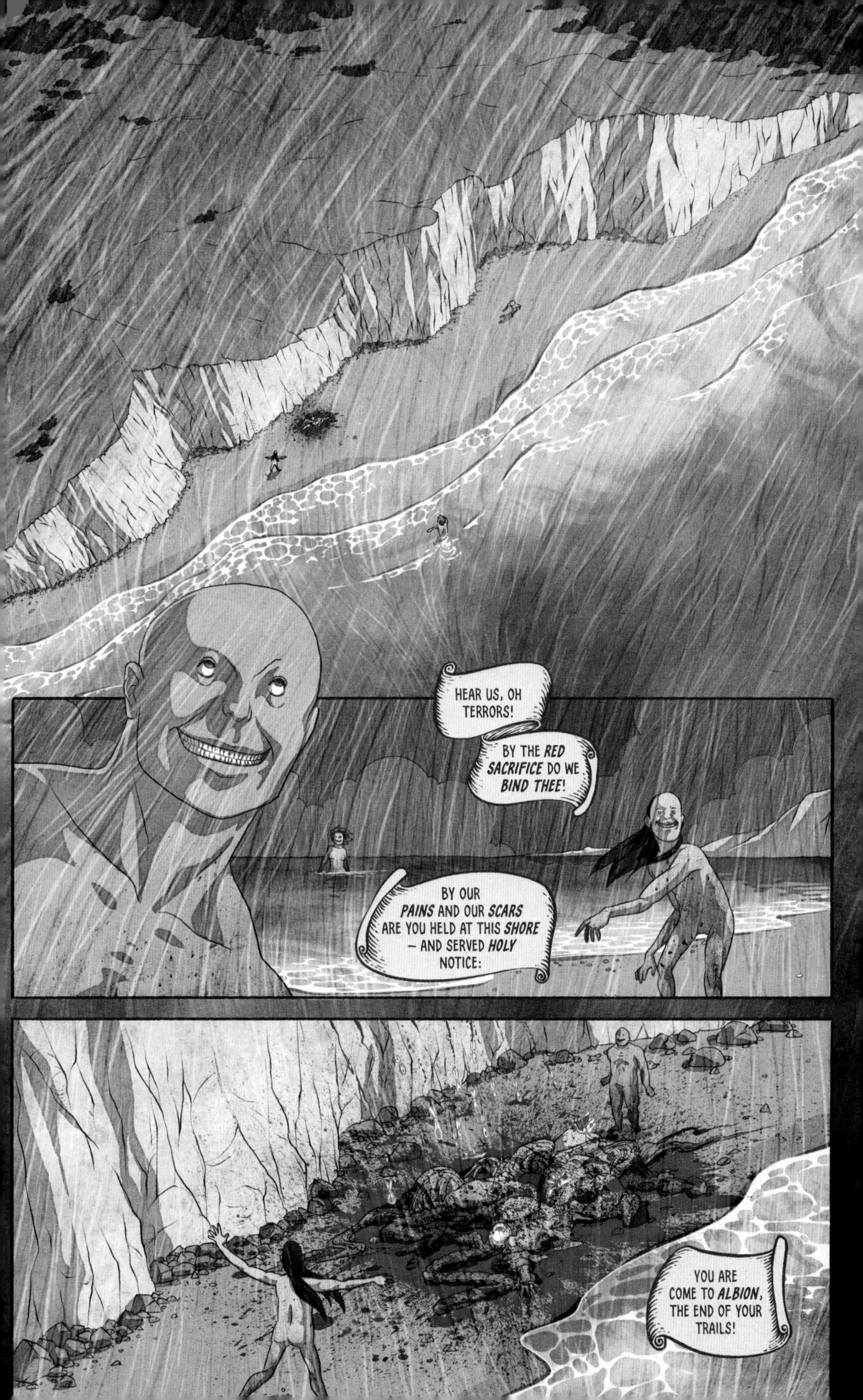
HEAR US, OH TERRORS!
BY THE *RED SACRIFICE* DO WE *BIND THEE*!
BY OUR *PAINS* AND OUR *SCARS* ARE YOU HELD AT THIS *SHORE* – AND SERVED *HOLY* NOTICE:
YOU ARE COME TO *ALBION*, THE END OF YOUR TRAILS!

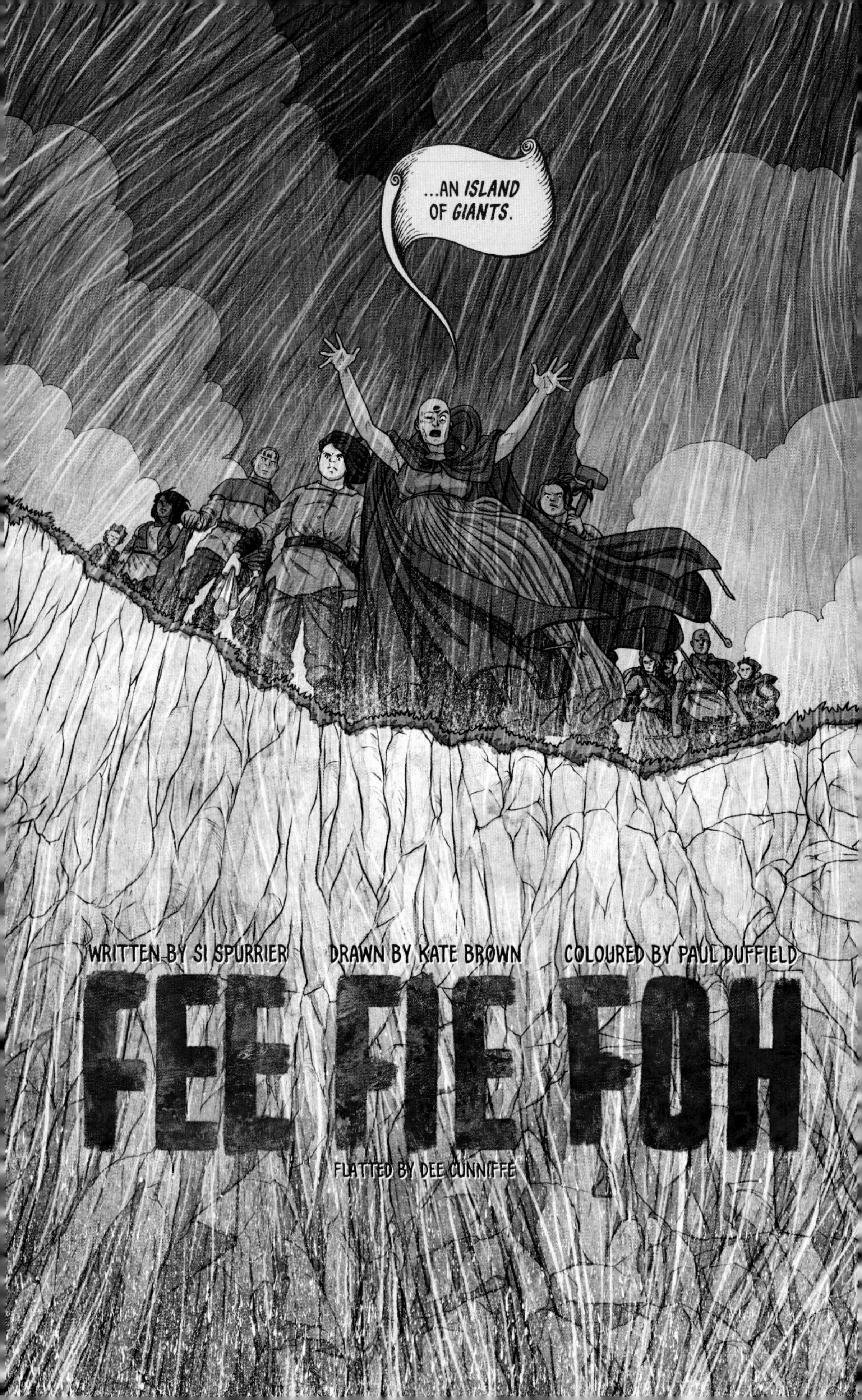
...AN ISLAND OF GIANTS.
WRITTEN BY SI SPURRIER
DRAWN BY KATE BROWN
COLOURED BY PAUL DUFFIELD
FEE FIE FOH
FLATTED BY DEE CUNNIFFE

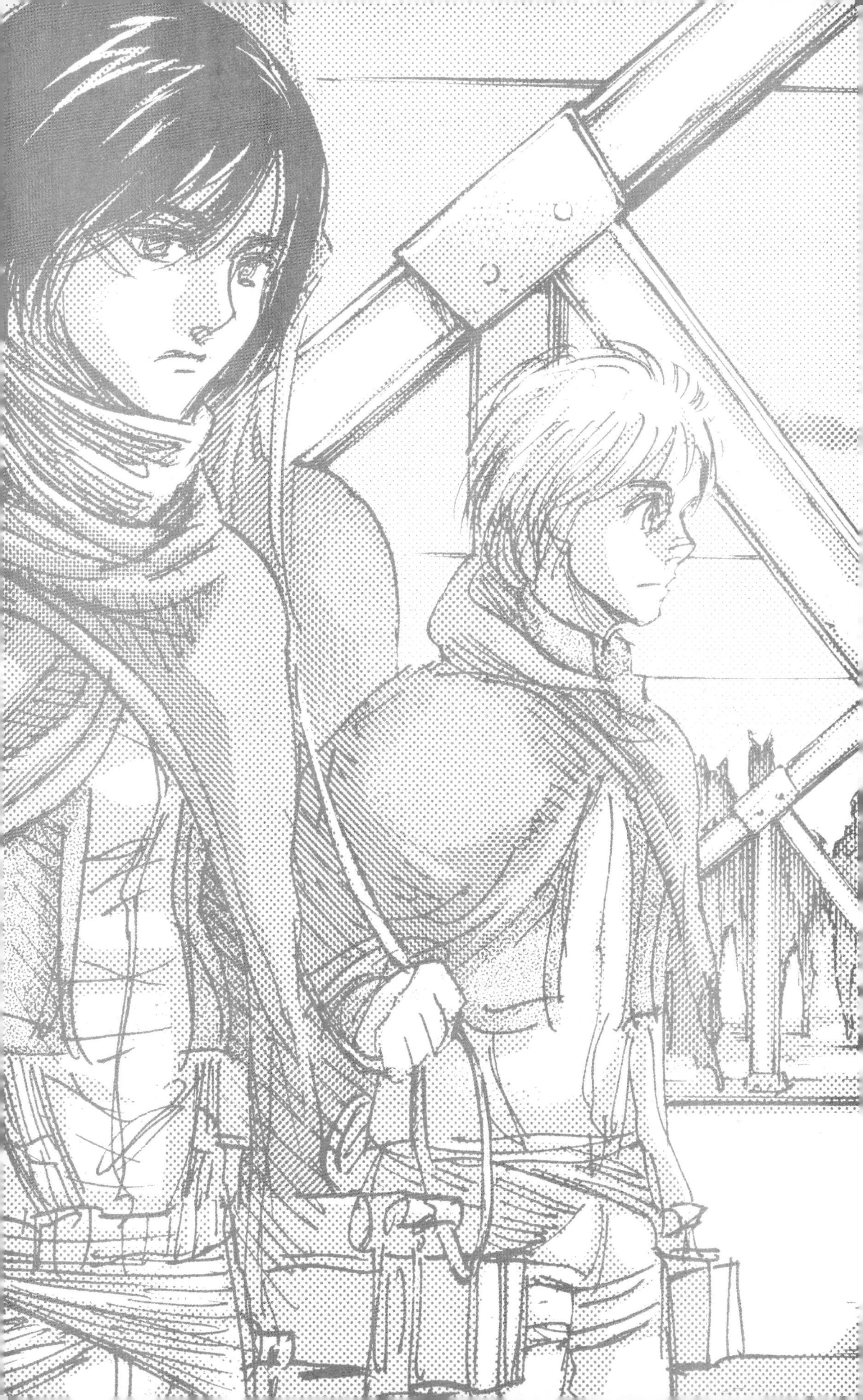

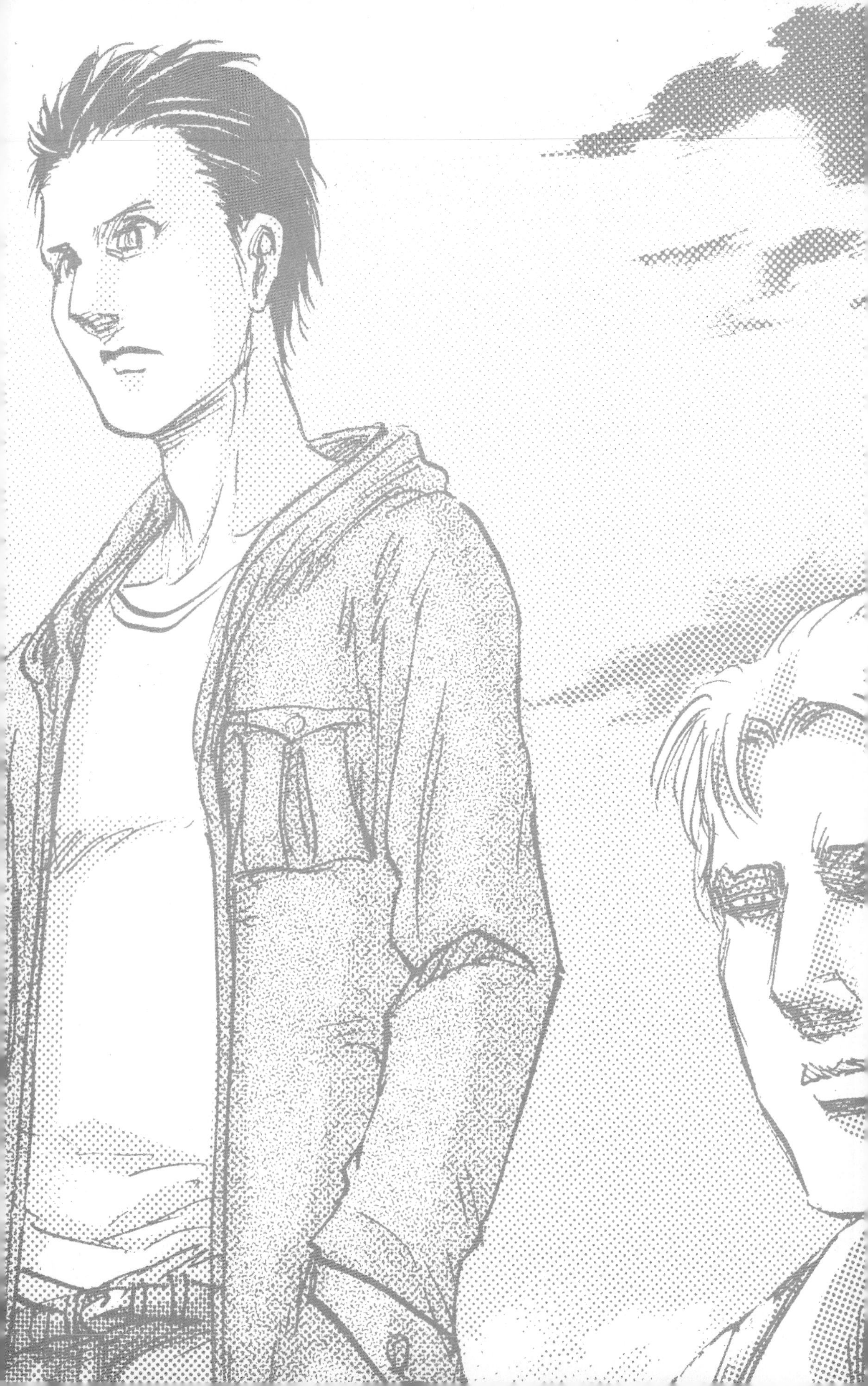

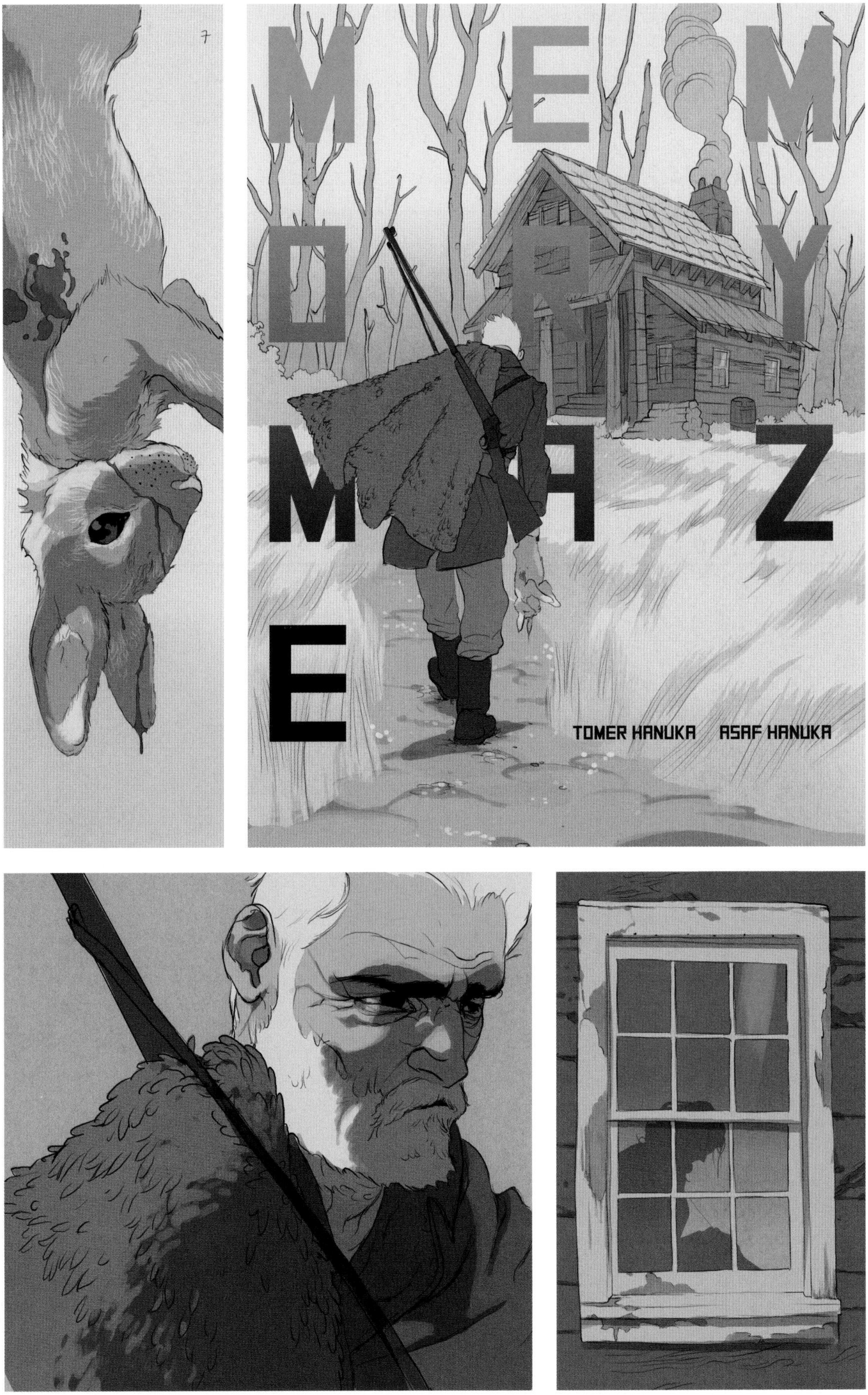
7
MEMORY MAZE
TOMER HANUKA
ASAF HANUKA

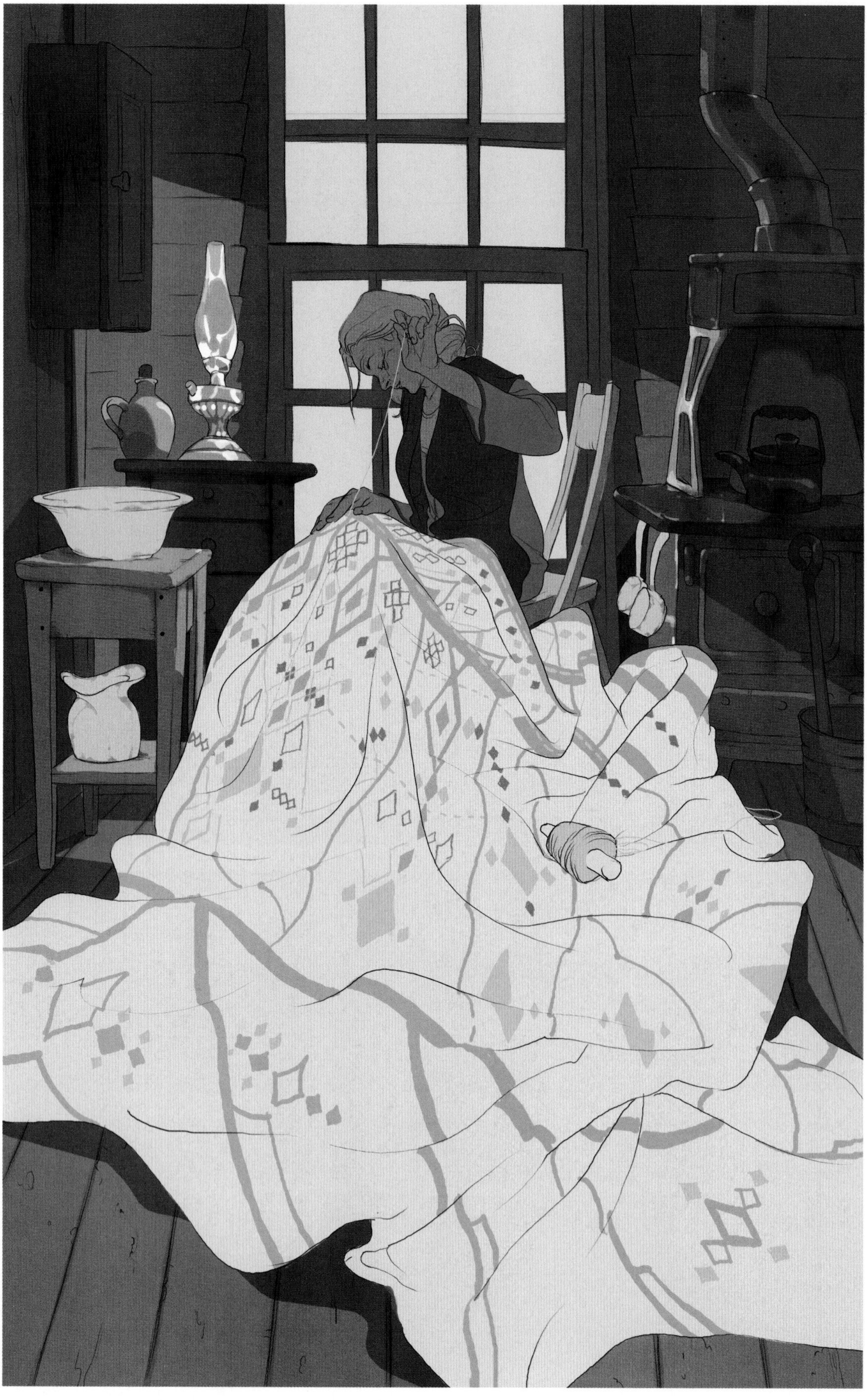

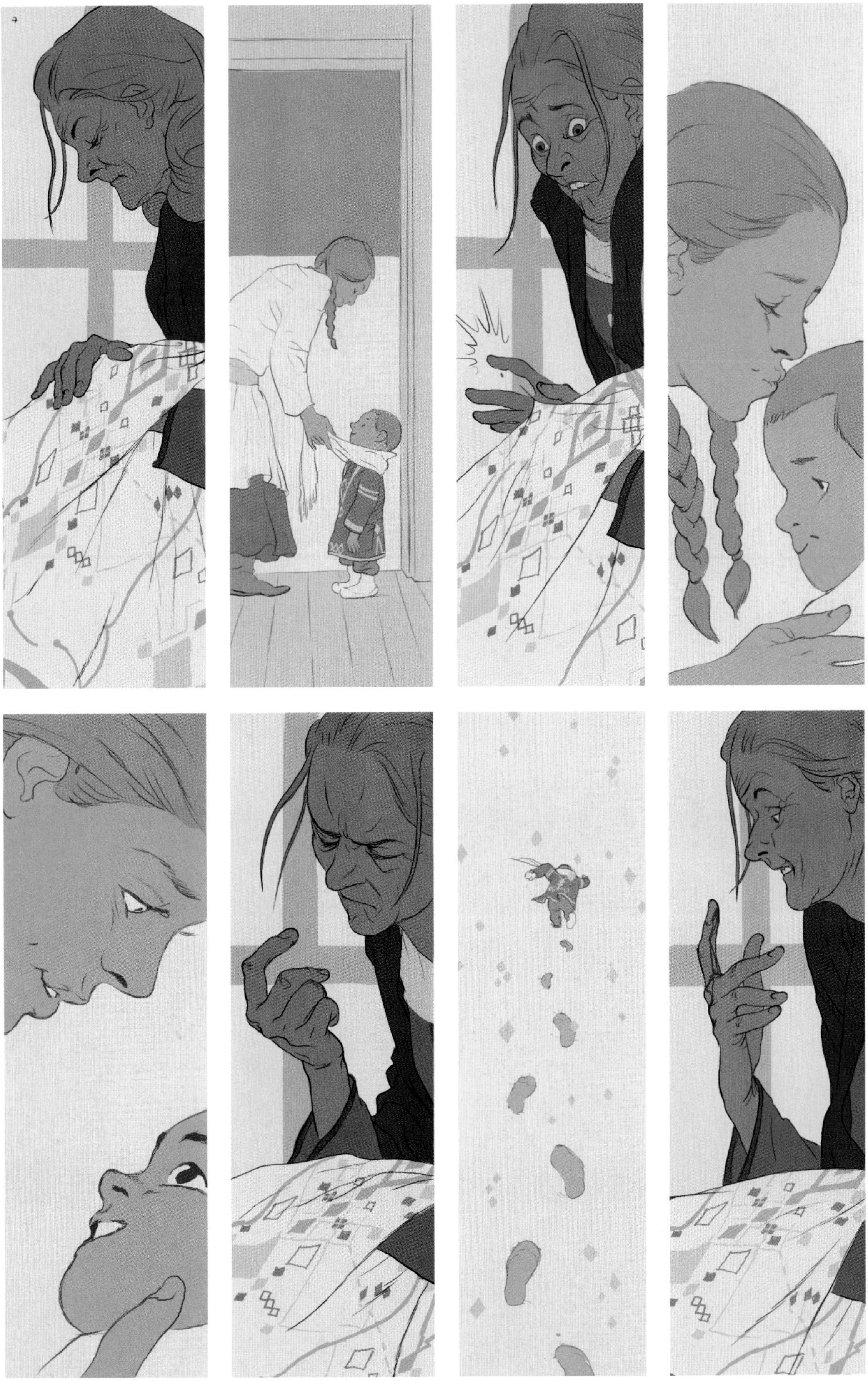

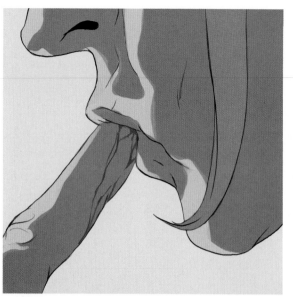

HE WILL LOVE THIS, WON'T HE, EDGAR?

HE'LL TELL US ALL ABOUT HIS JOURNEY WHEN HE COMES BACK.

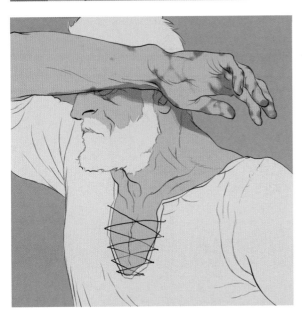

OF COURSE, LOVE.

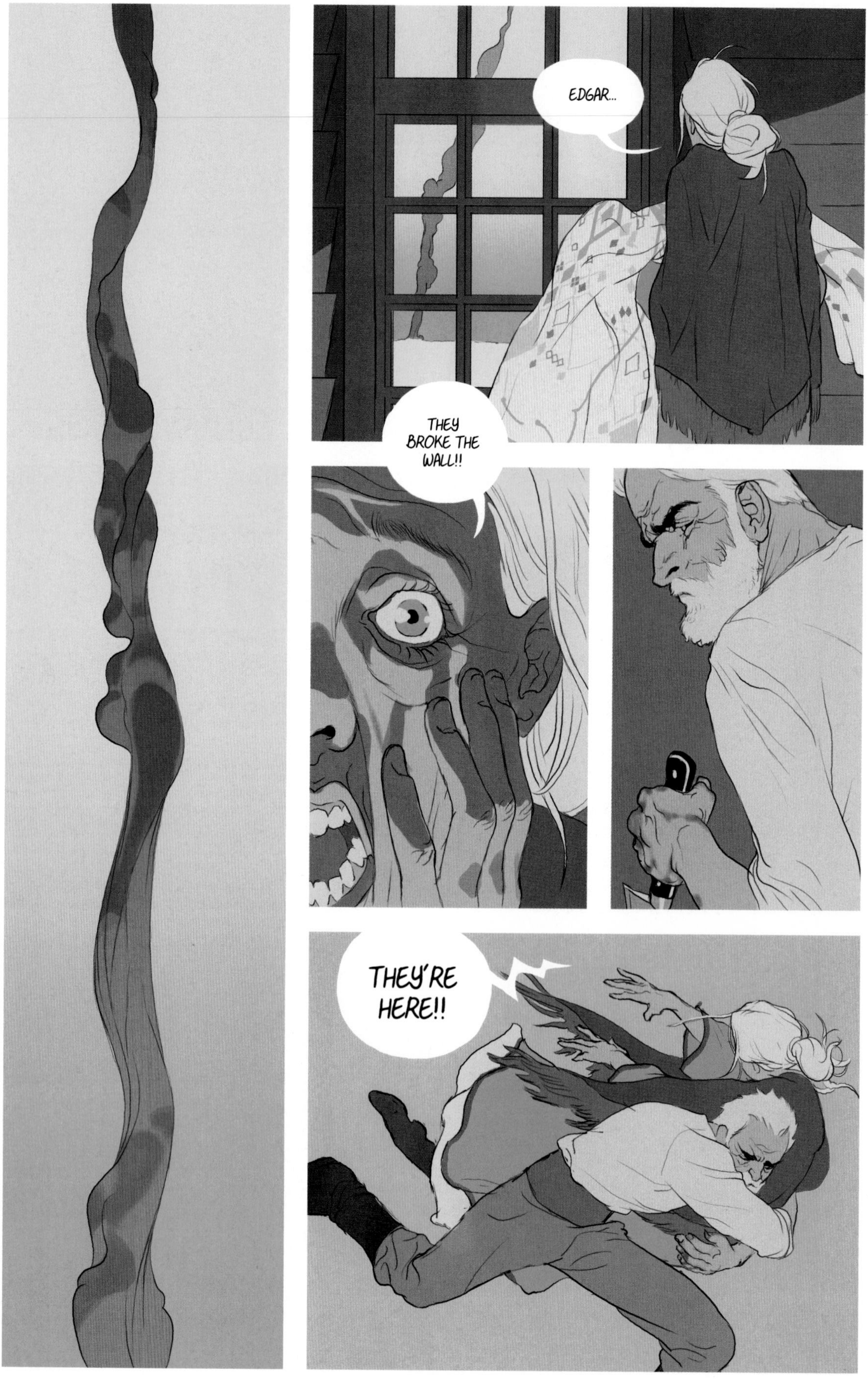
EDGAR...
THEY BROKE THE WALL!!
THEY'RE HERE!!

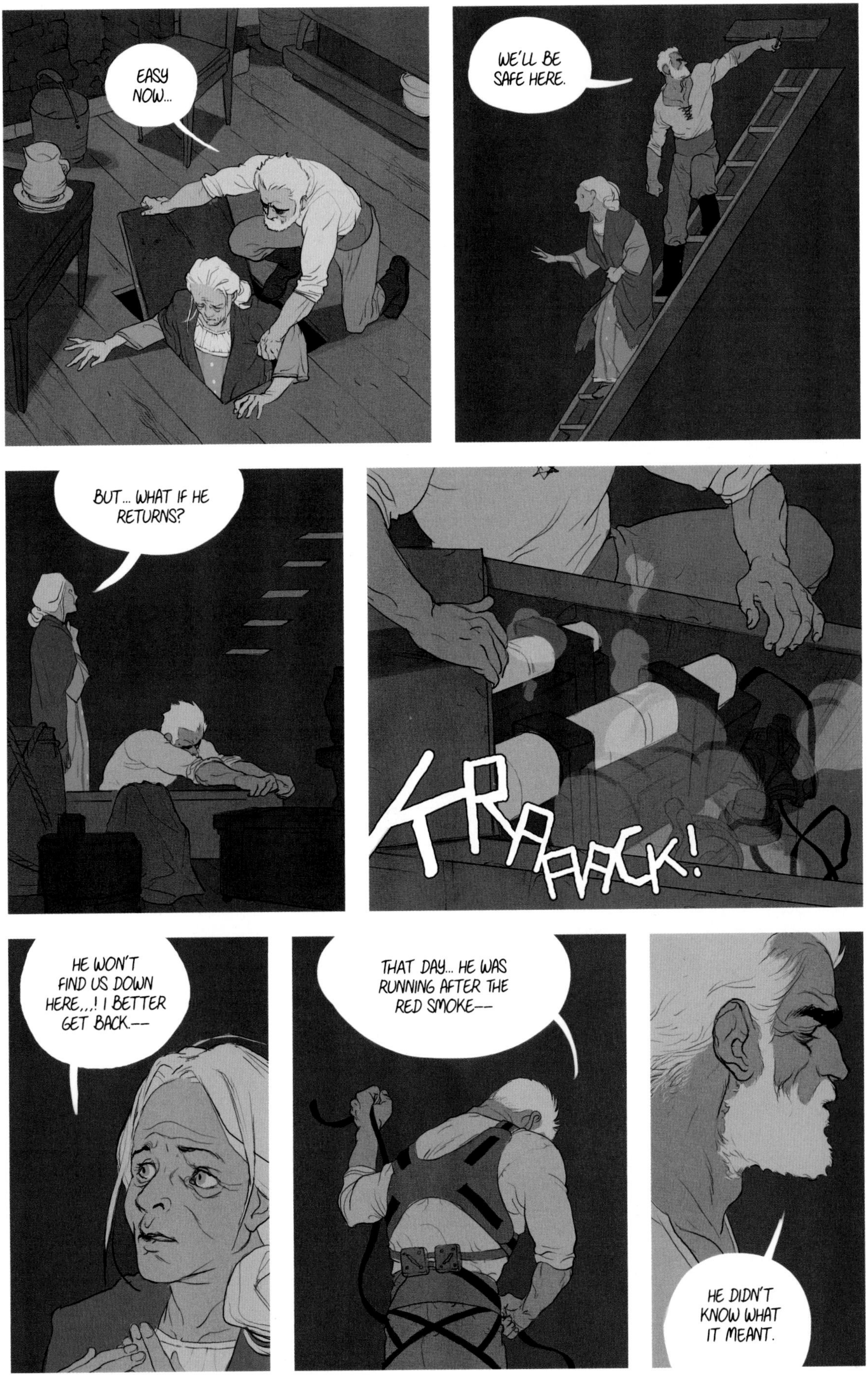
EASY NOW...
WE'LL BE SAFE HERE.
BUT... WHAT IF HE RETURNS?
KRAAACK!
HE WON'T FIND US DOWN HERE...! I BETTER GET BACK.--
THAT DAY... HE WAS RUNNING AFTER THE RED SMOKE--
HE DIDN'T KNOW WHAT IT MEANT.

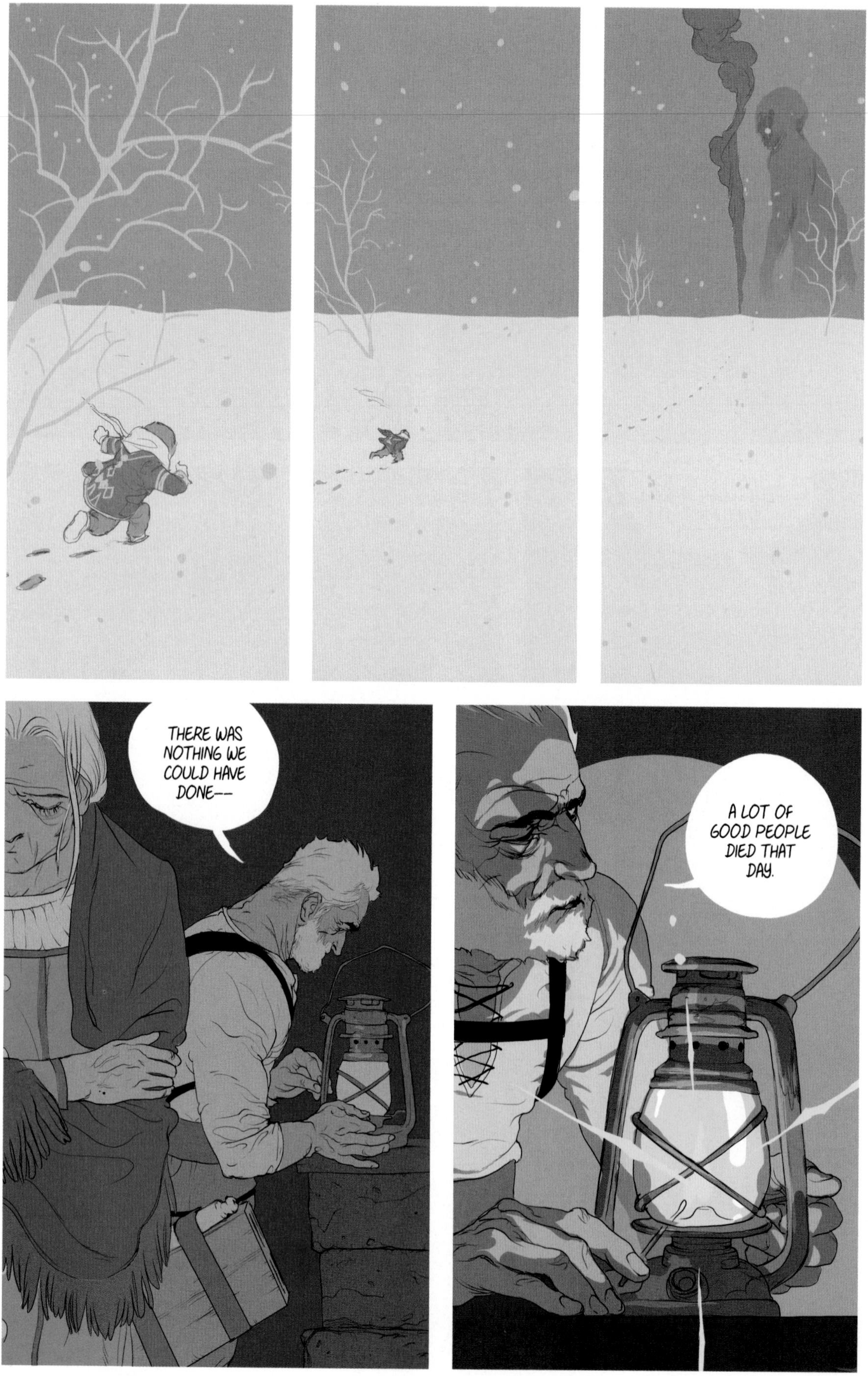
THERE WAS NOTHING WE COULD HAVE DONE--
A LOT OF GOOD PEOPLE DIED THAT DAY.

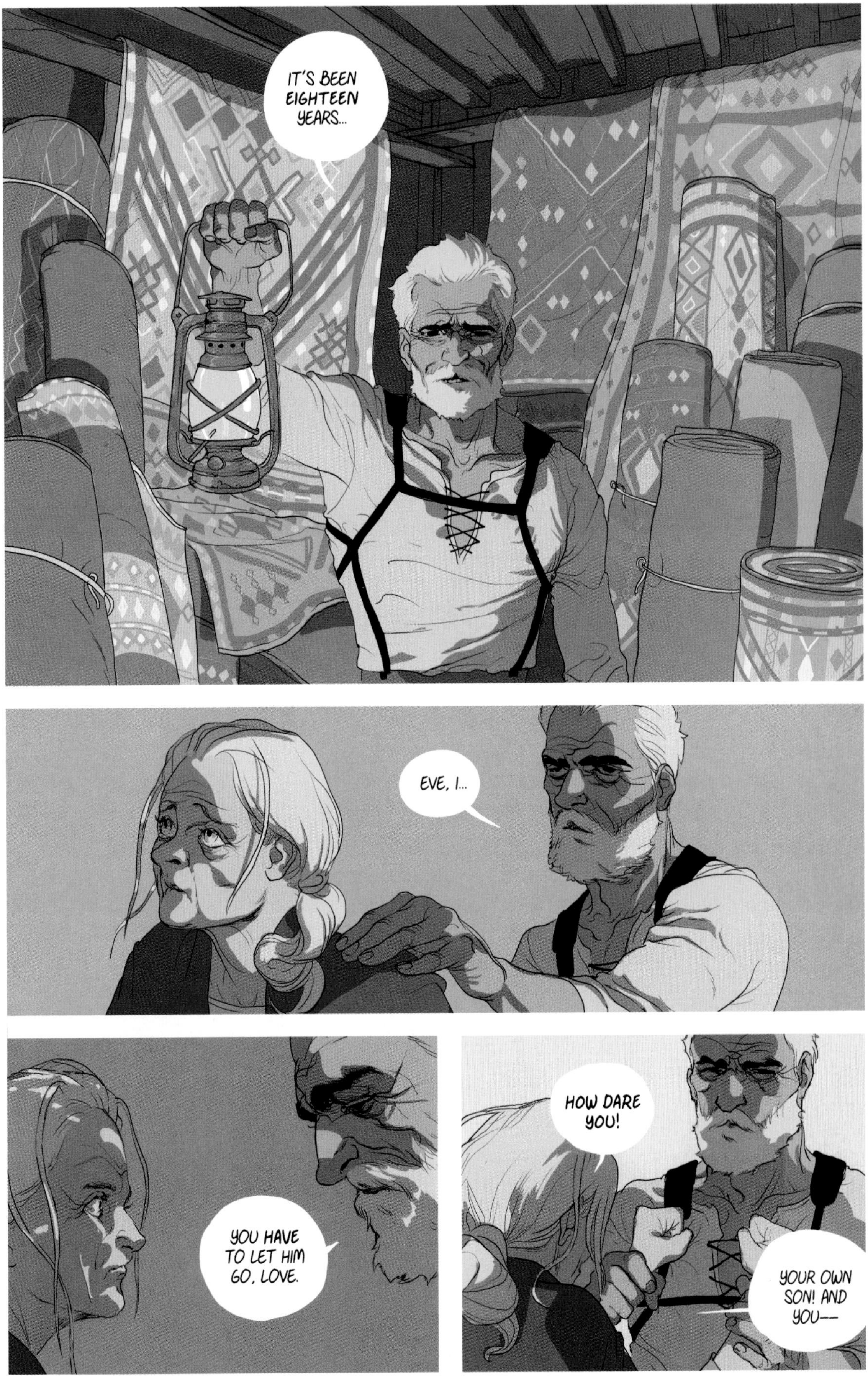
IT'S BEEN EIGHTEEN YEARS...
EVE, I...
YOU HAVE TO LET HIM GO, LOVE.
HOW DARE YOU!
YOUR OWN SON! AND YOU--

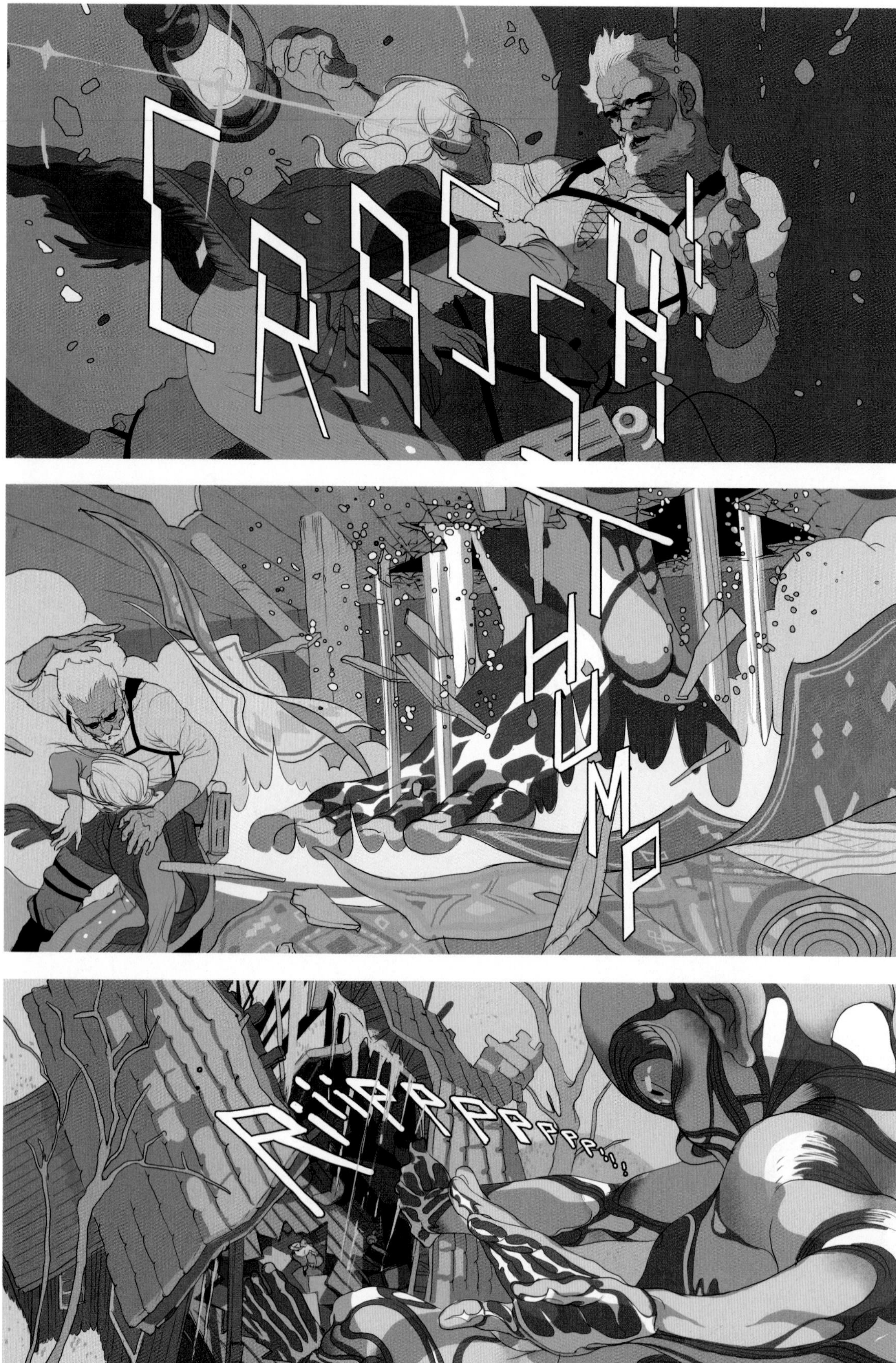
CRASCH!
THUMP
RIIIRRRRPPP!!!

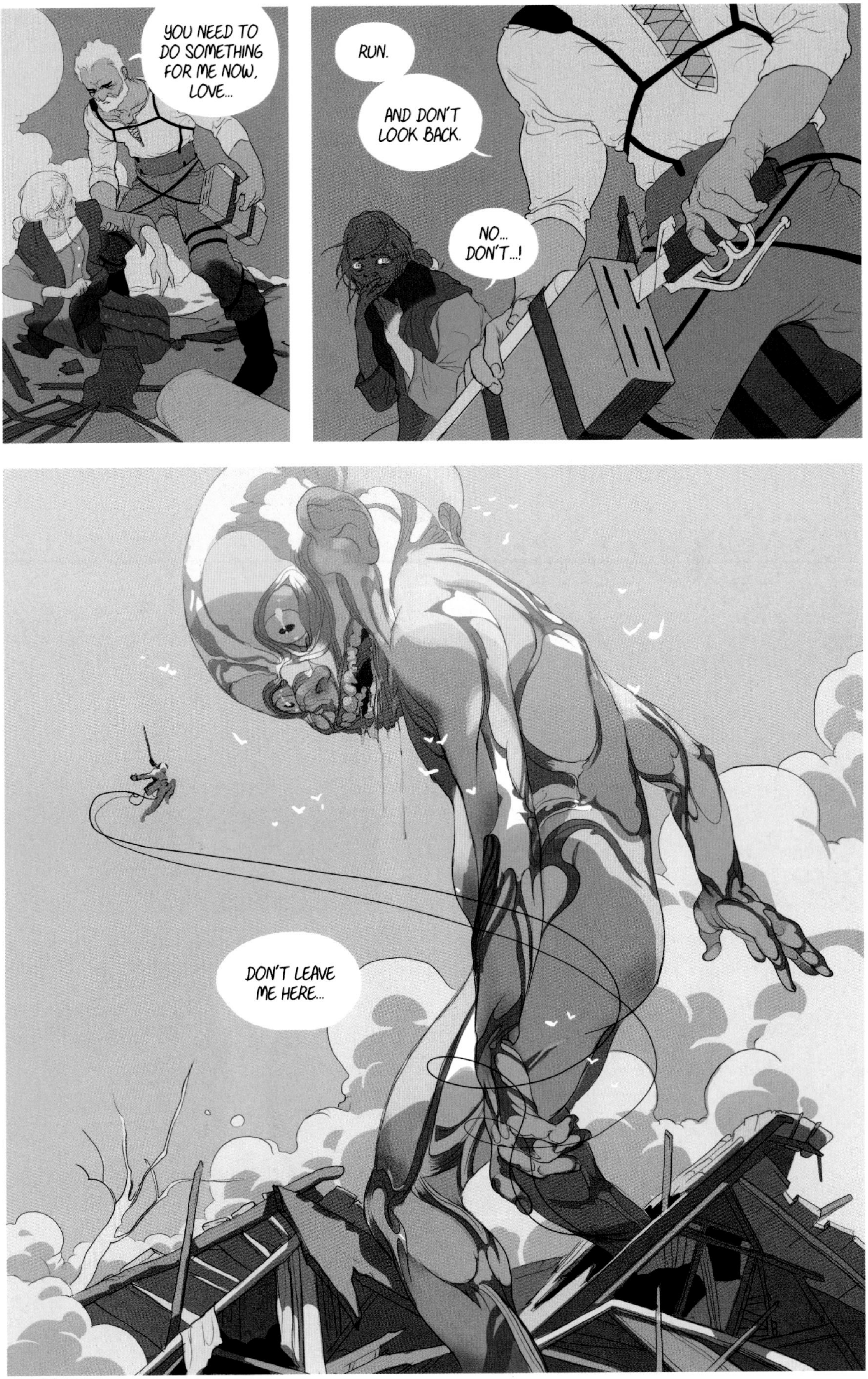
YOU NEED TO DO SOMETHING FOR ME NOW, LOVE...
RUN.
AND DON'T LOOK BACK.
NO... DON'T...!
DON'T LEAVE ME HERE...

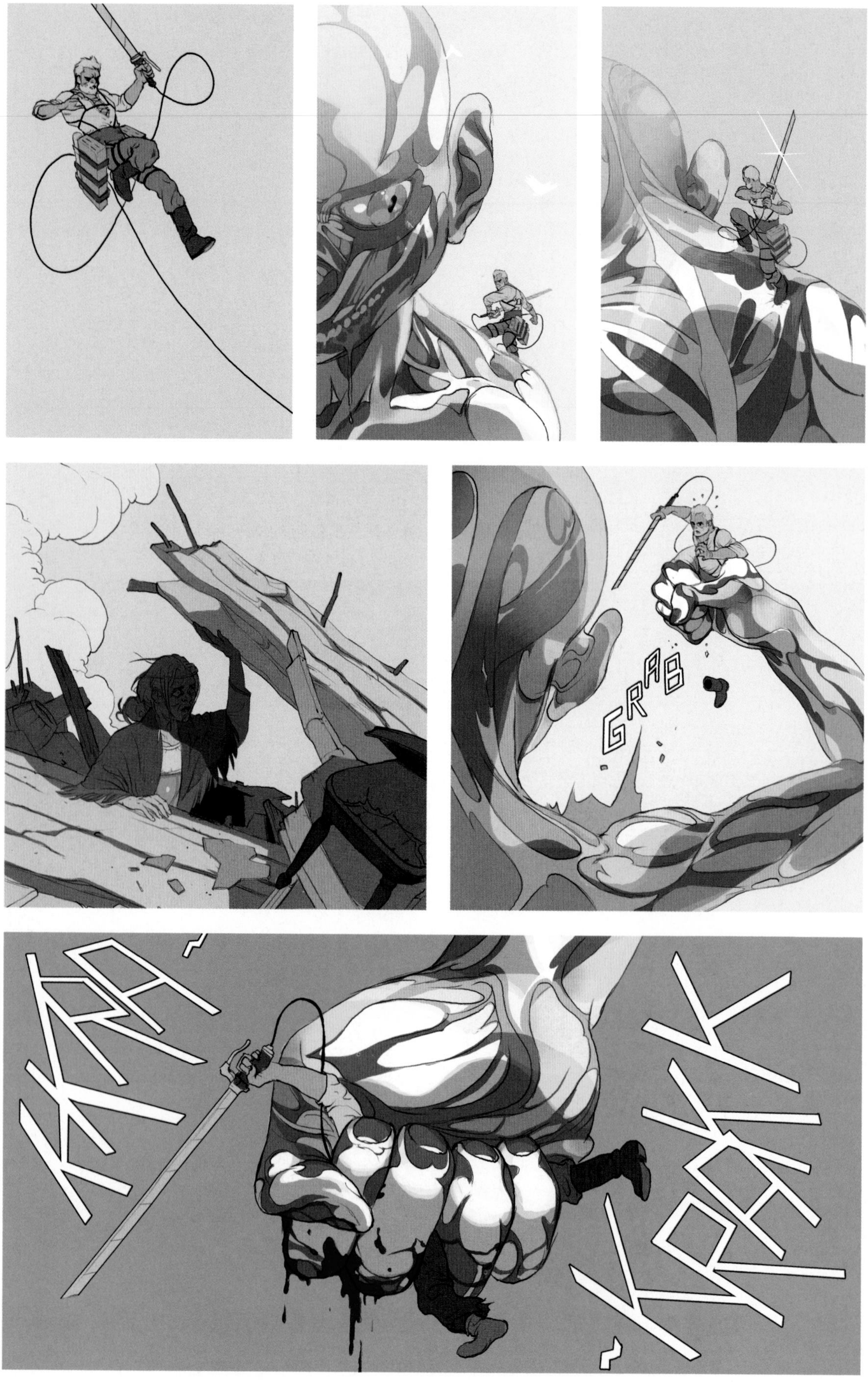
GRAB
KKRA~
~KRAKK

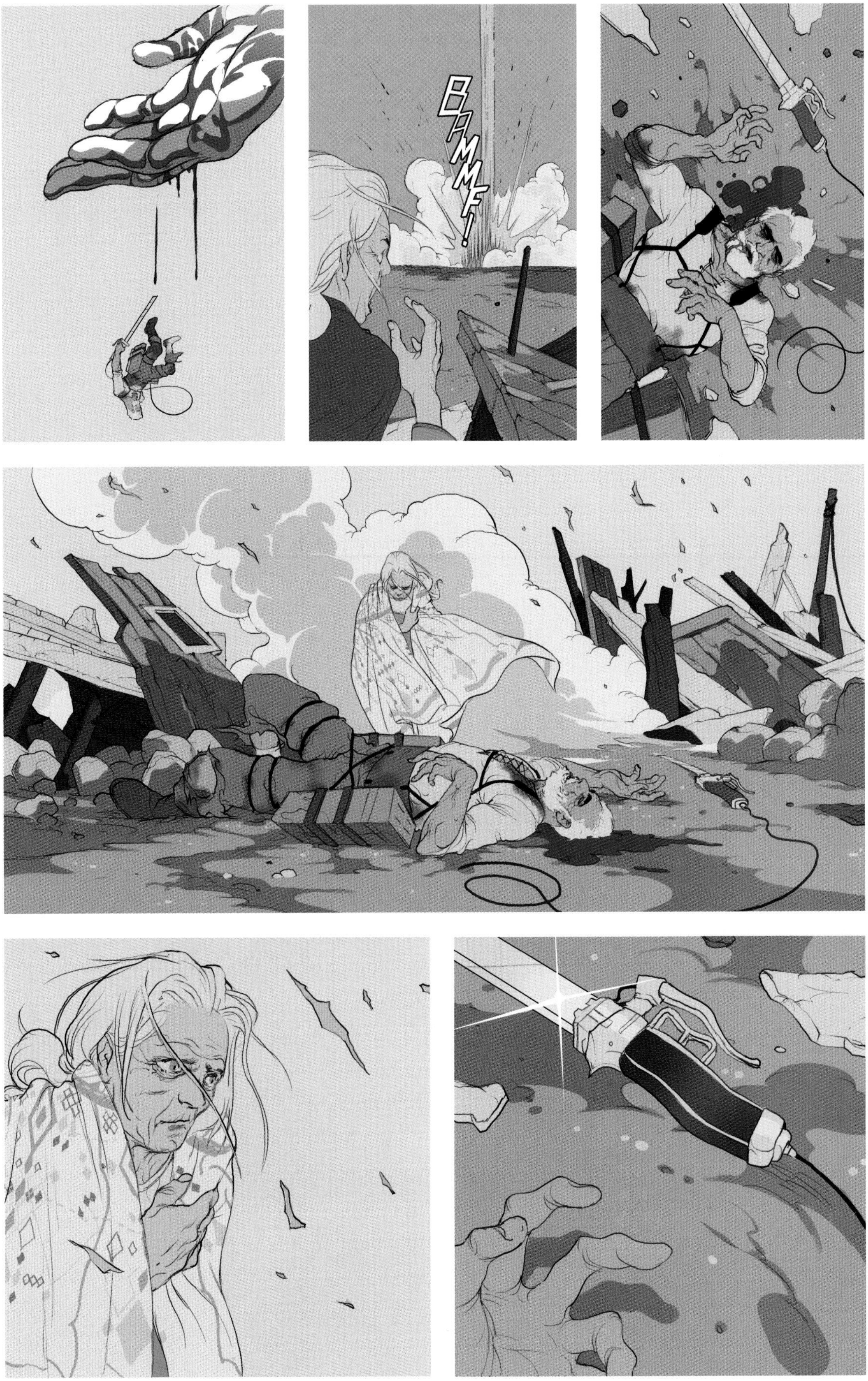
BAMMF!

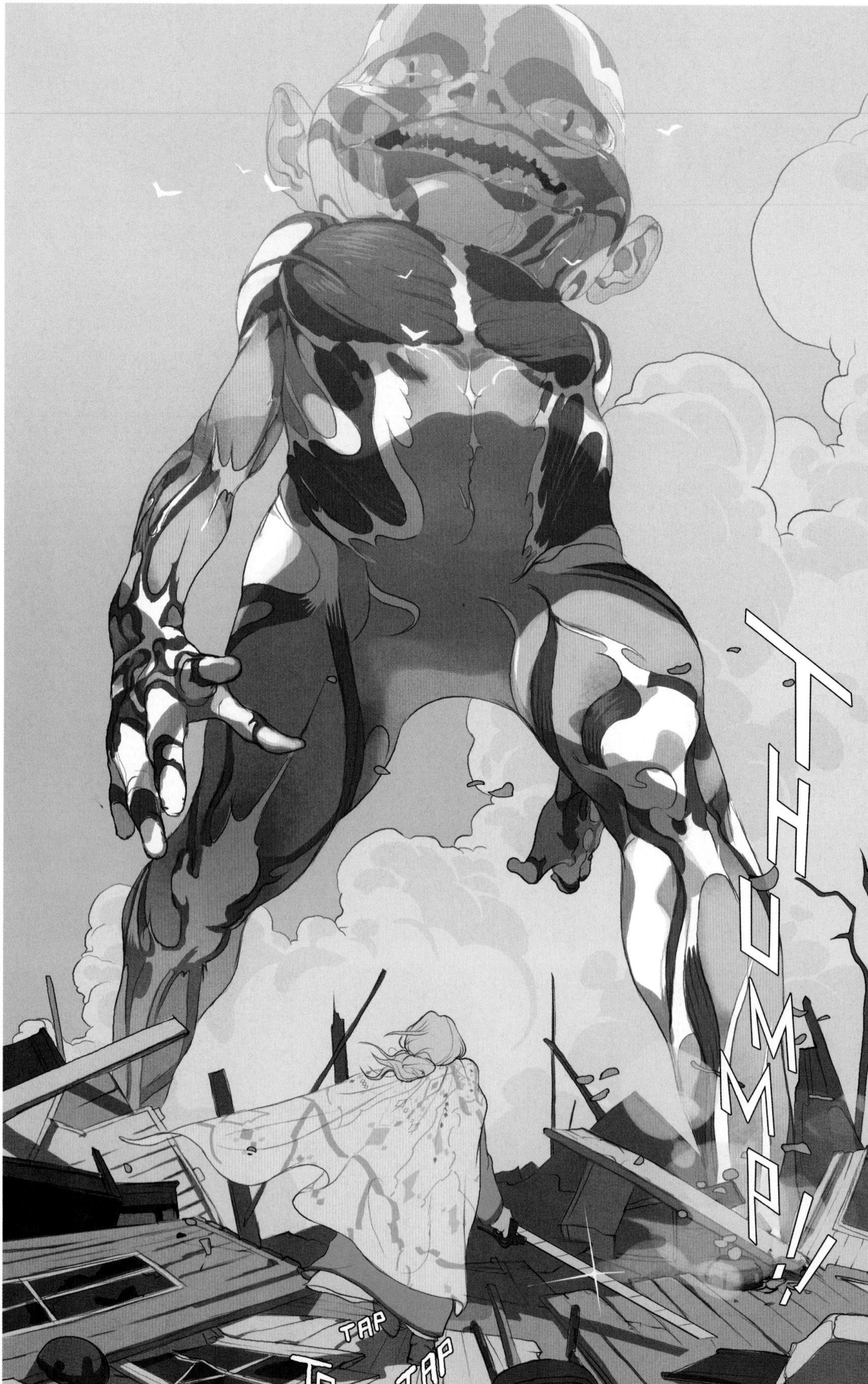
THUMMP!!
TAP
TAP TAP
TAP

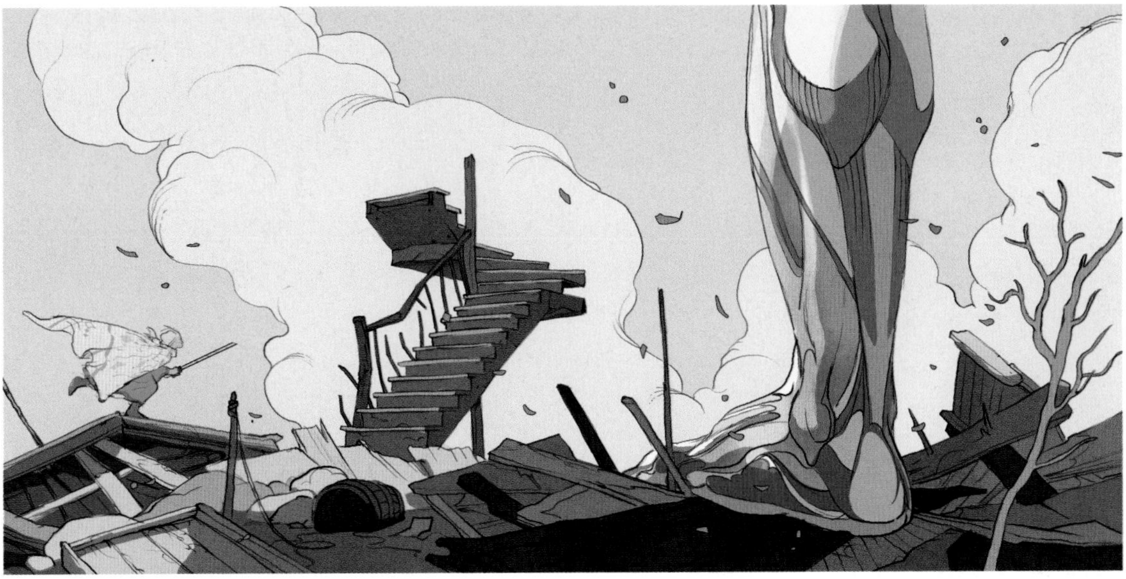

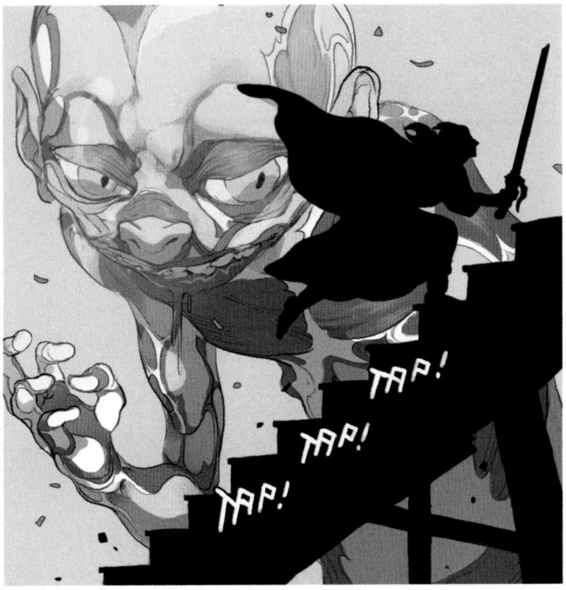
TAP!
TAP!
TAP!

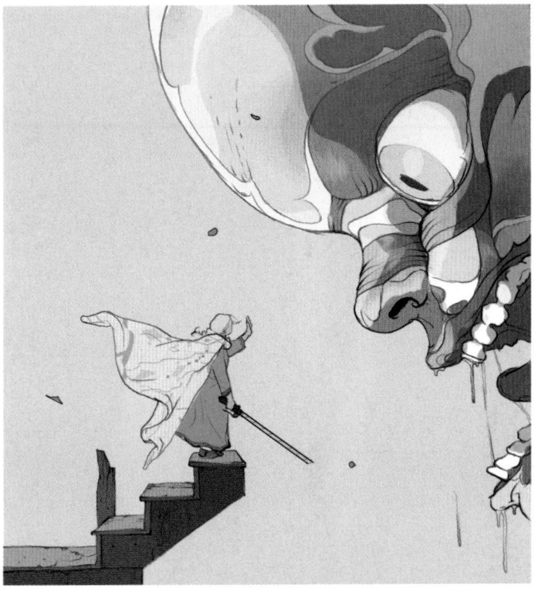

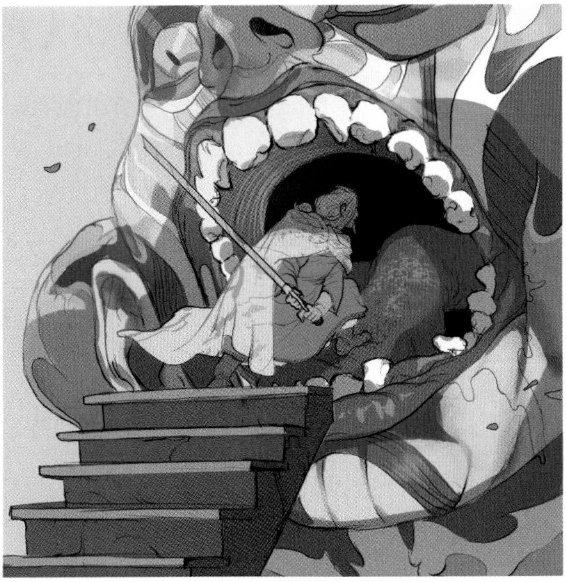

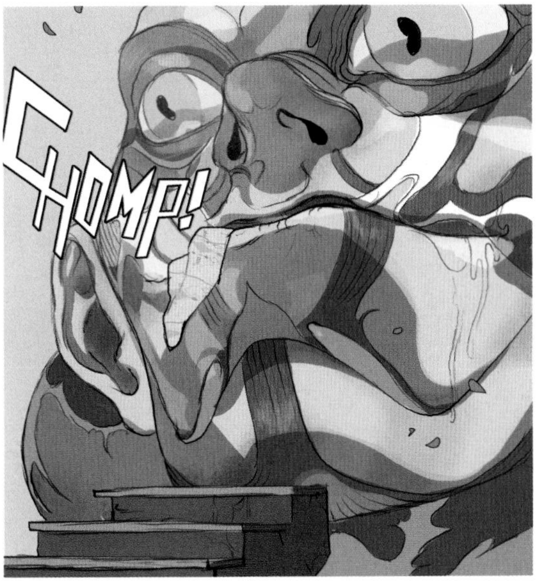
CHOMP!

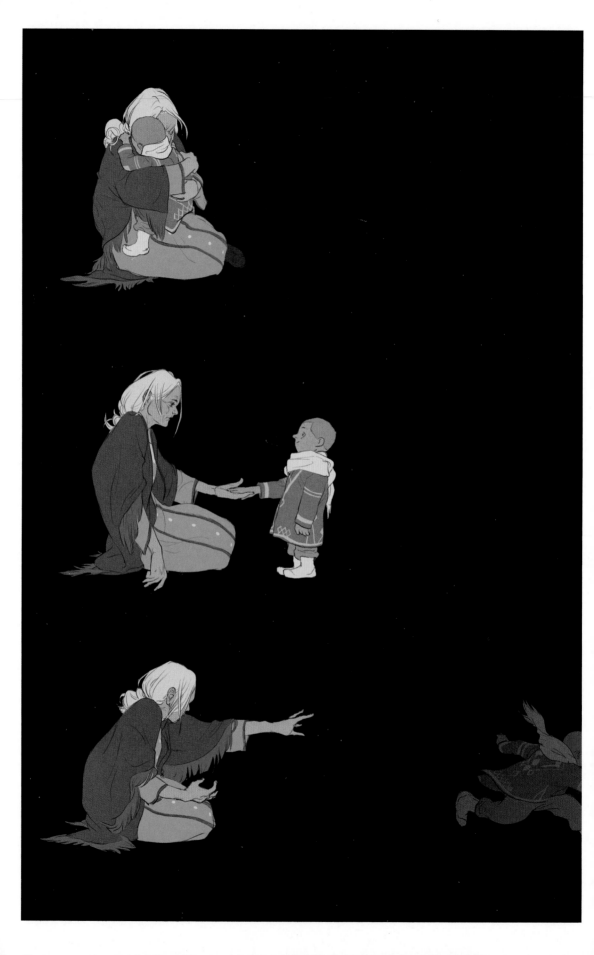

RIPPPPP

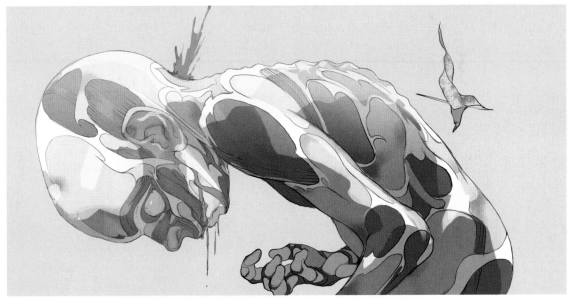

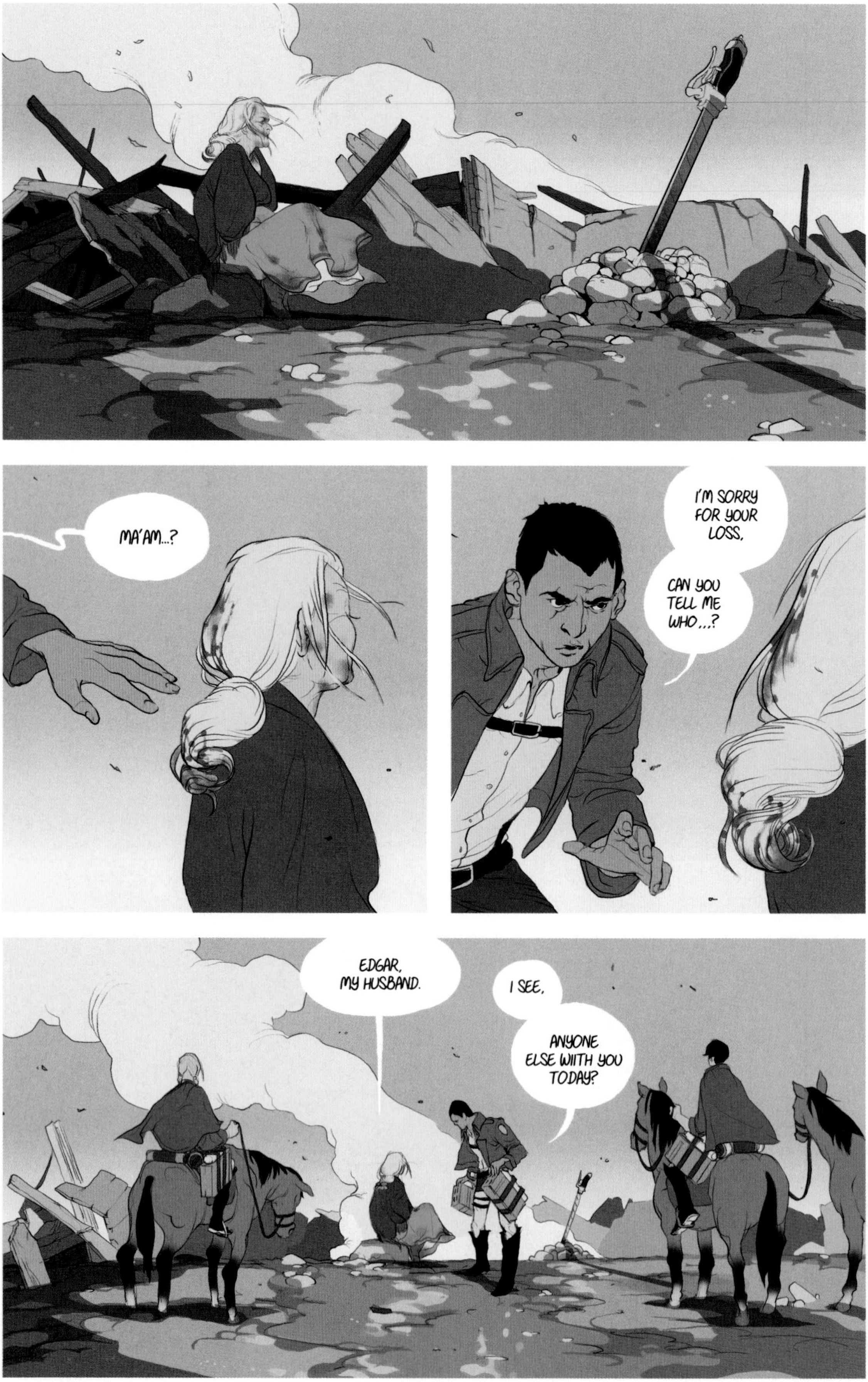
MA'AM...?
I'M SORRY FOR YOUR LOSS.
CAN YOU TELL ME WHO...?
EDGAR, MY HUSBAND.
I SEE.
ANYONE ELSE WITH YOU TODAY?

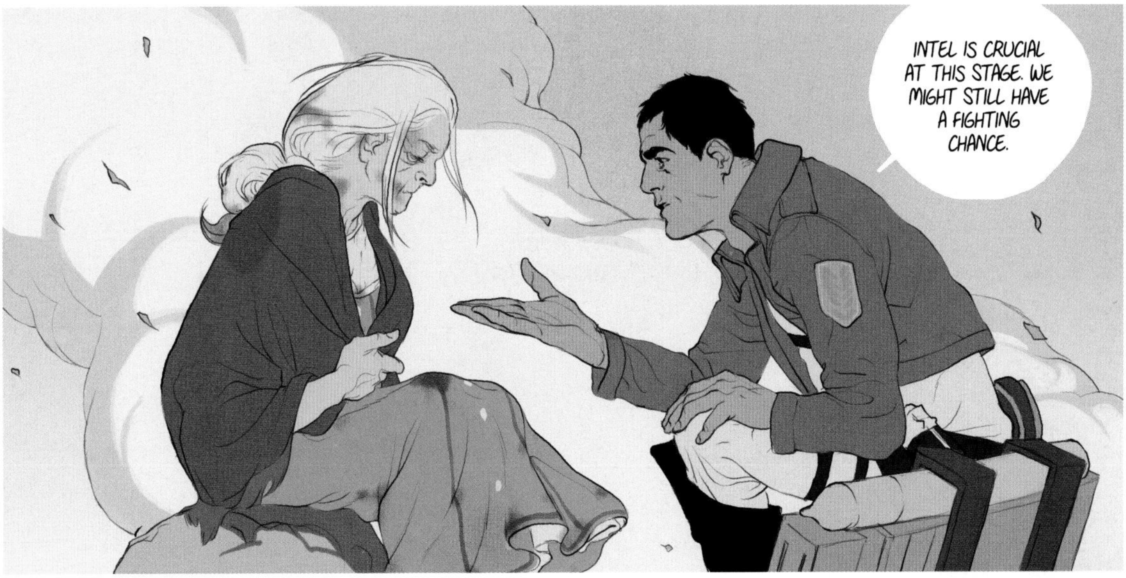
INTEL IS CRUCIAL AT THIS STAGE. WE MIGHT STILL HAVE A FIGHTING CHANCE.
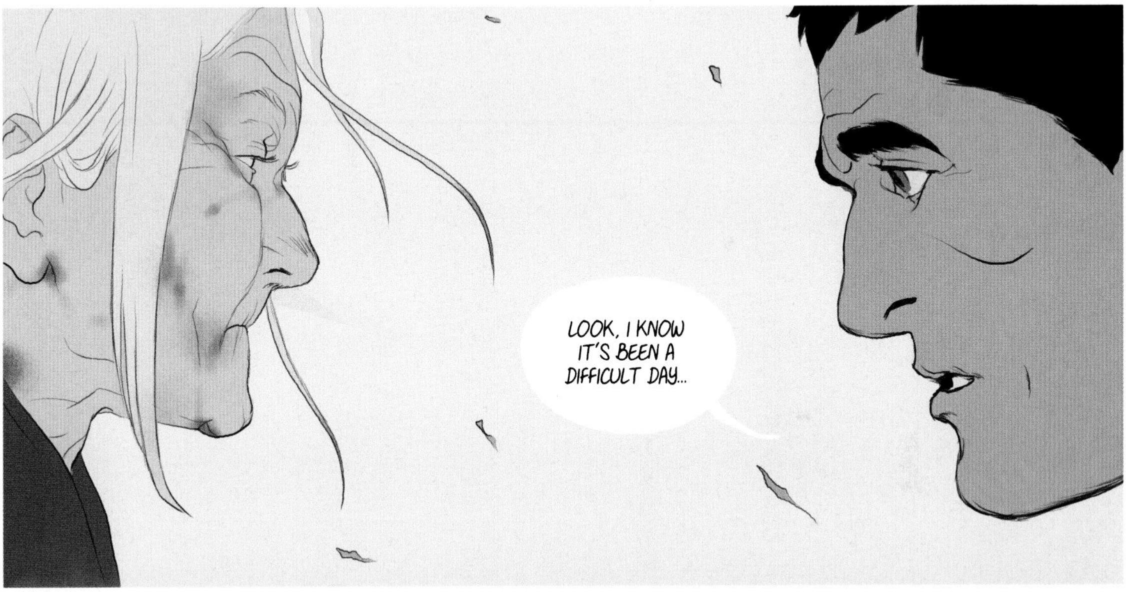
LOOK, I KNOW IT'S BEEN A DIFFICULT DAY...
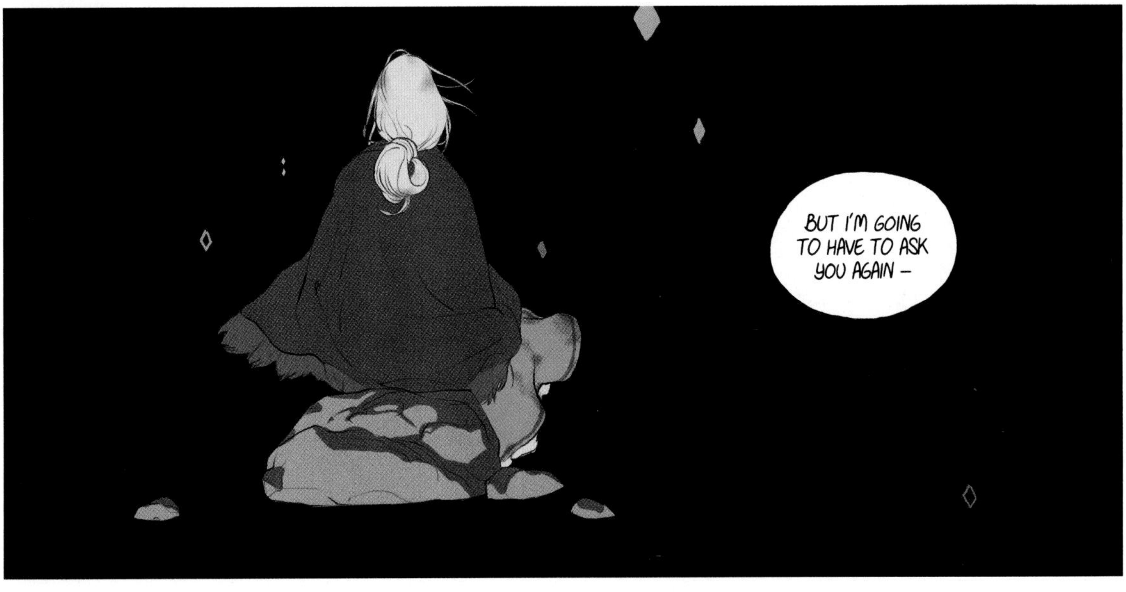
BUT I'M GOING TO HAVE TO ASK YOU AGAIN –

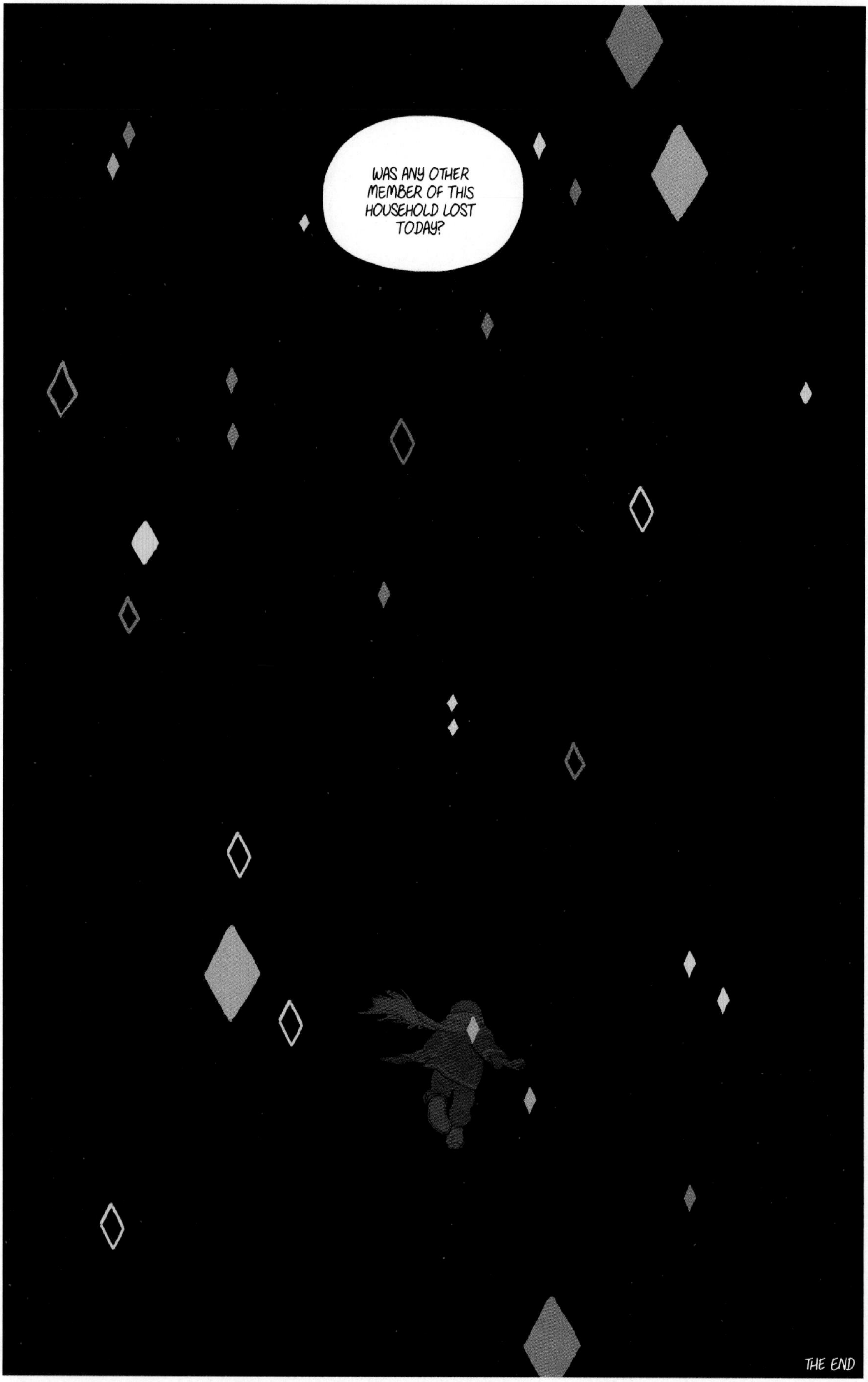
WAS ANY OTHER MEMBER OF THIS HOUSEHOLD LOST TODAY?
THE END

ATTACK on TITAN ANTHOLOGY

VARIANT COVER & CONCEPT ART GALLERY

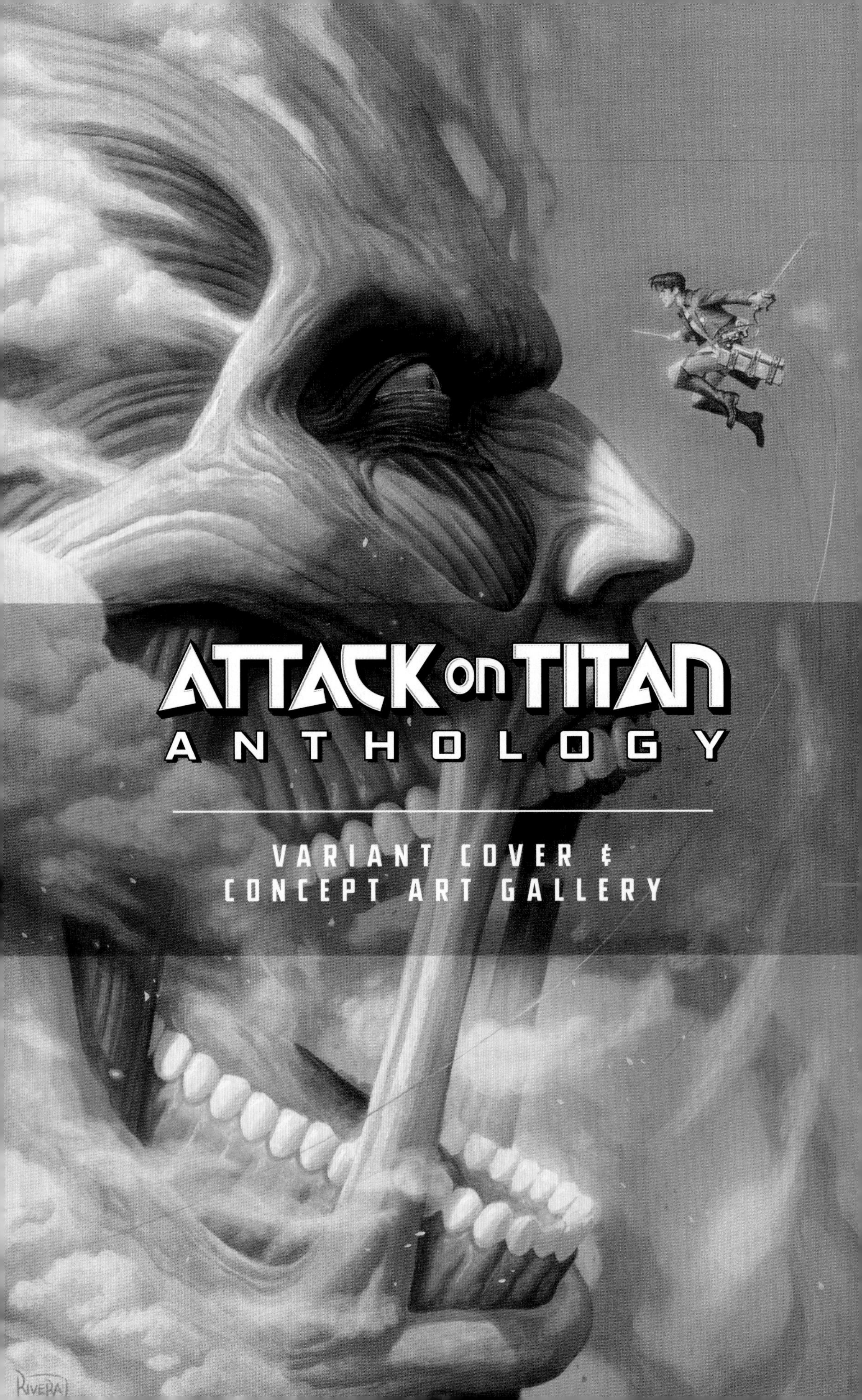
RIVERA

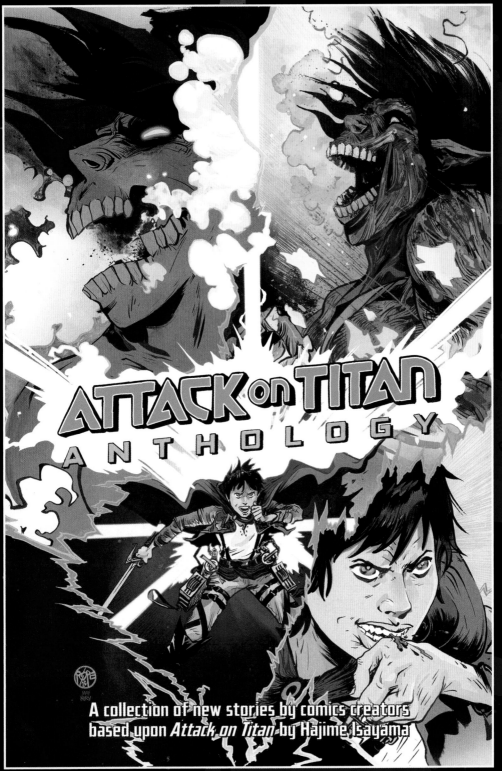

ATTACK on TITAN
A N T H O L O G Y

A collection of new stories by comics creators based upon *Attack on Titan* by Hajime Isayama

ATTACK ON TITAN ANTHOLOGY
FRIED PIE COMICS/BAM!
VARIANT COVER BY
PAUL POPE
AND PAUL MAYBURY

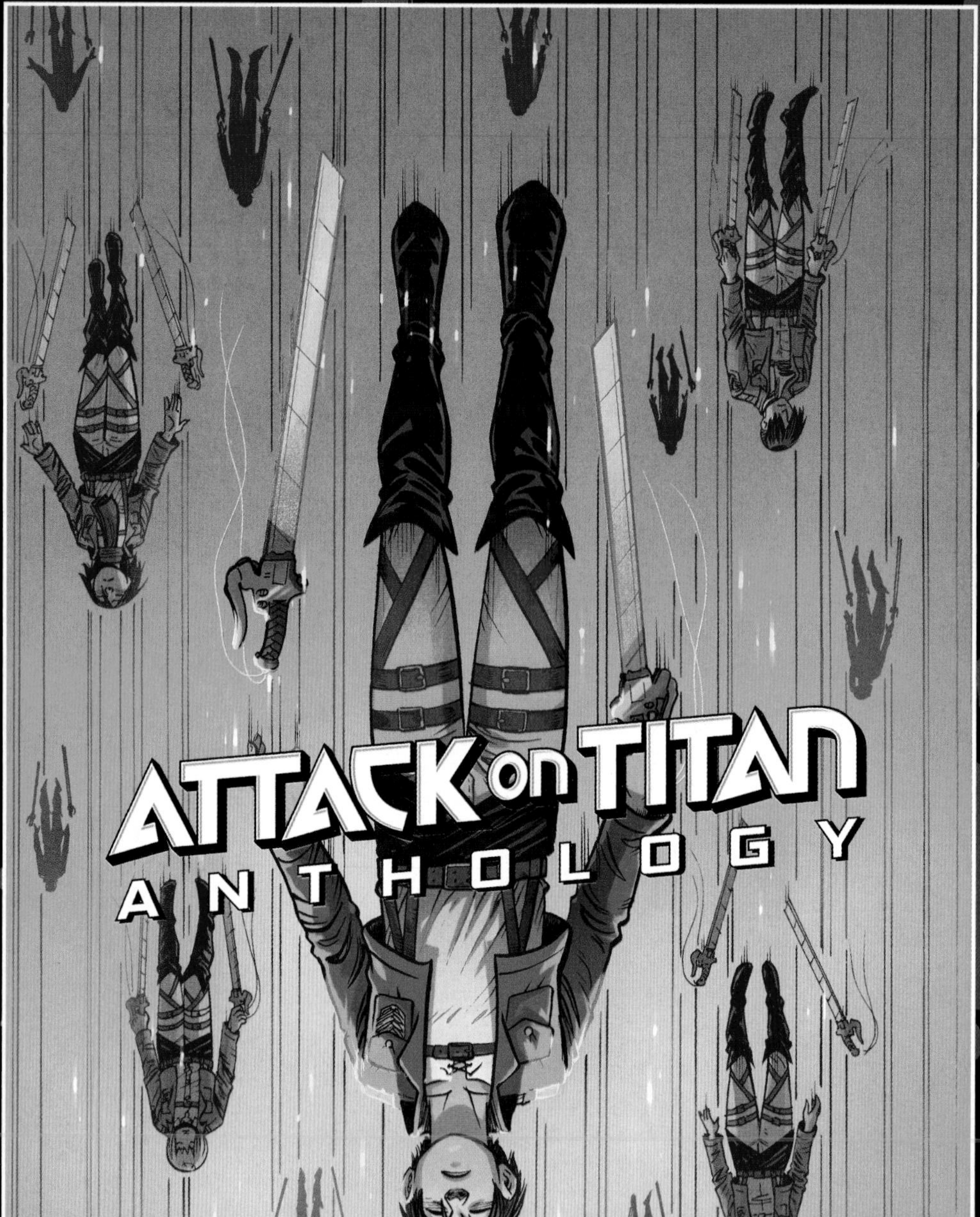
ATTACK on TITAN
ANTHOLOGY
A collection of new stories by comics creators based upon Attack on Titan by Hajime Isayama

ATTACK ON TITAN ANTHOLOGY
BARNES & NOBLE
VARIANT COVER BY
FAITH ERIN HICKS

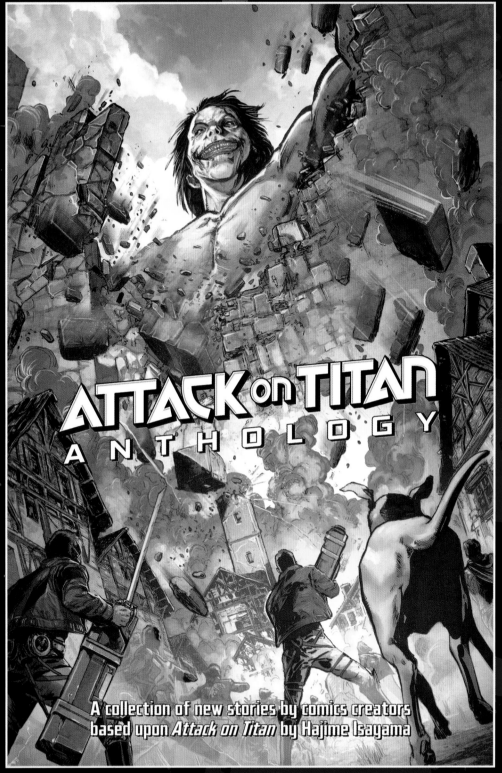

ATTACK ON TITAN
ANTHOLOGY

A collection of new stories by comics creators
based upon *Attack on Titan* by Hajime Isayama

ATTACK ON TITAN ANTHOLOGY
DIAMOND VARIANT COVER BY
PHIL JIMENEZ
AND ROMULO FAJARDO, JR.

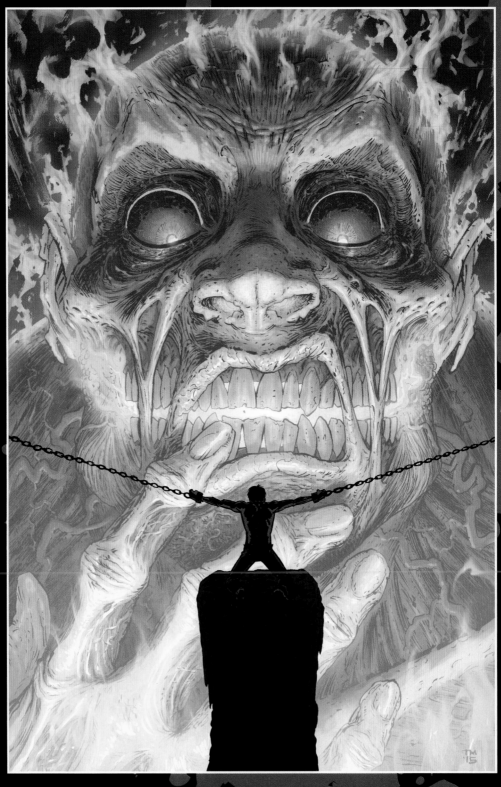

**ATTACK ON TITAN 16
SPECIAL EDITION WITH
PLAYING CARDS COVER BY
TONY MOORE**

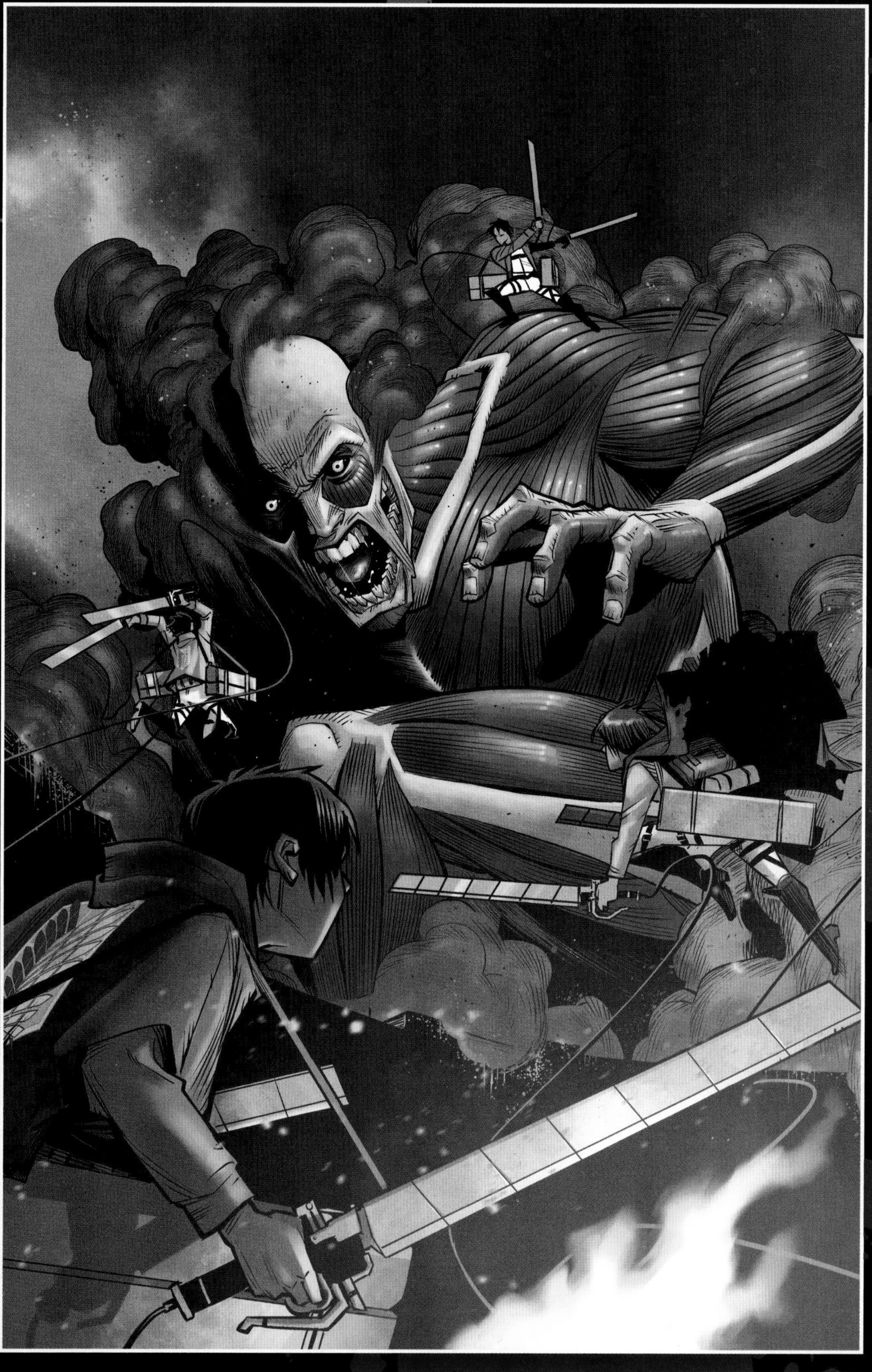

ATTACK ON TITAN 18
SPECIAL EDITION WITH DVD
COVER BY
CAMERON STEWART

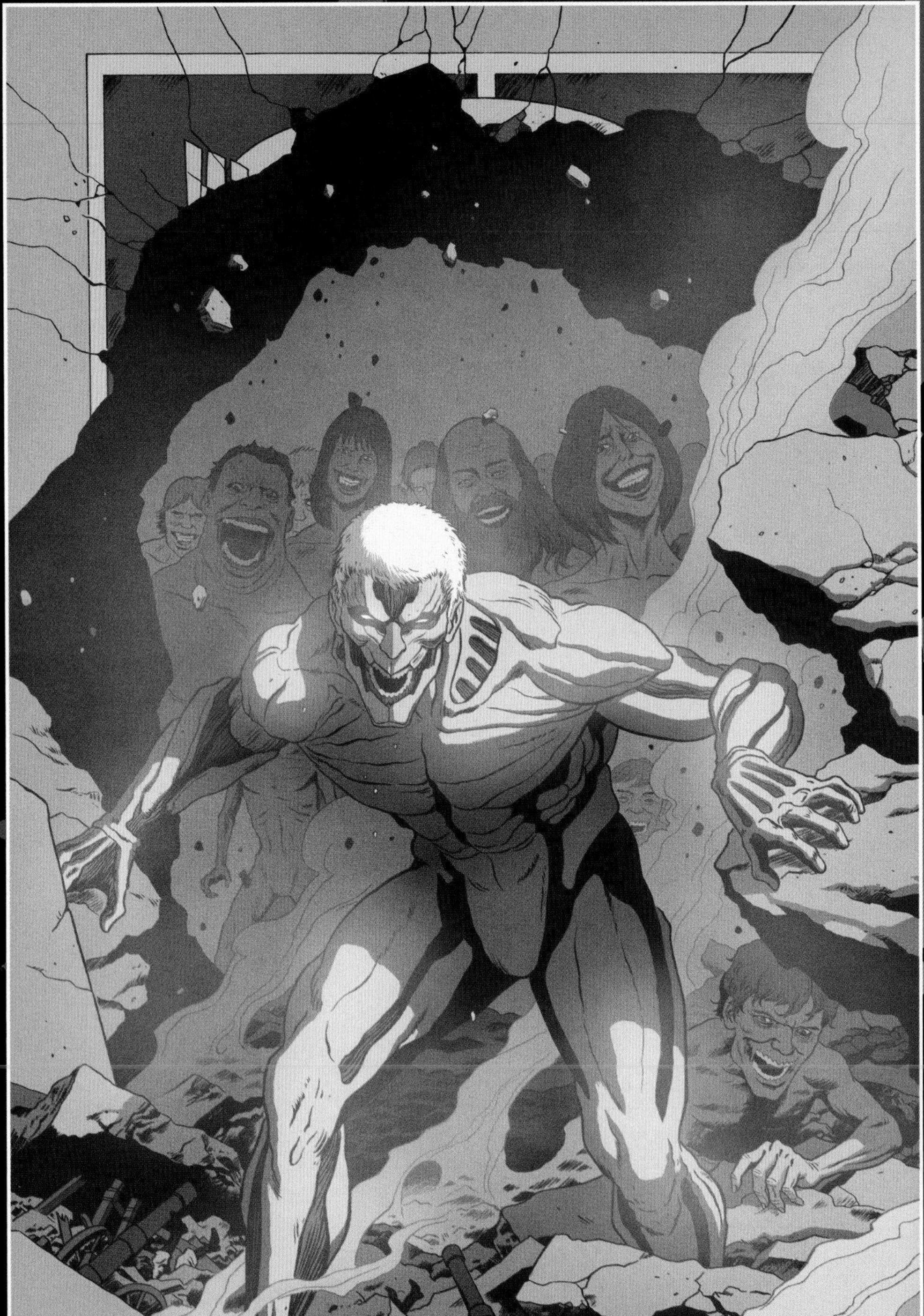
RIVERA

ATTACK ON TITAN 19
SPECIAL EDITION WITH DVD
COVER BY
PAOLO RIVERA

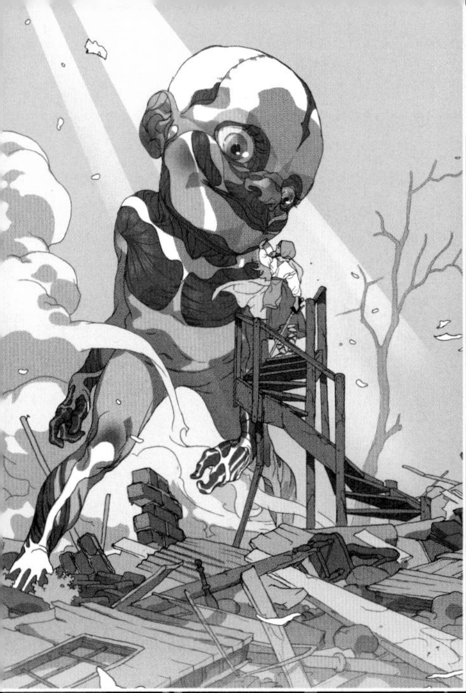
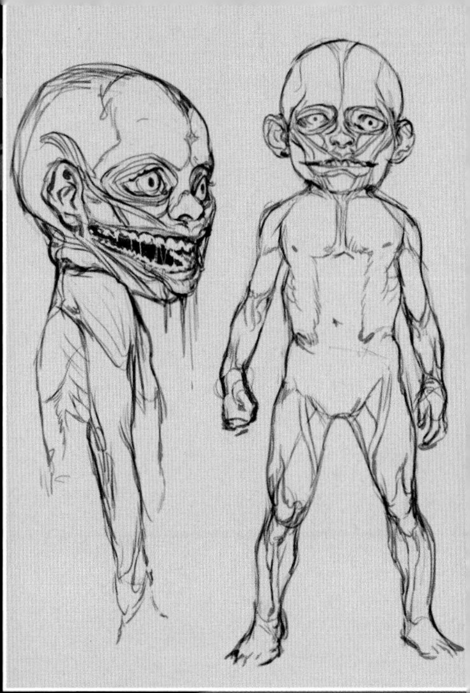
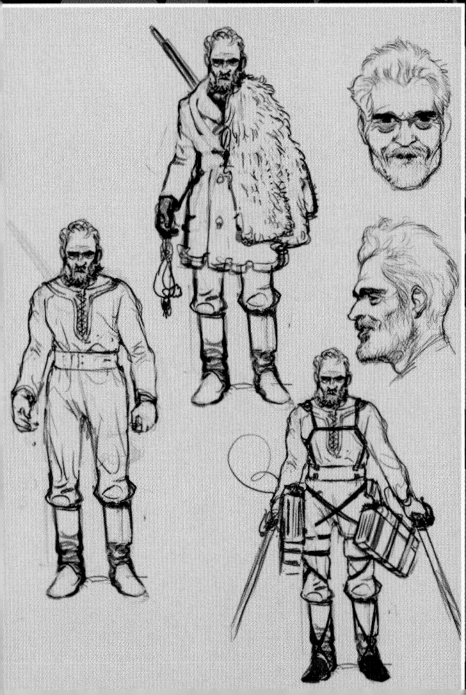
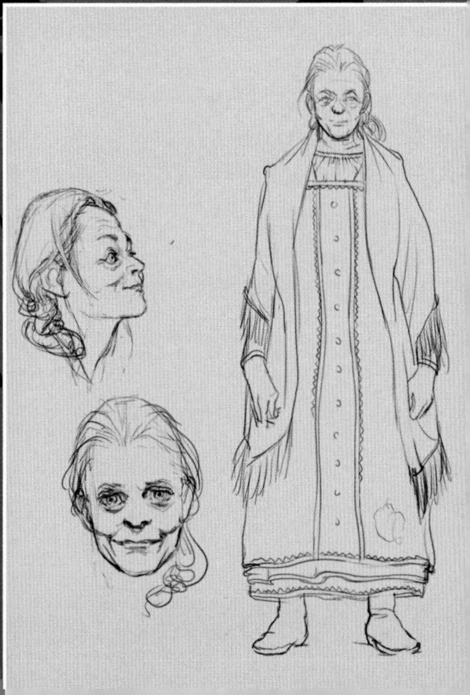

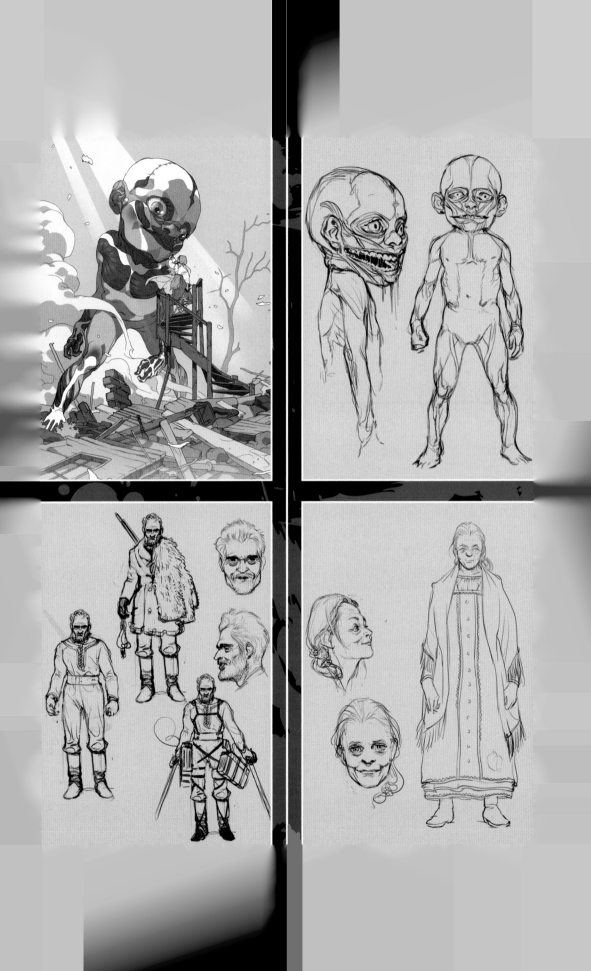

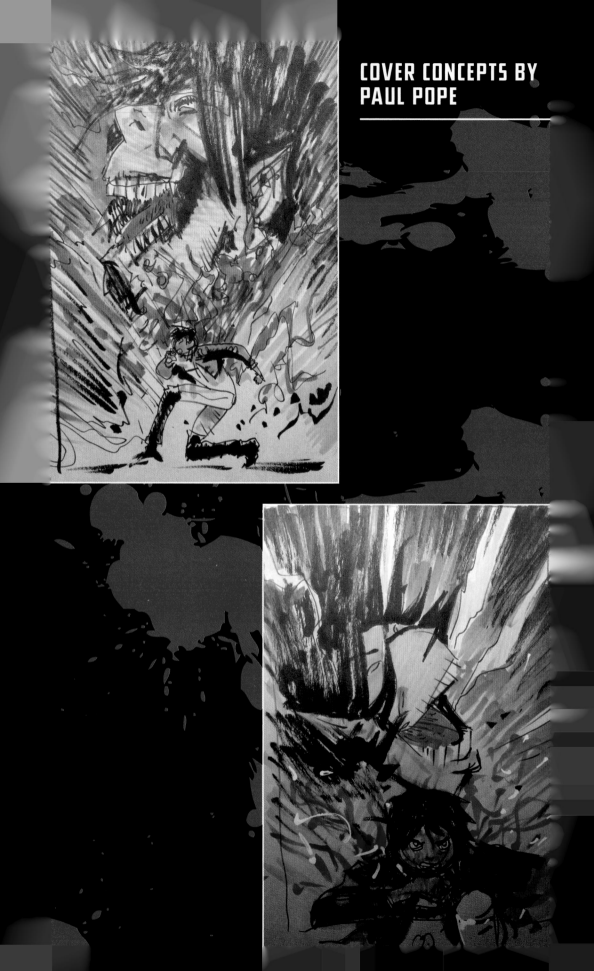

COVER CONCEPTS BY PAUL POPE

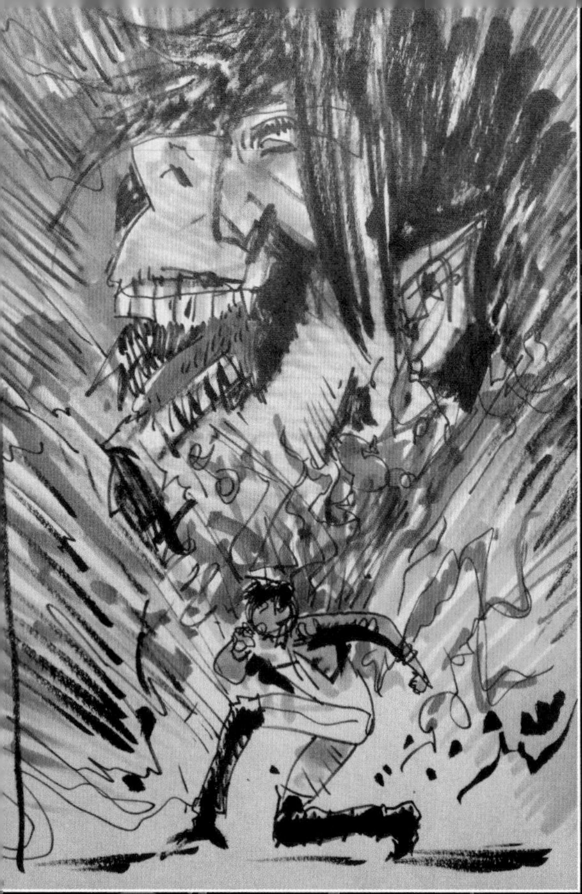

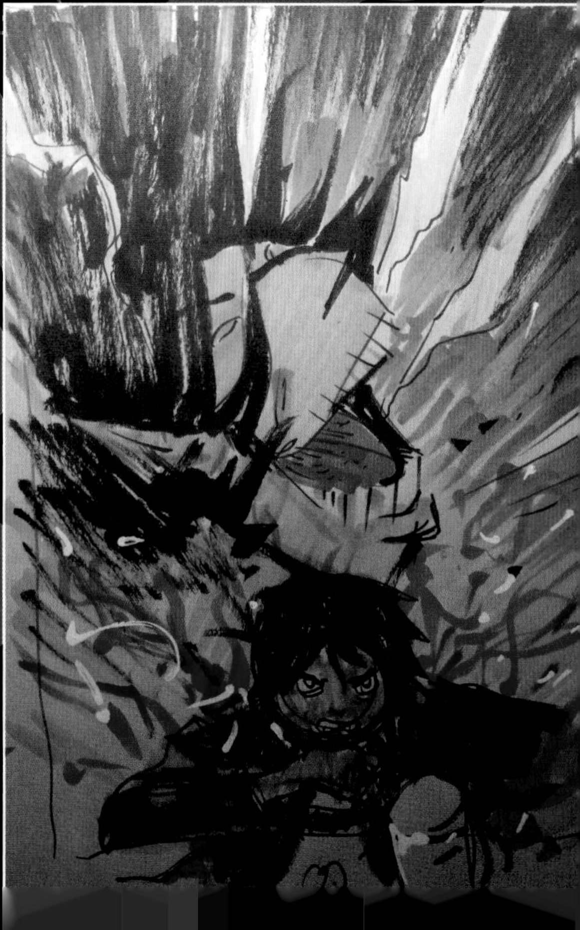

COVER CONCEPTS BY
PAUL POPE

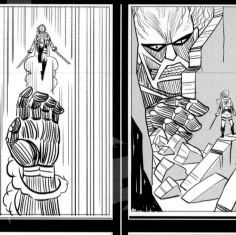

COVER CONCEPTS BY FAITH ERIN HICKS

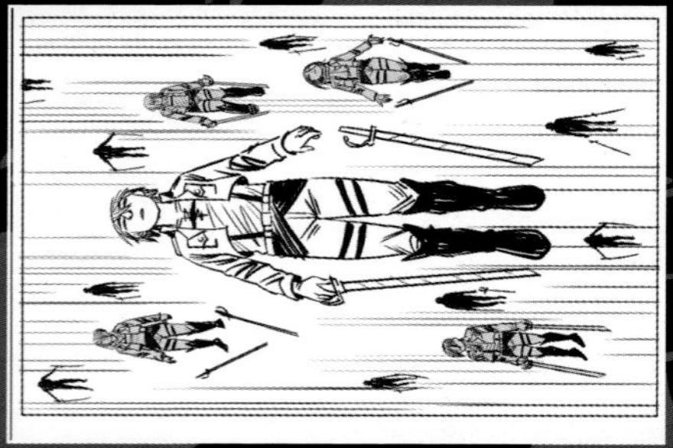

MICHAEL AVON DEMING CONCEPT ART

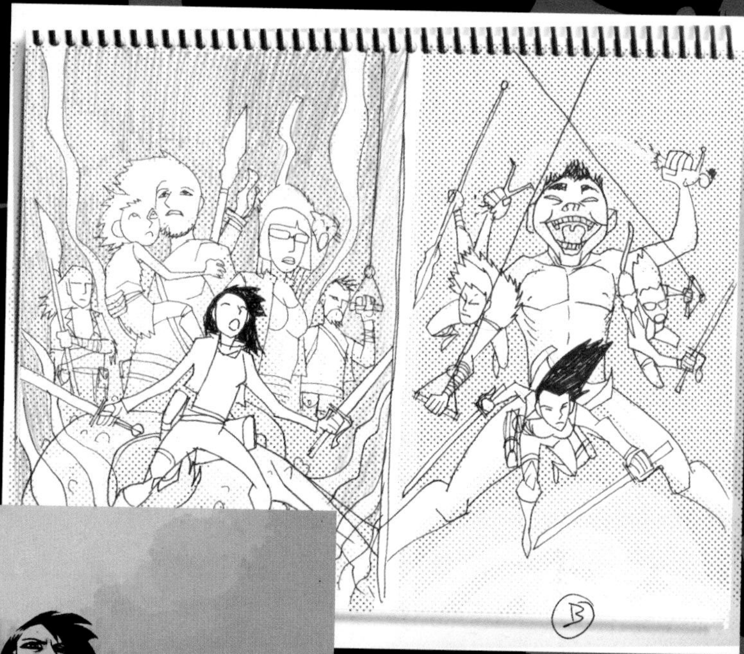
13

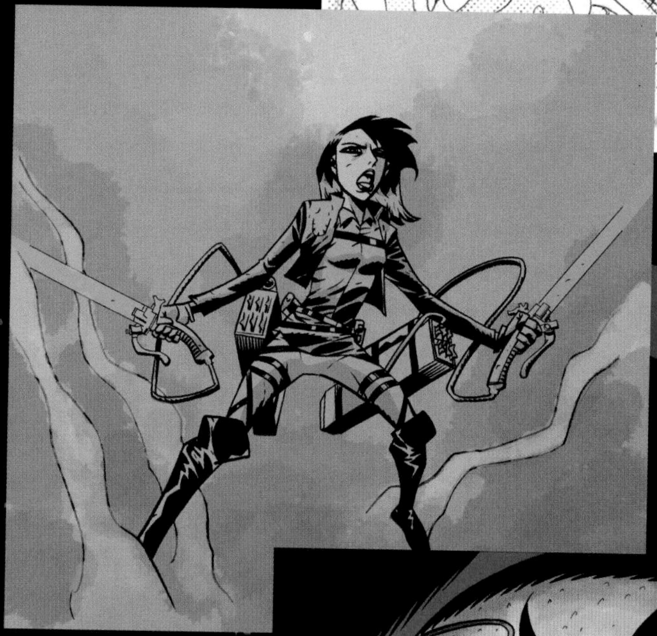

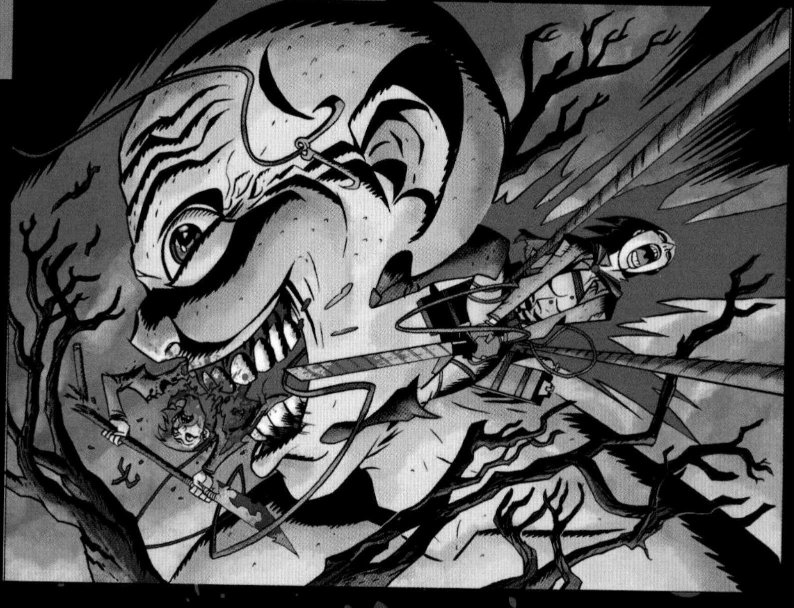

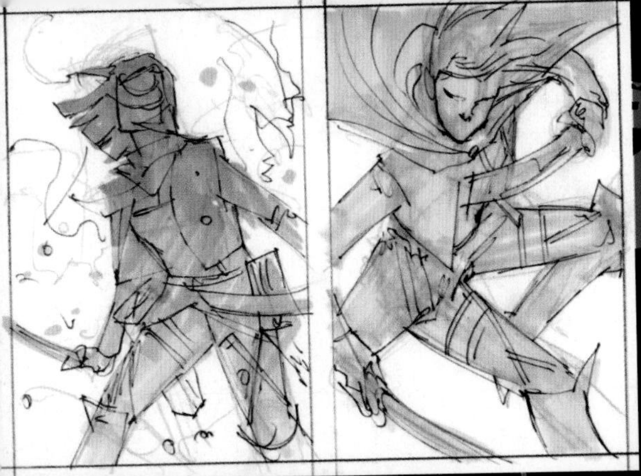

PAOLO RIVERA CONCEPT SKETCHES

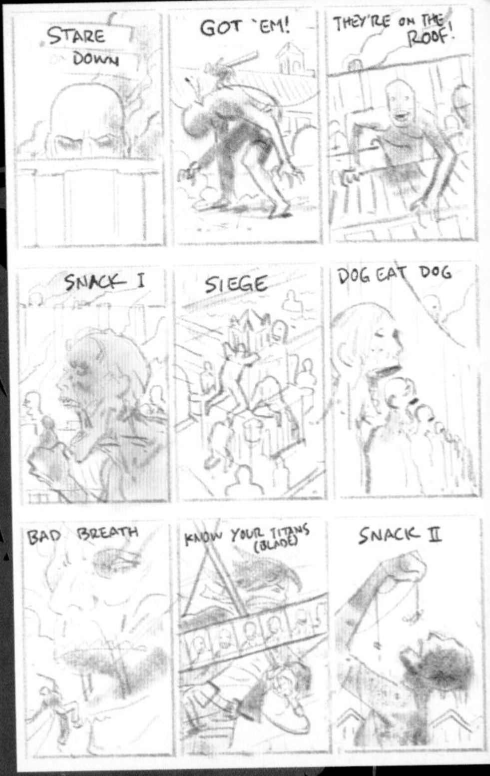

STARE DOWN
GOT 'EM!
THEY'RE ON THE ROOF!
SNACK I
SIEGE
DOG EAT DOG
BAD BREATH
KNOW YOUR TITANS (BLADE)
SNACK II

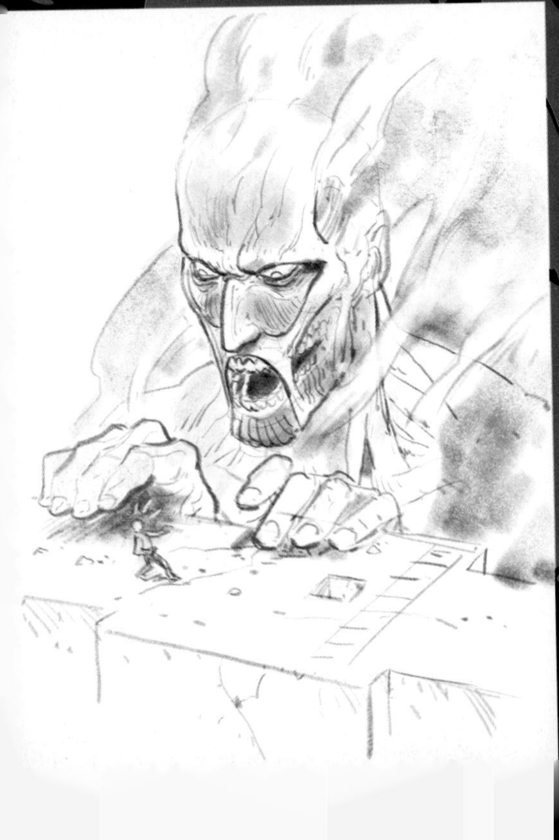

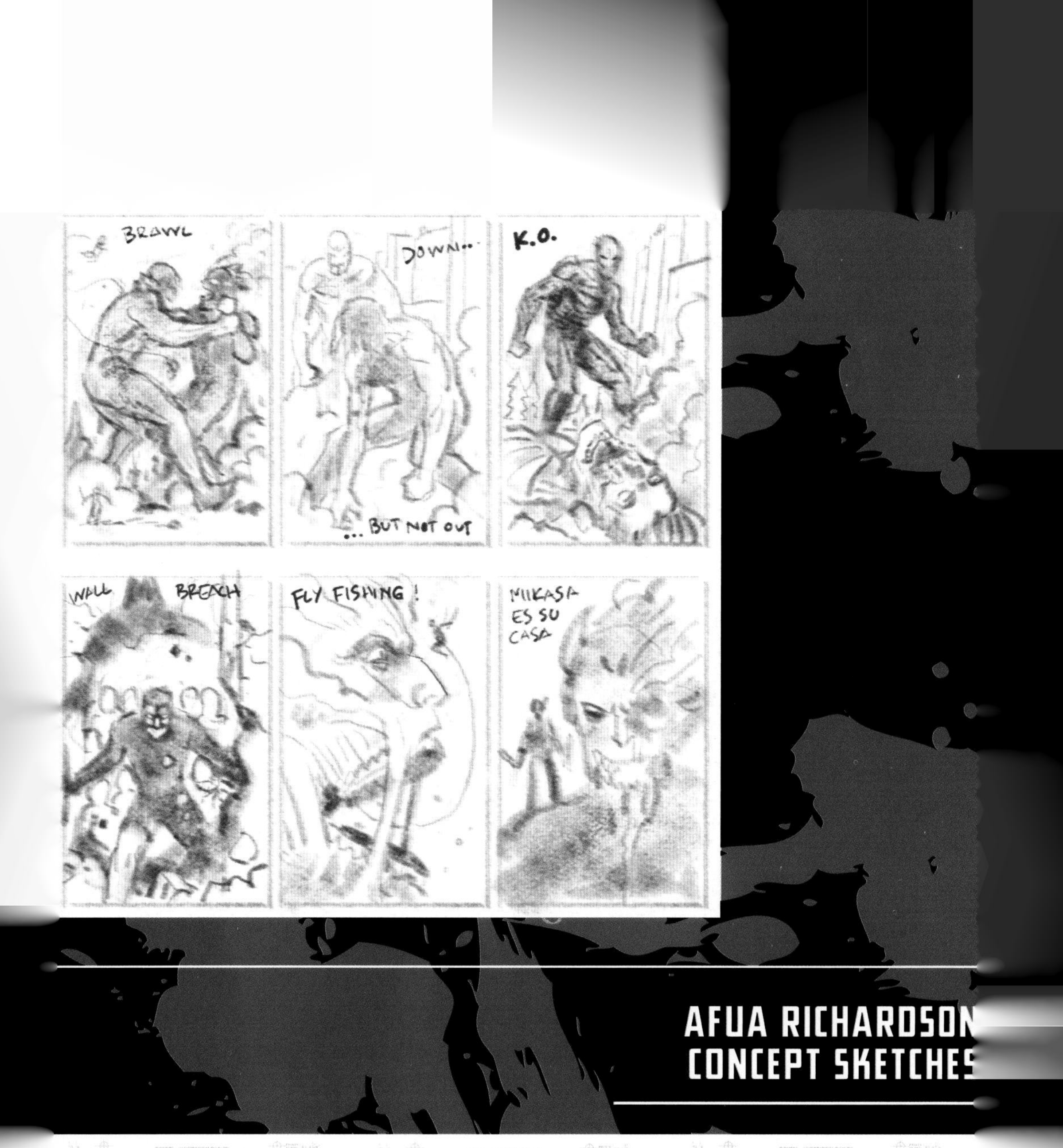
BRAWL
DOWN...
...BUT NOT OUT
K.O.
WALL BREACH
FLY FISHING!
MIKASA ES SU CASA

AFUA RICHARDSON
CONCEPT SKETCHES

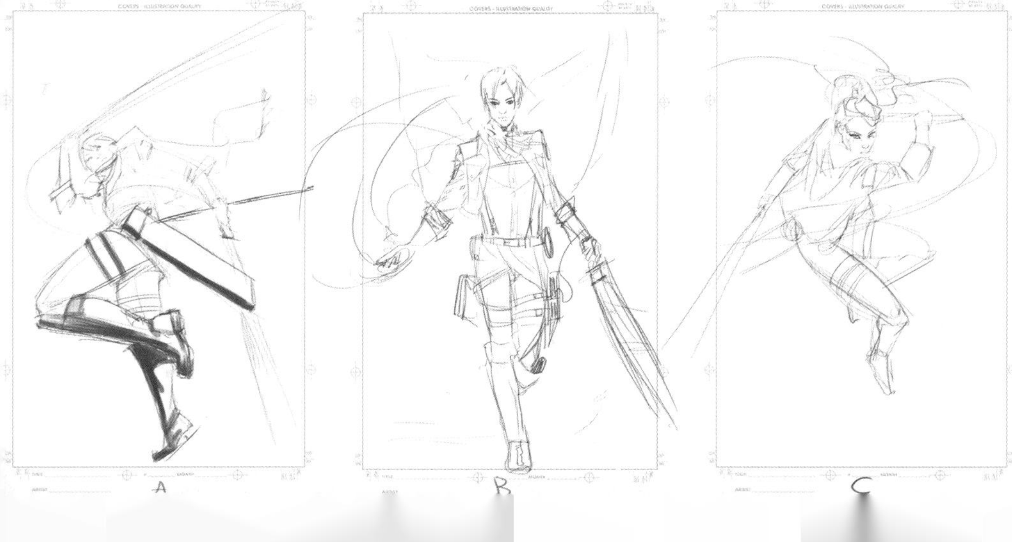
A
B
C

"UNDER THE SURFACE"
INKS TO COLOR
RAFAEL ALBUQUERQUE AND JOHN RAUCH

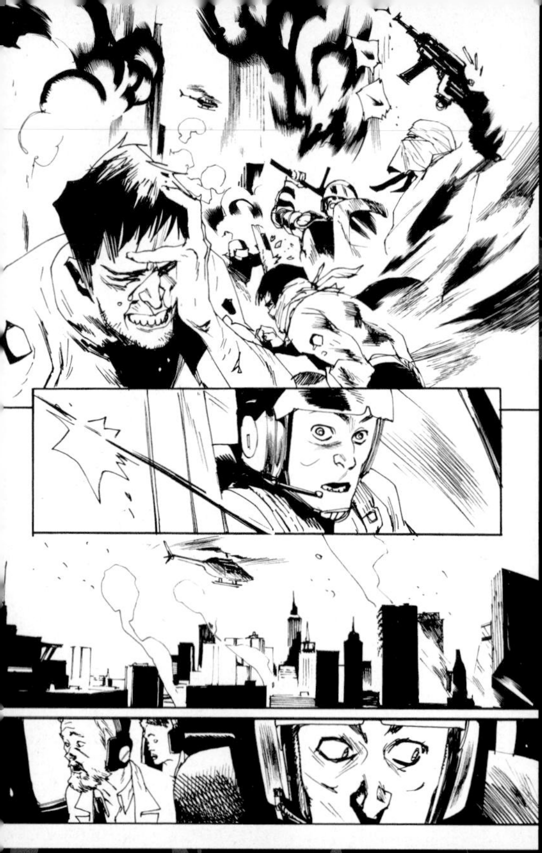

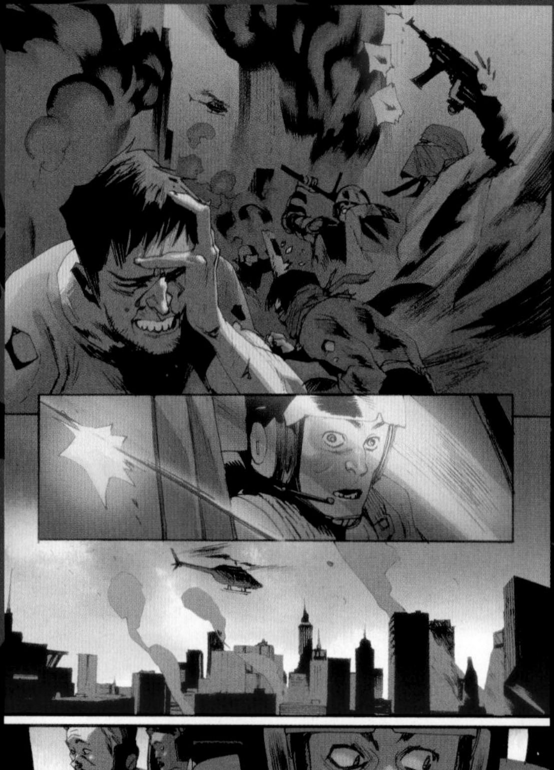

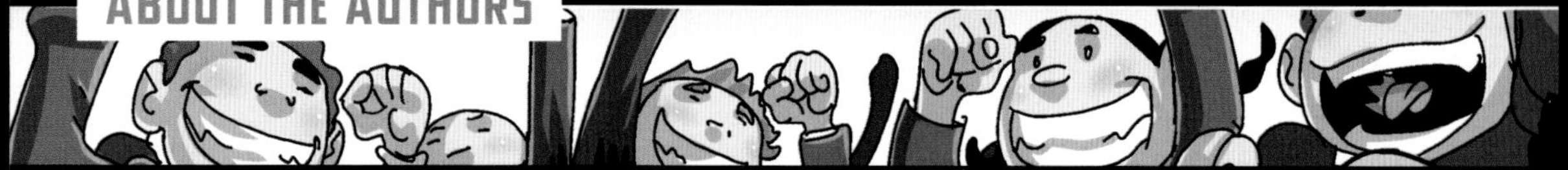

Rafael Albuquerque was born in Porto Alegre, Brazil. He has been working in the American comic book industry since 2005. Best known from his work on *Batman, Animal Man* and *Wolverine,* he has also published the creator-owned graphic novels *Crimeland* (2007), *Mondo Urbano* (2010) and *Eight* (2015). Rafael is an Eisner and Harvey Award-winner for the New York Times best seller *American Vampire* (DC Comics/Vertigo, 2010), written by Scott Snyder and Stephen King. He is currently working on *Batgirl* and *Hitgirl.*

Kate Brown lives & works full-time making comics in Oxford. In early 2010, she was awarded the Arts Foundation Fellowship for Graphic Novels. Her credits include her creator-owned titles, *Fish + Chocolate, The Unicorn and the Woodsman,* and British Comic Award-nominated *The Lost Boy.* She's currently working on the *Tamsin* series with Neill Cameron for UK weekly children's comic, *The Phoenix.* She provided art for *Young Avengers* Vol 2 and the guest arc of *The Wicked + The Divine,* and was a contributor to the British Comic Award-winning *Nelson.* She just loves drawing babies. And gore.

Jorge Corona is the Russ Manning Award-winning artist behind *Feathers, Goners* and *We Are Robin.* His body of work also includes titles such as *Bravest Warriors, Adventure Time, Jim Henson's Storyteller: Dragons, Power Rangers, Justice League Beyond,* and *Teen Titans GO!.* MFA in Sequential Arts from the Savannah College of Art and Design, Jorge is originally from Venezuela, where he grew up loving all things comics and animation.

Evan Dorkin is the Eisner, Harvey and Ignatz Award-winning creator of *Milk & Cheese, The Eltingville Club* and *Dork.* With his wife and frequent collaborator Sarah Dyer, he has written for several animated series including *Space Ghost Coast to Coast, Superman, Batman Beyond, Ben 10, DC Nation* and the children's television show *Yo Gabba Gabba.* Together they also created the Adult Swim animated pilot *Welcome to Eltingville,* based on the *Eltingville Club* comics. His work has appeared in comics published by Marvel, DC and Dark Horse, as well as *Mad Magazine, Spin, Esquire* and *The Onion.*

Paul Duffield is a comic creator, illustrator, animator and designer. He is currently working on *The Firelight Isle,* a long form graphic novel and webcomic, alongside a post at *The Phoenix Weekly Story Comic* as a designer and art director. Paul is best known for the art on Warren Ellis's *Freakangels,* which broke ground for being the first professionally published comic to be released for free online before being collected into trade, and for *The Tempest,* a manga-influenced adaptation of Shakespeare's play published by SelfMadeHero. His work has received

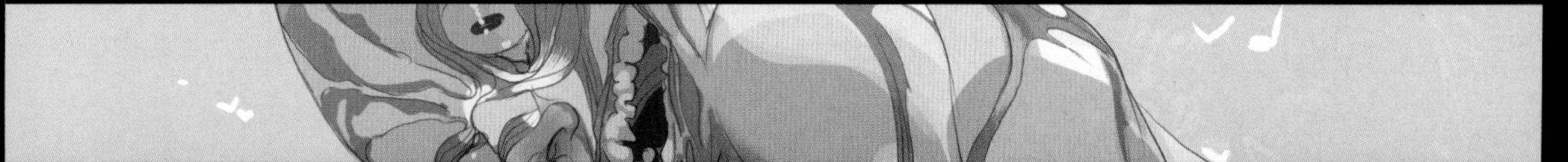

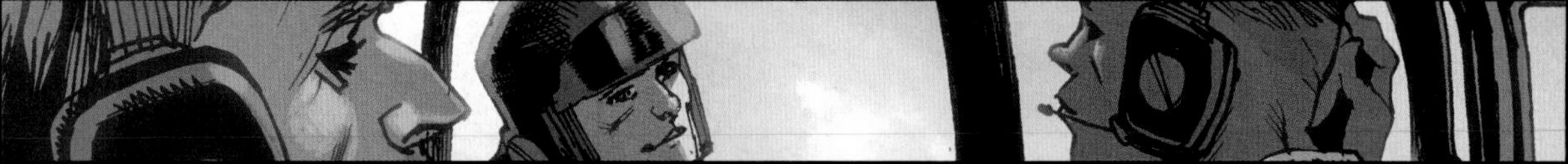

a number of awards, including an Eagle Award, first place in Tokyopop's first Rising Stars of Manga UK, and the International Manga and Anime Festival grand prize. paulduffield.co.uk

Sarah Dyer is the creator and editor of the *Action Girl Comics* anthology, which she also contributed stories and art to during its 19-issue run. She was nominated for an Eisner Award for her coloring work on David Lapham's *Amy Racecar Specials,* and wrote the English-localization scripts for the Tokyopop manga series *Kodocha, Snowdrop, President Dad* and *Paradise Kiss,* as well as a *Nathan Never* graphic novel published by Dark Horse.

Ray Fawkes is an award-winning writer and artist best known for his creator-owned graphic novels *One Soul, The People Inside, The Spectral Engine,* and *Intersect.* He has worked for DC Comics on *Batman: Eternal, Constantine,* and *Gotham by Midnight.*

Brenden Fletcher, Cameron Stewart, and **Babs Tarr** are the acclaimed team of creators behind *Batgirl* and *Motor Crush.* Artist **Babs Tarr** made her comics debut with *Batgirl.* She has also created illustrations for Hasbro, Disney, The San Francisco Chronicle, The Boston Globe, and many others. The Eisner and Shuster Award-winning artist and writer **Cameron Stewart** is a comics veteran, with art credits on *Fight Club 2, Batman & Robin,* and *Catwoman.* Well-known comics writer **Brenden Fletcher's** credits include the unique hit *Gotham Academy* with Becky Cloonan and Karl Kerschl, and *Black Canary* with Annie Wu.

Twin brothers **Tomer** and **Asaf Hanuka** are illustrators and comics creators living in Israel who often work as a team. Together they created the series *Bipolar* and, with Boaz Lavie, *The Divine,* which became a New York Times Bestseller and one of the most critically-acclaimed graphic novels of 2015. **Tomer Hanuka's** illustrations have appeared in The New Yorker, Rolling Stone, Time Magazine, and others. A collection of his illustrations, *OVERKILL,* was released in 2011. **Asaf Hanuka** has been documenting his life in comics form since 2009. A collection of this autobiographical work, *The Realist,* won an Eisner Award and has been translated into nine languages.

Jen Hickman is a Californian illustrator and colorist. Jen graduated from SCAD's Sequential Art master's program in 2012 and has been working in comics and illustration ever since.

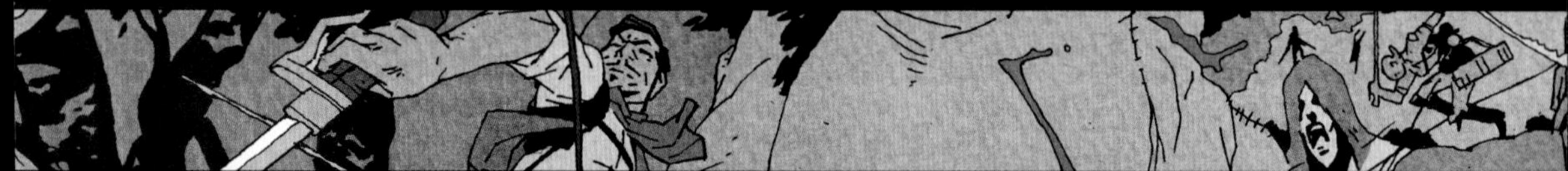

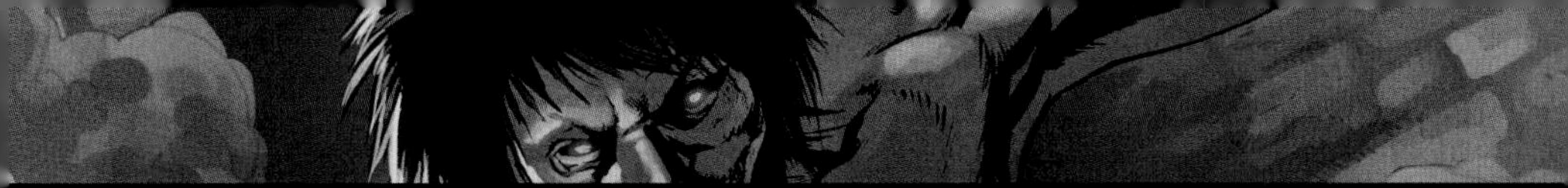

Faith Erin Hicks is a Canadian writer and artist based in Vancouver, British Columbia. She has written and drawn a number of graphic novels, including *The War at Ellsmere, Brain Camp* (with Susan Kim and Laurence Klavan), *Friends with Boys, Nothing Can Possibly Go Wrong* (with Prudence Shen), *The Adventures of Superhero Girl, The Last of Us: American Dreams* (with Neil Druckmann), and the *Bigfoot Boy* series (with J. Torres). She won an Eisner Award in 2014 for *The Adventures of Superhero Girl.* Her current project is a fantasy graphic novel trilogy called *The Nameless City.*

Sam Humphries is a comic book writer. He broke into comics with the self-published runaway hits *Our Love is Real* and *Sacrifice.* Since then, he has written high profile books such as *Legendary Star-Lord* for Marvel, and *Green Lanterns* for DC Comics, as well as co-created original hits like *Citizen Jack* and *Jonesy.* He lives in Los Angeles with his girlfriend and their cat, El Niño.

Phil Jimenez is an award-winning writer and artist who has worked for DC Entertainment and Marvel Entertainment for over 25 years. Best known for his work on *Tempest, JLA/Titans, The Invisibles, New-X-Men, Wonder Woman, Infinite Crisis, Amazing Spider-Man, Adventure Comics, The Transformers, DC: Rebirth,* and his creator owned project *Otherworld.* Jimenez has also worked in film, television, print media, and in design/packaging. He has created large-scale artworks for schools and museums, lectured at universities and the Library of Congress on identity and diversity in entertainment, and mentors young designers at the Cooper Hewitt National Design Museum. Considered one of the most prominent gay creators in mainstream comics, Jimenez also teaches life drawing at the School of Visual Arts in NYC. FB, Instagram, and Twitter @Philjimeneznyc

Jiji Knight was born and raised in Las Vegas and is a woman obsessed with illustration & fashion. Her work often features a variety of sassy ladies, geek chic redesigns, and all around promotes body positivity. She attended the Academy of Art University in foggy San Francisco and currently resides in her sunny, desert hometown of Vegas working as a part time freelance illustrator.

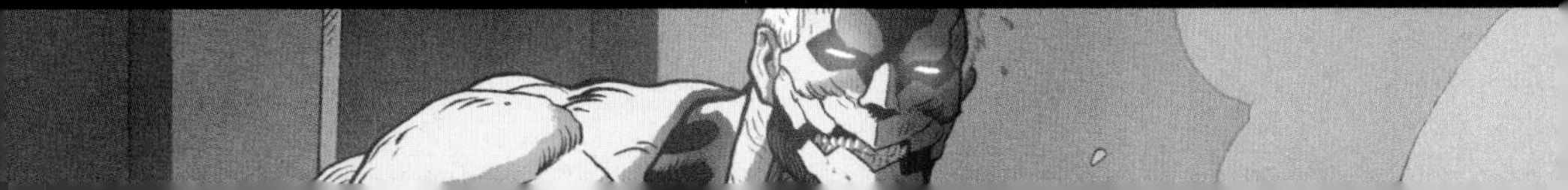

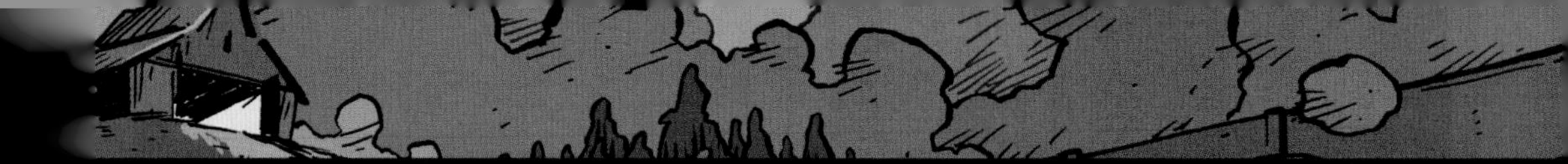

David López was born in the Canary Islands. He began his career with Espiral, a self published fanzine that moved later to Ediciones la Cúpula having national distribution there. He went on to draw *Fallen Angel* and *Catwoman* for DC Comics, and *X-Men, New Mutants, Hawkeye & Mockingbird,* the Eisner and Harvey Award-nominated *Mystic, Captain Marvel,* and *All New Wolverine,* among many others, for Marvel.

Alonso Nunez is a freelance comic artist and founder of Little Fish Comic Book Studio in San Diego, CA where he lives with his wife, two kids, and deadlines.

For decades, **Michael Avon Oeming's** art has been a pioneering, unique voice in comics. Co-creator of *Powers* (for which he won an Eisner Award), *The Mice Templar, Sinergy,* and many others, Oeming also led a team at Valve Software that created webcomics based on *Portal 2, Left 4 Dead,* and *Team Fortress.* He is an executive producer on the *Powers* TV series.

Cris Peter has been a comic book colorist for 14 years. She's worked for publishers like Dark Horse, Image, DC and Marvel Comics, and was nominated for an Eisner Award for Best Colorist for the title *Casanova,* written by Matt Fraction with art by Fábio Moon and Gabriel Bá. Cris lives in the south of Brazil, in a city called Porto Alegre, with her two dogs, where she finds time not only to color, but also to lecture about color and communication and write her own comic book projects.

Paul Pope is a 5-Time Eisner Award-winning American artist. He developed a number of manga projects for Kodansha's *Morning* magazine in the late '90s. His latest book, *Battling Boy* (:01) debuted at #1 on *The New York Times* Best Seller list. He lives and works in NYC.

Elmer Santos was born 1991 in Manila, and is a self-taught artist who started working professionally at age 15. He worked on various publications locally, as well as a brief stint as a Wardrobe Designer for a couple of feature films. He was 22 years-old when he decided to pursue a career as a colorist, and sought out his mentors Stephen Segovia and Philip Tan for help to be able to break into mainstream Western comics. He's now 25 and has worked on a handful of comic titles and various illustrating gigs.

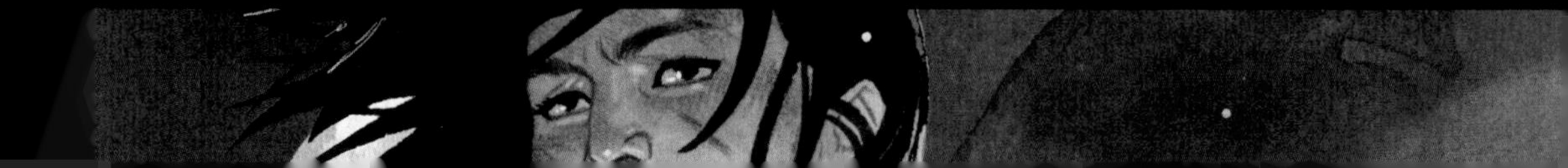

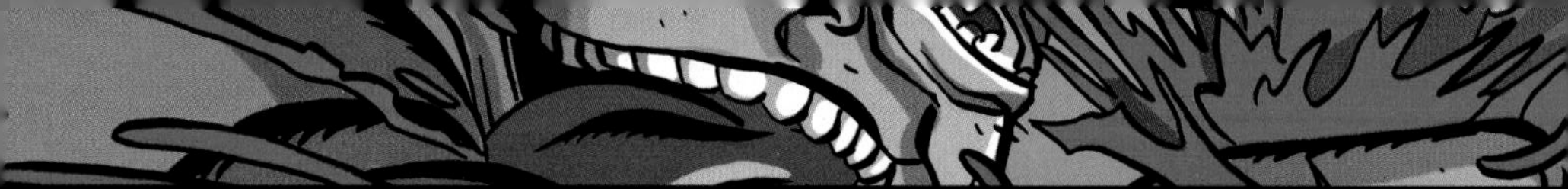

Rhianna Pratchett is an WGA award-winning writer who has spun tales for DC's *Mirror's Edge,* Dark Horse's *Thief: Tales from the City, Tomb Raider* and *Tomb Raider: The Beginning* and *Legends of Red Sonja* for Dynamite Entertainment. She also wrestles the wild beasts of narrative for videogames, film, TV, and short stories, with several novel-to-screen adaptations and a TV series in the works. Like most writers, she likes hard liquor and soft cats.

John Rauch is an American comic book colorist whose credits include: *The Beauty, Invincible, The Darkness, Teen Titans: Year One, Patsy Walker: Hellcat,* and a bunch of other stuff not worth bragging about. He enjoys speaking about himself in the third person and pretending he is more talented and relevant than he really is to fight off bouts of depression.

Afua Richardson [pronounced Ah FOO wah] is a comic book illustrator best known for her work in the politically potent, Reader's Choice-winning mini series Genius for Image/Top Cow. Her client list includes Marvel, DC, Dark Horse, Valiant, Disney, The New Yorker and many others. In addition to being a visual artist, Afua is a mentor, graphic designer, activist, singer, songwriter, commercial voice actor, musician, and writer. As recipient for the Nina Simone Award for Artistic Excellence, she was celebrated for being one of the few African/Native American women to work for Marvel, DC, and Image comics as a penciler, inker, and colorist. She has been called a "modern day renaissance woman" and a " Jane of all trades".

Paolo Rivera was born and raised in Daytona Beach, FL and graduated from the Rhode Island School of Design in 2003. He began his career at Marvel, working almost exclusively with them for a decade. He has since worked for every major publisher creating covers, posters, and comics. Ever since his run on Mark Waid's *Daredevil,* he has worked with his father, Joe Rivera, an award-winning inker. His most recent books include *The Valiant* and *Hellboy* and the *B.P.R.D. 1953.* He lives in San Francisco with his wife and daughter, blogging regularly at paolorivera.com

Damion Scott or "MOSH"0110 is a Jamaican/American comic book artist and writer. Scott is a graduate of The Kubert School. His drawing style is influenced by graffiti art and hip-hop culture. He has published a book entitled *How To Draw Hip-Hop* on the subject. Scott has worked on several DC Comics, including *Batman, Robin,* and *Raven,* and he was the featured artist in issue #10 of the *Solo* series (2006). Scott has also worked for Marvel comics on *Spider-Man, Deadpool* and *All New Ghost Rider.* He lives and works in his hometown of Brooklyn, NYC, but also has a residence in Tokyo, Japan, where he is heavily involved in the local art scene.

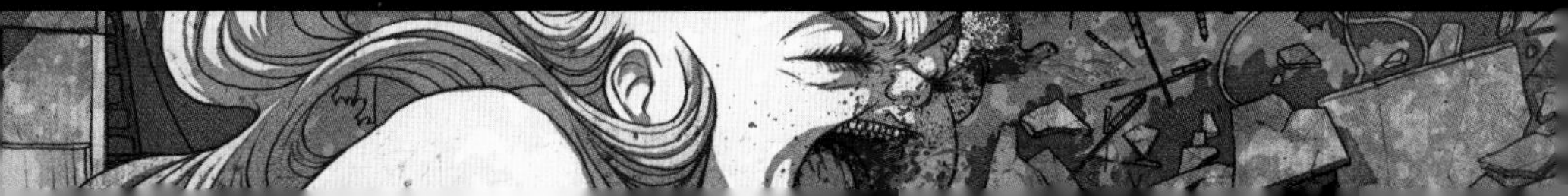

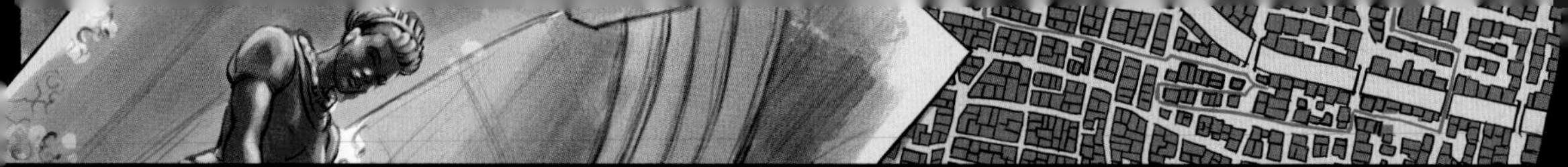

Gail Simone is a critically-acclaimed writer of comics, games and television, with groundbreaking runs on titles such as *Birds Of Prey, Batgirl, Deadpool, Wonder Woman* and *Secret Six,* as well as her creator-owned books, including *Leaving Megalopolis* and *Clean Room.* She currently resides on the Oregon coast with her family.

Scott Snyder is the New York Times best-selling author of *Batman, Swamp Thing,* the Eisner Award-winning *American Vampire, Wytches, The Wake, Severed,* and *After Death,* among other works. His book of stories, *Voodoo Heart,* was published in 2006 from The Dial Press. He lives in New York with his wife and two sons.

Simon "Si" Spurrier writes novels and comics. His work in the latter field stretches from award-winning creator-owned books such as *Numbercruncher, Six-Gun Gorilla* and *The Spire* to projects in the U.S. mainstream like *X-Men, Silver Surfer* and *Crossed.* His latest comic, *Cry Havoc,* is being published by Image Comics. His prose works range from the beatnik neurosis-noir of *Contract* to the occult whodunnit *A Serpent Uncoiled.* In 2016 he took a foray into experimental fiction with the e-novella *Unusual Concentrations: a tale of coffee, crime and overhead conversations.* He lives in London, regards sushi as part of the plotting process, and does not have a cat.

Sigmund Torre was born in the Philippines, raised in Canada, worked in Japan, then moved back to where he started. He started in comics in 2000 as a penciller then moved to coloring, working on books like *Transformers, TMNT, Raven, Star Wars Clone Wars Adventures, Streetfighter,* and most recently *Red Hill Billy.* See more of his work at sigmundtorre.com.

Genevieve Valentine is the author of novels *Mechanique, The Girls at the Kingfisher Club, Persona,* and *Icon.* Her essays and reviews have appeared at *The New York Times,* the *AV Club,* and *The Atlantic.* She's written *Catwoman* and *Batman and Robin Eternal* for DC Comics and *Xena: Warrior Princess* for Dynamite.

Kevin Wada is a freelance illustrator in San Francisco. His watercolor covers have been published by Marvel, DC, Boom!, Image, IDW and more.

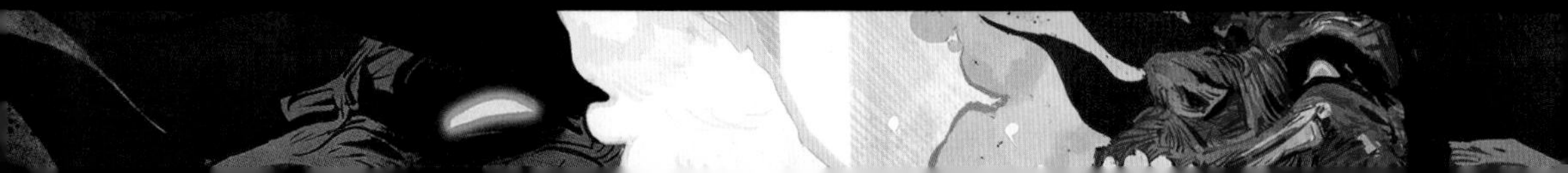

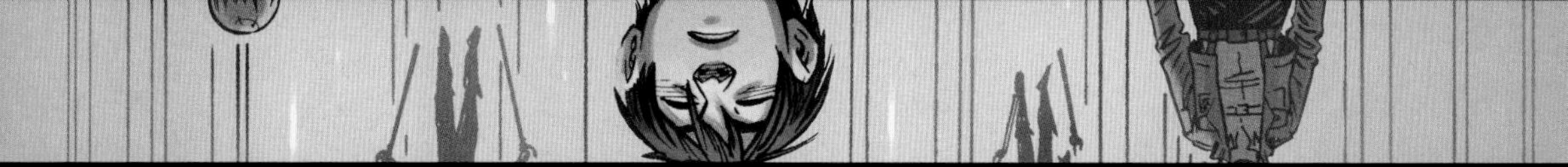

Ronald Wimberly is a designer based in NY city. He works primarily in narrative. He's worked with The New Yorker, Dargaud, DC, Marvel, Image, Darkhorse, Nike, Benetton and others. Some notable works are the Eisner Award-nominated *Sentences* for Vertigo, *Lighten Up for the Nib on Medium,* and *Prince of Cats.* He's been twice selected for the Maison des Auteurs residency in Angoulême and is the 2016 Columbus Museum of Art/Thurber House 2016 Graphic Novelist Artist in residence. He's exhibited in New York, Tokyo, and Paris.

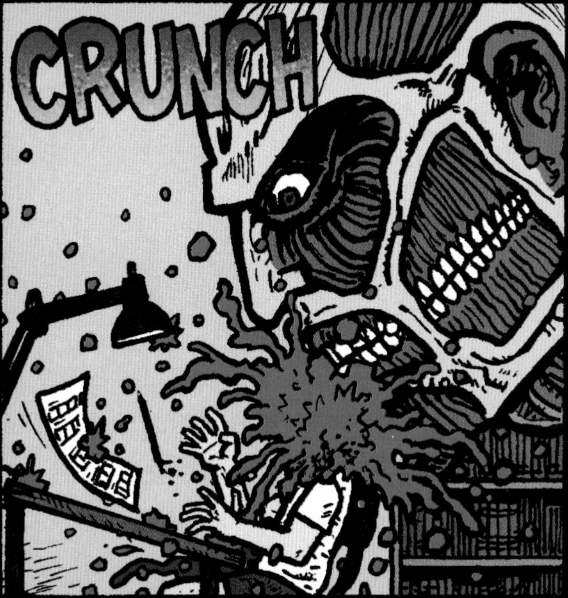
CRUNCH

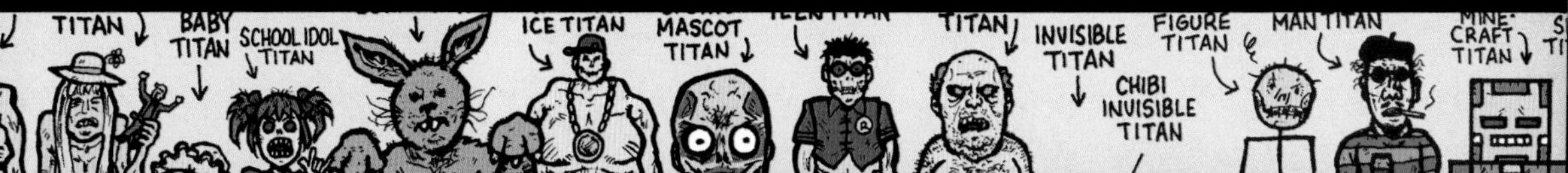
TITAN
BABY TITAN
SCHOOL IDOL TITAN
ICE TITAN
MASCOT TITAN
TITAN
INVISIBLE TITAN
CHIBI INVISIBLE TITAN
FIGURE TITAN
MAN TITAN
CRAFT TITAN

ATTACK on TITAN

A N T H O L O G Y

E X C L U S I V E
" A T T A C K   O N   T I T A N   M A N G A "
A P P   M O T I O N   B O O K   P R E V I E W

" B E R G H E I M "
W R I T T E N   B Y
K A T E   L E T H   &   J E R E M Y   L A M B E R T

A R T   B Y
A F U A   R I C H A R D S O N

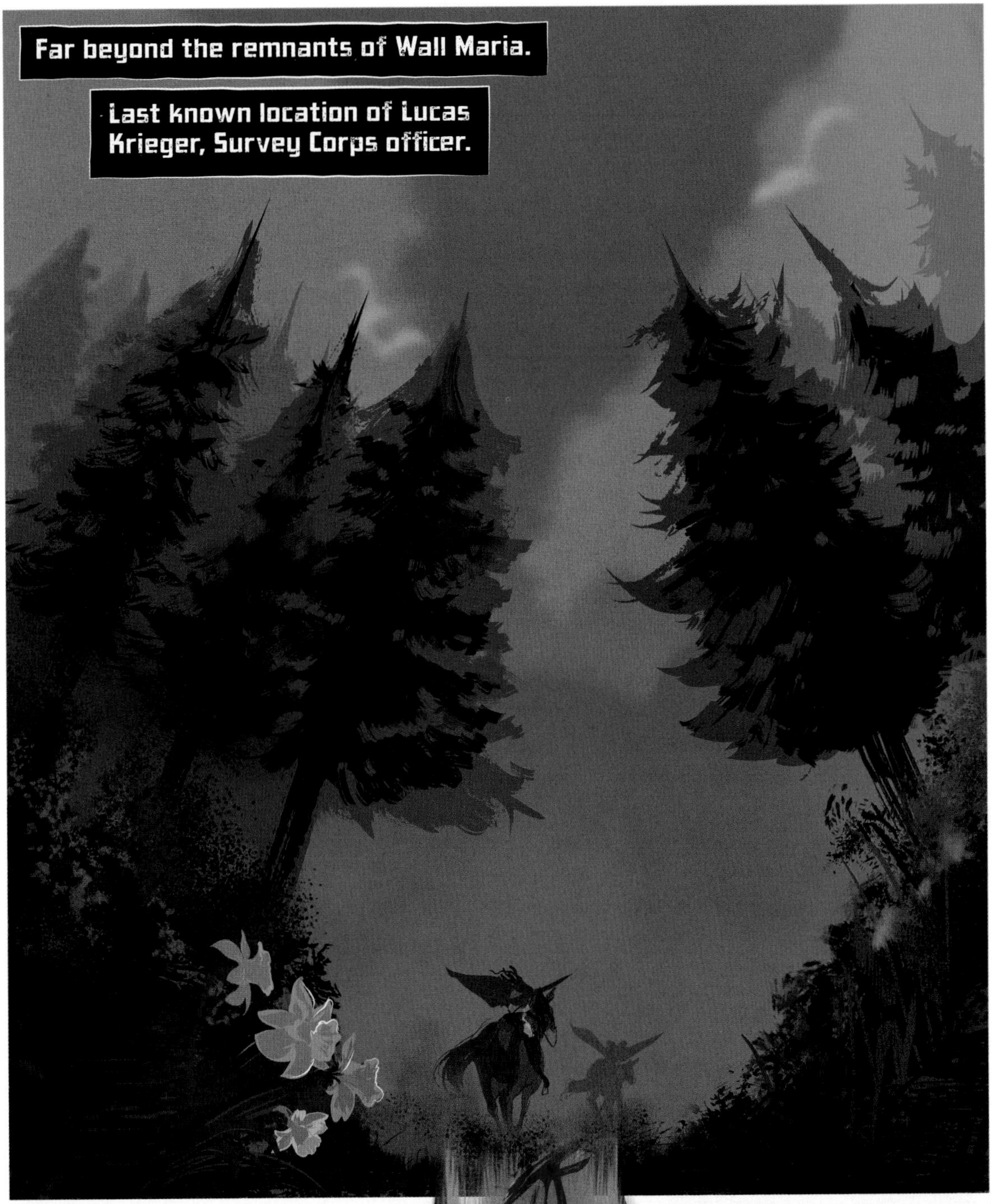
Far beyond the remnants of Wall Maria.
Last known location of Lucas Krieger, Survey Corps officer.
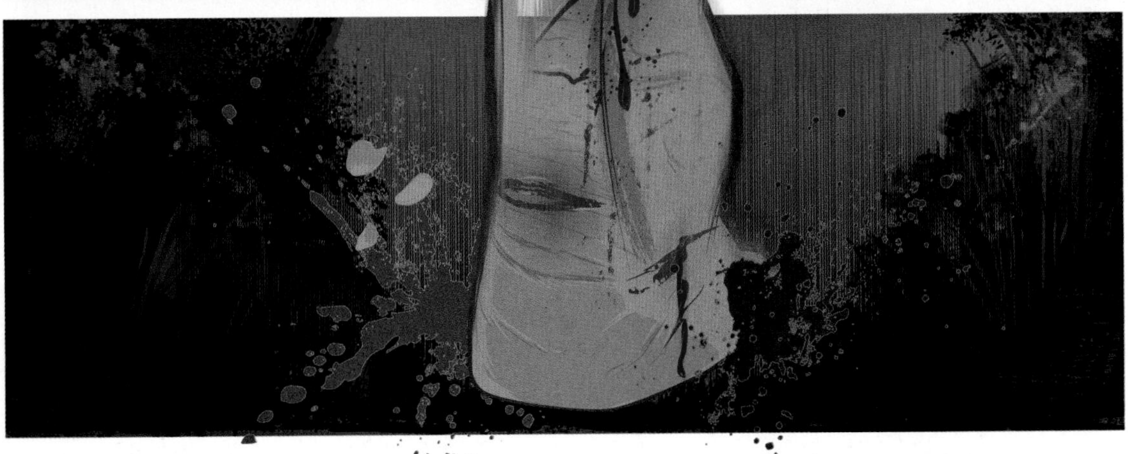

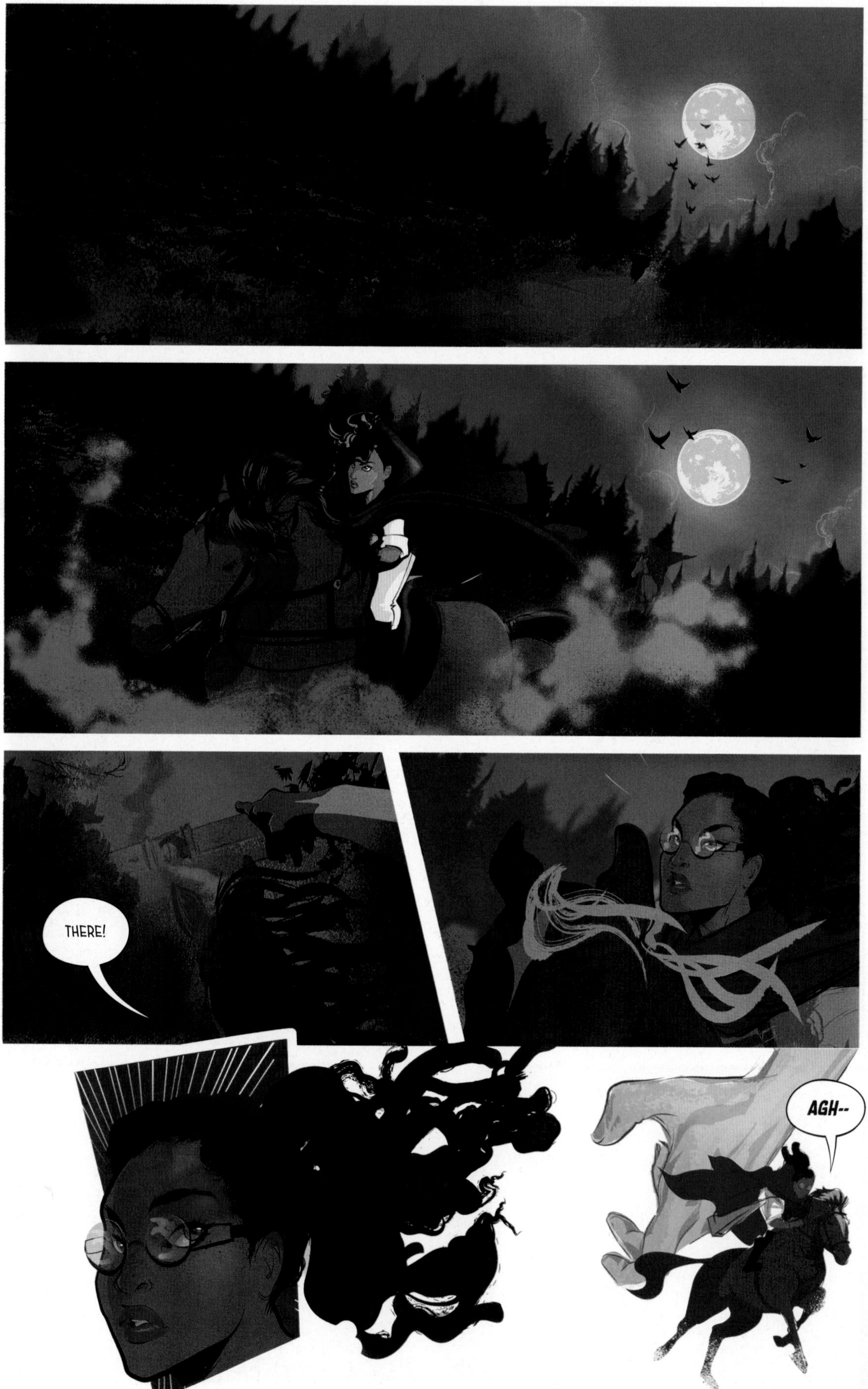
THERE!
AGH--

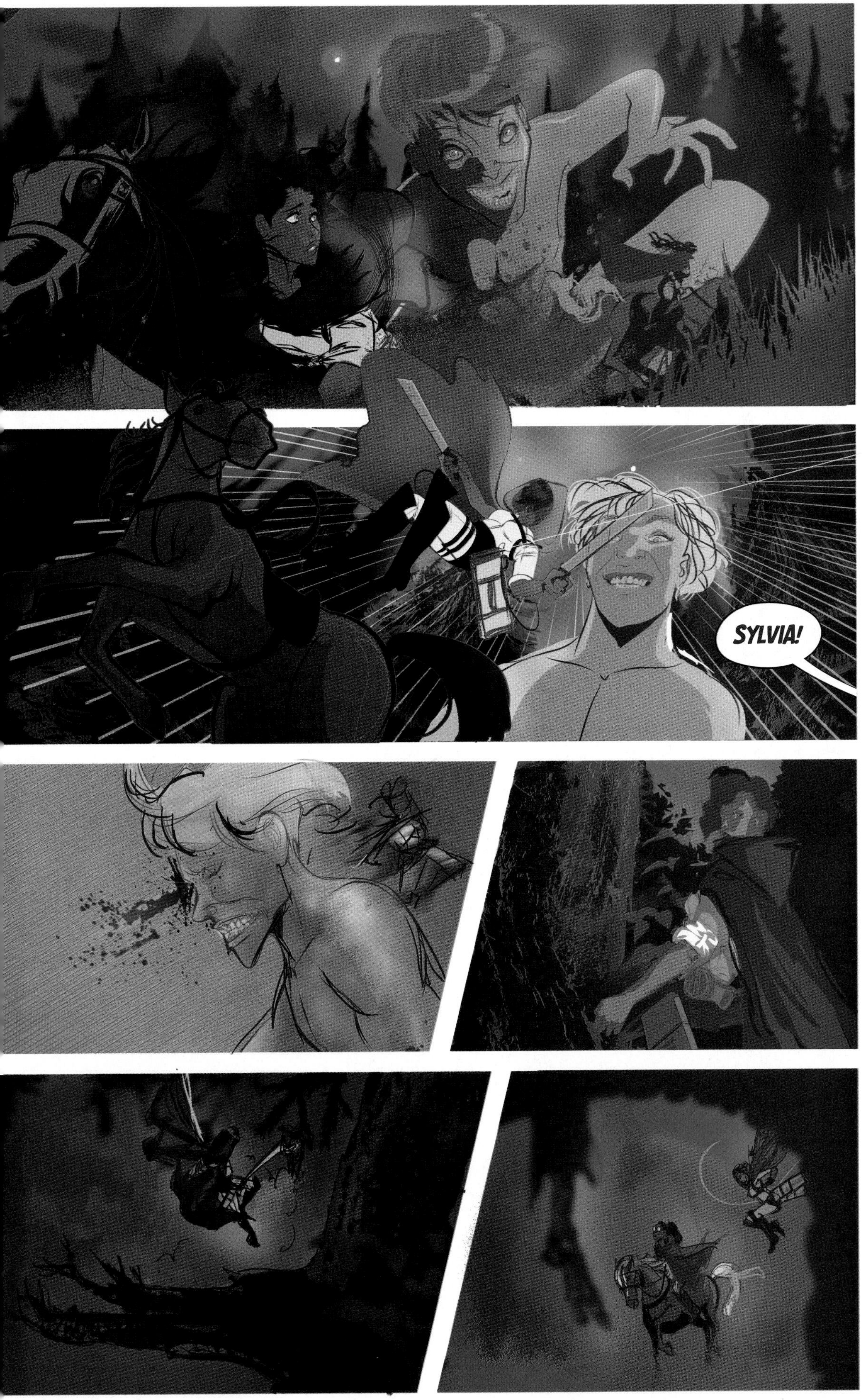
SYLVIA!

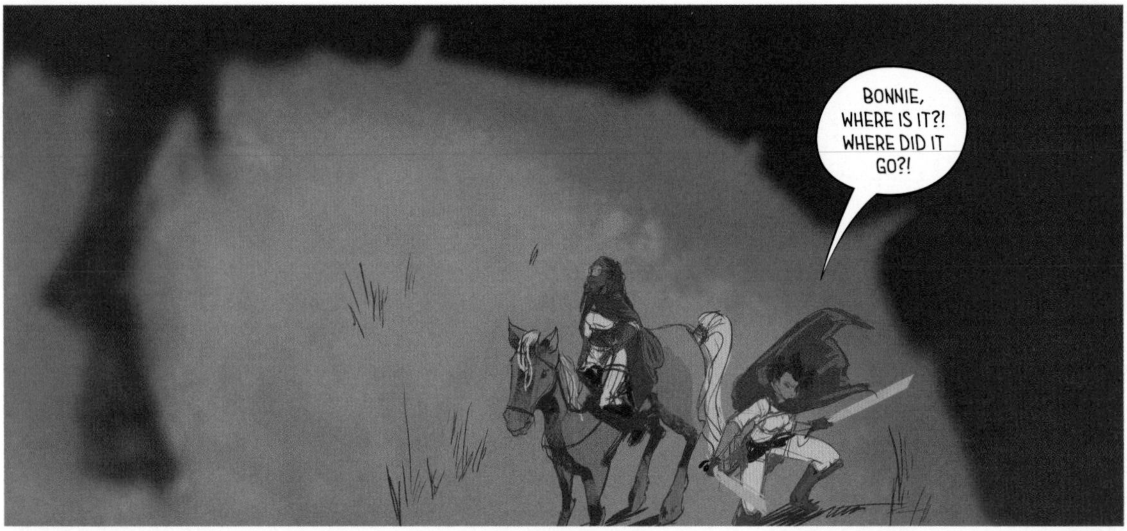
BONNIE, WHERE IS IT?! WHERE DID IT GO?!
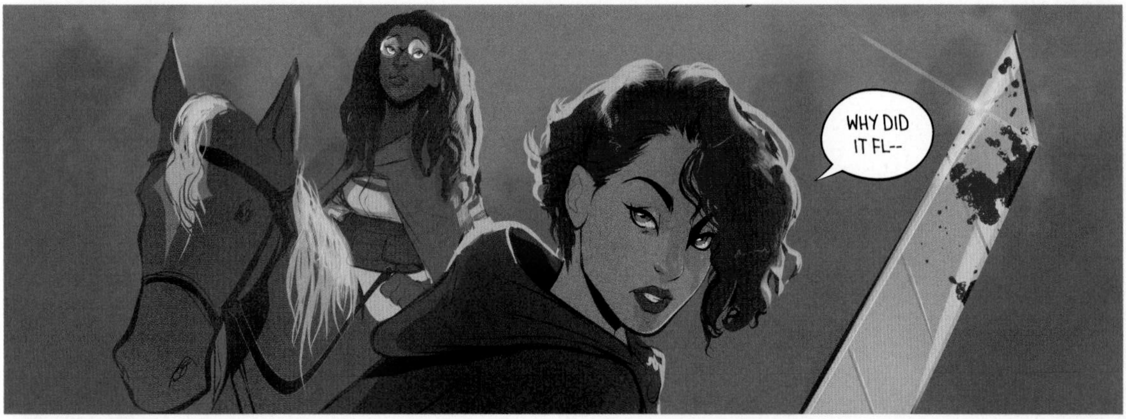
WHY DID IT FL--
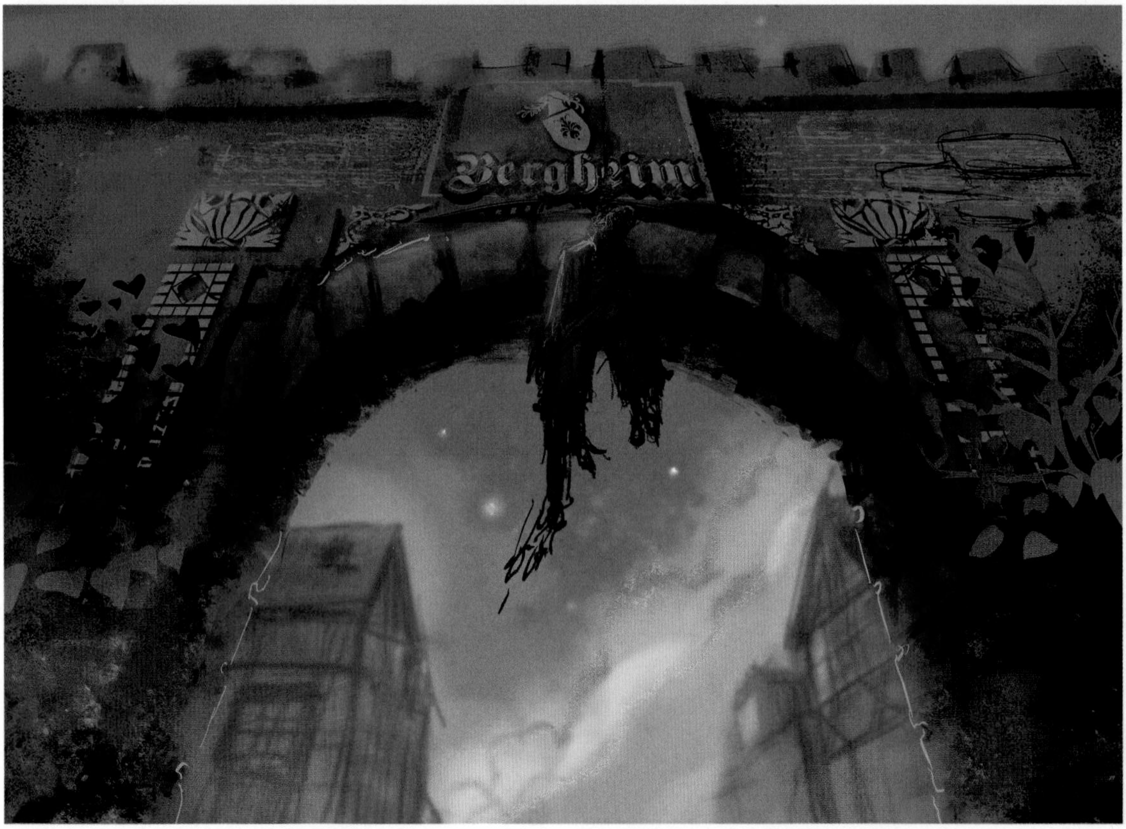
Bergheim

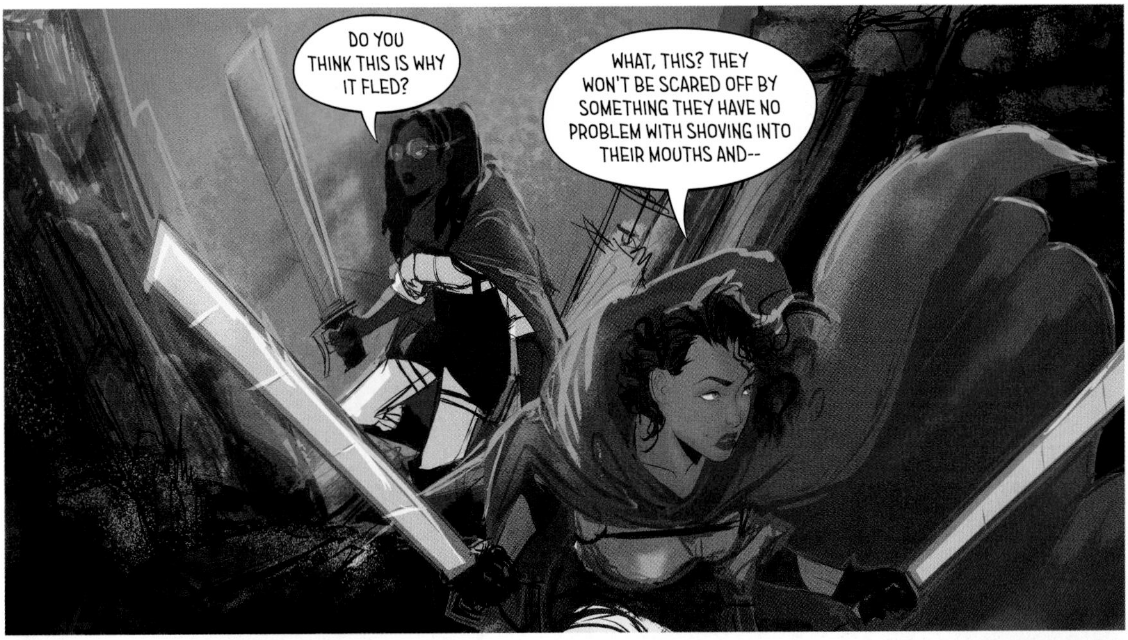
DO YOU THINK THIS IS WHY IT FLED?
WHAT, THIS? THEY WON'T BE SCARED OFF BY SOMETHING THEY HAVE NO PROBLEM WITH SHOVING INTO THEIR MOUTHS AND--

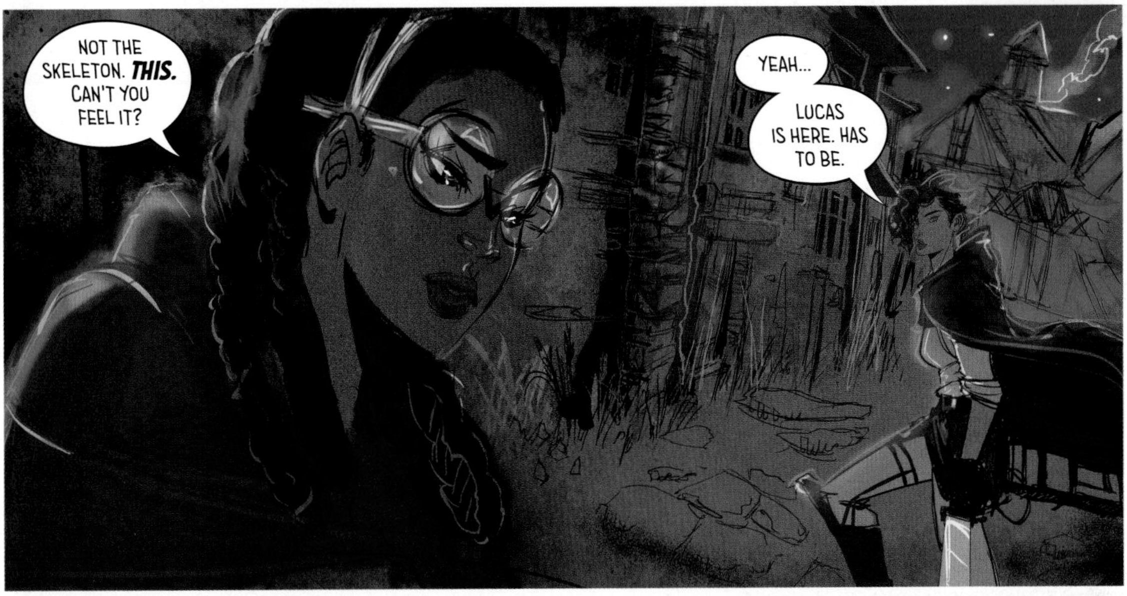
NOT THE SKELETON. ***THIS.*** CAN'T YOU FEEL IT?
YEAH...
LUCAS IS HERE. HAS TO BE.

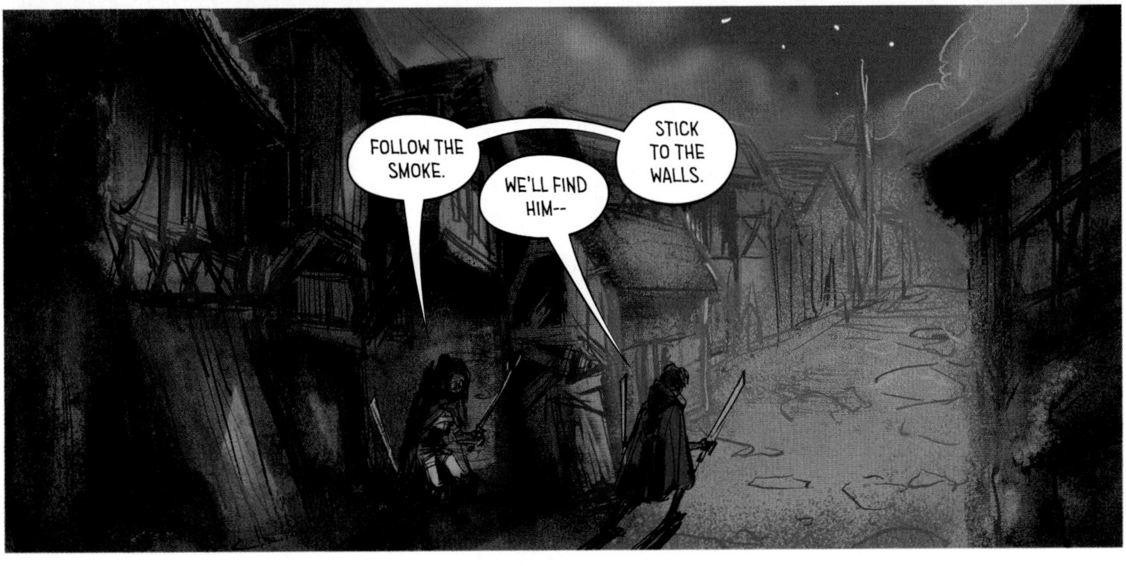
FOLLOW THE SMOKE.
STICK TO THE WALLS.
WE'LL FIND HIM--

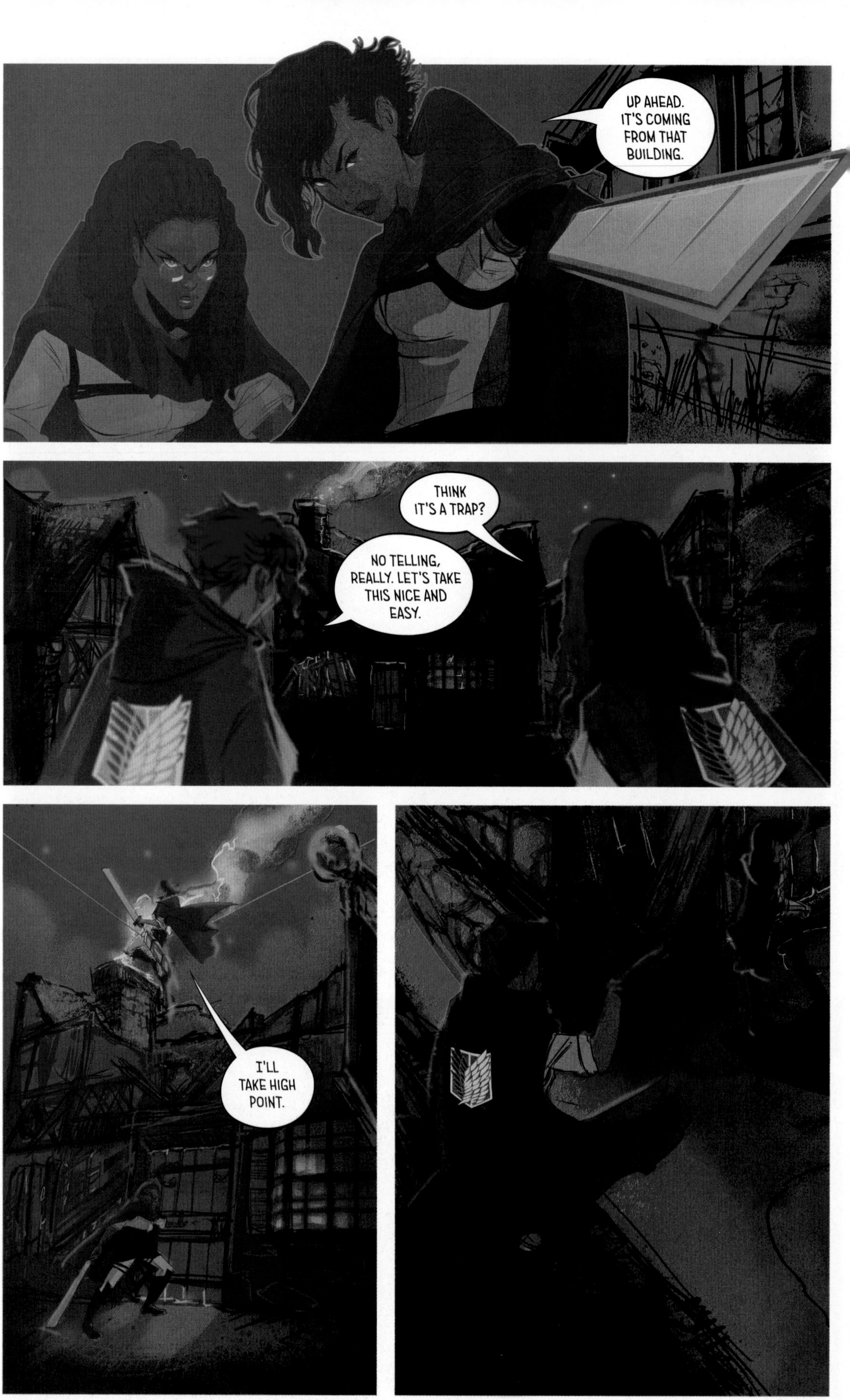
UP AHEAD. IT'S COMING FROM THAT BUILDING.
THINK IT'S A TRAP?
NO TELLING, REALLY. LET'S TAKE THIS NICE AND EASY.
I'LL TAKE HIGH POINT.

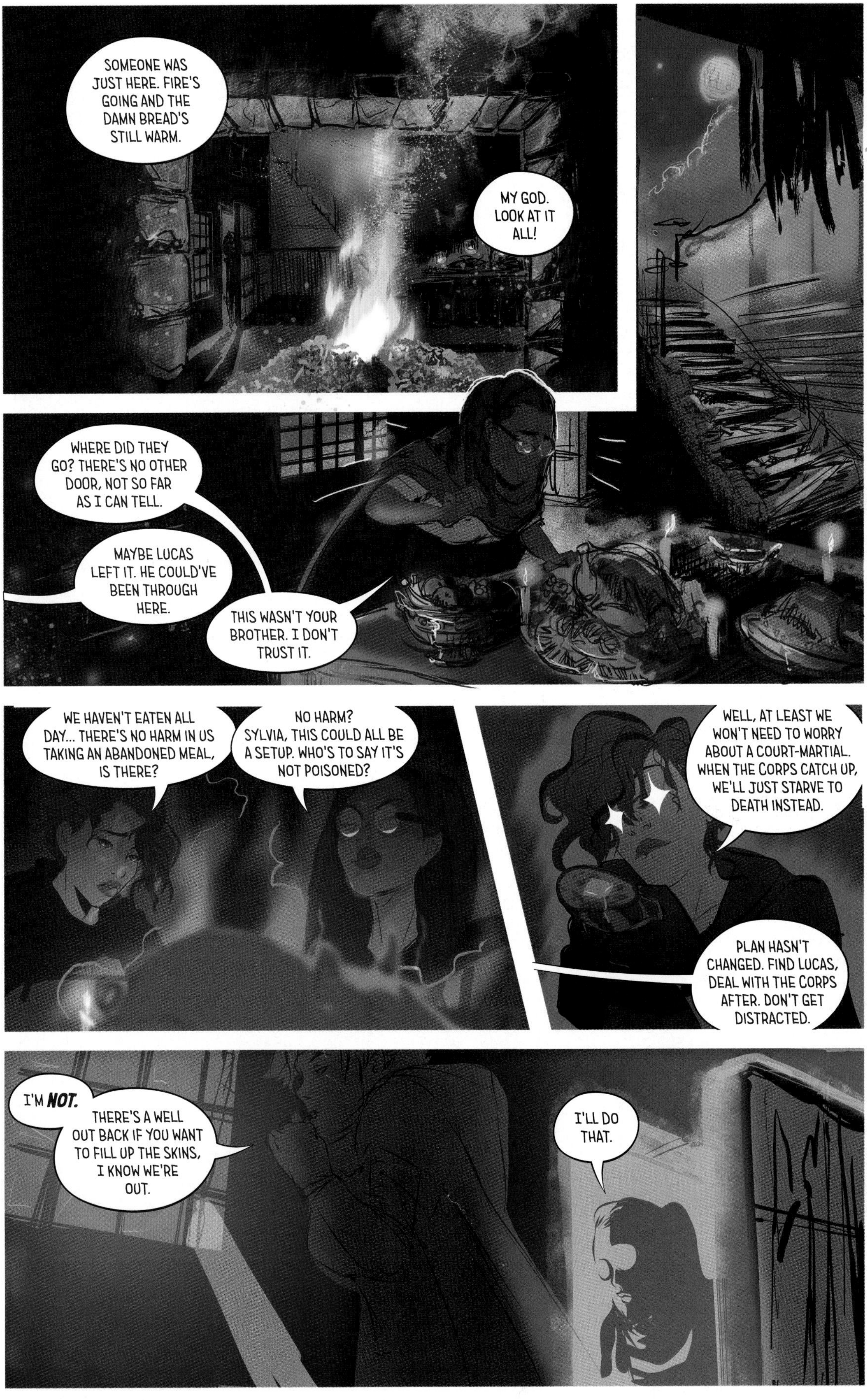
SOMEONE WAS JUST HERE. FIRE'S GOING AND THE DAMN BREAD'S STILL WARM.
MY GOD. LOOK AT IT ALL!
WHERE DID THEY GO? THERE'S NO OTHER DOOR, NOT SO FAR AS I CAN TELL.
MAYBE LUCAS LEFT IT. HE COULD'VE BEEN THROUGH HERE.
THIS WASN'T YOUR BROTHER. I DON'T TRUST IT.
WE HAVEN'T EATEN ALL DAY... THERE'S NO HARM IN US TAKING AN ABANDONED MEAL, IS THERE?
NO HARM? SYLVIA, THIS COULD ALL BE A SETUP. WHO'S TO SAY IT'S NOT POISONED?
WELL, AT LEAST WE WON'T NEED TO WORRY ABOUT A COURT-MARTIAL. WHEN THE CORPS CATCH UP, WE'LL JUST STARVE TO DEATH INSTEAD.
PLAN HASN'T CHANGED. FIND LUCAS, DEAL WITH THE CORPS AFTER. DON'T GET DISTRACTED.
I'M **NOT.**
THERE'S A WELL OUT BACK IF YOU WANT TO FILL UP THE SKINS, I KNOW WE'RE OUT.
I'LL DO THAT.

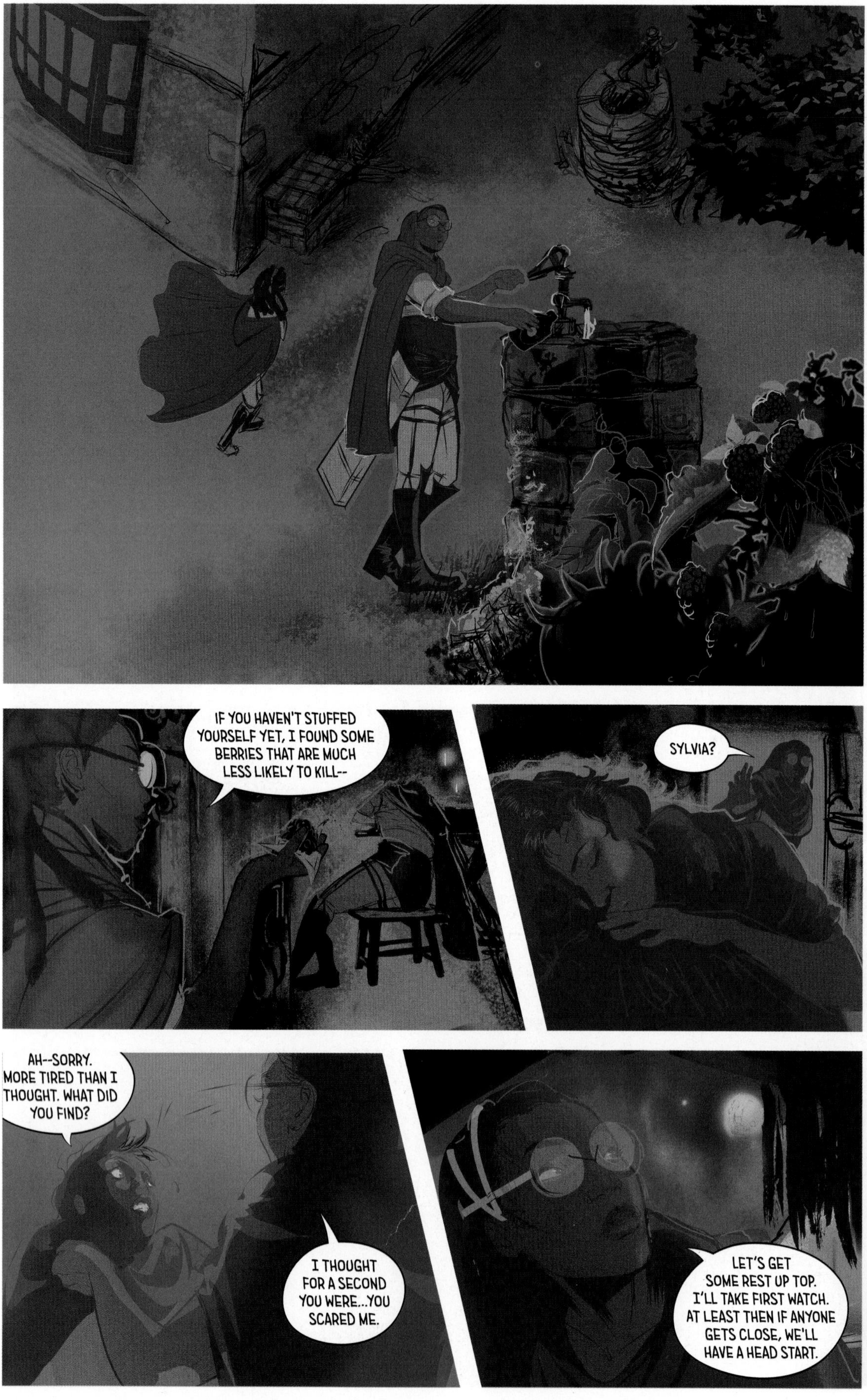
IF YOU HAVEN'T STUFFED YOURSELF YET, I FOUND SOME BERRIES THAT ARE MUCH LESS LIKELY TO KILL--
SYLVIA?
AH--SORRY. MORE TIRED THAN I THOUGHT. WHAT DID YOU FIND?
I THOUGHT FOR A SECOND YOU WERE...YOU SCARED ME.
LET'S GET SOME REST UP TOP. I'LL TAKE FIRST WATCH. AT LEAST THEN IF ANYONE GETS CLOSE, WE'LL HAVE A HEAD START.

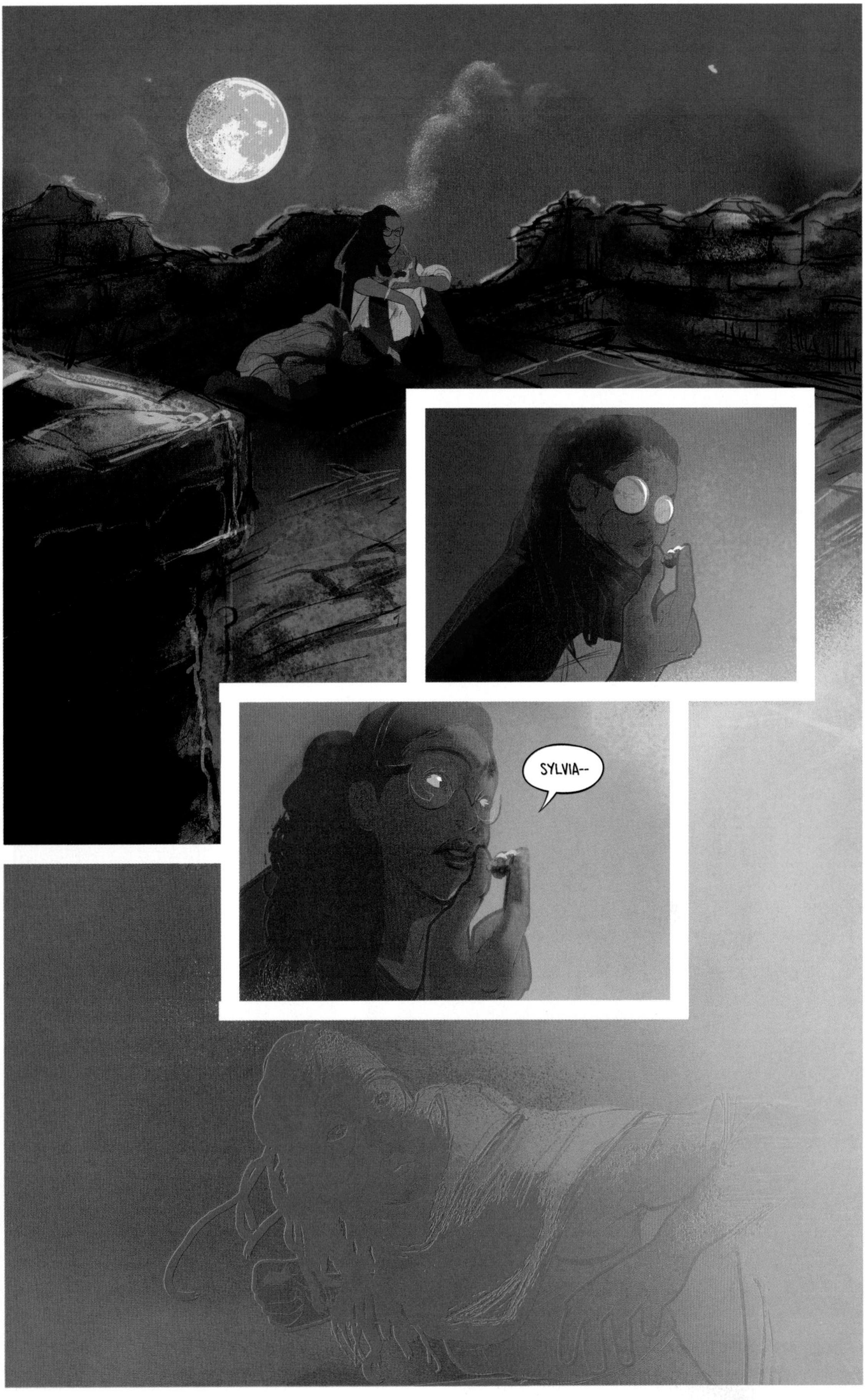
SYLVIA--

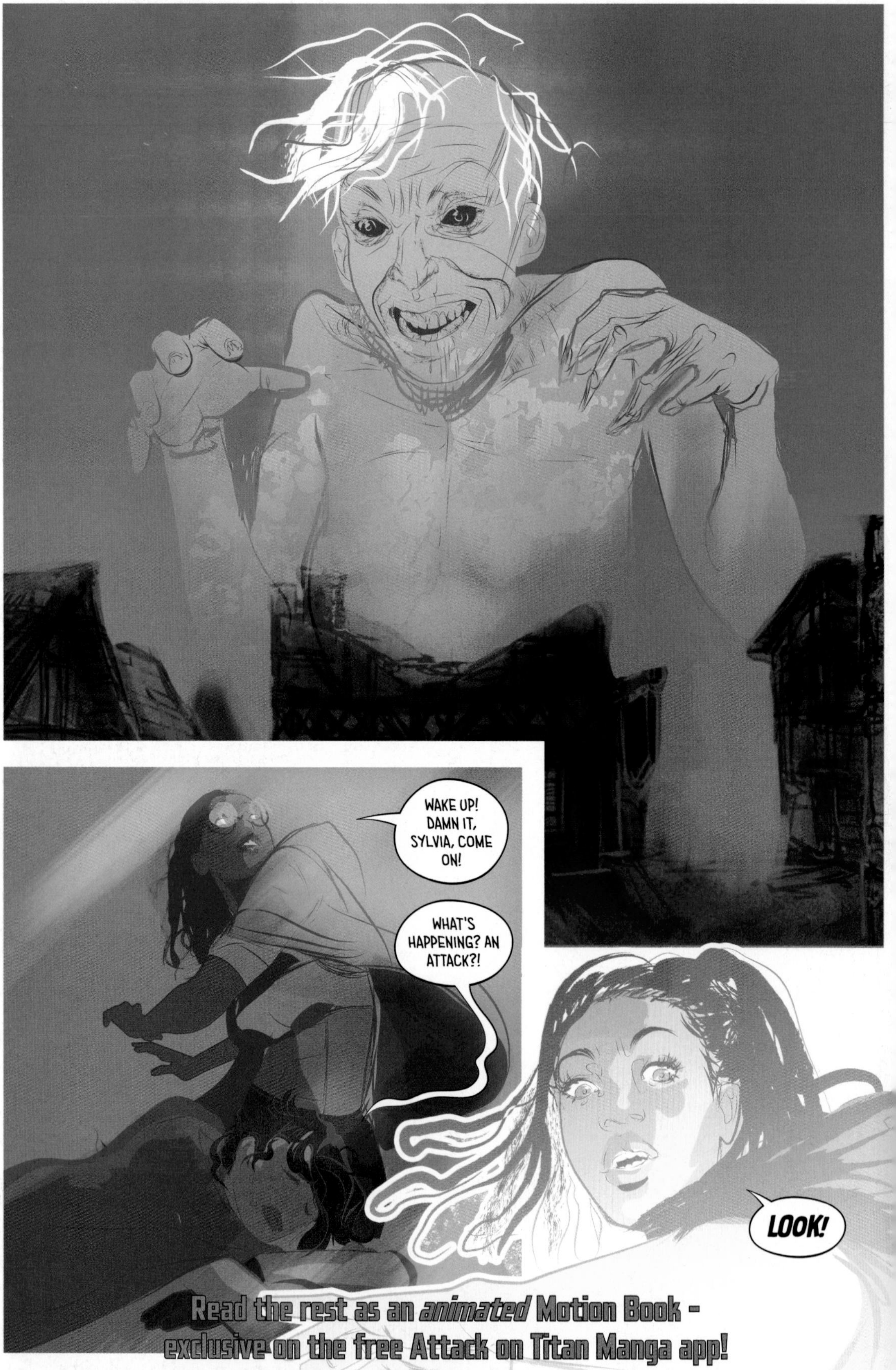
WAKE UP! DAMN IT, SYLVIA, COME ON!
WHAT'S HAPPENING? AN ATTACK?!
LOOK!
Read the rest as an *animated* Motion Book -
exclusive on the free Attack on Titan Manga app!
More info: kodanshacomics.com/series/attack-titan-anthology/

ATTACK on TITAN
ANTHOLOGY

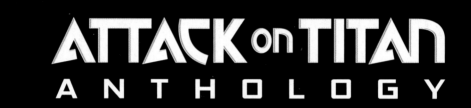